T0181931

Lecture Notes in Computer Science 13317

Founding Editors

Gerhard Goos
Karlsruhe Institute of Technology, Karlsruhe, Germany

Juris Hartmanis
Cornell University, Ithaca, NY, USA

Editorial Board Members

Elisa Bertino
Purdue University, West Lafayette, IN, USA

Wen Gao
Peking University, Beijing, China

Bernhard Steffen
TU Dortmund University, Dortmund, Germany

Moti Yung
Columbia University, New York, NY, USA

More information about this series at https://link.springer.com/bookseries/558

Jessie Y. C. Chen · Gino Fragomeni (Eds.)

Virtual, Augmented and Mixed Reality

Design and Development

14th International Conference, VAMR 2022
Held as Part of the 24th HCI International Conference, HCII 2022
Virtual Event, June 26 – July 1, 2022
Proceedings, Part I

 Springer

Editors
Jessie Y. C. Chen
U.S. Army Research Laboratory
Aberdeen Proving Ground, MD, USA

Gino Fragomeni
U.S. Army Combat Capabilities
Development Command Soldier Center
Orlando, FL, USA

ISSN 0302-9743 ISSN 1611-3349 (electronic)
Lecture Notes in Computer Science
ISBN 978-3-031-05938-4 ISBN 978-3-031-05939-1 (eBook)
https://doi.org/10.1007/978-3-031-05939-1

© The Editor(s) (if applicable) and The Author(s), under exclusive license
to Springer Nature Switzerland AG 2022
This work is subject to copyright. All rights are reserved by the Publisher, whether the whole or part of the material is concerned, specifically the rights of translation, reprinting, reuse of illustrations, recitation, broadcasting, reproduction on microfilms or in any other physical way, and transmission or information storage and retrieval, electronic adaptation, computer software, or by similar or dissimilar methodology now known or hereafter developed.
The use of general descriptive names, registered names, trademarks, service marks, etc. in this publication does not imply, even in the absence of a specific statement, that such names are exempt from the relevant protective laws and regulations and therefore free for general use.
The publisher, the authors and the editors are safe to assume that the advice and information in this book are believed to be true and accurate at the date of publication. Neither the publisher nor the authors or the editors give a warranty, expressed or implied, with respect to the material contained herein or for any errors or omissions that may have been made. The publisher remains neutral with regard to jurisdictional claims in published maps and institutional affiliations.

This Springer imprint is published by the registered company Springer Nature Switzerland AG
The registered company address is: Gewerbestrasse 11, 6330 Cham, Switzerland

Foreword

Human-computer interaction (HCI) is acquiring an ever-increasing scientific and industrial importance, as well as having more impact on people's everyday life, as an ever-growing number of human activities are progressively moving from the physical to the digital world. This process, which has been ongoing for some time now, has been dramatically accelerated by the COVID-19 pandemic. The HCI International (HCII) conference series, held yearly, aims to respond to the compelling need to advance the exchange of knowledge and research and development efforts on the human aspects of design and use of computing systems.

The 24th International Conference on Human-Computer Interaction, HCI International 2022 (HCII 2022), was planned to be held at the Gothia Towers Hotel and Swedish Exhibition & Congress Centre, Göteborg, Sweden, during June 26 to July 1, 2022. Due to the COVID-19 pandemic and with everyone's health and safety in mind, HCII 2022 was organized and run as a virtual conference. It incorporated the 21 thematic areas and affiliated conferences listed on the following page.

A total of 5583 individuals from academia, research institutes, industry, and governmental agencies from 88 countries submitted contributions, and 1276 papers and 275 posters were included in the proceedings to appear just before the start of the conference. The contributions thoroughly cover the entire field of human-computer interaction, addressing major advances in knowledge and effective use of computers in a variety of application areas. These papers provide academics, researchers, engineers, scientists, practitioners, and students with state-of-the-art information on the most recent advances in HCI. The volumes constituting the set of proceedings to appear before the start of the conference are listed in the following pages.

The HCI International (HCII) conference also offers the option of 'Late Breaking Work' which applies both for papers and posters, and the corresponding volume(s) of the proceedings will appear after the conference. Full papers will be included in the 'HCII 2022 - Late Breaking Papers' volumes of the proceedings to be published in the Springer LNCS series, while 'Poster Extended Abstracts' will be included as short research papers in the 'HCII 2022 - Late Breaking Posters' volumes to be published in the Springer CCIS series.

I would like to thank the Program Board Chairs and the members of the Program Boards of all thematic areas and affiliated conferences for their contribution and support towards the highest scientific quality and overall success of the HCI International 2022 conference; they have helped in so many ways, including session organization, paper reviewing (single-blind review process, with a minimum of two reviews per submission) and, more generally, acting as goodwill ambassadors for the HCII conference.

This conference would not have been possible without the continuous and unwavering support and advice of Gavriel Salvendy, founder, General Chair Emeritus, and Scientific Advisor. For his outstanding efforts, I would like to express my appreciation to Abbas Moallem, Communications Chair and Editor of HCI International News.

June 2022   Constantine Stephanidis

HCI International 2022 Thematic Areas and Affiliated Conferences

Thematic Areas

- HCI: Human-Computer Interaction
- HIMI: Human Interface and the Management of Information

Affiliated Conferences

- EPCE: 19th International Conference on Engineering Psychology and Cognitive Ergonomics
- AC: 16th International Conference on Augmented Cognition
- UAHCI: 16th International Conference on Universal Access in Human-Computer Interaction
- CCD: 14th International Conference on Cross-Cultural Design
- SCSM: 14th International Conference on Social Computing and Social Media
- VAMR: 14th International Conference on Virtual, Augmented and Mixed Reality
- DHM: 13th International Conference on Digital Human Modeling and Applications in Health, Safety, Ergonomics and Risk Management
- DUXU: 11th International Conference on Design, User Experience and Usability
- C&C: 10th International Conference on Culture and Computing
- DAPI: 10th International Conference on Distributed, Ambient and Pervasive Interactions
- HCIBGO: 9th International Conference on HCI in Business, Government and Organizations
- LCT: 9th International Conference on Learning and Collaboration Technologies
- ITAP: 8th International Conference on Human Aspects of IT for the Aged Population
- AIS: 4th International Conference on Adaptive Instructional Systems
- HCI-CPT: 4th International Conference on HCI for Cybersecurity, Privacy and Trust
- HCI-Games: 4th International Conference on HCI in Games
- MobiTAS: 4th International Conference on HCI in Mobility, Transport and Automotive Systems
- AI-HCI: 3rd International Conference on Artificial Intelligence in HCI
- MOBILE: 3rd International Conference on Design, Operation and Evaluation of Mobile Communications

List of Conference Proceedings Volumes Appearing Before the Conference

1. LNCS 13302, Human-Computer Interaction: Theoretical Approaches and Design Methods (Part I), edited by Masaaki Kurosu
2. LNCS 13303, Human-Computer Interaction: Technological Innovation (Part II), edited by Masaaki Kurosu
3. LNCS 13304, Human-Computer Interaction: User Experience and Behavior (Part III), edited by Masaaki Kurosu
4. LNCS 13305, Human Interface and the Management of Information: Visual and Information Design (Part I), edited by Sakae Yamamoto and Hirohiko Mori
5. LNCS 13306, Human Interface and the Management of Information: Applications in Complex Technological Environments (Part II), edited by Sakae Yamamoto and Hirohiko Mori
6. LNAI 13307, Engineering Psychology and Cognitive Ergonomics, edited by Don Harris and Wen-Chin Li
7. LNCS 13308, Universal Access in Human-Computer Interaction: Novel Design Approaches and Technologies (Part I), edited by Margherita Antona and Constantine Stephanidis
8. LNCS 13309, Universal Access in Human-Computer Interaction: User and Context Diversity (Part II), edited by Margherita Antona and Constantine Stephanidis
9. LNAI 13310, Augmented Cognition, edited by Dylan D. Schmorrow and Cali M. Fidopiastis
10. LNCS 13311, Cross-Cultural Design: Interaction Design Across Cultures (Part I), edited by Pei-Luen Patrick Rau
11. LNCS 13312, Cross-Cultural Design: Applications in Learning, Arts, Cultural Heritage, Creative Industries, and Virtual Reality (Part II), edited by Pei-Luen Patrick Rau
12. LNCS 13313, Cross-Cultural Design: Applications in Business, Communication, Health, Well-being, and Inclusiveness (Part III), edited by Pei-Luen Patrick Rau
13. LNCS 13314, Cross-Cultural Design: Product and Service Design, Mobility and Automotive Design, Cities, Urban Areas, and Intelligent Environments Design (Part IV), edited by Pei-Luen Patrick Rau
14. LNCS 13315, Social Computing and Social Media: Design, User Experience and Impact (Part I), edited by Gabriele Meiselwitz
15. LNCS 13316, Social Computing and Social Media: Applications in Education and Commerce (Part II), edited by Gabriele Meiselwitz
16. LNCS 13317, Virtual, Augmented and Mixed Reality: Design and Development (Part I), edited by Jessie Y. C. Chen and Gino Fragomeni
17. LNCS 13318, Virtual, Augmented and Mixed Reality: Applications in Education, Aviation and Industry (Part II), edited by Jessie Y. C. Chen and Gino Fragomeni

http://2022.hci.international/proceedings

Preface

With the recent emergence of a new generation of displays, smart devices, and wearables, the field of virtual, augmented, and mixed reality (VAMR) is rapidly expanding, transforming, and moving towards the mainstream market. At the same time, VAMR applications in a variety of domains are also reaching maturity and practical usage. From the point of view of the user experience, VAMR promises possibilities to reduce interaction efforts and cognitive load, while also offering contextualized information, by combining different sources and reducing attention shifts, and opening the 3D space. Such scenarios offer exciting challenges associated with underlying and supporting technologies, interaction and navigation in virtual and augmented environments, and design and development. VAMR themes encompass a wide range of areas such as education, aviation, social, emotional, psychological and persuasive applications.

The 14th International Conference on Virtual, Augmented and Mixed Reality (VAMR 2022), an affiliated conference of the HCI International conference, provided a forum for researchers and practitioners to disseminate and exchange scientific and technical information on VAMR-related topics in various applications. The presentations covered a wide range of topics, centered on themes related to interaction techniques, development issues, underlying technologies, and user experience and performance. With recent advances in robotics and artificial intelligence-based systems, topics of interest have expanded to include VAMR-based techniques for human-robot interaction and human interaction with intelligent systems. There are several emerging trends that are noteworthy. Increasingly, multimodal techniques are utilized to enhance VAMR effectiveness – ranging from interaction modalities to prediction of user behaviors. Multi-user and multi-platform paradigms are also explored in several studies.

Two volumes of the HCII2022 proceedings are dedicated to this year's edition of the VAMR conference, entitled Virtual, Augmented and Mixed Reality: Design and Development (Part I) and Virtual, Augmented and Mixed Reality: Applications in Education, Aviation and Industry (Part II). The first focuses on topics related to developing and evaluating VAMR environments, gesture-based, haptic, and multimodal interaction in VAMR, and social, emotional, psychological, and persuasive aspects in VAMR, while the second focuses on topics related to VAMR in learning, education and culture, VAMR in aviation, and industrial applications of VAMR.

Papers of these volumes are included for publication after a minimum of two single-blind reviews from the members of the VAMR Program Board or, in some cases, from members of the Program Boards of other affiliated conferences. We would like to thank all of them for their invaluable contribution, support, and efforts.

June 2022

Jessie Y. C. Chen
Gino Fragomeni

14th International Conference on Virtual, Augmented and Mixed Reality (VAMR 2022)

Program Board Chairs: **Jessie Y. C. Chen,** U.S. Army Research Laboratory, Aberdeen Proving Ground, USA and **Gino Fragomeni,** U.S. Army Combat Capabilities Development Command (DEVCOM) Soldier Center, Orlando, USA

- Shih-Yi Chien, National Chengchi University, Taiwan
- Tamara Griffith, U.S. Army DEVCOM Soldier Center, Orlando, USA
- Sue Kase, U.S. Army Research Laboratory, Aberdeen Proving Ground, USA
- Daniela Kratchounova, Federal Aviation Administration (FAA), Oklahoma City, USA
- Fotis Liarokapis, CYENS, Cyprus
- Phillip Mangos, Adaptive Immersion Technologies, USA
- Jose San Martin, Universidad Rey Juan Carlos, Spain
- Andreas Schreiber, German Aerospace Center (DLR), Germany
- Sharad Sharma, Bowie State University, USA
- Simon Su, National Institute of Standards and Technology (NIST), USA
- Denny Yu, Purdue University, USA

The full list with the Program Board Chairs and the members of the Program Boards of all thematic areas and affiliated conferences is available online at

http://www.hci.international/board-members-2022.php

HCI International 2023

The 25th International Conference on Human-Computer Interaction, HCI International 2023, will be held jointly with the affiliated conferences at the AC Bella Sky Hotel and Bella Center, Copenhagen, Denmark, 23–28 July 2023. It will cover a broad spectrum of themes related to human-computer interaction, including theoretical issues, methods, tools, processes, and case studies in HCI design, as well as novel interaction techniques, interfaces, and applications. The proceedings will be published by Springer. More information will be available on the conference website: http://2023.hci.international/.

General Chair
Constantine Stephanidis
University of Crete and ICS-FORTH
Heraklion, Crete, Greece
Email: general_chair@hcii2023.org

http://2023.hci.international/

Contents – Part I

Evaluating VAMR Environments

Gesture-Based, Haptic and Multimodal Interaction in VAMR

Social, Emotional, Psychological and Persuasive Aspects in VAMR

Contents – Part II

Industrial Applications of VAMR

Developing VAMR Environments

Integration of Augmented, Virtual and Mixed Reality with Building Information Modeling: A Systematic Review

Ahlem Assila[1]([⊠]) [iD], Amira Dhouib[2] [iD], Ziad Monla[1] [iD],
and Mourad Zghal[1]

[1] LINEACT, CESI Engineering School, Reims, France
{aassila, zmonla, mzghal}@cesi.fr
[2] Miracl Laboratory, Sfax, Tunisia

Abstract. Thanks to the digital revolution, the construction industry has seen a recognizable evolution, where the world has been heading towards modern constructions based on the use of Building Information Modeling (BIM). This evolution was marked by the integration of this paradigm with immersive technologies like Virtual Reality (VR), Augmented Reality (AR), and Mixed Reality (MR). During the last few years, the development of BIM started to emerge. This paper proposes a Systematic Literature Review (SLR) of recent studies about the integration of BIM with immersive environments using VR/AR/MR technologies. Four electronic databases were exploited to search for eligible studies, namely: Google Scholar, ACM Digital Library, IEEE Xplore, and Science direct. From an initial cohort of 239 studies, 28 were retained for analysis. The main findings of this review have been focused on stages of the projects' life cycle in which the immersive technologies are being implemented, approaches/techniques used to ensure the integration of BIM with the three immersive technologies, along with the current limitations and perspectives.

Keywords: Augmented reality · Virtual reality · Mixed reality · Immersive environment · Building information modeling

1 Introduction

In a world where technology is used in every industry sector, the Architecture, Engineering, and Construction (AEC) sector is no exception. Building Information Modeling (BIM) is a set of interacting policies, processes, and technologies that allow the development of infrastructures' models during and across their complete lifecycle [1, 2]. This process assists work teams to make the best decisions in construction projects by helping them to conceive, visualize, run simulations and collaborate easily [3, 4]. Although BIM is a paradigm shift that improves the traditional construction problems, its implementation and use remain a big challenge. As such, innovative tools to support BIM are in full development. These tools are based on immersive systems and interfaces that provide augmented, virtual or mixed environments [5].

In the context of the next-generation building, three immersive technologies can improve the BIM by allowing users to visualize the data of the developed 3D model

© The Author(s), under exclusive license to Springer Nature Switzerland AG 2022
J. Y. C. Chen and G. Fragomeni (Eds.): HCII 2022, LNCS 13317, pp. 3–19, 2022.
https://doi.org/10.1007/978-3-031-05939-1_1

and to connect to its data, virtually and/or in real-time [3]. The first technology concerns Augmented Reality (AR) which is used currently as one of the most promising technologies in the industry 4.0 context [6]. It allows the integration of virtual 3D objects with reality through devices such as smartphones, tablets, and augmented reality glasses or headsets [7]. The second technology concerns Virtual Reality (VR) which allows users to fully immerse themselves in a virtual environment, and to navigate to explore it and interact with 3D objects. This technology is generally achieved through advanced display devices, such as immersive helmets Head-Mounted Displays (HMD) [8]. The emergence of real and virtual realities has involved the creation of Mixed Reality (MR) technology [9]. The latter is characterized by its flexibility compared to the other technologies. As a consequence, it offers interactivity to the digital content with the real-world [10].

In the last few years, BIM-based immersive environments have emerged within the AEC sector, providing a wide range of applications in several fields, such as industry, construction, maintenance, engineering, and education [11]. However, a restricted number of systematic reviews currently exist on how researchers have integrated these advanced technologies with the BIM applied in the different phases of a building's lifecycle. In [5], for example, the authors have proposed a Systematic Literature Review (SLR) about tools and techniques of BIM-based virtual reality following the preferred reporting items for systematic reviews and meta-analyses (PRISMA-P) protocol. From an initial cohort of 2950 articles, 16 were retained for analysis and eleven research questions have been formulated. Their purpose was threefold: (1) present the immersive reality functionality, (2) identify the evaluation method of their applications, and (3) present the VR environments originated from BIM [5]. Numerous limitations of the existing works have been cited, such as software compatibility; the transition from the laboratory conclusions to the real-life context; the inability of the software to relay changes to the BIM model [5].

In another study, Sidani et al. [11] have proposed an SLR about tools and techniques of BIM-based augmented reality based on the PRISMA-P protocol. 24 articles were selected for the review and nine research questions have been formulated. These questions cover multiple aspects of BIM-based AR, mainly *the BIM dimensions, the target groups, the applied technologies, and the usability evaluation methods for AR* [11]. The analysis results have shown that AR implementation requires the development of more solutions to achieve the needed state. Additionally, several limitations have been presented such as the lack of non-geometric data, the localization problems, and the low connectivity levels regarding GPS connections and internet.

Our paper differs from these previous ones, in that it proposes a complete view of studies specifically focused on the integration of BIM with the immersive environments using virtual, augmented, and mixed reality. Accordingly, we propose an SLR about the recent advances proposed specifically during the last ten years in this field. The aim is to give researchers an overview of the stages of the projects' lifecycle in which the immersive technologies are being implemented, the main approaches/techniques used to integrate BIM with VR/AR/MR, the potential limitations, and the new perspectives.

The present paper is structured as follows: Sect. 2 describes the adopted research methodology. Section 3 reports the obtained review results in order to answer the defined research questions. Finally, Sect. 4 concludes the paper.

2   Methodology

The methodology applied to carry out this SLR is based on [12]. It consists of three phases, namely: planning, conducting, and reporting the review. Figure 1 illustrates the review process with a report of the outcomes obtained in each step.

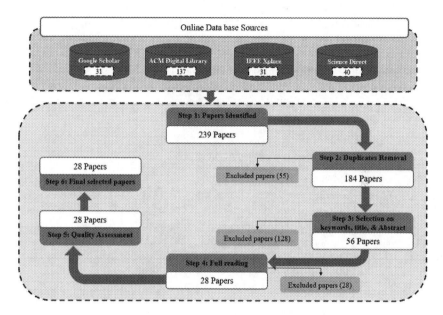

Fig. 1. Search and selection process

2.1   Planning the Review

The main goal of this systematic review is to undertake the integration of BIM with immersive environments using AR/VR/MR for improving the building process. The following subsections detail the Research Questions (RQs), the used electronic databases, the search string, along the inclusion/exclusion criteria applied to filter the studies.

Research Questions. Three RQs were formulated to conduct a detailed review of the present topic. These research questions are:

- **RQ 1.** At which stages of the project lifecycle are the AR/VR/MR technologies implemented?
- **RQ 2.** What are the applied techniques/approaches for combining BIM with AR/VR/MR technologies?
- **RQ 3.** What are the main limitations and new perspectives for BIM-based AR, BIM-based VR, and BIM-based MR?

Sources Selection

Search String. We start with the definition of the keywords and a simple string representing the three main aspects of this systematic review, namely; "B*uilding Information modeling"* AND *"augmented reality" OR "Virtual reality" OR "mixed reality"* AND *"Integration".* To ensure a more comprehensive search, alternate spelling and acronyms were added. In this way, we define the following search string;

("Building Information modeling" OR "BIM") AND ("augmented reality" OR "AR" "OR "Virtual reality" OR "VR" OR "mixed reality" OR "MR") AND ("Integration" OR "Integrating").

Electronic Databases. After the string definition, the search process was performed by searching for the studies published between January 2011 and December 2021. For this purpose, four electronic databases were selected: ACM Digital Library, IEEE Xplore, Science Direct, and Google Scholar. The search was carried out on the title, abstract, and indexed terms for journal papers and conference proceedings.

Table 1. Databases and search procedure

Database	String Query
Google scholar	allintitle: "Building information modeling" OR "BIM" AND "AR" OR "augmented reality" OR "VR" OR "Virtual reality" OR "MR" OR "mixed reality" AND "Integration" OR "Integrating"
ACM Digital Library	("Building information modeling" OR "BIM") AND ("AR" OR "augmented reality" OR "VR" OR "Virtual reality" OR "MR" OR "mixed reality") AND ("Integration" OR "Integrating")
IEEE Xplore	("Building information modeling" OR "BIM") AND ("AR" OR "augmented reality" OR "VR" OR "Virtual reality" OR "MR" OR "mixed reality") AND ("Integrat*")
Science direct	("Building information modeling" OR "BIM") AND ("AR" OR "augmented reality" OR "VR" OR "Virtual reality" OR "MR" OR "mixed reality") AND ("Integration" OR "Integrating")

Table 1 shows the used procedure to conduct string queries in each database.

Inclusion/Exclusion Criteria. A set of inclusion and exclusion criteria were used to filter studies that were not relevant to answer the research questions. The following inclusion criteria were defined in this review:

- Papers that tackle the integration of BIM with at least AR, VR, or MR technologies;
- Papers are written in English;
- Title, abstract, or keywords match the search query;
- Papers published between January 2011 and December 2021.

On the opposite, the exclusion criteria were:

- Papers are written in any other language than English;
- Papers not being available;
- Papers venue is not journals, conferences, or workshops;
- Papers in duplicity;
- Papers out of scope.

2.2 Conducting the Review

From the search in four databases, 239 studies were found. Next, the removal of duplicate studies reduced the studies to 184. After title, keywords, and abstract screening, 56 studies were retained. In the following, two authors have checked if the 56 papers address one or more of the RQs presented previously. Each paper was voted on anonymously based on three voting decisions: 'include', 'exclude', and 'maybe'. A paper was retained in the case that it received two 'include' votes or one 'include' and one 'maybe'. The paper that receives two 'exclude' votes or one 'exclude' and one 'maybe' vote was excluded. In the case of a conflict or two 'maybe' votes, a third author was involved in order to cast a deciding vote in excluding or including the paper.

This step revealed 28 papers. Lastly, the Quality Assessment (QA) of the studies was performed based on the study of [12]. The following QA questions were used to evaluate the relevance and completeness of the 28 studies.

- QA 1. Are the objectives of the research clearly stated?
- QA 2. Was the study designed to achieve these objectives?
- QA 3. Is the overall research methodology clearly described in the research?
- QA 4. Are the results of the conducted experiments clearly identified and reported?
- QA 5. Are the limitations of the current study adequately addressed?
- QA 6. Are new perspectives mentioned?

Three authors conducted the quality assessment of the studies. Each author was randomly assigned nine or ten studies to give a quality score to each question based on a three-point scale. These include: "Yes" referring to 1, "No" representing 0, and "Partially" representing 0.5. Next, the sum of the quality score of each paper was calculated. A threshold was defined such as if the total score was equal to or greater than three then the study was included. In the case when the study was less than three then it was excluded. Based on the QA, the quality criteria have been fulfilled by all of the preliminary retained studies. In this way, the 28 studies were qualified for further analysis.

2.3   Data Extraction

The final list of studies was used to extract the needed attributes to answer the set of research questions. These attributes include: (1) title, (2) list of authors, (3) stages of the project lifecycle, (4) used techniques/approaches for BIM-based AR, (5) applied techniques/approaches for BIM-based VR, (6) used techniques for BIM-based MR, (7) limitations and future works of BIM-based AR, (8) limitations and perspectives of BIM-based VR, and (9) limitations and perspectives of BIM-based MR.

3   Main Findings and Discussion

This section reports the findings of our SLR and synthesizes the final retained papers. The aim is to answer the RQs defined previously in Sect. 2.1 and discuss the relevant observations.

3.1   RQ 1. At Which Stages of the Project Lifecycle are the AR/VR/MR Technologies Implemented with BIM?

The BIM model can be deployed during the entire building lifecycle projects. It generally involves three main stages [13, 14]. The first stage concerns the *design or planning* stage which often involves a virtual collaboration between the architect/designer, structural engineer, and mechanical and electrical services engineer to ensure design clashes [14]. During this phase, BIM allows enhancing projects by offering a smart visualization and controlling the quality of the coordination between the different construction techniques. In this way, it reduces the project's cost without affecting its quality [14]. The second stage concerns the *construction* which is described as the implementation of a design envisioned by architects and engineers. During this stage, BIM allows facilitating the management of orders, deliveries, accounts, and progress reports as the work progresses. It can be used for construction monitoring, maintenance scheduling, and fabrication; as well as for the prefabrication and adjustment of elements [14, 15]. The last stage concerns the *operation*. It allows enhancing the building's lifespan and is used for maintenance and facility management operations [14]. In this stage, BIM can be used to link the model with management software [14].

To answer our research question, we firstly propose an analysis of the selected studies based on the combined technologies. Secondly, we examine them in accordance with the lifecycle stage. The aim is to determine in which stages of the project lifecycle, the AR/VR/MR technologies were implemented with BIM. The summary of studies in terms of these stages along with the BIM combined technologies are presented in Table 2.

Table 2. Selected studies: BIM combined technologies and building lifecycle stages

BIM combined technologies	References	Building lifecycle stages
BIM-AR	[16]	Operation (Maintenance)
	[17]	Operation (maintenance)
	[18]	Design
	[19]	Operation
	[20]	Construction
	[21]	Design Operation (Maintenance)
	[22]	Construction Operation (Maintenance)
	[2]	Operation
	[13]	Operation
	[23]	Construction
	[24]	Construction Operation (Maintenance)
	[25]	Operation (maintenance)
	[26]	Construction
BIM-VR	[27]	Design
	[28]	Design
	[29]	Design
	[30]	Design
	[31]	Planning
	[32]	Planning
	[33]	Construction
	[34]	Design
	[35]	Operation
	[36]	Design
BIM-MR	[37]	Operation (Maintenance)
	[10]	Design Construction
	[38]	Operation (Maintenance)
	[39]	Design
	[9]	Construction

As we can see from Table 2, a total of 13 studies out of 28 have focused on BIM-based AR technologies; 10 studies have been focused on the BIM-based VR and only 5 studies have been focused on the BIM-based MR. Concerning BIM-based AR studies, we note that most of the proposed solutions have been implemented for the operation stage (70% of the total studies), and construction stage than the design stage (two studies among 28). Regarding the BIM-based VR papers, 80% of studies focused on the design/planning stage. However, a few studies concern BIM-based MR solutions compared to BIM-based AR and BIM-based VR. An equitable distribution, which remains weak, between the three building lifecycle stages is noted.

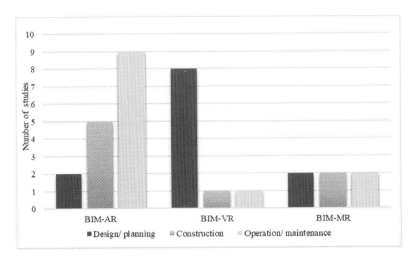

Fig. 2. Classification of the studies according to the combined technologies and their building lifecycle stage(s)

Some approaches have been applied simultaneously during two phases such as [10, 21, 22, 24].

Figure 2 shows the classification of the selected studies according to the combined technologies and their building lifecycle stage. After reviewing the 28 studies, the analysis indicated that BIM-based AR/VR/MR technologies could be involved in the three stages of the building lifecycle. Concerning the distribution of approaches according to the three building lifecycle stages, ten studies were directed to the design phase where 67% of them are focused on *BIM-based VR*. Also, twelve studies are related to the operation phase (*75% are focused on BIM-based AR*). Lastly, eight papers were related to the construction stage, where *62.5%* are related to *BIM-based AR*. To sum up, the BIM-based AR approaches were more developed in both the construction and operation stages. This can be explained by the benefits offered by the AR on the worksite through real-time construction review such as accuracy, limited errors, etc.

Concerning BIM-based VR, the approaches are more deployed in the design/planning phase. This can be explained by the fact that VR allows visualizing and enhancing the 3D contents created in the BIM models. Further, it is able to anticipate design errors before the construction phase, better communication between the various trades, the project and contracting authorities as well as the end operators. Regarding BIM-based MR, the development of approaches is in its infancy, since the application of mixed reality technology is still recent.

3.2   RQ 2. What are the Used Techniques/Approaches to Integrate AR/VR/MR with BIM?

In this section, we present a review of the used techniques/approaches regarding BIM coupled with immersive environments using AR, VR, and MR.

BIM-based AR Techniques/Approaches. Within the retained BIM-based AR studies, two major categories of approaches for integrating BIM with AR can be distinguished. The first category is based on *location-based systems*, using physical sensors to position objects and users such as Bluetooth Low Energy (BLE) beacons [2] or Wi-Fi positioning [22]. The second category concerns the approaches based on the *vision-based systems,* by applying feature points put on site and detected by cameras, such as markers [13, 19–23] or natural features tracking known as markerless based AR, which generally incorporates location-based systems [2, 13, 16, 17, 20, 24–26].

Approaches based on Located Systems. According to [22], the implementation of location-based systems requires two main techniques: (1) a Wireless Access Point (WAP) for Wi-Fi to locate workers indoor or within the workplace; a marker definition such as any building element (e.g., walls, floors, and windows), and (2) a BIM database (e.g., components models, tables, characteristics).

Once a location-based system is operated, a reference table that contains the BIM components and their corresponding rooms and markers will start downloading from the Apache Hbase database system (cloud). The reference table is arranged logically and organized in the form of columns and rows. Each row corresponds to a floor and all data of BIM components of this floor is classed in the same row. Each group of components is classed in a specific column. After loading the table, the indoor positioning system determines the position of the user by processing the wireless signals emitted by the wearable device and captured by the WAP. At this stage, the system maps between the determined Wi-Fi position and the reference table intending to locate the room and load all the BIM components corresponding to it. Finally, using the wearable video AR device, the system scans the marker inside the room. Then, it superimposes the virtual model of the BIM component on the real building element. The aim of using the positioning system is to reduce the number of used markers, taking an example of a multistory building. Each story has several rooms and each room contains a lot of architectural elements. In this case, a huge number of markers are needed, which will lead to difficulties in the implementation task. Accordingly, the adoption of these techniques allows us to use the same group of markers for different BIM components. Through a mapping between the user position and the reference table, the system can determine the specific story and room to determine the corresponding BIM component.

Approaches based on Vision-based systems.
Marker based-AR is the simplest and the easiest system. It requires a static image also known as a marker or a trigger photo that users can scan using an augmented reality application already installed in their mobile devices. After scanning the marker, the device gets or downloads additional content. A database is prepared and stored in advance on a cloud or the same device in order to experience Augmented Reality. Markers can be anything that has a unique visual point, like objects, images, packaging, and barcodes [40]. As mentioned earlier, several papers have adopted this technique. Among them, Chai et al. [13] have applied the marker-based AR technique using a tabletop AR-BIM technology. The goal of their proposed approach is to define an engineering plan as a marker. Through a SmartReality application installed on mobile

phones or iPad, we can overlay any 3D BIM model on the top of the building plan after scanning it. In another work [20], the marker-based AR technology is adopted and used in Liquified Natural Gas (LNG). In their study, the authors proposed an automatic positioning and tracking prototype. The latter allows visualizing massive 3D models of LNG plants and pipes characteristics by scanning corresponding specific barcodes.

Concerning Markerless augmented reality: AR technology does not depend on the presence of markers to be activated. By using this technique, users can scan horizontal and vertical surfaces such as tables, walls, and floors [40]. The system can, automatically, determine virtual coordinates of the real surrounding elements by analyzing and processing the real environment [40]. Markerless AR can be used usually and allows users to align any virtual content or object to the real world at the right place [40]. As mentioned above, this technique has been implemented in several papers. All the proposed approaches consist of four major components, namely: (1) BIM model, (2) AR platform, (3) tracking system, and (4) data transformation. In [24, 26], a new markerless AR implementation approach is proposed based on simultaneous localization and mapping (SLAM) technology. It allows solving issues of indoor positioning accuracy, understanding the surrounding environment during movement, determining positions, and constructing an accurate map of the location according to the observed feature points. In another work, Chai et al. [13] have proposed an approach based on a markerless AR. It consists of exporting the established BIM 3D model to Unity 3D. Communication has been ensured via a structured sensor that was developed to work as a mobile light system.

BIM-based VR Techniques/Approaches. Based on our review, BIM-based VR approaches usually follow the same architecture that consists mainly of three components. They include (1) *BIM model software* that allows providing both geometric and non-geometric information to the VR interfaces; (2) the *visual environment enhancement* which indicates the adopted software applied to ensure compatibility between game engines and BIM authoring tools; and (3) the *VR game engine* used to design and create virtual environments.

Table 3 presents a synthesis of the studies related to BIM-based VR approaches following four dimensions: (1) BIM software, (2) visual environment enhancement, (3) adopted VR game engine, and (4) used hardware in each solution to display VR. As seen in Table 3, the *Autodesk Revit* is the prominent software used to provide both geometric and non-geometric information to VR applications. Most of the retained studies related to BIM-based VR use this software for data modeling. In [31], the authors state that Autodesk Revit provides capabilities for creating and customizing parametric objects, which are more suitable for modeling dimensional and typological information related to activity workspaces.

Table 3. BIM-based VR studies' characteristics

References	BIM software	Visual environment enhancement	VR game engine	Hardware used to display VR
[31]	Autodesk Revit	Dynamo visual programming environment	Unity 3D	Mobile phone, Paired Bluetooth controller workers
[29]	Autodesk Revit	3Ds Max	OpenScene Graph (OSG)	Developed manipulator
[34]	Autodesk Revit	3Ds Max	Unity 3D	HTC Vive
[27]	Autodesk Revit	3Ds Max	Unity 3D	Oculus Rift head-mounted display
[35]	Autodesk Revit	TwinMotion	Unity 3D	HTC Vive
[33]	Autodesk Revit	3Ds Max	Unity 3D	Not available
[30]	Autodesk Revit	3Ds Max	Mars	Mobile phone, tablet, computer
[28]	Autodesk Revit	A real-time rendering engine developed by authors	A real-time rendering engine developed by authors	The Oculus Rift head-mounted display
[32]	Autodesk Revit	Not available	Unity 3D	HTC Vive
[36]	Autodesk Revit	3Ds Max	Unreal Engine or Stingray	Oculus Rift VR Headset

Regarding *the visual environment enhancement*, six studies use the 3Ds Max. The latter is known as a rich modeling environment for the development of professional-quality 3D models [41]. It solves the interoperability problems that may arise between the BIM software (component 1) and the VR game engine (component 3) [5]. Concerning the VR game engines, *Unity VR* can be considered as the most widely used one. According to our analysis, six studies out of ten have adopted Unity VR. This choice can be explained by several reasons. Firstly, this VR game engine allows the development of both immersive environments using VR and AR. In addition, it supports real-time multi-user collaboration and data sharing. Finally, it provides a package of tools that includes, for example, modeling, animation or other special effects [33, 38].

As illustrated in Table 3, the two most used hardware to display VR corresponds to: (1) the Oculus Rift head-mounted display [27, 28, 36], and (2) the HTC Vive [32, 34, 35]. The authors in [28] claim that although the Oculus Rift is an affordable device, it is characterized by a wide field of view, stereoscopic viewing, and physical rotation. In another approach, [34] highlighted that the use of HTC vive provides efficient visual reliability and input solutions.

Furthermore, the BIM-based VR approaches have been applied in several application domains related to the construction project such as the facility management field [34]. In the study of [34], VR has been implemented and integrated with BIM in order to allow maintenance personnel, facility managers and stakeholders to communicate effectively and to share comments, notes, lessons learned from the project execution and advice providing constructive feedback and database to enhance future designs. In another case, Petrova et al. [27] proposed a BIM-based VR solution applied in the building furnishing field. The proposed approach aims to help project staff to choose furniture for a building.

The Used Techniques/Approaches for BIM-based MR. Among the BIM-based MR studies, four main approaches/techniques have been used The study of [39] proposes an approach for the integration of MR into the design phase of BIM model with a focus on the recognition and avoidance of clashes. The approach requires the importation of the native Revit file (BIM model).rvt to Trimble Sketchup, then to Trimble Connect.

A second approach was proposed by [38]. Its aim is to facilitate work tasks and to improve workers' performance in the construction industry based on the collaboration between BIM and MR. In this way, a Collaborative BIM-based Markerless Mixed Reality Facility Management System to build virtual environments has been developed. The BIM model is transferred to Unity 3D as a.FBX file. Oculus Rift (HMD) with a touch controller is used to visualize the VE. In [10], the research aims to develop and conceptualize an integrative approach based on the IDEF0 methodology. During the pre-construction phase the planning stage consists of five steps as follows: developing a 3d model, developing an MR model, arranging schedule, updating and model reviewing. During the construction phase, the build stage consists of four steps as follows: (1) the BIM modeling, (2) Lean BIM-based meeting, (3) arranging a modifications list, and (4) execution. Moreira et al. [9] have proposed a new system that adopts MR, IoT, and BIM to manage and map risks for construction. As a result, a dynamic risk map that supports dynamic features is obtained providing an interactive visualization. Risks are grouped in rounded shapes markers, markers have different colors and sizes depending on risk magnitude.

3.3   RQ 3. What are the Main Limitations and Perspectives for BIM-Based AR, BIM-Based VR, and BIM-Based MR?

In this section, we present the main limitations and new perspectives for the integration of BIM-based AR, BIM-based VR, and BIM-based MR.

Limitations and perspectives for BIM-based AR. Within the 28 retained studies, 13 are related to BIM-based AR. Following the analysis of these studies, some drawbacks can be reported. First, some researchers have addressed data compatibility issues between the different components of augmented reality and BIM and other models and representations [3]. Often the input/output of BIM cannot be used as such by an AR application and must be processed or converted. Thus, most of the studies should be proposed to define a standardized BIM format (or extensions) that can easily adapt to AR applications. Secondly, some types of tracking tools must be used in the real world, (e.g., markers, beacons, or sensors) to locate and display AR objects [2, 22]. This means that if the number of AR objects to be displayed increases, more tracking tools will need to be put in the real world. Accordingly, more physical installations will be needed which can be a hindrance to the construction process. Furthermore, information about the real-world scene to be processed should be acquired to optimize physical, technical, and financial resources. In addition, all the necessary BIM information must be transmitted to the augmented reality application, which means that a sufficiently efficient network connection is required. BIM data must also be stored, so there is a need to have enough data storage to keep all the BIM models and information. Lastly, the BIM and AR's possible usage is still limited due to lack of real-time information and imprecise positioning during walkthrough [25].

Limitations and perspectives for BIM-based VR. Several limitations can be identified by using and implementing VR technology with BIM. Davila et al. [42] have reported that special and expensive requirements are needed to experience virtual environments such as HMD, controllers, high-end mobile phones, computers with a powerful processor, graphic card, and tracking sensors. This impacts the total cost of the project and requires a huge budget. Otherwise, we note that the multi-user capability, that allows multiple users to visualize the same virtual content from different physical places, is not fully developed. Thus, special attention to the development of collaborative virtual environments is required. In the study of Petrova et al. [27], the reported limitation concerns technical issues related to the required time and efforts to manage the required workflow between Revit and Unity. The researchers suggested, as future works, to improve the possibilities of optimizing processes. Furthermore, according to [28], the use of a specific room will naturally restrict visualization sessions and make users focus on a single location which leads to limiting their physical and mental accessibility. Thus, the development of a rendering engine able to manage large and complex 3D datasets in real-time is required. In the study of [43], the author pointed out that the existing BIM and VR libraries lack safety elements. This issue may be a major challenge in using these tools for such purposes.

Finally, [42] have proposed a well-organized roadmap to improve the adoption of VR in the AEC industry. The proposed roadmap sets out the best practices and states different actions that should be taken into account to guarantee a good adoption of VR technology. As an example, we state the importance of arranging training sessions to develop professional skills; facilitating access to experts' knowledge; increasing clients' awareness; developing a communication tool to exchange data and information, and encouraging the development of technology [42].

Limitations and perspectives for BIM based-MR. Despite all the benefits that MR provides, some barriers limit its ease of use and implementation. These limitations varied according to the following stages of the building lifecycle: (1) the design stage, and (2) construction/operation stages. Next, the existing challenges are categorized and presented according to these stages.

Limitations occurred during the design stage. According to [10], it is not possible to import the BIM model directly into the MR platform during the design stage. It is important to highlight that a game engine software is always needed in this stage to convert the material's texture and lighting features of the BIM model before importing it to the MR platform. Furthermore, in some cases, the design of the MR-ready model, saved on the cloud, is edited and changed randomly and automatically, which impacts the relevance of the downloaded data.

Limitations occurred during the construction and operation stages. During the construction and operation stages, [38] have presented some limitations while using mixed reality. The first challenge remains to track indoor the worksite. In this case, a well-distributed feature is needed to guarantee accurate tracking. Secondly, the mobility and voice commands are not supported by the majority of HMD which requires the implementation and integration of new scripts to integrate additional functionalities. In [38], the integration of MIT's SixthSense technology has been proposed as a technology to be considered for better integration with the AR module. In critical situations, the visualization of objects in mixed reality mode can cause workers confusion and affect their safety. In this way, the risk of having cybersickness problems may increase. To overcome this limitation, preliminary assessments are required to anticipate any problem related to the workers' health.

4   Conclusion

This SLR starts with January 2011 to December 2021 to identify the relevant studies in four electronic databases. The aim is to answer three research questions aiming to provide insight into the integration of BIM with three immersive technologies (VR, AR, and MR). This integration can benefit the construction industry, in the building process. It attempts to address specific research questions related to the stages of the projects' life cycle in which the immersive technologies are being implemented, the main approaches/techniques used to integrate BIM with VR/AR/MR, the potential limitations, and the new perspectives.

Our results indicated ten techniques/approaches that can be used for BIM-based VR. The majority of these techniques/approaches were based mainly on Autodesk Revit as a BIM software. The 3Ds max represents the most software applied to ensure compatibility between game engines and BIM authoring tools. Most of the retained studies related to BIM-based AR resort to the use of the vision-based systems by implementing either the marker-based AR or markerless AR techniques. Despite the limitations surrounding these technologies, the existing approaches/ techniques allow a good vision of the future realization of the infrastructure, which can improve the performance of the construction process. The conclusions, limitations, as well as perspectives presented in this article, could be beneficial for AEC practitioners and academics across the developed world.

References

1. Carneiro, J., Rossetti, R.J.F., Silva, D.C., Oliveira, E.C.: BIM, GIS, IoT, and AR/VR integration for smart maintenance and management of road networks: a review. In: 2018 IEEE International Smart Cities Conference (ISC2), pp. 1–7. IEEE, Kansas City, MO, USA (2018). https://doi.org/10.1109/ISC2.2018.8656978.

2. Schweigkofler, A., et al.: Development of a digital platform based on the integration of augmented reality and bim for the management of information in construction processes. In: Chiabert, P., Bouras, A., Noël, F., Ríos, J. (eds.) Product Lifecycle Management to Support Industry 4.0. pp. 46–55. Springer International Publishing, Cham (2018). https://doi.org/10.1007/978-3-030-01614-2_5.

3. Karji, A., Woldesenbet, A., Rokooei, S.: Integration of augmented reality, building information modeling, and image processing in construction management: a content analysis. In: AEI 2017. pp. 983–992. American Society of Civil Engineers, Oklahoma City, Oklahoma (2017). https://doi.org/10.1061/9780784480502.082.

4. Assila, A., Beladjine, D., Messaadia, M.: Towards AR/VR maturity model adapted to the building information modeling. In: Nyffenegger, F., Ríos, J., Rivest, L., Bouras, A. (eds.) Product Lifecycle Management Enabling Smart X, pp. 753–765. Springer International Publishing, Cham (2020). https://doi.org/10.1007/978-3-030-62807-9_59.

5. Sidani, A., et al.: Recent tools and techniques of BIM-based virtual reality: a systematic review. Arch Computat Methods Eng. **28**, 449–462 (2021). https://doi.org/10.1007/s11831-019-09386-0

6. Gattullo, M., Scurati, G.W., Fiorentino, M., Uva, A.E., Ferrise, F., Bordegoni, M.: Towards augmented reality manuals for industry 4.0: A methodology. Robotics and Comput.-Integrated Manuf. **56**, 276-286 (2019). https://doi.org/10.1016/j.rcim.2018.10.001.

7. de Almeida Pacheco, B., Guimarães, M., Correa, A.G., Farinazzo Martins, V.: Usability evaluation of learning objects with augmented reality for smartphones: a reinterpretation of nielsen heuristics. In: Agredo-Delgado, V., Ruiz, P.H. (eds.) Human-Computer Interaction, pp. 214–228. Springer International Publishing, Cham (2019). https://doi.org/10.1007/978-3-030-05270-6_16.

8. Assila, A., Plouzeau, J., Merienne, F., Erfanian, A., Hu, Y.: Defining an indicator for navigation performance measurement in VE Based on ISO/IEC15939. In: De Paolis, L.T., Bourdot, P., Mongelli, A. (eds.) Augmented Reality, Virtual Reality, and Computer Graphics, pp. 17–34. Springer International Publishing, Cham (2017). https://doi.org/10.1007/978-3-319-60922-5_2.

9. Moreira, L.C. de S., Mota, P.P., Machado, F.A.: BIM, IoT and MR integration applied on risk maps for construction. In: Toledo Santos, E., Scheer, S. (eds.) Proceedings of the 18th International Conference on Computing in Civil and Building Engineering, pp. 895–906. Springer International Publishing, Cham (2021). https://doi.org/10.1007/978-3-030-51295-8_62.

10. Alizadehsalehi, S., Hadavi, A., Huang, J.C.: BIM/MR-lean construction project delivery management system. In: 2019 IEEE Technology & Engineering Management Conference (TEMSCON), pp. 1–6. IEEE, Atlanta, GA, USA (2019). https://doi.org/10.1109/TEMSCON.2019.8813574.

11. Sidani, A., et al.: Recent tools and techniques of BIM-based augmented reality: a systematic review. J. Building Eng. **42**, 102500 (2021). https://doi.org/10.1016/j.jobe.2021.102500

12. Kitchenham, B., Charters, S.: Guidelines for performing Systematic Literature review in software engineering version 2.3, Engineering, **45**(4), 1051 (2007)

13. Chai, C., Mustafa, K., Kuppusamy, S., Yusof, A., Lim, C.S., Wai, S.H.: BIM Integration in Augmented Reality Model. IJTech. **10**(7), 1266 (2019). https://doi.org/10.14716/ijtech.v10i7.3278.

14. Olanrewaju, O.I., Kineber, A.F., Chileshe, N., Edwards, D.J.: Modelling the impact of building information modelling (BIM) implementation drivers and awareness on project lifecycle. Sustainability. **13**, 8887 (2021). https://doi.org/10.3390/su13168887

15. Olanrewaju, O., Ajiboye Babarinde, S., Salihu, C.: Current state of building information modelling in the nigerian construction industry. J. Sustain. Archit. Civ. Eng. **27**, 63–77 (2020). https://doi.org/10.5755/j01.sace.27.2.25142

16. Graf, H., Soubra, S., Picinbono, G., Keough, I., Tessier, A., Khan, A.: Lifecycle building card: toward paperless and visual lifecycle management tools. In: SpringSim (SimAUD), pp. 5–12 (2011)

17. Kahn, S., et al.: Beyond 3D "as-built" information using mobile ar enhancing the building lifecycle management. In: 2012 International Conference on Cyberworlds, pp. 29–36. IEEE, Darmstadt, Germany (2012). https://doi.org/10.1109/CW.2012.12.

18. Wang, X., Love, P.E.D., Kim, M.J., Park, C.-S., Sing, C.-P., Hou, L.: A conceptual framework for integrating building information modeling with augmented reality. Autom. Constr. **34**, 37–44 (2013). https://doi.org/10.1016/j.autcon.2012.10.012

19. Jiao, Y., Zhang, S., Li, Y., Wang, Y., Yang, B.: Towards cloud augmented reality for construction application by BIM and SNS integration. Autom. Constr. **33**, 37–47 (2013). https://doi.org/10.1016/j.autcon.2012.09.018

20. Wang, X., Truijens, M., Ding, L., Hou, L., Wang, Y., Lavender, M.: Integrating building information modelling and augmented reality for construction projects in oil and gas industry. In: Proceedings of the 19th CIB World Building Congress, Brisbane 2013: Construction and Society, pp. 1–2. RMIT University.

21. Wang, J., Wang, X., Shou, W., Xu, B.: Integrating BIM and augmented reality for interactive architectural visualisation. Constr. Innov. **14**, 453–476 (2014). https://doi.org/10.1108/CI-03-2014-0019

22. Chen, H.-M., Chang, T.-Y.: Integration of augmented reality and indoor positioning technologies for on-site viewing of BIM information. In: Presented at the 31st International Symposium on Automation and Robotics in Construction , Sydney, Australia July 8 (2014). https://doi.org/10.22260/ISARC2014/0082.

23. Hatem, W.A., Maula, B.H.: Improving project monitoring by integrating BIM with Augmented Reality. IRECE. **11**(6), 304 (2020). https://doi.org/10.15866/irece.v11i6.19358.

24. Liu, Y.-C., Chen, J.-R., Chen, H.-M.: System development of an augmented reality on-site BIM viewer based on the integration of SLAM and BLE indoor positioning. In: Presented at the 37th International Symposium on Automation and Robotics in Construction , Kitakyushu, Japan October 14 (2020). https://doi.org/10.22260/ISARC2020/0042.

25. Dudhee, V., Vukovic, V.: Integration of building information modelling and augmented reality for building energy systems visualisation. In: Energy and Sustainable Futures, pp. 83–89 (2021). Springer, Cham. https://doi.org/10.1007/978-3-030-63916-7_11

26. Wang, S.-K., Chen, H.-M.: A construction progress on-site monitoring and presentation system based on the integration of augmented reality and BIM. In: Presented at the 37th International Symposium on Automation and Robotics in Construction , Kitakyushu, Japan October 14 (2020). https://doi.org/10.22260/ISARC2020/0023.

27. Petrova, E., Rasmussen, M., Jensen, R.L., Svidt, K.: Integrating virtual reality and BIM for end-user involvement in building design: a case study. In: Joint Conference on Computing in Construction (JC3), pp. 699–709 (2017)

28. Johansson, M., Roupé, M., Viklund Tallgren, M.: From BIM to VR - Integrating immersive visualizations in the current design process. In: Fusion-Proceeding of the 32nd eCAADe Conference-Volume 2 (eCAADe 2014), pp. 261–269 (2014)

29. Sun, T., Xu, Z., Yuan, J., Liu, C., Ren, A.: Virtual experiencing and pricing of room views based on bim and oblique photogrammetry. Procedia Eng. **196**, 1122–1129 (2017). https://doi.org/10.1016/j.proeng.2017.08.071

30. Chen, L., Wang, J.: Application research of virtual reality technology in green building design. In: 2020 5th International Conference on Smart Grid and Electrical Automation (ICSGEA), pp. 249–253. IEEE, Zhangjiajie, China (2020). https://doi.org/10.1109/ICSGEA51094.2020.00060.

31. Getuli, V., Capone, P., Bruttini, A., Isaac, S.: BIM-based immersive Virtual Reality for construction workspace planning: a safety-oriented approach. Autom. Constr. **114**, 103160 (2020). https://doi.org/10.1016/j.autcon.2020.103160

32. Xu, S., Fu, D., Xie, Y., Hou, L., Bu, S.: Integrating BIM and VR for highway construction site layout planning. In: CICTP 2020. American Society of Civil Engineers, Xi'an, China (Conference Cancelled), pp. 1068–1079 (2020). https://doi.org/10.1061/9780784482933.093.

33. Lin, C.-C., Hsu, L.-Y., Tung, S.-H., Gao, R.-J., Wu, S.-M., Wang, K.-C.: Integrate BIM and virtual reality to assist construction visual marketing. In: 2020 IEEE 2nd International Conference on Architecture, Construction, Environment and Hydraulics (ICACEH), pp. 28–31. IEEE, Hsinchu, Taiwan (2020). https://doi.org/10.1109/ICACEH51803.2020.9366260.

34. Akanmu, A.A., Olayiwola, J., Olatunji, O.A.: Automated checking of building component accessibility for maintenance. Autom. Constr. **114**, 103196 (2020). https://doi.org/10.1016/j.autcon.2020.103196

35. Pour Rahimian, F., Seyedzadeh, S., Oliver, S., Rodriguez, S., Dawood, N.: On-demand monitoring of construction projects through a game-like hybrid application of BIM and machine learning. Autom. Constr. **110**, 103012 (2020). https://doi.org/10.1016/j.autcon.2019.103012

36. Davidson, J., et al.: Integration of VR with BIM to facilitate real-time creation of bill of quantities during the design phase: a proof of concept study. Front. Eng. Manag. **7**, 396–403 (2020). https://doi.org/10.1007/s42524-019-0039-y

37. Patti, E., et al.: Information modeling for virtual and augmented reality. IT Prof. **19**, 52–60 (2017). https://doi.org/10.1109/MITP.2017.43

38. El Ammari, K., Hammad, A.: Remote interactive collaboration in facilities management using BIM-based mixed reality. Autom. Constr. **107**, 102940 (2019). https://doi.org/10.1016/j.autcon.2019.102940

39. Prabhakaran, A., Mahamadu, A.-M., Mahdjoubi, L., Manu, P.: An approach for integrating mixed reality into BIM for early stage design coordination. MATEC Web Conf. **312**, 04001 (2020). https://doi.org/10.1051/matecconf/202031204001

40. Cheng, J.C.P., Chen, K., Chen, W.: Comparison of Marker-Based and Markerless AR: A case study of an indoor decoration system. In: Lean and Computing in Construction Congress - Volume 1: Proceedings of the Joint Conference on Computing in Construction, pp. 483–490. Heriot-Watt University, Heraklion, Crete, Greece (2017). https://doi.org/10.24928/JC3-2017/0231.

41. Jeginovic, S., Rizvic, S., Chalmers, A.: Interactive 3D models – From 3ds max to VRML. In: Proceedings of 8th Central European Seminar on Computer Graphics (CESCG 2004), Budmerice Castle, Slovakia (2004).

42. Davila Delgado, J.M., Oyedele, L., Beach, T., Demian, P.: Augmented and virtual reality in construction: drivers and limitations for industry adoption. J. Constr. Eng. Manag. **146**, 04020079 (2020). https://doi.org/10.1061/(ASCE)CO.1943-7862.0001844

43. Azhar, S.: Role of visualization technologies in safety planning and management at construction jobsites. Procedia Eng. **171**, 215–226 (2017). https://doi.org/10.1016/j.proeng.2017.01.329

Visualization of Macroscopic Structure of Ultra-high Performance Concrete Based on X-ray Computed Tomography Using Immersive Environments

Rajiv Khadka[✉] , Mahesh Acharya , Daniel LaBrier ,
and Mustafa Mashal

Idaho State University, Pocatello, ID 83209, USA
rajivkhadka@isu.edu

Abstract. Ultra-high performance concrete (UHPC) is a cementitious composite material which uses steel fibers, cement, silica fume, fly ash, water, and admixtures to provide better structural performance and durability compared to conventional concrete. UHPC is an attractive novel material because of its higher compressive strength, higher tensile capacity, and ultralow permeability. Currently in the United States, UHPC is batched in smaller quantities on-site with very strict quality control by representatives from the producer. This has significantly increased the cost (more than 15 times higher) of poured UHPC compared to conventional concrete. It is not studied if substituting the representatives from a commercial producer with trained concrete technicians from public and other entities, would actually yield into substantial defects in the structure of poured UHPC. Similar to conventional concrete, mechanical properties of UHPC, a heterogeneous material from various structural scales (microscopic, mesoscopic, and macroscopic) is expected to be different from each other. Past research has shown that defects that exist on smaller scales can dictate the performance of UHPC overtime. However, macroscopic structural analysis may be the most effective method to capture the defects and uncertainties due to quality of on-site workmanship. This research focuses on the X-ray computed tomography (XCT) of macroscopic structures. XCT is an effective analysis tool for structural components (e.g., beam, columns, walls, slabs) in civil and critical infrastructures. This paper presents a detailed overview outlining how the macroscopic structure of concrete characterized by XCT can be visualized in an immersive environment using virtual reality while capturing and recording the details of a scanned object for both current and future analysis. The high resolution two dimensional (2-D) tomographic slices, and 3-D virtual reconstructions of 2-D slices with subsequent visualization, can represent a spatially accurate and qualitatively informative rendering of the internal structure of UHPC components poured by individuals who are not necessarily representatives of a commercial producer. Results from this research are expected to reduce the cost of UHPC by modifying the guidelines for on-site pour. This can contribute to wider adoption of UHPC in future projects.

Keywords: X-ray computed tomography (XCT) · Visualization ·
Macroscopic · UHPC · Virtual reality

© The Author(s), under exclusive license to Springer Nature Switzerland AG 2022
J. Y. C. Chen and G. Fragomeni (Eds.): HCII 2022, LNCS 13317, pp. 20–33, 2022.
https://doi.org/10.1007/978-3-031-05939-1_2

1   Introduction

Concrete is the 2nd most consumed material in the world after water. In the last several decades many types of concrete have been developed that include high-strength concrete, ultra-high performance concrete (UHPC), high-early strength concrete, polymer concrete, and fiber-reinforced concrete. These concrete mixes include ingredients such as steel or polypropylene fibers, sophisticated admixtures, and resins (polymers) compared to conventional cement [1–3]. UHPC is an advanced cementitious composite material with exceptionally high strength and durability when compared to the conventional concrete. One of the unique features of UHPC is that it utilizes recycled products such as fly ash and silica fume as supplementary cementitious materials to reduce the portion of hydraulic cement (up to 70%) in the mix. Also, the addition of the steel fibers (Fig. 1) in the UHPC concrete can result in the added ductility in structures.

Fig. 1. Four-point bend testing of UHPC beam samples (left), steel fibers in UHPC (right)

In addition to applications in civil infrastructure such as bridges, the use of novel materials to support the development and qualification of advanced nuclear systems, such as portable microreactors and fission batteries, has become a recent thrust of research within the nuclear energy industry. In addition, use of novel concrete mixes for used fuel disposition, even for those fuel concepts that have not yet been fully vetted for deployment, may be considered if UHPC can provide superior performance in the areas of thermal and radiation resistance, or water impenetrability. New and lightweight shielding technologies for microreactors and fission batteries are areas of significant research interest for the nuclear community [4–7].

There are three different hierarchical structures of concrete materials: 1) microscopic; 2) mesoscopic; and 3) macroscopic. These structures correspond to quantum, materials, and engineering disciplines, respectively (Fig. 2). Use of three-dimensional (3-D) analysis tools such as XCT on concrete has primarily been focused at the microscopic and mesoscopic scales. However, it has been demonstrated in numerous studies that the underlying physics at the microscopic level, particularly with respect to propagation of damage mechanisms and presence of defects due to poor workmanship and quality control, can dominate the failure modes for materials such as concrete.

Issues related to embrittlement, cracking, and void collapse at the macroscopic level can all be traced to fundamental mechanical property analysis at the microscopic level.

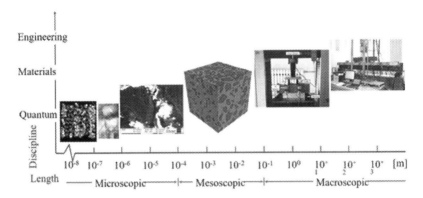

Fig. 2. Hierarchical structure of concrete materials [8]

One of the greater challenges is developing the proper models that can allow for information transfer amongst the three levels of analysis (microscopic, mesoscopic, and macroscopic). Similar to concrete, UHPC is a heterogeneous composite material, and it is likely the resulting mechanical properties from the three structural scales will differ from each other. The most accurate structure that can capture the global behavior/mechanical properties of concrete, including any defects/uncertainty due to quality of workmanship, is the "macroscopic." While previous literature exists for XCT characterization of concrete at the microscopic and mesoscopic structures, including for UHPC blends [9], this research focuses on the XCT of macroscopic structure which is relevant to structural components in civil and critical infrastructure (e.g., beams, walls, columns, slabs). Currently, microscopes are used to view and analyze the samples of macroscopic structure to understand the relationship of the features of interest which is time-consuming and inefficient. Herein, the researchers present a detailed overview outlining how the macroscopic structure of concrete characterized by XCT can be visualized in an immersive environment using virtual reality while capturing and recording the details of a scanned object for both current and future analysis. The high resolution two dimensional (2-D) tomographic slices, and 3-D virtual reconstructions of 2-D slices with subsequent visualization can represent a spatially accurate, and qualitatively informative rendering of the internal component and structure of UHPC. This paper also highlights present key challenges and limitations associated while visualizing the XCT of macroscopic structure in an immersive environment at various stages. Furthermore, we identify where improvements can be made and propose solutions to those existing problems while visualizing macroscopic structure of concrete materials such as UHPC.

2 Background and Related Work

UHPC is a new class of concrete that has been developed in recent decades. Typical ingredients in UHPC are shown in Fig. 3. UHPC offers higher compressive strength (9 times higher), superior mechanical properties, and excellent durability compared to conventional or high-strength concrete (Table 1). Similarly, the permeability for the UHPC is about 100 times less than that of conventional concrete, which is an important measure looking at the durability of the concrete. A summary of the mechanical properties for UHPC and conventional and high-strength concrete is provided in Table 1.

Table 1. Comparison of mechanical properties of UHPC with conventional and high-strength concrete [10].

Property	Normal concrete	High strength concrete	UHPC
Compressive strength	3,000–6,000 psi	6,000–14,000 psi	25,000–33,000 psi
Tensile strength	400–500 psi	-	1,000–3,500 psi
Elastic modulus	2,000–6,000 ksi	4,500–8,000 ksi	8,000–9,000 ksi
Poisson's ratio	0.11–0.21	-	0.19–0.24
Porosity	20–25%	10–15%	2–6%
Chloride penetration	> 2000	500–2000	< 100
Water-cement ratio	0.40–0.70	0.24–0.35	0.14–0.27

Note: 1 ksi = 1000 psi = 6.89 MPa; psi = pound per square inch; ksi = kips per square inch

The advantages associated with UHPC structures include but not limited to: eliminated transverse reinforcing, increased ductility, longer spans, shallower section depths, accelerated construction, and enhanced durability. Due to high shear strength of UHPC, transverse reinforcement (e.g., stirrups) can be completely eliminated in concrete structures which would reduce materials and labor costs. UHPC is a very durable product, and structures employing UHPC are expected to have a much longer service life and require less maintenance than structures built with conventional concrete which are typically designed for 50–75 years of service life.

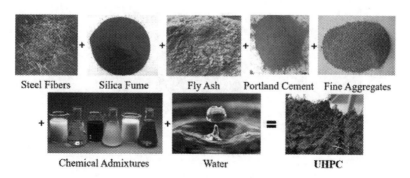

Steel Fibers   Silica Fume   Fly Ash   Portland Cement   Fine Aggregates

Chemical Admixtures   Water   UHPC

Fig. 3. UHPC composition

Cost seems to be the main disadvantage of considering UHPC over conventional concrete. A significant amount of research is currently being carried out on optimizing the use of proprietary and non-proprietary UHPC in civil infrastructure. These include topics such as reducing the thickness or height of new structural members, introducing new optimized structural shapes, and investigating applications of UHPC retrofitting of existing structures.

Piotrowski and Schmidt conducted a life cycle cost analysis of two replacement methods for the Eder bridge in Felsberg, Germany [11]. One method used precast UHPC box girders filled with lightweight concrete. The second method used conventional prestressed concrete bridge members. Although the UHPC had higher initial costs, the researchers predicted the life cycle cost over 100 years would be less for the UHPC bridge. The use of UHPC in highway bridge construction has increased over years in the United States. Figure 4 shows an interactive map of the in-service bridges in the United States that have employed UHPC. Majority of UHPC applications in bridges in the United States have been focused on using UHPC in closure-pour (Fig. 5) between precast/prestressed concrete elements.

Fig. 4. Bridge applications of UHPC in the United States [12]

Fig. 5. Application of UHPC in the closure-pour between precast bridge girders (Photo courtesy of New York State Department of Transportation)

X-ray computed tomography is a non-destructive analysis tool for composites and concrete materials such as UHPC. In recent years, there have been significant advances in XCT, high-performance computing, software algorithms and user-interfaces that communicate complex data from which scanning, and data analysis have benefitted in general. The schematic representation of a typical setup in the laboratory along with the data analysis procedure is presented in Fig. 6. Once the raw data is obtained by using x-rays to penetrate complex composites (e.g., UHPC) in 360-degree view, various state-of-the-art software can be used to process and analyze the images. The resolution achieved using XCT can be considered relatively better than other non-destructive analysis tools because of the high frequency in XCT.

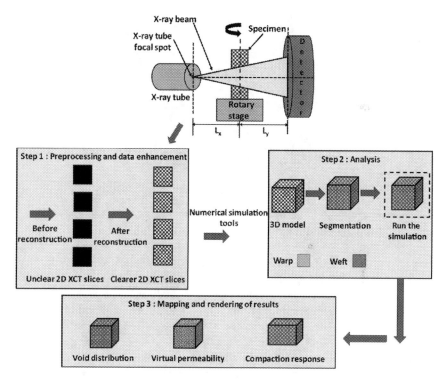

Fig. 6. Visualization of a material using XCT technique [13]

There have been several studies on the application of micro XCT to micro-structure characterization of concrete materials and their cracking process under different loading conditions (e.g., compression, tension). Studies have shown that micro-XCT tests and use of state-of-the-art image-based finite element modeling software could be an effective technique to study internal damage and cracking behavior of a composite material such as concrete [14]. Research has been carried out to investigate the freeze-thaw resistance of UHPC and explore the microstructural evolution of UHPC while undergoing freezing-thawing action. Microstructural observations seem to be a promising method to investigate the deterioration mechanism of the UHPC subjected to the freeze-thaw cycle. Compared to normal concrete, UHPC has a higher freeze-thaw resistance. However, the use of analysis tools such as the mercury intrusion porosimetry (MIP), scanning electron microscopy (SEM), along with XCT are needed to identify and describe the internal cracks and pore structures in the UHPC subjected to freeze-thaw cycle [15–17]. It is found that UHPC has a very dense microstructure, but large amounts of air voids are trapped in UHPC before freeze-thaw cycle. However, after the freeze-thaw cycle, cracks are prone to occur at the interfacial transition zone (ITZ) or the sand-paste interface of the UHPC [9]. The microcracks in plain UHPC after a freeze-thaw cycle is shown in Fig. 7.

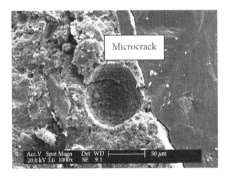

Fig. 7. Microcrack seen in UHPC after freezing-thawing action

3   Experimental Design for Visualization of UHPC

A proprietary UHPC that has been common in North America, Ductal JS1000 produced by Lafarge, has been selected for the experimental study. Ductal JS1000 is reinforced with steel fibers and is claimed by the producer to provide superior performance in terms of abrasion and chemical resistance, freeze-thaw, carbonation, and chloride penetration. The nanometer-sized non-connected pores located throughout UHPC's cementitious matrix is what makes the material attractive for its remarkable imperviousness and durability against adverse conditions. Material properties for Ductal JS1000 can be determined in accordance with ASTM C1856/C1856M-17 *"Standard Practice for Fabricating and Testing Specimens of Ultra-High Performance Concrete"* [18]. The components of Ductal JS1000 are summarized in Table 2. This type of UHPC should be batched in accordance with the Lafarge's Ductal Batching Procedure [19]. Most importantly, high-shear mixtures are recommended by the producer to properly and efficiently mix the UHPC. UHPC is self-consolidating and should not be vibrated to avoid the segregation of steel fibers.

In terms of micro-structure samples of UHPC, there could be models for prediction of mechanical properties from micro-structure, however, the results may not be reliable because the defects in the micro-structure are very hard to scale-up and have high uncertainty. Solid rectangular UHPC beam samples (15 in. × 10 in. × 4 in.) from a single batch shall be prepared as a benchmark specimen to study micro-structure, i.e., fiber distribution and orientation in the mix, and the voids in the mix. Also, a longer rectangular UHPC beam samples (20 in. × 10 in. × 4 in.) shall be prepared to have a cold joint in a longitudinal direction from one or two batches.

Table 2. Components of Ductal JS1000

Item	Properties
Premix (dark grey)	Pre-blended cement, sand, ground quartz, silica fume
Liquid admixture	High range water reducer
Steel fibers	0.008 in. diameter, 0.5 in. long, tensile strength > 290 ksi
Water	-

Note: 1 in. = 25.4 mm; 1 ksi = 6.89 MPa; ksi = kips per square inch

Meso-scale samples provide better results, but still fall short of reliable prediction for describing the macrostructure. These samples shall be extracted by slicing the 15 in. × 10 in. × 4 in. benchmark beam sample and 20 in. × 10 in. × 4 in. beam sample with a longitudinal cold joint or the potential defect plane. The visual representative of the samples is shown in Fig. 8.

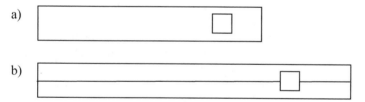

Fig. 8. UHPC samples a) solid rectangular beam, b) rectangular beam with a longitudinal cold joint

The beam samples should also be sliced for visualization. The beams can be sliced using a concrete saw to have a uniform slice for better comparison. There is not always a smooth shear surface nor some of the conventional concrete saws have the capability to obtain uniform samples; slices can also be obtained by carrying out the four-point bend test to break the beam samples as per Fig. 1. The samples then can be visualized in an immersive environment using virtual reality while capturing and recording the details of a scanned object for both current and future analysis. High resolution two dimensional (2-D) tomographic slices, and 3-D virtual reconstructions of 2-D slices and the subsequent visualization provides a spatially accurate, and qualitatively informative rendering of the internal component and structure of the concrete.

4   Challenges in Visualizing UHPC

One of the main objectives of this research is to investigate and explore the challenges of visualizing the macroscopic structure of UHPC and use visual representations of data and interaction techniques to gain a deeper understanding of potential defects in large-scale samples – partial or more complete – than would have been possible had it been explored in a non-immersive environment. To learn more about how to explore these challenges, the research proposes a UHPC slicing experiment as discussed in the previous section. This experimental design helps to identify the challenges currently posed for visualizing CT scanned slices of UHPC. This section attempts to summarize a number of challenges that need to be resolved for better results in the field of visualization of the UHPC macroscopic structure.

4.1   Porosity

One of the most popular applications of CT scan for concrete materials is porosity analysis: it refers to identifying porous spaces or voids in material, qualitatively visualizing, and analyzing the spatial distribution of porosity. Qualitative visualization of porosity in 2D slice images is simple and requires only basic (static) image contrast which has been developed several years ago and also used constantly [20]. Quantitative analysis which involves microstructural parameters requires selecting porous spaces by segmenting the image, usually using some form of threshold to sketch the boundary between the pores and the material. Furthermore, quantitative analysis can be used to measure volume, area, sphericity, and other parameters for each void space and analyze this statistical information of pores [21]. On-site mixing, quality control, and qualification tests are important considerations for pouring UHPC. If the correct procedure by the UHPC producer is not followed, the material will not have the specified and desired mechanical properties and durability. The aforementioned items have been the main drivers behind the high cost of UHPC. Therefore, it is important to investigate how the macroscopic structure of UHPC from large on-site pores compares to that of laboratory microscopic or meso-scale specimens. Currently, visualization of the macroscopic structure of UHPC using the CT scan in a two-dimensional display platform lack the support of visualizing all the diverse macrostructural parameters in combination and individually to discover and investigate the properties of the materials.

4.2   Composition Identification

Another important task in analyzing the macrostructure of the UHPC is identification of composition and components of the structure. The identification task is straightforward if there is information available regarding what constituents are involved in the mix, however, if the constituents are unknown, it requires image segmentation to accurately outline the materials and assign them. It is important to highlight that the X-ray CT scan does not allow for chemical analysis and the brightness that is used to differentiate the ingredients is a combination of the atomic mass and the density of the materials. While comparing multiple materials, the grey values represented during the visualization might be similar and the segmentation might be prone to errors. Therefore, there is a need for a high-quality scan and visualizing the information in a high-resolution platform to differentiate between the materials that are being used in the concrete. Currently, suppliers of UHPC in North America have proprietary UHPC materials that are pre-bagged with "secret" ingredients. They require a direct supervision of UHPC pour and testing by their personnel on-site for a designated project. This creates high costs. For instance, the cost of UHPC for pouring some recent bridge joints in the United States has been between $13,000-$20,000 per cubic yard. In contrast, high strength concrete costs would be between $800-$1,200 per cubic yard. The ability to compare, analyze and understand materials used across the different specimens in the macroscopic structure of UHPC poured under the direct supervision of a representative of the supplier and another person (e.g., contractor or trained concrete technician) against the microscopic and mesoscale might reduce the costs tremendously.

4.3   Data Generation

X-ray CT scan has become a mainstream tool in the field of concrete and each tomography of the UHPC generates large datasets. As a result, huge amounts of data have become available. Because this data is frequently collected for very specific purposes, the majority of the information contained within it remains untapped. Sharing this data across institutions, laboratories and researchers would allow for further investigation by other institutions; UHPC has a very high compressive strength which translates to a considerably high shear (slicing) strength compared to conventional or high strength concrete. For the macroscopic structure, a large UHPC sample will have to be sliced into pieces and the use of an X-ray CT scan would generate a large number of datasets. Therefore, sharing and visualization of these large datasets still is a challenge to the researchers. The researchers still lack the tools and interaction techniques to share and collaborate for better understanding and novel discoveries from large and complex datasets.

4.4   Resolution

The smallest interval correctly depicted in the image representation of the X-ray CT scan is referred to as resolution. Micron-scale image resolution enables accurate identification of individual fibers/materials in concrete. Spatial (voxel) resolution suggests the smallest sub-volume of the object captured in a tomogram. To visualize the individual fiber in a 3D space voxel width needs to be smaller than the fiber diameter. When the intricate details of the fibers for analysis are essential for instance shape of the fiber the voxel resolution must be adequately small to grab related curvatures and sharp edges. This specific requirement of spatial (voxel) resolution to be minimum for better visualization of the fibers in the specimens is still a challenge to the researchers.

4.5   Noise and Artifacts

The nature of the X-ray CT scan can introduce random noise while interacting with the UHPC specimens. More noise is frequently introduced into the detector and during image reconstruction. Although the signal-to-noise ratio can be increased by increasing the number of projections, exposure time, source of X-rays, or voxel size, this has an impact on the resolution. Furthermore, artifacts that are noisy artificial features inserted into images representation of the X-ray CT scan even though they are not present in the specimen. While artifacts are frequently insignificant in qualitative interpretations, they have a substantial impact on quantitative studies and can decrease the efficiency of the discovery. There still is a challenge in finding a balance between the noise and artifacts in the image representation of the X-ray scan of the macroscopic structure of UHPC.

5 Discussion

Though several research works have been conducted in the field of micro and meso-scale specimen of UHPC however, it still lacks investigation in the area of the macrostructure. The previous section describes the challenges associated with investigating and visualizing the macrostructure of UHPC. In addition, majority of the studies conducted on UHPC have been limited for applications in civil infrastructure. The availability of data/literature on UHPC at any structure level for application in critical infrastructure (e.g., after irradiation tests) can be considered very few to none.

Fig. 9. Example of immersive virtual environment (left) CAVE (right) virtual reality headset

There is some limited literature on microscopic or meso-scale structure of UHPC after thermal tests. The current meso-scale or microscopic model for thermal analysis does not consider moisture content, thermochemical behavior, variation in density and porosity from incorporation of steel fibers. However, study should be conducted on macroscopic structure change (e.g., due to fire, thermal heating/cooling etc.). This section discusses the use of 3D immersive environment and interaction techniques to provide potential solutions to solve some of the aforementioned challenges.

It is essential to investigate the intrinsic porosity of UHPC materials and the crucial role these pores can play in their mechanical and transport characteristics. Furthermore, the significant relationships between pore size distributions and concrete strength and transport qualities need to be analyzed. To understand the characteristics of the pores, quantification is critical. Visualizing the pores in UHPC using a 2D display platform might be a challenge due to the properties of the pore for instance volumes, size, and distribution. The complex structure of pores, materials, and cracks in UHPC might clutter the view of the scans in a 2D dimension. Therefore, volume visualization technique can be used in a 3D immersive environment (see Fig. 9) to support visualization and interaction for novel discoveries. With the X-ray scan of the macrostructure of UHPC, the scans can be used to develop 3D images to create pore networks. There might be a requirement for upscaling from the normally imaged volume to larger domains which might require the building of a statistically representative network of pores. This 3D visualization can support visualization and identifying the geometrical and topological characteristics of the pores and the network they are connected to. Furthermore, the availability of interaction techniques in a 3D immersive environment for instance slicing, clipping, and filtering can aid in interactive visualization of the macrostructure of the UHPC samples.

It is also essential to identify the composition of constituent materials in the UHPC samples. The 3D visualization coupled with the high-quality scan can be used to color-code the different materials based on the density. The absolute density determination of materials is anticipated to be beneficial, for example, in characterizing aggregates or bitumen independently. Also, the use of 3D interaction techniques like filtering, extracting components option might help to differentiate the constituents and identify various materials that have been used to develop the macrostructure of the UHPC sample.

The data generated using the X-ray CT scan can be large and complex. Therefore, there is a necessity for a tool to visualize large data without having any cognitive load while visualizing these complex datasets. To visualize the large and complex datasets, the use of a 3D immersive environment has shown to be more effective in comparison to the 2D display platforms. The 3D immersive environment can be connected to supercomputers or data servers for processing and analysis of the data and the visualization can be conducted using the 3D immersive environment. Furthermore, there is a need for sharing and collaborative visualization which might also help to overcome the challenge of the sharing of datasets across the network. The use of a 3D immersive environment to develop a remote collaboration that supports visualization of datasets in real-time while having the users either in the same geographical or different location. Also, the raytracing algorithm can be used to render the dataset such that the problem to load large datasets which might have computational and memory load can be lowered.

Local, non-linear techniques, in addition to low-pass filtering, can be employed to denoise the scanned images, as can an edge smoothing algorithm. Furthermore, anisotropic diffusion can be used to smooth images, ideally in weak gradient directions, without blurring the images. In block-matching, 3D algorithms can be utilized to represent scanned pictures using nonlocal patches. Furthermore, because it conducts weighted averages over similar pixels, non-local means filtering can be utilized to retain both edges and textures when producing the scanned images.

6 Conclusions

UHPC is an advanced material that has been gaining popularity for applications in civil infrastructure in North America. One of the main disadvantages of UHPC is the higher cost associated with qualification tests and supervision of the entire on-site mixing and pouring process solely by the representatives of the UHPC producer. This paper presents an overview of how the macroscopic structure of UHPC poured by trained concrete technicians from public or private entities, and defined by XCT, can be viewed in an immersive environment. The immersive environment is utilizing virtual reality while collecting and storing the minutiae of a scanned item for both current and future study. High resolution two-dimensional (2-D) tomographic slices, as well as 3-D virtual reconstructions of 2-D slices, can represent a spatially accurate and qualitatively informative portrayal of the internal component and structure of the concrete. This research also identifies challenges and limitations for preparation of large-scale UHPC samples and observations of XCT of macroscopic structure in an immersive environment at different phases. The research presented in this paper is part of an on-going research at Idaho State University.

References

1. Graybeal, B.: Behavior of ultra-high performance concrete connections between precast bridge deck elements. In: Proceedings, Concrete Bridge Conference, Phoenix, Arizona (2010)
2. Graybeal, B.: Fatigue response of an ultra-high performance concrete field-cas bridge deck connection. In: Proceedings, 2011 Transportation Research Board Conference, Washington D.C. (2011)
3. Li, M., Lim, I., Sawab, J., Mo, Y.L.: Self-Consolidating Ultra-High-Performance Concrete for Small Modular Reactor Construction, Transactions, SMiRT-23, pp. 10–14. Manchester, United Kingdom (2015)
4. Sawab, J. Lim, I., Mo, Y.L., Li, M., Wang, H., Guimares, M.: Ultra-High-Performance Concrete and Advanced Manufacturing Methods for Modular Construction, Summary Report, Project FY-ID 13–5282 (2016)
5. William, K., Xi, Y., Naus, D., Graves, H.: A Review of the Effects of Radiation on Microstructure and Properties of Concretes Used in Nuclear Power Plants, NUREG/CR-7171: ORNL/TM-2013/263 (2013)
6. American Nuclear Society: American National Standard Specification for Radiation Shielding Materials, ANSI/ANS-6.4.2–2006 (2016)
7. LaBrier, D., Mashal, M., Ebrahimpour, A., Mondal, K., Eidelpes, E., Johnson, D.: Evaluation of Novel High-Performance Concrete for Utilization in the Nuclear Industry. American Nuclear Society (ANS) Winter Meeting, Washington D.C., United States (2021)
8. Ren, W.Y.: In-situ X-ray Computed Tomography Characterisation and Mesoscale Image Based Fracture Modelling of Concrete, Doctor's Degree Thesis. The University of Manchester, UK (2015)
9. Gu, C., Sun, W., Guo, L., Wang, Q., Liu, J., Yang, Y., Shi, T.: Investigation of microstructural damage in ultrahigh-performance concrete under freezing-thawing action, Adv. Mater. Sci. Eng. (2018). https://doi.org/10.1155/2018/3701682
10. Ahlborn, T.M., Mission, D.L., Peuse, E. J., Gilbertson, C.G.: Ultra-High Performance Concrete for Michigan Bridges – Material Performance, Michigan Department of Transportation Report CSD-2008–11, Michigan (2008)

11. Piotrowski, S., Schmidt, M.: Life cycle cost analysis of a UHPC-bridge on example of two bridge refurbishment designs. In: Proceedings of Hipermat 2012 3rd International Symposium on UHPC and Nanotechnology for High Performance Construction Materials. Kassel University Press, Kassel, Germany, pp. 957–964 (2012)

12. Turner-Fairbank Highway Research Center: Deployments: Interactive Map, United States Department of Transportation Federal Highway Administration, McLean, Virginia (2022)

13. Naresh, K., Khan, K.A., Umer, R., Cantwell, W.J.: The use of X-ray computed tomography for design and process modeling of aerospace composites: a review. J. Materials Design **190**, 108553 (2020). https://doi.org/10.1016/j.matdes.2020.108553

14. Wenyuan, R., Zhenjun, Y., Rajneesh, S., Samuel, A.M., Paul, M.M.: Three-Dimensional In Situ SCT Characterisation and FE Modelling of Cracking in Concrete. Research Article, Hindawi, (2018) https://doi.org/10.1155/2018/3856584

15. Jacobsen, S., Marchand, J., Hornain, H.: SEM observations of the microstructure of frost deteriorated and self-healed concretes. Cement Concr. Res. **25**(8), 1781–1790 (1995)

16. Vegas, I., Urreta, J., Frias, M., Garcia, R.: Freeze-thaw resistance of blended cements containing calcined paper sludge. Constr. Build. Mater. **23**(8), 2862–2868 (2009)

17. Promentilla, M.A.B., Sugiyama, T.: X-ray micro-tomography of mortars exposed to freezing-thawing action. J. Adv. Concr. Technol. **8**(2), 97–111 (2010)

18. ASTM: Standard Practice for Fabricating and Testing Specimens of Ultra-High Performance Concrete. ASTM C1856/C1856M-17. West Conshohocken. PA (2017)

19. Lafarge North America: Product Data Sheet JS1000, chrome-extension. https://www.ductal.com/en

20. Rattanasak, U., Kendall, K.: Pore structure of cement/pozzolan composites by X-ray microtomography. Cem. Concr. Res. **35**(4), 637–640 (2005)

21. Ponikiewski, T., Gołaszewski, J., Rudzki, M., Bugdol, M.: Determination of steel fibres distribution in self-compacting concrete beams using X-ray computed tomography. Arch. Civil Mech. Eng. **15**(2), 558–568 (2014). https://doi.org/10.1016/j.acme.2014.08.008

Photographic Composition Guide for Photo Acquisition on Augmented Reality Glasses

Wonwoo Lee[✉], Jaewoong Lee, Deokho Kim, Gunill Lee, Byeongwook Yoo, Hwangpil Park, Sunghoon Yim, Taehyuk Kwon, and Jiwon Jeong

Samsung Research, Seoul 06765, South Korea
{wonw.lee,jw84.lee,deokho16.kim,gunill.lee,byeongw.yoo,hwangp.park,
sunghoon.yim,taehyuk.kwon,jiwon.jeong}@samsung.com

Abstract. Capturing meaningful moments by using cameras is a major application of Augmented Reality Glasses (AR Glasses). Taking photos with head-mounted cameras of AR Glasses bring a new photo acquisition experience to users because there are no viewfinders conventional cameras have. Users may experience difficulties to figure out the region the head-mounted camera will capture on AR Glasses. To address this issue, we propose a photographic composition guide for AR Glasses. The proposed method analyzes video streams from the camera and automatically determine the image region that has a high aesthetic quality score. Photos taken from the recommended position result in a better photographic composition. Our method achieved 4.03 in Mean-Opinion-Score (MOS) test, demonstrating that our method corresponds to human's expectation on aesthetic quality of photos.

Keywords: Augmented Reality Glasses · Photographic composition · Deep neural network

1 Introduction

Taking photos in a daily life sharing the with other people is a major application of smartphone cameras. Millions of users share their photos in social networks like Instagram[1] every day. Such a trend will continue with Augmented Reality Glasses (AR Glasses), a next-generation mobile device too. In conventional photo acquisition process on smartphones, users see a scene to capture through the display of a smartphone, decide a good photographic composition, and take a shot of the scene. Users of AR Glasses may expect similar user experience as they have done via smartphones. However, there are several differences between the experience on smartphones and AR Glasses.

Firstly, the display of AR Glasses is transparent and there may not be a preview of what to be taken because overlaying video on a transparent display through which a user see the real world is visually annoying. Secondly, there are

---

[1] https://www.instagram.com.

© The Author(s), under exclusive license to Springer Nature Switzerland AG 2022
J. Y. C. Chen and G. Fragomeni (Eds.): HCII 2022, LNCS 13317, pp. 34–44, 2022.
https://doi.org/10.1007/978-3-031-05939-1_3

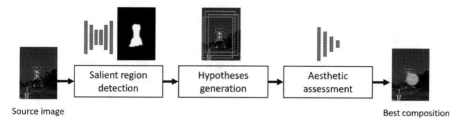

Fig. 1. Overview of our approach.

misalignment between the camera and the eyes. It is because not only they have different field-of-view but also the head-mounted camera sees the scene from a different viewpoint that is apart from the eyes. Consequently, it becomes difficult for a user to make decision on photographic composition on AR Glasses.

In this paper, we propose a photographic composition guide for AR Glasses in this paper. Our method analyzes video streams from a camera preview, and proposes the best position to take a photo with a good photographic compositions. Our method automatically identifies meaningful contents in an input image and provides photographic composition guide, i.e., a recommendation of position to take a photo, by evaluating aesthetic quality of image regions containing the identified contents. Our photographic composition guide is displayed as a yellow dot on the device screen, so that a user moves his/her head to capture the scene.

This paper is organized as follows. We review the existing researches on aesthetic assessment in Sect. 2. We present the details of our approach in Sect. 3 and experimental results in Sect. 4. We provide conclusions and future work in Sect. 5.

2   Related Work

Image aesthetic assessment have been actively researched as deep learning-based image analysis becomes popular. Early researches on aesthetic assessment have relied on implicit representations computed by deep neural network. A neural network learns an implicit representation of aesthetic score space by observing entire image [4,5,10].

Although deep features are better than hand-crafted feature representations, aesthetic assessment is still hard to generalize because it is highly subjective. Recent researches have focused on the contents in an image because aesthetic quality is closely related to the contents and their compositions [2,8]. On the other hand, there have been efforts to find meaningful information related to photographic compositions, such as dominant lines, and predict types of compositions directly from photos [1].

As a commercial solution of photographic composition guide, Samsung's Galaxy-S series smartphones provide a service called Shot Suggestion[2] in their

---

[2] https://www.samsung.com/global/galaxy/what-is/shot-suggestions/.

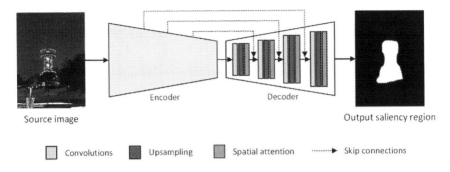

Source image   Output saliency region

☐ Convolutions   ▨ Upsampling   ▨ Spatial attention   ┈┈▶ Skip connections

Fig. 2. Architecture of salient region detection network.

camera App. The service uses artificial intelligence to analyze images and recommend a position where the camera moves to take a good photo, but it seems not considering photographic composition and tends to locate objects in a scene at the center of a photo.

3   Approach

Figure 1 shows the overview of our approach. Our method analyzes video streams from a camera preview, and proposes the best position to take a photo with a good photographic compositions. We find regions of meaningful objects from a preview by salient region detection. Then, we generate multiple hypotheses of boxes as region of interest to take a photo. Finally, aesthetic quality scores are measured over the image regions cropped to the hypotheses and we choose the crop box with the highest score.

3.1   Salient Region Detection

Salient region detection identifies the regions of what is considered as meaningful in an image. We use a neural network using encoder-decoder style, similar to U-Net [6]. Figure 2 shows a brief architecture of our network for salient region detection.

We adopt MobileNet-V2 as our encoder network because it has a good balance between the performance and computational complexity on mobile device platforms [7]. We take the output of *block_12_add* layer as encoded feature, which has 1/16 of the input image size. We also take the outputs of *expanded_conv_project_BN*, *block_2_add* and *block_5_add* layers[3] to transfer multi-scale features to the decoder network through skip connections.

The decoder network has 4 decode blocks. Each decode block consists of convolutions on lower resolution features, upsampling lower level features to

---

[3] The names of layers follow MobileNet-V2 implementation in Keras library (https:// keras.io/).

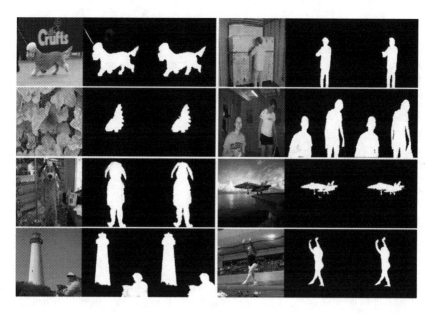

Fig. 3. Salient region detection results; from the left source image, detected salient regions, and ground-truth.

higher level, and spatial attention on the upsampled features. Upsampling is conducted by simple bilinear resize followed by convolutions. Spatial attention [3] refines the upsampled features so that the decoder network focuses more on critical contents in spatial dimensions. We use Inverted Residual Block [7] in all convolutions because it is efficient to carry saliency information in a reduced memory footprint.

The network is trained by minimizing the loss computed from Structural loss L_s [13] and Relaxed F-measure L_f [6]. Total loss is the linear combination of the two losses,

$$TotalLoss = w_s L_s(S, S^*) + w_f L_f(S, S^*)$$

where S and S^* are estimated and ground-truth salient regions. We set w_s and w_f to 1.0 and 2.0, respectively. Total loss is minimized by Adam optimizer with $\beta_1 = 0.9$ and $\beta_2 = 0.999$ and the learning rate is decayed from $5e-4$ to $1e-5$ exponentially in every 6000 steps. Training typically converges after $1,000k$ iterations.

We achieved mean absolute error 0.053 on DUTS-TE dataset [12], which is comparable to the existing researches [13]. It has only 0.5M parameters and runs very fast on modern mobile devices, so that it does not cause delay in photo acquisition process. Figure 3 depicts that our network successfully retrieves regions of interest from input images.

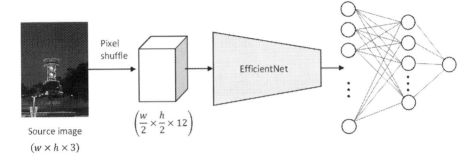

Fig. 4. Architecture of aesthetic quality assessment network.

3.2   Aesthetic Quality Assessment

Given a salient region mask and source image, we generate multiple crops of the original image to find high aesthetic quality and better compositions. To generate hypotheses of crop boxes, we adopt *Center* and *Rule of Thirds*, which are the most popular among many photographic composition rules. *Center* place the object of interest at the center of a photo, while *Rule of Thirds* generally align it to 1/3 in horizontal.

Given one or more salient regions, the crop boxes are generated around the salient regions so that they are located either at the center or 1/3 of the image according to the rules we use. In case that there is no salient region or the entire image region has a high saliency score, we use the pre-defined rules to generate the hypotheses. We set a moving window with the size of 60% of the image size and move it by 10% of the image with and height in horizontal and vertical, respectively. This results in 25 crop box locations.

The resulting cropped images are fed into our aesthetic quality evaluation network and we choose the one with the highest score as the final proposal to the user. We use EfficientNet-B0 [11] as a backend, which is followed by two fully-connected layers with 128 and 64 dimensions. The output of the network is a quality score ranging from $[0, 1]$. Figure 4 shows architecture of our aesthetic score evaluation network.

For training, we built a pseudo ground-truth dataset by using a pre-trained network [5] as reference. We collected images $47k$ images from *Pixabay*[4] and evaluate their aesthetic score through the reference network. To increase diversity of datasets, we apply geometric and pixel-wise color augmentations. The evaluation results are used as our ground-truth.

---

[4] https://pixabay.com/.

Fig. 5. Typical failure example of salient region detection; (left) source image, (center) detected salient regions, (right) ground-truth. The pattern in the background is dominant so that salient region detection failed to identify people in the photo.

As the loss function, we use mean-squared error L_s and pairwise-squared error L_p defined as

$$L_s = \frac{1}{N} \sum_{i}^{N} (s_i - s_i^*)^2 \tag{1}$$

$$L_p = \frac{2}{N(N-1)} \sum_{i}^{N} \sum_{j,j>i}^{N} ((s_i - s_j) - (s_i^* - s_j^*))^2, \tag{2}$$

where s_i and s_i^* are the predicted and the ground-truth scores, respectively. Pairwise-squared loss keeps the distances among training samples unchanged, so that the learned aesthetic score space remains similar to that of the reference network.

Total loss is computed as scaled sum of both losses. We set α to 0.5 in our experiments.

$$TotalLoss = \alpha L_s + (1 - \alpha)L_p \tag{3}$$

We set the initial learning rate to 0.002 and it is decayed for every 8000 steps with batch size of 32. The network typically converges after $1000k$ iterations. We use an input size of 224×224, The input image is further resized to 112×112 by applying Pixel Shuffle [9] to run inference faster and avoid delay in photo acquisition process. Pixel Shuffle transforms pixels in a 2×2 spatial block to channel dimension so that the spatial dimension is reduced without losing information.

3.3   Scene Context Identification

Photos have different characteristics depending on what they contain in their frames. Some subjects are important regardless of their size in a photo so that we need to keep them in the final output. For example, faces are important contents in a photo of a group of people although they occupy relatively small regions in the photo. On the other hand, there are photos that have no important contents or salient regions, e.g., a scene with plain textures and repetitive patterns. Saliency detection is tend to fail with such images, or resulting saliency information is not very useful as shown in Fig. 5.

Fig. 6. Scene categories; from the left *Scenery*, *Object*, *People*, and *None*.

To address such issues, we run scene context classification before salient region detection. A typical classification network based on MobileNet-v2 [7] is used to classify photos to 4 categories, i.e., *Scenery*, *Object*, *People*, and *None*. Figure 6 shows typical examples of them. We apply different strategies depending on classification results as follows.

- *Scenery*: Photos in Scenery class contain landscape scenes where all the contents inside images are important. We skip salient region detection and consider the entire image region as salient, i.e., filling the saliency mask with 1.
- *Object*: There are one or more objects and focused in a photo. In this case, we try to find salient regions considered as important in the image.
- *People*: A person or a group of people are captured in a photo and their faces are detected. We regard the regions of detected faces as salient regions without salient region detection.
- *None*: There are no physical objects or humans in a photo, e.g., plain or repetitive textures. In this case, we skip the entire recommendation process and leave the photo unmodified.

4   Experimental Results

We implemented our method on a smartphone platform to simulate AR Glasses environment. We used Tensorflow library[5] to implement deep neural networks for salient region detection and aesthetic quality assessment. The entire recommendation procedure takes about 110 ms on Samsung Galaxy S21 Ultra.

We evaluated qualitative performance of our method through Mean Opinion Score (MOS) tests. The purpose of MOS tests is how users feel about the recommended positions which they will see on the display of AR Glasses. Thus, we asked 10 subjects to evaluate how good the recommended locations are, instead of asking to evaluate the photos taken from the original and recommended positions. In our MOS test, the subjects rated the recommendations in discrete 5 scale; (1) Bad, (2) Poor, (3) Fair, (4) Good, (5) Excellent, as show in Fig. 7. We achieved MOS score of 4.03, which proves that our photographic composition recommendation corresponds to human expectation on aesthetic quality.

---

[5] https://www.tensorflow.org.

Fig. 7. Web interface for mean opinion score tests.

Figure 8 shows photos taken at the original and proposed positions on the left and right, respectively. The red lines represents the center and 1/3 and 2/3 of the image. As depicted in Fig. 8, target objects in the scene are relocated so that the photo has better photographic compositions. In Fig. 8(a) and (b), dominant objects are moved to center, while the ones in Fig. 8(c), (d), and (e) are aligned at 1/3 of the image region, keeping the *Rule of Thirds*. In Fig. 8(f), there is a person surrounded by several objects. In this case, the face of a person is detected in the scene context identification, so that our method focus on the human rather than the other objects in the photo. Finally, the person is located at the 1/3 of the photo taken from the recommended position. If we rely on saliency only, the objects will be dominant salient regions and our method will fail to align the person with a good composition.

Fig. 8. Photos taken before (left) and after (right) photographic composition recommendation; (a)(b) subjects are located at the center; (c)(d)(e) subjects are aligned with 1/3 locations; (f) thanks to face detection, the human is considered as a major contents, rather than the objects around it

5   Conclusions

In this paper, we proposed a photographic composition guide for Augmented Reality Glasses, where view-inconsistency between the camera and human eyes exists. Our method generates a recommendation to move a user's head to take photos with better quality by combining saliency detection and aesthetic quality evaluation. As we demonstrated, the proposed approach helps users to capture photos with improved quality, which corresponds to human perceptions. Currently our implementation and results are tested on smartphones and it requires more validation on the AR Glasses environment. We will continue our research in this direction as AR Glasses hardware is deployed in the market.

References

1. Lee, J.T., Kim, H.U., Lee, C., Kim, C.S.: Photographic composition classification and dominant geometric element detection for outdoor scenes. J. Vis. Commun. Image Represent. **55**, 91–105 (2018)
2. Liu, D., Puri, R., Kamath, N., Bhattacharya, S.: Composition-aware image aesthetics assessment. In: Proceedings of the IEEE/CVF Winter Conference on Applications of Computer Vision (WACV) (2020)
3. Liu, J., Zhang, W., Tang, Y., Tang, J., Wu, G.: Residual feature aggregation network for image super-resolution. In: IEEE Conference on Computer Vision and Pattern Recognition, pp. 2356–2365 (2020)
4. Mai, L., Jin, H., Liu, F.: Composition-preserving deep photo aesthetics assessment. In: IEEE Conference on Computer Vision and Pattern Recognition, pp. 497–506 (2016)
5. Murray, N., Marchesotti, L., Perronnin, F.: AVA: a large-scale database for aesthetic visual analysis. In: IEEE Conference on Computer Vision and Pattern Recognition, pp. 2408–2415 (2012)
6. Ronneberger, O., Fischer, P., Brox, T.: U-Net: convolutional networks for biomedical image segmentation. In: Medical Image Computing and Computer-Assisted Intervention, MICCAI 2015, May 2015 (2015)
7. Sandler, M., Howard, A., Zhu, M., Zhmoginov, A., Chen, L.C.: MobileNetV2: inverted residuals and linear bottlenecks. In: IEEE Conference on Computer Vision and Pattern Recognition, pp. 4510–4520 (2018)
8. She, D., Lai, Y.K., Yi, G., Xu, K.: Composition-aware image aesthetics assessment. In: IEEE Conference on Computer Vision and Pattern Recognition, pp. 8475–8484 (2021)
9. Shi, W., et al.: Real-time single image and video super-resolution using an efficient sub-pixel convolutional neural network. In: IEEE Conference on Computer Vision and Pattern Recognition, pp. 1874–1883 (2016)
10. Talebi, H., Milanfar, P.: NIMA: neural image assessment. IEEE Trans. Image Process. **27**(8), 3998–4011 (2018)
11. Tan, M., Le, Q.: EfficientNet: rethinking model scaling for convolutional neural networks. In: Proceedings of the 36th International Conference on Machine Learning, pp. 6105–6114 (2019)

12. Wang, L., et al.: Learning to detect salient objects with image-level supervision. In: IEEE Conference on Computer Vision and Pattern Recognition, pp. 3796–3805 (2017)
13. Wei, J., Wang, S., Huang, Q.: F^{3}net: fusion, feedback and focus for salient object detection. Proc. AAAI Conf. Artif. Intell. **34**(07), 12321–12328 (2020)

Method to Create a Metaverse Using Smartphone Data

Daehee Park, Jeong Min Kim, Jingi Jung, and Saemi Choi$^{(\boxtimes)}$

Samsung Research, Seoul 06765, Republic of Korea
saemi1.choi@samsung.com

Abstract. With the development of internet technology, several IT companies and users have become interested in virtual worlds, called metaverses. However, one of the main problems for a metaverse is the number of resources required to develop it. To reduce the burden of high computing power and other related resources, we propose a method that uses mobile phone functions and data to generate a personal virtual space as there is still a research gap in this area. In this study, we propose a method to intuitively generate a personal virtual space using smartphone data. We propose the development of a new type of metaverse application using the photo data saved on a smartphone. We hypothesized that using the new metaverse application induces more happiness and excitement than using the smartphone gallery application to view memorable photos. To evaluate the new metaverse application, we measured the emotional responses of users and compared the two applications. The results indicate that using the new metaverse application results in higher happiness and excitement.

Keywords: Metaverse · Smartphones

1 Introduction

With the development of internet technology, several IT companies and users have become interested in virtual worlds. Virtual worlds are regarded as persistent online computer-generated environments wherein multiple users in remote physical locations can interact in real time for work or play [1]. As various manufacturers have developed VR devices, and their functions and visual quality have improved, interest in virtual worlds has also increased. The concept of virtual worlds has been labeled metaverse. The word metaverse is a portmanteau of the prefix "meta" (meaning "beyond") and the suffix "verse" (shorthand for "universe"). Thus, it literally means a universe beyond the physical world [1]. Metaverse has become a popular topic, and many IT companies focus on developing virtual worlds, called metaverses, to provide users with a more innovative daily life. Facebook CEO Mark Zuckerberg was interviewed by the Verge about Facebook's future strategy. He emphasized that "Facebook would strive to build a maximalist, interconnected set of experiences straight out of sci-fi — a world known as the metaverse" [2]. In addition, the COVID-19 pandemic has changed our lives. We are required to avoid gathering in the same area and maintain social distancing. This accelerates the transformation of our society and development of technologies for the metaverse [2]. Doinisio et al. insisted that four features should be considered as the

© The Author(s), under exclusive license to Springer Nature Switzerland AG 2022
J. Y. C. Chen and G. Fragomeni (Eds.): HCII 2022, LNCS 13317, pp. 45–57, 2022.
https://doi.org/10.1007/978-3-031-05939-1_4

main components of the metaverse: realism, ubiquity, interoperability, and scalability [1]. To correspond to Doinisio et al.'s suggestions, it is necessary that developers possess high computing power and several types of data to generate a metaverse. To reduce the burden of high computing power and other related resources, we propose a method that uses mobile phone functions and data to generate a personal virtual space. There is still a research gap in the use of mobile phone functions and data to create a personal virtual space. In this study, we propose a method to intuitively generate a personal virtual space using a smartphone.

Fig. 1. Example of a personal virtual space (our creation)

To generate metaverse data by using smartphone data, we first defined the data that are applicable for generating the personal virtual space, by using work domain analysis (WDA) [3]. By conducting WDA using smartphone data, we found that photos, diaries, and GPS data are suitable for developing a private virtual space. We believe that a personal space developed using these data can be helpful for memory recall and provide memorable feelings. Second, we developed a personal virtual space by applying various machine learning techniques. In general, we focused on extracting meaningful keywords from noisy geographic information. In addition, we applied scene recognition to compensate for the weaknesses of noisy data. The extracted meaningful keywords were used to create a metaverse. Third, we developed a prototype based on the results for meaningful keywords using Unity (Fig. 1). The prototype indicates that the user can create a personal space based on the geographical data from the photos and diaries. For example, if the user possesses photos related to London, the personal space background is created as London, and some landmarks of London, such as Big Ben, are shown. Users can add more artifacts to their personal virtual space and share the space with friends. Finally, we conducted a case study to measure the user's affection level when using the new metaverse application. A self-assessment manikin (SAM) was used [4].

2   Application of Various Characteristics of Metaverse

Before we developed a method to create a metaverse using mobile phone data, we conducted various literature surveys to determine the core values of the metaverse. Through these surveys, we found that when researchers and commercial companies consider various approaches, the metaverse has the following characteristics compared to traditional media: interaction, immersion, and personalization. We focused on finding methods for maximizing these characteristics to provide an enhanced virtual experience for users.

The first characteristic of the metaverse is interaction. The metaverse is regarded as a combination of tight integration, interaction, and intertwining of the real and virtual worlds [5]. It is necessary to combine various new technologies to create novel internet applications and social forms [5]. According to Ning et al. (2021), it can be expected that the boundary between virtual reality (VR), augmented reality (AR), and mixed reality (MR) will not be concrete in the future, and the focus will be on more fusion products [5]. With the current technology, VR, AR, and MR are regarded as the primary interaction technologies that can be adopted by the metaverse to create a highly interactive virtual world for users [5]. Various digital media platforms have been developed to enhance interactivity. The level of interactivity has been increasing in texts, photos, and video clips. Video games are the most interactive digital content currently available [5]. The metaverse borrows multiple ideas and technologies from video games, making the metaverse the most interactive digital media so far. The increased interactivity of the metaverse provides advantages for several applications that require mutual communication. Education is one of the best areas that the metaverse can take advantage of. Schlemmer and Backes have already focused on the potential of the metaverse in interactivity and stated that more methodologies should be developed to maximize the potential in the educational process [6]. In a metaverse environment, it is crucial to manage persistent interactions with dynamic characteristics, such as specific sessions with multiple resource users. Furthermore, the real-time nature of a session can increase the level of user immersion [5].

The second characteristic of the metaverse is immersion. In this research, we suggest creating 3D objects from the data on the user's smartphone and providing them in the form of virtual objects in the metaverse. This gives users the chance to meet their own data in unexpected forms and is considered a more immersive approach, leading to a more immersive experience. Forbes pointed out that products could be more creative in metaverse spaces. Additionally, Gucci, a leading fashion brand, introduced its products in the metaverse space [7]. An increasing number of companies are attempting to introduce their products in the form of 3D objects in the metaverse space. Effective visual immersion involves removing this level of indirection [1]. In other words, a virtual world's visual presentation should provide sufficient information to our eyes, as in the real world. Then, the brain perceives imagery rather than synthesizing or recalling it, just as when reading text. [1]. Thus, it can be an important attribute to design visualization in the metaverse for users to receive it naturally and induce more immersion.

The third characteristic of the metaverse is personalization. Personalization is the extent to which a technology provides personal focus among people [8]. According to Ning et al., the metaverse acts as a bridge between digital and physical worlds [5]. They also insisted that it is crucial to make the user feel personalized after entering the virtual space [5]. Davis et al. emphasized that it is important for users to control their avatars and personalize their appearance [9]. In addition, users can become more immersive through direct contact with other avatars. Our research proposes a method for creating 3D objects by analyzing user data on a smartphone. Considering the modern usage of smartphones, the data on smartphones are highly personalized. Therefore, 3D objects created from personalized data represent the user's personality. When a user enters the metaverse space in this research, he/she can see that the space is familiar. This is possible because the space is created from the user's photos and location data. The photos on the smartphone are mostly taken at the locations that the user has visited. Thus, the space is more familiar to them.

Before our proposal, we identified the importance of the three major metaverse characteristics and applied them to our research. In the next section, we propose a new method for creating a metaverse by using smartphone data. In addition, we describe how we apply and increase interaction, immersion, and personalization in our metaverse system.

3 Method to Analyze Smartphone Data

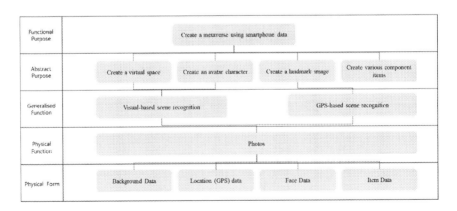

Fig. 2. Work domain analysis of creating a metaverse using smartphone data

To create a metaverse image using smartphone data, we conducted a cognitive work analysis, called work domain analysis (WDA), to determine the attributes required to create a metaverse. Lintern suggested that WDA could identify means-end relationships between functions at different levels of abstraction [3]. Many studies have used the WDA to consider means-end relationships at the initial stage of research [10, 11]. Figure 2 shows the results of the WDA. In general, we used various photos taken by smartphones. Photographs taken from smartphones include various types of data. In particular, we concentrated on the background, location, face, and item data contained in the photos. To analyze the photos, we considered both visual and GPS-based scene recognitions. Then, we created a 3D virtual space using the Unity application. This method is detailed in the following subsections.

3.1 Virtual Space Creation

Photographs taken during an event were used to create a virtual space by request. The group of photos is summarized as several keywords, and the corresponding memory spaces are recommended to users. Photographs captured during an event contain sufficient information to create virtual spaces. Famous sightseeing spots, such as historical monuments, provide clear information about the space in the picture. Some objects in the photo make it easier to identify the place where the photo was taken, and we can easily recognize a picture of a metal tower consisting of lattice girders with an exponential shape as the Eiffel Tower or running water flowing through sheer rock walls as a waterfall. However, not all photographs are useful. There may also be a food picture, group photo, or photo of interesting looking ornaments on a shelf. Because all of the information in the collection of photographs is noisy, it needs to be refined so that we can identify the place where the event occurred.

We propose a multimodal scene detection system to summarize photograph collections into several keywords by reducing noise. Figure 3 shows an overview of our system. We analyzed the content of a photograph using a visual scene recognition module. Furthermore, we used geographical information obtained from the Global Positioning System (GPS) about where the photo was taken. By integrating multimodal information, visual scene recognition and geographical information complement each other and reduce noise. In this section, we introduce the visual scene and GPS-based scene recognition modules, and describe how the noisy information obtained from the collection of photographs is summarized.

3.2 Visual-Based Scene Recognition

Suppose we are in a random place. Can we recognize where we are? Visual information helps us identify the place. For example, zoo, sea, etc., are composed of many objects, and we recognize these places by seeing these objects. Based on this intuition, we introduce a visual scene recognition model to automatically obtain the place information. Owing to recent advances in deep learning technology, specifically convolutional neural networks (CNNs) [12] and large visual datasets for visual object recognition, such as ImageNet [13], visual understanding has achieved remarkable progress. It has diversified with new tasks from image classification [14] to image generation [15]. Scene recognition is one of these tasks and its objective is to identify the place category in an image. The growth of publicly available large-scale datasets in scene recognition has also created new challenges, such as places people encounter in daily life [16], indoor specific datasets [17], and video scene classification [18]. Among the datasets, Place365-Standard [16] contains 1.8M scene photographs labeled with 365 scene semantic categories. Comparing ImageNet and scene understanding [19], Places365 is better in terms of the number of images per scene category and diversity of the categories. The training model with this dataset enabled better generalization performance and higher accuracy; therefore, we used this dataset. We compared performances of a variety of models [16, 20] and observed that ResNet50 [21], trained from scratch, is the best in terms of the top five error rates (14.71%) among the publicly available trained models.

Fig. 3. Overview of the analysing system

Figure 3 shows the procedure used to obtain the corresponding place names of the given collection of images in the visual scene recognition module. The visual scene recognition model outputs the top five place-names and the corresponding scores range from 0 to 1. All scores of the images were summed, and the place with the largest score became the corresponding place name.

3.3   GPS-Based Scene Recognition

Current digital image files of photos taken with smartphones record metadata such as GPS, shoot date and time, and focal length. The GPS information of the digital image file usually contains GPS coordinates, that is, latitude, longitude (or altitude), of where the photograph was taken. Even though the GPS coordinates are quite accurate (2.430 m error [22]), the numbers are not sufficient to precisely identify the location. We demonstrated that geographical information helps in recognizing places using Places API [23]. It converts the GPS coordinates into human understandable concepts. When GPS coordinates are given, it returns information about places such as establishments, which are prominent points of interest, using HTTP requests. The results not only consist of geo-graphical hierarchical structures (i.e., country, state, city) but also provide the type of that place (e.g., zoo, stadium). Because the city name could be a criterion for separating one memory from another, and most words describing a scene refer to entry-level names [16, 24], we focus on the city name and place type. In a real scenario, users request a place name with a collection of photographs, which returns noisy results owing to multiple results from multiple images. We refine the noisy results to obtain the corresponding place name (Fig. 3). Given a collection of photographs $C = \{I_1, I_2, \ldots, I_k\}$, the geographical coordinate is defined as $\phi(I_i)$, given image I_i. $T = \{t_1, t_2, \ldots t_{96}\}$ is a set of establishments with a size of 96 and is defined by the Place API beforehand (e.g., t_1 = amusement park, t_2= café). The Place API returns all the establishments in $T_D(I_i) = \{t_l, t_n, \ldots, t_m\}$, where $t_j \in T$. To deal with 96 dimensional categorical data, we transform the categorical data into one-hot encoding vector v. For example, given place category t_2 = café, v_2 is a column vector filled with zeros, except the second element being 1. The corresponding place of the given image collection C is defined as the place t that has the largest score, and it is formulated as:

$$Place(C) = \underset{t}{argmax} \sum_{i \in C} \sum_{t \in T} w_t^i \cdot v_t \tag{1}$$

$$w_t^i = \frac{D - d(\varphi(I_i), \varphi(t))}{D + d(\varphi(I_i), \varphi(t))}, \tag{2}$$

where ω_t^i is the weight related to the distance. If place t is closer to $\phi(I_i)$, it becomes 1 or 0, and vice versa. Here, $d(\cdot)$ is the Euclidean distance between two coordinates. A fractional equation was introduced to scale the range of w between 0 and 1. Using Eqs. (1) and (2), we obtained the corresponding place name of the given collection of photographs. The corresponding city name was determined by the frequently observed city names in the collection of photographs.

4   The New Metaverse Application Using Smartphones Data

In this section, we present an overview of metaverse system architecture, which is called Metabridge. Metabridge uses photos from a user's Android device to construct a space in metaverse and shows it on a mobile device through 3D rendering. Figure 4 shows the framework of the new metaverse application that uses smartphone data.

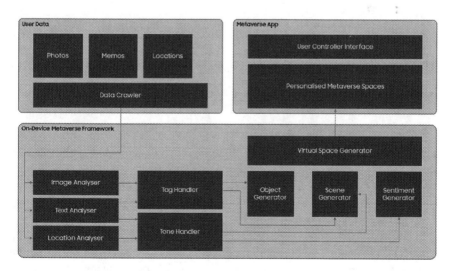

Fig. 4. Framework for the new metaverse application that uses smartphone data

To access the photos stored on the device, the Android SDK is used. We used Flask, a micro web framework written in Python, to provide an upload API. Based on the uploaded photo, it returns data that can compose the user's space. The data analysis is discussed in more detail in a later section. We built a metaverse space using Unity3D, a cross-platform game development software package. To use a user-generated avatar on the smartphone, we used the Emoji SDK for Unity. In our prototype, smartphone users can either use the emoji feature to create an animated avatar from a photo of their face or select from a few suggested characters. The SDK enables users to use their avatars on Metabridge. We used the Firebase Real-time Database to store and synchronize the data that compose the user space. It is a NoSQL cloud-based database in JSON format (Fig. 5).

Fig. 5. Screens of the new metaverse application

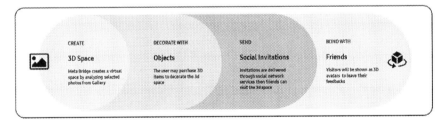

Fig. 6. Usage scenarios of the new metaverse application

Figure 6 depicts the main usage scenarios for the new metaverse application. First, the user can create a 3D virtual space by using photos on a smartphone. Thus, a virtual room is rendered with various objects, such as landmarks or other background objects. Second, the user can visit the store and purchase an item to decorate the virtual space. In the virtual space, the user can explore the space and view the photo gallery. Third, the user can send an invitation to their friends, and finally, the user's friends can join the virtual space. The friends can then see the user's photo gallery and interact with the user.

5   Case Study

To evaluate our new metaverse application, we measured and compared the emotional response between using the smartphone gallery application and the new metaverse application. To compare emotional responses, we used a self-assessment manikin (SAM). Initially, SAM was designed by Lang [25] to provide a solution for the problems that correspond to measuring emotional responses to advertising. SAM is a popular method for measuring emotional responses and has been used in various studies [10, 11, 26–28].

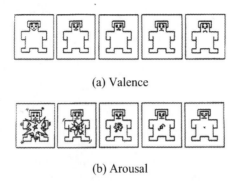

(a) Valence

(b) Arousal

Fig. 7.   Self-assessment manikin (SAM)

In general, SAM consists of pleasure, arousal, and dominance (PAD) dimensions. SAM measures each PAD dimension graphically on a nine-point scale [29] (Fig. 7). However, in our study, dominance was not relevant, so it was excluded from the experiment. Thus, we measured only the valence and arousal levels, and compared their scores. We measured the emotional responses after using the smartphone gallery application and the new metaverse application because we hypothesized that there would be a statistically significant difference between seeing memorable photos using the smartphone application and using the new metaverse application (Fig. 8). The participants were asked to see the memorable photos by using a smartphone gallery application and the new metaverse application in a random order, and were then asked to answer the SAM. On the valence scale, the closer the participant response was to 1, the happier the participant felt. Conversely, the closer the participant response was to 5, the unhappier the participant felt. On the arousal score scale, the closer the participant response was to 1, the more excited the participant felt. In contrast, the closer the participant response was to 5 on the scale, the calmer the participant felt.

We recruited 10 participants (8 males and 2 females) from Samsung Electronics employees who were not otherwise involved in this project (mean age = 39.6 years). Parkkola and Saariluoma suggested that 8–10 participants are sufficient to generate the majority of action types [30].

(a) Smartphone galley application   (b) New metaverse application

Fig. 8. Smartphone gallery application Vs. New metaverse application

6 Results

We measured the emotional responses when the user saw memorable photos using the two different applications (smartphone gallery application and the new metaverse application). Tables 1 and 2 list the results of the SAM. In the case of valence, Table 1 shows that there was a significant difference between using the smartphone gallery application and the new metaverse application. In the case of arousal, Table 2 shows the same.

Table 1. The result of SAM_Valence (Smartphone Gallery Vs. Metaverse Gallery)

Source	DF	Adj SS	Adj MS	F-Value	P-Value
Experience Type	1	5.000	5.000	18.00	0.000
Error	18	5.000	0.2778		
Total	19	10.000			
Experience Type	N	Mean	StDev	95% CI	
Smartphone Gallery	10	2.50	0.527	(2.150, 2.850)	
Metaverse Gallery	10	1.50	0.527	(1.150, 1.850)	

Table 2. The result of SAM_Arousal (Smartphone Gallery Vs. Metaverse Gallery)

Source	DF	Adj SS	Adj MS	F-Value	P-Value
Experience Type	1	18.050	18.0500	36.51	0.000
Error	18	8.900	0.4944		
Total	19	26/950			
Experience Type	N	Mean	StDev	95% CI	
Smartphone Gallery	10	3.40	0.843	(2.933, 3.867)	
Metaverse Gallery	10	1.50	0.527	(1.0330, 1.967)	

7 Discussion

Most participants felt greater pleasure and excitement when using the new metaverse application. We assume that using the smartphone gallery application was static and did not provide a new engagement experience. Conversely, using the metaverse application induced dynamics because the user could control and explore the virtual avatar. In addition, the background of the virtual space consists of the landmark obtained from the photo, so the participants felt happier when they saw the memorable photos using the new metaverse application. Furthermore, the metaverse application can send an invitation to friends. Thus, the friends of the participants could visit the virtual space and interact with each other. This might have helped the participants feel more excited when they saw memorable photos. In our future work, we will improve the metaverse application by collecting more diverse data from smartphones.

8 Conclusion

In this study, we proposed a method to generate a metaverse by using various types of smartphone data. We assumed that a personal space can be helpful for memory recall and providing memorable feelings. To build a metaverse model, we used various machine-learning techniques and concentrated on extracting meaningful keywords from the noisy geographic information. The extracted meaningful keywords were used to create a metaverse. We developed a prototype based on the results for meaningful keywords, using Unity. The prototype indicated that the user can create a personal space based on the geographical data from photos and diaries. To evaluate the new metaverse application, we conducted a case study to measure the user's emotional responses when using the metaverse application. The results show that using the metaverse application helps the user feel happier and more excited when they see memorable photos, than using the smartphone gallery application.

References

1. Dionisio, J.D.N., Burns, W.G., Gilbert, R.: 3D virtual worlds and the metaverse: current status and future possibilities. ACM Comput. Surveys (CSUR) **45**(3), 1–38 (2013)
2. The Verge: https://www.theverge.com/22588022/mark-zuckerberg-facebook-ceo-metaverse-interview, Accessed 25 Jan 2022
3. Lintern, G.: Tutorial: Work Domain Analysis (2011)
4. Desmet, P., Overbeeke, K., Tax, X.: Designing products with added emotional value: development and application of an approach for research through design. Des. J. **4**, 32–47 (2001)
5. Ning, H., Wang, H., Lin, Y., Wang, W., Dhelim, S., Farha, F., Daneshmand, M.: A Survey on Metaverse: the State-of-the-art, Technologies, Applications, and Challenges. arXiv preprint arXiv:2111.09673 (2021)
6. Schlemmer, E.: Learning in Metaverses: Co-Existing in Real Virtuality: Co-Existing in Real Virtuality. IGI Global (2014)

7. Forbes: https://www.forbes.com/sites/forbesbusinessdevelopmentcouncil/2021/12/21/why-the-metaverse-is-marketings-next-big-thing/?sh=69ee079325f0, Accessed 25 Jan 2022

8. Daft, R., Lengel, R.: Organizational information requirements, media richness, and structural design. Manage. Sci. **32**(5), 554–571 (1986)

9. Davis, A., Murphy, J.D., Owens, D., Khazanchi, D., Zigurs, I.: Avatars, people, and virtual worlds: foundations for research in metaverses. J. Assoc. Inf. Syst. **10**(2), 90 (2009)

10. Park, D., Park, H., Song, S.: Designing the AI developing system through ecological interface design. In: Ahram, T., Falcão, C. (eds.) AHFE 2020. AISC, vol. 1217, pp. 83–96. Springer, Cham (2020). https://doi.org/10.1007/978-3-030-51828-8_12

11. Park, D., Park, H., Song, S.: A method for increasing user engagement with voice assistant system. In: Marcus, A., Rosenzweig, E. (eds.) HCII 2020. LNCS, vol. 12201, pp. 146–157. Springer, Cham (2020). https://doi.org/10.1007/978-3-030-49760-6_10

12. Krizhevsky, A., Sutskever, I., Hinton, G.E.: Imagenet classification with deep convolutional neural networks. Adv. Neural. Inf. Process. Syst. **25**, 1097–1105 (2012)

13. Russakovsky, O., et al.: Imagenet large scale visual recognition challenge. Int. J. Comput. Vision **115**(3), 211–252 (2015)

14. Dosovitskiy, A., Beyer, L., Kolesnikov, A., Weissenborn, D., Zhai, X., Unterthiner, T., Houlsby, N.: An image is worth 16x16 words: Transformers for image recognition at scale. arXiv preprint arXiv:2010.11929 (2020)

15. Karras, T., Laine, S., Aittala, M., Hellsten, J., Lehtinen, J., Aila, T.: Analyzing and improving the image quality of stylegan. In: Proceedings of the IEEE/CVF Conference on Computer Vision and Pattern Recognition, pp. 8110–8119 (2020)

16. Zhou, B., Lapedriza, A., Khosla, A., Oliva, A., Torralba, A.: Places: a 10 million image database for scene recognition. IEEE Trans. Pattern Anal. Mach. Intell. **40**(6), 1452–1464 (2017)

17. Quattoni, A., Torralba, A.: Recognizing indoor scenes. In: 2009 IEEE Con-ference on Computer Vision and Pattern Recognition, IEEE, pp. 413–420 (2009)

18. Feichtenhofer, C., Pinz, A., Wildes, R.P.: Temporal residual networks for dynamic scene recognition. In: Proceedings of the IEEE Conference on Computer Vision and Pattern Recognition, pp. 4728–4737 (2017)

19. Xiao, J., Hays, J., Ehinger, K.A., Oliva, A., Torralba, A.: Sun database: Large-scale scene recognition from abbey to zoo. In: 2010 IEEE Computer Society Conference on Computer Vision and Pattern Recognition, IEEE , pp. 3485–3492 (2010)

20. Zhou, B.: https://github.com/CSAILVision/places365, Accessed 25 Jan 2022

21. He, K., Zhang, X., Ren, S., Sun, J.: Deep residual learning for image recognition. In: Proceedings of the IEEE Conference on Computer Vision and Pattern Recognition, pp. 770–778 (2016)

22. Global Positioning Team: Global Positioning System (GPS) Standard Positioning Service (SPS) Performance Analysis Report. GPS Product Team, Washington, DC, USA (2014)

23. Google: https://developers.google.com/maps/documentation/places/web-service/overview, Accessed 25 Jan 2022

24. Jolicoeur, P., Gluck, M.A., Kosslyn, S.M.: Pictures and names: making the connection. Cogn. Psychol. **16**(2), 243–275 (1984)

25. Lang, P.: The Cognitive Psychophysiology of Emotion: Fear and Anxiety (1985)

26. Park, D., Hwang, S., Ko, S., Lee, J., Lee, J.: Recording your stress, can it help to prevent job stress? In: Stephanidis, C. (ed.) HCI 2018. CCIS, vol. 851, pp. 429–435. Springer, Cham (2018). https://doi.org/10.1007/978-3-319-92279-9_57

27. Park, H., Lee, J., Bae, S., Park, D., Lee, Y.: A proposal for an affective design and user-friendly voice agent. In: International Conference on Human Systems Engineering and Design: Future Trends and Applications, Springer, Cham, pp. 249–255 (2018)

28. Park, D., Lee, C.: Method for viewing real-world scenes while recording video. Appl. Sci. **11** (10), 4617 (2021)
29. Morris, J.: Observations: SAM: the self-assessment manikin; an efficient cross-cultural measurement of emotional response. J. Advert. Res. **35**, 63–68 (1995)
30. Parkkola, H., Saariluoma, P.: would ten participants be enough for design of new services?, Qual. Impact Qual. Res. **86** (2006)

Development of Standards for Production of Immersive 360 Motion Graphics, Based on 360 Monoscopic Videos: Layers of Information and Development of Content

Jose Luis Rubio-Tamayo[1(✉)] ⓘ, Manuel Gertrudix[1] ⓘ, and Mario Barro[2] ⓘ

[1] Faculty of Communication, URJC, Camino del Molino 5, 28942 Fuenlabrada, Spain
{jose.rubio.tamayo,manuel.gertrudix}@urjc.es
[2] Universidad Nacional Autónoma de Mexico, Av. Constitución No 600 Bo. La Concha, C.P. 16210 Alcaldía Xochimilco, Mexico
mbarro@fad.unam.mx

Abstract. Virtual reality and immersive technologies are currently in full development. One of the most widely used formats in the medium are the 360 linear videos, which are proliferating thanks to the 360 cameras available today for the user. The forms of production, including filming and post-production, in this new medium have been transformed in many of their technical procedures. But what about computer-generated graphics, such as motion graphics? The creation of linear video content with the motion graphics technique, although increasingly common, requires specific procedures and techniques that differ from formats that do not fall into the category of 360, immersive or otherwise. In this paper, we aim to establish a series of mechanisms and standards, based on the knowledge gained from experience in filmed 360-degree videos, to help facilitate the development of motion graphics proposals, also considering the parameters of usability in virtual reality.

Keywords: 360 video · Motion graphics · Virtual reality · Digital technologies · Immersive video

1 Introduction

Virtual reality technologies have evolved notably over the last few decades, and exponentially in recent years. This has become a medium with its own characteristics and interaction mechanisms that has given rise to the development of contents of the most heterogeneous nature and purpose, and whose potential for production still has a long path to travel, whose end we cannot even begin to glimpse.

One of the booming formats, among many others, within the complexity of what we would call << immersive >>, is 360° video. Due to the proliferation of increasingly accessible filming technologies and the possibility offered by different platforms (such as Youtube or Facebook) for its access and reproduction, it is a medium that is in the

© The Author(s), under exclusive license to Springer Nature Switzerland AG 2022

J. Y. C. Chen and G. Fragomeni (Eds.): HCII 2022, LNCS 13317, pp. 58–73, 2022.
https://doi.org/10.1007/978-3-031-05939-1_5

process of consolidation, although there are still many technical issues that differ from traditional video production that have yet to be resolved.

360° video has its own peculiarities and features with respect to other formats within the category and the virtual reality medium, whether these are linear or interactive media. Moreover, as we have mentioned, it has its own peculiarities with respect to video production that does not fall into the 360-degree category. It also has certain advantages, as well as certain limitations, to which visual production has not been subject until the proliferation of these technologies.

Although this paper does not deal with 360 video filming as such, this, with its particularities, would be the starting point for establishing the guidelines that lead to the model proposed in this paper, which would focus on a technology that has been consolidated in recent years thanks to the evolution of digital technologies and means of production, which is already within the reach of many users. We are talking about the so-called motion graphics, which will be dealt with in this publication, based on the production of 360-degree videos, and the extrapolation of monoscopic video projections filmed on a map for the creation of visual content with the 2D motion graphic technique (although it will later be extrapolated to a 360° environment).

In this way, just as filmed cinema had elements that could later serve as a reference in the field of animation (although both also had their own creation mechanisms), the structure and projection of 360° videos can serve as a basis for the creation of animation content with motion graphics techniques based on projections, primarily 2D motion graphic techniques.

2   Literature Review

Recent scientific and academic literature related to immersive virtual reality has focused, in a particularly relevant way, and in recent years, on the applications of its different manifestations in different fields, to the extent that it has been revealed as a technology with significant potential for implementation in a broad spectrum of scientific and technological domains, or those related to the cultural and entertainment industries, in addition to education, dissemination and communication.

These studies in the field of different formats expressed in the medium of virtual reality are clearly reflected in applications in fields such as teaching and learning (Pan et al., 2006) [1] (Kavanagh et al., 2017) [2] (Parong and Mayer, 2018) [3], or in areas related to science, whether in the learning of science itself, or in the representation of the information it offers (Pottle, 2019) [4]. Also of spatial interest is the application of virtual reality technology in different fields of scientific production (Li et al., 2017) [5] (Ayoub and Pulijala, 2019) [6], or, in a reverse process, the use of science itself to study our behaviour in an immersive environment (Clay et al., 2019) [7], either by measuring factors such as presence in that immersive environment (Slater, 2018) [8], or, on the other hand, by studying cognitive factors such as empathy (Schutte, 2017) [9].

However, 360 video could be considered, to a certain extent, a subcategory within virtual reality, with a series of specific characteristics, derived, in turn, from the video format itself. This is manifested, primarily, through a linear narrative, where events follow one after the other and the spectator has no control over them, nor the ability to move around the environment[1]. The 360° video presents, however, the freedom to set the field of view or FOV in any section of the 360° that make up the scene, always taking into account the ergonomic limitations of the human body itself, such as, quite simply, the turning of the neck.

This feature of 360 video is of great interest for content development, because sometimes the nature of the content or the experience developed does not require that the user/viewer does not interact with the scene. And, just as other media such as literature, cinema, radio or theatre, to name the most classic ones, continue to exist in this context of ongoing media revolution, the emergence of new media of this category and, therefore, new communicative possibilities, offers us an unprecedented opportunity to develop content in media which, a priori, present less interactivity with the environ-ment/technology/history, and a lesser degree of agency[2].

That is why 360° videos, by presenting this specific feature, on the one hand, fit into the video category. However, they also fall into a subcategory of virtual reality, albeit, as we have already seen, with a limited level of interaction. Another key feature is that they do not require immersion (although they also offer that possibility) in order to be operational and efficient in their functions. Thus, they can be viewed with a device that does not allow immersion, such as a tablet or a mobile device without adaptation to vision, although, in these cases, the experience offered differs from the immersive one.

In reference to the studies on 360-degree video that can be found in the academic literature, these focus on different areas, both in terms of technical issues related to the filming of content, production and post-production, as well as on issues related to the high-quality reproduction of the content. Thus, we find recent studies such as Xu et al. (2020) [11] which address the issue of image processing in the medium (which requires a large amount of resources, due to the large amount of data that a 360 video has compared to a "traditional" video). Other authors such as David et al. (2017) [12] focus their research on the visual attention factor in 360-degree videos, reinforcing the importance of its study to gather information on our behaviour with our vision in a 360-degree environment, which in turn allows us to optimize the development of experiences and design them taking into account the variable of the focus on which we place our attention during the viewing experience. Along the same lines are the studies by

---

[1] That said, and based on the narrative levels established by Fonseca et al. (2021) [10], this paper proposes the existence of a potential format in which a total displacement through a given medium would be possible - albeit with established limits, which they categorize as Spatial Level 3 - and which, on the other hand, presents a linear narrative - which characterizes video, and which Durán Fonseca et al. (2021) [10] stipulate as Narrative Level 1 - implying that there is no possibility of influencing the medium. This description would be a kind of `free-scrolling video'. Curiously, there are hardly any creations in this format, precisely because of the technical differences in the creation of 360 videos, using cameras, but also motion graphics, and other formats with a higher level of interaction, for which game engine technologies are used, as in the case of Unreal.

[2] Agency refers to the ability of the viewer/user to influence the environment in a given digital technology. The term refers more specifically to the realm of virtual reality, although it can be extrapolated to any technology that potentially fits into the realm of extended reality.

Fan et al. (2017) [13], focusing on the prediction of the fields of vision (FoV) of users of virtual reality glasses or HMDs. Also, in the same year, Tran et al. (2017) [14], focused on the issue of quality metrics for 360 videos, proposing the development of parameters to establish these metrics that enable us to assess the quality of these videos. In addition to this, we can find publications that focus on aspects such as the importance of mobile devices for viewing (Broeck et al., 2017) [15] or mobile networks for accessing content through such devices (Mangiante et al., 2017) [16], stressing the constant need to optimize them, due to the amount of information that 360-degree videos handle.

As for the specific applications of the 360-degree video format within the field of virtual reality, these present an enormous degree of heterogeneity. This factor will be an element that will also take into account the possibilities offered to date by 360 video formats that are not necessarily immersive. Thus, the variety of fields of application of 360-degree video range from immersive 360 journalism (Van Damme et al., 2019) [17] to the evaluation of the effectiveness of learning in controlled experiments in areas such as health science education (Ulrich et al., 2019) [18], and the use of this 360-degree video technology for learning foreign languages (Repetto et al., 2021) [19], to give but a few examples.

Again, however, with regard to motion graphics produced with the same technology and projection base – although with a procedure that differs in some aspects, as we will see below – it is difficult to find literature focused on this modality. However, we have, for not so long, had relevant exponents of 360-degree videos created with animation and motion graphics techniques, such as TAS – The Canyon 360 4k VR (Tas Visuals, 2016) [20], the video clip *Show it 2 Me*, directed by Carter and Brooks (2016) [21] for the music project *Night Club* -and created in part with Tilt Brush-, or the already well-known *Pearl* (Google Spotlight Stories, 2016) [22], as well as other pieces that also have an informative vision, as is the case of *Dreams of Dali*, produced by The Dali Museum (2016) [23].

In this way, we can see that the technologies that already exist to produce 360° videos, such as 360-degree stereoscopic cameras, or 3D computational media, which make it possible to create immersive, rendered environments, can serve as a reference for working with other animation media based on 2D projection. This exponentially increases the possibilities for content development and, in turn, enables layered animation work, the use of more creative formats and, last but not least, the optimization of resources.

3   360 Video: Immersive and Non-immersive Typologies

The definition of 360-degree video is structured, however, by a series of characteristics and features that highlight the fact that we are dealing with a medium that incorporates the question of *immersiveness*, on the one hand, and the notion of belonging, on the other, taxonomically, to the category of virtual reality. But it also has some characteristic features which mean it has certain differences that make it a subcategory with respect to other manifestations of the virtual reality medium itself. This is true both when it comes to visualizing it and when it comes to producing it.

As far as the question of visualization is concerned, the following key differences can be found in relation to other formats that fall into the category of virtual reality. Among the differences we have found in this study are the following:

- In many cases, the use of immersive reality glasses or HMD (head-mounted display) is not essential. This is due to the very nature of the video itself, as there is no high level of interaction beyond the ability of the user/viewer to see within their field of vision what they want to see within the 360-degree angle.
- Preferably, the visualization of the story is always linear. A greater degree of interaction with the medium on the part of the viewer, beyond the occasional activation elements of other actions, would make the viewing experience more difficult, precisely because of the nature of the format. These two characteristics are interrelated, since the greater the degree of interaction, the greater the degree of user control necessary, and therefore the greater the degree of immersion required[3]. This correlation does not necessarily run in the opposite direction. Thus, a 360-degree video can have a high degree of immersion, as the user employs HMDs, without having to have a higher degree of interaction than the freedom of the user to view the part of the scenario he/she wants. On the other hand, a higher level of interaction would mean that the content could no longer be classified in the video category, because it has perfectly defined features.

On the other hand, among the fundamental differences found at the production level with other virtual reality formats are the following:

- The production does not require game engines. In fact, this option is normally used for other virtual reality formats, which require a higher degree of interactivity than video, but whose production processes are also more complex.
- The 360-degree video camera models are designed for 360-degree video production, but there are other techniques that do not necessarily require the use of a camera. Nor, as mentioned above, is it necessary to use game engines in the case of video. It is also possible to use 2D animation techniques.
- Another differentiating factor is that, although production layers can be superimposed, they are merged, with today's technology, into a single image. In other words, 360-degree camera filming technologies can be used, and then video effects (as in so-called conventional videos), 2D and 3D animation techniques can be applied in this order, although the latter two can be combined to varying degrees, depending on the needs for content development on the one hand, and the features of the techniques applied on the other.

The following image (Fig. 1) shows the subcategories of viewing and creation within the field of virtual reality, taking into account the interaction and the forms of production of virtual reality.

---

[3] This phenomenon only occurs in video format, as there are other media with a degree of immersion, not necessarily high, which provide a high degree of interaction with the story and the medium, such as video games.

Fig. 1. Subcategories of virtual reality, including 360-degree video, according to their production processes and the interaction capabilities they offer. Source: Own elaboration. The authors

Thus, knowledge of the specific features of 360-degree videos and the different layers of information they may contain is a vital tool for the division of video (combining filmed and animated elements) into production categories, in order to help optimize the content production process in this format.

4   Structural and Design Model of 360 Immersive and Non-immersive Video

The current model proposed is based on the projection presented by 360 photographs taken with cameras that make this function possible. In this way, the still image becomes the reference landscape for the creation of animations in immersive 360-degree videos. This is due to the type of projection it offers, usually referred to as equirectangular, or ERP, which would already have been addressed in studies such as those contributed by researchers such as Ray et al. (2018) [24], referring to the projection of a 360-degree physical world onto a flat rectangular image with a 2:1 aspect ratio. This implies, like other projections, a deformation in the position of objects. As can be seen in Fig. 2.

Fig. 2. 360° photography of the Church of San Pedro Apóstol, in the Polvoranca Park in the Community of Madrid, after some post-production adjustments. Source: Taken on 4–08-2021 by one of the authors. Own elaboration.

It is also important to differentiate the elements that make up a 360-degree image projection. This, with today's filming devices, will normally be represented as a 2:1 aspect ratio image, in 3840x1920 pixels, but it also allows other values, such as 1920x960, 4096x2048, or 8192x4096 (8K). In fact, the diversity of filming devices existing today will make an enormous amount of formats possible, with an increasingly higher image resolution. The elements that make up the scene are spread throughout the 360 images, and we can only see, at any given moment, those that are within our FOV or field of vision, which is normally 120 degrees on the device, although you can find devices that present 180 degrees, such as the HR VR Headset from XTAL, or even 200, such as the Pimax Vision 8K Plus VR Headset. These concepts are different from the human field of vision in physical reality, which is close to 180 degrees in binocular vision.

The correct levelling of the camera will allow the horizon, if there are no relevant geographical features, to be in the horizontal half of the recording, which would be called the Horizon. In contrast to traditional film cameras, the use of dipping and panning is counter-productive to the experience, as it distorts the natural interaction of the viewer/user with the virtual environment. However, it is possible, with the right knowledge and experience, and to ensure that the end result does not produce a counter-productive user experience for the viewer/user, that a certain degree of experimentation with respect to the potential camera position may take place.

The elements of the 360 experience should, in order to optimize it, also be structured in a certain way, taking into account that half of the image from the horizon downwards represents the ground, and half of the image from the horizon upwards, the elements that are related to the sky.

It is also important to establish a main target, which would be the most important element of the scene. This is already determined by studies such as those of Durán Fonseca et al. (2021) [10], in the so-called *Levels of Narrative Interest*, with Level A corresponding to the greatest importance of an element for the plot, Level B corresponding to the secondary elements, and Level C corresponding to the virtual landscape, which forms the basis of the plot. Thus, examples of the Main Target, the Horizon, and an approximation to the FoV, can be seen in Fig. 3.

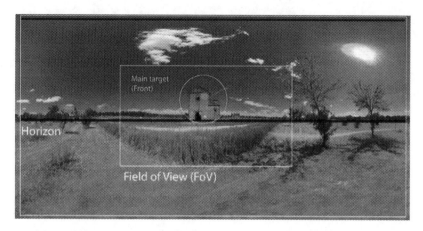

Fig. 3. 360° photograph of the Church of San Pedro Apostol, in the Polvoranca Park in the Community of Madrid, in which the main target, the Horizon, and the FoV are reflected. Source: Taken on 4–08-2021 by one of the authors. Own elaboration.

Other fundamental elements also appear, such as the equivalent of the poles, here called *Pole A* (up) or *Pole B* (ground or down), which are those that present a greater degree of distortion. This distortion is equivalent to that which relates to the equalization of the dimension of a point (the pole) with that of the equator, so that this image can be represented in a plane (Fig. 4). It is also important, and related to this, to note that what appears behind the user in the 360-degree experience, in the equirectangular projection, is on both sides (indicated by the back icon, Image 4). Also shown are the scene targets, corresponding to Level B within the Levels of Narrative Interest developed by Durán Fonseca et al. (2021) [10].

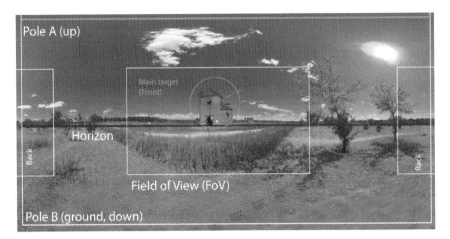

Fig. 4. 360° photograph of the Church of San Pedro Apostol, in the Polvoranca Park in the Community of Madrid, including secondary references. Source: Taken on 4–08-2021 by one of the authors. Own elaboration.

In the subsequent image (Fig. 5), this increase in distortion towards the poles is also shown in the previous paragraph. This is shown in the orange gradient, where a higher degree of orange illustrates a higher degree of horizontal length distortion, being more pronounced at the poles. Also shown - in green - are estimates of the approximate potential vanishing points of the image, estimates and calculations addressed by studies such as those of Youjin et al. (2018) [25] or Oh and Jung (2012) [26], which were among those that contributed to determining the estimates of vanishing points in equirectangular images taken with 360 filming devices, and which vary depending on the position in which it was taken, and the elements of the scene.

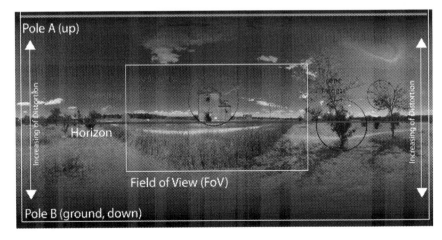

Fig. 5. Structure of the projection of components in a 360-degree image. Source: Taken on 4–08-2021 by one of the authors. Own elaboration.

Another fundamental component, which must also be taken into account when creating 360 videos with motion graphics techniques, is equivalence, which has already been mentioned in previous paragraphs. Although some 2D motion graphics editing software allows a view of the corresponding part of the user's field of vision, when making the equirectangular projection on a flat image, it would be necessary to take into consideration the correspondence of the elements in which this equivalence occurs, and which are cut off on the left and right in the equirectangular projection (Fig. 6).

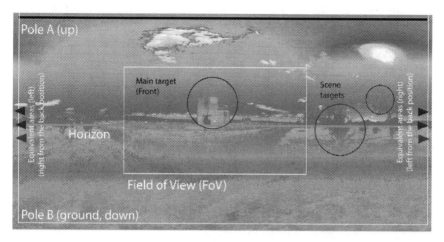

Fig. 6. Structure of the projection of the components in a 360 image, showing the horizontal equivalences. Source: Taken on 4–08-2021 by one of the authors. Own elaboration.

It is also important to take into account the layers of information that can be included in a 360-degree video creation, which would include the possibility of producing 360-degree videos partly with 2D and 3D motion graphic techniques.

These layers of information would basically be three, although it is possible to include as many layers of information as desired or necessary, always within these typologies. They can also have single-layer typology.

These layers correspond to the following, as can also be seen in Fig. 7:

- Layer A. This represents the part of the physical world filmed, the video. Any effects added to the video would also be included in this layer.
- Layer B. This represents a virtual world designed with 3D computational tools, or with single elements (characters, objects) that would be embedded in that virtual world (which would be a layer B frequency) or embedded in the physical world (which would be an insertion of a layer B within a main layer A).
- Layer C: This represents computer graphics created with 2D design tools. The creation process differs significantly from that of the elements belonging to layer C, since in this case it does not involve "modelling" with 2D tools. However, it is a projection of artificial two-dimensional elements onto a simulated three-dimensional world (360 video), but which is actually a projection (the equirectangular one). Another fundamental feature of Layer C is that it can contain elements

that have been previously designed in Layer A (from reality) and Layer B (from modelling), these 2D editing techniques being a kind of "final art" of the different elements that are going to be projected on a plane that will simulate a 3D experience.

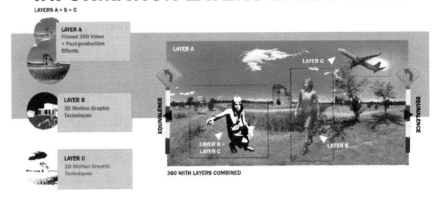

Fig. 7. Layers of information that can be included in a 360-degree video, composed of filming (Layer A), 3D computer graphics development (Layer B) and 2D computer graphics development (Layer C). Source: Own elaboration.

So, for example, a 360-degree video shot on film would represent a single layer (usually) within the Layer A category. A 360-degree motion graphics video created with 2D editing technologies would consist of a succession of C Layers, as these elements have been created from computer graphics with a limited level of reference to reality. A motion graphics video may also have been made with 3D computer graphics software, which would include a Layer B, if the rendering process has been done with such software, or a succession of Layers B, if it has been rendered in separate 3D computer environments. If this 3D environment generated by computational means with 3D creation software had a subsequent process of post-production in part, or the inclusion of graphics with other computational means, it would also include a Layer or succession of B Layers.

In this way, this whole procedure helps us to structure the information that must be present in a medium that is constituted as a 360-degree video, whose possibilities of representation are of great relevance, always taking into account its linear narrative features and the limitation in the interaction of the user/viewer with the virtual environment in comparison with other sub-categories of virtual reality.

5   Factors Related with User Experience in 360 Videos: What Do Spectators/Users Watch and Interact with?

One of the main questions relating to 360 video production is how the users interact with information and pictures shown in them. Factors such as agency or grounding are not variables to be taken into account. Nevertheless, 360 videos are an ERP projection of a position of the spectator/user in relation to the environment, which includes the time factor (events are occurring).

This ERP projection is going to allow the user, as explained, to look and pay attention to events or actions chosen by him/her. But what will the events or actions that are going to draw the attention of users be? And what will the facts which are going to help create atmosphere in the production be? Which factors should be adapted from the 2D cinema, and which ones from disciplines such as user experience?

One of the advantages of motion graphics is that it can also be produced by computational technologies, and, for that reason, it is not necessary to prepare the environment in the same way that we prepare to film a real environment with a 360 camera (with all the difficulties involved). However, this real-world filmed environment may also be a ground for researching the way users interact with real-world situations, and how that may be adapted to research in virtual reality, including 360 videos.

There has always been a need for user experience research in the field of virtual reality since this has been conceived as a medium. As the medium has evolved and became more accessible to users in the last decade, the 2010s, research into user experience in this area has increased dramatically. Rebelo et al. (2012) [27] identify the methods for evaluating user experience in the context of a virtual reality experience, as well as how research into UX may also take advantage of a virtual reality-based research methodology. Kuliga et al. (2015) [28] approach the medium of virtual reality as an empirical research tool in user experience, interaction design and human-computer interaction, by identifying some variables to be applied in research (environment, environmental appraisal, etc.). Meanwhile, researchers such as Rubio-Tamayo & Gertrudix (2016) [29] have also managed to design a taxonomy of levels of interaction between users and virtual reality environments, keeping in mind narrative factors and focusing on the interactive features of the medium in those levels. Kim et al. (2020) [30] identifies the diversity of types of interaction between users and devices in VR systems (which includes 360 videos), arguing, at the same time, that there is a significant lack of research on the taxonomy that may recognize the main features of virtual reality systems related with the factors that define the user experience. Shott & Marshall (2021) [31] explore, more recently, the effectiveness of virtual reality in fields such as education, by applying in their research a theoretical user experience framework. Wienrich et al. (2018) [32], on the other hand, undertake research giving relevant insights into relations between general aspects of user experience and virtual reality-specific ones. Those insights were obtained by applying the following four main research and analysis methods: the analysis of the evaluation requirements for a large-scale multi-user case, the relationship between evaluation concepts and features from the research fields of virtual reality, on the one hand, and user experience research, on the other. The other research and analysis methods applied by Wienrich et al.

(2018) [32] are the subsequent testing of the relation between user experience and virtual reality and the integration of measurements and standards from both research fields and, finally, the discussion of implications for a holistic evaluation framework in both domains.

User experience and interaction design have therefore been applied to the subcategory of virtual reality, represented by 360 videos and films. Authors such as Keskinen et al. (2019) [33] focus their research on exploring the spectator/user's viewing experience and determining that this experience may be affected by the user/spectator's ergonomic position itself, the proximity of actions happening in the story, and the camera height, whose optimal position is 150 cm above the ground. Fan et al. (2022) [34] focus their research on developing a model for watching 360 videos by aiming to quantify the named Quality of Experience (QoE), and identifying various factors, features and variables in the context of QoE. Broeck et al. (2017) [35] conduct a comparative study focused on user experience in 360 videos on mobile devices by using different interaction techniques between user and the virtual information shown via the device. Those interaction techniques, in contrast with those observed in interactive and immersive virtual reality (which does not include 360 videos) are focused on the spectator/user's view and points of interest for him/her, as those users do not have such a complete interaction as with information in 360 videos. On the other hand, other researchers such as Somrak et al. (2019) [36] conduct a study focusing on VR sickness by measuring the levels of discomfort in a virtual reality environment (based on 360 videos) and the user experience applied to those environments, showing a negative correlation between those factors: the increase of the user experience factor decreases the VR discomfort in an immersive experience.

Could all those factors determine what the optimal way to design motion graphics for 360 videos is? Of course, those factors should be kept in mind by content developers in creating experiences in 360 videos, and, also by researchers in getting users to interact more efficiently and comfortably with virtual environments and improving the factors determining the research into user experience.

In 360 videos, one of the main actions of the users/spectators is to look around the virtual environments while the events are happening. The user/spectator takes an active role, by looking around, and a passive role, as he/she cannot influence events or move freely around the virtual environment. And user experience for 360 videos should have specific features and take into account specific factors designed for user experience in virtual reality.

The user experience applied to 360 videos, in this case, as in interactive virtual reality, should also take into account different levels of interaction, by focusing on two main approaches: the user experience of the technology itself (related to the interaction between user and devices) and the user experience of the virtual environment (how information is represented by computational means and how users interact with it) (Fig. 8).

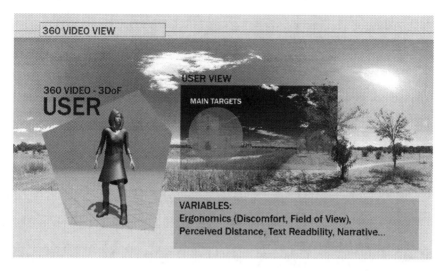

Fig. 8. Factors to take into count for user experience and interaction design when designing a virtual environment in the 360 video format. A model proposed by the authors. Source: Own elaboration.

6   Conclusions

360-degree videos are a format within virtual reality with its own characteristics, among which the linearity of the narrative and the possibility of viewing with or without complete audio-visual immersion stand out. Furthermore, the two senses involved, unlike other subcategories within virtual reality, are sight and hearing, although this does not mean that other senses cannot be added to the experience. On the other hand, there is the lower level of interaction with the medium with respect to other subcategories within the aforementioned virtual reality, and the aforementioned limitations of movement through virtual space (which are limited to a fixed position or a directed linear displacement, although the field of vision or FoV can be fixed in any desired position).

On the other hand, we have a wide range of creative and content development possibilities, taking into account the structural limitations of the video format. We also have a medium in which the potential creation of content, knowing the operating parameters, is relatively simpler than in other sub-categories of virtual reality, since it does not require such a sophisticated design of the potential interactions with the medium. Nevertheless, it is advisable, as this research shows, to be familiar with the operating structure and some of the elements in order to optimize the development of such content.

Just like the conventional video we have known so far, 360-degree video has a long way to go in terms of configuring itself as a medium with its own production, functioning and interaction dynamics with the user/spectator.

References

1. Pan, Z., Cheok, A.D., Yang, H., Zhu, J., Shi, J.: Virtual reality and mixed reality for virtual learning environments. Comput. Graph. **30**(1), 20–28 (2006)
2. Kavanagh, S., Luxton-Reilly, A., Wuensche, B., Plimmer, B.: A systematic review of virtual reality in education. Themes Sci. Technol. Educ. **10**(2), 85–119 (2017)
3. Parong, J., Mayer, R.E.: Learning science in immersive virtual reality. J. Educ. Psychol. **110** (6), 785 (2018)
4. Pottle, J.: Virtual reality and the transformation of medical education. Future Healthc. J. **6**(3), 181 (2019)
5. Li, L., Yu, F., Shi, D., Shi, J., Tian, Z., Yang, J., Jiang, Q.: Application of virtual reality technology in clinical medicine. American J. Transl. Res. **9**(9), 3867 (2017)
6. Ayoub, A., Pulijala, Y.: The application of virtual reality and augmented reality in oral & maxillofacial surgery. BMC Oral Health **19**(1), 1–8 (2019)
7. Clay, V., König, P., Koenig, S.: Eye tracking in virtual reality. J. Eye Mov. Res. **12**(1), (2019). https://bit.ly/3tGXyBR
8. Slater, M.: Immersion and the illusion of presence in virtual reality. Br. J. Psychol. **109**(3), 431–433 (2018)
9. Schutte, N.S., Stilinović, E.J.: Facilitating empathy through virtual reality. Motiv. Emot. **41** (6), 708–712 (2017)
10. Durán Fonseca, E., Rubio-Tamayo, J. L., Alves, P.: Niveles de diseño narrativo, espacial y de interacción para el desarrollo de contenidos en el medio de la realidad virtual. ASRI: Arte y sociedad. Revista de investigación, **19**, 96–111 (2021)
11. Xu, M., Li, C., Zhang, S., Le Callet, P.: State-of-the-art in 360 video/image processing: perception, assessment and compression. IEEE J. Sel. Topics Signal Process. **14**(1), 5–26 (2020). https://bit.ly/394U02P
12. David, E.J., Gutiérrez, J., Coutrot, A., Da Silva, M.P., Callet, P.L.: A dataset of head and eye movements for 360 videos. In: Proceedings of the 9th ACM Multimedia Systems Conference, pp. 432–437 (2018)
13. Fan, C.L., Lee, J., Lo, W.C., Huang, C.Y., Chen, K.T., Hsu, C.H.: Fixation prediction for 360 video streaming in head-mounted virtual reality. In: Proceedings of the 27th Workshop on Network and Operating Systems Support for Digital Audio and Video, pp. 67–72 (2017). https://bit.ly/393UQx0
14. Tran, H.T., Ngoc, N.P., Bui, C.M., Pham, M.H., Thang, T.C.: An evaluation of quality metrics for 360 videos. In: 2017 Ninth International Conference on Ubiquitous and Future Networks (ICUFN), IEEE, pp. 7–11 (2017). https://bit.ly/3lnFFoa
15. Broeck, M.V.D., Kawsar, F., Schöning, J.: It's all around you: Exploring 360 video viewing experiences on mobile devices. In: Proceedings of the 25th ACM international conference on Multimedia, pp. 762–768 (2017). https://bit.ly/3lsc4JZ
16. Mangiante, S., Klas, G., Navon, A., GuanHua, Z., Ran, J., Silva, M.D.: Vr is on the edge: How to deliver 360 videos in mobile networks. In: Proceedings of the Workshop on Virtual Reality and Augmented Reality Network, pp. 30–35 (2017). https://bit.ly/395UllZ
17. Van Damme, K., All, A., De Marez, L., Van Leuven, S.: 360 video journalism: Experimental study on the effect of immersion on news experience and distant suffering. Journalism Stud. **20**(14), 2053–2076 (2019). https://bit.ly/3AdxSiW
18. Ulrich, F., Helms, N.H., Frandsen, U.P., Rafn, A.V.: Learning effectiveness of 360 video: experiences from a controlled experiment in healthcare education. Interact. Learn. Environ. **29**(1), 98–111 (2021)

19. Repetto, C., Di Natale, A.F., Villani, D., Triberti, S., Germagnoli, S., Riva, G.: The use of immersive 360° videos for foreign language learning: a study on usage and efficacy among high-school students. Interact. Learn. Environ. **29**(1), 1–16 (2021). https://bit.ly/3ltAWkV

20. Tas Visuals: TAS – The Canyon 360 4k VR. Youtube (2016). https://bit.ly/2Xkjqa1

21. Carter, D., Brooks, M.: Show it to Me 360 Video for the Band Night Club. Youtube (2016). https://bit.ly/3zmkZlv

22. Google Spotlight Stories: Pearl. Youtube (2016). https://bit.ly/3Eclke5

23. The Dali Museum: Dreams of Dali (2016). https://bit.ly/2YWBRTg

24. Ray, B., Jung, J., Larabi, M.C.: A low-complexity video encoder for equirectangular projected 360 video contents. In: 2018 IEEE International Conference on Acoustics, Speech and Signal Processing (ICASSP), IEEE, pp. 1723–1727 (2018). https://bit.ly/3ElvyZq

25. Youjin, T., Wei, C., Xingguang, L., Lei, C.: A robust lane detection method based on vanishing point estimation. Procedia Comput. Sci. **131**, 354–360 (2018). https://bit.ly/2Xkr84g

26. Oh, S.H., Jung, S.K.: Vanishing Point Estimation in Equirectangular Images. In: Proceedings Int'l Conference Multimedia Information Technology and Applications, pp. 45–47 (2012). https://bit.ly/3k70apE

27. Rebelo, F., Noriega, P., Duarte, E., Soares, M.: Using virtual reality to assess user experience. Hum. Factors **54**(6), 964–982 (2012)

28. Kuliga, S.F., et al.: Virtual reality as an empirical research tool—Exploring user experience in a real building and a corresponding virtual model. Comput. Environ. urban Syst. **54**, 363–375 (2015)

29. Rubio-Tamayo, J.L., Gertrudix, M.: Realidad virtual (HMD) e interacción desde la perspectiva de la construcción narrativa y la comunicación: propuesta taxonómica. Icono14, **14**(2), 12 (2016)

30. Kim, Y.M., Rhiu, I., Yun, M.H.: A systematic review of a virtual reality system from the perspective of user experience. Int. J. Human-Comput. Interact. **36**(10), 893–910 (2020)

31. Schott, C., Marshall, S.: Virtual reality for experiential education: a user experience exploration. Australas. J. Educ. Technol. **37**(1), 96–110 (2021)

32. Wienrich, C., Döllinger, N., Kock, S., Schindler, K., Traupe, O.: Assessing user experience in virtual reality–a comparison of different measurements. In: International Conference of Design, User Experience, and Usability. Springer, Cham, pp. 573–589 (2018)

33. Keskinen, T., Mäkelä, V., Kallioniemi, P., Hakulinen, J., Karhu, J., Ronkainen, K., Turunen, M.: The effect of camera height, actor behavior, and viewer position on the user experience of 360 videos. In: 2019 IEEE Conference on Virtual Reality and 3D User Interfaces (VR) IEEE, pp. 423–430 (2019)

34. Fan, C.L., Hung, T.H., Hsu, C.H.: Modeling the user experience of watching 360 videos with head-mounted displays. ACM Trans. Multimedia Comput. Commun. Appl. (TOMM), **18**(1), 1–23, (2022)

35. Broeck, M.V.D., Kawsar, F., Schöning, J.: It's all around you: exploring 360 video viewing experiences on mobile devices. In: Proceedings of the 25th ACM International Conference on Multimedia, pp. 762–768 (2017)

36. Somrak, A., Humar, I., Hossain, M.S., Alhamid, M.F., Hossain, M.A., Guna, J.: Estimating VR Sickness and user experience using different HMD technologies: an evaluation study. Futur. Gener. Comput. Syst. **94**, 302–316 (2019)

Multi-user Multi-platform xR Collaboration: System and Evaluation

Johannes Tümler[✉][ID], Alp Toprak, and Baixuan Yan

Anhalt University of Applied Sciences, Köthen, Germany
johannes.tuemler@hs-anhalt.de

Abstract. Virtual technologies (AR/VR/MR, subsumed as xR) are used in many commercial applications, such as automotive development, medical training, architectural planning, teaching and many more. Usually, existing software products offer either VR, AR or a 2D monitor experience. This limitation can be a hindrance. Let's draw a simple application example: Users at a university shall join an xR teaching session in a mechanical engineering lecture. They bring their own xR device, join the session and experience the lecture with xR support. But users may ask themselves: Does the choice of my own xR device limit my learning success?

In order to investigate multi-platform xR experiences, a software framework was developed and is presented here. This allows one shared xR experience for users of AR smartphones, AR/MR glasses and VR-PCs. The aim is to use this framework to study differences between the platforms and to be able to research for better quality multi-user multi-platform xR experiences.

We present results of a first study that made use of our framework. We compared user experience, perceived usefulness and perceived ease of use between three different xR device types in a multi-user experience. Results are presented and discussed.

Keywords: Augmented reality · Virtual reality · Multi-user · Collaboration · Metaverse

1 Motivation and Goals

In the last 5–10 years, virtual technologies (AR/VR/MR, subsumed as xR) have matured from exotic expert tools to valuable industry standard. Sample commercial application fields are automotive development, medical training, architectural planning, teaching and many more [4,7,8,13].

The trend goes towards collaborative multi-user xR scenarios: Software allows synchronizing data between xR devices through local networks or cloud services[1].

---

[1] Examples: Microsoft Azure Spatial Anchors (https://azure.microsoft.com/en-us/services/spatial-anchors/), Vive Sync (https://sync.vive.com/), Mozilla Hubs (https://hubs.mozilla.com/).

© The Author(s), under exclusive license to Springer Nature Switzerland AG 2022
J. Y. C. Chen and G. Fragomeni (Eds.): HCII 2022, LNCS 13317, pp. 74–93, 2022.
https://doi.org/10.1007/978-3-031-05939-1_6

Social platforms and large companies propagate this as the "Metaverse": The next big step in xR. It shall be used to leverage social interaction and spatial cooperation in all kinds of xR use cases. Therefore, let us assume the following two sample use cases:

#1 University students physically join a lecture for mechanical engineering. The professor activates the xR session. Each student can join that session with their own xR devices (from Google Cardboard VR via handheld smartphone AR to see-through AR glasses). The teacher controls what the students can see, where virtual objects are located in the scene and which virtual objects can be used for interaction. If the students can't join the lecture hall ("co-location"), they can also join remotely using VR.

#2 The second application is a field engineer that needs to service a special purpose machine. He could use a mobile AR device (handheld, head-worn) to get servicing instructions. Meanwhile a backoffice engineer joins that servicing session using a VR device looking at the same machine (full virtual data). Both collaborate on the task to identify and solve problems of the machine.

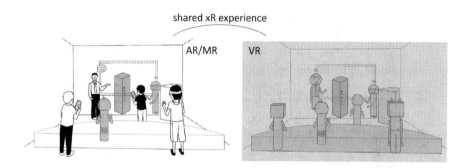

Fig. 1. Users join a university lecture co-located (left) and remotely (right) at the same time. Participants can interact with each other and with the lecturer, all xR content is synchronized and as interactive as necessary. *(pictures by Alistud)*

Figure 1 gives an example for use case #1. Independent of the actual application, users face the following questions:

- Can I use my own device to join a multi-user xR session?
- Do I have to use specific xR hardware or xR software?
- Do I have to use a VR device or an AR device?
- Can I switch between devices if I decide another device might work better?
- **Will my decision on the device limit my experience?**

The last question is particularly very important to answer because it helps find answers for the other questions. If in use case #1 the students pick the wrong device, they might achieve a bad learning outcome. If in use case #2 the wrong device was chosen, then maybe the interactions do not fit to the task, will take longer, thus result in higher cost for the action. A previous study has shown interesting differences in usability and user experiences between xR platforms [3].

It is necessary to understand the strengths and weaknesses of each xR device platform, of their interplay and how to support the users in their device decision. Decision makers, educators and users can create valuable concepts and procedures for such scenarios only if solid answers are available to the questions mentioned above. Here, for this paper we call these scenarios **multi-user multi-platform xR** or **cross-plattform xR** experiences.

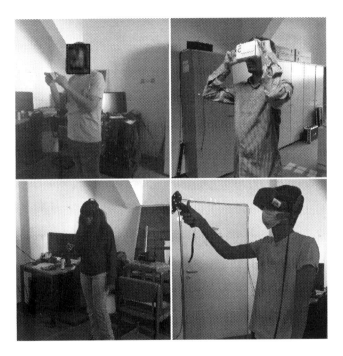

Fig. 2. Use of four xR platforms. Top left: AR-smartphone. Top right: VR Cardboard. Bottom left: Microsoft HoloLens 2. Bottom right: VR-PC with HP Reverb (G1) and VR controllers [3]

To better understand the named platforms we give the following example devices and configurations as shown in Fig. 2:

- *PC-VR*: Intel i7 processor equipped with nVidia RTX videocard, HP Reverb head mounted display with controllers.
- *standalone VR headset*: Oculus Quest or Vive Focus with its controllers or hand tracking
- *cardboard VR*: a stock Samsung Galaxy S10 smartphone put in a $5 cardboard with lenses

- *HoloLens 2*: the stock device as it is sold by Microsoft
- *Smartphone based AR*: a stock Samsung Galaxy S10

Table 1 presents major differences between these xR platforms. Most of the platforms can be used for 6 degrees of freedom experiences to include rotational and positional tracking, if correctly implemented.

Table 1. Overview of differences between xR device platforms

Platform	Computational performance	Interaction	Hand usage
PC-VR	High	Controllers or hand-tracked	Hold controllers or hands-free for interaction
Standalone VR headsets	Medium or low	Controllers or hand-tracked	Hold controllers or hands-free for interaction
Cardboard-VR (smartphone)	Medium or low	None or single button	Hold device and push button
HoloLens 2	Medium	hand-tracked	Hands-free for interaction
Smartphone based AR	Medium or low	Tap or swipe on screen	Hold device and touch screen

The computational performance is very different. A common measure is the number of polygons of 3D models that the devices are able to display at sufficient frames per second. For PC-VR this can range from 10 million to more than 100 million. For mobile devices like smartphones and standalone headsets, this is in a region between 100,000 to one or two millions.

The possible interactions are also very different and infer specific use of hands. For PC-VR and standalone VR headsets, hands usually need to hold and use controllers. That means, the controller is used as a medium or metaphor to achieve user's actual intended interaction. Some devices allow hands-free interaction without the need of controllers, such as the Vive Focus 3, Oculus Quest 2 or Microsoft HoloLens 2. Sometimes hands-free interaction can be achieved using extra devices like the LeapMotion. This allows a direct hand interaction with virtual content. With the VR cardboard, users must hold the device at least with one hand, usually with two, and press the single button that is available on some devices. For the smartphone, it is necessary to hold with at least one hand and use the other hand to interact on the touch screen.

In order to investigate user experiences in examples like #1 or #2, a cross-platform xR software framework must be used. This allows one shared xR experience for users of smartphones, AR/MR glasses and VR-PCs. The aim is to use such a framework to study differences between the platforms in multi-user sessions to be able to research for better quality of shared xR experiences.

2   Implementation of a Multi-user Multi-platform xR-Framework

2.1   Requirements

In order to evaluate properties of multi-user multi-platform xR experiences, systems used must allow multiple users to interact in the same scene with common xR devices in real time. The capabilities of each platform are different (Table 1). Rendering and computing power of the PC platform is the strongest. Up to a certain degree of data complexity, it is feasible to run the same virtual scene on different platforms. Our target smartphone is Google Pixel 3. For PC-VR, we selected the AltspaceVR recommended configuration [1] for comparison. As a head-worn device, we selected the Microsoft HoloLens 2 because it is the current industry standard. The Ubi-Interact framework[2] aims at distributed and reactive applications, but currently seems too complex for our purpose.

Table 2. MRTK v2.6.2 supported devices

Platform	Supported devices
OpenXR (Unity 2020.3.8+)	Microsoft HoloLens 2 Windows Mixed Reality headsets
Windows Mixed Reality	Microsoft HoloLens Microsoft HoloLens 2 Windows Mixed Reality headsets
Oculus (Unity 2019.3 or newer)	Oculus Quest
OpenVR	Windows Mixed Reality headsets HTC Vive Oculus Rift
Ultraleap Hand Tracking Mobile	Ultraleap Leap Motion controller iOS and Android

From the xR developer's perspective, each platform must use its own SDK. The PC-VR platform has VRTK[3] (and many more), the Android AR platform has ARCore[4], Apple iOS has ARKit[5] and finally Microsoft HoloLens 2 has MRTK[6]. One specialty about MRTK is, as shown in Table 2, that it not only supports HoloLens 2. It also allows to deploy to PC-VR headsets, Android smartphones, iOS smartphones and other platforms. MRTK is able to configure an xR application towards the platform specific requirements. But it does not support collaboration of multiple users on different xR platforms at the same time. Unfortunately, MRTK does not support the Google Cardboard VR platform,

---

[2] https://wiki.tum.de/pages/viewpage.action?pageId=190677154.
[3] https://vrtoolkit.readme.io/docs/summary.
[4] https://developers.google.com/ar/develop.
[5] https://developer.apple.com/documentation/arkit/.
[6] https://docs.microsoft.com/en-us/windows/mixed-reality/mrtk-unity/.

yet. Therefore for this paper, we decided to ignore Cardboard VR development even if it may be a popular device for students due to its low price.

Table 3. Data that must be shared between xR devices

Data type	Data source	Update requirements
Screen/head position	Coming from all devices	Real-time
Gaze direction	Coming from all devices	Real-time
Position and pose of controllers	Coming from VR	Real-time
Position and pose of hands and fingers	Coming from HoloLens 2	Real-time
Origin of world coordinate system	Registered between all devices	Once per start
Position and pose of spawned 3D objects	Coming from all devices	Real-time (interactive spawn object)/Once (static objects)
State of variables and function calls	Coming from all devices	Real-time
3D-Mesh of the "real world" around selected AR users	Coming from one selected AR user	Not necessary in realtime

Data transmission between users is required to allow for interaction and collaboration in the same scene in real time. Table 3 gives examples of shared and synchronized data, sources and update requirements, independent of the platform used. There are SDKs on the market to solve the data transmission problem, such as Photon [14] or Mirror [9]. They have powerful functions, provide a variety of data transfer methods and are either closed-source or complex to develop with. None of them allow cross-platform xR collaboration as per default.

One major requirement for all multi-user xR experiences is to work in a common shared coordinate system. Currently, if AR users start their application, the origin of their coordinate systems will differ. That is because, at the moment the application starts, each device builds its own map of spatial references. Therefore, the origin of each device's world coordinate system will be different. If, for example, co-located AR users use different coordinate systems, they will see the AR objects in different real-world positions. This would make it hard or impossible to collaborate. To solve this problem, it is possible to use:

- Cloud anchors [2]
- Fiducial markers such as QR codes [17]
- Additional tracking hardware on the device for referencing, such as active LEDs tracked by external tracking systems
- Use of an on-device referencing procedure that processes own tracking data with tracking data of a master device (see Sect. 2.5).

Finally, besides on-device computation, it would be possible to use cloud-based remote rendering. This is a foreseeable and valuable possibility to allow for high-quality real-time renderings on low-performance remote devices. For such scenarios it is also important to know and implement device-specific interaction metaphors and data sharing methods.

In order to understand differences between the named xR platforms it is necessary to create a suitable research platform that fulfills all previously mentioned requirements. Our aim is not to release such a system as a product. Instead, we want to use the system for experiments and research to help development of future multi-user multi-platform xR frameworks:

1. It should be ready for experiments as soon as possible. (simple architecture)
2. The data should be managed from one device. (simple management)
3. The number of users will be less than 10. (simple network system)
4. The future requirements and usage will remain similar. (static architecture)
5. The maintenance cost should be as low as possible. (simple code)

These are used as guidelines for our development. We are not sure if we shall call the developed tools a "framework", "development platform" or "system". In our eyes, it can be all that.

2.2   Concept

Users want to move around in the scene, interact with objects and observe other users' behavior. As shown in Fig. 3, users may use various inputs to control their avatars and interact with objects, while getting feedback from the scene.

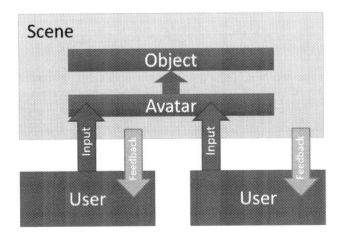

Fig. 3. Block chart for user's xR experience

Table 4. Input data of different platforms

Platform	Input data 1	Input data 2	Input data 3
VR-PC	Headset position and rotation	Controller position and rotation	Controller pointed at position
HoloLens 2	Headset position and rotation	Hand and finger position and rotation	Finger pointed at position
AR smartphone	Smartphone position and rotation	Screen tap position	Camera focus position and tapped object

The user's input data are different between devices. For example, VR headsets have tracking data from controllers, while smartphones do not. Their input data are summarized in Table 4.

If 3D objects are moved in the xR scene, they not only need to feed back the new position and rotation to the user. Instead, they also have to populate that data to other users. Even more, when some functions are triggered by one user, it is necessary to remotely trigger the same functions on other users' systems (remote procedure call, RPC). Ideally, this happens with close-to-zero latency. So for 3D objects in a multi-user scene, there are two kinds of data to be synchronized: First, object's pose data and second, RPC data. There are several basic network architectures to exchange data between devices:

1. Client-server model (C/S): The client directly accesses the server to obtain data, and the server also directly sends data to the client.
2. Three-tier and N-tier models derived from C/S model [15]: As shown in Fig. 4 (left), they divide different functions into different layers, and each layer performs its own duties to complete the user's request. This architecture is mostly used in complex systems.
3. Peer-To-Peer model (P2P): This is a completely different architecture from the C/S model, as shown in Fig. 4 (right), P2P emphasizes that no device is dedicated to providing services, but divides the work to each device, and each device acts as a peer. Peers can serve both as clients and as servers [18].

While these models apply to general problems in computer science, Peciva [12] gives a good overview on implications for xR. For example, some of the data needs real-time update (i.e. user's positions) while others don't (i.e. spawning of static geometry).

With regards to the guidelines of the last section, the C/S model and its derived architecture is a good choice [15]. For P2P, handing over the work to each device may affect the performance of less powerful devices (smartphone, HoloLens 2), thus result in a bad user experience. Besides, from the viewpoint of it being an experimental platform, monitoring data flow in the C/S model is much easier than with P2P. Therefore, the C/S model is very suitable for the development of our system.

One major challenge for any collaborative xR system is management of device-dependent coordinate systems: Microsoft Azure Spatial Anchors (Cloud

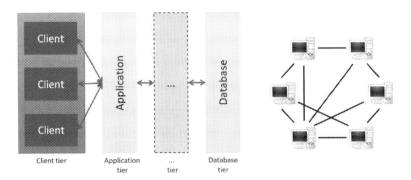

Fig. 4. N-tier model (left) and P2P model (right)

Anchors) require a paid account to log in and upload the anchor to the cloud database, then download it from the cloud to all devices, when in use. This increases maintenance costs and requires an internet connection. As an alternative, a QRcode anchor might be convenient. But it will cause problems in larger rooms when only one QRcode is used for positioning. The third possibility, additional hardware on the device would increase maintenance cost and complexity of the system. As a fourth possible solution, we used a simple calibration method based on 3D-point-set registration (see Sect. 2.5). It only requires the mobile AR user to send at least 4 shared point coordinates to a second mobile AR user to calibrate the coordinate system. A local WiFi network is required to share all data among the devices.

We developed a simple UDP data transmission system: The client connects to the server through the server's IP address and port. Data such as object positions or RPCs can be sent and received after connecting to the server. Data sent to the server will be forwarded to other connected clients. Finally, the conceptual diagram of the system is presented in Fig. 5.

The whole software is developed with Unity 2019.2 and C# programming language. PC-VR is selected as the VR device, HoloLens 2 as the head-mounted AR device, and an Android mobile phone as the handheld AR device. Because these platforms are all supported by MRTK but Google cardboard is not, Cardboard VR is temporarily abandoned. Because of the cross-platform feature of MRTK, all interactions are implemented with MRTK.

2.3   Acquisition and Transmission of Input Data

The transform component in Unity contains the position coordinates and rotation angle of the object in the scene. In Unity, the main camera represents the user's perspective into the 3D scene. For each platform, MRTK directly synchronizes the device's tracking data to the main camera to achieve the user's xR experience. Therefore, the main body of avatar can be synchronized by directly obtaining and sending the transform data of main camera to the server.

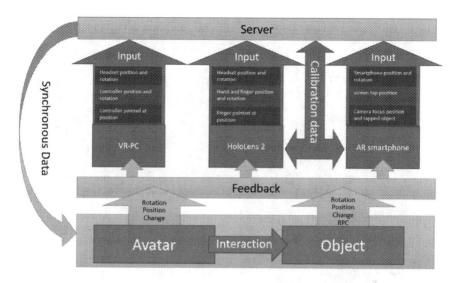

Fig. 5. System concept

But for users of PC-VR and HoloLens 2, there is still controller tracking data and hand tracking data to synchronize. As shown in Fig. 6 (top), both the user's controller and the hand are represented as pointers in MRTK [10].

To obtain the data of a pointer, MRTK's IMixedRealityPointer class is retrieved and saved, which contains the coordinates and rotation angle of the pointer to synchronize (see Listing 1.1). For the hand tracking of HoloLens 2, the following Listing 1.2 is be used to obtain the transform data of each joint of the palm (see Fig. 6, bottom).

Listing 1.1. Find all valid pointers

```
1   var pointers = new HashSet<IMixedRealityPointer>();
2
3   foreach (var inputSource in CoreServices.InputSystem.
        DetectedInputSources)
4   {
5       foreach (var pointer in inputSource.Pointers)
6       {
7           if (pointer.IsInteractionEnabled && !pointers.Contains
                (pointer))
8           {
9               pointers.Add(pointer);
10          }
11      }
12  }
```

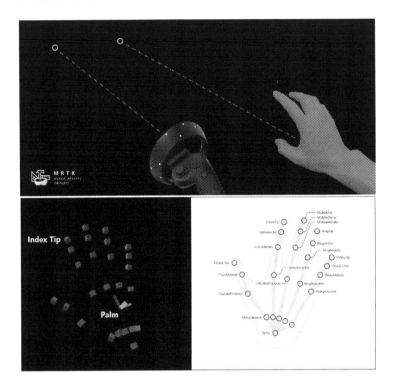

Fig. 6. MRTK Pointer (top) and hand tracking (bottom)

Listing 1.2. Get joint transform from hand joint service

```
1  var handJointService = CoreServices.GetInputSystemDataProvider
       <IMixedRealityHandJointService>();
2  if (handJointService != null)
3  {
4      Transform jointTransform = handJointService.
           RequestJointTransform(TrackedHandJoint.IndexTip,
           Handedness.Right);
5      // ...
6  }
```

After obtaining IMixedRealityPointer, the result in the IMixedRealityPointer class directly contains the coordinates of the position pointed at. Because smartphones don't have controllers or hand tracking, the smartphone's pointer defaults to the phone's camera. The focus point is the camera's focus point or where it points after tapping the screen.

The input data acquisition of each platform is summarized in Table 5.

Table 5. Input data acquisition of each platform

Platform	Main tracking data	Hand/controller tracking data	Focus point data
PC-VR	Main camera transform	IMixedRealityPointer	IMixedRealityPointer. result
HoloLens 2	Main camera transform	handJointService. RequestJointTransform	IMixedRealityPointer. result
Smartphone	Main camera transform		IMixedRealityPointer. result

2.4   Object Synchronization

The synchronization of the position and rotation angle of the object is the same as the synchronization of the main body of each device, and the data of the transform of the object can be used directly. But how is it possible to synchronize function states? For example, when a button is pressed, the function that makes a light bulb light up is triggered, and the light bulb will light up. How is it possible to trigger the light bulb function on all other user's devices? The concept of "reflection" is used here. When the function is called, the instance's index and MethodInfo are sent to the server, the server forwards it to other users, and other users use methodinfo.Invoke to trigger the corresponding function (Listing 1.3). This is what we refer to as RPC here.

Listing 1.3. Sample code for invoking remote procedure calls

```
1   using System.Reflection;
2
3   public void CallMethod(object instance, string methodName)
4   {
5       int index = -1;
6       MethodInfo methodToCall;
7       for (int i = 0; i < instanceList.Length; i++)
8       {
9           if (instance.Equals(instanceList[i]))
10          {
11              index = i;
12          }
13      }
14      if (index > -1)
15      {
16          Type instanceType = instanceList[index].GetType();
17          methodToCall = instanceType.GetMethod(methodName);
18          callMethodData.instanceIndex = index;
19          callMethodData.methodToCall = methodToCall;
20          objectUDPClient.DataEnqueue(callMethodData);
21      }
22  }
```

2.5   Coordinate System Registration

It is necessary to have all co-located AR users use a shared coordinate system. In our case this refers to users of HoloLens 2 and AR smartphone. The 3D-point-set registration method is inspired by the idea of the MPAAM see-through calibration [5]: It requires at least 4 pre-defined spatial input points to generate the required transformation matrix P and thus register the coordinate systems to each other. After P is obtained, any point can be converted between the two coordinate systems A and B:

$$
\begin{bmatrix} x_{3D_A} \\ y_{3D_A} \\ z_{3D_A} \\ 1 \end{bmatrix} = \mathbf{P} \cdot \begin{bmatrix} x_{3D_B} \\ y_{3D_B} \\ z_{3D_B} \\ 1 \end{bmatrix} \tag{1}
$$

To obtain P, several steps are necessary. One user must have two AR devices available, that shall be registered to each other. For example, a user carries the HoloLens 2 and an AR smartphone at the same time. Through the HoloLens 2 the user sees the pre-defined target position for the smartphone as a 3D representation. The smartphone and the target position are brought into overlay by moving the smartphone manually. By click of a button, the first 3D-3D correspondence is recorded. This step is done multiple times in different pre-defined positions. The positions must be widely spread to achieve good accuracy (Fig. 7).

Fig. 7. Image recorded from HoloLens 2 perspective: User trying to overlay the smartphone with the expected pose (blue 3D object) as good as possible. (Color figure online)

For each of the 3D-3D correspondences, the data is forwarded to the HoloLens through the server. At the same time, HoloLens 2 also sends the position coordinates of the target positions to the mobile client. HoloLens 2 and the mobile client calculate the calibration matrix through these sets of coordinates. After all points are recorded the 3D-3D projection matrix P can be calculated. Then, the next participating AR device can follow the same procedure. The expected error rates can be as high as 30 cm, depending on the tracking quality of the involved device's and the accuracy of user's device positioning.

2.6 Framework Test and Discussion

As a first test of the framework, we created an interactive cross-platform simulation using a 3D model of a lathe (see Fig. 8). The base Unity project was already available at our institution and had to be adjusted to work in the new framework. This was done in less than one work day, without the need to fully understand that existing (lathe) Unity project.

The following was tested with three users in the scene at the same time, to verify full functionality:

1. Grab and pass objects to each other
2. Operate the levers on the lathe alternately/simultaneously
3. Start drilling functions remotely on the 3D machine
4. Attach/detach objects from the machine by click of a button (RPC)

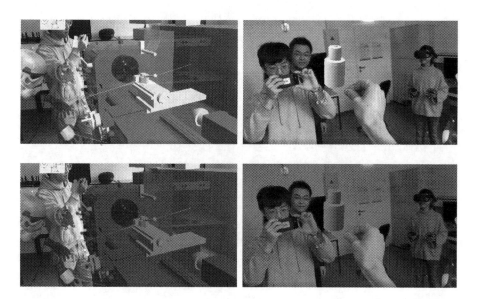

Fig. 8. Top: Screenshots from HoloLens 2 user perspective. Bottom: same images as top, but for better understanding with colored PC-VR user and avatar (yellow), smartphone user and avatar (green), 3D geometry (orange). The registration between smartphone and HoloLens 2 had an error of approximately 20 cm. (Color figure online)

A video of the test was recorded and is available online[7]. This confirms that the system can be used for research on interaction and cooperation of multiple cross-platform users in the same scene.

By developing this system, we learned:

1. what data is needed to synchronize avatars and objects, and how to obtain this data
2. Shared coordinate systems are very important for AR users to collaborate.
3. It is possible for users who use different interaction styles to work together.

There are also some questions waiting to be answered. Can users fully understand the behavior of other users? Is it necessary to synchronize all input data? For example, we could only synchronize one or two fingers of the HoloLens 2 user, only sync the controller position of the VR-PC user, or even sync only the focus point. Will these affect the collaboration between users? Following, we conducted preliminary research to start to work on these questions.

3   Evaluation

3.1   Study Goal

The collaborative multi-user multi-platform technology intends to enable collaborative work and social play, implying that we expand from a face-to-face scenario to one in which we collaborate in a virtual world. There is a danger that this new style of work degrades certain critical information for the collaborative process, such as understanding the partner's behavior, intentions and point of view [6].

Therefore, the aim of our first study with the new platform was to evaluate acceptance and usability among different xR device combinations. At the same time it should help us to get a first glimpse of understanding how to work with at least two different xR device types at the same time.

3.2   Method and Procedure

The user study implements three different experiments, always with two users at a time. At the beginning they filled out a demographic survey to assess age and previous xR experience. They were presented the different platforms and could try them out. After that, the experiments begun in randomized order (Fig. 9). Each participant took part in all three experiments:

1. HoloLens 2 *(user 1)* vs. PC-VR *(user 2)*
2. HoloLens 2 *(user 1)* vs. AR-smartphone *(user 2)*
3. AR-smartphone *(user 1)* vs. PC-VR *(user 2)*

After each run they filled out the user experience questionnaire (UEQ, [16]) and the technology acceptance model (TAM, [11]) questionnaire, both in English language.

---

[7] https://www.youtube.com/watch?v=iFT2G05fosU.

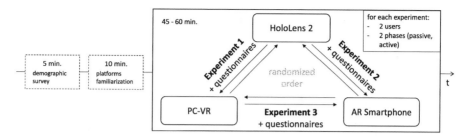

Fig. 9. Procedure of experiment

A puzzle of a 3D hand and arm skeleton had to be solved, similar to our previous work [3]. Eight 3D objects (bones) were spread around and the users had to put them in the right order. There was no need to explain the correct positions because measuring user's task performance was not a goal of the study. For each user there was an active and a passive phase: While *user 1* solved this puzzle with one xR platform, *user 2* passively watched the first user from a different xR platform. Then they changed their role, so that *user 2* had to solve the puzzle while *user 1* watched from afar. During their active and passive phase the participants could talk and help each other to solve the puzzle. They were co-located in the same room. Figure 10 shows a sample setting.

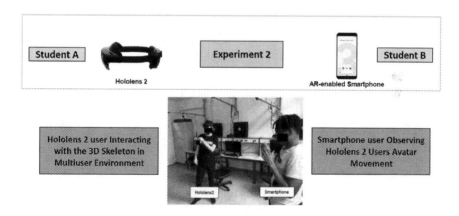

Fig. 10. Sample configuration

The study incorporated $n = 20$ students that participated without any compensation. They were international students of our engineering master degree programs such as Biomedical Engineering or Interactive Media. 30% of the participants were aged between 21–25 years and 70% between 26–30 years, according to the demographic questionnaire. 60% had prior virtual technology experience. Three had multi-user xR experience from school or virtual reality gaming. The majority of xR experienced participants employed virtual technologies for the purpose of studying. The remaining participants had no prior exposure to xR.

The UEQ captures a broad picture of the user's experience [16]. The user experience (originality and simulation) as well as classical usability (efficiency, perspicuity, and reliability) are evaluated. The participants were required to take a survey consisting of 26 constraint adjective pairs, each on a 7-point scale. The three UEQ measures are attractiveness, pragmatic quality (perspicuity, efficiency, reliability), and hedonic quality (stimulation, originality). Hedonic quality refers to non-task related elements of quality, whereas pragmatic quality refers to work related characteristics. We used the online version of "UEQ Data Analysis Tool" to analyze the data. It transforms data to values between -3 and $+3$.

Perceived usefulness and perceived ease of use are the two key variables used by the Technology Acceptance Model to determine if a computer system will be accepted by its users. This paradigm has a strong emphasis on the perceptions of potential users. A goal of the study was to investigate a possible link between university students' intentions to utilize two platform software systems and several characteristics such as perceived usefulness, perceived ease of use, attitude, software self-efficacy, subjective norm and system accessibility. Attitude has been identified as a cause of intention. Behavioral intention is a measure on how likely they are to utilize the system. The software self-efficiency is measured by the level of skills required to use this 2-platform multi-user system. Subjective norms as social influencing factors and system accessibility as an organizational factor were only measured by the difficulty of accessing and using this multi-user system in school.

3.3   Results

Matlab was used for statistical analysis. The data was not normally distributed, so we used the Wilcoxon signed rank test with an alpha level of 5%.

In UEQ the values between -0.8 and 0.8 reflect a neutral evaluation of the associated scale. Values larger than 0.8 up to 3.0 represent a positive evaluation, values from -3.0 to -0.8 represent a negative evaluation. From our data we see a positive evaluation in general (Fig. 11). On the other hand, the scores for novelty are notably lower than others. VR-PC and HoloLens 2 generally give better results in the evaluation compared to AR-smartphone.

From UEQ we did not find any significant differences between the evaluation of the individual platforms from other two platforms and the comparison of the platforms with one another in terms of the superior categories attractiveness, perspicuity, efficiency, stimulation or novelty.

Statistical analysis of the TAM reveals several significant differences:

- Between "HoloLens 2 vs. AR-smartphone" and "AR-smartphone vs. PC-VR" in the subjective norm ($Z = -2.365$, $p = 0.018$).
- "HoloLens 2 vs. PC-VR" compared to "AR-smartphone vs. PC-VR": significant differences for attitude questions 7 and 9 ($Z = -2.232$, $p = 0.026$) and ($Z = -2.588$, $p = 0.004$).

Groups:
1: Looking at VR-PC from HoloLens 2   2: Looking at VR-PC from AR-smartphone
3: Looking at HL2 from VR-PC   4: Looking at HoloLens 2 from AR-smartphone
5: Looking at AR-smartphone from VR-PC   6: Looking at AR-smartphone from HoloLens 2

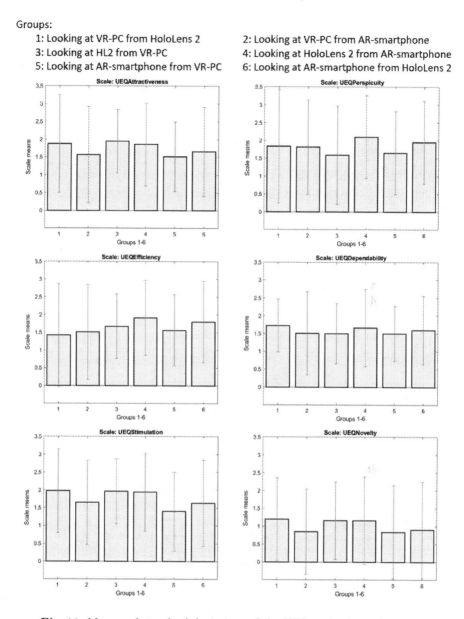

Fig. 11. Mean and standard deviations of the UEQ scales for each group

- "HoloLens 2 vs. PC-VR" compared to "AR-smartphone vs. PC-VR": significant differences for behavioral intention questions 10 and 11 ($Z = -2.019$, p $= 0.043$) and ($Z = -2.982$, p $= 0.003$)
- "HoloLens 2 vs. PC-VR" compared to "AR-smartphone vs. PC-VR": significant differences for subjective norm questions 13 and 15 with the results

of $(Z = -2.470, p = 0.013)$ and $(Z = -2.574, p = 0.010)$, and in software self-efficiency $(Z = -1.872, p = 0.061)$

– "HoloLens 2 vs. PC-VR" compared to "HoloLens 2 vs. AR-smartphone": significant differences between attitude questions 7 and 8 $(Z = -2.153, p = 0.031)$ and $(Z = -2.240, p = 0.025)$ and in the subjective norm $(Z = -2.365, p = 0.018)$.

3.4 Discussion of Study Results

By use of our novel multi-user multi-platform xR framework, it was possible to conduct a user study with three different xR device types. Users were able to see their partner's avatars and eventually interact with each other - but interaction between users was not part of the experiment.

With the study, we tried to assess how the user's experience, perceived usefulness and perceived ease of use differ if users collaborate through different xR device types. Based on the findings of the TAM questionnaire, we can say that PC-VR in combination with HoloLens 2 is the most suitable multi-user setting, compared to the other combinations tested. This is a combination that would likely be picked by users if they had freedom of choice.

4 Conclusion

It is foreseeable, that with the vision of a "Metaverse" the technological entry barrier must be low, if all people shall be able to access it. It should be possible to use any available xR device to collaborate and experience AR or VR sessions. Until now, there is no public software framework available that reflects the different xR device capabilities and their very different interaction metaphors.

A device-agnostic seamless xR development is not possible yet.

With this paper we present an approach to research on said multi-user multi-platform xR experiences. We developed an exemplary research software framework based on a simple client-server architecture and standard xR SDKs. We were able to use that platform to conduct a first study on xR device combinations from user's perspective. We found that a combination of VR-PC and HoloLens 2 is more likely to be used than other device combinations.

We will continue this work, to understand how to overcome disadvantages of specific xR device types and aim at equal possibilities for all xR users. We hope that in the near future existing xR SDKs such as MRTK will expand their functionality towards simple cross-platform xR collaboration.

References

1. AltspaceVR - minimum system requirements (2022). https://docs.microsoft.com/en-us/windows/mixed-reality/altspace-vr/getting-started/system-requirements
2. Azure spatial anchors documentation - azure spatial anchors (2022). https://docs.microsoft.com/en-us/azure/spatial-anchors/
3. Balani, M.S., Tümler, J.: Usability and user experience of interactions on VR-PC, HoloLens 2, VR cardboard and AR smartphone in a biomedical application. In: Chen, J.Y.C., Fragomeni, G. (eds.) HCII 2021. LNCS, vol. 12770, pp. 275–287. Springer, Cham (2021). https://doi.org/10.1007/978-3-030-77599-5_20
4. de Souza Cardoso, L.F., Mariano, F.C.M.Q., Zorzal, E.R.: A survey of industrial augmented reality. Comput. Ind. Eng. **139**, 106159 (2020). https://doi.org/10.1016/j.cie.2019.106159
5. Grubert, J., Tümler, J., Mecke, R., Schenk, M.: Comparative user study of two see-through calibration methods. VR **10**(269–270), 16 (2010)
6. Hrimech, H., Alem, L., Merienne, F.: How 3D interaction metaphors affect user experience in collaborative virtual environment. In: Advances in Human-Computer Interaction 2011 (2011)
7. Kavanagh, S., Luxton-Reilly, A., Wuensche, B., Plimmer, B.: A systematic review of virtual reality in education. Themes Sci. Technol. Educ. **10**(2), 85–119 (2017)
8. Martín-Gutiérrez, J., Mora, C.E., Añorbe-Díaz, B., González-Marrero, A.: Virtual technologies trends in education. Eurasia J. Math. Sci. Technol. Educ. **13**(2), 469–486 (2017)
9. Mirror networking (2022). https://mirror-networking.gitbook.io/docs/
10. Mixed reality toolkit | pointers (2022). https://docs.microsoft.com/en-us/windows/mixed-reality/mrtk-unity/features/input/pointers?view=mrtkunity-2021-05
11. Park, S.Y.: An analysis of the technology acceptance model in understanding university students' behavioral intention to use e-learning. J. Educ. Technol. Soci. **12**(3), 150–162 (2009)
12. Pečiva, J.: Active transactions in collaborative virtual environments. Ph.D. thesis, Faculty of Information Technology, Brno University (2007)
13. Perkins Coie LLP: 2020 augmented and virtual reality survey report. Technical report (2020). https://xra.org/wp-content/uploads/2020/07/2020-ar-vr-survey-report-0320-v4.pdf
14. Photon engine | realtime intro (2022). https://doc.photonengine.com/en-us/realtime/current/getting-started/realtime-intro
15. Reese, G.: Database Programming with JDBC and Java, Chapter 7: Distributed Application Architecture. O'Reilly (2000)
16. User experience questionnaire (2022). https://www.ueq-online.org/
17. van Schaik, J.: Positioning QR codes in space with Hololens 2 - building a 'poor man's Vuforia' (2021). https://localjoost.github.io/Positioning-QR-codes-in-space-with-HoloLens-2-building-a-'poor-man's-Vuforia'/
18. Vu, Q.H., Lupu, M., Ooi, B.C.: Peer-to-Peer Computing: Principles and Applications. Springer, Heidelberg (2010). https://doi.org/10.1007/978-3-642-03514-2

Using Multi-modal Machine Learning for User Behavior Prediction in Simulated Smart Home for Extended Reality

Powen Yao[✉] ⓘ, Yu Hou, Yuan He, Da Cheng, Huanpu Hu, and Michael Zyda

University of Southern California, Los Angeles, CA 90007, USA
{powenyao,houyu,heyuan,chengda,huanpuhu,zyda}@usc.edu

Abstract. We propose a multi-modal approach to manipulating smart home devices in a smart home environment simulated in virtual reality. Our multi-modal approach seeks to determine the user's intent in the form of the user's target smart home device and the desired action for that device to perform. We do this by examining information from two main modalities: spoken utterance and spatial information (such as gestures, positions, hand interactions, etc.). Our approach makes use of spoken utterance, spatial information, and additional information such as the device's state to predict the user's intent. Since the information contained in the user's utterance and the spatial information can be disjoint or complementary to one another, we process the two sources of information in parallel using multiple machine learning models to determine intent. The results of these models are ensembled to produce our final prediction results. Aside from the proposed approach, we also discuss our prototype and discuss our initial findings.

Keywords: Natural language processing · Virtual reality · Machine learning

1 Introduction

Users typically interact with existing Smart Home Devices (SHDs) in the market through the use of a 2D menu or through speech recognition via Smart Assistants. 2D menus and Smart Assistants leave out 3D spatial information that can potentially be used to interact with the SHD naturally, such as performing a pointing gesture to select a device. With speech recognition via Smart Assistants, the user also needs to rely on memory to choose the right SHD and the right interaction, or to resolve any mistake by dialoguing with Smart Assistants. These interaction techniques create redundant steps that force the user to temporarily detach from their objective and perform actions via proxies.

Our approach seeks to take advantage of the 3D spatial information that will become increasingly available through Augmented Reality (AR) technology (e.g. Ultra-wideband) that will allow the system to track the user and SHDs in

© The Author(s), under exclusive license to Springer Nature Switzerland AG 2022
J. Y. C. Chen and G. Fragomeni (Eds.): HCII 2022, LNCS 13317, pp. 94–112, 2022.
https://doi.org/10.1007/978-3-031-05939-1_7

3D space. We propose using the user's spoken utterances and body information together with position and rotation data from the SHD, and take a multi-modal approach to improve the SHD interaction into a more continuous, natural, and immersive experience. Specifically, we use natural language processing (NLP) technologies to extract information from the user's utterance, allowing the user to speak naturally and express their intents without having to be precise.

This approach allows the user to freely mix speech and gestures as needed. For example, the user could simply look towards the microwave and say "turn on" to turn on the microwave. Alternatively, the user could say "microwave" and then perform a gesture to open the microwave. We also consider how the user can differentiate wearable smart devices from stationary smart home devices. For example, if the user is wearing headphones, saying "play music" will result in the music coming from their headphones instead of a boombox near the user. However, if the user is looking at the boombox, "play music" is more likely to target the boombox absent any other input from the user.

We simulate this proposed smart home experience in a virtual reality environment for three reasons. First, the VR devices make it possible for us to intuitively and efficiently capture all the required information and data and test the outcome. Second, it frees us from the technical details of the differences in application programming interfaces and functionality across existing SHDs. Third, it enables us to simulate SHD functionalities that may not be common or available today (Fig. 1).

Fig. 1. Simulated smart home environment in virtual reality. Cyan head in the middle represents the user

2   Related Works

Virtual Control Interface (VCI) [4,5] has used the user's body information as well as NLP in a virtual smart home environment. When the user looks at the environment in a VCI, the user is presented with indicator points for each SHD. When the user selects an indicator point through hand interaction, the VCI provides the user with the corresponding user interface for that device. The user can then use a simple two axis slider menu to fine-tune the settings, access the advanced menu, or use voice commands to interact with the SHD. VCI's approach is limited to using user's hands for selection and interaction with NLP is only used to select from a list of existing commands. In contrast, our approach aims to allow the user to perform the selection or interaction via either NLP or hand interaction or a combination of the two. We address the potential for ambiguity through the use of machine learning and ensemble.

There are already explorations on learning relationships between natural language instructions and indoor vision [1,3]. However, due to the 2D task limitations, these explorations are all focusing on using computer vision technologies without considering real environment spatial information. Our work focuses on exploring smart home interaction through a multi-modal approach that makes use of natural language processing and spatial information from the user and devices to improve on traditional voice commands.

A previous work demonstrating a Dynamic Predictive Modeling Approach of User Behavior in Virtual Reality [2] utilizes the body interactions of a user to predict the user's future behaviour. In this application, real-time data communication is employed to track the accurate location and orientation of a head-mounted display device worn by the user. This work's methodology for predicting future movements of the user inspired us to consider a user's related spatial information when predicting the user's intended interaction with smart home devices.

3   Smart Home Device Interaction

3.1   Types of Smart Devices

For a smart home scenario, we envision three categories of devices: Stationary Exocentric Devices, Mobile Exocentric Devices, and Egocentric Devices. These distinctions among devices allow for more detailed interactions and allow for optimization in the design of our prediction system.

Stationary Exocentric Devices: Stationary exocentric devices are what generally comes to mind when discussing SHDs. These devices are stationary when in operation and they are exocentric as they do not move when the users move. Examples include light fixtures, ovens, and microwaves. Due to their generally stationary nature, the position and rotation of these devices do not need to be constantly sent to the server.

Mobile Exocentric Devices: Mobile exocentric devices are mobile when in operation and they are exocentric as they move on their own as part of their operation. Examples include autonomous robotic vacuum cleaners and grocery delivery robots. In addition to the potential need to select the device spatially, the user may also need to instruct these devices spatially. For example, the user may point to a location and instruct the selected robot to "clean here". Due to their mobile nature, their current spatial information will need to be updated while in operation.

Egocentric Devices: Egocentric devices are equipped by or otherwise move alongside the user. Examples include smart phones, glasses, watches, and earphones. Egocentric devices also include kitchen devices that are held by the user, such as a handheld mixer or a blowtorch. Although some of these devices are currently not smart devices and require hand-operated buttons, it's not hard to imagine a smart handheld mixer where the user might say, "mix on low for 30 s".

For our research, while predicting the specific object the user wants to interact with, we can take the intrinsic differences between these three categories into account. Obvious differences include size and mobility. Stationary exocentric devices are often larger because they do not need to be mobile, and exocentric devices in use are always mobile whenever the user is moving. A less obvious intrinsic difference is that a selected egocentric device is normally very close to the user's position if it is outside of the user's eyesight. By defining these prominent characteristics of devices, we can identify more relevant data to train the model more efficiently.

3.2   Types of Smart Devices Interaction

We examined common functionalities among SHDs and grouped them into sets of common actions that are shared between different devices. See Table 1.

We also found it useful to think of these functionalities as either states or processes. Many functionalities to alter the state of the SHD can be changed into a process by introducing a timer. For example, commanding the oven to "bake" or "start" will change its state to baking. However, the user can also say "bake for 60 min" which will change the command from a state change into a process.

Open/Close: Open and close are common actions related to any SHD with a door, cover or lid. When the user says "Open the microwave", the door of the targeted microwave should open. However, if the door of microwave is already open, the command should not have any effect.

Start/Stop: Start and stop are typically associated with the primary default function of the device. When the user says "start" to a dishwasher, the dishwasher starts the wash cycle. Some SHDs are multi-purposed and a simple "start" command is only able to start its default function. For example, a typical oven can bake or broil, and "start" would only be able to start baking at a default temperature. Additional information can be provided through NLP or hand interaction to handle more complicated cases such as "broil for five minutes" or "start baking at 200 F".

Table 1. Type of smart home interaction

	Open-Close	Start-Stop	Turn Light On-Off	Start-Stop Timer	Device-unique action
Light			X		
Counter sink	X	X			
Oven	X	X	X	X	Grill
Refrigerator	X	X	X	X	
Boombox	X				Play music
Microwave	X	X	X	X	
Dishwasher	X	X			
Rubbish bin	X				
Cabinet	X		X		

Turn Light On/Off: Control the primary light for the device, such as the light in an oven, microwave, or cabinet. In the case of a light fixture where the primary purpose is lighting, start/stop would have the same effect as turn light on/off.

Start/Stop Timer: Control the timer associated with the device. This is normally associated with SHDs like ovens and microwaves. With AR, however, we can create a virtual timer and associate it with any SHD and attach additional SHD interactions, allowing any SHD to operate on a timer.

Add/Remove/Edit/View Notes: Similar to Start/Stop Timer, the user can associate information with a SHD using AR. This could be supported on the Operating System level. This allows the user to associate recipes with an oven or a grocery list with the fridge.

Device-unique Action: Any action that is not covered by the interaction above is considered a device-unique action. For example, having the refrigerator dispense ice or having the oven perform its clean operation.

To allow more natural speech, we implemented a synonym transformation method to recognize the synonyms users express. For example, if the user says, "turn on the microwave", our NLP model will detect 'turn on' as the user intent and transform it into 'start' in order to match our predefined actions. In this way, the system can be flexible instead of requiring users to speak specific commands.

3.3   Ways to Target a Device

We evaluated common SHD interactions and identified eight likely ways to target a smart home device.

By SHD Name: The user can choose a device by explicitly referring to the device's unique name or predefined nickname, e.g. "open oven 01". This is the most common and straightforward way to interact with a device, but requires extra precision and the user must refer to a device by a specific name which the user may not be familiar with.

By SHD Type: The user can choose a device by explicitly referring to the device's type, e.g. "open the microwave". This makes it easy to choose the device if there is only one copy of this particular type of device. If there are more, however, we will require a prediction from our model to differentiate between the devices.

By SHD Type and Spatial Reference: Additional spatial information regarding the intended SHD target could be provided to help identify it, e.g. "open the cabinet to the left of the fridge". Here, we evaluate positional data to select a device.

By Gaze: The user could interact with a device via looking at[1] a SHD and saying commands such as "open it". Our model uses Euclidean distance and cosine distance to determine which SHD is closest to the user's line of sight.

By Hand Direction: The user could interact with a device via pointing[2] at it and saying commands such as "open that". We determine which device is pointed at in a similar way to a gaze.

By Recent Process Completion: The user could interact with a device that has recently finished a task, either by saying "open the microwave which just finished" or simply "open". If a SHD has recently finished an operation, it is more likely that the user may want to interact with it. Our model assigns higher priority to these devices when instructions lack an obvious target.

By Special Command Set: The user could interact with a device via its unique function with a command such as "start the timer for 5 min" which includes both start and stop instructions. We can add more weight to those SHDs bundled with specific timer commands when we choose the target.

By User Equipment: The user could interact with a device they are currently equipped with. For example, the user may want to take a picture of the food with a high-end camera (exocentric) setup on the table, with smart glasses, or with a smartphone. In these cases, spatial relationships between these devices and the user can be used for disambiguation.

For example, if the user is looking at the exocentric camera, that camera would take precedence even though the user is wearing smart glasses. If the user is currently holding a smartphone, and looking at a plate of food near the exocentric camera, the distance between the user's hand and the smartphone would suggest that the user is using the smartphone and that should take precedence. At any other time, "take a picture" will activate the camera on the user's smart glasses. In the case that the user wants to use an egocentric device over an exocentric device, the user can include key words in the utterance to signify an egocentric device over an exocentric device, such as "take a picture with my glasses".

---

[1] In the absence of a VR headset with eye-tracking features, we approximate this with a simple head gaze based on the headset position and rotation.

[2] We use VR controller's position and rotation to simulate user pointing.

4   System Architecture

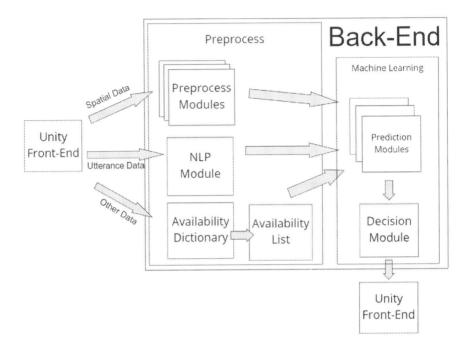

Fig. 2. System architecture overview

4.1   Pipeline Flow

Figure 2 is a high level flow chart of our system. Each interaction cycle contains the following steps:

1. Front-End: We collect the spatial information of the user and SHDs. We also get the user's speech audio in order to use natural language processing to convert it into utterance text for the NLP module to use.
2. Data to Back-End: The Front-End makes API calls to the Back-End to send spatial data, utterance data, and any other relevant data such as SHD states.
3. Preprocessing Modules: Spatial algorithms on the server preprocess the spatial data by calculating various distances and other information used to evaluate the 3D space.
4. NLP module: The NLP module runs intent classification on utterance text and generates intent and entities. If the utterance was not sent to the Back-End in the form of a text string, the conversion would also happen here.

5. Availability Dictionary & Module: The dictionary simply stores information on all the devices available to the user. The dictionary does not need to be updated constantly. The Availability List, however, can change constantly based on the current SHD states.

6. Prediction Modules: The data, intent, and entity information is then processed by our Prediction Modules to determine the user's target device and action. Each Prediction Module is a different multi-modal machine learning model in our implementation.

7. Decision Module: This module takes the output of the Prediction Modules and determines the final output to send back to the front end.

8. Response: The finalized response that contains the target device and target intent is then sent back to Front-End as a API response.

9. Action: The Front-End performs the user's intent on the predicted SHD.

4.2   Preprocessing Modules

We process the raw environment and user information into different lists for the Prediction Modules to use. The NLP Module also preprocesses information, but is listed separately due to our emphasis and reliance on NLP.

Two different distance lists are used to represent spatial information (e.g. User Gaze)[3]. A cosine distance list measures which devices are in front of the user and how far away they are from the user's orientation. A Euclidean distance list measures the spatial distance between the SHDs and the user in 3D space. Both are necessary, as neither list by itself can capture all kinds of distance relationships.

We can also generate cosine distance and Euclidean distance list for different parts of the user's body, such as the head and hands. In addition, the user may also want to interact with a SHD that has just completed a process. These lists can be utilized by the machine learning model to make predictions and are provided below for the sake of completeness.

– Object to Head Cosine Distance List (Directional)
– Object to Head Euclidean Distance List (Far or near)
– Object to Left Hand Cosine Distance List (Directional)
– Object to Left Hand Euclidean Distance List (Far or near)
– Object to Right Hand Cosine Distance List (Directional)
– Object to Right Hand Euclidean Distance List (Far or near)
– Recently Interacted SHD List

Implementation of Preprocessing Modules. In our model, we implement several Preprocessing Modules, each with distinct algorithms.

---

[3] The same process can be used on the user's other body-related information, such as a hand direction.

Object to Head/Hand Cosine Distance List. Cosine distance is used in predictions where we need to determine which devices are in the front of the user or measure the angle between the user's gaze and each individual SHD.

$$Cosine\ Distance = 1 - \cos(\mathbf{u}, \mathbf{v}) = 1 - \frac{\mathbf{uv}}{\|\mathbf{u}\|\|\mathbf{v}\|} \tag{1}$$

where u is the head heading vector and v is the smart home device vector.

Object to Head/Hand Euclidean Distance List. Euclidean distance is used in predictions where we need to determine which devices are near or far away from the user. We measure this distance in the 3D space for each individual SHD.

$$d\,(p,q) = \sqrt{\sum_{i=1}^{n} (q_i - p_i)^2} \tag{2}$$

where p is the head position and q is the smart home device position.

4.3   NLP Module

The NLP module handles the user's utterance and processes it for the multi-modal machine learning module. First, the user's speech is processed and converted into text. In our current implementation, we are using the speech recognition service in Windows 10 through Unity to convert the user's utterance into a text string on the Front-End. However, this can also be done with any chosen NLP solution on the Back-End as well as by outside servers. For example, we could send the user's utterance to the Back-End as a WAV file to accommodate other speech recognition services and allow a way to double-check the results if needed.

The second step is making sense of the converted text string. The goal of the NLP module is to parse as much relevant information as possible to determine the user's target device and intent. We can view this as trying to fill in a simple sentence in the grammatical form of subject-verb-object where the subject is assumed to be the user, the verb is the intent or the desired action, and the object is the desired smart device.

Other information in the sentence is used to better identify the verb and object. We could also parse the text to get additional information and therefore achieve the different ways to choose a device as mentioned in Subsect. 3.3.

Implementation of NLP Module. Similar to how the Preprocessing Modules provide two lists based on spatial algorithms, the NLP module provides an intent availability list and an entity list in conjunction with the Availability Dictionary & Module.

This intent availability list, see below Fig. 3, makes use of the intent recognized by the NLP model. Since there is a static list of what an object can do,

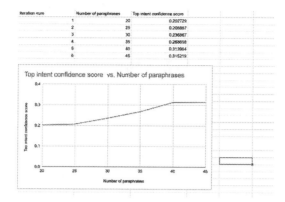

Fig. 3. NLP model result

after receiving the intent, we can generate a list with the keys being the unique identifiers of the SHDs, and the values being Boolean values indicating whether the intent can be performed on that SHD.

Entity List. Since the NLP Module has the ability to recognize predefined entities from the utterance, we can generate a list with the keys being the unique identifiers of the SHDs and the values being Boolean values indicating whether an object was directly mentioned in the user's original utterance.

Examples of Utterances Providing Additional Information Example 1: If the user says "open this," the keyword 'this' will be picked up from the utterance, and the objects closer to the user will get additional weight during target prediction.

Example 2: The NLP model stores a list of object names and customized nicknames. For example the object named 'Microwave 1' could be associated with a nickname "Tiger Microwave". If the user mentions either of these names by saying, "open Microwave 1," or "open Tiger Microwave," both utterances will be interpreted as the entity 'Microwave 1'.

Example 3: If the user mentions any number that's not part of an object name in their utterance, such as "open these three" the NLP module could return the top three results from our target prediction models instead of only returning the default single result. Similarly, if the user says "turn on these two stoves", we could filter the target prediction model result down to only stove type objects and then follow a similar procedure.

Example 4: If the user uses any transitional words like "open this and that, then play music", our NLP module will split up the utterance at the transitional words and process each part separately. In this specific case, the utterance will be split into three segments: "open this", "that", and "play music". If no intent is found in a segment but a target SHD is identified, it will be associated with the same intent found in the previous segment.

Example 5: If the user says, "Open the cabinet to the left of the fridge," the module should recognize that the object is a cabinet. The additional keywords 'left' and 'fridge' should be recognized and used so that the cabinets near the refrigerator and on the left will get additional weight during the prediction.

Implementation with RASA Framework. For the proof of concept and prototype, we are using the RASA framework to train and make inferences. We focus on simple cases with one verb and one noun, but allow for user ambiguity.

RASA is originally designed for conversational agents such as chatbots. This conversational approach includes tools for recognizing entities and predicting intents based on a text utterance. Specifically, RASA uses the SpacyFeaturizer, which provides pre-trained word embeddings. For intent recognition, we are using the Bag-of-Word (BoW) algorithm. Below is an example:

- (1) Turn on the microwave.
- (2) Turn off the oven.

The BoW algorithm will construct the list of words: ["turn", "on", "off", "the", "microwave", "oven"]. Since there are a total of 6 unique words here, each utterance will be converted to a vector of length 6.

- (1) [1, 1, 0, 1, 1, 0]
- (2) [1, 0, 1, 1, 0, 1]

For entity recognition, we are using a Conditional Random Field (CRF) algorithm. CRFs are a class of statistical modeling methods often applied in pattern recognition and machine learning and used for structured prediction. A CRF algorithm can take context into account to quickly identify parts of speech.

Data Preparation. Before training the model, we cast our data into the RASA data formats

- Regex-features. This is less important for the purpose of our model, but can contain pattern information for identifying special entities such as zip codes or oven temperatures.
- Entity-synonyms. This is where we define the entities and their synonyms. For example the value "pan" can be associated with synonyms ["pan", "pot", "wok"]. This way, the user could say "grab the pan" or "grab the wok", and the entity extracted will always be "pan".
- Common-examples/paraphrases. This is where we put the training utterances, their intents, and the included entities. For example for the intent "open", the training utterances or paraphrases would be "open this", "make this open", "open it", etc.

Inference. At inference time, the model will output the prediction result in three lists:

- **Entities** will contain a list of all entities recognized from the utterance.
- **Intent** will contain the name and confidence score of the intent with highest prediction confidence.
- **Intent-ranking** will contain a full list of intent names and their corresponding prediction confidence, ranked from highest to lowest.

4.4   Prediction Modules

This module consists of multiple ML models. Each of the ML models takes the multi-modal information provided and tries to predict the target device and action. As the provided input may be missing parts, the goal is to let different machine learning models evaluate the data and combine their strengths for our final result.

Implementation of Prediction Module. Using a pre-defined object availability list, the distance lists from the Preprocessing modules, and the entity list and predicted intent from the NLP module, we train three different ML models: multiple linear regression, decision tree, and naive Bayes. Each of these models is given randomly split collected data.

Multiple linear regression is an extension of simple linear regression. With input lists, the model is trained to assign weights to each list and uses the best weight to get the most likely target.

Decision tree uses an adopted CART algorithm to learn a series of if-else decision rules and uses these rules to predict the final target.

Naive Bayes considers the input lists as different probable features of the classifier and the predicted target will be returned based on the highest calculated probability.

Implementation of Multiple Linear Regression. Multiple regression is an extension of simple linear regression. It is used when we want to predict the value of a variable based on the value of two or more other variables. The variable we want to predict is called the dependent variable (or sometimes, the outcome, target or criterion variable). This model suits our needs since we have multiple lists of weights and want to make a prediction based on all of them.

For implementation, the multiple linear regression model takes four lists as inputs: cosine distance, Euclidean distance, object availability, and entities. At training time, the pre-processed data is split randomly into two groups, in a 7:3 ratio, where 70% of the data is used for training and validation, while the rest is used for testing.

Training. For this model, we are making a general assumption:

$$X = a * x_1 + b * x_2 + c * x_3 + d * x_4$$

The meaning of each parameter is as followed:

- x_1 is the euclidean distance, a is the weight of x_1;
- x_2 is the cosine distance, b is the weight of x_2;
- x_3 is the entity list value, c is the weight of x_3;
- x_4 is the availability value, d is the weight of x_4;
- X is a value that indicates the likelihood of an object being the target.

Based on the above assumption, the model's job is essentially finding the correct weight a, b, c, and d, or the alpha vector [a, b, c, d].

Here, x_1 and x_2 are distance values, and we make the assumption based on common sense that the smaller the distance value is, the more likely an object is the target. On the other hand, if a SHD is available for an operation, or if it is directly mentioned in the user's utterance, the model should recognize it as being a more likely target. Therefore, we initialize the alpha vector to be [−1, −1, 1, 1].

Below is an outline of each epoch:

1. Randomly sample validation-batch-size length data from the training data set, and test-batch-size length data from the test data set.
2. Randomly change one of the four weights in the alpha vector by learning-rate.
3. Using the current alpha vector, compute the X current value and use it to rank the list of objects in the validation set.
4. If the validation result is positive (defined as having correct inferences for more than half of the data in the validation set), then maintain the current alpha vector and proceed.
5. If the validation result is negative, reverse the change by 0.5 * learning rate.
6. Perform the same ranking on the test-data set, and maintain the result.

Currently, the best training accuracy we achieved is 0.923. After increasing the batch size to 71 and collecting more data from Unity, we have also added a strategy which decreases the learning rate from 0.1 to 0.05 after epoch 300. The model converges to about 0.9 accuracy after epoch 400.

Implementation of Decision Tree. Decision tree models can be used to predict the target SHD with a classification problem using decision rules, which is suitable for predicting the target object that the user wants to interact with. Moreover, decision tree models can be visualized in order to help us better understand how the model is processing our data.

The decision tree model takes four data sets as inputs: cosine distance, Euclidean distance, intent availability, and entities.

An illustration of a preprocessed dataframe is presented (Tables 2 and 3):

Table 2. Decision tree data format

	Cosine distance	Euclidean distance	Availability	entity
0	1.3901	2.4835	0	1
1	1.3898	2.4833	0	1
2	1.3877	2.4828	0	1
3	1.3860	2.4826	0	1
...	...	...	...	...
27393	1.7267	3.1056	0	0
27394	1.7300	3.1057	0	0
27395	1.7317	3.1058	0	0

At training time, the preprocessed data was split randomly in different ratios to train and validate the model, including a 7:3 ratio and a 8:2 ratio and we adopted a CART algorithm to train our model.

At each decision step, we want to find for each variable, i.e. cosine distance&euclidean distance&availability list&entity list, which variable provides the largest information gain. By applying the CART algorithm, the variable with the largest information gain at each node will be found and set as the tree node. In general, we make the following assumption:

$$p_{mk} = 1/N_m \sum_{y \in Q_m} I(y = k)$$

Since we are solving a classification problem, the proportion of class k for each node m is represented by our assumption formula. For the entropy calculation at each node, we are making the assumption with the following formula:

$$H(Q_m) = \sum_k p_{mk}(1 - p_{mk})$$

The model initially achieved 100% accuracy when predicting with the test data split from the whole dataset. Since decision trees are susceptible to over-fitting during the training process, we implemented different methods to control the tree size. The accuracy was reduced to 94% on the test data after these adjustments.

Implementation of Naive Bayes. Naive Bayes classifiers are a supervised learning method. This model will produce a probability for each instance based on weights of selected features in the training data. Naive Bayes models require less training data with short training time and can handle both continuous and discrete data. This model suits our needs, since our training dataset includes both continuous and discrete data. Additionally, since our smart home application should react quickly, the shorter training time makes a naive Bayes approach an ideal choice.

The Naive Bayes classifier model takes two preprocessed lists as inputs: cosine distance and intent availability list. At training time, the preprocessed data is split randomly into two groups in a 7:3 ratio, where 70% of the data is used for training and validation, while the rest is used for testing. For this model, we are making a general assumption:

$$P(c|X) = P(x_1|c) * P(x_2|c) * P(x_3|c) * P(x_4|c) * P(c)$$

- $P(c|X)$ is a value that indicates the likelihood of an object being the target;
- $P(x1|c)$ is the likelihood which is the probability of Cosine Distance given class c;
- $P(x2|c)$ is the likelihood which is the probability of Euclidean Distance given class c;
- $P(x3|c)$ is the likelihood which is the probability of intents given class c;
- $P(x4|c)$ is the likelihood which is the probability of entity given class c;
- $P(c)$ is the prior probability of class c.

Approximately 27,000 collected utterances were used for training and testing the naive Bayes model with 97% overall accuracy on the test data.

4.5   Decision Module

The output from the Prediction Modules is processed in the Decision Module. In this module, we propose the use of an ensemble method to improve the results of our ML module, though other methods could be used.

Implementation of Decision Module. For our implementation, we adopt the voting ensemble strategy to decide the final target. Each model has one vote regarding the target prediction, and this strategy uses the majority vote to decide the final target. If there is no majority, our final prediction relies on the single model with the best test accuracy. In our simple scenario, this strategy was sufficient. A more robust Decision Module could also be based on majority voting, weighted voting, simple averaging, weighted averaging, and so on.

5   Preliminary User Study

To prove the concept, we designed experiments based on Stationary Exocentric Devices and focusing on interactions via SHD Name, SHD Type, Spatial References, and Gaze. We believe our method could be easily extended to more complex scenarios with other types of SHDs and forms of interaction.

5.1   Setup

We built our virtual environment in Unity 2019.4.29f1. We used Unity's XR Interaction Toolkit (XRITK) for interacting with objects using VR hardware. We used XRITK in place of a platform-specific solution such as SteamVR or Oculus for multi-platform support. For VR Hardware, we used HTC Vive (2016), but any VR equipment with 6 Degree of Freedom Headset and Controllers can work.

For the purposes of this project, we deployed our NLP & Machine Learning server on a local Flask server, such that each time a REST API request and user utterance is received from the Unity Front-End, the NLP & Machine Learning server processes it and returns the inference result.

5.2   Procedure

Overall, there are two roles in the data collection process: A VR smart home user and the experiment host. Under our instruction, participants were asked to enter the scenario through VR devices and were prompted with tasks such as opening and closing the microwave ten times while standing at different locations and instructed to give commands in various ways. The process is listed below:

- Host starts the experiment via pressing the 2D button on the PC with a mouse;
- User, equipped with the headset and controllers, enters the VR kitchen;
- User takes on the role of a smart home user and follows our instructions to finish different tasks;
- After all tasks are completed, the host stops the experiments and saves the results into a file that contains all position, rotation, utterance, target and gesture status information.

5.3   Collected Data for Training

As a result, we collected about 27k records of intents to open and close smart home devices, including three cabinets, a dishwasher, a freezer, a microwave, and an oven. Each record contains user and environment information. Data breakdowns are shown in Table 1.

Table 3. Data statistic

UID	Device	Open	Close
1	Cabinet	1966	1803
4	Cabinet	1768	2443
5	Cabinet	2316	1886
7	DishWasher	1933	1886
10	Oven	1744	1782
15	Microwave	1983	2023
20	Freezer	1786	1826

5.4   Data Format Detail

For user information, we track the current position and rotation of the user's head through the VR headset and the current position and rotation of the user's hands through the VR controllers. We also record the user's utterance as a WAV file and as a recognized text string[4]. Finally, to ensure that only relevant data was collected for training, we asked the user to push a button on the controller, which generates a timestamp and indicates the start of the user's utterance for speech recognition purposes.

For environment information, we assign each SHD a unique ID to identify it across sessions. For each SHD, we also track its position, rotation, appliance type, device state (including whether it is opened, whether it is started, whether its timer is started, whether its light is on, and any other applicable properties), and the times of its last user interaction and last completed action.

Since we are using the built in speech-to-text function in Unity and our NLP model has been performing well, we designed experiments to evaluate the performance of three machine learning models under real user cases.

5.5   Evaluation

The core idea of the evaluation is to test the performance of the system under real life scenarios. To simulate a full kitchen, we included seven target SHDs, including three cabinets at different positions, a dishwasher, an oven, a microwave and a freezer. We instructed the participant to look at five different gaze points for each device to mitigate user biases (different users might have different preferences when interacting with a device) and to repeat two operations: open and close. Details are as follows:

Intent: Open, Close
Target: 3 cabinets + dishwasher + oven + microwave + freezer
Gaze point: Center + near the target (left, right, top, bottom)

Then, we monitored the results and marked if the trial was successful or not for all combinations.

Our final count was 7 targets * 5 gaze points * 2 intents, i.e. 70 combinations. Multiple Linear Regression succeeded 60 times, Decision Tree succeeded 66 times, and Naive Bayes succeeded 68 times, with accuracy 85.71%, 94.29% and 97.14% respectively. With the ensemble strategy, the final accuracy was 100%, which is as expected because the current task does not contain many complicated cases like "open the left oven" or "play music using the earphones instead of the boombox".

---

[4] The speech recognition service in Windows 10 is used in Unity.

6 Limitations and Future Work

Our preliminary experiment shows promise, but is very limited. It only considers a few simple cases suggested by our proposed approach. Aside from the low number of use cases, we also did not collect a large amount of data to thoroughly test our current models. Thus, the current model may not be able to properly respond to situations that were not included in the training data or use cases it was not designed to handle.

For future work, we would like to support interactions with egocentric devices such as being able to look at the microwave while saying "play music" for the user's smartphone to start playing music. We would also like to support more complicated utterances to further make use of any additional data embedded in the user's utterance.

We also see opportunities to enhance smart devices on an Operating System level. For example, implementing the aforementioned ability to associate a timer to any state changing interaction to turn it into a process (e.g. turn off light for 3 min).

Lastly, we also look to apply this approach to contexts other than a smart kitchen or even a smart home. Users should be able to interact with virtual objects and tools using natural speech and hand interactions, whether they are in AR, VR, PC desktop, or mobile phone environments.

7 Conclusion

To interact with a smart home environment more naturally, we propose a multi-modal approach, where the user's intent is determined from the spoken command along with spatial information from the user and the various smart devices. We explored how various interaction cases can be handled by our proposed approach and verified our idea via preliminary experiments. We found our current approach is flexible and could be used to design more intelligent future extended reality homes. Although more experiments and studies are needed to make the system robust enough to be used in real life, we see this as a promising basis for future work in smart homes, along with other use cases that involve 3D user interaction within virtual workspaces.

References

1. Kolve, E., et al.: AI2-THOR: an interactive 3D environment for visual AI. CoRR abs/1712.05474 (2017). http://arxiv.org/abs/1712.05474
2. Köse, A., Tepljakov, A., Petlenkov, E.: Dynamic predictive modeling approach of user behavior in virtual reality based application. In: 2019 27th Mediterranean Conference on Control and Automation (MED), pp. 57–62 (2019). https://doi.org/10.1109/MED.2019.8798521
3. Shridhar, M., et al.: ALFRED: a benchmark for interpreting grounded instructions for everyday tasks. CoRR abs/1912.01734 (2019). http://arxiv.org/abs/1912.01734

4. Xu, Z., Lympouridis, V.: Virtual control interface: discover and control IoT devices intuitively through AR glasses with multi-model interactions. In: 2021 IEEE Conference on Virtual Reality and 3D User Interfaces Abstracts and Workshops (VRW), pp. 763–764. IEEE (2021)

5. Xu, Z., Yao, P., Lympouridis, V.: Virtual control interface: a system for exploring AR and IoT multimodal interactions within a simulated virtual environment. In: Stephanidis, C., Antona, M., Ntoa, S. (eds.) HCII 2021. CCIS, vol. 1420, pp. 345–352. Springer, Cham (2021). https://doi.org/10.1007/978-3-030-78642-7_47

Virtual Equipment System: Toward Bag of Holding and Other Extradimensional Storage in Extended Reality

Powen Yao⬥, Zhankai Ye(✉)⬥, and Michael Zyda

University of Southern California, Los Angeles, CA 90007, USA
{powenyao,zhankaiy,zyda}@usc.edu

Abstract. The term 'storage' in real life typically refers to a container that occupies physical space, such as rooms, closets, warehouses, etc. Our interactions with items stored within are constrained by physics in real life. However, Virtual Reality allows us to ignore certain rules. Inspired by a Bag of Holding from Dungeons & Dragons and other entertainment media, we envision a storage which can store more items than the physical space the container occupies by linking it to another dimension. Users can interact with the stored item as they would with containers in VR or physically enter the storage. We refer to this approach as 'Extradimensional Storage'. During our design and implementation of Extradimensional Storage, we identified five core components of a generic storage system, which are storage space, container, access, stored items and interactor. By altering the properties associated with the core components, we are able to implement Extradimensional Storage. We further applied the five core components to reinterpret the inventory taxonomy proposed by Cmentowski et al. Thus, our contributions include a general framework for storage, an implementation of a specialized version known as Extradimensional Storage, additions to the inventory taxonomy, and how properties of the core storage components can be utilized for different scenarios.

Keywords: Virtual Reality · Inventory · Game design · Taxomony · Human-computer interaction

1 Introduction

In current Virtual Reality (VR) games, there are three common ways to interact with storage:

1. **Real World Model**: Items stored in their original sizes and placed in an appropriately sized container in the world.
2. **2D Layout Model**: Multiple items stored as their miniature versions (for instance, icons) in a 2D grid layout as backpacks, chests, etc.
3. **Single Symbolic Model**: A single item stored as its miniature and placed in a storage location.

© The Author(s), under exclusive license to Springer Nature Switzerland AG 2022
J. Y. C. Chen and G. Fragomeni (Eds.): HCII 2022, LNCS 13317, pp. 113–130, 2022.
https://doi.org/10.1007/978-3-031-05939-1_8

We use the following terms to analyze these three storage solutions:

Egocentric vs. Exocentric. Egocentric and Exocentric describes the storage with respect to its location in space and how its spatial relationship is defined.

Egocentric refers to objects that are positioned in relationship to the user. Egocentric storage moves as the user moves. Examples of egocentric storage include holsters, pockets, messenger bags, etc.

Exocentric refers to objects that are positioned in relationship to the environment. Exocentric storage stays in the same location when the user moves, though it may be moved by other means. Examples of exocentric storage include closets, chests, sconces, etc.

Original vs. Symbolic. Original and Symbolic refer to the representations of the objects stored inside the container. Original, as its namesake suggests, is when the object is in its original, unmodified form. Symbolic is when the stored object is represented by a symbolic representation. This symbolic representation could be a 2D icon, a miniature version of the original 3D representation, or a line of text.

Single vs. Multiple. Single and multiple refers to the quantity of stored items that the storage solution can handle.

Table 1. Examples of storage solutions as characterized by size and egocentricity

Size/Ego-Exo	Egocentric	Exocentric
Original	Holstered weapon	Closet
Symbolic	Backpack	Chest with 2D layout

In the real world model, interactions with the stored item work the same way as they do in real life. The users have interactors, such as hands in real life or VR controllers in games, with which they can interact with the storage. Users must be close to the container and move their interactors to select and interact with the stored items. This allows the user to utilize their spatial memory. The 2D Layout Model uses less physical space. It allows users to retrieve their items with less effort. However, users are less able to utilize their spatial sense and memory with a 2D grid layout. It is particular difficult to utilize spatial memory if the content shifts around based on adding or removing an item.

In the single symbolic model, such as the wrist pocket in Half-Life: Alyx [3] or guns stored in holster in many VR games, objects occupy less space while in storage. Given that there is only one object, the storage and the stored item share the same location and users can utilize spatial sense to retrieve the object easily, especially if the storage is located on the user's body. However, the problem with this approach is that it cannot store more than one item. It is designed for storing and retrieving the most frequently used item only.

Additionally, item management, particularly with 2D User Interfaces, is common in games. However, there aren't many examples that apply spatial memory

Fig. 1. Examples of different storage techniques from Cmentowski et al., showcasing a 2D grid layout, a 3D grid layout, and an alternate 3D layout.

to item management, which is an important distinction. Users should be able to interact with the stored objects in 3D using a multitude of techniques, especially techniques that allow users to utilize their spatial sense.

As stated above, all three approaches have their own advantages and disadvantages. To bridge the gap between the three common but different cases of interaction, we propose a storage technique that allows the user to easily switch between the different approaches. This storage would occupy less physical storage space than the items stored inside while offering the user the ability to enter the storage as a room to utilize their spatial senses and spatial memory if needed. This approach and series of techniques would enable us to realize an Extradimensional Storage, commonly found in fantasy media, for instance, the bag of holding in Dungeons & Dragons, in virtual reality.

2   Related Work

The work of Cmentowski et al. [1] as shown in Fig. 1 illustrates a method to manage items in VR using a grid layout. This kind of technique help users manage their items efficiently since items can be placed in order. However, its disadvantages are also clear. It works like the bag systems in non-VR games, using icons or models to replace the real item.

Additionally, according to the work of Wegner et al., there is another approach which allows users to place items on their body, for instance, waist [8]. This approach brings spatial memory into the field. Also, it is easy to use because it works like real world. However, its disadvantage is that the number of items it can hold is limited since there aren't many spots on users' body that can be used to store items (Fig. 3).

Fig. 2. User in the game Fantastic Contraption seeing two different locations. On the left, we see the user's hand interacting with the world inside the helmet. On the right is the world the user and the helmet resides in.

Fig. 3. Approach made by Wegner et al. Items are placed around users' waist.

The game Fantastic Contraption motivated us to think about extradimensional space. Figure 2 shows the user looking at the world inside the helmet alongside the world the user and their helmet reside in. In this game, the player is able to put a helmet on the user's head in order to travel to a different location. That location essentially functions as a settings menu, including options such as level selection. When the helmet is removed from the player's head, the player's view will revert back to the original world. The helmet provides the user access to another space without having to physically relocate.

According to Tavanti et al., it is feasible to sustain a general superiority of the 3D display for the chosen spatial memory task, even when compared to a 2D non-scrolling display [2]. Thus, in order to bring spatial memory into VR, we combine the existing techniques of storage interaction and world interaction together. For some scenarios where efficiency is the top priority, the user will utilize the traditional class of storage interaction techniques. At the same time, user have the option of entering into a different world and fine-tuning their storage interaction techniques or making full use of their spatial sense to interact with objects in personal, peripersonal or extrapersonal space from within the storage space, similar to how the user can enter another location as in Fantastic Contraption.

3   Extradimensional Storage

Extradimensional Storage (EDS) refers to a storage system where the storage space is much larger than the space the storage container takes up. The extra space does not exist in the 3D world that the user occupies and no amount of movement in the 3D space will bring the user to that location. Thus, the storage exists in a separate dimension or a parallel universe and we refer to it as extradimensional based on the popular culture definition. Other similar concepts are hammerspace [7] where objects can be pulled out of containers that couldn't possibly fit the object. Finally, there's the concept of a pocket dimension. This concept utilizes a separate dimension, but the available space isn't so vast that one would consider it as a parallel universe [6].

3.1   Core Components of a Storage Framework

In our design and implementation of the Extradimensional Storage, we have identified five core components and their associated properties that make up a storage system. They are:

1. Interactor
2. Access
3. Container
4. Storage Space
5. Stored Item

Of the five core components, an implementation of an individual storage system (instance) would require three of the components, the container, the storage space within, and the access. Stored Item and interactor are required for the framework as a whole to function and to interact with the system, but is not needed.

In the case of EDS, the storage instance is made up of three components: the outside container, the inner Extradimensional Storage space, and the access via a physical manifestation called an entry. The entry is the physical space that connects the container and the storage space.

When users move their interactors through the entry, the interactors will enter the storage's dimension and cease to interact with the dimension the user was originally in. Instead, the user will be able to access the stored items within.

Each of the five components can be represented differently and have unique properties that greatly affect how the users can interact with the storage.

3.2   Taxonomy of Inventory Systems

The taxonomy proposed by Cmentowski et al. [1] can be linked to our proposal of the five core components of a storage framework. Figure 5 and Fig. 6 are figures we modified based on the original figure. We replicated the original figure with different background colors applied to the open codes, concepts, and building blocks to illustrate how the core components fit in and how it can be implemented. Further, we propose new additions to the taxonomy, which is shown with a different border.

3.3   Gestures Using Physical Objects

Of the five components, the interactor, container, and stored item exist as physical objects and can utilize motion gestures and surface gestures. Given an interactor such as hand or controller and a interacted object such as a container or a stored item, motion gesture refers to the movement of the interacted object due to the interactor. In the case of the surface gesture, the interacted object itself will not move, but the interactor will be in contact with the interacted object's surface and moving to perform a surface gesture. For example, on a mobile phone, we recognize shaking the phone as motion gesture and swiping on the screen as surface gesture. Figure 4 from Ze Dong et al.'s paper [9] clearly shows the difference between motion gesture and surface gesture.

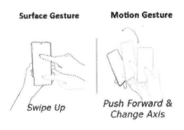

Fig. 4. Differences between motion gesture and surface gesture.

Unlike the real world, in virtual reality, players don't need a dedicated devices with accelerometers and gyroscopes. Any object can have its own motion gesture. Also, instead of needing a touch surface that can detect interactor, anything can have surface gesture. Thus, motion and surface gestures will be very easy to implement in VR.

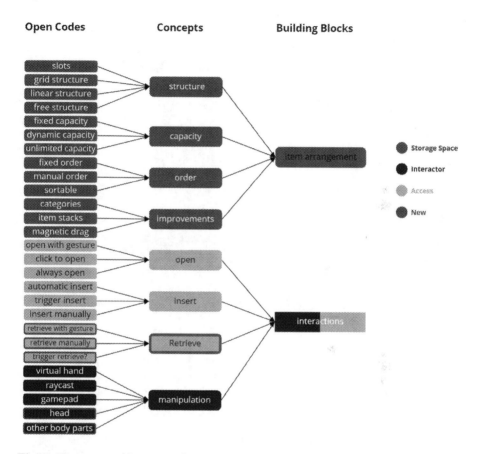

Fig. 5. Taxonomy of Inventory System Part I, modified to reflect the five core components of storage

3.4   Interaction Zones

On the other hand, the storage space and access are not physical objects. They are areas in space that can define new behaviors for interactions with physical objects. Whereas performing a controller gesture of up might not do anything in one space, it might retrieve the last item placed in the storage when performed inside entry space.

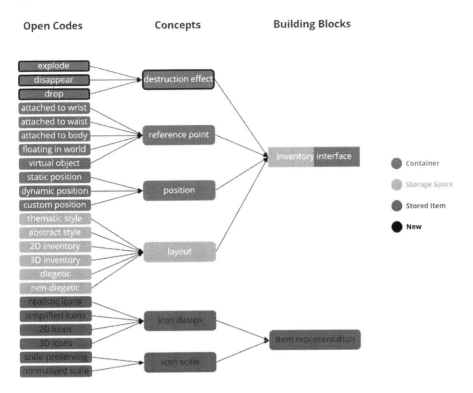

Fig. 6. Taxonomy of Inventory System Part II, modified to reflect the five core components of storage

We refer to these areas with different interactions opportunities as Interaction Zones. In other words, the interactor, container, and stored item can interact differently when inside the storage space (Storage Interaction Zone), inside the entry space (Entry Interaction Zone), or outside of either space (Default Interaction Zone).

The interactions users can perform in an Interaction Zone are thus referred to as Zone Interactions. In particular, Zone Gestures are a subset of Zone Interactions that we focus on in EDS.

4   Core Components of Extradimensional Storage

In this section, we describe each of the five core components and their associated properties, with emphasis on the implementation of EDS. We discuss some of the most representative properties as well as special cases or alternate usages to illustrate the potential of this storage framework.

The examples we have mentioned in Table 1 are actually properties belonging to different components. By analyzing the different properties of these different components of a storage framework, we can design and implement other storage solutions for different purposes by manipulating these properties.

4.1   Interactor

An interactor is a representation of the user that is able to interact with the storage. While it is common to use the user's hands or to substitute VR controllers as interactors, it is also possible for other body parts to be used as interactors, such as the user's head.

Interactor Properties

1. Direct vs. Remote Interaction
2. Physics Collider
3. Motion Gesture
4. Surface Gesture

For example, when the interactor is inside the storage space, its motion gesture may be adapted to retrieve multiple items. When the interactor is inside the Entry Interaction Zone, the motion gestures are replaced with a different set of motion gestures that allow user to retrieve items known as quick access, which we will describe in detail next.

4.2   Access

Access is the component that determines whether an interactor can interact with the storage system.

In the case of EDS, the entry area between the inside of the container and the outside world serves as the physical manifestation of Access. The entry is a representation of what allows users access to the storage, in this case, to access the EDS with their hands or the whole body.

The entry could be a bag opening, a mirror surface, or even a tattoo. The concepts of Interaction Zones and EDS allow the user to have much more user interaction within a small confined area, allowing these unusual objects to serve as both the container and the entry for storage.

The user only needs to be able to move their interactors to the entry in order to interact with the stored contents.

Access Properties. Access properties determine whether the storage is available for interaction. Access properties also includes what happens when an interactor interacts with a physical manifestation of the access such as the entry. A storage system can also have multiple different ways of accessing the storage, such as via different entry.

As the entry is an area of space, it provides modifiers to interactions that can be performed by physical interactors. These new interaction opportunities are called Entry Zone Interactions. Entry Zone Interactions allow for new interaction opportunities or colloquially as quick access and modification of its associated properties.

1. Entry Effect (Fig. 7)
   (a) Regular size
   (b) Enlarged
   (c) Non-linear mapping
2. Quick Access
   (a) First In First Out (FIFO)
   (b) Last In Fist Out (LIFO)
   (c) Gesture Based
   (d) Voice Recognition
3. Manual Management
   (a) Grab spatially only
   (b) Grab sockets only

Access Properties on Different Interactors. When the user enters the entry with either the hand or the whole body, the entry properties may apply and may change based on the interactor.

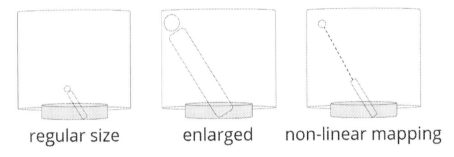

regular size   enlarged   non-linear mapping

Fig. 7. Three different settings for users to access items stored in the storage space, rectangles stand for users' arms and circles stand for users' hands/controllers

Like Fig. 7 illustrated, in the case of the user's hands (or controllers), the user's hand may be regular size, leaving the user only able to grab objects near the entry. The user's hand may be enlarged so that when the user's arm is all the way in the container, it will be just far enough to grab the item at the end of the storage. Alternatively, the arm size may remain unchanged, but we could allow for reach bounded, non-linear input amplification based on the work of Wentzel [4].

Similarly, while outside using quick access, the user may want to use different strategies or even multi-modality to access the items. By modifying the entry properties for quick access, we can allow the users to use gestures, voice recognition, or other means to access stored items (Fig. 8).

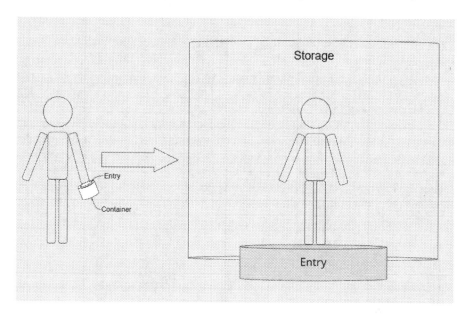

Fig. 8. While user is outside of the extradimensional space, the container is the size of a handbag. After the user enters the space through the entry, the user may find the storage space is large enough to stand inside.

4.3   Container

The container represents the part of storage that exists in the user's original dimension. It could be a bag, a cup, or even an pack mule. The container would follow physical rules in its original dimension.

Container Properties. Container Properties describe what happens to the container (and optionally its content) when the container is affected.

1. Egocentric vs Exocentric
2. Damage
3. Damage Propagation
4. Destruction
5. Weight
6. Motion Gesture
7. Surface Gesture

Egocentric vs Exocentric: Whether the container is attached to or follows the user or whether the container is attached to a location in the world.

Damage: Whether the container can be damaged, how it can be damaged, and the feedback to being damaged such as visual, sound, or haptic feedback.

Damage Propagation: When the container is hit or otherwise damaged, the contents stored inside could be unaffected, randomly damaged, equally damaged, etc.

Destruction: When the container is destroyed, what happens to the items stored inside. The items could either disappear, be dropped on the floor, or explode into pieces.

Weight: When users put a new item into the container, the weight of the container could increase based on the weight added, increase based on a fraction of the weight added, or remain unchanged.

Motion Gesture: When the user grabs the container and moves it around to perform gestures such as shake, jerk, etc. For example, the user may turn the container upside down with entry pointing down, then do a shake gesture in order to pour the contents of the EDS out.

Surface Gesture: When the user uses an interactor to draw a gesture on the surface of the container. For example, the user may draw a lock symbol to lock the container and prevent it from being accessed.

4.4   Storage

Storage may also be referred to as storage space, storage dimension, or storage world. It is the extradimensional space that is connected to the user's dimension via the Entry.

Storage Properties. Represent the forces that influence the storage space and thus affect the items stored within. These forces could be the standard laws of physics, or it could be other properties that will affect how the user will use this storage. For example:

1. Gravity
2. Drag Coefficient
3. Oxygen

Gravity, drag coefficient, and oxygen are all examples of properties that the storage space could have. These properties can then interact with any physical objects that enter the storage space. In the case of gravity, the storage space could have the standard 1G gravity, zero gravity, or other values of gravity. The different values of gravity could also affect different objects differently, so that normal gravity is exerted on the user while zero gravity applies to the stored objects.

In the case of drag coefficients, it would affect whether the object in motion will stay in motion or come to an immediate stop. This is particularly useful in combination with zero gravity so that stored objects would float in the air and stay in the air unless the user explicitly interact with them.

As for oxygen, it is often an important factor in our tabletop role-playing game inspiration. Some Extradimensional storage may contain oxygen, some may not. Oxygen levels may affect flammable items such as matches and torches. It may also affect whether a creature can stay alive inside the storage. The user may enter the extradimensional space to evade enemies, but would have limited time before suffocating to death. These has high relevance in VR game scenario.

Storage Properties also provide opportunities to implement features that a user may find useful in a work environment, allowing Extradimensional Storage to be used beyond VR games. In this case, the storage serves as a tool to modify properties of the stored items.

For example, a container could function as a sorting machine. Similar to folders in PC environment, the user can sort the items inside the storage based on parameters such as name, modified time, or size. Alternatively, the container could function as a translation machine. Any items that contain text elements such as documents would be translated to a different language, depending on the container used.

4.5   Stored Item

An item that is placed in a storage system is considered to be a stored item. A stored item often takes on different properties or interaction based on the current interaction zone. The stored item's own properties may also interact with the storage space's property.

1. Response to Oxygen
2. Response Gravity
3. Motion Gesture
4. Surface Gesture

The existence of oxygen in the storage space may affect the stored item as mentioned in the storage properties. As a physical object, we could use motion gesture or surface gesture with stored item. An example of a motion gesture with stored item would be a shake gesture on an item stored inside storage space to send it outside. An example of a surface gesture would be to draw an x on an item in storage space to send it outside.

4.6   Storage Sockets and Storage Queues

To aid the user with retrieving objects from outside the storage space, the user can make use of storage sockets and storage queues. These storage sockets and storage queues are not a core component of the storage system. Rather, they can be viewed as a limited version of the storage system that is used to make interaction with EDS easier (Fig. 9).

Storage sockets hold an item in space. This guarantees an item to be in a specific spatial location for the user to retrieve. Certain storage sockets could also be associated with the user's gesture actions instead of a spatial location.

Storage queues are an alternate version of storage sockets. It provides a track for users to place multiple items with one end of the track functioning as a socket. When the user interacts with the storage queue from the outside, the user will grab the item at the end of the track and the next item will fill in for the grabbed item. This allows the user to repeatedly grab multiple items from the same location or using the same gesture.

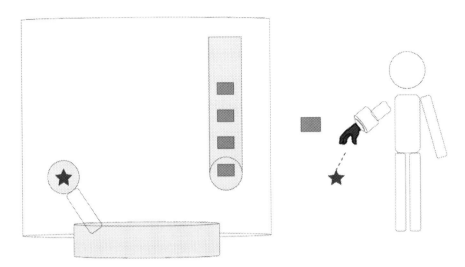

Fig. 9. Difference between storage sockets and storage queues

5   Interaction with Extradimensional Storage

In addition to the typical storing and retrieving that a storage has, EDS has additional storage and retrieving interaction based on whether the user is inside the storage space or outside. In this section, we will describe some of the main interactions that EDS is designed for.

5.1   Entering and Leaving

The user's hands can enter the Extradimensional Storage through the entry in order to retrieve items. What sets the EDS technique apart, however, is that the user can also enter the Extradimensional Storage as if it was a room (Fig. 10).

By placing the container with the entry side facing the user over the user's head, the user can enter the Extradimensional Storage space as if entering an attic, a closet, or a storage room.

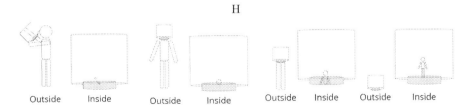

Fig. 10. Process when the user enters the storage space.

As the container moves from the top of the user's head down, the user goes through different states of entry. The first state is just outside of the head or part partially over the head. The user can see into the container, but any head rotation would not influence the world within the container. The user can get a better view by changing the angle between the head and the container. The user can use the other hand to retrieve any item in sight. This is a quick way to retrieve an item.

The user can then move the container further down to the neck position or even further down to the waist. The user can leave it there as if equipping the container on the head as a helmet or an article of a shirt covering the user to the waist. In this state, the user's head has entered the storage space, and rotation will affect what the user sees inside the storage space. With the container equipped, the user can use both hands to interact with the storage space or the outside world, depending on whether the hands are above or below the head/entry. In this state, other users would see the user with their upper body covered by the container.

Finally, the user can drag the container completely down to the feet. The user fully enters the Extradimensional Storage with a translucent view of the outside world at their feet. From the perspective of the outside world that the user came from, the only thing remaining is the container on the floor (Fig. 11).

To leave the bag, the user can grab the edge of the entry and pull up. Then the user will return to their previous position in the original world.

5.2   Storing and Retrieving

When storing and retrieving items, the user can either be outside of the storage space or inside the storage space.

Storing While Outside

1. store in the bag anywhere
2. store in a specific position in the bag

The user can either place an object at the opening of the bag or move the bag and any eligible objects will be sucked into the bag. In this scenario, the user will not be able to decide where any items will be placed and stored. The new items will be stored in automatic sequence, whether by LIFO, FIFO or a customized sequence. If the user would like to place the item in a specific place, they can place the item in a storage socket or any other specific location. The default position and sequence for the items can be configured by users.

Retrieving While Inside. There are three ways for users to retrieve items from inside. First, the user can grab an object and bring it to the outside world. However, this method can only retrieve one item each time. Second, if the user wants to take more than one item, they can grab each object and drop it through the entry. These objects will show up in the outside world at the user's feet.

Finally, users can perform a double grip action on any number of objects to tag or untag them. Tagged objects will have an outline applied to them. When the user leaves the bag of holding, the tagged items will be retrieved from the EDS.

Retrieving While Outside. For retrieving items from outside, the most basic way is to move a hand inside the entry and grab. At this moment, the user's hand will disappear in its original dimension. Also, only a user who owns the space is able to view and retrieve the items inside. If the storage space is large, a non-linear mapping hand-movement can be applied to the user's hand. While the user's hand is in the entry, a floating minimized 3D model will appear in front of the user's head to help users retrieve items precisely. Similar to the world in miniature technique, the 3D miniature world to help players view the storage space more clearly [10]. Instead of a representation of the space that the user is in, however, it represents the world within the container. Players' interactors will be minimized as well and the interactors can move freely in the miniature world. The position of this miniature world can be adjusted as needed. Nevertheless, if the user do not select anything while putting their controllers into the access, quick access functions will be activated. The user can either grab the next item placed in the queue, take the first item in FIFO or LIFO order, or just say the object's name. Furthermore, the user can reach a hand inside and point in a specific direction to retrieve a pre-selected item, which is a form of gesture based access. These methods are designed the maximize the efficiency of retrieval. Once the user becomes familiar with these options, the speed of retrieval is significantly buoyed.

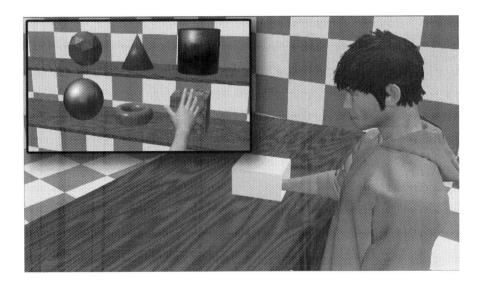

Fig. 11. Rendering image of extradimensional storage

Finally, the user can also turn the bag upside down and shake. As the user continues to shake, items fall out in a FIFO sequence until the storage space is empty.

5.3   Object Organization

Depending on the Storage Properties and how the user has arranged the Storage, objects inside the EDS may be floating in the air, on the floor, or held in place by additional storage system such as shelves or other constructs. Aforementioned constructs such as Storage Sockets and Storage Queues can further aid the user in organization in addition to storing and retrieving items. By allowing the user to place objects in 3D space, the user can rely on muscle memory or spatial memory to retrieve items.

Additionally, if the user chooses to arrange their items automatically, there are many sorting strategies available to be applied, for instance, items can be arranged by their categories such as tools, weapons, etc.

6   Conclusion

In this paper, we propose a framework to expand the capability of existing VR storage solution based on our inspiration from Extradimensional Storage. In order to create an extradimensional storage, we ended up designing and building a storage system with five core components. We then interpreted and matched the five core components with Cmentowski's Ground Theory analysis work and made some additions of our own. The five core components model provides us with an alternative perspective to think about and design a storage system. Each component of the storage system can have unique properties that change how the user may utilize the storage, transforming simple storage systems an Extradimensional Storage of fantasy works or into productivity tools. Our work results in a highly generalizable storage framework as well as its specialized implementation in the form of Extradimensional Storage. With EDS, users have the ability to retrieve and store items quickly and efficiently as with a normal storage container, but can also enter the container as a storage room to make use of different interaction techniques. As the concept of a 'Metaverse' is frequently mentioned and implemented, our approach has applications not only for games, but also for work and XR interactions.

References

1. Cmentowski, S., Krekhov, A., Krüger, J.: I packed my bag and in it I put...": a taxonomy of inventory systems for virtual reality games (2021)
2. Tavanti, M., Lind, M.: 2D vs 3D, implications on spatial memory. In: IEEE Symposium on Information Visualization, INFOVIS 2001, pp. 139–145 (2001)
3. Games, V.: Half Life: Alyx. ([CD-ROM] (2020)

4. Wentzel, J., D'Eon, G., Vogel, D.: Improving virtual reality ergonomics through reach-bounded non-linear input amplification. In: Proceedings of the 2020 CHI Conference on Human Factors in Computing Systems, pp. 1–12 (2020)
5. Khadka, R., Banic, A.: Prop-based egocentric and exocentric virtual object storage techniques, pp. 779–780 (2020). https://doi.org/10.1109/VRW50115.2020.00240
6. Pocket Dimension. https://tvtropes.org/pmwiki/pmwiki.php/Main/PocketDimension. Accessed 4 Feb 2022
7. Hammerspace. https://tvtropes.org/pmwiki/pmwiki.php/Main/HammerSpace. Accessed 4 Feb 2022
8. Wegner, K., et al.: Comparison of two inventory design concepts in a collaborative virtual reality serious game. In: Extended Abstracts Publication of the Annual Symposium on Computer-Human Interaction in Play, pp. 323–329 (2017). https://doi.org/10.1145/3130859.3131300
9. Dong, Z., Zhang, J., Lindeman, R., Piumsomboon, T.: Surface vs motion gestures for mobile augmented reality. In: Symposium on Spatial User Interaction (2020). https://doi.org/10.1145/3385959.3422694
10. Stoakley, R., Conway, M., Pausch, R.: Virtual reality on a WIM: interactive worlds in miniature. In: Proceedings of the SIGCHI Conference on Human Factors in Computing Systems, pp. 265–272 (1995). https://doi.org/10.1145/223904.223938

Virtual Equipment System: First Evaluation of Egocentric Virtual Equipment for Sensory Settings

Powen Yao[1]([⊠])(ID), Shitong Shen[2], and Michael Zyda[1]

[1] University of Southern California, Los Angeles, CA 90007, USA
{powenyao,zyda}@usc.edu
[2] Pittsburgh, USA
https://viterbischool.usc.edu/

Abstract. Virtual Equipment System is a system in extended reality that provides the user with equipment slots and equipment that serve as an interface for further interactions. The equipment slots are storage locations for equipment that is associated with the user spatially (egocentric). Due to the virtual nature of the system, these egocentric equipment slots do not have to be attached to the user's body; they can instead belong in the user's personal, peripersonal, or extrapersonal space, which greatly expands the potential space for storage. Virtual Equipment are virtual objects that fulfill specific roles or functions. Their look and feel provide cues for how to interact with them as well as potential functionalities associated with them. In this paper, we present our first results from an experimental evaluation of the Virtual Equipment System. We compare different interaction techniques available in our Virtual Equipment System with the standard technique for adjusting audio volume as well as look at the effect of having the same Virtual Equipment in different egocentric equipment slots located in the three different spaces.

Keywords: Virtual Reality · Hyperphysicality · Virtual Equipment System · Egocentric equipment

1 Introduction

In extended reality, one can easily interact with virtual objects. As the objects are virtual, many of the restrictions that apply to real-world objects such as the laws of physics no longer apply. Instead, these objects can follow rules of physics different from our real world, such as an object floating in mid-air or appearing out of nowhere. We refer to this quality as hyperphysicality and interfaces that take on that quality as hyperphysical user interfaces.

Thus, when a user in extended reality is working and in need of equipment, we can use hyperphysicality as a lens for design and create a better equipment

---

S. Shen—Independent.

© The Author(s), under exclusive license to Springer Nature Switzerland AG 2022
J. Y. C. Chen and G. Fragomeni (Eds.): HCII 2022, LNCS 13317, pp. 131–149, 2022.
https://doi.org/10.1007/978-3-031-05939-1_9

system than what is available in the real-world. However, whereas hyperphysicality encourages us to think of new and unusual ways that an interface can work, we need something to ground our design in the practical and useful. For that, we use whole-body interaction as our other design lens. Anything is possible with hyperphysicality, but whole-body interaction grounds us to the practical.

From these design lenses came our Virtual Equipment System (VES). Virtual Equipment System [12] is a system in extended reality that provides the user with equipment slots and equipment that serve as an interface for further interactions. The equipment slots are egocentric storage locations for the equipment that are virtual and attached to the user's spatial location. Virtual equipment are virtual objects that fulfill some role or function. There are unique and common interactions that users can perform with each Virtual Equipment. Finally, pieces of Virtual Equipment are organized into collections of equipment known as Equipment Sets [10]. Each Equipment Set can be oriented toward a particular purpose, such as sensory options [9] or privacy settings [11].

Equipment and equipment slots would seem very familiar to their real-world counterparts. However, hyperphysicality affects the system on all levels. There are Virtual Equipment where there is no equivalent in the real world. Virtual Equipment Slots can float in mid-air or allow retrieval of multiple equipment from the same spatial location. Users can perform interactions such as surface gestures with these Virtual Equipment that would not be possible or feasible without additional costs. Equipment Sets can be worn simultaneously as well as be switched on and off at a moment's notice. This makes our Virtual Equipment System a very powerful tool at the user's disposal.

To evaluate our Virtual Equipment System, we try to utilize the design lens of whole-body interaction. A faster technique may not always be better in XR due to the many contexts and settings that the user may be in. For example, the user may not be able to do large sweeping gestures or may not wish to speak aloud. We must also consider how the user's body interact with the interface by measuring factors such as the user's head and hand movement and rotation.

1.1   Background

Skeuomorphism can be used to a greater extent in Virtual Reality. Instead of having a small flat 2D icon that represents a particular collection of functionalities, we can have a 3D representation that mimics its real-world equivalent and allows for interactions similar to real-world interfaces. This can aid the user in associating the functionality of a piece of Virtual Equipment with its shape. The shape may further aid the user in associating it with a spatial location, allowing the user to utilize proprioception and spatial memory to interact with their equipment.

Prior work such as Body Mnemonics [1, 2] by Ängeslevä et al. have examined the possibility of utilizing the user's body image as a mnemonic device. This idea seeks to reduce the user's cognitive load by using the user's body image as a frame of reference. The user moves a handheld mobile device to different parts of the body to activate and store information, namely apps. Whereas Ängeslevä et al. primarily deal with mobile devices and use the body location as a starting point to access additional functionalities, our approach allows the user to utilize the equipment stored at the location directly for multiple interactions.

By encapsulating a collection of related functionalities into a virtual object, this allows us to retrieve detailed information as needed while also drawing upon techniques from mobile device interactions such as mobile gestures, surface gestures [4], and other customized gestures [8].

In contrast, works by Khadka et al. [5] utilize physical props to enable using different body parts as storage. They also compared the use of egocentric and exocentric storage techniques and found that egocentric storage techniques take less time to complete than exocentric storage techniques [6]. However, due to the physical nature of the props, the storage locations are limited to where they could be placed physically in the real-world. Their work also focused on using the location as simple storage and not a potential area for further interactions.

2 Virtual Equipment System

Previously, we have proposed and created a demonstration of a set of Virtual Equipment known as the Sensory Equipment Set or simply as Sensory Set. Sensory Set provides the user with a universal way to quickly adjust sensory settings through a body-centered 3D user interface.

What this means is that if the user wants to adjust the audio settings for the VR experience, the user can simply interact with the Virtual Headphones to do so. If the user wants to adjust the visual setting, the user would interact with Virtual Goggles, and so on.

While our initial work dealt exclusively with egocentric equipment in personal space, our recent work [7] has also introduced Egocentric Equipment that resides in peripersonal space (space reachable by the user) as well as extrapersonal space (space reachable by the user with a tool). We initially chose to use headphones to represent a piece of equipment that can alter the audio setting and place it next to the users' ears. Instead of headphones by the users ear to adjust audio settings, we could represent the same equipment as a music player and place it in a different location in the personal space or even in the peripersonal space.

2.1 Qualities

Each equipment within the Virtual Equipment System can exhibit different qualities relative to the user's body position and influence its interactions with the surrounding space. To better illustrate and discuss the different equipment, we introduce the following categories and concepts.

Egocentric vs Exocentric. This pair of qualities describe whether an object is spatially attached to the user or to something other than the user.

Egocentric Equipment are objects that belong to and follow the user as the user moves. Real-life examples of egocentric equipment are backpacks, tools, watches, and so on. They may also be referred to as body-locked, body-stabilized, body-fixed, or body-anchoring in existing works.

In contrast, the positions of Exocentric Equipment are not related to the user spatially. They may remain fixed as the user move or move while the user remains stationary. They are also referred by world-locked or world-anchoring.

Using real-life as an analogy, egocentric equipment would be a knife in the user's hand or a worn apron while exocentric equipment would be a kitchen oven, microwave, or a fridge.

Personal, Peripersonal, and Extrapersonal Equipment. Personal, peripersonal, and extrapersonal space are terminologies in the field of proxemics to describe objects in relationship with the user's body [3].

The space around the user can be divided into personal space, peripersonal space, and extrapersonal space. Personal space is the area immediately bordering the body. Peripersonal space constitutes the area that is within the distance of the user's reach. Finally, extrapersonal space indicates the area beyond the user's reach.

In real life, egocentric equipment typically resides in the user's personal space. However, Virtual Egocentric Equipment can reside in these different spaces relative to the user. Thus, we use these terminologies to describe the user's equipment based on the equipment's storage location.

As personal, peripersonal, and extrapersonal space describe objects in space, the spatial relationship between the user and a given equipment can change very rapidly, regardless of whether the equipment is egocentric or exocentric. In this paper, when we refer to personal equipment, peripersonal equipment, or extrapersonal equipment, we are referring to egocentric equipment that is stored in personal, peripersonal, or extrapersonal space, respectively.

Qualities Summary. From the qualities introduced, a piece of equipment can be described by [Egocentric/Exocentric] and if it is egocentric, it can be further described by the quality [Personal/Peripersonal/Extrapersonal]. For example, a machete stored on the user's back would be described as a personal egocentric equipment. A bookshelf would be an exocentric equipment. A hammer always floating right by the user's 9 o'clock position within the user's reach would be a egocentric peripersonal equipment. In this particular analysis, however, we primarily focus on evaluating egocentric equipment. Thus, we simply refer to it as personal equipment, peripersonal equipment, and extrapersonal equipment.

However, a more accurate descriptor would be [Egocentric/Exocentric] Equipment stored in [Personal/Peripersonal/Extrapersonal] slot.

2.2   Interaction Techniques

There are many ways that the user can utilize Virtual Equipment within the Virtual Equipment System. In this paper, we evaluate some of the interaction techniques in order to assess their effectiveness against traditional interactions as well as against each other.

Grab Equipment. The most common method of interaction would be grabbing a Virtual Equipment. As the user moves the VR controller close to the Virtual Equipment, they would feel a vibration to indicate that they can interact with the Virtual Equipment. Then, the user can use the Grip Button to grab the Virtual Equipment. To illustrate, the user can move the controller next to the user's ear where the Virtual Headphone is equipped. After feeling the vibration, they can use the grip button to grab the Virtual Headphone. This interaction is introduced as it forms the basis of other interactions, thus it is not evaluated by itself but as a part of other techniques.

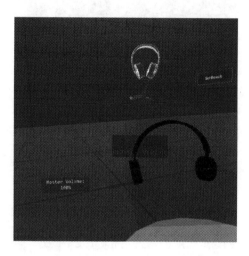

Fig. 1. The right controller (not visible from user's perspective) is performing a motion gesture. The user has visual feedback from text of the current volume, text of the current detected gesture, and a mirrored copy of the Virtual Equipment at the ear in front of the user.

Equipment Motion Gesture. An Equipment Motion Gesture can be performed while a Virtual Equipment is grabbed. We refer to the term Motion gestures from work with mobile devices. With mobile devices, the user can grab the device and then move it in 3D space to perform 3D spatial gestures.

In the case of an Equipment Motion Gesture, the user can grab the equipment and move the controller in different directions and, as a result, the equipment would follow along with it. We compare the new position of the equipment with respect to its stored location to determine if the user has perform an gesture in one direction.

For example, the user can grab Virtual Headphones by the user's ear. As the user move the controller up and down, the Virtual Headphones would move up and down along with it, triggering the Virtual Headphones' Equipment Motion Gesture. The up and down gesture corresponds to increasing or decreasing the system's volume.

Due to the stored location of certain equipment, it may be difficult for the user to visualize what they are doing. To address this, we provided visual feedback in the form of a mirrored copy of the grabbed Virtual Equipment in front of the user while showing the currently recognize gesture as shown in

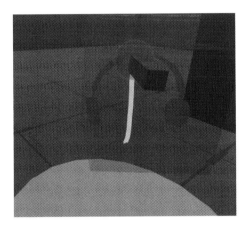

Fig. 2. The user moving the controller up in the peripersonal equipment's interaction zone to perform an up surface gesture.

Equipment Surface Gesture. An Equipment Surface Gesture is an alternative way to interact with a Virtual Equipment. Surface Gesture typically refers to drawing on a surface with a finger, as is the case in mobile phones.

In this particular implementation, the user will use the trigger to start a surface gesture. The user will first move the controller near the equipment. When the controller is close enough to perform an interaction, the user will feel a vibration. At this stage, the user can hold down the trigger button and move the controller in different direction. This interaction will not pick up the Virtual Equipment.

To provide further visual feedback, we have added a trail to trace the movement while the trigger button is held down as shown in Fig. 2. To illustrate, the Virtual Headphone could support Equipment Surface Gesture as an alternate way of interaction. In this case, the user would use the VR controller to draw up or down on the hear the Virtual Headphones to increase or decrease the audio volume, respectively.

An important distinction to note is that the current implementation of the Surface Gesture is different from a Surface Gesture on a mobile phone. Unlike a normal surface gesture, the VR controller does not necessarily move along the surface of the Virtual Equipment. Instead, the VR controller performs a gesture within a zone defined by the Virtual Equipment. This was implemented due to the lack of haptic feedback for the surface of a Virtual Equipment. In the paper and in the experiment, we refer to this gesture as Surface Gesture for simplicity.

Alt Node Interaction. Finally, the last interaction in the Virtual Equipment System being tested is the Alt Node interaction. Inspired by the alt key on a traditional PC keyboard, the alt node provides a modifier to existing interactions.

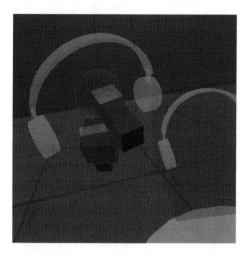

Fig. 3. User dragging and dropping a Virtual Equipment into the Alt Node in order to access the associated detailed menu.

Fig. 4. An example of a detailed Virtual Equipment menu associated with the Virtual Headphones.

With regards to Virtual Equipment, it provides a way to quickly access a detailed menu specific to that equipment. With a virtual equipment grabbed, the user can move it to the Alt Node and release it as shown in Fig. 3. Upon detecting a released Virtual Equipment in its area, the alt node will open the setting menu associated with the Virtual Equipment. For example, bringing Virtual Headphones to the Alt Node will bring up a detailed audio menu, including specific volume settings such as sound effect volume, music volume, etc. This is shown in Fig. 4.

This provides the user with an alternative to access sensory settings instead of the current standard of pushing the menu button, then navigating to the general setting menu and finally to the appropriate specific setting menu.

3   Experiment

We evaluate the Virtual Equipment System through a series of experiments and comparisons. Specifically, we seek to assess the performance of the different interaction techniques.

We perform a within-subjects study and evaluate the user on adjusting the audio settings with equipment motion gesture, equipment surface gesture, alt node interaction, and menu button interaction.

We also compare whether the user prefers having the audio adjustment equipment next to the ear in personal space, in other locations in the personal space, or in peripersonal space. The user is evaluated on motion gesture as well as surface gesture for each equipment.

In total, there are eight different tasks that the user need to perform.

– Personal Equipment (Ear) Motion Gesture
– Personal Equipment (Ear) Surface Gesture
– Personal Equipment (Waist) Motion Gesture
– Personal Equipment (Waist) Surface Gesture
– Peripersonal Equipment Motion Gesture
– Peripersonal Equipment Surface Gesture
– Moving a slider on a 2D Menu for Audio, through the use of Alt Node
– Moving a slider on a 2D Menu for Audio, through a menu button on the VR Controller

To represent equipment in different spaces, we place the equipment in different locations with respect to the headset as shown in Fig. 5. The personal equipment by the right ear is placed 15 cm to the right and 7 cm to the back of the headset. The personal equipment by the waist is placed at 60 cm below below the headset. The peripersonal equipment is placed 20cm to the front, 20 cm and 60 cm in front of the headset.

Due to time constraints, these values are pre-determined to roughly represent equipment in the respective areas. The only customization allowed is how far in front of the headset the peripersonal equipment is placed. The user is able to calibrate user's arm reach by moving the arm in front of the user, parallel to the floor, and selecting the 'Set Reach' button with the ray controller.

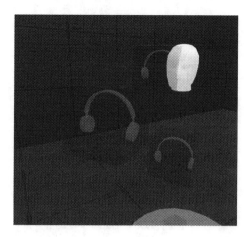

Fig. 5. Next to the cyan head is the personal equipment stored by the ear, to the very left is the peripersonal equipment stored at 1 o'clock with respect to the user's head. At the bottom is the personal equipment stored by the waist.

Table 1. Equipment X, Y, Z position offset from VR headset in meters

Location	x	y	z
Personal Equipment (Ear)	0.15	0	−0.07
Personal Equipment (Waist)	0	−0.6	0
Peripersonal Equipment	0.2	0.2	0.6

3.1   Setup

We have written a program using Unity to guide our testers through the experiment. They are asked to perform a series of tasks with various tools from the Virtual Equipment System. When first initiating the program, a virtual panel on the right side guides the user through the tutorial section and encourages them to familiarize themselves with the various interaction techniques. The user can move through the tutorial at their own pace. This typically takes about 10 min.

Once the user finishes the tutorial section, they will move onto the experiment portion where they will be shown prompts for the user to perform a certain action.

When the user is ready, they can initiate a task by placing both of their controllers inside the pink translucent cube in front of them as shown in Fig. 6. While both controllers are within the cube, a timer on the top of the pink cube will count down from 1 s to 0 s. If the user moves the controller away before the timer hits 0, the timer will revert to 1 s.

This pink cube is meant to represent a neutral starting position and a way for the user to indicate that they are ready for the next task. To avoid giving any technique too much advantage, it is placed 40 cm below and 20 cm in front of

Fig. 6. Pink cube in front of the user near the chest area. It is used to confirm user's readiness. (Color figure online)

the user's headset. This roughly place the pink cube 49.5 cm away from the ear, 28 cm away from the waist, and 48.9cm away from the peripersonal location.

Once the timer finishes count down to 0, a random interaction technique would show up in front of the user. The user would need to adjust the volume with the indicated method. This is considered a single task. When the user has performed each technique once, the user is then presented with the option to choose any technique as the 9th task. After this 9th task is completed, a block of interaction has been completed and the process repeats. The user will perform 9 tasks in each block with 10 blocks in total, meaning that the user will have completed 90 tasks.

The eight tasks are described in short-hands to the user

- Headphones + Motion
- Headphones + Surface
- Waist + Motion
- Waist + Surface
- Peri + Motion
- Peri + Surface
- Alt Node + Slider
- Menu Button + Sliders

Hardware. Our development device and targeted device is HTC Vive. However, due to COVID-19, we asked for volunteers to participate in the experiment remotely. As such, a variety of different VR devices were used in the experiment including HTC Vive, HTC Vive Cosmos, Valve Index, Oculus Rift S, and Oculus Quest 1 and 2.

We used Unity 2019.4.29f1, Unity's older Built-In XR system, and XR Interaction Toolkit to support VR devices from different vendors. However, there are minor discrepancies between the different devices and our implementation that may have affected the results. There are a few known issues: HTC Vive vibration only results in a small blip, and HTC Vive's menu button corresponds to Oculus family device's face button and not the menu button that Oculus users are familiar with. In addition, the different controllers have slightly different setup that resulted in the ray used to select menu to have slightly different orientation that we did not account for.

3.2   Quantitative Data

The same set of quantitative data are measured for each interaction technique. It constitutes of the time taken to complete the task, the cumulative positional movements for the head and the VR controllers, as well as the cumulative rotational movements for the head and the VR controllers while performing the task.

While leaving the headset stationary on a flat surface, we observed that the positional numbers remain fixed before the third decimal place. To filter out the noise, we discard any detected changes below a millimeter.

We performed the same tests for rotational numbers and decided to discard any changes below 0.1f. After the experiment, all of the recorded data are saved to a comma separated value (CSV) file.

3.3   Qualitative Data

After the experiment, we ask our volunteers to complete a post-experiment questionnaire to give us more insights on the Virtual Equipment System and help us assess what areas can be further improved. They were first asked to evaluate Motion Gesture, Surface Gesture, and Alt Node Interaction in the following three areas: how mentally demanding was the task, how physically demanding was the task, and how much do they like completing the tasks using those specific interaction techniques. They are asked to choose a number between one (very low) and five (very high).

Then, they are asked to assess Personal Equipment by the Ear, Personal Equipment by the Waist, and Personal Equipment in the Peripersonal Space using the same three evaluation categories and rating system. Finally, they are encouraged to share any thoughts specific to the overall experiment as well as each interaction technique in written form.

4   Data and Results

Eleven participants (N=11, mean age: 27.1, SD: 4.43, male/female, 9/2) volunteered for the experiment.

The participants are given email instructions, link to pre-experiment questionnaire, a build of the experiment, and a post-experiment questionnaire.

For all eight interaction techniques, we computed the average number of the different measurements and compared them within each criteria to find out the best performing method. We also collected data through a post-experiment questionnaire to get a sense of how people feel about the different interaction techniques.

4.1 Pre-experiment Questionnaire Results

Due to COVID-19, the experiment is conducted remotely with the participants own VR equipment. The VR equipment include 4 HTC Vive, 2 HTC Vive Pro, 1 HTC Vive Cosmos Elite, 1 Oculus Quest, 1 Oculus Quest 2, and 2 Oculus Rift S.

The participants report themselves as having high familiarity with VR (mean of 4.09, lowest of 3) on a scale of 1–5 between not familiar to very familiar. They also report of commonly using VR equipment (mean of 3.36, lowest 2) on a scale of 1–5 between never to very often.

4.2 Experiment Data

We removed the first block of data collected out of 10 blocks as users are still getting familiar with the system. We also removed any obvious outliers such as when a task takes over a minute due to the user going back to read the instructions.

Table 2. Duration

Source	Type	Duration (in seconds)	stdev
Personal Equipment (Ear)	Surface	2.61	1.17
Peripersonal Equipment	Motion	2.96	1.55
Personal Equipment (Ear)	Motion	3.03	2.09
Personal Equipment (Waist)	Motion	3.10	1.78
Peripersonal Equipment	Surface	3.32	1.94
Personal Equipment (Waist)	Surface	3.37	2.42
Alt Node	Slider	5.25	2.25
Menu Button	Slider	5.39	1.34

Duration. The duration records the time taken to complete a task. It starts when a task is prompted and ends when the user successfully adjusts the volume with the correct interaction technique.

We can see that Personal Equipment (Ear) Surface Gesture has the lowest average value of 2.61 s. It is closely followed by Peripersonal Equipment Motion Gesture with an average of 2.96 s and other motion gestures, then by the rest of the surface gestures. The interaction method that has the longest duration is the Controller Menu Button, averaging around 5.39 s. The Alt Node Button interaction barely beats the menu button with an average duration of 5.25 s.

This is in line with our expectation that having direct access to modifying volume through gestures would be much faster than going through a series of menus. What is interesting to note is that although Surface Gesture with Personal Equipment by the Ear is the fastest result in this experiment, the other surface gestures are much slower in comparison.

Table 3. Head movement and rotation

Source	Type	Accumulated head movement (in meters)	stdev	Accumulated head rotation (in degrees)	stdev
Personal Equipment (Ear)	Surface	0.03	0.06	36.60	44.04
Personal Equipment (Ear)	Motion	0.03	0.06	40.85	53.18
Menu Button	Slider	0.04	0.07	37.78	44.78
Peripersonal Equipment	Surface	0.05	0.14	53.82	68.39
Peripersonal Equipment	Motion	0.07	0.12	62.78	70.19
Alt Node	Slider	0.08	0.11	85.69	54.66
Personal Equipment (Waist)	Surface	0.16	0.19	85.46	81.91
Personal Equipment (Waist)	Motion	0.16	0.18	90.88	75.60

Head Movement. The head movement records how much the head has moved during each task. We would calculate the head position difference at each frame, adding up to the total distance travelled by the head.

We observe that both Personal Equipment (Ear) gestures recorded the least head movement, followed closely by the Controller Menu Button interaction. The interaction technique requiring most head movements were the Personal Equipment (Waist) gestures.

Head Rotation. The head rotation records how much the head has turned during each task. We would calculate the head rotation difference at each frame, adding up to the total rotation angle by the head.

The Personal Equipment (Ear) Surface gesture exhibits the least head rotation, with an average total rotation angle of 36.6°C. It is closely followed by the Controller Menu Button which is 37.78°C. Both Personal Equipment (Waist) gestures and the Alt Node Button require the most with a total rotation at least two times bigger than the Personal Equipment (Ear) Surface gesture.

Two Hands Movement. The two hand movement records how much the two hands have moved during each task using the same method to calculate the total path for the head movement.

We observe a big disparity between the button gestures. The Controller Menu Button records the least hand displacements, while the Alt Node Button has the longest average distance travelled. The Alt Node Button interaction (2.46 m) has roughly 2.8 times more displacements than that for the Controller Menu Button interaction (0.87 m).

Table 4. Two hands movement and rotation

Source	Type	Accumulated two hands movement (in meters)	Accumulated two hands rotation (in degrees)
Menu Button	Slider	0.87	454.07
Personal Equipment (Ear)	Surface	1.63	813.18
Personal Equipment (Waist)	Surface	1.80	835.74
Personal Equipment (Waist)	Motion	1.89	653.86
Personal Equipment (Ear)	Motion	1.91	876.68
Peripersonal Equipment	Motion	1.96	515.26
Peripersonal Equipment	Surface	2.02	538.18
Alt Node	Slider	2.46	1,051.32

Two Hands Rotation. The two hand rotation records how much the two hands have rotated during each task using the same method to calculate the total rotation angle for the head rotation.

The three interaction methods with the least amount of hand rotation angle are respectively the Controller Menu Button, the Peripersonal Equipment Motion Gesture, and the Peripersonal Equipment Surface Gesture, ranging between 454.07 and 538.18°C. The Alt Node Button records the largest rotation angle of 1051.32°C.

Total Movement. The total movement adds up the head movement data and the two hands movement data to give a holistic view of the total amount of physical movements when completing a task.

After combining the numbers, we can see that the Controller Menu Button requires the least amount of movement, while the Alt Button requires the most.

Total Rotation. The total rotation sums up the head rotation data and the two hands rotation data to compute the total amount of physical rotation when completing a task.

Similar to total position, the Controller Button Menu takes the lead with the least total rotation angle, in contrast to the Alt Button that records the most total rotation angle. The second and third place are taken by the two Peripersonal Equipment Gestures.

Table 5. Total movement and rotation

Source	Type	Accumulated total movement (in meters)	Accumulated head rotation (in degrees)
Menu Button	Slider	0.90	491.86
Personal Equipment (Ear)	Surface	1.66	849.78
Personal Equipment (Ear)	Motion	1.94	917.53
Personal Equipment (Waist)	Surface	1.96	744.74
Peripersonal Equipment	Motion	2.02	578.04
Personal Equipment (Waist)	Motion	2.05	921.20
Peripersonal Equipment	Surface	2.07	592.00
Alt Node	Slider	2.54	1,137.01

4.3   Post-Experiment Questionnaire Data

In the first section of the post-experiment questionnaire, the volunteers are asked to evaluate the four different interaction gestures (Surface Gesture, Motion Gesture, Alt Node+Slider, and Menu Button+Slider) on three aspects: Mental demand, physical demand, and their preference. The user rate each on a 1–5 point scale from very low to very high.

Table 6. Post-experiment questionnaire: interaction technique

Technique	Mental demand	Physical demand	Preference
Motion Gesture	1.55	1.82	3.82
Surface Gesture	1.73	1.55	3.55
Alt Node + Slider	2.27	2.45	2.45
Menu Button + Slider	2.09	2.00	2.27

Motion Gesture turns out to be the least mentally demanding (1.55) whereas Surface gesture is the least physically demanding task (1.55). Motion Gesture is the most preferred interaction method (3.82). Surface Gesture is the second favorite interaction method (3.55), closely following the first place with a difference of only 0.27. Alt Node+Slider is the most mentally (2.27) and physically (2.45) demanding method. Interestingly, it is still slightly more preferred than the Menu Button+Slider, the least favorable out of all four.

The second section of the questionnaire asks the volunteers to assess the different locations of the interaction techniques.

Of the three locations, we can see that the waist position is the most demanding position both mentally (2.36) and physically (2.27). It is also the least preferred method.

Table 7. Post-experiment questionnaire: location

Location	Mental demand	Physical demand	Preference
Ear	1.82	1.82	3.91
Waist	2.36	2.27	2.45
Peripersonal	1.55	1.82	3.55

Of the other two, Virtual Equipment at the peripersonal location is the least mentally (1.55) and physically (1.82) demanding location. While Virtual Equipment at the ear location is tied in terms of how physically demanding it is (1.82), it is slightly more mentally demanding (1.82).

However, of the three, the most preferred location is not the location with the least mental and physical demand. The ear location is more preferred (3.91) than the peripersonal location (3.55).

5   Analysis

From the data, we observe that on average all the volunteers completed the volume adjusting task faster when using the interaction methods from the Virtual Equipment System compared to the traditional controller menu button access method or the Alt Node method. This makes sense as these are really different classes of techniques. Motion gesture and surface gesture allow change of volume with one movement and one button click. Alt Node and Menu Button require more effort but allow the user to fine tune settings.

Out of all the locations for a equipment, the peripersonal location is reportedly to be the least physically and mentally demanding location with the ear location being slightly more mental demanding, according to the questionnaire. Nonetheless, the ear location is the most preferred location. This suggests that physical association of the location and the actual task goal (ear and headphone) aids the volunteer to process and complete the task faster. Participants also reported preferring peripersonal equipment simply because it is always visible, which would explain the lower mental load.

In contrast, although the waist location is actually the closest to the pink cube, it is rated to be the most physically demanding location during the experiment. Despite its proximity, its lack of association to the task and being outside of the field of view might have caused it to become the least favorable interaction location in this specific experiment. The power of association should be taken into consideration when designing future expansions for the Virtual Equipment System.

We also observed that surface gesture is faster for the ear location but motion gesture is faster for the waist and peripersonal location. Feedback from the questionnaire suggest that this might be an implementation issue. They state that the interaction volume of the surface gesture sometimes cannot be detected, causing them to move aggressively. In the current implementation, however, the same collider volume is used to determine when a user can initiate a surface gesture or a motion gesture. It may be possible that users intentionally move their controller more to the center of the collider volume to grab the equipment in the case of motion gesture. For surface gesture, they may intentionally move less toward the center to interact with the surface, which would be presumed to be further away. In the case of equipment at the ear, given that there is no way to see, the user relied completely on their proprioception and thus had no issue with surface gesture. Another possibility is that the difference may be a result of how the brain interpret personal, peripersonal, and extrapersonal space differently. Further investigation is needed.

By tracking the head movement and rotation, we learned that users are spending a lot of time looking at the waist location and when utilizing alt node. Given that these locations are stationary with respect to the user's body (waist and left hand), the user could have used proprioception to perform these techniques, but instead they relied heavily on visual feedback. Similarly, by looking at the accumulated hand movement and rotation, we note that Alt Node had the greatest movement and rotation while Menu Button had the least. Nonetheless, Alt Node is about the same speed as Menu Button and slightly preferred in the post-questionnaire survey. Given that Alt Node is currently a two-handed technique, perhaps it could be better as a single-hand technique, which can be done by placing it in the user's peripersonal space with respect to the user's body.

Overall, the results suggest that the Virtual Equipment System allows the usage of multiple different interaction techniques that are fast, easy to use, and liked by the participants.

6   Limitations and Future Work

This experiment was designed to measure speed more than precision. The task is considered completed as soon as the user changes the volume in any direction. This was done to eliminate any difference that can result from the implementation of a given technique. For example, the motion gesture could also be implemented so that the gesture is determined based on the difference between the position at which the equipment is picked up instead of the position where the equipment is stored. The equipment could also be used as a slider handle so that the user would be setting the volume from min to max instead of making increments to the current volume. We aim to conduct future work comparing the precision of different techniques.

Precision aside, we would also like to examine variations of a given technique. In the comparison of Alt Node and Menu Button, Alt Node did not seem particularly advantageous. With the current implementation of the technique and of the experiment, an user can easily navigate to the audio menu as the setting menu is the first item on the general menu and audio menu the first item on the setting menu. Without the need to look through the 2d menu, much of the advantage is lost. While some participants still recognize the potential for alt node and overall prefer Alt node in spite of higher mental and physical demand, we plan to make a full evaluation of the alt node technique. The user would interact with Virtual Goggles for visual setting, Virtual Headphones for audio setting, Virtual Microphone for audio recording setting, and so on.

The feedback we provide to the user also appear to be lacking from the questionnaire answers we have gotten. In particular, while we have visual feedback for the Motion Gesture that resides in the space by user's ear and by the waist, but we did not implement the same mirrored equipment feedback for the surface gesture. We also noticed that the user has much more trouble initiating a surface gesture compared to the motion gesture. Additional feedback, especially in terms of spatial cues, could alleviate some of the difficulties users face.

We also noted that the user spends a lot of time looking around when interacting with the Virtual Equipment at the waist or with the Alt Node when they should have been able to perform these actions without looking. One of the main advantages of peripersonal equipment cited by participants was the fact that it's in front of the user and thus fully visible. We are interested in comparing peripersonal equipment in different locations as well as evaluating virtual equipment in general while encouraging the users to rely less on their sight.

7   Conclusion

By using the design lenses of hyperphysical interfaces and whole-body interaction, we have proposed and built a Virtual Equipment System for Extended Reality. Hyperphysicality provided us with new ways to categorize and think about Virtual Equipment in terms of different qualities such as egocentric or exocentric Equipment, and location in personal, peripersonal, and extrapersonal space. We then utilize whole body interaction as a lens to aid us in evaluating user interaction with the Virtual Equipment System. In this first preliminary testing of the Virtual Equipment System, we found that while the experiment is not comprehensive and some results were inconclusive due to our implementation of the Virtual Equipment System, there are many interesting findings that support our initial theories and results from background work. We plan on using the results of this experiment to improve our implementation and conduct additional experiments that pinpoint and test specific parts of our Virtual Equipment System.

References

1. Ängesleva, J., Oakley, I., Hughes, S., O'Modhrain, S.: Body mnemonics portable device interaction design concept. In: Proceedings of UIST, vol. 3, pp. 2–5 (2003)
2. Ängesleva, J., O'Modhrain, S., Oakley, I., Hughes, S.: Body mnemonics. In: Physical Interaction (PI03) Workshop on Real World User Interfaces. p. 35. Citeseer (2003)
3. Di Pellegrino, G., Làdavas, E.: Peripersonal space in the brain. Neuropsychologia **66**, 126–133 (2015)

4. Dong, Z., Zhang, J., Lindeman, R., Piumsomboon, T.: Surface vs motion gestures for mobile augmented reality. In: Symposium on Spatial User Interaction, pp. 1–2 (2020)

5. Khadka, R., Banic, A.: Body-prop interaction: evaluation of augmented open discs and egocentric body-based interaction. In: 2019 IEEE Conference on Virtual Reality and 3D User Interfaces (VR), pp. 1705–1710. IEEE (2019)

6. Khadka, R., Banić, A.: Prop-based egocentric and exocentric virtual object storage techniques. In: 2020 IEEE Conference on Virtual Reality and 3D User Interfaces Abstracts and Workshops (VRW), pp. 778–779. IEEE (2020)

7. Miller, M., Yao, P., Jothi, A., Zhao, A., Swieso, S., Zyda, M.: Virtual equipment system: toward peripersonal equipment slots with machine learning. In: Symposium on Spatial User Interaction, pp. 1–2 (2021)

8. Ruiz, J., Li, Y., Lank, E.: User-defined motion gestures for mobile interaction. In: Proceedings of the SIGCHI Conference on Human Factors in Computing Systems, pp. 197–206 (2011)

9. Yao, P., Lympouridis, V., Zhu, T., Zyda, M.: Interfacing with sensory options using a virtual equipment system. In: Symposium on Spatial User Interaction, pp. 1–2 (2020)

10. Yao, P., Lympouridis, V., Zyda, M.: Virtual equipment system: expansion to address alternate contexts. In: Stephanidis, C., Antona, M., Ntoa, S. (eds.) HCII 2021. CCIS, vol. 1420, pp. 353–360. Springer, Cham (2021). https://doi.org/10.1007/978-3-030-78642-7_48

11. Yao, P., Lympouridis, V., Zyda, M.: Virtual equipment system: face mask and voodoo doll for user privacy and self-expression options in virtual reality. In: 2021 IEEE Conference on Virtual Reality and 3D User Interfaces Abstracts and Workshops (VRW), pp. 747–748. IEEE (2021)

12. Yao, P., Zhu, T., Zyda, M.: Designing virtual equipment systems for VR. In: Stephanidis, C., Antona, M. (eds.) HCII 2020. CCIS, vol. 1225, pp. 137–144. Springer, Cham (2020). https://doi.org/10.1007/978-3-030-50729-9_19

Evaluating VAMR Environments

Effect of Personality Traits and Stressor Inducers on Users' Cognitive Load During Interactions with VR Environments

Aaron Cecil-Xavier[1], Avinash Gupta[2(✉)], Shelia Kennison[3],
and Miguel Pirela-Cruz[4]

[1] University of Wisconsin-Madison, Madison, USA
[2] University of Illinois Urbana-Champaign, Champaign, USA
avinashg@illinois.edu
[3] Oklahoma State University, Stillwater, USA
[4] Creighton University, Phoenix, USA

Abstract. In this paper, HCI-based design criteria focusing on managing the cognitive load of users during their interaction with Virtual Reality (VR) based training environments are presented. The design criteria explored in the paper help lay a foundation for the creation of Human Centric VR environments to train users in two healthcare domains. The first domain is orthopedic surgery, and the second domain is related to the Covid-19 pandemic. The HCI-based perspective presented in the paper investigates criteria such as personality traits and stress inducers and their impact on cognitive load. The paper delineates the implementation of the VR based environments and a set of attributes that guide and influence the content of the environments. Testing and assessment strategy is described and results are also included which provide insights into the impact of such HCI-based criteria on participants' acquisition of skills and knowledge during interactions with the VR environments.

Keywords: Cognitive load · Human Computer Interaction · Virtual Reality

1 Introduction

The use of Virtual Reality (VR) based technologies in the design and development of training simulators in fields such as manufacturing, space systems, education, and healthcare have been increasing rapidly [1–10]. As the number of platforms supporting VR such as HoloLens, HTC Vive Pro, and Magic Leap is increasing, the application of such platforms in creating simulators for various surgical domains such as laparoscopic surgery, orthopedic surgery, brain surgery, eye surgery among others, [11–15] is also rising. The focus of current research is primarily on the software and hardware related issues arising during the development of surgical simulator.

Researchers have not aimed at understanding the human centric aspects during the design of VR based environments for surgical context. This paper focuses on understanding the impact of human computer interaction (HCI) based criteria during the design, development, and assessment of an VR based simulator for orthopedic surgical training. HCI focuses on the design of a computer system, particularly in the interaction

© The Author(s), under exclusive license to Springer Nature Switzerland AG 2022

J. Y. C. Chen and G. Fragomeni (Eds.): HCII 2022, LNCS 13317, pp. 153–164, 2022.
https://doi.org/10.1007/978-3-031-05939-1_10

between the users and the system. It is a broad field covering various types of systems such as desktops, handheld devices, VR devices, and wearables. The catalog of research focused on understanding the HCI centric aspects of the VR platform and devices is relatively small [16, 17]. In [18], common HCI based design principles such as affordance, cognitive overhead, user satisfaction, learnability, among others and their impact on AR system design is discussed.

Cognitive load refers to the working memory load utilized by a user when performing a particular task. In learning complex tasks such as flying airplanes and performing surgeries, the cognitive load becomes a crucial factor. Working memory is a limited resource and differs from one person to another. If a certain task's complexity is greater than the working memory of a person, the learning is negatively affected, and the person is cognitively overloaded. Learning systems should be designed in a way that provides appropriate levels of cognitive load to their users. Cognitive load theory categorizes cognitive load into two broad types: intrinsic and extraneous load. Intrinsic load refers to the load imposed by the nature of the topic to be learned. Extraneous load refers to the load imposed by the manner in which the information or instructions are provided to the users.

Researchers have developed and utilized a number of subjective methods to measure cognitive load. Some of the methods are the NASA TLX test [19], Paas Scale [20], among others. The Paas Scale measures the mental load of a person during a task; it consists of a Likert chart ranging from 1 (very, very low mental effort) to 9 (very, very high mental effort). The NASA TLX test measures the mental, physical, temporal demand, effort, and frustration using a 21-point Likert scale. The cognitive load can also be measured objectively by using a test called Dual-Task Measures [21]. In this test, it is assumed that when the learning task becomes overloading, the level of performance in the secondary task decreases. Some researchers have measured cognitive load by measuring physiological parameters such as pupil dilation, electroencephalography (EEG), and heart rate [22, 23].

Previous research focused on assessing the load using various subjective and objective methods; however, researchers have not focused on developing scenarios within the XR environment that would impose additional cognitive load on the user. Dual-task measures have been used by few researchers in which basic tasks such as identifying letters, reacting to a sound, etc., have been used. Such tasks are unrelated to the target process being performed in the VR environment. In this paper, two studies have been presented which focus on understanding the impact of two criteria on the cognitive load experienced by the users during the interaction with VR based training environments.

1.1 Personality Traits

A major focus of research within the area of Human-Computer Interaction (HCI) is the design of 3D Virtual Reality (VR) environments. VR-based immersive training environments are becoming more widely used in many occupational settings (e.g., medicine [24]). To further improve the quality of virtual training environments, it is important to consider how differences in how users' experience of immersive media and whether these individual differences affect one's ability to learn from these environments.

A growing number of studies have examined the role of individual differences in performance using VR environments [29–32] with mixed results. In the present study, we aimed to investigate further whether individual differences in absorption, a personality trait related to how readily users adapt to the VR environment predict users' stress levels while using an immersive training environment as well as comprehension of information encountered during training.

Absorption is defined an individual's disposition to become completely attended to a real or imagined experience event. This results in an "altered sense of self" wherein individuals engage in intense perspective taking while remaining impervious to distractors outside the attended stimulus [25]. Sacau et al. (2005) demonstrated that absorption involves an element of fascination with media, and that it should be considered in research on virtual environments [26]. Findings from this study suggest that absorption is a strong predictor of spatial presence, which refers to one's feeling of being physically present in a simulated experience [27]. Absorption has also been found to be a strong predictor of this "feeling" of presence in VR [28]. Despite absorption's strong relationship with presence, there has been little research on absorption's relationship with learning outcomes in VR.

Previous studies on learning outcomes in immersive learning environments have focused on the relationship between presence and learning, but this body of research has yielded inconsistent results [29–31]. Even with more recent findings that support the idea that presence contributes to learning gain [32], researchers still struggle to understand what mechanisms underlie this relationship. This gap in understanding also exists in findings where presence has been associated with negative learning outcomes [30]. A better understanding of individuals' emotional experiences while using virtual reality may help us understand how immersive environments can be better implemented.

1.2   Stress Inducers

The focus is on studying the relationship between users' knowledge and skills acquisition and the cognitive functioning of a human. Working memory, in general, may vary across users; we plan to design the environments for such varying user capabilities. If the complexity of a certain task is greater than a user's cognitive load, it negatively affects the learning outcomes resulting in cognitive overload. Learning systems should be designed in a way that provides appropriate levels of cognitive load to their users. In this paper, the stress inducers were imposed on the user to study the impact of such load on users' knowledge and skills acquisition.

2   Design of VR Based Environments

The VR based environments for training users in two domains related to healthcare. The first domain was orthopedic surgical training and the second was training healthcare personnel for Covid-19 pandemic. The orthopedic surgical procedure in focus was condylar plating surgery which is performed to treat the fractures of the femur bone. The healthcare personnel were trained in procedures related to safely donning and doffing the PPE kit and performing nasal swabbing for sample collection.

The VR based environments were developed for Vive Pro immersive platform The VR environments were developed using the Unity 3D engine. Only one of the environments from each of the domain are discussed in this paper for brevity.

2.1   Plate Assembly Training Environment

The focus of this training environment is to help users (medical residents) become familiar with the procedure of assembling the condylar plate before inserting it in patient's leg.

In the training environment, the residents pick up the parts and assemble them using the wireless controllers. The buttons on the controllers can be used for several purposes such as picking up objects, drilling, positioning, etc. The residents need to complete the following steps to complete the training in this environment. The resident needs to first position the insertion handle on the condylar plate correctly and then insert the locking bolt through the hole of the insertion handle. The resident tightens the nut next. Subsequently, the resident attaches the aiming arm to the insertion handle and secures the connection bolt to the insertion handle. The resident inserts the guide sleeve and subsequently inserts the wire guide through the guide sleeve. Finally, the resident tightens the nut on the locking bolt to complete the training. A view of a user wearing the Vive headset and interacting with the VR environment is shown in Fig. 1. The view of the plate assembly training environment is shown in Fig. 2.

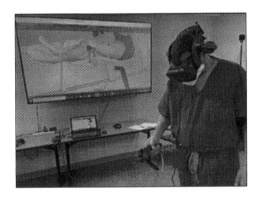

Fig. 1. View of a user interacting with the VR based Training Environment

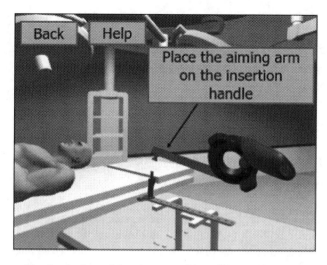

Fig. 2. A view of the plate assembly training environment

2.2 Swabbing Training Environment

The Swabbing Training VR environment consists of an entryway, a hallway that leads forward, and the room on the user's right is labeled "room 1" and the two rooms at the end of the hallway are labeled "room 2" and "room 3". Room 1 features a 3D model of a nurse in full PPE gear and a patient sitting on a hospital bed, with another whiteboard utilizing the same button scheme, text, and audio narration describing the proper nasopharyngeal swab sampling procedure (shown in Fig. 3).

Fig. 3. A view of swabbing training environment showing a nurse inserting the swab inside the patient's nose

This layout can be removed and replaced at will with a simple patient on a hospital bed between two tables, one with a swab and one with a set of test tubes. The user can pick up the swab on the table, grasp and tilt the patient's head back, and insert the swab into the patient's nose, causing green or red dots to appear nearby indicating that the swab is in the correct region of the nasal cavity. Outside of the room is another 3D model of a nurse performing swab sampling on a patient, but one step is done incorrectly, in this case, the nurse does not tilt the patient's head back.

3   Method

3.1   Effect of Personality Traits

A total of 34 undergraduate and graduate college students (25 men, 9 women) enrolled in computer science courses at Oklahoma State University were recruited for this study. Participants completed a series of questionnaires via Qualtrics, completing demographic information and the Tellegen Absorption Scale (TAS), a 34-item self-report measure that measured absorption. The TAS utilized a 7-point Likert scale (1 = *Strongly Disagree* to 7 = *Strongly Agree*), with higher scores representing a more absorbed participant.

Participants were then asked to engage with two target stimulation environments of varying complexities via an HTC Vive, a fully immersive VR headset. These environments were created for the HTC Vive by members of the Center for Cyber-Physical Systems. Environment 1 featured the assembly of a surgical tool called a condylar plate. Instructions on how to assemble this tool were displayed throughout the environment. Environment 2 featured a more complex scenario, requiring participants to observe and execute the procedure for nasal swab collection. Instructions were administered via previously recorded verbal guidance within the environment.

Participants were informed that the purpose of these environments was to memorize the names of the individual parts, the order of the assembly, and reasoning for certain steps. They were also informed that following VR engagement with each environment, they would answer questions testing their ability to retain this knowledge.

While engaging with these environments, stress levels were measured with a NEULOG galvanic skin response (GSR) sensor that was placed on participants' nondominant hands to measure sweat gland activity. Participant GSR readings were measured in neutral conditions to attain an average baseline reading. Each participant's average baseline reading would be compared to their average readings while engaging with the learning environment.

3.2   Effect of Stress Inducers

A total of eighty participants from four medical centers and nursing schools were recruited for this study. The eighty participants were divided into two groups consisting of forty participants. The first group interacted with the environments without any stress inducers and the second group interacted with the environments with stress inducers. For the skills assessment, the participants interacted with the in-simulator challenge scenarios after completing the training. For the knowledge assessment, the users took a pre-test before interacting with the environments; subsequently, they took a post-test to assess the improvement in knowledge. The heartbeat of the participants was also measured during the interactions using a pulse oximeter. Questionnaire-based pre and post-test method was used to assess the knowledge gained by the users after the interactions with the VR-based environment. In this method, the users first take a pre-test in which their knowledge regarding the condylar plate surgical procedure is assessed through a set of questions. Subsequently, they interact with the VR-based simulator performing the training activities. Finally, the users take the post-test in which the same set of questions asked in the pre-test is asked again. The knowledge gained is calculated by the difference in the score of post-test and pre-test. The knowledge assessment is used for both cognitive load and comparison studies. The users learn different skills in the training environments. After the user completed the training, they completed the 3 challenge scenarios based on Training environments 1, 2, and 3. No voice or text cues were provided during the challenge session. Users could ask for a hint which would reduce their score. Only one of the skills assessment scenarios (Drilling Skills Assessment) is presented for brevity. Drilling is a crucial step in condylar plate surgery. In the skills assessment, the users were asked to drill the bone marked with yellow and red zone. The yellow light warns the user when he/she is too close to the no-go zone, The Red-Light flashes when the user enters the no-go zone. The score calculation follows.

α is the initial score of the user

β is the number of times the user goes close to the no-go zone

The final score (τ) is calculated as

$\tau = \alpha - \beta$

where α was set to 100 after discussions with the expert surgeons

The overarching goal was to understand the impact of stressors on users' skills and knowledge acquisition. For the study, the users were divided into two groups. The first group interacted with the training environments without the stress inducers and the second group interacted with the training environments with the stress inducers. The stressors were chosen after consultation with an expert surgeon. The first stressor was the rapid deterioration of the virtual patient's vitals accompanied by continuous blinking of red light and fast beeping sound. The second stressor was excessive blood loss of the patient (blood hemorrhage) when the user is interacting with the virtual drilling procedure. Two variants of training and challenge scenarios were created; the first with stress inducers and the second without the stress inducers. The focus was on analyzing the effect of such stress inducers on knowledge and skills acquisition in the users.

4 Results

4.1 Results of Personality Traits Assessment

To test the hypotheses, a Pearson product-moment correlation coefficient to investigate the relationship between absorption, stress, and comprehension for environment was utilized. This statistical technique reveals whether a relationship exists between two variables, as well as the intensity. Table 1 displays a summary of the correlation results. There was a trend supporting the hypothesis that those experiencing higher levels of absorption would perform better on the comprehension questions. This trend was observed for participants in Environment 1 ($r = .328$, $p = 0.06$). The results also supported the second hypothesis that when stress was high, absorption would be low. This pattern was observed for participants in Environment 2 ($r = -.386$, $p = 0.04$).

Table 1. Correlational matrix

	1	2	3	4	5
1.**TA**	1				
2.**SE1**	−0.100	1			
3.**SE2**	**−0.386****	0.532**	1		
4.**CE1**	**0.328***	0.146	−0.230	1	
5.**CE2**	0.110	−0.175	0.023	−0.094	1

* *Correlation is significant at the 0.1 level (2-tailed)*
** *Correlation is significant at the 0.05 level (2-tailed).*

TA, Tellegen Absorption; SE1, GSR Stress Reading (Environment 1-Baseline); SE2, GSR Stress Reading (Environment 1-Baseline); CE1, Comprehension Question Performance (Environment 1); CE2, Comprehension Question Performance (Environment 2).

These results suggest that the ability to immerse oneself leads to less stress in environments and a better ability to recall information about the learning environment. The negative correlation between absorption and stress being limited to Environment 2 may be due to the environment's more demanding nature. Having to balance multiple tasks in scene, a more visually dense environment, and attempting to remember scene information for a posttest may be too demanding for individuals who are not able to employ appropriate attentional resources. The lack of a significant correlation between absorption and comprehension questions in Environment 2 could be attributed to users habituating to the novel, rich learning environment. This could demonstrate that differences in spatial presence may only influence learning in initial stages of VR interaction.

4.2   Results of Cognitive Load Assessment

The results of the cognitive load study for VR environments are shown in Fig. 4. As seen in Fig. 4, the participants who were introduced to stress inducers received lower scores in both skills and knowledge assessment during the interactions with VR based environments.

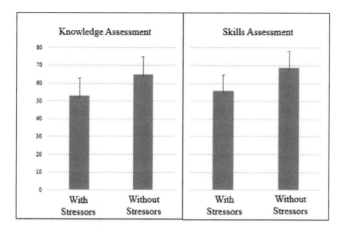

Fig. 4. Results of knowledge and skills assessment

To test the hypothesis, two T-tests were also performed to test if there was a significant difference in the means of the two groups (with stress inducers and without stress inducers). The results from the t-test for the skills assessment show a significant difference in mean in the group interacting with stress inducers (M = 55.75, SD = 9.08) and the group interacting without stress inducers (M = 68.82, SD = 9.30), t (78) = 6.35, p = 0.001. The results from the t-test for the knowledge assessment also show a significant difference in mean in the group interacting with the stress inducers (M = 53, SD = 10) and the group interacting without the stress inducers (M = 65, SD = 10.04), t (78) = 5.35, p = 0.001.

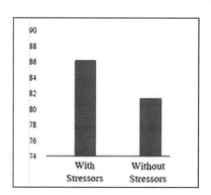

Fig. 5. Heart rate during interactions with the VR environments

The results from the t-tests (for skills and knowledge assessments) conducted for VR training environments show that stress inducers affect the knowledge and skills acquisition during the interactions with VR environments. Furthermore, the heart rate of the group interacting with VR environments with stressors is higher compared to the other group (Fig. 5). This validates that the participants were imposed to additional cognitive load during the interactions with the stressors.

5 Conclusion

The HCI-based design criteria focusing on the cognitive load imposed on the users during interactions with Virtual Reality (VR) based training environments was discussed in this paper. The design criteria laid the foundation for the creation of Human Centric VR environments to train users in two domains viz. orthopedic surgery, and Covid-19 pandemic management. The HCI criteria such as personality traits and stress inducers and their impact on cognitive load experienced by the users during interactions with the VR based training environments were delineated in the paper. A detailed discussion of the testing and assessment strategy was also included in the paper. Finally, the results from the testing studies were presented which provided insights into the impact of such HCI-based criteria on cognitive load experienced by the users.

References

1. Gonzalez-Franco, M., et al.: Immersive mixed reality for manufacturing training. Front. Robot. AI **4**, 3 (2017)
2. Vellingiri, S., McMahan, R.P., Prabhakaran, B.: SCeVE: A component-based framework to author mixed reality tours. ACM Trans. Multimedia Comput. Commun. Appl. (TOMM), **16** (2), 1–23 (2020)
3. Kaluschke, M., Weller, R., Zachmann, G., Pelliccia, L., Lorenz, M., Klimant, P., Möckel, F.: A virtual hip replacement surgery simulator with realistic haptic feedback. In: 2018 IEEE Conference on Virtual Reality and 3D User Interfaces (VR), pp. 759–760. IEEE (2018)
4. Turini, G., Condino, S., Parchi, P.D., Viglialoro, R.M., Piolanti, N., Gesi, M., Ferrari, V.: A microsoft hololens mixed reality surgical simulator for patient-specific hip arthroplasty training. In: International Conference on Augmented Reality, Virtual Reality and Computer Graphics, pp. 201–210. Springer, Cham (2018)
5. Cecil, J., Kauffman, S., Gupta, A., McKinney, V., Pirela-Cruz, M.M.: Design of a Human Centered Computing (HCC) based virtual reality simulator to train first responders involved in the COVID-19 Pandemic. In: 2021 IEEE International Systems Conference (SysCon), pp. 1–7. IEEE (2021)
6. Cecil, J., Kauffman, S., Cecil-Xavier, A., Gupta, A., McKinney, V., Sweet-Darter, M.: Exploring Human-Computer Interaction (HCI) criteria in the design and assessment of next generation VR based education and training environments. In: 2021 IEEE Conference on Virtual Reality and 3D User Interfaces Abstracts and Workshops (VRW), pp. 524–525. IEEE (2021)
7. Cecil, J., Sweet-Darter, M., Gupta, A.: Design and assessment of virtual learning environments to support STEM learning for autistic students. In: 2020 IEEE Frontiers in Education Conference (FIE), pp. 1–9. IEEE (2020)
8. Gupta, A., Cecil, J., Pirela-Cruz, M.: A cyber-human based integrated assessment approach for orthopedic surgical training. In: 2020 IEEE 8th International Conference on Serious Games and Applications for Health (SeGAH), pp. 1–8. IEEE (2020)

9. Cecil, J., Albuhamood, S., Ramanathan, P., Gupta, A.: An Internet-of-Things (IoT) based cyber manufacturing framework for the assembly of microdevices. Int. J. Comput. Integr. Manuf. **32**(4–5), 430–440 (2019)

10. Cecil, J., Krishnamurthy, R., Huynh, H., Tapia, O., Ahmad, T., Gupta, A.: Simulation based design approaches to study transportation and habitat alternatives for deep space missions. In: 2018 IEEE International Conference on Systems, Man, and Cybernetics (SMC), pp. 1439–1444. IEEE (2018)

11. Panait, L., Akkary, E., Bell, R.L., Roberts, K.E., Dudrick, S.J., Duffy, A.J.: The role of haptic feedback in laparoscopic simulation training. J. Surg. Res. **156**(2), 312–316 (2009)

12. Huber, T., Paschold, M., Hansen, C., Wunderling, T., Lang, H., Kneist, W.: New dimensions in surgical training: immersive virtual reality laparoscopic simulation exhilarates surgical staff. Surg. Endosc. **31**(11), 4472–4477 (2017)

13. Echegaray, G., Herrera, I., Aguinaga, I., Buchart, C., Borro, D.: A brain surgery simulator. IEEE Comput. Graphics Appl. **34**(3), 12–18 (2014)

14. Choi, K.S., Soo, S., Chung, F.L.: A virtual training simulator for learning cataract surgery with phacoemulsification. Comput. Biol. Med. **39**(11), 1020–1031 (2009)

15. Pedersen, P., Palm, H., Ringsted, C., Konge, L.: Virtual-reality simulation to assess performance in hip fracture surgery. Acta Orthop. **85**(4), 403–407 (2014)

16. Ashtari, N., Bunt, A., McGrenere, J., Nebeling, M., Chilana, P.K.: Creating augmented and virtual reality applications: Current practices, challenges, and opportunities. In: Proceedings of the 2020 CHI Conference on Human Factors in Computing Systems, pp. 1–13 (2020)

17. Sutcliffe, A.G., Poullis, C., Gregoriades, A., Katsouri, I., Tzanavari, A., Herakleous, K.: Reflecting on the design process for virtual reality applications. Int. J. Human-Comput. Interact. **35**(2), 168–179 (2019)

18. Dünser, A., Grasset, R., Seichter, H., Billinghurst, M.: Applying HCI principles to AR systems design. In: Mixed Reality User Interfaces: Specification, Authoring, Adaptation (MRUI'07: 2nd International Workshop at the IEEE Virtual Reality 2007 Conference), 11 Mar 2007. Mixed Reality User Interfaces: Specification, Authoring, Adaptation (MRUI 2007) Workshop Proceedings, Charlotte, NC, USA, pp. 37-42 (2007)

19. Hart, S.G., Staveland, L.E.: Development of NASA-TLX (Task Load Index): results of empirical and theoretical research. In: Advances in Psychology, vol. 52, pp. 139–183. North-Holland (1988)

20. Lox, C.L., Jackson, S., Tuholski, S.W., Wasley, D., Treasure, D.C.: Revisiting the measurement of exercise-induced feeling states: the Physical Activity Affect Scale (PAAS). Meas. Phys. Educ. Exerc. Sci. **4**(2), 79–95 (2000)

21. Andersen, S.A.W., Frendø, M., Sørensen, M.S.: Effects on cognitive load of tutoring in virtual reality simulation training. MedEdPublish, **9** (2020)

22. Shi, Y., Ruiz, N., Taib, R., Choi, E., Chen, F.: Galvanic skin response (GSR) as an index of cognitive load. In: CHI'07 Extended Abstracts on HUMAN FACTORS in Computing Systems, pp. 2651–2656 (2007)

23. Nemani, A., Sankaranarayan, G., Roberts, K., Panait, L,M., Cao, C., De, S.: Hierarchical task analysis of hybrid rigid scope natural orifice translumenal endoscopic surgery (NOTES) Cholecystectomy Procedures. In: Proceedings of the 2013 Medicine Meets Virtual Reality Conference (NEXTMED/ MMVR20), February 20–23, San Diego, CA, pp.293–297 (2013)

24. Mao, R.Q., Lan, L., Kay, J., Lohre, R., Ayeni, O.R., Goel, D.P.: Immersive virtual reality for surgical training: a systematic review. J. Surg. Res. **268**, 40–58 (2021)

25. Tellegen, A., Atkinson, G.: Openness to absorbing and self-altering experiences ("absorption"), a trait related to hypnotic susceptibility. J. Abnorm. Psychol. **83**(3), 268 (1974)

26. Sacau, A., Laarni, J., Ravaja, N., Hartmann, T.: The impact of personality factors on the experience of spatial presence. In: The 8th International Workshop on Presence (Presence 2005), pp. 143–151 (2005)
27. Slater, M., Wilbur, S.: A framework for immersive virtual environments (FIVE): Speculations on the role of presence in virtual environments. Presence Teleoperators Virtual Environ. **6**(6), 603–616 (1997)
28. Kober, S.E., Neuper, C.: Personality and presence in virtual reality: does their relationship depend on the used presence measure? Int. J. Human-Comput. Interac. **29**(1), 13–25 (2013)
29. Persky, S., Kaphingst, K.A., McCall, C., Lachance, C., Beall, A.C., Blascovich, J.: Presence relates to distinct outcomes in two virtual environments employing different learning modalities. Cyberpsychol. Behav. **12**(3), 263–268 (2009)
30. Makransky, G., Terkildsen, T.S., Mayer, R.E.: Adding immersive virtual reality to a science lab simulation causes more presence but less learning. Learn. Instr. **60**, 225–236 (2019)
31. Buttussi, F., Chittaro, L.: Effects of different types of virtual reality display on presence and learning in a safety training scenario. IEEE Trans. Visual Comput. Graphics **24**(2), 1063–1076 (2017)
32. Ratcliffe, J., Tokarchuk, L.: Presence, embodied interaction and motivation: distinct learning phenomena in an immersive virtual environment. In: Proceedings of the 28th ACM International Conference on Multimedia, pp. 3661–3668 (2020)

The Development and Validation
of an Augmented and Mixed Reality Usability
Heuristic Checklist

Jessyca L. Derby[(✉)] and Barbara S. Chaparro

Embry-Riddle Aeronautical University, Daytona Beach, FL, USA
derbyj1@my.erau.edu, chaparbl@erau.edu

Abstract. Augmented Reality (AR) and Mixed Reality (MR) are new emerging technologies that are becoming increasingly popular. Because these technologies are so new, there is a lack of standards and consistency in application and hardware design. This can make it difficult to learn and frustrating for users. One way to standardized design and enhance the usability of a product is through the use of heuristic evaluations. General heuristics, such as Nielsen's 10 or Schneiderman's 8 usability heuristics have been used to evaluate these technologies. These heuristics are a useful starting point because they bring attention to many crucial aspects of the usability of a product. However, additional aspects that could alter the users' experience may not be assessed due to the uniqueness of AR and MR. There are very few validated AR and MR heuristics in the literature for practitioners to use. The purpose of this study was to create and validate a heuristic checklist that can be used to assess and inform design changes that influence the user experience of an AR or MR application and/or device. We followed an established and comprehensive 8-stage methodology developed by Quiñones, Rusu, & Rusu to create and validate our AR and MR usability heuristic checklist [4]. This included a search and summary of the current literature, formally defining heuristics based on this literature search, and validating through heuristic evaluations, expert reviews, and user testing. Our final revised heuristic checklist included 11 heuristics and 94 checklist items that encompasses usability aspects for AR and MR technologies.

Keywords: Human factors · User experience · Augmented Reality · Mixed Reality · Usability · Design guidelines

1 Introduction

Augmented Reality (AR) and Mixed Reality (MR) are new emerging technologies that are becoming popular in enterprise and consumer markets. These have been defined in many ways by individual companies and academic scholars. It has been defined by Milgram et al. using a Reality-Virtuality Continuum [1] (see Fig. 1). One side of the continuum is reality, while the other opposite side is full virtuality, such as virtual reality (VR) where the user is completely immersed in a virtual environment and interacting with virtual objects. AR differs from this because virtual elements are introduced to a real environment. Mixed Reality can appear anywhere on the spectrum

© The Author(s), under exclusive license to Springer Nature Switzerland AG 2022

J. Y. C. Chen and G. Fragomeni (Eds.): HCII 2022, LNCS 13317, pp. 165–182, 2022.
https://doi.org/10.1007/978-3-031-05939-1_11

between real and virtual, as it integrates these aspects together in many ways. For example, in a VR application, a user may wear a headset and headphones. Everything that the user sees or experiences is virtual, the objects they interact with, the background environment, etc. For an AR application, a user may wear a headset (also called a head mounted display, or HMD) with a see-through display, or use a mobile device with a functioning camera. The user can see their real environment through these displays, but 2D or 3D elements is overlayed onto their environment. These can often be interacted with through gestures, voice commands, or tapping on their mobile device's screen. MR applications can be a mix anywhere between these two areas. A real object may be placed into a virtual environment, virtual objects may be placed into real environments, virtual audio may be tethered to a real location, etc.

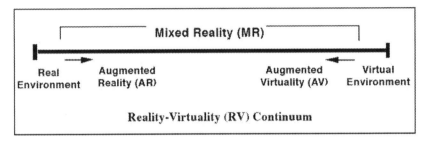

Fig. 1. Reality-Virtuality Continuum [1].

In addition to this, AR has been defined by three characteristics, 1) Combines the real and virtual 2) Interactive in real time 3) Registered in 3-D [2]. MR has been defined as a, "blend of digital and virtual worlds, unlocking natural and intuitive 3D human, computer, and environment interactions," and must involve "computer processing powered by the cloud, advanced input methods, and environmental perceptions," [3]. This definition encompasses visual and auditory MR technology. The difference between AR and MR often lies in whether the virtual object behaves as if it were physically present in the real world or not [3]. In MR applications, virtual elements follow the rules of physics, occlusion, and will adapt to the environment around it (e.g., a virtual picture that will hang onto a wall, or a virtual table that will stay on the floor and is unable to attach itself to a wall). In AR applications, virtual objects are only overlaid on top of the real world and these rules of physics are not followed (e.g., a table will float on top of any environment it is placed). For the purpose of this paper, we will be using these definitions of AR and MR.

One challenge that users face is that there is a lack of consistency in AR and MR application interfaces. User interactions and experiences can differ from one application or device to the next, making these difficult to learn and frustrating to use. One way that developers and human factors practitioners can standardize design is to evaluate their product to use usability heuristics. Usability heuristics are a set of best practices that practitioners can follow to enhance the ease-of-use and are often seen as rules of thumb for product development [4, 5]. These can be generalizable, such as Nielsen's 10 Usability Heuristics or Shneiderman's 8 Usability Heuristics [6, 7]. These heuristics have become a standard when evaluating web applications, software tools and interfaces [8]. They have also been used more recently to evaluated AR, MR, or even virtual reality [9, 10]. These heuristics are a useful starting point to evaluate these technologies because they bring attention to many crucial aspects of the usability of a product. However, additional aspects that could alter the users' experience may not be assessed due to the uniqueness of AR and MR. These could include the accuracy of the tracking technology, integration of virtual objects onto the real world, intuitiveness of gesture interactions, or the physical comfort and safety of a user [9]. More specific heuristics can be created to assess these contributing factors to the overall usability of AR and MR applications.

1.1 Literature Review

Heuristics and design guidelines have been created for general AR applications [11–13] as well as for several AR use cases. Heuristics have been created for mobile AR games [14, 15], mobile AR user interfaces [16–18], wearable AR applications [19], collaborative AR environments [20], applications geared towards children [21, 22], and older adult users [23]. Very few heuristics or guidelines have been established for MR applications [24–27] thoughcompanies and organizations themselves have taken on the task of creating best practices and guidelines for their developers [3, 28, 29].

Many of these heuristics included aspects of Nielsen's 10 and Schniderman's 8 Heuristics such as visibility of system status, user control & freedom, help & documentation, aesthetic & minimalistic design, recognition rather than recall, consistency & standards, error prevention, simple error handling, and reduce short-term memory load [6, 7]. However, many of these heuristics also added aspects that were specific to the user experience of AR and MR. For example, physical comfort [11, 12, 17, 19] relationship between the virtual and physical world, specifically the quality the integration of augmented objects onto the real world and distinction between virtual and real objects [11–14, 18, 23]; sensory aspects [20]; collaboration, and user privacy [20, 23].

Despite this effort, very few of these heuristics and guidelines have been validated [13, 23]. Many heuristics are created with the authors' biases and past experiences and not based on the research literature. To reduce these biases, it is recommended that heuristics follow a validation process. This can be done by evaluating the research literature and asking experts in the field of interest to evaluate the ease-of-use, usefulness, and comprehensiveness of the heuristics and checklist items. Formalized methodologies also have been documented so those who are creating heuristic checklists can follow a step-by-step guide to validate their heuristic set. One such methodology that is well established and is very comprehensive has been developed by Quiñones, Rusu, & Rusu [4]. Their methodology involves a standardized search through the literature, formalized definitions, validation through suggestions from experts from the field, comparison of heuristic evaluation scores, and user testing, to refine a final heuristic checklist.

1.2   Purpose

The purpose of this current study is two-fold: 1) to create a comprehensive heuristic checklist that can be used by practitioners to assess and inform design and user experience of their AR or MR application or device and 2) to validate these heuristics using expert review, comparison to existing heuristics, and user testing with two applications.

2   Method

We followed Quiñones, Rusu, & Rusu's 8-stage methodology for developing usability/user experience heuristics [4] (see Fig. 2).

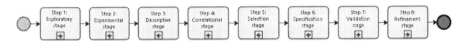

Fig. 2. Stages of the methodology developed by Quiñones, Rusu, & Rusu [4].

2.1   Steps 1–4: Exploratory through Correlational Stages

Step 1: Exploratory Stage involved completing a review the current literature. This was done to compile definitions and features about the domain (Augmented Reality), current heuristics, and usability and user experience (UX) principles related to AR applications and devices. We completed a literature search using the following search terms: "Augmented Reality" OR "AR" AND "Heuristics", "Augmented Reality" OR "AR" AND "Guidelines", "Mixed Reality" OR "MR" AND "Heuristics", and "Mixed Reality" OR "MR" AND "Guidelines". We found twenty articles that proposed new heuristics, or guidelines, for AR and MR experiences. Fifteen of which were specific to AR, four that were specific to MR, and one that described guidelines for both AR and MR. More details about these articles were discussed previously in the literature review above and in Table 1.

Table 1. Summary of the literature found after step 1

Authors	Area of focus	Type
Aultman, et al. [14]	Mobile AR game user interfaces	Heuristics
Endsley et al. [11]	AR applications	Heuristics
Santos et al. [16]	Mobile AR graphical user interfaces	Guidelines
Gale et al. [19]	Wearable AR applications	Heuristics
Kalalahti [12]	AR applications	Heuristics
Guimarães et al. [13]	AR applications	Heuristics
Franklin et al. [20]	AR remote collaborative systems	Heuristics
Ko et al. [17]	Mobile AR applications	Guidelines

(continued)

Table 1. (*continued*)

Authors	Area of focus	Type
Ganapathy [18]	Mobile AR applications	Guidelines
XR Association [27]	AR & MR devices and applications	Guidelines
Liang [23]	AR applications for older adults	Guidelines
Apple [28]	AR devices and applications	Guidelines
Microsoft [3]	MR devices and applications	Guidelines
Magic Leap [29]	MR devices and applications	Guidelines
Tuli [21]	AR applications for children	Guidelines
Masmuzidin [22]	AR applications for children	Heuristics
Gotsis et al. [24]	MR games	Heuristics
De Belen [25]	MR applications for elderly people	Guidelines
Miracle Handbook [26]	MR applications	Guidelines
Wetzel et al. [15]	AR games	Guidelines

Step 2: The Experimental Stage involved an in-depth analysis of the current experimental literature to gain insight about what important usability attributes are missing from currently published heuristic sets. From this, new checklist items and heuristic categories were created in the new heuristic set to fill in these gaps. For this study, researchers organized details from each article, such as the heuristics/guidelines proposed or important usability attributes discovered in experimental studies and organized these into a spreadsheet. Many of these paralleled with Nielsen's 10 Usability Heuristics [6] with the addition of the following for AR and MR devices: integration of physical & virtual worlds, user interactions, physical comfort, collaboration with others, and privacy.

Step 3: Descriptive Stage, the information gained from the literature search was organized even further. Important information from the domain, heuristics, and usability and user experience (UX) principles were selected and prioritized. In this study, the information that was rated somewhat important included: Usability & UX attributes such as those defined by ISO standards, Nielsen, Morville, and the Usability Body of Knowledge [6, 30–33] and known usability problems for AR and MR such as the lack of standards for developers, layout and navigation of apps, reliability of controls, accessibility, and accuracy of tracking technology. No information was rated not important for this study.

Step 4: Correlation Stage. Features were matched to either existing or newly created heuristics. These included a subset of heuristics from Nielsen's 10 Usability Heuristics, an established set of usability heuristics [6], as well as any other relevant heuristics found from the literature that were not previously included.

2.2 Step 5: Selection Stage

During the Selection Stage, heuristics and checklist items were adapted, added, or discarded. In this study, this was done in three iterations. The first resulted in a draft developed by the researchers in this study (17 heuristics, 82 checklist items). This draft was then evaluated by experts who have completed heuristic evaluations in the past. The researchers reworded and discarded a subset of checklist items based on these expert evaluators' comments (15 heuristics, 80 checklist items). This second draft was then evaluated by experts in the AR or MR domain. Based on these domain experts' comments and suggestions (see Table 2 for an example), checklist items and heuristic categories were regrouped, reworded, added, and discarded. This resulted in a third draft of the heuristic checklist (11 heuristics, 87 checklist items).

Table 2. Example of a comment that resulted in a revised heuristic checklist item.

Heuristic	Original checklist item	Comment	Revised checklist item
Integration of Physical & Virtual Worlds	Do virtual elements act as the user would expect them to in the real world?	"We should probe the device's ability to register virtual content in their real world. Address issues such as jitter, drift, fly away, anchoring to a plane, etc. Maybe we can combine this into one and describe issues or add separate items?"	Additional items: 1. Does the device and/or application avoid lag, delays, jitter, drift, and other forms of virtual element malfunctions? 2. Are virtual elements accurately placed on the real environment?

2.3   Step 6: Specification Stage

The Specification Stage incorporated the information gathered from stages 3–5. Formalized heuristics were defined and mapped to the following: ID, priority level, definition, explanation, application feature, examples, benefits that could come out of following the heuristic, problems that may occur if the heuristic is not satisfied, checklist items (if applicable), usability attributes, UX factors, and similar sets of heuristics that were found from the literature. Clearly defined heuristics were created through the completion of this stage. The final set resulted in 11 heuristics (see Table 3).

Table 3. Definitions of the proposed usability heuristics for augmented (AR) & mixed reality (MR).

Heuristic	Definition
Unboxing & Set-Up	Getting started with the AR device/application should be easy to identify, complete, and a positive experience
Help & Documentation	Help and documentation for the app and device should be easily accessible. Instructions and error messages should give users clear feedback
Cognitive Overload	The application should minimize cognitive overload by easing the user into the environment and avoiding unnecessary clutter

(continued)

Table 3. (*continued*)

Heuristic	Definition
Integration of Physical & Virtual Worlds	It should be easy to identify virtual elements and which virtual elements are interactable. Virtual elements should not obstruct physical objects in the users' environment that are crucial for the completion of their goals
Consistency & Standards	The application should be consistent and follow design standards for text, audio, navigation, and other elements
Collaboration	It should be clear what AR content is able to be viewed by the public and what content is private (only viewable to the specific user or device). It should also be clear to a user what content others can see and manipulate and what content is only for their personal use
Comfort	The application and device should be designed to minimize user discomfort
Feedback	The application and device should provide adequate feedback to the user to explain what is currently going on
User Interaction	All interactions that the user has with the device/application should be simple, easy to understand, and easy to complete
Recognition Rather than Recall	The application should be designed in a way that promotes the use of recognition rather than recall to minimize the user's memory load
Device Maintainability	The device should be designed in a way that makes it easy to maintain. This includes reusability, storage, cleaning, and the ability to fix/replace parts

2.4   Step 7: Validation Stage

In the validation stage, three different activities were completed to investigate user perceptions and show that the new heuristics are effective, easy to use, and necessary. These included 1) heuristic evaluations 2) expert judgements and 3) user tests.

For each of these tests, participants were asked to evaluate two applications, an AR puzzle game (PuzzlAR) and an educational AR anatomy application (Insight Heart). They were asked to explore each app by completing tasks and evaluate them using either a head-mounted display (HMD) (either the Microsoft HoloLens 1 or 2, or Magic Leap 1), or a mobile device (iOS or Android phone).

Test 1: Heuristic Evaluation. The set of heuristics that were developed in the specification stage were compared with a set of control heuristics. Heuristics developed by de Paiva Guimarães [13] AR heuristics were chosen as the control set. Some items were slightly altered to generalize the terminology across different technologies. This included rewording items that mentioned "markers" such as, "Is it easy to remember the application's functionalities? (i.e., is it easy to memorize the functionalities of each marker?)" to "Is it easy to remember the application's functionalities? (i.e., is it easy to memorize the functionalities of each button or gesture?)". This set of heuristics were chosen over other, more general, heuristics such as Nielsen's 10 since they focused on usability aspects specific to AR, such as accuracy of tracking technology, layout of virtual elements, and navigation using novel interactions.

Six experts evaluated both the AR puzzle game and AR anatomy application using the control heuristics [13], three of which used a mobile phone (iOS or Android), and three used an HMD (Microsoft HoloLens 2 or Magic Leap 1). Another six experts evaluated both apps using the new, proposed, heuristics. Again, three used a mobile phone and three used an HMD. A total of 12 evaluators performed two heuristic evaluations each and provided comments about how the heuristics could be improved.

Overall, a larger percentage of heuristic violations were found for the new proposed heuristics than the control heuristics. For the Insight Heart application, only 4.7%-19.1% (mobile and HMD) of the items were marked as violations using the control set of heuristics, whereas 15.9%-18.2% of the items from our proposed heuristics were marked as violations. For the PuzzlAR application, 9.5–14.3% (mobile and HMD) of the items were marked as violations fromthe control heuristics, and 17.8–19.3% (mobile and HMD) of the items were marked as violations from our proposed heuristics (see Table 4). Some common violations from both heuristic sets included: interactions were difficult to learn (the proposed heuristics specified that this was due to the lack of a clear tutorial), instructions were vague, menu items did not include any affordance, and no error prevention or error methods occurred. The proposed heuristics additionally revealed that it was unclear which virtual elements the user could interact with and which they could not. As well as the concern that there were no indications regarding whether the information the user provides is private or open to the public. Evaluators mentioned this was especially important for the anatomy application that could sync information from the user's fitness watch regarding heart rate and other biological information. One final area that the proposed heuristics revealed was that virtual objects and text were too small to read and differentiate from one another. No additional violations were discovered from the control heuristics.

Table 4. Comparing the average number of violations found across applications for each of the two heuristic checklists used.

	Control heuristics [13] (21 questions)		Proposed heuristics (88 questions)	
	Insight Heart	PuzzlAR	Insight Heart	PuzzlAR
HMD	4/21 (19.1%)	2/21 (9.5%)	16/88 (18.2%)	16/88 (18.2%)
Mobile	1/21 (4.7%)	3/21 (14.3%)	14/88 (15.9%)	17/88 (19.3%)

Test 2: Expert Judgement. Six experts, separate from the twelve described above, evaluated the new, proposed, heuristic checklist based on its utility, clarity, ease of use, necessity, importance of each heuristic, completeness, and likelihood of using it in the future. These experts also provided comments about how to improve checklist items and heuristics. Three of these experts evaluated the checklist using an HMD application (either HoloLens 1 or 2, or Magic Leap 1) and three used a mobile application (iOS or

Android). No differences in the ratings between technology used or application were found, so the following summary data describes all six experts' ratings.

On a scale of 1–5, 5 being the best, each of the 11 heuristics were rated as useful, clear, necessary to include a detailed checklist, and easy to complete. All of the averages for these ratings were above a 3.5 on a scale of 1–5. Experts also rated each heuristic on importance using a scale of 1–3, 1 being useful, 2 being important, and 3 being critical. The most important heuristics included Set-Up and Comfort. The least important, but still useful, heuristic was Maintainability (see Fig. 3).

On a scale of 1–5, 5 being best, the entire heuristic checklist was rated easy to complete ($M = 4$, $SD = 0.6$), experts stated that they would be likely to use it in the future ($M = 4.5$, $SD = 0.52$), and the items were rated as mostly complete ($M = 4.2$, $SD = 0.72$), (see Fig. 4).

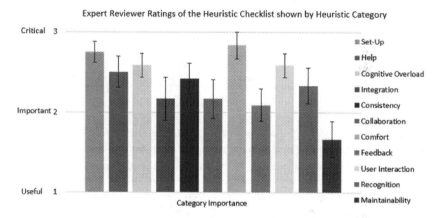

Fig. 3. A summary of the expert reviewer ratings of importance by proposed heuristic.

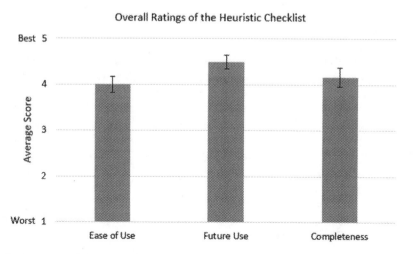

Fig. 4. A summary of the overall ratings of the proposed heuristic checklist regarding ease of use, intended future usage, and completeness.

Experts also provided recommendations about (1) the wording of checklist items, (2) additional examples to further clarify each checklist item, and (3) suggestions for new checklist items. A representative quote for each of these types of recommendations is provided in Table 5.

Table 5. Examples of recommendations experts provided about the heuristic checklist items.

Type of Recommendation	Quote
Wording of Checklist Items	The negative wording makes this difficult to answer. Consider rewording, "does the app avoid making the user feel uncomfortable or nauseous during use," to, "Is the user able to remain physiologically comfortable DURING use? (e.g., not in pain, discomfort or nauseous)"
Additional Examples	I am unsure what this checklist item means, "Is information organized in an understandable manner?" this is too vague. Please write an example to clarify this
New Checklist Items	I think a checklist item on immersion is missing and possibly alignment for overlays

Test 3: User Test. A total of 12 users were asked to complete tasks with the two AR apps described previously. These tasks were specific to each of the applications and covered all areas of the application including the application's features, important functions, and experience using gestures and in-app interactions. Six users completed these tasks using an HMD (Microsoft HoloLens or Magic Leap), and six used a mobile device (iOS or Android). Eleven of the users had very minimal experience with the AR and MR devices they were asked to use (less than 4 h of experience with the AR or MR device). One user in the mobile device group reported that they had spent over 100 h using AR on their mobile device. The following metrics were gathered: task success, task difficulty, user comments, and a self-report measure of perceived usability (System Usability Scale) [34].

Task success, difficulty, and user comments. The most difficult tasks for the HMD version of the applications involved manipulating objects with novel interactions, viewing small virtual elements (holograms) or text, and tasks that involved many steps to complete. Poor depth perception cues, lag, and inaccurate scaling were also mentioned by users. The most difficult tasks for the mobile version of the applications involved finding settings that required the use of buttons that did not show affordance, and interactions that were not consistent with other mobile apps (such as swiping on a virtual object to move it rather than controlling it with buttons). This difference between the mobile and HMD version of the PuzzlAR app was especially apparent. This could have been due the interactions and gestures that novice users had to learn when interaction with 3D aspects on a 2D phone screen, rather than being able to walk up and touch a 3D object like what was done in the HMD version of the applications.

Perceived usability. Most of the applications scored fairly well on the System Usability Scale (SUS), with the exception of the mobile PuzzlAR application. Insight Heart received "good" scores for both the mobile (M = 71.88, SD = 18.7) and HMD (M = 74.38, SD = 23.86) versions of the application [35]. PuzzleAR received a "Ok" score for the mobile version of the application (M = 41.56, SD = 25.63) and a "Excellent" score for the HMD version of the application (M = 74.38, SD = 23.86) [35] (see Fig. 5).

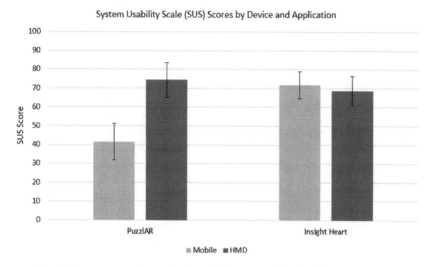

Fig. 5. A summary of perceived usability scores of each of the applications.

2.5   Step 8: Refinement Stage

The Refinement Stage further finalized the heuristic set. Heuristics were reworded, added, or removed based on the results found in the validation stage. Before this stage, our list consisted of 11 heuristics and 88 checklist items. After this refinement, our list consisted of 11 heuristics and 94 checklist items. Seven checklist items were added, 37 were revised, and 1 was omitted. The final set of heuristics and checklist items are shown in the appendix.

3   Discussion

By following Quiñones, Rusu, & Rusu's 8-stage methodology for developing usability/user experience heuristics, we have created and validated a usability heuristic checklist that can be used by practitioners to assess and inform design changes that could enhance the user experience of their AR application or device [4]. These heuristics incorporate elements that have not been established in a validated heuristic checklist such as items from Unboxing & Set-Up, Integration of Physical & Virtual Worlds, Collaboration, and Device Maintainability. Additionally, we have integrated these checklist items into a standalone auto-calculating tool. This spreadsheet separates each heuristic into a separate tab and allows practitioners to easily check off whether or not a checklist item is satisfied using a dropdown list. It also includes additional information for each checklist item by including definitions, examples, descriptive statistics (overall scores and scores for each heuristic), and summary graphs. This resource can be found at https://www.ruxresearch.com/heuristic-development. It is recommended that multiple raters conduct the heuristic evaluation individually and then convene to discuss their findings and user experience. This allows for more comprehensive recommendations for improvement.

It is also important to note that no heuristic evaluation will discover every usability problem of an application. During user tests, users may interact with the application in a more natural way, may not encounter a usability problem that is addressed by the heuristics, may have less experience with the application subject matter, or may not be as skilled using the device as a heuristic evaluator. It is important to be aware of this distinction and always use both heuristic evaluation and user testing as complementary methods. Results from this study's user tests and heuristic evaluations demonstrates how this may vary. For example, the mobile version of the PuzzlAR application was shown to be more difficult than what heuristic evaluations initially showed. A summary diagram of usability issues that were found in both the heuristic evaluations and user testing is shown in Fig. 6.

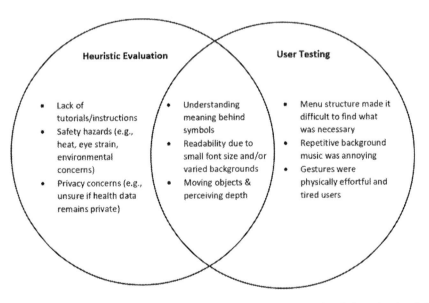

Fig. 6. Usability issues found with Insight Heart and PuzzlAR through heuristic evaluation (left) and user testing (right). Items in the overlapping portions of the circles were discovered with both methods. Comparing Heuristic Evaluation and User testing results.

3.1   Limitations and Future Research

This heuristic checklist was validated with just two applications, a puzzle game and an educational anatomy application, and with four devices, the HoloLens 1 and 2, Magic Leap 1, and mobile phones. Future work should focus on further validating and adapting the heuristic list to make it more comprehensive and applicable to the wide range of devices and applications available in enterprise and commercial environments. For example, further research could be done to investigate how inclusion/accessibility, haptics, and integration with other systems (for example, a collaborative AR application that allows one user to wear an AR headset while a secondary user join using a VR headset or desktop computer).

Appendix

Derby & Chaparro AR and MR Usability Heuristic Checklist
Unboxing & Set-Up

1. Is the unboxing process a positive experience?
2. When the user interacts with the device for the first time, are they introduced to the user interface, basic interaction methods, and basic features/content?
3. Is a quick start guide available with the device?
4. Is a call to action (QR code, instructions to use AR, etc.) clearly marked in the physical space?

   Help & Documentation

5. Is there the option of a tutorial upon first use of the device and/or application?
6. Does the tutorial explain all of the necessary actions/mechanics to use the device and/or application?
7. Is the tutorial easy to understand?
8. Are required interactions easy to learn?
9. Is help or documentation easily accessible for the application?
10. Are instructions easy to understand?
11. Do instructions provide actionable feedback?
12. If auditory instructions are given, do these instructions match what the user is seeing in the application?
13. Are error messages easy to understand?
14. Do error messages provide actionable feedback?
15. Does the device's user interface and/or application avoid irreversible errors?
16. Is there a way for the user to report errors or crashes to the developer?

    Cognitive Overload

17. Is the user eased into the virtual environment?
18. Does the device's user interface and/or application avoid clutter, as appropriate?
19. Does the device's user interface and/or application avoid large amounts of text?

20. Does the screen space focus on the virtual elements rather than controls or other non-AR features, as appropriate?
21. Is information organized in an understandable manner?
22. If the quantity of information is large, is it organized in a layered or hierarchical manner so it is easy to understand?
23. Does the device's user interface and/or application avoid tasks that involve a large amount of steps to complete?
24. Does the application make use of all of its AR functions (including information that is visual, auditory, and involved other sensory modalities)?

Integration of Physical & Virtual Worlds

25. Are physical (real-world) elements easily distinguishable from virtual elements?
26. Is it clear which virtual elements can be interacted with and which cannot?
27. Does the device's user interface and/or application avoid obstructing physical or virtual elements that are necessary for the users' goals?
28. Does the device's user interface and/or application avoid obstructing virtual navigation elements?

Consistency & Standards

29. Are virtual elements easy to delete or close out of?
30. Can the user pause the application at any point?
31. Are all aspects of the device's user interface and/or application (virtual elements, controls, text, etc.) clear and readable?
32. Are virtual elements sized appropriately?
33. Are virtual elements rendered a reasonable distance away from the user's targeted point?
34. For mobile devices, are the controls based on known interactions for mobile devices?
35. For mobile devices, are landscape and portrait mode supported?
36. For mobile devices, is the application responsive?
37. Do virtual elements act as the user would expect them to in the real world?
38. Are virtual elements accurately placed on the real environment?
39. Does the device and/or application avoid lag, delays, jitter, drift, and other forms of virtual element malfunctions?
40. Is the navigation consistent throughout the device and/or application?
41. Can the user navigate freely throughout aspects of the device and/or application?
42. Does the device adjust to the environment it is used in?
43. Are environmental requirements clearly defined?
44. Does the device and/or application remind users to be aware of their surroundings?
45. Does the device and/or application avoid jargon?
46. Are sans serif font types used, as appropriate, throughout the device and/or application?
47. Is the contrast between the background and text sufficient enough that the text can be read easily under a range of normal lighting conditions?
48. If the text background is transparent, is the text visible across different backgrounds and under a range of normal lighting conditions?

49. Is the volume adjustable so the user can hear audio, even in noisy environments?
50. Are auditory features understandable?
51. Are captions available for auditory features as appropriate?

Collaboration

52. Does the device and/or application allow for the user to control privacy-related content?
53. Is it clear what information is private or public content?
54. Does the application allow users to preserve virtual elements from others users' changes?
55. Is it clear which virtual elements can be interacted with and which cannot for each person?
56. Is content consistent across all users, as it is appropriate?

Comfort

57. Can the user experience the device and/or application without pain, discomfort, nausea, etc. DURING use?
58. Can the user experience the device and/or application without pain, discomfort, nausea, etc. AFTER use?
59. Is the device's weight light enough to feel comfortable?
60. Does the device avoid overheating to the point that it is uncomfortable to use?
61. Are physical interactions with the application safe and comfortable?
62. Does the application avoid making the user walk backwards, pull their head back, or push their head downwards to see virtual elements?
63. Do interactions with the device and/or application avoid tiring the user?
64. Does the device and/or application avoid causing the user eye strain?
65. Are users reminded to take breaks to prevent eye strain and fatigue?
66. Does the device easily adjust its size for different users?
67. Does the device accommodate users with eyeglasses?
68. Does the device accommodate for personal protective equipment?

Feedback

69. Does the device and/or application provide feedback on its status?
70. Does the device and its accessories provide feedback about battery levels and charging state?
71. Does the device and/or application provide feedback for user input?
72. Does the device and/or application respond quickly to user input?
73. Does the device and/or application provide the user feedback after automatic selections?
74. If an automatic selection occurs, does the device and/or application suggest what to do next?

User Interaction

75. Does the user feel in control?
76. Are user interactions simple and easy to understand?

77. Does the device and/or application include multiple forms of interaction so users can choose based on ability, preference, & skill?
78. Are the forms of interaction direct when it is appropriate to use this form of interaction?
79. Does the device and/or application avoid interactions that force the user to make large or sudden movements?
80. Does the device and/or application accommodate for the user to complete other necessary real-world tasks?
81. Does object manipulation work well in all instances?
82. Do virtual elements adapt to the users' position appropriately?
83. Does the device and/or application avoid input overloading by assigning distinct functions to buttons or gestures?

Recognition Rather than Recall

84. Are virtual elements and icons self-explanatory (does their form communicate function)?
85. Are virtual elements and controls placed near objects they reference?
86. If a virtual element is related to an object that is in motion, is the virtual element tightly coupled with object in motion appropriately?
87. Are virtual elements that are outside of the field of view easy to find?
88. Are available user actions identifiable?
89. If voice commands are included, are text labels for voice commands given?

Device Maintainability

90. Is the device sturdy enough to withstand multiple uses?
91. Does the device have a sturdy storage case?
92. Is it easy to clean the lenses, cameras, and other components on the device?
93. Are device parts fixable and replaceable as needed?
94. Does the device's battery life last long enough to perform necessary tasks of the application?

References

1. Milgram, P., Kishino, F.: A taxonomy of mixed reality displays. IEICE Trans. Inf. Syst. **77** (12), 1321–1329 (1994)
2. Azuma, R.T.: A survey of augmented reality. Presence Teleoperators Virtual Environ. **6**(4), 355–385 (1997)
3. Microsoft Docs: Mixed Reality Design Start designing and prototyping, https://docs.microsoft.com/en-us/windows/mixed-reality/design/design, Accessed 10 Feb 2022
4. Quiñones, D., Rusu, C., Rusu, V.: A methodology to develop usability/user experience heuristics. Comput. Stan. interfaces **59**, 109–129 (2018)
5. Nielsen, J., Molich, R.: Heuristic evaluation of user interfaces. In: Proceedings of the SIGCHI Conference on Human Factors in Computing Systems, pp. 249–256, Association for computer machinery, New York, NY (1990)
6. Nielsen, J.: Ten Usability Heuristics (2005)

7. Schneiderman, B., Plaisant, C., Cohen, M.S., Jacobs, S., Elmqvist, N., Diakopoulous, N.: Designing the User Interface: Strategies for Effective Human-Computer Interaction. Pearson, Hoboken, NJ (2016)

8. Gonzalez-Holland, E., Whitmer, D., Moralez, L., Mouloua, M.: Examination of the user of Nielsen's 10 usability heuristics & outlooks for the future. In: Proceedings of the Human Factors and Ergonomics Society Annual Meeting, pp. 1472–1475 (2017)

9. De Paiva Guimarães, M., Martins, V.F., Corrêa, A.G.D.: Usability Evaluation of Learning Objectives with Augmented Reality for Smartphones: A Reinterpretation of Nielsen heuristics. Human-Computer Interaction, pp. 214–228 (2019)

10. Usability Heuristics Applied to Virtual Reality: https://www.nngroup.com/articles/usability-heuristics-virtual-reality/, Accessed 11 Feb 2022

11. Endsley, T., Sprehn, K., Brill, R., Ryan, K., Vincent, E., Martin, J.: Augmented reality design heuristics: designing for dynamic interactions. In: Proceedings of the Human Factors and Ergonomics Society Annual Meeting, pp. 2100–2104 (2017)

12. Kalalahti, J., Porras, J.: Developing Usability Evaluation Heuristics for Augmented Reality Applications (2015)

13. De Paiva Guimarães, M., Martins, V.F.: A checklist to evaluate augmented reality applications. In: 2014 XVI Symposium of Virtual and Augmented Reality, pp. 45–52. IEEE (2014)

14. Aultman, A., Dowie, S., Hamid, N.: Design heuristics for mobile augmented game user interfaces. In: CHI EA '18: Extended Abstracts of the 2018 CHI Conference on Human Factors in Computing Systems, pp. 1–5. Association for Computing Machinery, New York, NY (2018)

15. Wetzel, R., McCall, R., Braun, A., Broll, W.: Guidelines for designing augmented reality games. In: Proceedings of the 2008 Conference on Future Play: Research, Play, Share, pp. 173–180. Association for Computing Machinery, New York, NY (2008)

16. Santos, C., Miranda, B., Araujo, T., Carneiro, N., Marques, A., Mota, M., Morais, J., Meiguins, B.: Guidelines for graphical user interface design in mobile augmented reality applications. In: Lackey, S., Shumaker, R. (eds.) VAMR 2016, LNCS 9740, pp. 71–80 (2016)

17. Ko, S.M., Chang, W.S., Ji, Y.G.: Usability principles for augmented reality applications in a smartphone environment. In: International Journal of Human-Computer Interaction 29(8), 501–515 (2013)

18. Ganapathy, S.: Human Factors in Augmented Reality Environments. Springer Science + Business Media, New York, NY (2013)

19. Gale, N., Mirza-Babaei, P., Pedersen, I.: Heuristic guidelines for wearable augmented reality applications. In: Proceedings of the 2015 Annual Symposium on Computer-Human Interaction in Play, CHI PLAY, Association for Computing Machinery, New York, NY (2015)

20. Franklin, F., Breyer, F., Kelner, J.: Usability heuristics for collaborative augmented reality remote systems. In: Proceedings of the 16th Symposium on Virtual and Augmented Reality, SVR, pp. 53–62. IEEE, Piata Salvador, Brazil (2014)

21. Tuli, N., Mantri, A.: Usability principles for augmented reality based kindergarten applications. Procedia Comput. Sci. 172, 679–687 (2020)

22. Masmuzidin, M., Aziz, N.: The adaptation of Shneiderman's golden rules and Nielsen's heuristics on motivational augmented reality technology design for young children. In: 2019 IEEE 9th International Conference on System Engineering and Technology, ICSET, pp. 62–67, IEEE, Shah Alam, Malaysia (2019)

23. Liang, S.: Design principles of augmented reality focusing on the aging population. In: Pr4oceedings of the 30th International BCS Human Computer Interaction Conference, pp. 1–7. BCS Learning and Development Ltd, Swindon, England (2016)
24. Gotsis, M., Lympouridis, V., Turpin, D., Tasse, A., Poulos, I.C., Tucker, D., Swider, M., Thin, A.G., Jordan-Marsh, M.: Mixed reality game prototypes for upper body exercise and rehabilitation. In: Coquillart, S., Feiner, S., Kiyokawa, K. (eds.) 2012 IEEE, Virtual Reality Workshops (VRW), pp. 181–182 (2012)
25. de Belen, R.A., Bednarz, T.: Mixed reality and the internet of things (MRIoT) Interface design guidelines for elderly people. In: Wyeld, T.G., Banissi, E., Ursyn, A., Bannatyne, M., Datia, N., Sarfraz, M. (eds.) International Conference In Information Visualization, Imaging and Visualization, CGIV, pp. 82–85. Adelaide, SA, Australia (2019)
26. Helle, S., Lehtonen, T., Woodward, C., Turunen, M., Salmi, H. (eds.): Miracle Handbook: Guidelines for Mixed Reality Applications for Culture and Learning Experiences. University of Turku, Turku, Finland (2017)
27. XR Association: XR primer 2.0: a starter guide for developers. https://xra.org/research/xr-primer-1-0-a-starter-guide-for-developers/, Accessed 11 Feb 2022
28. Apple: getting started with AR: https://developer.apple.com/news/?id=c6vr1ag2, Accessed 11 Feb 2022
29. Magic leap: design principles: https://developer.magicleap.com/en-us/learn/guides/design-principles, Accessed 11 Feb 2022
30. ISO   9241-11:2018:   https://www.iso.org/standard/63500.html#:~:text=ISO%209241%2D11%3A2018%20provides,services%20(including%20technical%20and%20personal, Accessed 11 Feb 2022
31. Usability 101: Introduction to usability: https://www.nngroup.com/articles/usability-101-introduction-to-usability/, Accessed 11 Feb 2022
32. User Experience Basics: https://www.usability.gov/what-and-why/user-experience.html, Accessed 11 Feb 2022
33. Principles for Usable Design: https://www.usabilitybok.org/principles-for-usable-design, Accessed 11 Feb 2022
34. Bangor, A., Kortum, P.T., Miller, J.T.: An empirical evaluation of the system usability scale. Intl. J. Human-Comput. Interaction **24**(6), 574–594 (2008)
35. Bangor, A., Kortum, P., Miller, J.: Determining what individual SUS scores mean: adding an adjective rating scale. J. Usability Stud. **4**(3), 114–123 (2009)

A Vibrotactile Reaction Time Task to Measure Cognitive Performance in Virtual and Real Environments

Markus Jelonek$^{(\boxtimes)}$ (ID), Lukas Trost, and Thomas Herrmann (ID)

Ruhr University Bochum, 44780 Bochum, Germany
{markus.jelonek, lukas.trost, thomas.herrmann}@rub.de

Abstract. Cognitive load is an important concept to understand people's cognitive processing performance of information. To assess cognitive load, several methods can be applied. For performance-based measure, Reaction times (RT) tasks can be used. Compared to physiological measures such as electroencephalography, RT tasks can be easily implemented and can be used as an alternative to subjective questionnaires, like NASA-TLX. In this paper we present two evaluation studies of a vibrotactile wearable for RT tasks. The first study evaluates its potential for Choice Reaction Time (CRT) tasks to compare real and virtual settings, the second study uses a simple Reaction Time (RT) task to evaluate cognitive effort on two different VR locomotion techniques while working on tasks in VR. The system is based on a vibrotactile wearable for the cues/stimuli and is suited for VR settings as well as real environments. We argue that such systems allow to compare cognitive performance between real and virtual tasks and discuss the limitation of the system.

Keywords: Vibrotactile feedback · Virtual Reality · Locomotion · Reaction Time Task · Dual-task paradigm · Wearable computing · Cognitive load

1 Introduction

As humans, we have limited cognitive resources that allow us to perform in our environments. Cognitive load refers to the amount of mental activity needed to process the amount of given information. With increasing cognitive load, a person's performance might decrease [1–4]. Findings in the research of cognitive load has had many implications for the design of today's information systems, as poorly designed user interfaces might result in user's confusion and cognitive overload [2]. With the widespread availability of consumer hardware for Virtual Reality (VR) and the resulting developments for immersive training and educational simulations, measuring cognitive load has also become a relevant area for VR [5, 6].

Cognitive load measurement can be achieved with different methods [7]. In [8], Chen provides an overview of four different measurable aspects of cognitive load: the subjective feeling of effort, the interpretation of performance, physiological arousal, and interpreting task characteristics. For example, an often used subjective questionnaire which allows to measure mental load is the NASA-Task Load Index (NASA-TLX) [8, 9].

© The Author(s), under exclusive license to Springer Nature Switzerland AG 2022
J. Y. C. Chen and G. Fragomeni (Eds.): HCII 2022, LNCS 13317, pp. 183–198, 2022.
https://doi.org/10.1007/978-3-031-05939-1_12

It uses six subscales: mental demands, physical demands, temporal demands, performance, effort, and frustration. A physiological measure of cognitive load can be done with electroencephalography (EEG) [10, 11].

For performance-based measures, reaction time (RT) measurements can be used to assess the cognitive effort of processing information [12]. A reaction time is defined as the time that elapsed between the appearance of a stimulus (or cue) to the point of a person's reaction to that stimulus. Measurements of reaction time are applied in the procedure of the *dual-task paradigm*. While subjects perform a main (or primary) task, a reaction time measurement to one or more stimuli is performed as a *secondary task* [13]. The design of the secondary task's complexity has an impact on the performance for this task. For example, in simple RT tasks participants only need to react to one reappearing cue, whereas in Choice-Reaction Time (CRT) tasks, multiple cues are used and each cue needs a different response [14].

Reaction times are widely used in experimental psychology to uncover all kinds of different research questions. For example, research has shown that reaction times become slower with increasing age [15], that performance in reaction tasks correlate with intelligence [12, 14], and that reaction times correlate with impulsivity [16].

Compared to methods like electroencephalography, RT tasks need, besides a computer, no additional hardware and are lightweight to implement. However, RT tests are mostly relying on a visual interface, as most RT tests are designed for desktop applications, which limits their usage to static testing and prohibiting the use in mobile settings or settings in which participants are physically active, like daily routines, making them also unusable for testing in VR simulations.

Fig. 1. With consumer VR hardware, participants usually are wearing a head mounted display (HMD) and controllers for interaction inside the VR scene.

One example of a RT task for mobile scenarios is shown in [17, 18]. Here, a watch-like wearable device is used for the generation of haptic stimuli. The responses are recognized by the participants' hand movement. Although this approach is promising for use in mobile settings, it is only partially suitable for VR simulations, as the unnatural hand movement would likely interfere with the controller interaction needed in VR (see Fig. 1).

In our approach, we use an abdominal belt equipped with multiple vibration motors for the RT task. By using the tactile sensory channel, the RT test does not interfere with any visualization inside the VR simulation and does not add any artificial sounds the VR soundscape. The vibrotactile wearable allows to be used in mobile settings and in tasks that require physical activity. Additionally, the interface of the wearable can be connected to and controlled by an Android application (as hotspot), without relying on available Wi-Fi networks. This enables the vibrotactile belt to be used for measuring RT tasks in VR as well as in real settings anywhere on earth.

In this paper, we present two studies with RT tasks to measure reaction time performance. The first study uses the RT task while participants use free walking in a virtual environment as well as a real environment, showing that both settings result in comparable RT. The second study investigates the impact of locomotion techniques on the performance in the RT task by comparing room-scale based and controller-based locomotion in three tasks inside VR. Results show, that the locomotion technique had no effect on the RT performance whereas the tasks had. The results of this paper contribute to the research of cognitive load measurement in VR settings and the comparison of cognitive effort used in VR to real environments.

2   Related Work

2.1   Locomotion in Virtual Reality

When developing VR games or simulations, one eventually reaches the point where it is necessary to decide how players/participants should move around in the virtual environment. For VR, there are different ways to implement locomotion, including, for example controller-based movement [19], walking-in-place [20], redirected walking [21], free movement [22] or teleporting [19]. An overview of different VR locomotion techniques can be found in the typology provided in [23]. In this typology, VR locomotion types are distinguished between the interaction type (physical or artificial), the motion type (continuous or non-continuous), and the interaction space (open or limited). For example, a controller-based locomotion technique would be classified as *artificial* interaction type, which allows *continuous* motion to interact in an *open* VR interaction space, whereas real-walking (or room-scale based) locomotion in VR would be classified as *physical, continuous* locomotion that has a *limited* VR interaction space (cf. [23]).

The type of VR locomotion technique might influence the participants VR experience [19]. For example, moving in VR by using teleportation could minimize the effect of realism of VR experiences and VR trainings, whereas free movement limits the interaction space of VR experiences. Although there are many approaches to address this challenge (e.g. [21, 23, 24]), in many cases participants stay on the spot during a VR simulation (e.g. controller-based motion, walking-in-place, gesture-based, etc.) [23].

When considering VR training simulations, standing still while moving in VR limits the comparability of real-world and VR settings. For example, the tactile perception of humans is reduced under movement, due to the mechanism of tactile suppression [25]. Tactile suppression refers to minimizing the amount of input of somatosensory information and leads to a reduction of tactile perception under physical activity. In order to transfer results of VR to the real-world, knowledge would be needed about to what extent vibrotactile cues are recognized and how recognition differs under movement in a real setting and during the experience of a VR simulation. To gain knowledge about the differences in recognizing tactile cues, this paper presents results of two studies comparing the perception of vibrotactile cues under different locomotion techniques in VR.

2.2   Vibrotactile Feedback Cues

There is a lot of research work in which tactile or vibrotactile signals have been tested for diverse use cases. Besides the use of vibration in the entertainment sector (e.g. smartphones or force feedback in game controllers), tactile warnings are already used in the automotive sector, e.g. in the lane warning assistant [26–28]. As soon as a vehicle with the lane warning assistant switched on changes lanes, a short vibration signal is presented to the driver via the steering wheel. Other applications investigated the use of vibration as a navigation control for pedestrians [29–32], cyclists [33], motorcycles [34] or cars [35]. In the field of intensive care, tactile warnings have been tested, e.g., to relieve the auditory sensory channel [36, 37]. In the field of Human Augmentics, the tactile channel has been used for augmented cognition, for example, to give users feedback about distance to a target destination [38].

Using the tactile channel to present information is particularly suitable when the visual and auditory systems are already under load or in which these sensory systems are impaired [39]. Inside VR, the visual and auditory system are occupied with the VR scene. Adding additional, artificial sounds or visualizations for the RT task could minimize the feeling of presence or disturb the VR experience. The tactile channel is the ideal candidate for RT testing as the vibrotactile on-body cues are identical in both real and virtual environments, thereby also increasing the comparability of cognitive load in both settings.

2.3   Example Use Case: Construction Site Work

As a contextual use-case for the virtual environments, their visualization and the tasks inside VR, we used the case of construction site work, as there can be found a lot of research on the use of VR in the construction industry. For example, it is anticipated that the use of VR will lead to training applications in the area of safety and health, as the industry has been facing high accident and fatality rates for many years (e.g. [40–44]). Research in this area has shown that, compared to conventional training, VR supports maintaining concentration and attention of trainees [45]. Experiencing potential accident hazards in VR safety trainings has also shown that it can trigger reflection processes in the participants by comparing the VR content to prior experiences with hazards [46]. With Building Information Modeling (BIM) it is possible to use construction states of the model and use them for VR simulations (e.g. [47, 48]). This allows to explore hazardous sections of the construction site in advance by using VR.

However, it should be noted that the vibrotactile reaction time task presented in this paper is not limited to this use case or depending on it, but can be used in any context to measure cognitive effort.

3   Vibrotactile Choice-Reaction Time Task in VR and Reality

In this study, we implemented a Choice-Reaction Time (CRT) task using vibrotactile cues that were presented participants around an abdominal belt. The research goal was to built a mobile apparatus that allowed to do the CRT in VR as well as in a real environment. We used a within-subjects design and invited 12 participants for the evaluation of the system and compared their RT data among four settings: standing or moving in either the real world ('static-R', 'move-R') or in VR ('static-VR', 'move-VR').

In the move-settings, a simple transporting task had to be fulfilled (primary task), as such tasks occur in a variety of jobs, e.g. in logistics or on construction sites. In the move-R condition, participants transported office material on a serving cart on a planned route inside a university building, whereas in the static-R condition they stood still while doing the CRT. In the VR conditions, participants used an HTC Vive Pro. During the static-VR condition participants did the CRT while experiencing a neutral VR environment, whereas in the move-VR condition they had to transport red and blue cement bags from one pallet to pallets for either red or blue cement bags in a construction site scenario (see Fig. 2). To transport the bags, they used the same serving cart as in all other conditions, which had an almost identical digital twin in VR, and moved physically inside the boundaries of the room-scale VR setting.

In order to minimize a bias of learning effects in the results, the sequences of the four conditions were balanced and participants were randomly assigned to each sequence. Additionally, participants filled out the NASA-TLX for each setting. After each session, a semi-structured interview was conducted with each participant.

Fig. 2. In the move-VR condition participants transported cement bags between pallets by moving a real serving cart physically through the virtual environment while doing the choice-reaction time task. Image showing a participant with (a) the experiment apparatus and (b) the corresponding view in the VR simulation.

3.1   Technical Solution and Apparatus

The developed system is based on an Android app that performs the CRT and triggers eight different vibration motors that are attached to an abdominal belt (see Fig. 2 and Fig. 3). (two motors for each direction: front, right, left, back). To trigger the motors, a NodeMCU-ESP32 board was used for the communication with the app. The input to react to a signal was attached to a serving cart, which was used by the participants in the study (see Fig. 3).

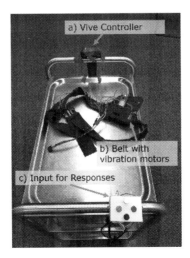

Fig. 3. The mobile apparatus used in the study, showing a serving cart with an attached Vive Controller (a) to track the cart inside VR. Vibro-tactile stimuli were triggered via the belt (b) which was connected by cable with the response unit (c) and transferred data to the smartphone of the experiment facilitator.

To investigate whether the perception of vibro-tactile cues is comparable during a VR-experience as to a real-world setting, we used the CRT to measure and compare the elapsed time between randomly applied vibro-tactile cues (stimulus) and the identification of the stimulus (response) in four conditions with a mobile apparatus. Findings of this study provide information on whether controller-based locomotion in VR environments [24] is sufficient to test vibro-tactile warnings in order to draw conclusions about real environments, or if perception differs between VR and real environments.

3.2   Participants, Data and Ethics

Twelve participants (10 male, 2 female) took part in this experiment with a mean age of 24.33 (SD = 3.14). Due to an unnoticed technical mishap during one experiment session, four CRT data sets had to be withdrawn as partly or totally corrupt, leaving a resulting data set of 8 participants (7 male, 1 female) with a mean age of 23.5 years (SD = 1.22). For the analysis of the qualitative data, however, the semi-structured interviews of all participants were considered, as their comments might still uncover relevant aspects, even if their CRT data was not usable for analysis.

Before taking part in this study voluntarily, the informed consent was handed out, the study was explained and participants had the chance to ask questions anytime. Participants were also informed that they could stop their participation at any time, especially as soon as signs of motion sickness would appear.

3.3   Results

For analyzing reaction time data, we followed approaches suggested in [49, 50] and removed very short RTs (<200 ms) as well as RTs slower than two standard deviations above the mean. Due to the small sample, we have not performed any statistical tests but limited ourselves to descriptive data.

Reaction Times and Cognitive Load. The results have shown that RTs required longer time when participants were doing the transportation tasks (move-R: M = 965.9, SD = 272.29; move-VR: M = 967.06, SD = 156.29) compared to the neutral conditions (see Fig. 4). Furthermore, the spread of reaction times was higher in the moving conditions, indicating it was more difficult to recognize the vibro-tactile cues during movement.

The TLX results did also show higher values for the moving conditions. In the interviews, participants mentioned that the task was easy to complete, but it was more difficult to identify the correct directional cue in the moving conditions. The overall TLX scores were M = 32.08 for move-R and M = 33.65 for move-VR. For the static conditions: M = 18.65 for static-R and M = 18.02 for static-VR. Additionally, the mental demand subscale of the TLX results show that participants' mean mental demand was higher in the move-R (M = 41.25) and move-VR (M = 43.75) conditions than in static-R (M = 19.37) or static-VR (M = 21.25).

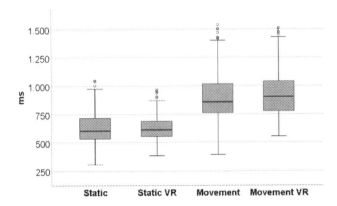

Fig. 4. Box-plot diagram of reaction times for each condition, showing a higher spread of CRT when participants were moving

Evaluating Directional Vibrotactile Cues. To evaluate our vibrotactile CRT, we analyzed the rates of correct responses to the cues. Aggregated by cue direction, the correct interpretation of the cues on the back seemed to be more difficult than the others, leaving the lowest rate of correct reactions to 91.56% (see Table 1).

Table 1. Rate of reactions to vibrotactile cues and rate of correct interpretation of the cues direction during the Choice-Reaction Time Task aggregated by cue direction.

Cue direction	Reaction to stimulus	Correct reaction to stimulus direction
Left	99.30%	97.89%
Right	99.61%	98.52%
Back	99.53%	91.56%
Front	98.91%	97.03%

Furthermore, we analyzed the correct reactions per condition (see Table 2). During the transport task, the detection rate of vibrations was comparable to that in the static conditions. However, the identification of the correct direction of the cue was noticeably more difficult, as can be seen from the drop in correct responses. This was also confirmed in the interviews with the participants. Several participants said that during the transport task, they sometimes guessed from which direction the cue came.

Table 2. Rate of reactions to vibrotactile cues and rate of correct interpretation of the cues direction during the Choice-Reaction Time Task aggregated by condition.

Condition	Reaction to stimulus	Correct reaction to stimulus direction
Static-R	94.79%	91.25%
Static-VR	99.69%	92.19%
Move-R	97.5%	80.94%
Move-VR	97.5%	86.25%

3.4 Discussion

The results and observations made have shown that the system of vibrotactile CRT has worked but needs adjustments. The high error rates in all four conditions indicate that vibration cues are sometimes not noticed and that it is difficult to identify them correctly, especially the cues presented at the back.

Additionally, participants stated that the task complexity was perceived as low for both settings, the VR environment and in the real environment. No participant criticized the use of a serving cart on the virtual reality construction site nor the usability of the system. Instead, the serving cart was accepted as a "given" artifact to fulfill the task. When asked, all participants would rather have expected a wheelbarrow on a construction site. In terms of the VR experience, participants reported a very positive user experience in the move-VR setting, as the free movement in the setting made the whole scenario seem more real.

4   Comparing Artificial vs Physical Locomotion Techniques

Based on the experiences of the first study, we built a new virtual environment with more complex tasks and repeated the study with two different locomotion techniques for VR: Motion Tracking/Room-Scale based vs. Controller-based Locomotion. Whereas controller-based locomotion allows exploration of an open world, room-scale based locomotion is subject to the limitations of the game area. The comparison is interesting in that room-scale based locomotion is the most natural movement technique for VR whereas controller-based movement is completely artificial in sense of moving around but one of the easiest locomotion techniques to implement in VR.

4.1   Virtual Environment and Technical Setup

Vibrotactile Belt. To increase the detection and identification rate of the cues, we have developed an updated abdominal belt. The number of vibration motors has been doubled (from 2 to 4 motors) and they have been distributed to the side of the spine rather than in the center. The vibration belt was tested in several pre-tests until a sufficiently well-functioning version was achieved.

To ensure that the vibration motors can be positioned precisely even with different body and abdominal sizes, the motors for left, right and front cues can be repositioned using Velcro (Fig. 5).

Fig. 5. Updated version of the vibrotactile belt, using two motors for left, right, front and four motors for back (two motors on each side of the spine).

Reaction Time Task. Based on the results and the experiences of the first study, we changed the Choice Reaction Time (CRT) task to a simple Reaction Time task, so that it wouldn't interfere with the interaction methods used in the study. As the controller-based locomotion technique is dependent on the controller's touchpad, we did not want to overload the user by giving them two controllers with two different touchpad functions. Instead, a button above the controller was used as input for reaction to a directional vibrotactile cue (see Fig. 6). We mirrored the controllers, so that both offered the same functionality and participants could decide themselves with which hand they navigated through the scene and which hand they used to react to the vibration cues.

Compared to the technical solution in the first study, we implemented the RT task directly in the unity game engine which sent commands to the abdominal belt, without using the Android application as external controller.

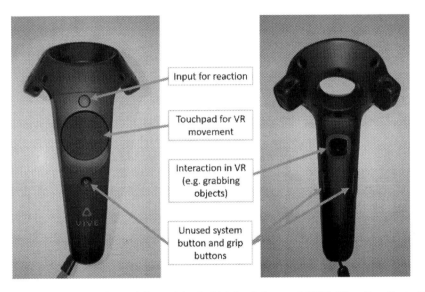

Input for reaction

Touchpad for VR movement

Interaction in VR (e.g. grabbing objects)

Unused system button and grip buttons

Fig. 6. Picture of the front (left) and back (right) of the used HTC Vive Pro Controller explaining its implemented functionalities.

Virtual Reality Simulation and Primary Tasks. Based on the results of the first study, we implemented a more dynamic VR experience in which participants had to fulfill three tasks: adding mortar to bricks and building a wall, drilling hole into a wall with a drill hammer, and mixing cement (see Fig. 7). In the VR environment we used a soundscape of a construction site and added some dynamics to make the environment more vivid.

The tasks differed in terms of complexity. While mixing cement, participants were standing still, interacting only with the controllers, whereas drilling holes and building a wall needed slightly more physical movement. Prior to the tasks, participants did a baseline RT measurement. Additionally, participants filled out the NASA-TLX after each task.

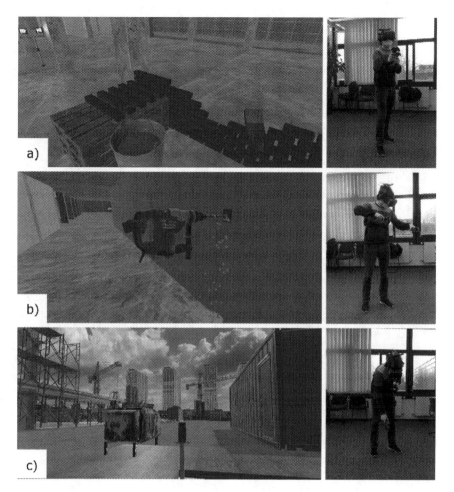

Fig. 7. Participants had to fulfill three tasks in VR during the study while wearing the vibrotactile belt and doing the reaction time task: a) adding mortar to bricks and building an unfinished wall, b) drilling holes with a drill hammer, and c) mixing cement.

4.2   Participants, Data and Ethics

We invited 16 participants (15 male, 1 female) to take part in this study. The mean age was 30.06 (SD = 13.77). Three of the participants stated they were very experienced with VR, three stated they had some experience and 10 participants had no prior experience with VR.

Participants were informed again about the study and the technical equipment. They were handed an informed consent and had the chance to ask questions at any time. Additionally, they were reminded that they could withdraw from the study at any time during or after the study.

4.3   Study Procedure

Prior to the study, participants were handed out the informed consent and a short questionnaire about demographics. After that, the study facilitator explained the technical equipment and the controls for moving and interacting in the VR scene. To reduce fatigue or practice effects during the study, we balanced the locomotion technique (controller-based vs. free walking) with which participants started as it was randomly assigned.

When participants were ready, they could try out and learn the required control in a tutorial at their leisure and without time pressure. After finishing the tutorial, the VR construction scene started and participants first performed a baseline measurement of reaction time. After the baseline measure, the first task started, building a wall. By starting the task, the RT task started automatically. After finishing all three tasks, participants removed the HMD and completed the NASA TLX. The same procedure was followed for the two remaining tasks (drilling holes and mixing cement). After successful completion of all tasks, participants repeated all tasks with the other locomotion technique.

4.4   Results

Reaction Time and Cognitive Load. Based on the results, it can be seen that compared to the baseline survey, all RTs in the tasks were longer. That suggests that each of the tasks is responsible for an increase in cognitive load compared to the baseline measurement. The median RTs are highest on average for the Controller+Bricks and Controller+Drill tasks, followed by Walking+Bricks and Walking+Drill. The cement mixing task required little interaction in the virtual environment, thus the shorter RTs can be explained by reduced task complexity.

The NASA-TLX results have shown no difference in the rating of both locomotion techniques.

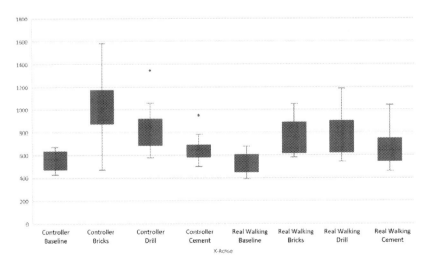

Fig. 8. Box-plot diagram of reaction times in the different conditions, showing higher RT for the two tasks 'drill' and 'brick' compared to 'cement' and the baseline measure.

Correct Reactions. For the rate of correct reactions, we have analyzed the logged timeouts, meaning, meaning how often cues were not noticed by subjects. The rate of correct reactions to vibrotactile cues shows lower values for the 'bricks' task in both locomotion types as well as for Controller+Cement, although for this task we measured comparably shorter reaction times than Controller+Bricks and Walking+Bricks. The highest rate was achieved in the baseline conditions, when participants could concentrate fully on the RT task (Table 3).

Table 3. Rate of correct reactions to vibrotactile cues during the simple Reaction Time Task aggregated by condition.

Condition	Rate of correct reactions
Controller, Baseline	98.44%
Controller, Bricks	88.28%
Controller, Drill	92.97%
Controller, Cement	87.50%
Moving, Baseline	99.22%
Moving, Bricks	86.72%
Moving, Drill	95.31%
Moving, Cement	94.53%
Total	**92.87%**

5   Discussion and Outlook

In this study, we addressed the possibility of RT tasks to measure cognitive load in VR settings. For this purpose, a system was presented that allows comparative studies to be conducted in mobile or static settings in VR or reality. The tactile channel was used as the sensory channel for the dual-task because it is the least disruptive to interaction in VR compared to the auditory or visual sensory channel. For the evaluation of the system, two consecutive studies were carried out, which led to adjustments to the belt and the virtual environment.

In the first study it was shown that the perception of vibrations in the real setting was comparable to the virtual settings, independent of the movement (move-R & move-VR vs. static-R & static-VR). In the semi-structured interviews, the system was confirmed to have a good usability and a positive user experience overall.

In the second study, two locomotion modes in VR were tested with respect to each other over three tasks. Here, higher reaction times could be measured for the tasks in which the interaction was more complex. An effect between the mode of locomotion was not demonstrated. This could indicate that the effect of the locomotion mode in VR does not have a large influence on the cognitive load. However, it has to be noted that the reaction times differed greatly from one another (see Fig. 8). This may have been due to the fact that the participants had different levels of prior experience with VR systems.

VR allows testing of scenarios that otherwise cannot or should not be tested without further ado. For example, for VR training, hazard scenarios can be mapped in VR that cannot and should not be tested in reality. VR is also suitable as a testbed for new ideas and prototypes for Human Augmentics that are not yet feasible due to technical barriers. In addition, new applications in mixed reality for instructional learning are being developed. The system presented here could be used and adapted for all mixed reality applications.

References

1. Cooper, G.: Cognitive load theory as an aid for instructional design. AJET **6** (1990). https://doi.org/10.14742/ajet.2322
2. Albers, M.J., Tracy, J.P.: Measuring cognitive load to test the usability of web sites 6 (2006)
3. Sweller, J.: Cognitive load during problem solving: Effects on learning. Cogn. Sci. **12**, 257–285 (1988). https://doi.org/10.1207/s15516709cog1202_4
4. Sweller, J.: Cognitive load theory, learning difficulty, and instructional design. Learn. Instr. **4**, 295–312 (1994). https://doi.org/10.1016/0959-4752(94)90003-5
5. Albus, P., Vogt, A., Seufert, T.: Signaling in virtual reality influences learning outcome and cognitive load. Comput. Educ. **166**, 104154 (2021). https://doi.org/10.1016/j.compedu.2021.104154
6. Armougum, A., Orriols, E., Gaston-Bellegarde, A., Marle, C.J.-L., Piolino, P.: Virtual reality: A new method to investigate cognitive load during navigation. J. Environ. Psychol. **65**, 101338 (2019). https://doi.org/10.1016/j.jenvp.2019.101338
7. Sweller, J.: Measuring cognitive load. Persp. Med. Educ. **7**(1), 1–2 (2017). https://doi.org/10.1007/s40037-017-0395-4
8. Chen, S.: The construct of cognitive load in interpreting and its measurement. Perspectives **25**, 640–657 (2017). https://doi.org/10.1080/0907676X.2016.1278026
9. Hart, S.G.: Nasa-Task Load Index (NASA-TLX); 20 years later. In: Proceedings of the Human Factors and Ergonomics Society Annual Meeting vol. 50, p. 5 (2006)
10. Kumar, N., Kumar, J.: Measurement of cognitive load in HCI systems using EEG power spectrum: An experimental study. Procedia Comput. Sci. **84**, 70–78 (2016). https://doi.org/10.1016/j.procs.2016.04.068
11. Antonenko, P., Paas, F., Grabner, R., van Gog, T.: Using electroencephalography to measure cognitive load. Educ. Psychol. Rev. **22**, 425–438 (2010). https://doi.org/10.1007/s10648-010-9130-y
12. Jensen, A.R.: Clocking the Mind: Mental Chronometry and Individual Differences. Elsevier (2006)
13. Schoor, C., Bannert, M., Brünken, R.: Role of dual task design when measuring cognitive load during multimedia learning. Educ. Tech. Res. Dev. **60**, 753–768 (2012). https://doi.org/10.1007/s11423-012-9251-8
14. Deary, I.J., Liewald, D., Nissan, J.: A free, easy-to-use, computer-based simple and four-choice reaction time programme: The Deary-Liewald reaction time task. Behav Res. **43**, 258–268 (2011). https://doi.org/10.3758/s13428-010-0024-1
15. Deary, I.J., Der, G.: Reaction time, age, and cognitive ability: Longitudinal findings from age 16 to 63 years in representative population samples. Aging Neuropsychol. Cogn. **12**, 187–215 (2005). https://doi.org/10.1080/13825580590969235
16. Edman, G., Schalling, D., Levander, S.E.: Impulsivity and speed and errors in a reaction time task: A contribution to the construct validity of the concept of impulsivity. Acta Physiol. (Oxf) **53**, 1–8 (1983). https://doi.org/10.1016/0001-6918(83)90012-4

17. Cinaz, B., Vogt, C., Arnrich, B., Tröster, G.: A Wearable user interface for measuring reaction time. In: Keyson, D.V., et al. (eds.) AmI 2011. LNCS, vol. 7040, pp. 41–50. Springer, Heidelberg (2011). https://doi.org/10.1007/978-3-642-25167-2_5

18. Cinaz, B., Vogt, C., Arnrich, B., Tröster, G.: Implementation and evaluation of wearable reaction time tests. Perv. Mob. Comput. **8**, 813–821 (2012). https://doi.org/10.1016/j.pmcj. 2012.06.006

19. Frommel, J., Sonntag, S., Weber, M.: Effects of controller-based locomotion on player experience in a virtual reality exploration game. In: Proceedings of the 12th International Conference on the Foundations of Digital Games, pp. 1–6. Association for Computing Machinery, New York (2017). https://doi.org/10.1145/3102071.3102082

20. Slater, M., Usoh, M., Steed, A.: Taking steps: the influence of a walking technique on presence in virtual reality. ACM Trans. Comput.-Hum. Interact. **2**, 201–219 (1995). https://doi.org/10.1145/210079.210084

21. Auda, J., Pascher, M., Schneegass, S.: Around the (Virtual) World: Infinite walking in virtual reality using electrical muscle stimulation. In: Proceedings of the 2019 CHI Conference on Human Factors in Computing Systems, pp. 431:1–431:8. ACM, New York (2019). https://doi.org/10.1145/3290605.3300661

22. Nilsson, N.C., Serafin, S., Steinicke, F., Nordahl, R.: Natural walking in virtual reality: A review. Comput. Entertain. **16**, 8:1–8:22 (2018). https://doi.org/10.1145/3180658

23. Boletsis, C.: The new era of virtual reality locomotion: A systematic literature review of techniques and a proposed typology. Multimodal Technol. Interact. **1**, 24 (2017). https://doi.org/10.3390/mti1040024

24. Boletsis, C., Cedergren, J.E.: VR locomotion in the new era of virtual reality: An empirical comparison of prevalent techniques. Adv. Hum. Comput. Interact. **2019**, 1–15 (2019). https://doi.org/10.1155/2019/7420781

25. Juravle, G., Binsted, G., Spence, C.: Tactile suppression in goal-directed movement. Psychon. Bull. Rev. **24**(4), 1060–1076 (2016). https://doi.org/10.3758/s13423-016-1203-6

26. Hwang, S., Ryu, J.-H.: The haptic steering wheel: Vibro-tactile based navigation for the driving environment. In: 2010 8th IEEE International Conference on Pervasive Computing and Communications Workshops (PERCOM Workshops), pp. 660–665 (2010). https://doi.org/10.1109/PERCOMW.2010.5470517

27. Suzuki, K., Jansson, H.: An analysis of driver's steering behaviour during auditory or haptic warnings for the designing of lane departure warning system. JSAE Rev. **24**, 65–70 (2003). https://doi.org/10.1016/S0389-4304(02)00247-3

28. Ho, C., Reed, N., Spence, C.: Assessing the effectiveness of "intuitive" vibrotactile warning signals in preventing front-to-rear-end collisions in a driving simulator. Accid. Anal. Prev. **38**, 988–996 (2006). https://doi.org/10.1016/j.aap.2006.04.002

29. Erp, J.B.F.V., Veen, H.A.H.C.V., Jansen, C., Dobbins, T.: Waypoint navigation with a vibrotactile waist belt. ACM Trans. Appl. Percep. **2**, 106–117 (2005). https://doi.org/10.1145/1060581.1060585

30. Asseman, F., Bronstein, A.M., Gresty, M.A.: Guidance of visual direction by topographical vibrotactile cues on the torso. Exp Brain Res. **186**, 283–292 (2008). https://doi.org/10.1007/s00221-007-1231-6

31. Li, Y., Jeon, W.R., Nam, C.S.: Navigation by vibration: Effects of vibrotactile feedback on a navigation task. Int. J. Ind. Ergon. **46**, 76–84 (2015). https://doi.org/10.1016/j.ergon.2014.12.008

32. Meier, A., Matthies, D.J.C., Urban, B., Wettach, R.: Exploring vibrotactile feedback on the body and foot for the purpose of pedestrian navigation. In: Proceedings of the 2nd international Workshop on Sensor-based Activity Recognition and Interaction - WOAR '2015. pp. 1–11. ACM Press, Rostock (2015). https://doi.org/10.1145/2790044.2790051

33. Pielot, M., Poppinga, B., Heuten, W., Boll, S.: Tacticycle: supporting exploratory bicycle trips. In: Proceedings of the 14th International Conference on Human-Computer Interaction with Mobile Devices and Services - MobileHCI 2012. p. 369. ACM Press, San Francisco (2012). https://doi.org/10.1145/2371574.2371631

34. Kiss, F., Boldt, R., Pfleging, B., Schneegass, S.: Navigation systems for motorcyclists: Exploring wearable tactile feedback for route guidance in the real world. In: Proceedings of the 2018 CHI Conference on Human Factors in Computing Systems, pp. 617:1–617:7. ACM, New York (2018). https://doi.org/10.1145/3173574.3174191

35. Asif, A., Boll, S.: Where to turn my car? Comparison of a Tactile Display and a Conventional Car Navigation System under High Load Condition, p. 8 (2010)

36. Cobus, V., Heuten, W., Boll, S.: Multimodal head-mounted display for multimodal alarms in intensive care units. In: Proceedings of the 6th ACM International Symposium on Pervasive Displays, pp. 26:1–26:2. ACM, New York (2017). https://doi.org/10.1145/3078810.3084349

37. Cobus, V., Boll, S., Heuten, W.: Requirements for a wearable alarm distribution system in intensive care units. Zukunft der Pflege, p. 5 (2018)

38. Mateevitsi, V., Haggadone, B., Leigh, J., Kunzer, B., Kenyon, R.V.: Sensing the environment through SpiderSense. In: Proceedings of the 4th Augmented Human International Conference, pp. 51–57. ACM (2013)

39. van Erp, J.B.F., Verschoor, M.H.: Cross-modal visual and vibrotactile tracking. Appl. Ergon. **35**, 105–112 (2004). https://doi.org/10.1016/j.apergo.2003.12.004

40. Jelonek, M., Herrmann, T.: Attentiveness for potential accidents at the construction site: Virtual reality test environment with tactile warnings for behavior tests in hazardous situations. In: Proceedings of Mensch und Computer 2019, pp. 649–653. Association for Computing Machinery, New York (2019). https://doi.org/10.1145/3340764.3344885

41. Albert, L., Routh, C.: Designing impactful construction safety training interventions. Safety. **7**, 42 (2021). https://doi.org/10.3390/safety7020042

42. Abdelhamid, T.S., Everett, J.G.: Identifying root causes of construction accidents. J. Constr. Eng. Manag. **126**, 52–60 (2000). https://doi.org/10.1061/(ASCE)0733-9364(2000)126:1(52)

43. Hilfert, T., König, M.: Low-cost virtual reality environment for engineering and construction. Visual. Eng. **4**(1), 1–18 (2016). https://doi.org/10.1186/s40327-015-0031-5

44. Gibb, A., Lingard, H., Behm, M., Cooke, T.: Construction accident causality: learning from different countries and differing consequences. Constr. Manag. Econ. **32**, 446–459 (2014). https://doi.org/10.1080/01446193.2014.907498

45. Sacks, R., Perlman, A., Barak, R.: Construction safety training using immersive virtual reality. Constr. Manag. Econ. **31**, 1005–1017 (2013). https://doi.org/10.1080/01446193.2013.828844

46. Fiala, E., Jelonek, M., Herrmann, T.: Using virtual reality simulations to encourage reflective learning in construction workers. In: Zaphiris, P., Ioannou, A. (eds.) HCII 2020. LNCS, vol. 12206, pp. 422–434. Springer, Cham (2020). https://doi.org/10.1007/978-3-030-50506-6_29

47. Graham, K., Chow, L., Fai, S.: From BIM to VR: Defining a level of detail to guide virtual reality narratives. ITcon. **24**, 553–568 (2019). https://doi.org/10.36680/j.itcon.2019.031

48. Teizer, J., et al.: Digitalisierung der Arbeitssicherheit auf Baustellen. In: Bauer, W., Mütze-Niewöhner, S., Stowasser, S., Zanker, C., Müller, N. (eds.) Arbeit in der digitalisierten Welt, pp. 399–414. Springer, Heidelberg (2021). https://doi.org/10.1007/978-3-662-62215-5_26

49. Whelan, R.: Effective analysis of reaction time data. Psychol Rec. **58**, 475–482 (2008). https://doi.org/10.1007/BF03395630

50. Harald Baayen, R., Milin, P.: Analyzing reaction times. Int. J. Psych. Res. **3**, 12 (2010). https://doi.org/10.21500/20112084.807

Assessing User Experience of Text Readability with Eye Tracking in Virtual Reality

Tanja Kojic[1]([⊠]), Maurizio Vergari[1], Sebastian Möller[1,2], and Jan-Niklas Voigt-Antons[2,3]

[1] Quality and Usability Lab, Technische Universität Berlin, Berlin, Germany
`tanja.kojic@tu-berlin.de`
[2] German Research Center for Artificial Intelligence (DFKI), Berlin, Germany
[3] Immersive Reality Lab, University of Applied Sciences Hamm-Lippstadt, Lippstadt, Germany

Abstract. Virtual Reality (VR) technology is mostly used in gaming, videos, engineering applications, and training simulators. One thing which is shared among all of them is the necessity to display text. Text reading experience is not always in focus for VR systems because of limited hardware capabilities, lack of standardization, user interface (UI) design flaws, and physical design of Head-Mounted Displays (HMDs). With this paper, key variables from the UI design side were researched that can improve text reading user experience in VR. Therefore four important points for reading in VR application were selected to be focused on: 1) Difference in canvas type (flat/curved), 2) Contrast on virtual scene (light/dark), 3) Number of columns in layout (1 column/2 column/3 column) 4) Text distance from the subject (1.5 m/6.5 m). For a user study a VR app for Oculus Quest was developed, enabling the possibility to display text while varying some of the features important for readability in VR. This user experiment has shown parameters that are important for text reading experience in VR. Specifically, subjects performed very well when the text was on a 6.5-meter distance from the subject with font size 22pt, on a flat canvas with one column layout. When it comes to physiological variables, the conditions measurements were behaving similarly, as all of the selected parameters were in line with the design guidelines. Therefore, selection on final settings should be more oriented towards user experience and preferences.

Keywords: User experience · Virtual Reality · Text readability · Eye tracking

1 Introduction

In recent years, the use of VR equipment has become quite common in both commercial and academic spheres. There are several compelling reasons to make VR devices popular, including infinite virtual space with a feeling of presence

© The Author(s), under exclusive license to Springer Nature Switzerland AG 2022
J. Y. C. Chen and G. Fragomeni (Eds.): HCII 2022, LNCS 13317, pp. 199–211, 2022.
https://doi.org/10.1007/978-3-031-05939-1_13

and immersion. Because of the growing usage of VR devices in our everyday lives, it has become important to determine which aspects contribute to a comfortable and coherent reading experience in a VR environment.

In general, there are few different elements and categories that contribute to a better reading experience such as software, hardware, and humans themselves [20]. UI layout, text location, font size, distance from the text, UI color scheme, and how easy it is to interact with the text are all software considerations. Hardware considerations include the screen resolution of the HMD, the field of depth, the HMD design, weight, and so on. Human elements are usually more difficult to observe because they are constantly based on an individual's personality and talents.

VR technology is still developing, but nevertheless VR can produce 360-degree scenes and allow users to interact with them. However, when it comes to reading text, sometimes an inappropriate viewing angle, or text that is not positioned precisely on the canvas with insufficient contrast, leads to overall low quality and text can be hard to read. All of this adds up to a less pleasant VR experience for consumers and results in some discomfort. Therefore, in this paper, we chose the most important criteria that directly effect text readability based on past research to determine the most critical elements to improve the reading experience in VR.

2   Related Work

According to 2021 VR adoption statistics, 27% of VR industry professionals believe that user experience is a barrier to broad adoption of VR technology [3]. In addition, 19% of respondents mentioned a lack of content from the VR sector as an impediment. Text is an integral part of the user experience, and readability (see definition below) is a fundamental requirement to ensure that all on-screen components blend in a way that optimizes UX while communicating the message. When incorporating text in a user interface, generally it should be made sure that users can read it easily and make excellent use of the information that it is trying to express.

2.1   Text and Readability

Readability can be described as a measure of how straightforward it is to read a piece of text [11]. This can be observed as well on human behavior with technology and text. For example if the typical user finds the material on a website too difficult to read, they will leave the web-page and won't use the offered service. Furthermore, readability was recognized to be so important that even Google considers it a Search Engine Optimization (SEO) key ranking factor. These rankings are used to rank website to the top of the list in Google [24].

Columns Layout. Writing text in more than one column saves space and speeds up reading since your eyes do not have to travel along long lines [15]. In terms of empirical research, the presence of additional columns allows small line lengths to be compared against larger ones with the same quantity of text per screen. In terms of column text, this study supports both long single columns of text and many short columns of text [16].

Contrast. For text representation, there are two forms of contrast: positive contrast and negative contrast. The text is written in light colors on a dark background in positive contrast, whereas the dark text is written on a lighter background in negative contrast. Preferences about positive or negative studies are still in research depending on the media [5]. According to one research study, there are no differences in performance or preferences for positive and negative contrast in general. However, another study has reported that positive contrast is commonly utilized for computer screen displays since flicker is less noticeable at conventional repetition rates than negative contrast [25].

Typeface. A typeface is the overall design of letters; variants include extra bold, bold, regular, light, italic, condensed, extended, and so on, and it has already been established that typography is an important role in readability [11]. Many investigations have been undertaken in order to discover the optimal font for readability and reading. San serif fonts are claimed to be ideal for computer displays since they are considerably easier and faster to read [7], while serif typefaces include features that make them simpler to read, which is why most books, periodicals, and newspapers use serif fonts like Times New Roman [2].

Line Spacing. The insertion of a space between lines is referred to as line spacing. Reading efficiency has also been found to improve when text on a computer screen is double spaced rather than single spaced [22, 23]. More fixations per line are necessary with single spacing. However, due to new, superior displays and technologies, current consensus is that line spacing of 130% to 150% is best for reading for web applications.

Line Length. There are two ways to define line length: Character density and Character count per line. The maximum number of characters shown in a horizontal line is referred to as character density. Density of a computer display character is typically between 40 and 80 [18]. On the other hand, the maximum number of spaces utilized to show information is defined by the number of characters per line. Overall, medium to short line lengths may result in better understanding [4], and rich text presentation are generally chosen since reading smaller letters requires fewer fixations [22].

2.2   VR and Readability

A lot of research has been conducted to improve text reading on digital screens, but when it comes to VR it is not possible to assume that reading in VR will provide the same results. Even thouguh VR does not need to be only with head mounted displays (HMDs) in scope of this paper, this option will only be considered. The key distinctions in readability between VR and traditional digital screens [30] include immersive, 360-degree, 3D infinite universe, movement of the whole 3D space with your head movement, depth of field, the distance between eyes and display, and the HMDs themselves. Until today, research on readability in VR has been quite restricted since this technology has not been widely available to the general public and has been employed only for scientific purposes on a limited scale. However, with the growth of technology in recent years, VR technology research has also followed. In one study [29] focusing on a reading in VR, participants were instructed to read some material in virtual reality. Using HTC Vive on flat and curved canvas, it was reported that the most practical mean character size for reading was 23.0 dmm and 23.8 dmm, respectively. When the same experiment was repeated and carried out using the Pimax 5K Plus VR headset, the mean comfortable character size for flat and curved canvas were reported to be 20.6 dmm and 22.1 dmm.

Another study was carried out with the Oculus Rift CV1 HMD and user interactions were carried out with the Xbox controller [13]. The UI was created using the typefaces Arial and Times New Roman, which were also utilized throughout the experiment. There were three factors in focus: font size, distance, and angular size, all of which are connected to one another. Other options were dark vs. bright backgrounds, text box size, and font size. According to the findings of these investigations, 13 people chose a dark backdrop, a vertical text box position of $-1.0 +/- 2.6$ degrees, and a reported font size of 237.8 dmm. According to research reporting about crucial characteristics that should be included while developing and designing for VR [9], curved canvas improves the overall VR experience. As for immersive and interactive data visualization, curved canvas is preferable. This research has added several additional helpful features that improved the VR experience, such as pointing, clicking, zooming, rotating, and grabbing objects from the collection.

Another study was conducted using two HMDs, Oculus Go and Oculus Quest, where participants were requested to read some text [21]. Additionally, participants had to change the variable as per their comfort level for short (2 words), medium (21 words), and long (51 words) text. Users could choose the distance of text (between 0 and 10000 mm), font size (from 5 pt to 40 pt), and contrast ratio (from 1:1 to 21:1). The study was conducted to determine which text properties individuals rated as the best and worst for reading in virtual reality. The findings indicated that the mean angular size for short, medium, and long text was 27.48 dmm, 17.17 dmm, and 16.01 dmm (Oculus Go), 32.06 dmm, 16.18 dmm, and 17.87 dmm (Oculus Quest); while the mean contrast ratio for short, medium, and long text was reported as 11.89, 10.47, and 11.02 (Oculus Go) and 10.12, 8.71, and 9.37 (Oculus Quest), respectively.

Because VR is still a developing technology, there are not precise rules when it comes to UI and VR design principles. Some companies provide internal guidelines, standards, or best practices to follow. For example, during Google I/O '17 [12], a set of standards for building Virtual Reality interfaces was presented. They reported on testing several units of measurement when it comes to size items in a virtual space. Oculus has also established certain "VR Design Best

Practices" [30], where they discussed general user experience, vision, user inputs, hand tracking, audio, user orientation, avatars, and other topics.

2.3   Eye Tracking and Readability

Our eyes, brain, and psychology all play a role in making the VR text readability experience more enjoyable and efficient. Our capacity to read is intimately related to the functioning of our eyes and brain. The most associated physiological characteristics for text reading are blink rate, eye activities, pupil confidence, and pupil size [6]. Several studies had already been conducted in which eye-tracking was employed while reading text, but mainly these trials were conducted for conventional screens, not for VR.

The human eye has limited mobility and focus, it can only see 114° [19]. As in VR there is a 360° perspective, therefore when a user looks at the text from an angle other than 0°, that user might experience some distortion, and reading distorted text can lower reading performance, which can lead to the effect that at some angles it will be difficult to read the text. By knowing the position of eye with eye tracking in VR, several effects on user experience can be explained. Further more, reading is a cognitive task that stimulates the brain, resulting in longer inter-blink intervals [26]. While reading, the typical person blinks 4.5 times per minute [28]. This drop in blink rate might be due to intense attention on the job at hand, or it could be due to a relatively narrow range of eye movement. Eye tracking in virtual reality is a smart approach that combines the advantages of traditional laboratory settings with fixed monitor panels with the actual environment [10].

3   Method

3.1   Design and Test Setup

For this user study, an app in which users read a text and answer a question based on that content was developed. There are a total of 26 scenes/screens in the VR app. Except for the instruction and concluding scenes, each scene contains 4-5 lines of text and one question. Users had to read the material, mark the correct answers about text to ensure text was fully read, and then go to the next scenario by clicking on the "Next" button as shown with Fig. 1. Every scenario had a mix of our chosen factors, and all possible combinations of factors were tested. The design factors of choice include contrast, distance, number of columns, and canvas type. The initial screen has instructions for reading the material, answering the question after each scene, clicking on buttons to choose responses, and moving on to the next scene. All scenarios have a Wikipedia paragraph with a standard English vocabulary, and questions are designed to be simple to understand. The topics for texts are chosen in a way that users do not require any additional expertise to answer the question. If an error occurs, the user can resume the experiment by clicking on the "Restart" button. Oculus Controls are used by users to interact with the app.

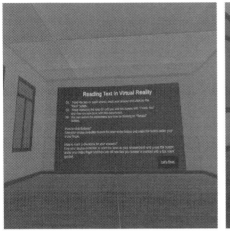

(a) First scene

(b) Reading scene

Fig. 1. Example of reading scenes in VR applications a) on boarding first scene for users, b) reading scene as one of the conditions during experiment.

By the standard-setting, Oculus Quest currently does not support any eye-trackers. A converter/holder for holding the HTC Vive Binocular add-on[1] had to be built that can be mounted to the display lens of Oculus Quest as it is shown with Figs. 2 and 3. This was done in order to gather eye-tracking data with Oculus Quest. The HTC Vive Binocular add-on was used to collect eye-tracking and physiological data from the subject's eyes, such as blink rate, pupil diameter, pupil activity, and pupil confidence. Further on, a customized raw data exporter plugin was written in the Python programming language to extract all raw data. It was possible to extract timestamps, blinks, pupil activity, pupil confidence, and pupil diameter as data sets that were later analyzed. Additionally, the VR gameplay was synced with eye tracker data with the help of timestamps and calculated the number of blinks, average pupil activity, confidence, and diameter for each scene.

3.2 Procedure

To begin with the experiment, each participant had to sign a consent form, which described the procedure and data usage policy for all the data collected during this whole experiment. Afterwards, moderator of the study has given a brief introduction to users of how to handle VR headset and once the users knew how to perform this experiment, they could click on the "Let's Start" button. The user started with the first text paragraph, and they had to read the material and answer the question at the conclusion of the paragraph before clicking the "Next" button. The process had to be repeated until all of the 24 scenes with various variables were completed. All 24 scene screens were presented in a random order

---

[1] https://docs.pupil-labs.com/vr-ar/htc-vive/.

and contained distinct content with no duplication. This randomization ensured that first-hand experience was gained for all of these scenarios, without getting incorrect biased data. After reading all of the content in the app and answering all of the questions, users could see the final scene of the VR app, which displayed a "thank you" message and asked them to remove their headsets. During this experiment, an eye tracker collected user gameplay and eye activity data. Data points collected during the VR gameplay were: 1. Total time spent in reading the whole text 2. Time spent reading each paragraph. 3. Environment Variables for each scene(Canvas Type, Contrast, text layout, and distance from subject).

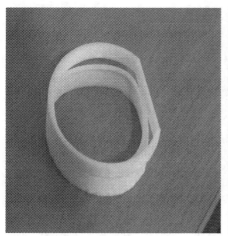 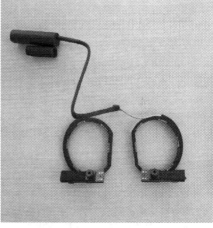

(a) 3D Printed Eye Tracker   (b) HTC Vive Binocular Add-on

Fig. 2. Example of reading scenes in VR applications a) oD Printed Eye Tracker Holder/Converter, b) HTC Vive Binocular Add-on Eye Tracking hardware.

Fig. 3. HTC Vive fitted with 3D printed Eye Tracker Holder and the eye tracker.

The users completed a questionnaire at the end of the experiment. This questionnaire was divided into five sections: 1. Demographics 2. Affinity for Technology Interaction (ATI) Scale [17] 3. System Usability Scale (SUS) [8] 4. IPQ Questionnaire [1] 5. Overall experience and open-end questions. The demographics section gathered information such as users' age, gender, and reading preferences. The ATI Scale section was used to measure how familiar individuals are with technologies in general and how eager they are to learn about new ones. The SUS score was chosen since it covers questions on VR user experience, whereas the IPQ part is also4 relevant to VR experience, as users were asked about spatial presence, engagement, and experienced realism.

3.3   Participants

A sample of 15 participants took part in the experiment, due to the unpredictability of Covid-19 situation. The experiment was done following all current regulations and hygiene measures. Everyone who took part in the experiment did so voluntarily. Participants ranged in age from 22 to 41 years old, with 66.7 % being male and 33.3 % female. Majority of participant were students by profession (80%), with the remaining of participants being employed and working (20%). Participants have reported that majority of them spent 2-4 hours reading (53.3 %) text on digital devices such as computers, mobile phones, while around one third of participants reads less than 1 hour per day (33.3%). Minority reported reading around 5-7 hours (6.7%) and more than 11 hours a day (6.7%). When it comes to eyesight majority of participants (73.3%) were not using any sort of vision improvement assistance such as glasses, lenses, or laser surgery, while the others reported (20%) reported that they were wearing glasses and eyesight aid, and the remaining (6.7%) were using another type of eyesight improvement aid.

4   Results

Corresponding to the structure of the measured parameters, the results of the research will be presented in two separate sections with the first one focusing on the text distance and the differences between canvas types, and the second focusing on the number of columns and different theme modes. Overall, for reading a paragraph in a study that contained 4-5 lines of text and answering the one question from that paragraph was done on average in 40.24 s (SD=17.81, min=5, max=102). When it comes to overall accuracy of all answered questions about the text topic, 98% of the questions were answered correctly.

According to the questionnaire, 73.3% of individuals preferred to read the text in VR when it was 6.5 m away from them as it can be seen in Table 1. Reading one paragraph is also quicker (by 7.08 seconds per paragraph) than reading text from a distance of 1.5 m. Except for the blink rate, all physiological characteristics (such as pupil diameter, pupil confidence, and movements) remained nearly constant throughout both distances.

Table 1. Results show preferred setting by users and eye tracking parameters per condition of text distance (1.5 m away text and 6.5 m away text from user) and canvas type (text displayed on flat or curved canvas).

Parameter	1.5 m	6.5 m	Flat canvas	Curved canvas
Preferred setting by users (%)	26.7	73.3	73.3	26.7
Time reading a paragraph (s)	43.75	36.67	41.87	38.76
Blink rate per minute	13.79	14.49	12.75	15.85
Answer accuracy (%)	97.39	98.89	96.87	99
Pupil size (mm)	3.82	3.94	3.95	3.72
Pupil confidence (%)	95.18	95.16	95.40	95.94
Pupil activity	0.43	0.43	0.43	0.43

Exception is when the test is performed at 6.5 m, the blink rate rises (0.7 blinks), however, this is around one blink per minute less than 1.6 m. Further on, when it comes to comparison of flat and curved canvas for text reading in VR, 73.3% of individuals reported that they preferred to read text on a flat canvas. This can be confirmed as well with reading times that was also found to be faster with flat canvas (by 3.11). Further more, the blink rate was reduced for flat canvas condition for 3.1 blinks per minute. Other physiological factors are very similar, with very minor changes and don't go in favour of flat or curved canvas type as it is shown with results presenting in Table 1.

Table 2. Results show preferred setting by users and eye tracking parameters per condition of number of columns (text displayed in 1 column view, 2 column view or 3 column view) and theme (light theme background with dark text and dark theme background with bright text).

Parameter	1 col	2 col	3 col	Light	Dark
Preferred setting by users (%)	46.7	40.0	13.3	60.0	40.0
Time reading a paragraph (s)	37.78	38.17	44.68	39.88	40.61
Blink rate per minute	13.53	15.03	13.85	14.59	13.49
Answer accuracy (%)	100.00	96.00	98.00	98.00	97.00
Pupil size (mm)	3.75	3.74	3.96	3.90	3.87
Pupil confidence (%)	92.27	95.44	95.08	95.68	94.22
Pupil activity	0.43	0.43	0.43	0.43	0.43

According to the survey, 46.7% of respondents preferred a one-column style, while 40% preferred a two-column layout as it is shown with Table 2. Only 13.3% of participants preferred the three column reading arrangement. The average reading time was 37.78, 38.17, and 44.68 s, respectively. All other variables remained constant with minor variations.

Lastly, according to the survey and as shown with Table 2, 60% of the subjects preferred the light theme. The difference between dark and light themes in terms of average time spent reading each paragraph is at 0.73 s, while the accuracy of correct responses is 1% different. All of the other measures indicate minor variations, such as a 0.03 mm difference in pupil diameter size and a 1.46% difference in pupil confidence, but the eye movement stays constant.

5   Discussion and Conclusion

With the aim to explore text settings for the best readability in VR experiences, not only based on user experience questionnaires but also based on results from eye-tracker, a study with several different scene options was designed. Depending on the condition of the study, users had to read some text on two different distances (1.5 m or 6.5 m) where text was placed on a flat or curved canvas. Further on, text was presented to users in 1-, 2- or 3- columns, and there were two different themes light (where dark text was presented on a background) and dark theme (where light text was presented on dark background). Overall, it can be noticed that as all conditions were designed inside of the scope of current limitations and design guidelines, and aim was to explore if there were any strong preferences to users based on their preferences or based on physiological indicators measured via eye-tracking.

Users stated their preferences after reading the text with all possible scene options. The most voted scenario for presenting text was to show text on a flat canvas that is 6.5 m away from the user, on 1- or 2-column layout with a light theme. Interesting is the fact that users were quite strongly agreeing on selecting a distance and the canvas type. In contrast, results for the amount of columns was not as clear. This could be due to the fact that the number of columns is not as important for readability. It seems that users rather prefer no or a small number of columns, but a clear differentiation here is not as easy as for the other parameters.

However, when observing the physiological data, there were no big differences reported. The fact that there are only marginal differences of eye-tracking parameters could be due to the fact that all conditions were designed inside of the guidelines, and none of them made the user feel fully unconformable. Also the experimental condition were selected so that physical safety was always maintained. For example, the light theme was not using a full white background in order not to be too bright on users' eyes. Therefore, according to eye-tracking data, contrast adjustment appears to be a matter of personal choice. Some people favour dark contrast, while others prefer bright contrast. These results are in line with other tests conducted in the past for standard computer screens as they also indicate that there is no change in reading performance [5], but people preferred dark themes on PCs in general since flicker is less evident with dark colors [25].

While prior studies focused on reading performance on digital displays and traditional books, these findings show that the same ideas apply to VR as well.

It demonstrates that reading in VR follows the same performance principles as reading on a digital display screen or a printed book, as previously demonstrated by researchers [14]. Column layout, contrast, and blink rate factors, for example, provide an almost similar result. Because physiological indications are directly proportionate to cognitive activity in the brain. In fact, when it comes to text layouts for VR within well selected design parameters, our cognitive processes as measures by eye-tracking seem to not deviate significantly between conditions.

The findings from this study might be one of the first steps in understanding and designing good VR reading experiences, making them more accessible in general. However, these results should be read with their limitations, as there is no eye-tracking device that can currently be used with Oculus Quest. Therefore, the HTC Vive eye tracker and then 3D design a device that holds an eye tracker in Oculus Quest was used, while with the use of an embedded eye tracking system for Oculus Quest, the physiological data could have been more precise. Further on, when it comes to the accuracy of preferred solutions based on user experience, it is important to notice that in this study, many of the individuals were experiencing VR for the first time, so their feedback may have been biased [27]. In addition, the rather smaller sample size could also be a limiting factor.

The results demonstrated and reported by this paper indicate some of the preferred settings for reading in virtual reality, but they do not report how comfortable long time reading scenarios for users are. When it comes to how comfortable VR devices are for longer usage, a lot of research and improvements has been done, but for reading it is especially important. Therefore, it's not only about the design of an application, but also hardware itself can be an important influencing factor. In future works, it would be interesting to try out several different devices and include more different text options. Also, it is known that physiological and cognitive processes such as cognitive load rather accumulate over time. Which makes the usage of longer stimuli with a wider range of physiological measures a promising direction.

Acknowledgements. This work would not have been possible without the effort of Zohaib Hassan, who took part in the gathering of results for this paper.

References

1. igroup presence questionnaire (ipq) overview. http://www.igroup.org/pq/ipq/index.php
2. Ali, A.Z.M., Wahid, R., Samsudin, K., Idris, M.Z.: Reading on the computer screen: does font type have effects on web text readability? Int. Educ. Stud. **6**(3), 26–35 (2013)
3. Alsop, T.: Top obstacles to mass adoption of vr technologies 2019 (2022). https://www.statista.com/statistics/1098566/obstacles-to-mass-adoption-of-vr-technologies/
4. Baker, J.R.: Is multiple-column online text better? it depends. Usability News **7**(2), 1–8 (2005)
5. Baldwin, T.S., Bailey, L.J.: Readability of technical training materials presented on microfiche versus offset copy. J. Appl. Psychol. **55**(1), 37 (1971)

6. Bayat, A., Pomplun, M.: The influence of text difficulty level and topic on eye-movement behavior and pupil size during reading. In: 2016 2nd International Conference of Signal Processing and Intelligent Systems (ICSPIS), pp. 1–5. IEEE (2016)

7. Berninger, V.W., et al.: Comparison of faster and slower responders to early intervention in reading: differentiating features of their language profiles. Learn. Disabil. Q. **25**(1), 59–76 (2002)

8. Brooke, J., et al.: Sus-a quick and dirty usability scale. Usability Eval. Ind. **189**(194), 4–7 (1996)

9. Cao, L., Peng, C., Hansberger, J.T.: A large curved display system in virtual reality for immersive data interaction. In: 2019 IEEE Games, Entertainment, Media Conference (GEM), pp. 1–4. IEEE (2019)

10. Clay, V., König, P., Koenig, S.: Eye tracking in virtual reality. J. Eye Movement Res. **12**(1) (2019)

11. Dale, E., Chall, J.S.: The concept of readability. Elementary Eng. **26**(1), 19–26 (1949)

12. Developers, G.: Designing screen interfaces for VR (google i/o'17) (2017)

13. Dingler, T., Kunze, K., Outram, B.: VR reading UIS: assessing text parameters for reading in VR. In: Extended Abstracts of the 2018 CHI Conference on Human Factors in Computing Systems, pp. 1–6 (2018)

14. Dyson, M.C.: How physical text layout affects reading from screen. Behav. Inf. Technol. **23**(6), 377–393 (2004)

15. Dyson, M.C., Haselgrove, M.: The influence of reading speed and line length on the effectiveness of reading from screen. Int. J. Hum. Comput. Stud. **54**(4), 585–612 (2001)

16. Dyson, M.C., Kipping, G.J.: The effects of line length and method of movement on patterns of reading from screen. Vis. Lang. **32**(2), 150 (1998)

17. Franke, T., Attig, C., Wessel, D.: A personal resource for technology interaction: development and validation of the affinity for technology interaction (ati) scale. Int. J. Hum. Comput. Inter. **35**(6), 456–467 (2019)

18. Hooper, S., Hannafin, M.J.: Variables affecting the legibility of computer generated text. J. Inst. Develop. **9**(4), 22–28 (1986)

19. Howard, I.P., Rogers, B.J.: Binocular vision and stereopsis. https://oxford. universitypressscholarship.com/view/10.1093/acprof:oso/9780195084764.001. 0001/acprof-9780195084764

20. ITU-T: Influencing factors on quality of experience for virtual reality services. https://www.itu.int/rec/T-REC-G.1035

21. Kojić, T., Ali, D., Greinacher, R., Möller, S., Voigt-Antons, J.N.: User experience of reading in virtual reality-finding values for text distance, size and contrast. In: 2020 Twelfth International Conference on Quality of Multimedia Experience (QoMEX), pp. 1–6. IEEE (2020)

22. Kolers, P.A., Duchnicky, R.L., Ferguson, D.C.: Eye movement measurement of readability of CRT displays. Hum. Fact. **23**(5), 517–527 (1981)

23. Kruk, R.S., Muter, P.: Reading of continuous text on video screens. Hum. Fact. **26**(3), 339–345 (1984)

24. Lewandowski, D., Sünkler, S., Yagci, N.: The influence of search engine optimization on google's results: a multi-dimensional approach for detecting SEO. In: 13th ACM Web Science Conference 2021, pp. 12–20 (2021)

25. Mills, C.B., Weldon, L.J.: Reading text from computer screens. ACM Comput. Surv. (CSUR) **19**(4), 329–357 (1987)

26. Orchard, L.N., Stern, J.A.: Blinks as an index of cognitive activity during reading. Integrat. Physiol. Behav. Sci. **26**(2), 108–116 (1991)
27. Pan, X., Hamilton, A.F.D.C.: Why and how to use virtual reality to study human social interaction: The challenges of exploring a new research landscape. British J. Psychol. **109**(3), 395–417 (2018)
28. RK, R., et al.: Real-time attention span tracking in online education. arXiv preprint arXiv:2111.14707 (2021)
29. Solum, H.H.: Readability in Virtual reality, an investigation into displaying text in a virtual environment. Master's thesis, NTNU (2019)
30. Yao, R., Heath, T., Davies, A., Forsyth, T., Mitchell, N., Hoberman, P.: Oculus VR best practices guide. Oculus VR **4**, 27–35 (2014)

Virtual Reality is Better Than Desktop for Training a Spatial Knowledge Task, but Not for Everyone

Matthew D. Marraffino[1]([⊠]), Cheryl I. Johnson[1],
and Allison E. Garibaldi[2]

[1] Naval Air Warfare Center Training Systems Division, Orlando, FL 32826,
USA
mfino242@gmail.com
[2] University of Central Florida, Orlando, FL 32816, USA

Abstract. Advances in virtual reality (VR) technology have resulted in the ability to explore high-resolution immersive environments, which seem particularly useful for training spatial knowledge tasks. However, empirical research on the effectiveness of training in VR, including for spatial knowledge-based tasks, has yielded mixed results. One potential explanation for this discrepancy is that key individual characteristics may account for differences in who benefits most from VR-based training. Previous research has suggested that immersive VR imposes high cognitive load on learners and thus impedes learning, but the amount of cognitive load experienced may be dependent on an individual's video-game experience (VGE). Therefore, the goal of this experiment was to explore the effects of VGE on learning in VR versus a desktop-based training environment, since VGE has been demonstrated to affect performance in previous spatial navigation studies in virtual environments. In this experiment, 62 participants trained in a virtual scavenger hunt task to learn the locations of different equipment in a submarine's machinery room. After training, participants' spatial knowledge was assessed in a drawing task of the room's layout. The results showed no differences overall for experimental condition (i.e., Desktop or VR) or VGE, but there was a significant interaction between these two variables. The high-VGE participants in the VR condition outperformed low-VGE participants in both the Desktop and VR conditions. This suggests that VR may be particularly useful for training experienced gamers, but both VR and Desktop seem to be equally effective for less experienced gamers in a spatial task.

Keywords: Virtual reality · Video game experience · Individual differences · Spatial knowledge

1 Introduction

In light of the rapid advances in virtual reality (VR) there has been a recent surge in the availability of cost-effective virtual reality systems, making VR-based training an attractive medium for education and training. VR can deliver fully immersive experiences using tracked head-mounted displays (HMD) and provide visually rich

© The Author(s), under exclusive license to Springer Nature Switzerland AG 2022
J. Y. C. Chen and G. Fragomeni (Eds.): HCII 2022, LNCS 13317, pp. 212–223, 2022.
https://doi.org/10.1007/978-3-031-05939-1_14

environments, which many argue leads to positive learning outcomes relative to traditional desktop training interfaces (e.g., Bailey et al. 2017; Cummings and Bailenson 2016; Makransky and Petersen 2021; Pollard et al. 2020). However, research exploring whether VR is a more effective training technology relative to traditional approaches is mixed (for a review, see Abich et al. 2021). One potential explanation for the discrepancy in findings may be due to individual differences, such as video game experience (VGE), which may play a critical role in determining who benefits from VR and who does not. Therefore, the goal of this experiment was to investigate the role of VGE in a comparison of VR and Desktop-based training in the context of a spatial knowledge task.

VR appears well-suited to train spatial knowledge tasks due to the immersive properties afforded by high resolution, motion-tracked HMDs that allow users to explore virtual spaces with natural movements, stereoscopic visual cues, and realistic environments (Cummings and Bailenson 2016). For instance, proprioceptive cues from head and body rotations afforded by VR interfaces have been shown to improve spatial understanding within virtual and physical environments (Cherep et al. 2020; Klatzky et al. 1998; Wraga et al. 2004). Notwithstanding, the evidence for whether VR-based training leads to better learning outcomes than Desktop-based interfaces for spatial tasks is mixed. Some studies report better learning outcomes from VR-based training (e.g., Krokos et al. 2019; Pollard et al. 2020), while others report no differences (Li and Giudice 2013; Srivastava et al. 2019; Zhao et al. 2020) or higher learning outcomes from Desktop-based training (Srivastava et al. 2019). The contrasting findings from these studies may stem from the potential of VR to induce higher levels of cognitive load than less immersive environments, resulting in fewer available cognitive resources for learning and retention (Han et al. 2021; Makransky and Petersen 2021; Moreno and Mayer 2002; Parong and Mayer 2021).

The Cognitive Theory of Multimedia Learning (CTML; Mayer 2020) can help explain the effects of cognitive load within VR environments. Assuming that individuals have a limited working memory capacity, CTML highlights the importance of designing instructional systems in a way that effectively manages a learner's cognitive resources. To summarize, the cognitive processes involved with learning include selecting relevant information, organizing the information into coherent mental models, and integrating the information into long-term memory. These processes must be managed effectively to produce positive learning outcomes. If cognitive resources are exceeded during the instructional episode, learners may experience cognitive overload, negatively affecting learning outcomes. CTML identifies three types of cognitive processing that occur during instruction: *essential, extraneous, and generative.* *Essential processing* is the cognitive processing related to the difficulty of the material with more complex material inducing higher levels of essential processing. *Extraneous processing* is any cognitive processing that does not support the learning task, such as distracting information or sounds that are not germane to the task. *Generative processing* is the cognitive processing that supports selecting, organizing, and integrating information. Effective multimedia instruction aims to manage *intrinsic processing*, limit *extraneous processing* and promote *generative processing*.

Previous research has suggested that VR environments may induce extraneous processing demands on individuals for two reasons. First, VR may increase extraneous processing demands as a result of highly immersive content that distracts learners from the educational goal of the lesson. For instance, in an experiment by Makransky et al. (2019), students learned a biology task in either a fully immersive VR simulation or an equivalent desktop version. The results of the study indicated that the VR condition yielded inferior learning outcomes and higher levels of cognitive load as compared to the Desktop condition. The authors posited that the added perceptual realism in the VR condition acted as a seductive detail (Moreno and Mayer 2002) which distracted learners from engaging in generative processing. Second, using unfamiliar controls to interact with the virtual environment may also lead to higher extraneous processing demands. In the same experiment, the authors pointed to the controller interface used with the VR and suggested that it may have been less intuitive than the mouse and keyboard used in the Desktop condition, and this less familiar interface acted as additional source of extraneous processing. In other words, learners had to expend cognitive resources to figure out how to interact with their environment, which could have otherwise been directed to more productive cognitive processing related to the educational goal. Overall, compared to desktop-based training, VR may lead to increased extraneous processing that that reduces learners' cognitive capacity for productive cognitive processing, which in turn leads to reduced learning outcomes. However, individual differences, such as VGE, may play a role in how much cognitive load interferes with learning and VR and may help determine which individuals may benefit most from VR-based training.

Given the potential for higher levels of cognitive load when learning in VR, VGE may be a critical factor in determining how well individuals can learn in this environment Given the paucity of research directly investigating the effect of VGE and learning from VR, it may be reasonable to consider desktop-based research to make VR learning outcome predictions since cognitive skills acquired with VGE may translate to performance in the two learning environments similarly. Previous research has linked VGE with higher performance in navigation tasks within desktop-based virtual environments (e.g., Smith and Du'Mont 2009, Murias et al. 2016; Santos et al. 2009; Ventura et al. 2013). This link suggests that individuals with high VGE may have more cognitive resources available to encode information from virtual environments leading to better spatial knowledge of the surrounding location. These additional cognitive resources may stem from a variety of acquired cognitive skills from video game play. For instance, individuals with high VGE are more familiar with video game controllers (Murias et al. 2016; Richardson et al. 2010; Waller 2000) and likely would not need to expend cognitive resources on figuring out how to operate the controls in the environment, whereas less experienced video gamers would. Likewise, individuals with high VGE may be better able to select relevant information by attending to the task-related elements and ignoring irrelevant information, thereby reducing extraneous processing of seductive details (Green and Bavelier 2006; Mayer and Moreno 2002; Sungur and Boduroglu 2012). Finally, experienced gamers may use more efficient navigational strategies as compared to low-VGE individuals. To illustrate, in a study by

Murias et al. (2016), participants navigated a virtual museum on a desktop computer using an Xbox 360 controller. Participants were tasked with moving room to room within the museum using the shortest route possible. Their results indicated that higher VGE was significantly correlated with more efficient paths within the virtual environment. Additionally, they found that those with high VGE utilized more efficient navigational strategies than individuals with low VGE (e.g., used cognitive maps in lieu of landmarks). The findings from this study show that experienced gamers can take advantage of their experience by using more efficient strategies to navigate, which frees up cognitive resources to perform other tasks in the virtual environment. Taken together, several studies have demonstrated that higher VGE is associated with better learning outcomes in desktop-based navigation tasks, suggesting that high-VGE individuals may be less susceptible to the cognitive load of learning spatial knowledge tasks within immersive VR and demonstrate higher learning outcomes.

1.1   Current Study

Although VGE has been shown to predict performance in VR (e.g., Madden et al. 2020), it has not to our knowledge been explored in a VR media-comparison study examining learning outcomes in a spatial knowledge task. Furthermore, VGE may help explain conflicting findings in the VR training literature when comparing training effectiveness in VR versus desktop-based training environments. To these ends, the current experiment compared training in VR to an equivalent desktop interface, in which participants learned the locations of important equipment throughout a submarine's machinery room. Participants were later tested on whether they acquired spatial knowledge through this experience by drawing the layout of the pathways within the machinery room. Because of the contrasting findings in the literature, we did not define a specific hypothesis regarding whether VR or desktop-based training would lead to better learning outcomes overall. However, based on predictions from the CTML, we hypothesized that participants with high VGE would have higher learning outcomes on a measure of spatial knowledge acquisition (measured by a map drawing test) than individuals with low VGE (H1). We further hypothesized an interaction such that high-VGE participants would have better learning outcomes than low-VGE participants in the VR condition in particular (H2).

2   Method

2.1   Participants and Design

The data reported in this experiment are a subset of a larger experiment investigating the effects of interfaces used within VR. Sixty-two (32 women, Age: $M = 22.2$, $SD = 4.52$) participants were recruited from a large university population. Using a between-subjects design, participants were randomly assigned to either the VR or Desktop condition. The entire experiment took approximately 90 min to complete, and participants were compensated $30 for their time.

2.2   Materials

VR and Desktop Equipment. In the VR condition, participants trained using an HTC Vive Pro headset and two Vive controllers. The Vive was powered by an HP VR Backpack G2 and tracked with two base stations spaced approximately 10 feet apart. Participants selected items within the environment using the trigger button on the Vive controller. Participants could control their viewpoint by moving their head and rotating their body, however, they could not walk. Travel through the environment used a teleport metaphor where participants pointed the controller to a location on the floor while holding the center button. Upon release, the participant immediately 'jumped' to that location.

In the Desktop condition, participants trained using a 17-in gaming laptop and selected items in the environment using the "A" button on an Xbox controller. Viewpoint and travel were controlled by the left and right joysticks, respectively.

Virtual Environment and Task. In this experiment, participants learned the layout of a virtual auxiliary machinery room located inside a submarine. The virtual machinery room is approximately 900 square feet and the environment was created using a modified version of the Virtual Interactive Shipboard Instructional Tour (VISIT), which is a training platform used to introduce and orient sailors to the location of critical safety equipment onboard ships and submarines. Participants in both conditions learned the layout of the room by completing a series of five scavenger hunts to find 16 items. Starting at the entrance of the room, the scavenger hunts required traversing the room multiple times. As the scavenger hunts progressed, they became more difficult due to the amount of assistance participants received to find the items being reduced. Figure 1 illustrates the first two scavenger hunts, which had participants find the items in a fixed order and included a blue path that led to the item, and the item was highlighted with a blue box. Items to find were presented one at a time. Once the participant found the item and selected it, the system moved on to the next item for participants to find. The third scavenger hunt had participants locate the equipment in the same order, and the item was still highlighted in blue, but the blue path was no longer present. If participants failed to locate the target item on the list within 30s, the blue path appeared for assistance. In the fourth scavenger hunt, participants received five minutes to find the items in any order and were provided no assistance. Finally, the fifth scavenger hunt was identical to the fourth except the room was full of smoke that obscured the participants' vision. At the end of each scavenger hunt, participants received feedback on the number of items they found and the time it took them to complete the task. In the fourth and fifth scavenger hunts, the hunt would end promptly at the five minute mark if participants did not find all of the items in time.

Fig. 1. A screenshot from the first two scavenger hunts, which guided participants to find the item highlighted by a blue box.

2.3   Measures

Map Drawing Test. The primary performance measure in this experiment was a paper-based map drawing test where participants were evaluated on their spatial knowledge of the machinery room. This test was administered after all scavenger hunts were completed. For this test, participants were given a grid of dots and asked to draw the layout of the pathways within the machinery room as if they were drawing a map of the room. Participants were instructed to use single, straight line segments to denote pathways and that the lines could be drawn up, down, left, or right, but not diagonally. The starting location was marked at the bottom of the page indicating where the participant began each scavenger hunt.

Surveys. Participants filled out a general demographics questionnaire that included basic biographic information (e.g., age, sex) and a 5-point question asking how frequently they played video games (i.e., 5-Daily, 4-Weekly, 3-Monthly, 2-Less than once a month, 1-Never), which was used as our measure of VGE.

2.4   Procedure

Upon arrival, participants read an informed consent and were asked if they agreed to participate in the study. Upon consent, they began by filling out the general demographics questionnaire. Next, participants reviewed a short PowerPoint slideshow that described the task, the machinery room, and the basics of how to navigate around the virtual environment based on the assigned condition. In the VR condition, the experimenter assisted the participant in putting on the VR headset and backpack, and reiterated how to travel within the virtual environment using the teleport metaphor. Participants were further instructed that they could rotate their body and bend but not walk. In the Desktop condition, participants were seated in front of the gaming laptop and were instructed to put on headphones while the experimenter reiterated how to use the Xbox controller. Once the participant was familiar with the equipment, the experimenter initiated the training in the VISIT virtual environment. In both conditions, participants completed a pier-side familiarization module to allow participants to get comfortable with the controls and the virtual environment. In this module, participants located orange briefcases scattered about a virtual pier. When participants found a briefcase, they selected it and received a "ding" sound to indicate they correctly located an item. If they selected the wrong item (or an item that was previously found), they heard a "buzzer" sound. Once all briefcases were located, participants were given an opportunity to spend additional time traveling around the space as desired to ensure they were confident with the controls before beginning the scavenger hunts in the machinery room. Once the familiarization module was complete, participants moved on to the main training task. During the training phase, participants completed the first three scavenger hunts in the virtual machinery room to locate items throughout the space. After this set of scavenger hunts, participants filled out surveys outside the virtual environment (not reported in this paper) before completing the final two scavenger hunts. After the final two scavenger hunts were completed, participants exited the virtual environment and completed the SUS and the paper-based map drawing test. Finally, they were debriefed and thanked for their time.

3   Results

3.1   Data Coding

Map Drawing Test. Performance on the map drawing test was assessed via two independent coders, who rated each map on its subjective similarity to the correct map (rated on a scale from 1–7), as well as objective criteria. These objective criteria were based on the number of correct vertical and horizontal lines (i.e., pathways), as well as correct intersections between pathways. A penalty of one point was given to any incorrect pathways (i.e., a pathway placed where one did not exist in the machinery room). Room scale was not taken into consideration. Overall, participants could score a maximum of 36 points on the objective assessment. To ensure the reliability of the paper map test scoring, a subset of 19 paper maps were scored independently by the two raters. The correlation between the raters was $r(17) = 0.92$ for subjective scores and $r(17) = 0.97$ for objective scores. The scores for this subset were then reviewed until the coders came to agreement on the scores for each of the maps. The remaining maps were then split evenly between the coders and independently scored. To check the validity of the objective score, it was correlated with the subjective score. Both scoring methods were highly correlated, $r(60) = 0.94$, indicating high level of convergent validity. Therefore, the objective score was used as the primary performance metric during analysis. Figure 2 includes a map of the machinery room with samples of scored map drawing tests.

Video Game Experience. VGE scores were recoded into high and low groups using a median split (median = 3). Participants responding with a score greater than three were placed into the high VGE group, and those who scored three or less were placed into the low VGE group.

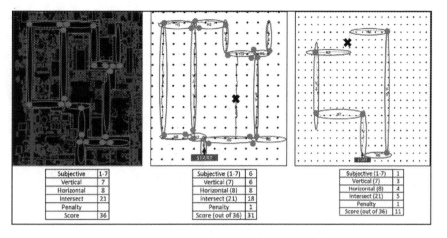

Fig. 2. The left image is a map of the machinery room detailing the number of vertical (red circles) and horizontal paths (green circles), and the locations of intersections (blue dots) used for scoring. The center (high score) and right (low score) images are example maps drawn by participants with their associated scores. (Color figure online)

3.2   Spatial Knowledge Learning Outcomes

This experiment focused on the effects of VGE (low vs. high) for learning a spatial knowledge task in VR and desktop-based interfaces. Previous research has indicated that sex differences may affect navigation task performance in virtual environments, (e.g., Murias et al. 2016; Santos et al. 2009; Ventura et al. 2013; Woolly et al., 2010) although the effects of sex are highly correlated with VGE (see Madden et al. 2020). Therefore, we checked the distribution of sex across the four conditions, and we found that sex was not evenly distributed across conditions (see Table 1). As a result, we included sex in the primary performance analysis. To that end, we conducted a 2 Condition (VR or Desktop) x 2 VGE (high or low) x 2 Sex (Male or Female) ANOVA using the map drawing test objective score as the dependent variable. Means and standard deviations are reported in Table 1.

The ANOVA revealed no main effect for condition, $F(1,54) = 2.11$, $p = .152$, and no main effect for VGE, $F(1,54) = 1.19$, $p = .281$. However, these results were qualified by a significant condition by VGE interaction, $F(1,54) = 4.63$, $p = .036$, $\eta^2_{partial} = .079$. As illustrated in Fig. 3, for the VR condition, those in the low VGE group performed worse on the map drawing test than those in the high VGE group. Overall, high-VGE participants in the VR condition had the highest average scores on the map drawing test. A post-hoc test revealed that this group scored significantly higher than high-VGE participants in the Desktop condition, $t(54) = 3.01$, $p = .004$, $d = 1.05$, and low-VGE participants in the VR condition, $t(54) = 2.30$, $p = .025$, $d = 0.94$), supported by large effect sizes. Looking at the effects of sex, a main effect, supported by a large effect size, was found such that males scored higher ($M = 26.5$, $SD = 8.10$) than females ($M = 18.8$, $SD = 8.89$), $F(1,54) = 11.4$, $p = .001$, $\eta^2_{partial} = .174$. However, there was no condition by sex interaction, $F(1,54) = 0.13$, $p = .712$, $\eta^2_{partial} = .003$, sex by VGE interaction, $F(1,54) = 0.002$, p = .965, $\eta^2_{partial} < .001$ or condition by sex by VGE interaction, $F(1,54) = 0.74$, $p = .394$, $\eta^2_{partial} = .013$. These results suggest that sex may have contributed to overall performance outcomes. Overall, the results do not support H1 that those with high VGE would perform better across both Desktop and VR conditions than those with low VGE. However, the results provide support for H2 that individuals with high VGE would perform better than those with low VGE in the VR condition.

Table 1. Means and standard deviations for the map drawing test (objective score).

| Condition | Sex | VGE | | | | | Total |
| | | Low | | High | | | |
		n	M (SD)	n	M (SD)	M (SD)	M (SD)
Desktop	Female	5	18.8 (8.11)	6	14.2 (5.49)	**16.3 (6.87)**	**22.0 (8.60)**
	Male	4	25.5 (6.95)	16	25.1 (8.30)	**25.2 (7.88)**	
	Total		**21.8 (7.97)**		**22.1 (9.02)**		
VR	Female	12	16.0 (8.26)	9	25.6 (9.02)	**20.1 (9.67)**	**23.0 (10.10)**
	Male	3	25.0 (12.12)	7	30.7 (6.65)	**29.0 (8.35)**	
	Total		**17.8 (9.41)**		**27.8 (8.25)**		

Note. Maximum possible score was 36.

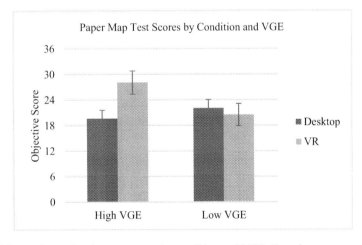

Fig. 3. Means of map drawing test scores by condition and VGE. Error bars represent standard error.

4   Discussion

This experiment investigated whether VGE affects learning outcomes differently in VR versus a traditional desktop-based virtual environment to explore VGE as a potential explanation for the mixed results in media comparison studies. Consistent with previous research (Li and Giudice 2013; Srivastrava et al. 2019; Zhao et al. 2020), the results of this experiment revealed no differences between the Desktop and VR conditions in terms of performance on the spatial test without considering VGE.

With regard to VGE, the data did not support our first hypothesis that overall, individuals with high VGE would display higher scores on the map drawing test. Nevertheless, we did find support for our second hypothesis that individuals with high VGE in the VR condition would display higher learning outcomes than individuals with low VGE. Furthermore, high-VGE participants in the VR condition also outperformed high-VGE participants in the Desktop condition, indicating that for some people VR-based training is advantageous. Consistent with CTML, this finding suggests that extraneous processing demands are reduced for experienced gamers freeing up cognitive resources to select, organize, and integrate relevant information in spite of the extraneous processing demands imposed by the highly immersive VR environment. We failed to detect a similar pattern for the low-VGE participants. However, future research should further investigate the hypothesis that extraneous demands implicit with VR-based training may offset the potential benefits of a fully immersive environment (e.g., stereoscopic vision, physical rotation cues; Makransky et al. 2019; Moreno and Mayer 2002; Parong and Mayer 2021).

It is surprising that high VGE did not lead to higher scores compared to low VGE in the Desktop condition given the findings from previous research suggesting VGE predicts performance within desktop-based virtual environments (Smith and Du'Mont 2009; Murias et al. 2016; Ventura et al. 2013). This could imply that the Desktop condition did not impose as much extraneous processing demands on individuals, such that those with low VGE could perform similarly to those with high VGE. Furthermore, the fact that high-VGE participants had higher map drawing scores in the VR condition than the Desktop condition supports the hypothesis that the immersive properties of VR provide added value when the individual is able to overcome the extraneous processing demands of the media.

The experiment also found that men performed better on the map drawing test than women overall. This result is consistent with previous research documenting an advantage for men in navigation-related simulations (Murias et al. 2016; Ventura et al. 2013). However, the data in the present experiment did not reveal any significant interactions with VGE or condition providing no evidence that that the advantage men had over women was due to the media with which the individual trained (i.e., VR vs. Desktop). Some potential explanations for why men outperformed women overall in the spatial task include using different navigational strategies during training or other sex-related individual characteristics (e.g., spatial ability). Future research could explore other individual differences that may impact how people learn in immersive environments which may also explain the mixed results in the VR vs. desktop-based training literature.

Overall, there were some limitations in the reported experiment. For instance, different types of controllers were used in each condition, an Xbox controller for Desktop and Vive controllers for VR. These controllers were chosen because they are typical for that particular platform. It could be the case that the different controllers imposed different levels of extraneous processing that may have contributed to the lack of differences between the VR and Desktop conditions. Future studies may consider holding the type of controller constant across conditions to cleanly compare VR to Desktop. Finally, the Vive Pro HMD used a teleport metaphor to travel around the environment. Teleporting prevents individuals from experiencing optic flow as they traverse through the environment. In the Desktop condition, participants could see the room pass by them as they traversed, although, this was without available physical cues, such as turning one's head and body, that were present in the VR condition. However, research suggests that head and body rotations are more important during spatial updating than optic flow (Klatzky 1998). Future research may explore the effects of VGE on other means of locomotion in VR, such as walking freely in the space or treadmills (Boletsis 2017; Cherep et al. 2020; Zhao et al. 2020), in which visual and physical cues may be critical to forming a better mental map of the space.

5   Conclusion

This experiment investigated the effects of VGE in Desktop and VR-based training systems on learning the layout of a large room. Overall, there were no differences in spatial knowledge scores across the two conditions, but significant differences emerged when considering participants' VGE. Individuals with high VGE in the VR condition performed the best, indicating that individual differences play an important role in how people learn from immersive training environments. When designing immersive learning environments, considerations of learners' prior experience in video games may play a critical role in how effective the training is overall.

Acknowledgments. We gratefully acknowledge Mr. Marc Prince and Mr. Kevin Cuong for their assistance with testbed development. This work was funded under the Naval Innovative Science and Engineering program established by the National Defense Authorization Act, Section 219. Presentation of this material does not constitute or imply its endorsement, recommendation, or favoring by the U.S. Navy or the Department of Defense (DoD). The opinions of the authors expressed herein do not necessarily state or reflect those of the U.S. Navy of DoD.

NAWCTSD Public Release 22-ORL001 Distribution Statement A – Approved for public release; distribution is unlimited.

References

Abich, J., Parker, J., Murphy, J.S., Eudy, M.: A review of the evidence for training effectiveness with virtual reality technology. Virt. Reality **25**(4), 919–933 (2021). https://doi.org/10.1007/s10055-020-00498-8

Bailey, S.K., Johnson, C.I., Schroeder, B.L., Marraffino, M.D.: Using virtual reality for training maintenance procedures. In: Interservice/Industry Training, Simulation, and Education Conference (I/ITSEC), vol. 17108, pp. 1–11 (2017)

Boletsis, C.: The new era of virtual reality locomotion: A systematic literature review of techniques and a proposed typology. Multimodal Technol. Interaction **1**(4), 24 (2017). https://doi.org/10.3390/mti1040024

Cherep, L.A., et al.: Spatial cognitive implications of teleporting through virtual environments. J. Exp. Psychol. Appl. **26**(3), 480–492 (2020)

Cummings, J.J., Bailenson, J.N.: How immersive is enough? A meta-analysis of the effect of immersive technology on user presence. Media Psychol. **19**(2), 272–309 (2016)

Green, C.S., Bavelier, D.: Effect of action video games on the spatial distribution of visuospatial attention. J. Exp. Psychol. Hum. Percept. Perform. **32**(6), 1465–1478 (2006)

Han, J., Zheng, Q., Ding, Y.: Lost in virtual reality? Cognitive load in high immersive VR environments. J. Adv. Inform. Technol. **12**(4), 302–310 (2021)

Klatzky, R.L., Loomis, J.M., Beall, A.C., Chance, S.S., Golledge, R.G.: Spatial updating of self-position and orientation during real, imagined, and virtual locomotion. Psychol. Sci. **9**(4), 293–298 (1998)

Krokos, E., Plaisant, C., Varshney, A.: Virtual memory palaces: Immersion aids recall. Virtual Reality **23**(1), 1–15 (2019)

Li, H., Giudice, N.A.: The effects of immersion and body-based rotation on learning multi-level indoor virtual environments. In: M. Tomko, S. Bell, K.-J. Li (Eds.), ACM International Conference Proceedings Series, ISA 2013: Proceedings of the Fifth ACM SIGSPATIAL International Workshop on Indoor Spatial Awareness: November 5, 2013, Orlando, Florida, USA, pp. 8–15. Association for Computing Machinery, New York

Madden, J., Pandita, S., Schuldt, J.P., Kim, B.S., Won, A., Holmes, N.G.: Ready student one: Exploring the predictors of student learning in virtual reality. PloS ONE**15**(3), e0229788 (2020)

Makransky, G., Petersen, G.B.: The cognitive affective model of immersive learning (CAMIL): A theoretical research-based model of learning in immersive virtual reality. Educ. Psychol. Rev. **33**, 937–958 (2021)

Makransky, G., Terkildsen, T.S., Mayer, R.E.: Adding immersive virtual reality to a science lab simulation causes more presence but less learning. Learn. Instr. **60**, 225–236 (2019)

Mayer, R.E.: Multimedia Learning, 3rd edn. Cambridge University Press, Cambridge (2020)

Moreno, R., Mayer, R.E.: Learning science in virtual reality multimedia environments: Role of methods and media. J. Educ. Psychol. **94**(3), 598–610 (2002)

Murias, K., Kwok, K., Castillejo, A.G., Liu, I., Iaria, G.: The effects of video game use on performance in a virtual navigation task. Comput. Hum. Behav. **58**, 398–406 (2016)

Parong, J., Mayer, R.E.: Cognitive and affective processes for learning science in immersive virtual reality. J. Comput. Assist. Learn. **37**(1), 226–241 (2021)

Pollard, K.A., et al.: Level of immersion affects spatial learning in virtual environments: results of a three-condition within-subjects study with long intersession intervals. Virtual Reality **24**(4), 783–796 (2020). https://doi.org/10.1007/s10055-019-00411-y

Santos, B.S., et al.: Head-mounted display versus desktop for 3D navigation in virtual reality: A user study. Multimedia Tools Appl. **41**(1), 161–181 (2009)

Smith, S.P., Du'Mont, S.: Measuring the effect of gaming experience on virtual environment navigation tasks. In: 2009 IEEE Symposium on 3D User Interfaces, pp. 3–10. IEEE

Srivastava, P., Rimzhim, A., Vijay, P., Singh, S., Chandra, S.: Desktop VR is better than non-ambulatory HMD VR for spatial learning. Front. Robot. AI **6**, 50 (2019)

Sungur, H., Boduroglu, A.: Action video game players form more detailed representation of objects. Acta Physiol. (Oxf) **139**(2), 327–334 (2012)

Ventura, M., Shute, V., Wright, T.J., Zhao, W.: An investigation of the validity of the virtual spatial navigation assessment. Front. Psychol. **4**, 852 (2013)

Waller, D.: Individual differences in spatial learning from computer-simulated environments. J. Exp. Psychol. Appl. **6**(4), 307 (2000)

Wraga, M., Creem-Regehr, S.H., Proffitt, D.R.: Spatial updating of virtual displays. Mem. Cognit. **32**(3), 399–415 (2004)

Zhao, J., et al.: Desktop versus immersive virtual environments: Effects on spatial learning. Spat. Cogn. Comput. **20**(4), 328–363 (2020)

Is Off-the-Shelf VR Software Ready for Medical Teaching?

Angela Odame and Johannes Tümler

Anhalt University of Applied Sciences, Köthen, Germany
`johannes.tuemler@hs-anhalt.de`

Abstract. Over the last decade, the use of computerized three-dimensional (3D) models in a virtual environment has become widespread to enhance medical teaching and learning, particularly in anatomy. Technologies such as Virtual Reality (VR) offer large potential to enhance medical training processes.

The research focus of this paper is to investigate the effectiveness of using predesigned off-the-shelf VR software to teach medical knowledge in comparison with a conventional teaching method. Also investigated was the degree of satisfaction associated with using VR to learn. The teaching example focuses on the anatomy of the human heart because it is one of the most challenging topics to teach and comprehend due to its complex three-dimensional nature.

A randomized controlled study was conducted with forty participants. They were equally distributed into two groups: 20 in control (non-VR) and 20 in experimental (VR) group. Two learning methods were used to study the heart. The non-VR group used PowerPoint presentation, whereas the VR group used immersive VR from off-the-shelf software.

This study subsequently gives insight on three main aspects: First, there was significant difference in anatomy knowledge within the two groups. Second, the VR group found the learning experience to be significantly more engaging, enjoyable, and useful. Third, non-customizable predesigned software can be suitable and effective for medical training tasks and applications.

Keywords: Virtual Reality · Cardiac anatomy · Computer-generated 3D-model · Training

1 Background, Motivation and Goals

The health and medical education system has begun to incorporate more interactive media and online materials as new learning tools become available. The use of computer-generated 3D models in anatomy education has become increasingly popular in recent years [14]. Anatomy, in particular, focuses on the detailed structure of the different systems of the human body. A variety of descriptive models to provide an in-depth understanding have been used to facilitate this. This visual science is considered a crucial foundation for medical education as this is important

© The Author(s), under exclusive license to Springer Nature Switzerland AG 2022
J. Y. C. Chen and G. Fragomeni (Eds.): HCII 2022, LNCS 13317, pp. 224–237, 2022.
https://doi.org/10.1007/978-3-031-05939-1_15

for the accurate diagnosis in organs and human systems [6]. Learners should be able to identify structures and their spatial relationships when learning anatomy. Despite this, medical students frequently struggle to grasp three-dimensional (3D) anatomy from visual images in textbooks and PowerPoint presentations [16,18]. These struggles exist by virtue of several challenges associated with traditional medical education. These are limited spatial understanding obtained from lectures and restricted anatomic dissections [2]. Also, traditional modalities' grasp of spatial relationship is unclear; it needs expertise to explain and lacks sufficient depth to demonstrate a specific teaching point. Some examples are textbooks, two-dimensional (2D) images, and medical imaging modalities such as CT, MRI and ultrasound. Furthermore, the human cadaver, one of the pioneer teaching anatomy method, is also associated with several limitations such as the rising expenses, decreasing availability, and the decay in quality [7,8].

Consequently, it has become critical to develop modern methodologies such as computer-generated interactive 3D models in Virtual Reality (VR) that focus on efficient and high-quality anatomy education and learning to overcome these challenges. This enables visualization of the spatial relationships between structures from various viewpoints, is reusable, is of changeable size, and allows explorative details which improve understanding [2]. VR has shown to actively promote reforms of teaching concepts, teaching methods, teaching contents and teaching measures [17]. Virtual anatomy is a technology tool that allows users to visualize and learn anatomy in an interactive and motivating manner. Learners, educators and professionals can use this digital anatomy to study, teach and better understand the human body. The tools include 3D models, videos, informative labels, animations, quizzes and more [3]. Presently, as every iPhone or Android smartphone can be used as a VR headset in combination with cardboard VR devices, one could argue that practically everyone now has potential for their own VR device, which can be used anywhere other than in the classroom [20].

Today's VR technology is simple to set up and use, has intuitive controls and user-friendly software [20]. However, this technology sometimes needs a lot of effort and resources to create new, realistic and high-quality scenarios and training software for medical teaching - but at the same time, now off-the-shelf VR software exists. These are 'ready-to-use', and it might be easier to implement such software than to create new ones [9]. They are usually easily accessible, downloadable, inexpensive and could be used for medical training. Medical schools would be willing to use VR, but the lack of money to design for specific training prevents leveraging potentials of VR technology. Instead of spending time and resources to make new medical content, why not use off-the-shelf software?

This paper assessed the effectiveness of using non-customized, predesigned VR software to teach specific biomedical knowledge: The structure of the human heart in comparison to a non-VR teaching method. Hence, it aimed at two main objectives: (1) to find the effectiveness of using sample off-the-shelf VR software to teach the heart using pre-post-quizzes, and (2) to assess VR learner experience. To be able to discuss the expected results, the following research questions served as guidance to reach the goal:

- **RQ1:** Are the quiz scores improved after intervention in both groups?
- **RQ2:** Are the quiz scores more improved using VR education as compared to the other non-VR teaching method?
- **RQ3:** Is VR a more effective way to improve learner's level of cardiac anatomy knowledge?
- **RQ4:** Is the students' perceived learning and effectiveness of using VR for cardiac anatomy education a positive, negative or neutral experience?

These questions will help answer if off-the-shelf VR software is ready for medical teaching and subsequently conclude on the usefulness of such software for (bio-) medical training and applications. The following sections aim at finding answers to these research questions.

2   Use Case and Implementation

The study implemented a biomedical use case where the heart was taught through two learning approaches: VR and Non-VR. The human heart was chosen because it is a complicated topic to teach and understand due to its complex three-dimensional nature. Several teaching methods currently used to study anatomy, for example, dissection, textbooks, medical imaging and plastic models, have some drawbacks in explicitly displaying the true 3D nature of the heart [5]. But through VR, a computer-generated 3D human anatomical model, heart inclusive, can be easily taught and studied in an immersive, interactive virtual environment with and/or without assistance anywhere other than the classroom.

The content of the learning materials in both teaching approaches was a comprehensive overview of the human heart, the heart exterior and interior: the heart chambers and heart valves, heart blood circulation, heart conduction system and a few heart pathologies. The structure of teaching was given in an orderly manner as above in both groups.

The VR teaching method utilized educational material from predesigned software, Sharecare YOU VR, purchased from Steam store. This product was used because it provides an accurate cardiac virtual environment that has 3D heart content and videos including anatomy, physiology, conditions, and treatments, informative labels and contextual information with voice-over pronunciation and interactive tools and functionality to dissect, handle, customize and explore the heart in 360°C as seen as examples in Fig. 1. The VR participants used all these functionalities and tools as instructed by the investigator to study the learning content. Also, the price-performance ratio of Sharecare YOU VR software seemed incomparable to other software available for us because of the low cost, high quality and realistic contents it provided. The non-customizable version was used [12] (Price 07/2021: 29,99 €).

A Varjo VR-2 [15] headset was used because it offers resolution equivalent to human eye vision with advanced integrated eye-tracking technology. HTC Vive controllers were used for interaction with the 3D heart model and navigation in the software. Varjo VR-2 supports SteamVR tracking, hence two base stations were set up to track the headset and the controllers. For comfortable use of VR

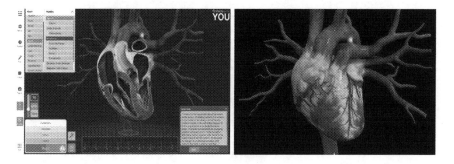

Fig. 1. Sharecare YOU VR - virtually dissected heart (left) and outside view of the heart as seen in VR (right)

Head-mounted display (HMD), the computer used had specifications of an Intel Core i7-8700 CPU, 64 GB RAM, NVIDIA GeForce RTX 2080 GPU at default HMD rendering resolution and Microsoft Windows 10 (64-bit) operating system.

The Non-VR teaching method used Microsoft PowerPoint 2016 presentation that contained similar educational texts from the Sharecare You VR software with 2D and 3D images. The lecture was delivered by the same investigator on the same learning content.

For measurable results and statistical analysis, an assessment via quiz gave insight on heart knowledge in the study.

An experienced medical doctor served as an expert to make sure the learning content of the Non-VR is similar to the VR experience as well as assess its medical relevance. Quiz questions and answers were also verified for accuracy and relevance by the same expert.

3 Procedure

Forty participants took part in the study without compensation. They were primarily students from the biomedical engineering graduate program at Anhalt University of Applied Sciences. To follow a between-subject study design, they were randomly and equally allocated into two groups: an experimental (VR) and a control (Non-VR) group to study the heart.

Each participant completed a demographic survey, which contained questions regarding age range, gender, prior cardiac anatomy knowledge and previous VR exposure. They also completed the pre-intervention quiz to test their baseline knowledge of the heart. Then a 25–30 min learning session took place using either VR or PowerPoint, PPT learning modes. The learning materials were as identical as possible in teaching content. At the end of the lesson, each participant immediately took the post-intervention quiz. The pre- and post- intervention quiz was the same and consisted of twenty multiple-choice questions: Eleven conventional (e.g. "Which of the following is correct regarding the flow of blood in reference to the left side of the heart?" with four given possible answers)

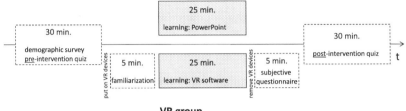

Fig. 2. Diagram of the study design

and nine heart diagram labelling questions. In addition, the VR participants filled out a subjective questionnaire [5]. It asked for their learner experience and degree of satisfaction in using VR to study the heart. It was done to assess their thoughts and opinions on VR implementation in the study of the heart. The feedback recorded ranged from strongly agree to strongly disagree (with a five-point Likert scale). The overall study took about 80–100 min for each participant. Figure 2 provides an overview of the study design.

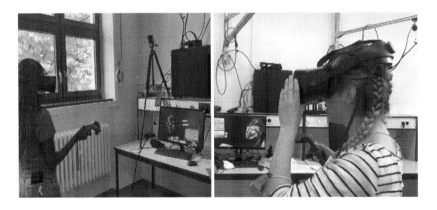

Fig. 3. VR group participants learning the heart

As seen in Fig. 3, all participants who were exposed to the VR experience were outfitted with Varjo VR-2 headset and HTC Vive controllers. Eye-tracking values were recorded but not analyzed for this paper.

Participants were subsequently given a five minute tutorial on VR device familiarization, how to view and interact with the VR platform, and how to use the controllers to manipulate other organs on the software, for example, the liver, in three dimensions. This included explanations of how to toggle between different views and menus in order for them to easily and uninterruptedly interact with the 3D heart model from the Sharecare YOU VR application. The investigator instructed the VR participants on what to learn based on the study's learning content. Interference happened if a participant requested technical assistance with the VR device.

Fig. 4. Non-VR group participants learning the heart with PowerPoint and a teacher

Participants in the control group were exposed to a conventional way of studying the heart thus with PowerPoint presentation delivered by the same investigator as illustrated in Fig. 4.

4   Results

For statistical analyses, the number of correct answers pre- and post- teaching session expressed as a percentage of the total number of questions were calculated. The between-individual factor was the two groups of participants (PowerPoint, VR) and the within-individual factor was the two time points in each group (pre versus post teaching session). Evaluation of differences was done using Wilcoxon Signed Rank Test because the data was not normally distributed. Pearson Correlation coefficient, r, was used for correlation analysis. All the results have been normalised to 100, thus the values are between 0% and 100%, where 0 means low and 100 means high. The significance level (Sig./p) for all analyses was 0.05.

According to the demographic survey, out of the 40 enrolled participants in the study, 23 (57.5%) were male and 17 (42.5%) female. Their ages ranged from 21–35 years, with the majority (82.5%) between the ages of 26–30 years. 23 (57.5%) participants answered having no to low cardiac anatomy knowledge, 16 (40%) responded to having medium cardiac knowledge and 1 (2.5%) responded to having high knowledge in cardiac anatomy. Out of the 20 participants in the VR group, eleven (55%) had never tried VR prior to this experiment, eight (40%) rarely used VR, one (5%) used VR on a weekly basis and none used it on a daily basis. However, none of the participants had the experience of using VR to learn anatomy. No significant differences were observed regarding the demographics; age, gender, responded prior cardiac knowledge and prior VR experience between the groups.

Table 1. Summary of test results between both groups

	Non-VR group pre intervention vs. post intervention results	VR group pre-intervention vs. post intervention results	Non-VR group post intervention vs. VR group post intervention results
Mean difference	25.25	34.75	5.0
Z	3.630	3.927	−1.557
Significance level	$p < 0.001$	$p < 0.001$	$p = 0.12$

For the knowledge assessment analysis, the number of correct answers pre and post- teaching session expressed as a percentage of the total number of questions were calculated. Table 1 presents the results. On the pre-intervention quiz, before the learning phase, the students scored on average $51.5\% \pm 17.85\%$ in the PPT group and $47\% \pm 20.55\%$ in the VR group. On the post-intervention quiz, the students scored on average $76.75\% \pm 11.73\%$ on PowerPoint content and $81.75\% \pm 9.64\%$ on VR content. Both groups demonstrated an overall significant increase in post-intervention quiz scores. The PPT group demonstrated a (25.25%, $p < 0.001$), while the VR group participants demonstrated a (34.75%, $p < 0.001$.) On the post-intervention quiz between the experimental and control group, the students exposed to VR scored on average 5% ($p = 0.12$) higher than the students exposed to the conventional content, PPT. In terms of the normal heart diagram labelling part that comprised of 9 questions in the quiz, 13 (65%) students out of 20 in the VR group had a perfect score, compared to the PowerPoint group where 5 students (25%) out of 20 had a perfect score in the post-intervention quiz ($p = 0.107$).

The bar plot in Fig. 5 presents mean values (grey bars) and standard deviation (orange line). The horizontal axis represents the pre- and post intervention results in both groups. 1 and 2 represent the pre- and post-intervention mean value in the non-VR group respectively as 3 and 4 represent VR pre- and post-intervention mean value respectively. All show the correspondent standard deviation. The vertical axis represents the mean scale between 0 and 100 with 0 being the lowest value and 100 being the highest value.

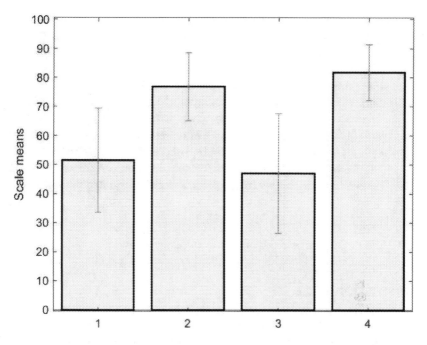

Fig. 5. Bar chart with error bars illustrating test result summary in both groups (1: pre- 2: post-intervention non-VR group; 3: pre- 4: post-intervention VR group)

The subjective questionnaire performed in the VR group was done to measure the degree of satisfaction and students' perceived learning and effectiveness of using VR to study the heart. All the twenty VR participants returned the questionnaire (Fig. 6). Nineteen students (95%) agreed or strongly agreed that "seeing the heart from the inside reinforced my knowledge of cardiac anatomy", that "the anatomic relationship between different structures in the heart is easily seen in Cardiac VR". Five students (25%) strongly agreed and 15 students (75%) agreed that "Cardiac VR enhances anatomic integration skills", however, ten students (50%) strongly agreed, nine students (45%) agreed and one student (5%) disagreed with the statement that "Cardiac VR can improve visual-spatial skills". Eleven students (55%) strongly agreed and nine students (45%) strongly agreed that "Cardiac VR provides useful 3D interaction and I enjoy it". To the statement "Cardiac VR assisted me in appreciating size differences of different structures", fourteen (70%) strongly agreed and six (30%) agreed. "Cardiac VR is useful for my learning", eight (40%) strongly agreed, nine (45%) agreed and three (15%) somewhat agreed. To the statement "I enjoyed Cardiac VR" sixteen (80%) strongly agreed, three (15%) agreed and one (5%) somewhat agreed. To the statement "I learn more when I have fun" five (25%) strongly agreed, 9 (45%) agreed and six (30%) somewhat agreed. Sixteen (80%) strongly agreed, three (15%) agreed and one (5%) somewhat agreed with the statement "I like the idea of VR and would like to see more of it in my education." No student strongly disagreed with any statement.

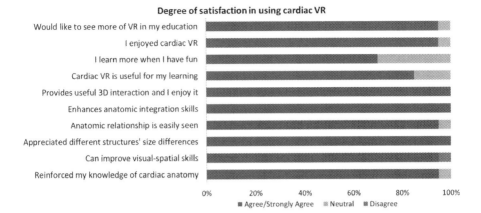

Fig. 6. Subjective questionnaire in the experimental (VR) group

5   Discussion

Within the field of medical education, the use of VR has been validated as an effective way to improve the learners' level of anatomy knowledge and previous research has demonstrated the utility of 3-dimensional learning with evidence relating to medical education, particularly in the cardiovascular system [11,19]. Apart from the issues associated with the acquisition, storage, and disposal of potentially biohazardous tissue specimen, another advantage VR has over cadaveric dissection is the ability to cut back or 'clip' the three-dimensional model in a variety of planes, and then reassemble the anatomic model once virtually clipped. An essential lesson that can also be gained from VR is to appreciate the relative size and proximity of distinct heart structures. The typical anatomic relationships of heart chamber interiors are distorted after dissection. In medical education, physically interacting with a three-dimensional model is critical for comprehending its physical build and gaining a sense of confidence and familiarity with it. This is certainly relevant for medical students studying anatomy or surgery [1,10]. Hence the objective of this study to assess the educational effectiveness of using VR to teach medical knowledge, the heart compared to a conventional approach. To achieve this, two different teaching methods - a conventional approach with PowerPoint presentation and an immersive VR 3D cardiac model approach with an off-the-shelf VR software was used. The study incorporates the use of the Varjo VR-2 HMD system to provide a completely immersive experience of a 3D heart model with human eye resolution.

It was found that no significant differences existed in the age groups and gender. In the experimental, VR group, the average pre-intervention score was 47% with an average score increment of 34.75% to reach an average of 81.75% at the post-intervention scores ($Z = 3.927$, $p < 0.001$). This finding indicates that there was a statistically significant difference in quiz scores after the intervention, hence the VR simulation from the software was an effective way of increasing the learners' level of heart anatomy knowledge. All the participants had increment on the post-intervention quiz. In terms of the Pearson correlation coefficient, the relationship (r = 0.38, p = 0.098) between the pre-intervention and post-intervention quiz scores show a weak and positive correlation. This positive correlation is statistically not significant. Also the relationship (r = 0.686, p < 0.001) between the students' responded prior cardiac anatomy knowledge and their performance on the pre-intervention quiz scores show a statistically significant moderate positive correlation. This implies that their responses on prior cardiac knowledge truly reflected on their pre-intervention quiz performance.

In the control group, the average pre-intervention score was 51.50% with an average score increment of 25.25% to reach an average of 76.75% at the post-intervention scores (Z = −3.630, p < 0.001). This indicate that there was a statistically significant difference in quiz scores after the intervention, hence the PowerPoint presentation was also an effective way of increasing the learners' level of heart anatomy knowledge. Three students scored same on pre- and post-intervention quiz. In terms of Pearson correlation coefficient, the relationship (r = 0.37, p = 0.108) between the pre-intervention and post- intervention quiz scores show a weak and positive correlation This positive correlation is statistically not significant. Also the relationship (r = 0.471, p = 0.036) between the students' responded prior cardiac anatomy knowledge and their performance on the pre-intervention quiz scores show weak to moderate positive correlation but not statistically significant. This implies that even though a correlation existed between their responses on prior cardiac knowledge and pre-intervention quiz score, it may not have necessarily reflected on their performance.

Altogether, no student retrogressed and scored lower on the post-intervention quiz in both groups. Quiz scores improved in both groups. This provided an answer to the **RQ1**. The students who gained the most information were those who had a low baseline level of the relevant knowledge, especially seen in the experimental group. That participant in the VR group exhibited a 65% knowledge increment from 35% on the pre-intervention quiz to 100% on the post-intervention quiz. Two students from the VR group scored 100% compared to none in the non-VR group students. It was observed that, the VR participants took shorter duration to complete the post-intervention quiz as compared to the non-VR participants but the time was not recorded.

Between the control and experimental group, the mean increment was 5% (Z = −1.557, p= 0.12). This indicate that there was no statistically significant difference of anatomy knowledge gain in the post-intervention quiz between the two groups even though on average the VR group scored 5% higher than the PowerPoint group. A larger number of participants might show a significant result. The negative z values recorded within and between both groups indicate that the raw data value was a number of standard deviation times below the mean value: 3.630 in Non-VR group, 3.927 in VR group and 1.557 between the groups. This paragraph gives response to **RQ2** and **RQ3** that quiz scores were more improved using VR but the improvement was not statistically significant. Also both teaching methods are effective ways of improving learner's level of cardiac anatomy knowledge even though the results obtained does not explicitly indicate that VR is a more effective method.

The subjective questionnaire performed in the VR group to ascertain the degree of satisfaction as a secondary outcome for this study was positive, answering **RQ4**. This was done to evaluate the students' perceived learning and effectiveness of using VR to study the heart. 95–100% of the students agreed or strongly agreed to 8 out of the 10 statements.

The VR participants who took part in the study overwhelmingly appreciated the ability to dissect and resect an anatomically realistic heart in VR, appreciated the anatomic relationships and relative sizes between heart structures, as well as enjoyed cardiac VR and the useful 3D interaction it offered. Cardiac VR improves visual-spatial skills statement was clearly evident in the post-intervention quiz scores when 13 out of 20 VR group students had a perfect score compared to just 5 of their peers in the PowerPoint group. The 2 exceptions were statements "I learn more when I have fun" and "Cardiac VR is useful for my learning", where 30% and 15% of the students respectively were neutral and somewhat agreed. Despite the aforementioned exceptions, 95% of the students agreed or strongly to the statement "I like the idea of VR and would like to see more of it in my education".

In summary, these results indicate that VR was as effective as the traditional method,PowerPoint presentation to study the heart. This study's insignificant but positive results was rather found significant by other studies when using the VR to study the heart [2,5,20] but support a study where VR was applied in the study of the brain [13].

However, some limitations could have led to the unexpected shortcomings of the study, particularly the small sample size. A higher number of students would have further supported the goal of this study. An indirect possible weakness of the study could have resulted from some students acting under stress while completing the task and not being motivated enough due to the no compensation scheme for participation.

The results presented here are only valid for Sharecare YOU VR software, as used in the experiment. Other medical off-the-shelf VR teaching software might produce different results. Nevertheless, due to its low cost, high performance and good availability this software can be seen as a good representative of that software class. Similar results can be expected from other off-the-shelf software if their content and interactivity are similar.

6   Conclusion

VR is efficient and raises students' motivation. It is not clear whether the better learning effect comes from "better spatial explanation" or if it is a combined effect coming from better spatial explanation and higher technology motivation. The students were motivated to try out the new technology, thus might influence their learning.

It also demonstrated that VR can be at least as effective as the traditional PowerPoint presentation in teaching cardiac anatomy, in terms of students' quiz scores yielding a performance increase of 5% in the experimental group over the control group. A positive VR learner experience and enhanced student motivation were achieved. This was evident in several subjective measurements: engagement, enjoyment, usefulness, and learner motivation. Also, non-customizable predesigned off-the-shelf VR software is ready, suitable and effective for (bio) medical training tasks and applications, as shown with the example of the Sharecare YOU VR software. Another study, that is specifically designed to assess self-learning with VR could be done with less to no 'teacher' interference or instructions.

While cardiac anatomy can be difficult to grasp due to its complicated three-dimensional form, VR provides an immersive and intuitive experience that allows users to appreciate the size variations between distinct heart structures as well as contextualize the links between them [5]. Despite the potential substantial overhead in terms of setup time, the software and hardware costs, as well as training of both students and educators that can be incurred in utilizing VR solutions in the classroom, institutes and so on [4], VR has gained popularity in medical education and this cost-benefit ratio may sway in the favour of VR.

Although our results are encouraging, more research is required to establish the best and effective way to deliver this VR immersive medical content to students, alongside using a larger sample size to undertake the study task. A follow-up post-intervention quiz, several weeks after the training might be helpful to assess knowledge retention, cost-effectiveness and adverse reactions such as blurred vision and disorientation when evaluating the teaching effectiveness of VR in medical education, is encouraged. Also, the recorded eye tracking data from this study is currently under investigation and will be reported in the future.

In conclusion, VR technologies are improving in quality and becoming more widely available. As these trends continue, it will be easier to integrate virtual reality into anatomy classes and in medical training in general. Its usefulness in biomedical applications cannot be left out.

Acknowledgement. We thank Dr. med. C. Schadow from St. Marienstift hospital (Magdeburg, Germany) for the great support with our project, especially with compilation of the non-VR teaching material.

Conflict of Interest Statement. The software and hardware used in this study was purchased at the regular price. The authors have no connection to Varjo or Sharecare, Inc. The results presented here are based on the sole actions of the authors and are in no way related to Sharecare, Inc or Varjo.

References

1. Cooper, J., Taqueti, V.: A brief history of the development of mannequin simulators for clinical education and training. Postgrad. Med. J. **84**(997), 563–570 (2008)
2. Falah, J., Charissis, V., Khan, S., Chan, W., Alfalah, S.F.M., Harrison, D.K.: Development and evaluation of virtual reality medical training system for anatomy education. In: Arai, K., Kapoor, S., Bhatia, R. (eds.) Intelligent Systems in Science and Information 2014. SCI, vol. 591, pp. 369–383. Springer, Cham (2015). https://doi.org/10.1007/978-3-319-14654-6_23
3. HealthySimulation.com. Virtual anatomy | healthcare simulation | healthysimulation.com (2021). https://www.healthysimulation.com/virtual-anatomy/
4. Kavanagh, S., Luxton-Reilly, A., Wuensche, B., Plimmer, B.: A systematic review of virtual reality in education. Themes Sci. Technol. Educ. **10**(2), 85–119 (2017)
5. Maresky, H., Oikonomou, A., Ali, I., Ditkofsky, N., Pakkal, M., Ballyk, B.: Virtual reality and cardiac anatomy: exploring immersive three-dimensional cardiac imaging, a pilot study in undergraduate medical anatomy education. Clin. Anat. **32**(2), 238–243 (2019)
6. McLachlan, J.C., Patten, D.: Anatomy teaching: ghosts of the past, present and future. Med. Educ. **40**(3), 243–253 (2006)
7. Nicholson, D.T., Chalk, C., Funnell, W.R.J., Daniel, S.J.: Can virtual reality improve anatomy education? a randomised controlled study of a computer-generated three-dimensional anatomical ear model. Med. Educ. **40**(11), 1081–1087 (2006)
8. Petersson, H., Sinkvist, D., Wang, C., Smedby, Ö.: Web-based interactive 3d visualization as a tool for improved anatomy learning. Anatom. Sci. Educ. **2**(2), 61–68 (2009)
9. Pixo. Off-the-shelf XR solutions for every organization (2021). https://pixovr.com/off-the-shelf-xr-solutions/
10. Privett, B., Greenlee, E., Rogers, G., Oetting, T.A.: Construct validity of a surgical simulator as a valid model for capsulorhexis training. J. Cataract Refract. Surg. **36**(11), 1835–1838 (2010)
11. Sajid, A., et al.: Cardiology patient simulator and computer-assisted instruction technologies in bedside teaching. Med. Educ. **24**(6), 512–517 (1990)
12. Sharecare Inc. Sharecare YOU (2021). https://www.sharecareyou.com/
13. Stepan, K., et al.: Immersive virtual reality as a teaching tool for neuroanatomy. Int. Forum Allergy Rhinol. **7**, 1006–1013 (2017)
14. Sugand, K., Abrahams, P., Khurana, A.: The anatomy of anatomy: a review for its modernization. Anatom. Sci. Educ. **3**(2), 83–93 (2010)
15. Varjo Technologies Oy. System requirements - varjo.com (2021). https://varjo.com/use-center/get-started/system-requirements/#hardware
16. Wainman, B., Wolak, L., Pukas, G., Zheng, E., Norman, G.R.: The superiority of three-dimensional physical models to two-dimensional computer presentations in anatomy learning. Med. Educ. **52**(11), 1138–1146 (2018)
17. Xiaoying, L., Xianbo, S.: The application of virtual reality technology in teaching reform. In: Advanced Technology in Teaching, pp. 149–156. Springer, Heidelberg (2012). https://doi.org/10.1007/978-3-642-29458-7_24
18. Yammine, K., Violato, C.: The effectiveness of physical models in teaching anatomy: a meta-analysis of comparative studies. Adv. Health Sci. Educ. **21**(4), 883–895 (2015). https://doi.org/10.1007/s10459-015-9644-7

19. Zhao, J., Xu, X., Jiang, H., Ding, Y.: The effectiveness of virtual reality-based technology on anatomy teaching: a meta-analysis of randomized controlled studies. BMC Med. Educ. **20**(1), 1–10 (2020)
20. Zinchenko, Y., Khoroshikh, P., Sergievich, A., Smirnov, A., Tumyalis, A., Kovalev, A., Gutnikov, S., Golokhvast, K.: Virtual reality is more efficient in learning human heart anatomy especially for subjects with low baseline knowledge. New Ideas Psychol. **59**, 100786 (2020)

Ease of Use and Preferences Across Virtual Reality Displays

Lisa Rebenitsch[1]([✉]), Delaina Engle[1], Gabrielle Strouse[2],
Isaac Egermier[1], Manasi Paste[1], and Morgan Vagts[1]

[1] South Dakota Mines, Rapid City, SD 57701, USA
lisa.rebenitsch@sdsmt.edu
[2] University of South Dakota, Vermillion, SD 57069, USA

Abstract. Head mounted displays have become popular, but it is uncertain whether the interactive quality of these systems is sufficient for educational and training applications. This work is a longitudinal study into a variety of VR systems, which examines interface restrictions, ease of use, and user preferences with an emphasis on educational settings. Four different systems were examined with a range of interaction elements. Certain interactions failed in some systems and users did not necessarily prefer the highest-end systems. Overlapping interaction elements were also discovered, which may direct future work in later interaction test suites.

Keywords: Virtual reality · Displays · Education · Interaction

1 Introduction

Virtual reality (VR) has become widely available. While head-mounted displays (HMDs) have become the most popular option for VR, there remain questions on the interface capabilities of these systems, and whether the additional cost of HMDs is acceptable, given lower-cost alternatives. This is particularly important in an educational setting where potentially a few dozen individuals need access to a VR system simultaneously. The authors present a longitudinal study into a variety of VR systems, which examine interface restrictions, learnability, ease of use, and user preferences. The intent was to provide guidance for future projects requests, with an emphasis on educational settings.

There are several challenges in selecting a VR system for a project. The primary challenge is the initial, substantial cost. Another is that some systems are not suitable for particular applications due to variations in the support for different interactions and ease of learning may vary with hardware. For example, an Oculus Rift controller provides 6° of freedom (DOF) in tracking in two controllers, but an Oculus Go only provides 3 DOF (orientation) on one controller. However, the Go is substantially less expensive.

In the experiment presented, four different VR systems were compared using consistent virtual environments along with a variety of interaction methods to examine how easily different types of interactions would be learned across different hardware restrictions. To provide the most general guidance for selecting VR hardware, the

© The Author(s), under exclusive license to Springer Nature Switzerland AG 2022
J. Y. C. Chen and G. Fragomeni (Eds.): HCII 2022, LNCS 13317, pp. 238–260, 2022.
https://doi.org/10.1007/978-3-031-05939-1_16

interaction and systems were selected to be as varied as possible, but still usable in the classroom. As a result, the four systems were selected to include a variety of input methods, displays, and additional hardware peripherals to enhance VR experience. Given the emphasis on educational settings, the four systems were also selected with a wide cost range in order to consider cost benefit ratios. In addition, the experiment considered success rate, ease of use, and user preference.

We found the ease of interaction did vary across systems. An Oculus Rift with rumble tactile feedback showed had higher ease of use ratings than other systems across several factors.. However, other systems may have better success rates or higher preference in some contexts. The details of the results are in the Sect. 5 Results. There were also many behaviors and comments on the system from the users that present additional preference and acceptance of the systems as stated in Sect. 5.4 Preferences and Informal Participant Responses. Given the rapid changes in availably of HMDs, the results were further analyzed to narrow the tasks needed for future comparison, shown in Sect. 5.5 Refinement of Interaction Tasks. By reviewing these results, we provide some guidance in which contexts lower end systems are still useful, and what features of higher end systems may be worth the additional cost.

2 Background

Good computer interface design has been under investigation since before the first monitor, and VR introduces new challenges. The WIMP (window, icon, menu, pointer) paradigm has been predominant in desktops for decades. Given the new context of VR, there were reasonable questions of what parts of WIMP still applied. The window is now 360° and the pointer has moved from 2 DOF to 6 DOF. The development of standard user interfaces in VR is much younger than the standard desktop. This is clearly shown by examining the input devices over time. Some early devices were little more than a rotatable sphere with a few mouse buttons, or a large 3D tracked pointer with a single button [1]. Over time, the controllers have begun to consolidate into a left and right controller with a similar number of buttons to a standard modern game console. While controllers are becoming standardized, the way users interact using them are still extremely varied. As time has progressed, there has been increasing focus on interaction usability as the "awe" of VR wanes [2].

In the context of education, a meta-analysis of virtual education studies supports a steady result of improvement in learning outcomes, particularity in knowledge of procedural tasks [3]. VR training has also resulted in better motivation in VR [4, 5]. Prior research has also shown that virtual reality training can be superior to other methods of training in a variety of domains [6–9]. These systems may also be perceived by learners as more useful, easier to use, and may result in a greater sense of presence [10], leading to greater engagement with the material and better learning [11].

One caveat is that there can be time lost learning a new system rather than the content. Moreover, since the goal in education is to support the ability to remember, build, and transfer knowledge, ideal input methods may vary. For example, learning may be better in some contexts with a projector VR compared to an HMD [12]. Counter to that, researchers have argued that higher-end systems may be the best for promoting transfer of newly acquired skills because they provide VR learning opportunities that are most similar to the visual and physical real-world environments in which learners must apply their skills [11, 13].

Given the change on interaction from 2DOF to 6DOF, classic pointing options are not viable in many contexts. Instead, alternatives such as leaning, gestures, and 6DOF points are considered. Leaning navigation is possible with just an HMD although chair or balance boards are common. Leaning or pointing that lends itself towards natural behaviors also tends to be more easily learned and allows for better navigation around corners [14, 15, 16]. This type of interaction provides some of the missing tactile feedback. Sound and vibration feedback tend to improve experience [17, 18]. This was one motivation in including additional feedback options in the experiment.

Gestural interfaces have the benefit of not requiring additional devices, but have tracking, fatigue, and gesture selections limitations [19]. Fine tracking of the fingers is difficult for most systems as it requires sub-centimeter accuracy. As a result, larger motions are more common and full hand gripping is more available. However, these motions must be selected to meet two opposing conditions. 1) The meaning of the gesture must be intuitive. 2) The gesture is rare so as to not accidently cause an event with normal motion. Larger motions also result in swift fatigue if used for more VR interactions than the natural world. Should these conditions all be met, there is good success [20, 24] In the reference study, gripping with two hands is atypical except when carrying items, but it is a natural and intuitive motion. It is also not a long-term interaction. This was one motivation in including full hand tracking in the experiment.

3   Methodology

There were two questions of focus in the study. 1) Does lower cost hardware support VR interactions as well as higher cost hardware? 2) What are the well supported interactions in various systems to aid in future educational applications?

With these goals in mind, the study selected the best available VR systems with restricted display and interaction capacities, within some cost limits. Interactions were selected by reviewing past VR educational and training applications as mentioned in the background. Outcomes measured included success rates, ease of use, preferences, and informal responses. In addition, some transfer of knowledge of the system and distances were also collected and are part of a continuing project.

We examined these systems over 2 years due to the COVID pandemic interfering with in-person activities. Due to the pandemic occurring mid-experiment, we split the study into comparing the Vive versus the Go, and the Rift versus the 3D projector system. We refer to the comparison studies as the Vive+Go and the Rift+Projector sets. Within these sets, we perform within-subject analysis, although we did have a few participants that had sessions in all four systems. For the final analysis of all four systems, we used between-subject statistical tests that allows for non-parametric data and uneven groups (Kruskal-Wallis) of participants across sets.

3.1 Environment

The environment was intended to be a simple environment with multiple objects with which to interact as shown in Fig. 1. The room area was bounded by a low wall and allowed a view to the horizon. The shelves had one long range object. The control panel had a twist knob, three buttons, two levels, and a slider. The table had several blocks, a cabinet that contained a hammer, and a square pitcher with blue spheres inside. The table also contained a drawer underneath. Lastly, there were two bullseye cubes with a stake, and a floating capsule that changed color when tapped.

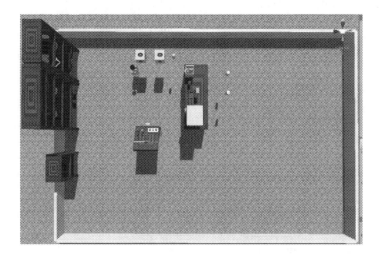

Fig. 1. Environment

To provide the most general and widest guidance for selecting VR hardware, the following four systems were selected:

1. A Vive Pro with Leap Motion hand tracking, and a KatMini 2D treadmill.
2. An Oculus Rift S with a mirrored controller, and a swivel chair on a rumble platform.
3. An Oculus Go with a swivel chair and the chair's controller.
4. A 3D projector system with the user standing, and with a wireless Xbox controller.

Although 3D projectors have fallen out of favor, there are a few benefits to them. One is that prior research by Srivastava et. al. suggest that learning may be better in some contexts with a projector VR compared to an HMD. Another is the substantial cost decrease for a classroom. The controllers were selected to achieve a wide range of common input methods. The chair, rumble platform, and treadmill were used to identify if these additional peripherals could improve the quality of the experience while improving safety of the system.

3.2   Interaction Selection

The interaction list was selected from commonly used paradigms in VR applications, which includes prior lists of suggested interactions, and a focus on educational needs. There is not a standard set of interactions to test a new method, but prior sets have been proposed. The VEPAD is relatively established, and provides an overview of items that most navigation\interaction systems need to consider [21]. In reviewing prior work, as noted in Sect. 2 Background above and VR applications, the following categories were selected:

1. Interaction with constraints (e.g., buttons, sliders, door)
2. Long distance interactions (e.g., interaction with an out of arm reach object)
3. "free" object manipulation interactions (e.g., grab and place an object)
4. 2-handed interaction (when feasible with the hardware)

The final list of interactions is listed in Table 1. Unfortunately, due to the tap capsule being out of range depending on where the participant turned the camera, and the pitcher breaking part apart in the Rift, the tap capsule and the pitcher were both removed from most of the analysis.

Constrained elements were selected to confirm if there were certain translation movements that may be difficult in some systems. Long distance interaction is a common need in VR environments. Free interaction includes the common grab and carry interaction. The 2-handed interaction was to see if more complicated interactions were feasible. To place a stake, a participant needed to grip a stake and then tap it with a hammer. The picture contained several small blue spheres that the user was instructed to put into the drawer. This required either fast coordination as the drawer closed slowly or two-handed interaction where the participant held the drawer and pitcher at the same time. Interactions were as similar as possible across systems.

Table 1. Interaction set

"Free" object	Constrained	Long distance	2-handed (when applicable)
1. Gravity-affected cubes	5. Cabinet door	11. Out of reach cylinder	12. Hammer with stake and bullseye
2. Floating cubes	6. Knob		13. Pour spheres into a drawer
3. Tap capsule*	7. Drawer		
4. Pitcher*	8. Slider		
	9. Button		
	10. Lever		

* *The tap capsule and pitcher were removed from analysis due to difference in interaction abilities in the systems and a software\hardware problem.*

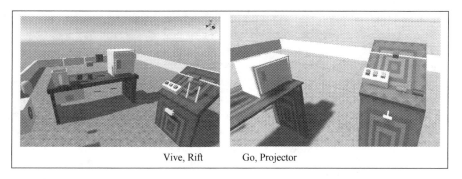

Vive, Rift   Go, Projector

Fig. 2. Changes in environment to meet system limitations

After these items were selected, and environment was built and then ported to all 4 hardware systems. However, there were some variations due to limitations in the systems. These included the following:

- The Go and Projector did not support positional information for the controllers. This meant a change in interaction where placing an item required selection of the final location for the small box placement, lever, and stake.
- The hammer was 2-handed in the Vive and Oculus but controlled by buttons in the Go and Projector.
- Movement was restricted to node-based navigation in the Go and Projector due to the decrease in display quality.
- Some object sizes, such as the buttons, were increased in the Vive due to lack of sensitivity in the finger tracking.

Example differences are presented in Fig. 2. This variation was predicted to affect success rates, ease of use, preference, and informal responses. For success rates, the participants' activity was monitored and the screen recorded. Then, the number of attempts to complete a required interaction was recorded. In some cases, this also included a complete failure, and the task was marked as incomplete.

For learnability and ease of use, we examined surveys suggested by Nielsen's 10 Heuristics [22] and Lund's USE questionnaire [23]. Given this was a preliminary study, not all questions were viable. Moreover, we wished to limit survey fatigue. We selected the following:

1. Feels natural to use
2. Consistent
3. Visual/tactile feedback useful
4. I learned to use it quickly
5. It is easy to learn to use it
6. Interaction methods are easy to remember

For preference, we asked the participants which system was preferred over another, and their general opinion of the variation in the systems and their components. This was intended to be exploratory for features that may require additional study.

Success rates included tracking the number of times each participant took to use each object during their session for a total of 13 data points per participant, per system.

The ease of use ratings consisted of subjective responses as well as objective. There were 16 questions using Likert data, per system. Ten of these were rating the objects tested in each environment. While there were 13 interaction objects in each system, the cabinet, hammer, and tap capsule were removed due to limitations in one or more systems. The hammer and cabinet were 2-handed in some systems. The tap capsule was removed due to a software glitch in the projector system that made it unavailable for several participants. The six remaining questions were overall use questions listed in Methodology to determine how easily a participant was able to use the system. Likert data was on a scale of 7 with the best positive responses corresponding to "strongly agree" and the worst negative responses corresponding to "strongly disagree."

3.3 Alpha Testing and Refinement

Alpha testing was performed to both improve quality and to determine if there were immediate differences in the quality of the system that affect development. Initial alpha testing was done with Oculus Go and the Vive. Originally, participants were not instructed to do anything specific beyond "try things out."

Alpha testing revealed that additional tutorials on use were needed along with a guided walkthrough to locate all interactable elements. The Go's lack of position tracking was difficult to understand at first. Also, an additional teleportation node for the Go was needed to jump behind the desks after frustration was mentioned by some of the alpha testers in some items not being visible after dropping them.

The KatMini 2D treadmill straps in a participant to a harness that could spin 360° and kept the participant centered above the platform below. The user could then walk in any direction and they would move in the virtual world. However, alpha testers noted that the walking method the 2D treadmill required was not natural and that the friction was too high. Custom low-friction shoes were created and additional instructions on the walking motions were added. The low-friction shoes were cotton-bottomed slippers with Teflon tape on 90% of the sole.

Several items were also noted to be too small or short to readily access. This was more pronounced in the Vive system, but alpha testers noted difficulty in pointing with the Go, as well. Small and thin items, such as buttons and handles, were enlarged slightly to compensate. Short items were an issue on the projection system, so some items were raised to be more visible.

3.4 Procedure

The same procedure was applied for all systems and the order of the systems within the set were randomized. Before the experiment, participants completed the motion sickness susceptible questionnaire (MSSQ) [24], viewed a consent form, and were given an overview of the purpose and content of the experiment. The MSSQ was primarily used to determine who may be particularly sensitive to cybersickness.

When a participant arrived, they were given an overview of the system and controls before using the system. The participant then put on the system. The session lead then led the participant though the different interaction elements in a specified order. During use, the session lead recorded how many attempts were needed to complete each interaction task. To allow for testing for transfer of positional information, there was a matching object in the real and virtual world, on shelves that were in the same relative placement in the real and virtual world. Half of the participants were asked to find the object in the real world after VR use, and half were asked to look around the lab before VR use, and then find the object in the virtual world. The session lead timed how long this search took. This was done in random order.

After the session completed, the participant confirmed how they were feeling to ensure safe usage of the next system. Participants then completed a survey of the first system while the session lead set up the next system. The first survey only had the distance and location questions. The participant then put on the new system and performed the same interaction tasks.

3.5   Participants

The experiment had 46 users. 27 were female, and 19 were male. The Vive+Go set consisted of 33 participants. The Rift+Projector set consisted of 24 participants. The users were primarily college age. Given the short time spent in the virtual environment, no participant withdrew before completing the second system in the set. However, only 12 participants were able to complete both sets as the experiment required 2 years to complete due to interruption by the COVID pandemic. This project was performed with the approval of the local IRB and all participants gave consent before beginning.

3.6   Device Details

There were four systems tested in the experiment to provide a range of hardware. Example differences are shown in Fig. 3.

Lowest End, (3D Projector). The 3D projector was a 20ft diagonal screen with the participant positioned 6 feet from the screen, which resulted in a 120° field of view (FOV). The 3D system used active shutter glasses set to a 110 Hz refresh rate. While 120 Hz would have been ideal, the computer in use could only supply the 110 Hz frame rate. For this system, the participants stood and used a wireless Xbox controller for input. The system was selected for its cost effectiveness, familiarity of input, and prior research that suggested it may be better for education [12]. Movement was accomplished by resetting the viewpoint to the four cardinal directions upon a button press as shown in Fig. 3 A. Some side-to-side motion was permitted with the joystick.

Low-End HMD (Oculus Go). The Oculus Go has a 60 Hz frame rate and a 101° FOV. Its controller was the original Oculus go controller, which permitted orientation tracking only. Participants sat in a swivel chair for safety. This system was tested due to its low cost. Translation movement was accomplished with node-based teleportation that cycled through 4 nodes as shown in Fig. 3 B and rotation was done by tracking the head.

A) Projector's camera locations and approximate view angles

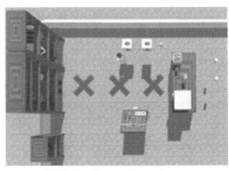

B) Go's teleportation nodes

C) Rift's in-house rumble pad

D) Vive's hand-tracking view

Fig. 3. Examples of the four systems

Mid-end (Oculus Rift with rumble pad). The Oculus Rift S has a 110° FOV and an 80 Hz refresh rate. Its controller had both Oculus Rift controllers with the button commands mirrored to allow for both left and right-handed individuals. For safety, participants were seated on a swivel chair. Course translation movement was accomplished with sliding navigation with a forward press on the joystick. Fine translation and rotation were accomplished by tracking the head. The swivel chair was placed on a rumble platform that vibrated when the participant moved. This system was selected due to it wide availability and more standard design of HMDs. The rumble platform was developed in-house and was comprised of four motors mounted to a 4x4ft platform as shown in Fig. 3 C. While not standard, vibration is corrected to affect perception and cybersickness [18], and it is a far less costly means to provide this tactile feedback than a 2D treadmill.

High End (Vive Pro Eye with 2D Treadmill and Hand Tracking). The Vive Pro Eye has a 110° FOV with a 90 Hz refresh rate. Controls were provided with full hand tracking with the Leap Motion infrared camera, as shown in Fig. 3 D. Movement was provided by using the KatMini 2D treadmill as shown in Fig. 3 D. This system was selected to see if there were notable benefits of better realism within a 6x6ft bounded area.

4   Analysis

The experiment consisted of two within-subject designs entailing the Vive + Go set and the Rift + Projector set. There were 13 interaction objects tested in each environment. The useability elements tested were success rates and perceived ease of use collected with a post-use survey. Between-subject design was later used to compare all four systems using the Kruskal-Wallis test. Finally, exploratory factor analysis was used to refine analysis. All hypotheses tested were evaluated with an α of 0.05.

Participant success results were initially analyzed for normality using histograms. Almost all histograms showed strong positive skewing, which is expected due to a lot of participants being able to use an object after only one or two attempts. No further analysis was used to look for normality in success rates, and non-parametric methods of analysis were used to analyze success rates. Each set of systems originally consisted of 13 tests, one for each interaction object. However, due to the glitch in the tap capsule and pitcher, the number of tests was decreased to 11 tests. This resulted in a total of 22 paired Wilcoxon tests completed.

Binomial tests were also used to determine the probability of success for each object and for each of the four systems. This resulted in a total of 50 binomial tests (13 objects tested for the Oculus Go and the Vive, and 12 objects tested for the 3D Projector and the Oculus Rift due to the tap capsule failing in the Projector). To perform this analysis, the number of attempts to use each object was converted to a 0–1 scale, where 0 indicated the participant took more than one attempt to use the object, and a 1 otherwise.

Participant ease of use responses were also analyzed for normality. There were 16 different categories plotted for all four systems. When plotted as histograms, these graphs suggested little indication of normality. As a secondary measure, Shapiro-Wilk's normality tests were used for all categories and all systems. Out of the 64 total tests, a large majority were statistically significant, meaning those categories were not normally distributed. Although there were a few that did not show significant results, this only meant that it cannot be concluded that they are not normally distributed and is not an indication that they are. Thus, in order to simplify analysis, all perceived ease of use tests were done using non-parametric methods of analysis.

A non-parametric version of the ANOVA test, the Kruskal-Wallis test, was used when comparing data across all four systems. The non-parametric paired Wilcoxon test was used when analyzing responses between sets of participants, and all correlations were tested using the Spearman correlation test.

5   Results

5.1   Success Rates

Results of the paired Wilcoxon tests for each set of systems are shown in Table 2. For the paired Wilcoxon tests between the Vive and Oculus Go, only three objects showed statistical significance, while tests between the 3D projector and the Oculus Rift showed six objects showing statistical significance. This may be indication that there are greater differences between the 3D projector and the Rift than with the Vive and the Oculus Go.

The binomial test results are shown in Table 3. Based on the binomial tests, the Vive was the system to have the least number of objects with success rates statistically greater than 50%. Two objects were had a probability of success greater than 50%, as well as having the most objects with success rates statistically less than 50%. The Oculus Go and Oculus Rift both had the highest number of objects to have success rates statistically greater than 50%, with the Rift at 8 objects and the Go at 9. However, the Oculus Rift had zero objects with a success rate statistically lower than 50%, while the Oculus Go had one. The 3D projector had similar results to the Oculus Go and Oculus Rift, and this is most likely due to the simplicity of the controls on the game controller.

Table 2. Paired-Wilcoxon tests for success rates

Vive+Go

Gravity-affected cubes (**)	Floating cubes (ns)	Cabinet door (ns)	Knob (*)	Drawer (ns)	Slider (ns)
Button (ns)	Lever (*)	Hammer (ns)	Stake (ns)	Out of reach cylinder (ns)	

Rift+Projector

Gravity-affected cubes (ns)	Floating cubes (ns)	Cabinet door (ns)	Knob (**)	Drawer (***)	Slider (*)
Button (***)	Lever (**)	Hammer (ns)	Stake (ns)	Out of reach cylinder (*)	

*** $p < 0.001$ ** $p < 0.01$ * $p < 0.05$ (ns) not significant

Table 3. Binomial tests for success

Probability of success	Vive	Go	Projector	Rift
Gravity-affected cubes	36% (ns)	55% (ns)	50% (ns)	92% (***)
Floating cubes	90% (**)	74% (*)	75% (*)	92% (***)
Pitcher	26% (*)	87% (***)	67% (ns)	N/A
Cabinet door	45% (ns)	55% (ns)	83% (**)	88% (***)
Knob	52% (ns)	81% (***)	100% (***)	75% (*)
Drawer	45%(ns)	84% (***)	71% (ns)	88% (***)
Slider	36% (ns)	61% (ns)	88% (***)	75% (*)
Button	19% (***)	87% (***)	71% (ns)	54% (ns)
Lever	52(ns)	81% (***)	92% (***)	58% (ns)
Hammer	26% (*)	68%	96% (***)	96% (***)
Stake	13(***)	26% (*)	67% (ns)	71% (ns)
Out of reach cylinder	61% (ns)	84% (***)	75% (*)	58% (ns)
Capsule Tap	90% (***)	97% (***)	N/A	92% (***)

*** $p < 0.001$ ** $p < 0.01$ * $p < 0.05$ (ns) not significant

The Kruskal-Wallis tests were used between all systems and used for all objects. This resulted in a total of 11 Kruskal-Wallis tests, and are shown in Table 4. Eight of the 11 tests came back statistically significant, which is not surprising as it was already shown in the paired-Wilcoxon tests that there were statistical differences between systems.

Table 4. Kruskal Wallis tests between all systems for ease of use responses

Feels natural to use (***)	System is consistent (*)	Knob (ns)	Learned to use system quickly (*)	System is easy to learn (*)	Interaction methods easy to remember (**)	Button (**)	Lever (ns)
Slider (ns)	Out of reach cylinder (ns)	Pitcher (*)	Gravity-affected cubes (***)	Floating cubes (**)	Visual/tactile feedback useful (***)	Drawer (ns)	Stake (***)

*** p < 0.001 ** p < 0.01 * p < 0.05 (ns) not significant

5.2   Ease of Use

Responses from the usability survey were employed to compare specific elements between systems. Elements included each individual object (10 total) as well as 6 different 'overall use' responses. When comparing all four systems at once (Kruskal-Wallis), almost all objects showed significance (11 out of 16). This indicates that at least one system was showing different responses from the other three systems but does not conclude which. To further compare, paired-Wilcoxon tests were used between sets of systems (Oculus Go & Vive and 3D Projector and Oculus Rift) for those 11 elements that showed statistical significance. For the button and pitcher, the Go was statistically shown to have better participant responses. Ironically, these are the only two categories that the Rift was not shown to have statistically better responses. Thus, for 9 out of 16 categories the Rift was statistically significant in showing higher participants responses on ease of use than the other three systems. This may indicate that participants found this system easiest to use or they preferred this system more than the projector.

All question responses were averaged for further analysis as shown in Table 5. All variables were split into categories to determine which system had higher responses in each category. The categories analyzed were: overall use (questions relating to how participants felt overall about the system), objects that required simple touching, grabbing or picking up objects, and objects that required pushing or pulling. It was found that the Oculus Rift had the highest responses on average for almost all variables in all categories, while the lowest responses were evenly distributed between the other three systems. In particular, for the overall use category and the push/pull objects, the Oculus Rift had the highest responses for every variable. This would give indication that this system was favored more than the other systems and this it was easier to use.

Finally, Wilcoxon tests were used between all remaining pairs of systems to test ease of use. This includes Wilcoxon tests between the Oculus Go & Rift, the Oculus Go & 3D Projector, the Vive & Oculus Rift, and the Vive and 3D Projector. The same 11 variables from the with-in subject tests were examined, with four post-hoc tests performed for each pair of systems. This resulted in 44 Wilcoxon tests performed.

Using these tests along with the paired Wilcoxon tests performed earlier, it was possible to conclude that the Oculus Rift showed statistically higher responses than any other system for six of the 11 categories as shown in Table 6. No other system showed statistically greater responses in any category. The Oculus Rift showed statistically higher responses for three of the five overall use variables as well as three of the five grab/pick up objects. For objects that required pushing or pulling, not a single system showed statistically higher responses. Also, there was not a single system that showed statistically lower responses than any other system.

Table 5. Averages of participant ease of use responses

Category	Variable	Vive	Go	Projector	Rift
Overall use	Feels natural to use	5.39	4.61	4.13	6.22
Overall use	System is consistent	4.97	5.00	5.35	6.09
Overall use	Visual/tactile feedback useful	5.52	4.88	4.87	6.43
Overall use	Learned to use system quickly	6.03	6.12	5.59	6.65
Overall use	System is easy to learn	5.84	5.88	5.27	6.52
Overall use	Interaction methods easy to remember	6.19	5.85	4.86	6.57
Touch	Button	5.81	6.57	6.18	5.70
Push/Pull	Lever	5.97	6.19	6.10	6.59
Push/Pull	Slider	5.94	5.68	6.05	6.52
Push/Pull	Drawer	5.52	5.68	5.77	6.09
Push/Pull	Knob	5.43	5.73	5.86	6.09
Grab	Gravity-affected cubes	5.71	5.32	5.45	6.70
Grab	Floating cubes	5.47	5.65	5.45	6.70
Grab	Pitcher	5.06	6.06	5.45	4.78
Grab	Out of reach cylinder	5.61	6.10	6.05	5.87
Grab	Stake	4.48	4.21	5.77	6.23

Table 6. Wilcoxon tests between systems for ease of use responses

	Vive/Go	Rift/Projector	Vive/Projector	Vive/Rift	Rift/Go	Go/Projector
Feels natural to use	(ns)	(***)	(*)	(***)	(***)	(ns)
System is consistent	(ns)	(*)	(ns)	(**)	(*)	(ns)
Visual/tactile feedback useful	(ns)	(***)	(ns)	(**)	(***)	(ns)
Learned to use system quickly	(ns)	(**)	(ns)	(*)	(ns)	(ns)
System is easy to learn	(ns)	(**)	(ns)	(*)	(ns)	(ns)
Interaction methods easy to remember	(ns)	(**)	(*)	(ns)	(*)	(ns)
Button	(**)	(ns)	(ns)	(ns)	(ns)	(*)
Gravity affected cubes	(ns)	(**)	(ns)	(***)	(***)	(ns)
Floating cubes	(ns)	(**)	(ns)	(***)	(**)	(ns)
Pitcher	(***)	(ns)	(ns)	(ns)	(ns)	(*)
Stake	(ns)	(*)	(**)	(***)	(***)	(**)

5.3   Secondary Analysis

Two other secondary factors of analysis were considered. Participant self-reported weekly hours of game play was used to determine if there was a correlation between the number of hours participants spent in a week playing video games and how successful they were at using VR. To perform these Spearmen correlation tests, an average was found for the number of attempts it took one individual participant to use each object for one system.

Based on this analysis, the Vive was the only system to statistically show indication of a correlation. The correlation test showed statistical significance of a negative correlation between video game hours and number of attempts ($p = 0.018$, rho = -0.422), indicating that those who play more video games showed better success rates when using the Vive. The other three systems showed little to no trends and very low correlations, which indicated prior video game experience was not associated with a participant's ability to use these systems.

Participants were also asked to estimate distances in the virtual environment due to prior research showing distance estimation discrepancies [25]. This was done somewhat informally as it was not the primary focus of the research. However, since the same environment was used in all four systems, it was possible to use these distance estimates to determine how participants perceived the environment during use. The averages for the Vive and the Oculus Go were close to the actual distance in the environment. The Oculus Rift, however, showed to be the furthest off with participant underestimating.

5.4   Preferences and Informal Participant Responses

In addition to formal measures, the experiments collected informal responses from the participants via verbal comments and notable behaviors. This showed a wide range of expressed factors to have impacted their experience.

At a high level, we asked participants to order their preference of device for that set. For the Vive + Go set, 11 selected the Go over the Vive, and 21 selected the Vive over the Go. The reason given was primarily that the Go was easier to use if selected. For the Vive, most stated it felt more natural when selected. For the Rift + Projector set, 3 selected the projector as their preferred choice and largely stated familiarity as the reason. The Rift largely won due to ease of use and immersiveness.

While in the 2D world, participants did not expect additional tactile feedback when pressing a button, rotating about a pivot, or a slider. In a 3D world, participants expected actions to mimic the real world more accurately. This showed dramatically in difficulty gripping and throwing, and moving a lever which required following an arc with no tactile feedback in the Vive. One participant phrased it the best, "with the [hand tracking], people expected the actions to be natural." In the Go, many of the participants felt it was unnatural for the slider to slide and twist knobs to rotate upon touch and wanted to slide or rotate the items themselves. On the other hand, the Go and projector provided feedback via button press. Even if these systems felt less real, they preferred the ease of using a button to complete the action.

However, many participants seemed to favor hand tracking. Quite a few stated that it felt very immersive and that using their hands was a great experience. They also commented that using their hands allowed for a lot more control of objects, such as easy rotation and the ability to poke objects, rather than having to grab the item first. There were remarks about the newness of the system when some initial troubles arose from getting the hands calibrated, but after this, the participants were very happy using these systems.

Participants also expressed graphics on the Oculus Go as a pain point compared to the Vive Pro Eye used with the 2D treadmill. This was likely due to the higher resolution and refresh rate available with the Vive Pro Headset.

The treadmill had mixed reviews. Most participants really enjoyed using it and said it felt great to walk through the world, rather than to move by teleporting. It also had the benefit of a feeling of "safety" that participants would not walk into a wall. Others said the treadmill movement was "jumpy," and that they would move farther or shorter than they anticipated when making a step, and that trying to move on the base of the treadmill with the low friction shoe attachments was difficult. Participants who said they preferred Oculus Go felt it was easier to get started rather than "fighting" the 2D treadmill, which took a while to get used to walking on. People who preferred the 2D treadmill felt it was a natural extension of human motion, whereas the Oculus Go had restrictions on what they could do with its controller. Interactability and immersiveness were also two important factors for which the participants felt the 2D treadmill was preferable over the Oculus Go.

Many of the observations had to do with the participants' familiarity with similar devices (likely through gaming). Depending on how the participant acted throughout the study, the lead could, very accurately, determine if the participant had played video games before, played video games frequently, or played video games often with experience using a VR. The first noticeable difference was whether the participant would try to use both hands to pick up an object on the Vive. If the participant had infrequently or never played video games, the participant almost always attempted to pick up the first object with both hands. Perhaps even more interesting, the participant would then continue to try and pick up the object with two hands by trying to grab it more firmly or from different angles before alerting the session instructor. Those that had more experience with gaming, especially VR, would almost never reach for an object with both hands. Another difference was the persistence between participants. Those without experience would attempt an action 2–3 times before alerting the session instructor. Those without gaming experience demonstrated the hardest adjustment to VR. Currently, it is unlikely that a person would take up VR without having previous experience with gaming, but as VR becomes more popular, this may prompt developers to create interactions that are more realistic.

Users with gaming experience were more likely to "play" in the virtual world. Instead of simply completing the task and moving on, they would appear to be almost testing the object for other uses (for example, instead of picking up an object and setting it back down, they might throw it in the air and try to catch it or bounce it on the ground). One might assume that those with less experience would be more inclined to "play" and try all the different new possibilities VR brings. Instead, it seems that comfortability is a big factor in "playing" in a virtual world. Participants that had previous gaming/VR experience were comfortable enough to try new ways to interact with items without instruction.

Overall, it seemed that the lower end systems were favored for ease of use and simplicity, and the higher end systems were favored for their immersion and natural control scheme. The Rift was a compromise between these options and may be why it had higher preference.

5.5   Refinement of Interaction Tasks

Repeating this experiment for each new interaction method or hardware would be constrained due to the time needed to build, test, and analyze each new system. Success rate analysis used data points for 13 different variables over four different systems, and ease of use analysis used data points for 16 different variables over four systems. Since the data consisted of two different within subjects' data sets, Kruskal-Wallis tests and paired Wilcoxon tests had to be used for each test employed, not only to look for differences across participants, but to also look for differences across systems. Between success rates and ease of use over all four systems, there were a total of 116 variables to be tested. Besides the large amounts of data, it was also found that some data were not useful. For instance, there were certain variables that showed the number of attempts for all participants was one. This means that every participant who used that particular object on one particular system was able to use the object on the first try. Variables that only had one number for each participant are not recommended for use in most tests. Therefore, it would be beneficial if the number of interaction tasks could be reduced without sacrificing the range of motions that may be needed in applications.

5.6   Selection and Application of Exploratory Factor Analysis

The goal of the post analysis was to identify any features that had highly correlated results, and thus at least one of the features could be removed while limiting the decrease in explanation power. Exploratory factor analysis (EFA) is a statistical approach used to determine the correlation among variables in a dataset. In EFA, 'factors' are created by grouping variables based on strong correlations. These factors can help to create a clean structure for modeling. By using EFA, we are also able to see what variables do not correlate with the others, and those variables can be eliminated completely from analysis.

The assumptions that were assessed prior to the analysis are listed in Table 7. The first assumption assessed was missing data. EFA works best when less than 10% of the dataset is missing. Here, we looked at missing data as a percent of the entire dataset as well as a percent for each participant. Participants with more than 50% of the data missing were completely removed from analysis. The next assumption was sample size. Typically, EFA works best with a 10:1 ratio of observations to response variables. However, the minimum ratio is considered to be 3:1. For success rates, outliers were also considered. Since ease of use responses came from a questionnaire, outliers were not assessed. Normality was also considered. However, previous analysis concluded that all data was not normally distributed. Thus, non-parametric means of analysis were used during EFA. Finally, additivity was assessed to initially analyze the correlations among variables and determine if the datasets are well suited for EFA. Correlation matrices were used. It is optimal to see a mixture of correlations between 0 and 1 without being equal to 1 (variables completely correlated).

Table 7. Assumptions for EFA

	Success rates	Ease of use responses
Missing data	11/1210 data points missing (0.91%) 0 participants removed	44/1760 data points missing (2.5%) 3 participants removed from analysis
Sample size	110 participants over 11 variables (10:1)	107 participants over 16 variables (6.7:1)
Outliers	No outliers removed	N/A
Normality	All variables non-normal	All variables non-normal
Additivity	All correlations between 0 – 0.6	All correlations between 0 – 0.8

After initially assessing correlations using a correlation matrix, correlation adequacy was assessed using Bartlett's test and Kaiser-Meyer-Olkin factor adequacy (KMO). These results are shown in Table 8. Bartlett's test is used to statistically assess correlations among variables. A significant p-value indicated that data is correlated enough to perform EFA. Typically, Bartlett's test requires multivariate normal data. However, this test can also use a correlation matrix as input. Thus, correlation matrices were created using Spearman correlations and then used as input for Bartlett's test. KMO further assesses adequacy of data for EFA. Typically, an overall MSA (mean sampling adequacy) value above 0.7 is optimal for EFA. Again, correlation matrices created using Spearman correlations were used as input for this test.

Table 8. Correlation adequacy for EFA

	Success rates	Ease of use responses
Bartletts Test	p < 0.0005	p < 0.0005
KMO	Overall MSA = 0.67	Overall MSA = 0.89

After the initial assessment of data to ensure that it is fit to use in EFA, the factors can be created and analyzed. To determine how many factors are best for the dataset, graphical and statistical analysis can be used. During this analysis, the results may be somewhat ambiguous. Multiple rounds of EFA can be performed using different numbers of factors to determine which model performs best. To determine the number of factors to use, scree plots and parallel analysis were used. A scree plot is a graphical representation of the eigenvalues for the data. Eigenvalues correspond to how much of the data is explained by that factor. The optimal number of factors to use is the location where the eigenvalues level off and no longer explain a significant amount of data. The plots can be subjective and require judgment to determine the optimal number of factors to use. Scree plots for ease of use responses and success rates are shown in Fig. 4 and Fig. 5, respectively. For ease of use responses, the scree plot indicates that 2 factors explain a large majority of the data. For success rates, the plot does not have a great elbow but indicates between 2 – 4 factors. Parallel analysis results for ease of use responses indicated 2 factors, while parallel analysis for success rates indicated 4 factors.

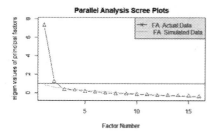

Fig. 4. Scree plot for ease of use responses

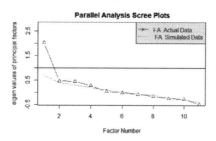

Fig. 5. Scree plot for success rate

Finally, EFA can be used. The rotation method used for both sets of analysis was Varimax, which is the most common type of orthogonal rotation. An orthogonal rotation assumes that factors are independent. The fitting estimation also must be included, as it is how the analysis is performed. Maximum likelihood is commonly used in EFA. However, this works best with normally distributed data. Thus, both sets of analysis used principal axis factoring. After running EFA, a factor matrix is created. This matrix contains loadings for each variable onto each factor. A variable is said to load onto a factor if the loading is greater than 0.3 or less than -0.3. In these factor matrices, variables should load onto only one factor. If a variable loads onto more than one factor, that indicated cross-loading. These variables should be eliminated from analysis. Non-loading variables should also be eliminated from analysis as they do not correlate with the rest of the data. After analyzing the factor matrix, cross-loading and non-loading variables are removed from the data set, creating a new correlation matrix, and then another round of EFA is performed. This process is repeated until a model is created without cross-loading or non-loading variables.

5.7 EFA Results

This analysis is preliminary but aids in refinement of future interaction work. Multiple sets of EFA were employed to determine the best suited model for the data. Initially, separate EFA models were created for the success rate and ease of use for both individual sets. After little success with this analysis, all four systems were examined, which resulted in two models: one for success rates over all participants on all four systems, and one for ease of use responses over all participants on all four systems. These models were better suited for EFA as one of the assumptions in EFA is an adequate sample size.

After finding the best fit model, model adequacy can be tested, and the results can be interpreted. For model adequacy analysis, goodness of fit statistics were used along with residual statistics and reliability. The tests used along with the results for both sets of EFA are listed in Table 9. As seen is Table 10, both of our models produced values that were either excellent or acceptable, which indicated the models are good.

Table 9. Model adequacy analysis for EFA models

Category of analysis	Test used	Success rates	Ease of use responses
	Total proportion of variance explained by final model	0.45	0.57
Goodness of fit statistic	*Tucker Lewis Index*	1.099	0.919
Goodness of fit statistic	*CFI*	1.016	0.963
Residual statistic	*RMSEA*	0.00	0.098
Residual statistic	*RMSR*	0.02	0.04
Reliability	*Cronbach's alpha*	Factor #1 = 0.84 (Factor #2 only has one variables loaded) Factor #3 = 0.48 Factor #4 = 0.35	Factor #1 = 0.87 Factor #2 = 0.62

The prime models found for success rates and ease of use responses are shown in Table 9. For success rates, it was found that four factors best explained the data. This model only resulted in two variables being eliminated from analysis. The slider and long distance selection were eliminated from analysis. This could possibly be due to how simple the interactable objects were to use. The remaining eleven variables split over four different factors left only one to three variables per factor. For ease of use responses, it was found that two factors best explained the data. Contrary to the results with success rates, this model eliminated 8 of the 16 total variables. However, with the remaining variables split over only two factors, this model can be interpreted well and provide useful results.

For success rates, the model produced has only a few variables eliminated but produces good model adequacy. The first factor consists of only objects from the podium environment. However, this factor could be useful in showing that objects on the podium have similarities. All objects have simple motions along a standard degree of freedom. All had up-down motions or similar. While the knob rolled, most participants used an up-down motion to "whack" it rather than grab and turn. The second factor with the drawer had a fore-aft motion. The third factor with the floating cubes and cabinet had left-right motions. While the floating cubes had more motion, most participants moved the cubes left-right. The last factor was free 6DOF motion.

For ease of use results, there was an adequate number of variables loaded onto each factor. The first factor consists of all 'overall use' variables. This factor contains five out of the six overall use variables with the last one being eliminated from analysis. The second factor consists of only objects. However, these objects do not have as much in common as with the first factor. The button is a touch object, the pitcher is a grabbing/pick up object, and the drawer is a pulling object. Although the second factor is not as useful in interpreting results, the first factor gives great insight into how useful those specific questions for ease of use were.

Although this analysis is very preliminary in the current analysis, it will primarily be helpful for future test suite development. Success rate seems to follow the common degree of freedoms in motion, but a wider set of interaction objects would be needed to confirm. Not only do the factors produced help to explain which variables have similarities, but the factors eliminated also give insight to the variables that may not be worth adding to future test environments.

Table 10. Results of exploratory factor analysis

	Success rates	Ease of use responses
Factor #1	Button, Lever, Knob	Feels natural to use, Visual/tactile feedback useful, Learned to use system quickly, System is easy to learn, Interaction methods easy to remember
Factor #2	Drawer	Button, Pitcher, Drawer
Factor #3	Floating cubes, Cabinet	N/A
Factor #4	Gravity-affected cubes, Hammer Stake	N/A
Variables eliminated	Slider, Out of reach cylinder	System is consistent, Gravity-affected cube, Floating cube, Out of reach cylinder, Slider, Stake, Level, Knob

6 Discussion

In this study we focused on interaction quality across a variety of systems with a focus towards the needs of educational applications. We considered four systems which included 4 different displays, four different input devices, and a few additional peripherals to examine if these improved the quality of interaction. We then considered the quality of the interaction in terms of success rates, ease of use, preferences, and informal responses.

We found that an Oculus Rift with its standard controllers, a swivel chair, and a rumble platform was the best performer overall. Following the Rift, in order of preference and quality were the Vive, the Go, and the Projector. However, other systems sometimes had better individual scores among the items tested. The Go and projector, in general, had better success rates. This is partially due to the absolute interaction of a controller button activating an event rather than needing to position the controller first. However, the point option in the Go resulted in a faster success rate. The hand-tracking testing in the Vive system was of keen interest but had a higher error rate. However, comments suggested that this would be highly desirable if improved.

During the sessions we noted several additional user behaviors and comments that were either surprising or could affect future selection of interaction methods.

As a result of this study, we propose the following:

1. The Go, or a single controller, can be used in some contexts, primarily, especially those contexts that are predominately viewing with most interactions being basic selection.
2. Hand tracking is highly desirable with a few caveats. The primary desire is improved accuracy and range. A secondary concern is that the interaction cannot require more than the natural motion of the real world as fatigue can rapidly occur.
3. 2D treadmills, unless naturalness is improved, merely serve as better safety hardware.
4. Regular Xbox controllers have the advantage of familiarity, but 3D tracking controllers with a similar button format are learned as swiftly and are preferred for their position capabilities.
5. Swivel chairs allow for easy and natural rotation. This seems to be preferred over most other rotation options.

6.1   Limitations and Future Work

The work was preliminary to determine if there was a notable effect by the systems at some level. The range of systems lessens the power of comparisons as there could be interactions between the controller, seating\standing arrangement, and display. The sessions were very short and had few repeated movements to gain an average case. We implemented the input as closely as possible across systems, but this could mean that one input method doesn't transfer well to a new system. We saw this particularly with the Xbox controller. The "trigger" button was used regularly in the HMDS, so we used the "bumper" on the Xbox control to have the same hand position. However, those with moderate game play instinctively used the 'A' button near the thumb instead out of familiarity. Another restriction of using the Xbox controller is the rotation interaction was restricted. This caused surprising difficulty.

Despite this, the variety of system allowed a better overview of the general benefits and limitations of the VR system that we otherwise would be unable to see. This presented us with several future directions. While preliminary analysis says we can decrease the number of different types of interactions, repeated tests of one type of interaction would be necessary to ensure reliability. This is paired with the fact that the minimal size of the controls seems to vary with each system. For example, buttons of varying sizes are needed. Navigation techniques were also not included in the system, and movement and interaction can interact. Combined, a larger test suite is needed for further analysis.

Acknowledgements. This project was run at the VR lab at South Dakota Mines. The project was only successfully completed with several volunteers and the aid of several undergraduate researchers, including Raiza Soares and others in the author list.

References

1. Bowman, D., Coquillart, S., Froehlich, B., Hirose, M., Kitamura, Y., Kiyokawa, K., Stuerzlinger, W.: 3D user interfaces: new directions and perspectives. IEEE Comput. Graphics Appl. **28**(6), 20–36 (2008)
2. Porter, J.I., Robb, A.: Thoughts, An Analysis of Longitudinal Trends in Consumer on Presence and Simulator Sickness in VR Games. In: CHI PLAY, Barcelona, Spain (2019)
3. Papastergiou, M.: Digital game-based learning in high school computer science education. Comput. Educ. **52**, 1–12 (2009)
4. Checa, D., Bustillo, A.: A review of immersive virtual reality serious games to enhance learning and training. Multimedia Tools Appl. **79**, 5501–5527 (2019)
5. Howard, M.C.: A meta-analysis and systematic literature review of virtual reality rehabilitation programs. Comput. Hum. Behav. **70**, 317–327 (2017)
6. Hamilton, E.C., Scott, D.J., Fleming, J.B., Rege, R.V., Laycock, R., Bergen, P.C., Tesfay, S. T., Jones, D.B.: Comparison of video trainer and virtual reality training systems on acquisition of laparoscopic skills. Surg. Endosc. Other Interv. Tech. **16**(3), 406–411 (2002)
7. Jang, S., Vitale, J.M., Jyung, R.W., Black, J.B.: Direct manipulation is better than passive viewing for learning anatomy in a three-dimensional virtual reality environment. Comput. Educ. **106**(106), 150–165 (2017)
8. Webster, R.: Declarative knowledge acquisition in immersive virtual learning environments. Interact. Learn. Environ. **24**(6), 1319–1333 (2016)
9. Vora, J., Nair, S., Gramopadhye, A.K., Duchowski, A.T., Melloy, B.J., Kanki, B.: Using virtual reality technology for aircraft visual inspection training: presence and comparison studies. Appl. Ergon. **33**(6), 559–570 (2002)
10. Lee, E.A.-L., Wong, K., Fung, C.: How does desktop virtual reality enhance learning outcomes? a structural equation modeling approach. Comput. Educ. **55**(4), 1424–1442 (2010)
11. Slater, M., Wilbur, S.: A framework for immersive virtual environments five: Speculations on the role of presence in virtual environments. Presence Teleoperators Virtual Environ. **6** (6), 603–616 (1997)
12. Srivastava, P., Rimzhim, A., Vijay, P., Singh, S., Chandra, S.: Desktop VR is better than non-ambulatory HMD VR for spatial learning. Front. Robotics. AI **6**, 50 (2019)
13. Kozak, J.J., Hancock, P.A., Arthur, E.J., Chrysler, S.T.: Transfer of training from virtual reality. Ergonomics **36**(7), 777–784 (1993)
14. Riecke, B.E., Feuereissen, D.: To move or not to move: can active control and user-driven motion cueing self-motion perception ("Vection") in virtual reality?. In: SAP ACM Symposium on Applied Perception, Los Angeles California (2012)
15. Tregillus, S., Al Zayer, M., Folmer, E.: Handsfree omnidirectional VR navigation using head tilt. In: Human Factors in Computing Systems. Denver (2017)
16. Rebenitsch, L., Delaina, E.: The effects of steering locomotion on user preference and accuracy in virtual environments. Presence, p. accepted (2021)
17. Kruijff, E., Marquardt, A., Trepkowski, C., Lindeman, R.W., Hinkenjann, A., Maiero, J., Riecke, B.E.: On your feet! enhancing vection in leaning-based interfaces through multisensory stimuli. In: Proceedings of the 2016 Symposium on Spatial User Interaction, Tokyo, Japan (2016)
18. Peng, Y.-H., Yu, C., Liu, S.-H., Wang, C.-W., Taele, P., Yu, N.-H., Chen, M.Y.: WalkingVibe: reducing virtual reality sickness and improving realism while walking in vr using unobtrusive head-mounted vibrotactile feedback. In: Conference on Human Factors in Computing Systems, Honolulu HI USA (2020)

19. Vivian, R.: Propositions for a mid-air interactions. In: Distributed, Ambient, and Pervasive Interactions, Vancouver, BC, Canada (2017)
20. Dias, P., Cardoso, J., Quintino, B.F., Ferreira, C., Santos, B.S.: Freehand gesture-based 3D manipulation methods for interaction with large displays. In: International Conference on Distributed, Ambient, and Pervasive Interactions, Las Vegas, NV, USA (2017)
21. Lampton, D.R., Knerr, B.W., Goldberg, S.L., Bliss, J.P., Moshell, M.J.: The Virtual Environment Performance Assessment Battery (VEPAB): Development and Evaluation, Alexandria (1994)
22. Nielsen, J.: 10 Usability Heuristics for User Interface Design. 15 Nov 2020. [Online]. Available: https://www.nngroup.com/articles/ten-usability-heuristics/. [Accessed 18 Nov 2021]
23. Lund, A.M.: Measuring usability with the USE questionnaire. STC Usability SIG Newsletter **8**(2), 3–6 (2001)
24. Golding, J.F.: Motion sickness susceptibility questionnaire revised and its relationship to other forms of sickness. Brain Res. Bull. **47**(8), 507–516 (1998)
25. Stanney, K.M., Kennedy, R.S., Drexler, J.M., Harm, D.L.: Motion sickness and proprioceptive aftereffects following virtual environment exposure. Appl. Ergon. **30**(1), 27–38 (1999)

Objective Quantification of Circular Vection in Immersive Environments

Debadutta Subudhi$^{(\boxtimes)}$ ⓘ, P. Balaji ⓘ, and Manivannan Muniyandi

Touch Lab, Department Applied Mechanics, Indian Institute of Technology Madras, Chennai 600 113, India
dev.subudhi49@gmail.com, mani@iitm.ac.in

Abstract. Human interaction in the computer environment requires conduciveness with minimal cybersickness. One such sickness is vection, where the subjects undergo illusory perception of self-motion in response to visual stimulus. The present research quantifies the perceptual parameter. An optokinetic drum (OKD) is used to induce circular vection on a virtual reality (VR), and the inertial measurement unit (IMU) in a head-mounted display (HMD) is used to track the head rotation about x, y, z axes. The study quantifies the vection in terms of the vection index (VI). The VI depends on the ratio of the angular velocity of HMD to the angular velocity of OKD. There is a significant difference from resting state to higher angular speeds in clockwise (CW) as well as anticlockwise (ACW) direction ($p < 0.05$). Also, the circular vection along the y-axis imparts the motion along the x and z axes. The magnitude of vection increases with speed in CW and ACW directions till the optimum speed of OKD. The vection is absent during very low and high speeds of OKD. Most participants experience the self-motion in an angular displacement range of 30–97°/s in both CW and ACW directions. The vection in ACW compensates for the vection in CW direction about x, y and z axes.

Keywords: Motion sickness · OKD · VI · IMU

1 Introduction

Motion sickness (MS) is a general experience of discomposure in response to motion stimuli present in a real or virtual environment. The MS depends on the ocular and vestibular organs that sense the motion and stabilize the gaze in real-world through vestibulo-ocular reflex (VOR) [19]. However, in a virtual environment, motion sickness is predominantly visually induced, known as visually induced motion sickness (VIMS). According to the Ebenholtz hypothesis, exposing individuals to various visual movements causes VIMS [16]. The VIMS depends on several factors, such as the conflict in VOR and somatosensory graviceptor[11] inputs. The magnitude of the phase difference between these sensory inputs causes a higher probability of VIMS [49].The other reasons of VIMS

Supported by organization IITM.

© The Author(s), under exclusive license to Springer Nature Switzerland AG 2022
J. Y. C. Chen and G. Fragomeni (Eds.): HCII 2022, LNCS 13317, pp. 261–274, 2022.
https://doi.org/10.1007/978-3-031-05939-1_17

are optokinetic nystagmus (OKN) [15] and body posture disability [51]. Conflict in VOR is effectively perceived by humans [5]. Researchers create vestibulo-ocular conflict by a rotating chair [61], flow field video [57], an off-vertical axis [9], a parallel swing [65], and a driving simulator [35], to trigger the vestibular system. However, the VIMS depends on eye movement in different directions, saccades and eye blinks [10]. The effect of VIMS on the eye leads to minor postural changes in the head that transmits to the semicircular canal sensing the changes in angular velocity of the head. This oculo-vestibular reflex (OVR) is not explored in literature.

1.1   Vection

The vection is an illusory perception of self-motion in real and virtual immersive environments. The nature of vection can be circular, linear or a combination of linear and circular. The OKD is a general apparatus used to discover many properties of perception of self-motion [1,29,47]. Different input modalities can induce vection, such as auditory-induced vection (AIV) [33], Hapto-kinetic Vection (HKV) is induced by applying tactile motion on the body [14,42], Biomedical vection (BMV) is induced from treadmill motion [7,52], visually induced vection (VIV) from computer display [64] by OVR. The intensity of vection depends on the flow, and apparent depth of the objects in the visual field [40]. It also depends on the time of exposure, and literature shows that a visual stimulus for 10 s is enough to induce illusory self-motion [14]. Also, the characterization of vection depends on which part of the body perceives self-motion. Most subjects experience VIMS reported vection; however, VIMS can happen in the dearth of vection [38]. The vection in virtual environments deteriorates the immersion. Therefore, nullifying the cause of vection is primary for the design of most of the head-mounted displays (HMD). It requires objectification and measurement of vection in VR.

1.2   Vection Measurement Methods

There is both subjective and objective measurement of vection in literature. However, the objective measurements are more effective in vection quantification compared to subjective measurements [44] as it aids in control and validation. Yet, the subjective measurements provide an insight towards the parameters resulting in self-motion. Subjective measure reports onset/offset of self-motion and it's strength from joystick button [20], rotation of circular knob in response to spinning OKD at $0.1—100°/s^2$ in real environment[41] or in VR [37], magnitude estimation (ME) ratings on a 10 or 100-point scale [2,8,36,46]. Eye movement and eccentric gaze conditions also objectify the vection strength at slower eye velocity [34]. The alpha power in electroencephalogram (EEG) during spatial disorientation due to vection increases variably among the subjects [58]. Other objective parameters such as heart rate (HR), blood pressure (BP) and skin conductance level (SCL) measures vection [10]. There is greater variability among subjects due to vestibular and somatosensory control of the autonomic nervous system while quantifying vection [3]. The literature shows the neural response of vection from positron emission tomography(PET) [13], Magnetoencephalography (MEG) [63], and functional magnetic resonance imaging (fMRI) [54].

Measurement of Vection from EEG: EEG is independent of subjective response and has a higher temporal resolution in the order of milliseconds and can sense the vection from time-frequency analyses of event-related brain potentials (ERP) [32]. There is an increase 10 Hz alpha wave activity at 14 s followed by a decrease in beta and delta activity as the ten participants subjected to linear vection with two types of optic flow display, which constitutes of 1000 blue circular dots of $0.36°$ in diameter moving at a 1 m/s on a black background [45]. Studies show that negative inflection $N230$ at O_1 (left occipital), and O_2 (right occipital) is more pronounced to visual stimuli producing stronger vection during longer 45 s stimulus exposure [31]. Literature also suggests that the EEG may be informative about inducing potential towards vection by optic flow. At the same time, stimulus exposure of 2.5–3.5 s is minimal to cause vection during EEG recording [45]. EEG can indicate cortical processing towards vection onset or offset and magnitude of vection. However, EEG measures can reflect parameters that are not purely vection-related [32].

Measurement of Vection from EGG: Vection causes an increase in gastric tachyarrhythmia, an increase in sympathetic activity, and a decrease in parasympathetic activity. Exposure to the virtual environment through OKD causes more stomach contraction activity [24]. Optokinetic stimulation causes a rise in frequency of EGG from 3.0 cycles/min to "tachygastric" frequencies (4–9) cycles/min [56]. However, various research studies scored tachygastric condition differently [55].

Measurement of Vection from EOG: The EOG parameters from the eye tracker in a few HMDs, such as the number of eye blinks, eye movement, pupil diameter and pupil position, are some factors showing the level of vection in VR. The mean eye blinking rate (number/min) is lower in the initial minutes of visual stimulus exposure, and it is considerably higher during the middle of the trials [35]. The blinking rate per epoch is more in HMD than display monitor [12]. Also, the foveal retinal slip velocity is an essential parameter towards the level of VIMS [21]. However, some studies in OKD rotation claims that unnatural and random eye motion can distort VIMS and eye fixation can nullify the effect of it [28,56,67].

Measurement of Vection from SCL: Skin conductance level is the tonic part of electrodermal activity (EDA), responsible for autonomic changes in the electrical conductance of the skin. It depends on autonomic arousal due to emotional and cognition loads. Compared to the baseline, SCL is high during the final minutes of experience in VR using the driving simulator as well as OKD rotation [35]. The OKD rotating at 60^0 per second (10 cycles per minute (cpm)) for 12 min causes an increase in both tonic and phasic levels at both palm and forehead sites (sensitive) with a positive Pearson correlation coefficient of 0.62 at forehead site than 0.48 at palmer site [59].

Measurement of Vection from Heart Rate Variability(HRV), BP and Breath Rate (BR): The HRV provides a measure for the autonomic nervous system activity [6]. Most of the study shows that vection causes a higher heart rate of 1.54 Hz [26]during OKD simulator [23,66] with higher low frequency (0.04–0.15 Hz) power in the RR-interval, which results in higher sympathetic outflow during computer graphics (CG) and real roller coaster movie scene [62]. BP shows an upward trend when subjects are VR driving simulators [39] and OKD simulator[23]. Oscillatory scenes in displays play a significant role in enhancing the BP as well as BR [22] to 0.365 Hz [26].

1.3   Gaps in the Measurements of Vection and Present Research

The assessment of vection through methods in the literature is cumbersome from a practical point of view. These methods require additional hardware that might reduce immersion which is the main objective of VR systems. Therefore, the current study focuses on measuring the vection through elegant and straightforward methods without requiring additional hardware. The current research proposes that mild head movements can be recorded from IMUs in most HMDs. The authors propose a novel parameter, Vection Index (VI), for measuring the vection from the IMU data. The objective of the study is to quantify circular vection from the kinematic analysis of OKD and HMD. The hypothesis is that the drum velocity reflects in head velocity. The authors also emphasise perceiving the self-motion to the direction of drum rotation.

2   Method

2.1   Participants

A total of 18 postgraduate students ($Mean_{AGE}$ = 26, SD_{AGE} = 4.2) $Mean_{Weight}$ = 76 Kg, SD_{weight} = 22.6 kg participate in the study. One participant did not participate in the experiment because of slight nausea, leaving 17 participants (11 male, six female) in the final analysis. There is no history of vestibular disorders among the participants, and they report the display is clear.

2.2   Apparatus

An Oculus Quest-2 VR headset has a horizontal field of view of $89°$ and a vertical field of view of $93°$. The refresh rate 60 Hz. The virtual environment simulates the OKD with a 200 cm diameter. The camera viewpoint is 100 cm away from the inner surface of the OKD [37]. Each stripe in OKD has a width of 49.1 cm.

The width is kept wider than 33 cm [37] to avoid spatial convergence at higher angular velocity. The VR headset is set with an inter-ocular distance (IOD) of 64 mm for all participants [37]. To confirm that the participants perceive the interior of OKD, they are asked about the stimulus appearance as flat, convex, or concave at the beginning of the experiment. All participants observe the drum in a concave shape in game mode. The subjective measurement for the participants is about the perception of self-motion during CW and ACW directions of virtual drum rotation at the end of the experiment.

2.3 Stimuli

The OKD for graphical display is built in Unreal Engine 4.8. The vertical stripe pattern in the VR display moves with six speeds in CW and ACW directions. The experiment runs on a computer with an Intel Core i7 processor,3.6GH, NVIDIA GeForce GTX980ti graphics card and 32 GB RAM.

2.4 Design

The experiment has six drum speed from slow to fast angular velocity in CW and ACW directions ($0°/s$, $5°/s$, $30°/s$, $70°/s$, $97°/s$, $110°/s$, $115°/s$, $0°/s$, $-5°/s$, $-30°/s$, $-70°/s$, $-97°/s$, $-110°/s$, $-115°/s$, $0°/s$) constituting 14 experimental conditions with 14 time intervals. Each time interval lapses for 16 s which is close to the mean vestibular adaptation time constant during perception of real rotation [53]. The total duration of the experiment is 240 s. The subjects go through a trial before the experiment to familiarise the participants with the VR environment. The angular velocities follow a fourth-order logistic function (Sigmoid function) to mimic the naturally occurring events as shown in Fig. 1a. The angular acceleration is shown in Fig. 1b.

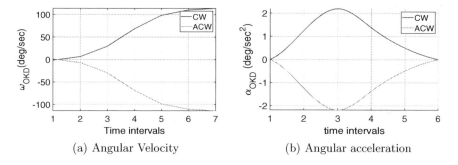

(a) Angular Velocity   (b) Angular acceleration

Fig. 1. Input angular velocity and acceleration from the OKD in VR fixed throughout the experiment

The authors define Vection Index (VI) as ratio of input angular velocity from virtual drum (ω_{OKD}) to angular velocity of HMD (ω_{HMD}) as shown in following equations.

$$VI_{x,y,z} = \frac{[\omega_{OKD}]_y}{[\omega_{HMD}]_{x,y,z}} \qquad (1)$$

$$VI = \sqrt{VI_x^2 + VI_y^2 + VI_z^2} \qquad (2)$$

2.5   Procedure

Participants are seated upright on a grounded wooden chair in a dark room with their feet on the ground and heads unconstrained. Once participants are seated, the display is adjusted with 'Guardian' in the oculus-VR headset to get it in front of them. The participants are positioned at the centre of the virtual OKD by the camera setting. Participants go through one practice trial to get comfortable with the VR headset, stimulus, and task. The experiment begins with OKD starting from zero angular velocity in CW and ACW directions. The experimental setup is shown in Fig. 2.

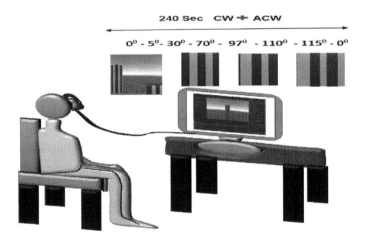

Fig. 2. Experimental set up showing various angular speeds of the virtual drum in both CW and ACW direction with head being unconstrained with body being grounded. The vertical stripes are for slow, medium and higher angular velocities.

3   Results

The vection strength is quantified from the angular displacement of HMD about X, Y, Z axes, which provides respective angular velocity and angular acceleration of HMD. The positional analysis is neglected as the stimulus here is rotational in nature. The t-test with 95% confidence intervals [27] is used to find the significant difference between different angular velocities.

3.1   Angular Displacement

The angular displacement of HMD for 16 s for a particular subject at each angular velocity of OKD is shown in Fig. 3. At zero angular velocity of OKD, the angular velocity of HMD has some flutters as the head can not be absolutely still. The head flutters get streamlined at lower speeds of OKD.

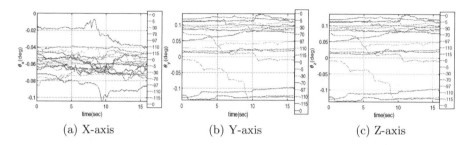

| (a) X-axis | (b) Y-axis | (c) Z-axis |

Fig. 3. Angular displacements($\theta_x, \theta_y, \theta_z$) of HMD for a typical sybject at various speed of OKD

The box plot of the angular displacements in Fig. 4 shows that the rotation of HMD about the y-axis follows a similar pattern of the inherent y-axis rotation of OKD. Also, the stimulus imparts rotation magnitude about other axes increase or decrease monotonously due to vection and weight of the HMD. There is a significant difference $p < 0.05$ between angular displacements at $70°$/s in CW and $97°$/s, $110°$/s in ACW than other angular velocities.

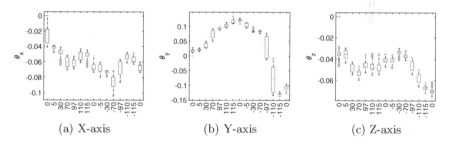

| (a) X-axis | (b) Y-axis | (c) Z-axis |

Fig. 4. Box-plot of angular displacement for a typical subject considering various speeds of OKD about a. X-axis, b. Y-axis, c. Z-axis

3.2   Angular Velocity and Acceleration

The angular velocity is obtained by differentiating angular displacement of HMD with respect to a time interval, which is shown in Fig. 5.a. The angular velocity of HMD increases as the speed of the virtual drum rises and decreases after reaching an optimal value in both CW and ACW directions of the drum about the y-axis of HMD than other axes. The peak value of the angular velocity of HMD about the y-axis occurs at 46 °/s in CW and 70 °/s in ACW direction.

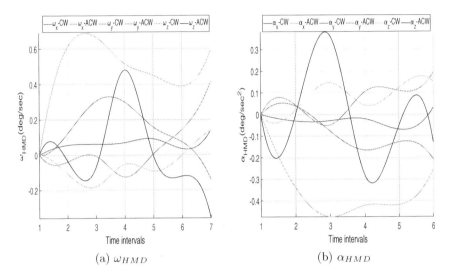

(a) ω_{HMD} (b) α_{HMD}

Fig. 5. a. Scaled median angular velocity (Scaling factor of 10^3) about X,Y,Z axes in both CW and ACW directions of HMD for all subjects b. Scaled median angular acceleration (scaling factor of 10^4) about X,Y,Z axes in both CW and ACW directions of HMD considering all subjects.

The angular acceleration is obtained by differentiating the angular velocity of HMD with respect to a time interval, which is shown in Fig. 5.b. The angular acceleration of HMD increases uniformly after 30 °/s of ω_{OKD} about the y-axis signifying that the vection happens after a speed of 30 °/s.

3.3   Vection Index

The intensity of HMD motion increases as the speed of OKD increases. However, the vection happens at the acceleration of the drum (maximum slope region of the sigmoid (Fig. 1). The vection index follows the sigmoidal input velocity pattern of OKD (Fig. 6b). At very low and high speeds, the participants do not show vection. The perception of self-motion has lower and upper bound from 30–97 °/s. However, the slope of the sigmoid for CW and ACW direction HMD is 0.5147 and 0.5138, respectively. This reflects in response from participants as most of the participants (47%) perceive vection in CW direction than in ACW direction as shown in Fig. 6c. This is the response for the sigmoidal input velocity of OKD, which is fixed throughout the experiments and has a slope of 0.5938 for both CW and ACW directions as shown in Fig. 1.

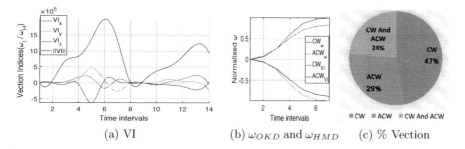

Fig. 6. a. Vection indices about x, y, z axes and magnitude of vection with a scaling factor of 0.001 for number of experimental conditions in x-axis, b. Normalised angular velocity of OKD and VI, c. Percentage of participants getting vection for different direction of motion pattern of OKD as in (b).

4   Discussion

4.1   Kinematic Analysis

The current paper has used the OKD to induce vection in an immersive VR environment and IMU readings from HMD as a method to quantify circular vection speed. However, the vection speed and strength is more complex since it involves multi-sensory inputs apart from visual input.

The kinematics of the HMD accurately depicts vection on the display's y-axis, and the impact may also be observed on other axes, albeit not as prominently as on the y-axis. The rate of change of angular velocity determines the vection strength, which is represented in the ω_y of HMD (CW_y, ACW_y) as in Fig. 5a, which mimics the angular acceleration of OKD (Fig. 1b). It may be due to the absence of vection at very low and high speeds of OKD and ω_y of HMD reaches a maximum magnitude close to maximum acceleration of OKD.

In contrast to the literature, which shows that vection is proportional to display speeds [41, 43, 47], the finding that the VI may have a derivative relationship with the motion of OKD is surprising. However, as evidenced by the current study, this is not always the case. Furthermore, greater speeds obscure peripheral vision, lowering vection since peripheral vision affects vection while central vision affects motion sickness, according to [61].

4.2   Vection Index

In both CW and ACW directions, VI is proportional to OKD speed. In Fig. 6b the current study reveals that the slope of the magnitude of the VI is smaller in the ACW direction than in the CW direction. As seen in Fig. 6a, the vection strength in the ACW compensates for the vection strength in the CW direction. This might be reversed if the OKD rotation starts with ACW and then CW. The study shows that the vection strength in ACW compensates for the vection strength in the CW direction as in. This could be reversed if rotaion of OKD starts with ACW followed by CW. The pi-chart in Fig. 6c indicates a similar finding, with 47% of participants perceiving vection during CW rotation than ACW rotation, as seen by the slope of normalized-VI magnitude, which is larger for CW rotation. In contrary to the literature, where the vection speed from turning knob is higher than the speed of OKD [37], the slope of normalized-VI is lower than the slope of the OKD. This might be due to the fact that the knob is operated by hand, and during vection, skin conductance activity is greater at the palm location, but during the evaluation of vection via an HMD, the visual information travels through a complicated neural pathway, dampening head motion.

Moreover, in this study, the authors found that vection may occur in axes other than the Y-axis, such as X and Z, which are not the axes of rotation of the OKD (Y-axis), and that the weight of the HMD is a major contributor. As a result, the authors assess vection magnitude in terms of VI, considering motion across all axes. There is compensatory activity taking place to eliminate vection between axes. For example, in CW, vection about the y-axis is more than vection about the x and z axes in the CW direction, whereas in ACW, vection about the y-axis is less than vection about the x and z axes in the ACW direction.

The current work is unique in that the data are taken directly from the HMD, which will aid in forecasting vection speed and likely occurrence time in a dynamic scenario in diverse media such as water [18] or space. In essence, the slope of the vection index on a normalised scale is equivalent to the slope of display speed. Other research investigations have shown the same thing, albeit with various stimuli and measurements: vection speed is similar to display speed. In dynamic situations, further study is needed to determine the transfer function between display and vection indices, as well as a mathematical model.

5   Conclusion

The current study proposes a simple method of measuring the vection without requiring additional hardware. It shows that mild head movements can be recorded from IMUs in most HMDs. The study finds that vection intensity depends on the specific range of visual display motion and slope of the motion. The head response because of vection is a differential operator on the display acceleration. The vection is relatively dependent of the axis of rotation of the visual field, and it has a cross balancing property about other axes of rotation of HMD. The study proposes a novel parameter Vection Index (VI) from which vection intensity can be found in the dynamic virtual environments. The link between VI and display speed has practical implications for applications such as all types of motion simulation in air, water, space. Several sensory cues such as audio, smell, and tactile input from the environment enhance the realism, hence play a role in affecting VI due to sensory mismatches in simulators [4,17,25,30,48,50,60]. The VI can better aid in calibrating display speeds to auditory and vestibular cueing speeds in motion simulators and games. The multi-sensory effects on vection can be filtered with help of VI and can help in enhancing the immersion.

In this study the subjects are seated with motion of head alone. The body movements during standing or walking while navigating VR might distort the VI and the accuracy of vection detection may be erroneous. Future study could involve subjects with unconstrained body movements.

References

1. Aitken, J.: 2. On a new variety of ocular spectrum. Proc. Royal Soc. Edinburgh **10**, 40–44 (1880)
2. Allison, R.S., Zacher, J.E., Kirollos, R., Guterman, P.S., Palmisano, S.: Perception of smooth and perturbed vection in short-duration microgravity. Exp. Brain Res. **223**(4), 479–487 (2012)
3. Aoki, M., Thilo, K.V., Burchill, P., Golding, J.F., Gresty, M.A.: Autonomic response to real versus illusory motion (vection). Clin. Auton. Res. **10**(1), 23–28 (2000)
4. Aykent, B., Merienne, F., Guillet, C., Paillot, D., Kemeny, A.: Motion sickness evaluation and comparison for a static driving simulator and a dynamic driving simulator. Proc. Inst. Mech. Eng. Part D J. Autom. Eng. **228**(7), 818–829 (2014)
5. Barnett-Cowan, M., Harris, L.: Perception of simultaneity and temporal order of active and passive head movements paired with visual, auditory and tactile stimuli. In: 9th International Multisensory Research Forum (IMRF 2008), p. 168 (2008)
6. Berntson, G.G., et al.: Heart rate variability: origins, methods, and interpretive caveats. Psychophysiology **34**(6), 623–648 (1997)
7. Bles, W.: Stepping around circular vection and coriolis effects. In: Attention and Performance IX, pp. 47–61 (1981)
8. Brandt, T., Dichgans, J., Koenig, E.: Differential effects of central versus peripheral vision on egocentric and exocentric motion perception. Exp. Brain Res. **16**(5), 476–491 (1973). https://doi.org/10.1007/BF00234474
9. Chelen, W., Kabrisky, M., Rogers, S.: Spectral analysis of the electroencephalographic response to motion sickness. Aviat. Space Environ. Med. **64**(1), 24–29 (1993)
10. Cheung, B., Hofer, K., Heskin, R., Smith, A.: Physiological and behavioral responses to an exposure of pitch illusion in the simulator. Aviat. Space Environ. Med. **75**(8), 657–665 (2004)
11. Cheung, B., Howard, I., Nedzelski, J., Landolt, J.: Circularvection about earth-horizontal axes in bilateral labyrinthine-defective subjects. Acta oto-laryngologica **108**(5–6), 336–344 (1989)
12. Dennison, M.S., Wisti, A.Z., D'Zmura, M.: Use of physiological signals to predict cybersickness. Displays **44**, 42–52 (2016)
13. Deutschländer, A., Bense, S., Stephan, T., Schwaiger, M., Dieterich, M., Brandt, T.: Rollvection versus linearvection: comparison of brain activations in pet. Human Brain Mapp. **21**(3), 143–153 (2004)
14. Dichgans, J., Brandt, T.: Visual-vestibular interaction: effects on self-motion perception and postural control. In: Held, R., Leibowitz, H.W., Teuber, H.L. (eds.) Perception, pp. 755–804. Springer, Heidelberg (1978). https://doi.org/10.1007/978-3-642-46354-9_25
15. Ebenholtz, S.M.: Motion sickness and oculomotor systems in virtual environments. Pres. Teleoper. Virtual Environ. **1**(3), 302–305 (1992)

16. Ebenholtz, S.M., Cohen, M.M., Linder, B.J.: The possible role of nystagmus in motion sickness: a hypothesis. Aviat. Space Environ. Med. **65**(11), 1032–1035 (1994)

17. Ehrlich, J.A., Kolasinski, E.M.: A comparison of sickness symptoms between dropout and finishing participants in virtual environment studies. In: Proceedings of the Human Factors and Ergonomics Society Annual Meeting, vol. 42, pp. 1466–1470. SAGE Publications, Los Angeles (1998)

18. Fauville, G., Queiroz, A., Woolsey, E.S., Kelly, J.W., Bailenson, J.N.: The effect of water immersion on vection in virtual reality. Sci. Rep. **11**(1), 1–13 (2021)

19. Fetter, M.: Vestibulo-ocular reflex. Neuro-Ophthalmol. **40**, 35–51 (2007)

20. Fischer, M., Kornmüller, A.: Optokinetisch ausgelöste bewegungswahrnehmungen und optokinetischer nystagmus [perception of motion based on the optokinetic sense and optokinetic nystagmus]. J. für Psychologie und Neurologie **41**, 273–308 (1930)

21. Guo, C., So, R.: Effects of foveal retinal slip on visually induced motion sickness: a pilot study. In: Proceedings of the Human Factors and Ergonomics Society Annual Meeting, vol. 56, pp. 2565–2569. SAGE Publications, Los Angeles (2012)

22. Himi, N., Koga, T., Nakamura, E., Kobashi, M., Yamane, M., Tsujioka, K.: Differences in autonomic responses between subjects with and without nausea while watching an irregularly oscillating video. Auton. Neurosci. **116**(1–2), 46–53 (2004)

23. Holmes, S.R., Griffin, M.J.: Correlation between heart rate and the severity of motion sickness caused by optokinetic stimulation. J. Psychophysiol. **15**(1), 35 (2001)

24. Hu, S., Grant, W.F., Stern, R.M., Koch, K.L.: Motion sickness severity and physiological correlates during repeated exposures to a rotating optokinetic drum. Aviat. Space Environ. Med. **62**, 308–314 (1991)

25. Jaekl, P., Jenkin, M., Harris, L.R.: Perceiving a stable world during active rotational and translational head movements. Exp. Brain Res. **163**(3), 388–399 (2005)

26. Jäger, M., Gruber, N., Müri, R., Mosimann, U.P., Nef, T.: Manipulations to reduce simulator-related transient adverse health effects during simulated driving. Med. Biol. Engi. Comput. **52**(7), 601–610 (2014)

27. Jarmasz, J., Hollands, J.G.: Confidence intervals in repeated-measures designs: the number of observations principle. Can. J. Exp. Psychol./Revue canadienne de psychologie expérimentale **63**(2), 124 (2009)

28. Ji, J.T., So, R.H., Cheung, R.T.: Isolating the effects of vection and optokinetic nystagmus on optokinetic rotation-induced motion sickness. Human Fact. **51**(5), 739–751 (2009)

29. Jongkees, L.: Physiologie und pathophysiologie des vestibularorganes. Archiv für klinische und experimentelle Ohren-, Nasen-und Kehlkopfheilkunde **194**(1), 1–110 (1969)

30. Kennedy, R.S., Stanney, K.M.: Postural instability induced by virtual reality exposure: development of a certification protocol. Int. J. Human-Comput. Interact. **8**(1), 25–47 (1996)

31. Keshavarz, B., Berti, S.: Integration of sensory information precedes the sensation of vection: a combined behavioral and event-related brain potential (erp) study. Behav. Brain Res. **259**, 131–136 (2014)

32. Keshavarz, B., Campos, J.L., Berti, S.: Vection lies in the brain of the beholder: EEG parameters as an objective measurement of vection. Front. Psychol. **6**, 1581 (2015)

33. Keshavarz, B., Hettinger, L.J., Vena, D., Campos, J.L.: Combined effects of auditory and visual cues on the perception of vection. Exp. Brain Res. **232**(3), 827–836 (2013). https://doi.org/10.1007/s00221-013-3793-9
34. Kim, J., Palmisano, S.: Eccentric gaze dynamics enhance vection in depth. J. Vision **10**(12), 7 (2010)
35. Kim, Y.Y., Kim, H.J., Kim, E.N., Ko, H.D., Kim, H.T.: Characteristic changes in the physiological components of cybersickness. Psychophysiology **42**(5), 616–625 (2005)
36. Kirollos, R., Allison, R.S., Palmisano, S.: Cortical correlates of the simulated viewpoint oscillation advantage for vection. Multisensory Res. **30**(7–8), 739–761 (2017)
37. Kirollos, R., Herdman, C.M.: Measuring circular vection speed in a virtual reality headset. Displays **69**, 102049 (2021)
38. Koohestani, A., et al.: A knowledge discovery in motion sickness: a comprehensive literature review. IEEE Access **7**, 85755–85770 (2019)
39. Kothgassner, O.D.: Salivary cortisol and cardiovascular reactivity to a public speaking task in a virtual and real-life environment. Comput. Human Behav. **62**, 124–135 (2016)
40. LaViola Jr., J.J.: A discussion of cybersickness in virtual environments. ACM Sigchi Bull. **32**(1), 47–56 (2000)
41. Melcher, G.A., Henn, V.: The latency of circular vection during different accelerations of the optokinetic stimulus. Percept. Psychophys. **30**(6), 552–556 (1981)
42. Nilsson, N.C., Nordahl, R., Sikström, E., Turchet, L., Serafin, S.: Haptically induced illusory self-motion and the influence of context of motion. In: Isokoski, P., Springare, J. (eds.) EuroHaptics 2012. LNCS, vol. 7282, pp. 349–360. Springer, Heidelberg (2012). https://doi.org/10.1007/978-3-642-31401-8_32
43. Owens, D.A., Gu, J., McNally, R.D.: Perception of the speed of self-motion vs. object-motion: another example of two modes of vision? Conscious. Cogn. **64**, 61–71 (2018)
44. Palmisano, S., Allison, R.S., Schira, M.M., Barry, R.J.: Future challenges for vection research: definitions, functional significance, measures, and neural bases. Front. Psychol. **6**, 193 (2015)
45. Palmisano, S., Barry, R.J., De Blasio, F.M., Fogarty, J.S.: Identifying objective EEG based markers of linear vection in depth. Front. Psychol. **7**, 1205 (2016)
46. Palmisano, S., Burke, D., Allison, R.S.: Coherent perspective jitter induces visual illusions of self-motion. Perception **32**(1), 97–110 (2003)
47. Palmisano, S., Gillam, B.: Stimulus eccentricity and spatial frequency interact to determine circular vection. Perception **27**(9), 1067–1077 (1998)
48. Reason, J.T.: Motion sickness adaptation: a neural mismatch model. J. Royal Soc. Med. **71**(11), 819–829 (1978)
49. Reason, J.T., Brand, J.J.: Motion Sickness. Academic press, Cambridge (1975)
50. Rebenitsch, L., Owen, C.: Review on cybersickness in applications and visual displays. Virtual Reality **20**(2), 101–125 (2016). https://doi.org/10.1007/s10055-016-0285-9
51. Riccio, G.E., Stoffregen, T.A.: An ecological theory of motion sickness and postural instability. Ecol. Psychol. **3**(3), 195–240 (1991)
52. Riecke, B.E., Feuereissen, D., Rieser, J.J., McNamara, T.P.: Spatialized sound enhances biomechanically-induced self-motion illusion (vection). In: Proceedings of the SIGCHI Conference on Human Factors in Computing Systems, pp. 2799–2802 (2011)
53. St George, R.J., Day, B.L., Fitzpatrick, R.C.: Adaptation of vestibular signals for self-motion perception. J. Physiol. **589**(4), 843–853 (2011)

54. Stephan, T.: Functional MRI of galvanic vestibular stimulation with alternating currents at different frequencies. Neuroimage **26**(3), 721–732 (2005)
55. Stern, R., Koch, K., Leibowitz, H., Lindblad, I., Shupert, C., Stewart, W.: Tachygastria and motion sickness. Aviat. Space Environ. Med. **56**(11), 1074–1077 (1985)
56. Stern, R.M., Koch, K.L., Stewart, W.R., Lindblad, I.M.: Spectral analysis of tachygastria recorded during motion sickness. Gastroenterology **92**(1), 92–97 (1987)
57. Strychacz, C., Viirre, E., Wing, S.: The use of EEG to measure cerebral changes during computer-based motion-sickness-inducing tasks. In: Biomonitoring for Physiological and Cognitive Performance during Military Operations, vol. 5797, pp. 139–148. International Society for Optics and Photonics (2005)
58. Tokumaru, O., Kaida, K., Ashida, H., Yoneda, I., Tatsuno, J.: EEG topographical analysis of spatial disorientation. Aviat. Space Environ. Medicine **70**(3 Pt 1), 256–263 (1999)
59. Wan, H., Hu, S., Wang, J.: Correlation of phasic and tonic skin-conductance responses with severity of motion sickness induced by viewing an optokinetic rotating drum. Percept. Motor Skills **97**(3_suppl), 1051–1057 (2003)
60. Watson, G.: A synthesis of simulator sickness studies conducted in a high-fidelity driving simulator. In: Proceedings of Driving Simulation Conference, pp. 69–78 (2000)
61. Webb, N.A., Griffin, M.J.: Optokinetic stimuli: motion sickness, visual acuity and eye movements. Aviat. Space Environ. Med. **73**(4), 351–358 (2002)
62. Wibirama, S., Hamamoto, K.: Investigation of visually induced motion sickness in dynamic 3d contents based on subjective judgment, heart rate variability, and depth gaze behavior. In: 2014 36th Annual International Conference of the IEEE Engineering in Medicine and Biology Society, pp. 4803–4806. IEEE (2014)
63. Wiest, G., Amorim, M.A., Mayer, D., Schick, S., Deecke, L., Lang, W.: Cortical responses to object-motion and visually-induced self-motion perception. Cogn. Brain Res. **12**(1), 167–170 (2001)
64. Wright, W., DiZio, P., Lackner, J.: Vertical linear self-motion perception during visual and inertial motion: more than weighted summation of sensory inputs. J. Vestib. Res. **15**(4), 185–195 (2005)
65. Wu, J.P.: EEG changes in man during motion sickness induced by parallel swing. Space Med. Med. Eng. **5**(3), 200–205 (1992)
66. Yang, X., Wang, D., Hu, H., Yue, K.: P-31: visual fatigue assessment and modeling based on ECG and EOG caused by 2D and 3D displays. In: SID Symposium Digest of Technical Papers, vol. 47, pp. 1237–1240. Wiley Online Library (2016)
67. Yang, J., Guo, C., So, R., Cheung, R.: Effects of eye fixation on visually induced motion sickness: are they caused by changes in retinal slip velocity? In: Proceedings of the Human Factors and Ergonomics Society Annual Meeting. vol. 55, pp. 1220–1224. SAGE Publications Sage CA, Los Angeles (2011)

Are You There? A Study on Measuring Presence in Immersive Virtual Reality

Reiya Tamaki[✉] and Tatsuo Nakajima

Department of Computer Science and Engineering, Waseda University,
Tokyo, Japan
{t-reiya, tatsuo}@dcl.cs.waseda.ac.jp

Abstract. With the recent development of virtual reality (VR) technologies, we can create a virtual environment that exceeds the constraints of the real environment. A concept called "presence" is one of the most important elements of a VR experience. To provide more interesting VR experiences, we need to measure how much the users feel their presence in the VR experiences is important. However, when we measure this presence by a questionnaire inside or outside the VR, the subjects' sense of presence in virtual reality environments is disrupted by the transition from the VR experience to the questionnaire. Therefore, in this study, we propose a method to integrate questionnaires into VR experiences. We conduct two comparative experiments between the proposed method and the existing method to validate the effectiveness of our proposed method. From the results of the two experiments, although we cannot determine the optimal design for the proposed method and cannot say our proposed method can measure presence more accurately, we confirmed the partial effectiveness of the proposed method.

Keywords: Virtual reality · Presence · Questionnaire · Person perspective

1 Introduction

With the recent development of virtual reality (VR) technologies, many VR applications and VR games have been developed [3, 9, 14, 20]. By using VR technologies, it is possible to create a virtual environment that exceeds the constraints of the real environment, and such virtual environments can provide experiences and enjoyment that cannot be realized by the constraints of the real environment [18]. In particular, games that produce the feeling of "being there" in an artificial world are expected to be highly entertaining [27].

One of the most important elements of a VR experience is a concept called "presence" [5, 8]. Presence is commonly defined as "the subjective feeling of being there" [26] or "the perceptual illusion of nonmediation" [13]. While playing VR games, gamers are likely to encounter various types of unexpected impediments. These distractions are known to degrade the feeling of presence experienced by gamers.

The concept of a break in presence (BIP) is also an important element of a VR experience [24]. A BIP occurs when participants who enjoy VR experiences become

© The Author(s), under exclusive license to Springer Nature Switzerland AG 2022
J. Y. C. Chen and G. Fragomeni (Eds.): HCII 2022, LNCS 13317, pp. 275–288, 2022.
https://doi.org/10.1007/978-3-031-05939-1_18

aware of the real-world setting when realizing experiences, and their sense of presence in virtual reality environments is disrupted [2, 19].

If a BIP occurs during a user questionnaire of a VR experience, the VR experience before conducting the questionnaire becomes a discontinuous experience and may adversely affect the questionnaire results [17]. Therefore, in recent studies, some methods have been proposed to conduct a questionnaire in VR environments to suppress the BIP by eliminating the transition between the virtual environment and the real environment [11, 16, 22, 23]. However, even with these methods, the BIP that occurs when transitioning from a VR experience to a questionnaire has not been suppressed [17].

This paper proposes a method to integrate questionnaires into VR experiences and shows a practical example using this method by comparing first-person shooting (FPS) and third-person shooting (TPS) as the VR experiences. We conduct two comparative experiments to validate the effectiveness of our proposed method and its practical application. From the results of these two experiments, we confirm the partial effectiveness of the proposed method, but we cannot say our proposed method can measure presence more accurately, and we cannot determine the optimal design for the proposed method. We believe that further research will help us establish a more accurate method for measuring presence.

2 Related Work

Several methods for measuring presence have been proposed. The simplest and most common method is measurement via a questionnaire [12]. Popular questionnaires used for measuring presence include the Presence Questionnaire [26], the Slater-Usoh-Steed Questionnaire [25], and the Igroup Presence Questionnaire (IPQ) [21]. These questionnaires are mainly conducted on paper media or on a PC. Therefore, when measuring presence in a VR experience, the VR device for displaying a virtual environment, which is a head-mounted display (HMD), is removed to answer the questionnaires [10]. When participants return to the real environment to answer questionnaires, a BIP occurs. Due to the occurrence of the BIP, the VR experience up to that point becomes a discontinuous experience. Therefore, a user has to answer the questionnaire by recollecting his or her experiences, which may adversely affect the results.

Therefore, in recent research, as in Schwind et al., a method of conducting a questionnaire inside VR just after experiencing a VR application has been adopted [11, 16, 22, 23]. According to the results of Schwind et al., there were no significant differences between the results of the questionnaire conducted inside VR and the questionnaire conducted outside VR. However, it was concluded that the variance of the results is significantly lower in the questionnaire conducted inside VR; thus, reliable and consistent results can be obtained. However, Putze et al. argued that a questionnaire conducted inside VR can suppress the generated BIP more than a questionnaire conducted outside VR, but BIPs still occur during the transition to the questionnaire [17]. In terms of measurement methods other than a questionnaire, there are also methods for measuring and analyzing heart rate, galvanic skin reaction and physiological data of human beings to measure presence. Since presence can be measured at the same time with the VR experience, Skarbez et al. stated that these methods are the most objective [24]. However, there are many restrictions, such as preparing the measuring equipment.

On the other hand, Frommel et al. proposed a method to integrate a questionnaire into a game, thereby conducting the questionnaire while maintaining the game experience, and showed that the approach was significantly more enjoyable for the game experience [7]. By unifying the game environment and the questionnaire environment, it is possible to conduct a questionnaire while maintaining the game experience. However, the integration of the game content and the questionnaire needs to be solved individually for each game's content, and there are still many restrictions, such as the integration itself, which may be difficult depending on each game's content.

3   First Experiment

In our first experiment, we investigated a method that can maintain presence and proposed the method for integrating a questionnaire into a VR experience. To integrate a questionnaire into a VR experience, we created an FPS game, in which drones are shot with a pistol, by using Unity3D, and we used Oculus Quest2 as the HMD to present the VR game.

In this study, we used a questionnaire created in Japanese based on the IPQ [21] to measure presence during a VR experience. In the IPQ, each question item is answered using a 7-point Likert scale, and there are four subscales: general presence, spatial presence, involvement, and realism. The reason for adopting the IPQ is that Schwind et al. compared the Presence Questionnaire [26], the Slater-Usoh-Steed Questionnaire [25], and IPQ inside and outside a VR environment and recommended the IPQ as the best questionnaire for measuring presence [22].

3.1   Game Design

In the FPS game used in the first experiment, a calculation formula using four arithmetic operations is displayed at the top of the screen. The player calculates and answers them by shooting down as many drones as the answer. Regardless of whether the answer is correct or incorrect, another formula will be displayed after answering. The answer was set to be an integer between 0 and 6 because we used a 7-point Likert scale questionnaire. The left picture of Fig. 1 shows the VR game view.

3.2   Questionnaire Design

In the proposed method, we assigned the questionnaire text to the calculation formula and the Likert scale to the number of drones. The proposed method can match the flow of the game, which is to read and calculate a formula and shoot down the drones, as well as the flow of the questionnaire, which is to read and answer a questionnaire and shoot down the drones. Therefore, we were able to maintain the consistency of the control and presentational data, as shown by Frommel. The middle picture of Fig. 1 shows the proposed method for answering a questionnaire.

To have a contrast, we used the VR Questionnaire Toolkit[1] (VRQT) created by
Feick et al. [6] as the existing method for establishing questionnaires inside VR.
Since VRQT is implemented based on the research by Alexandrovsky et al. [1], it is
useful for the questionnaire design of the existing method. The right picture of Fig. 1
shows this method being used in the actual VR space. In Fig. 1, the screenshots present
the questionnaire in English, but the experiment conducted in this study used Japanese
in the actual questionnaire.

Fig. 1. Screenshots of the actual VR spaces in the first experiment

3.3   Experimental Conditions

Participants. There were 12 subjects (10 males, 2 females) in our first experiment.
The age of the subjects ranged from 21 to 28 (M = 23.9, SD = 1.84), and all of them
were university students. The subjects answered each of the displayed questions using
our proposed method and the existing method in random order to eliminate the order
effect.

Analysis. We performed the Wilcoxon signed-rank test, which is a nonparametric test,
using the mean value of the total IPQ score and each subscale score in the IPQ obtained
from each subject. The reasons regarding why we selected this test are as follows. The
number of subjects was small, and the results from the Shapiro–Wilk test, which is a
test of normality, showed that there was no normality in some scores.

3.4   Results and Discussion of the First Experiment

Figure 2 shows the mean values of each IPQ subscale (general presence, spatial
presence, involvement, and realism) and the total IPQ scores measured by the proposed
method and existing method. From the results of the Wilcoxon signed-rank test, there
was a significant difference in the mean values of the total IPQ scores ($p < 0.01$,
$r = 0.86$), in the mean values of the spatial presence ($p < 0.01$, $r = 0.83$), and in the
mean values of the involvement ($p < 0.01$, $r = 0.88$). The results of the Wilcoxon
signed-rank test are also shown in Fig. 2.

The result from each IPQ score shows that the questionnaire of the proposed
method was able to measure presence while maintaining it. However, some opinions

---

[1] https://github.com/MartinFk/VRQuestionnaireToolkit.

obtained from the subjects, such as "the existing method was easy to answer because it was the same as a usual questionnaire" and "I felt I wanted to shoot down the drones a lot because of the count-up method" in the proposed method, indicate some problems in the method of answering the questionnaire. Therefore, as described below, we modified our proposed method to make it easier to answer the questionnaire, and we conducted a second experiment.

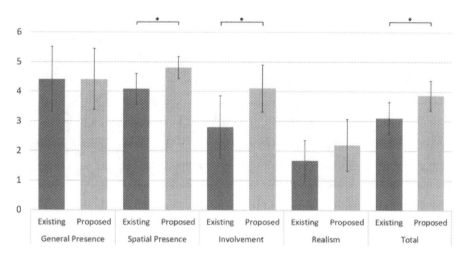

Fig. 2. Results of the IPQ score measured in the first experiment. The statistical significances evaluated by Wilcoxon signed-rank test are marked with stars ($* = p < 0.01$)

4 Second Experiment

There are two purposes of the second experiment. The first is to validate the effectiveness of the modified method. The second is to compare the first-person perspective and third-person perspective in a VR experiment as a practical example of using the proposed method. For the first-person perspective, we used the FPS game as in the first experiment, whereas we developed a new TPS game for the third-person perspective. In the second experiment, there are two independent variables, *Person Perspective* and *Methodology*. Therefore, the subjects experienced all four conditions: FPS and Proposed Method (FP condition), FPS and Existing Method (FE), TPS and Proposed Method (TP), TPS and Existing Method (TE).

4.1 Game Design

In the second experiment, subjects performed the same task as in the first experiment. However, the answer method for the task question in the second experiment was changed from shooting down the number of drones to hitting a balloon with number. This change aimed to make it easier to answer the Likert scale questionnaire. The balloons have an integer between 0 and 6 and float around the user. The number of balloons hit by the user is used as the user's answer to the task or questionnaire. The position of the balloons is randomized for each task or question to prompt the user to look around in the VR space.

In TPS, the character in front of the user holds a pistol, and the user can aim at the balloons by changing the direction of the character or moving the character with controllers.

The left picture of Fig. 3 shows a task in the FPS game, and the right picture shows a task in the TPS game.

Fig. 3. Screenshots of the actual VR spaces in the task of the second experiment

4.2   Questionnaire Design

In the proposed method, the answering method for the questionnaire was changed in accordance to the change of the answering method in the task. Subjects selected the number for the questionnaire directly instead of by the count-up method (i.e. by shooting down drones, as in the first experiment). In addition, the proposed method is designed to be performed using the first-person perspective in the FPS task and the third-person perspective in the TPS task.

On the other hand, in the existing method, we used VRQT as in the first experiment. However, the existing method was designed to be performed in the first-person perspective regardless of whether it appeared in the FPS game or TPS game.

The left picture of Fig. 4 shows usage of the proposed method in the FPS game, the middle picture of Fig. 4 shows usage of the proposed method in the TPS game, and the right picture of Fig. 4 shows usage of the existing method. In Fig. 4, the screenshots present questionnaire in English, but the experiment conducted in this study used Japanese in the actual questionnaire.

Fig. 4. Screenshots of the actual VR spaces in the questionnaire of the second experiment

4.3   Experimental Conditions

Participants. There were 12 subjects (11 males and 1 female) in our study. The age of the participants ranged from 21 to 29 (M = 23.8, SD = 2.36), and all of them were university students. Among the subjects, 5 had extensive VR experience, 7 had some VR experience, and no subject had no VR experience.

Experimental Procedure. In this study, each subject experienced the FP, FE, TP, and TE conditions and answered a question regarding the method in each condition. At this time, to eliminate the order effect between each condition, the order of experiencing the four conditions was randomly determined for each subject by using a Latin square design.

As shown in Fig. 5, our study flow consisted of the following seven states: 1. Explanation: We explained the contents and the flow of the experiment to the subjects in writing and verbally. 2. Training: We explained how to play the FPS and TPS games, and we trained the subjects on each operation until they displayed competency with the controls of the game. 3–6. Questionnaire condition: The subjects played the game and answered the IPQ in each method. 7. Conclusive questionnaire: The subjects answered the conclusive questionnaire on a PC after all VR experiences. In the conclusive questionnaire, we asked about the operability and gameplay in FPS and TPS and the ease of answering the questionnaire of the proposed method (FPS), proposed method (TPS) and existing method with a 7-point Likert scale.

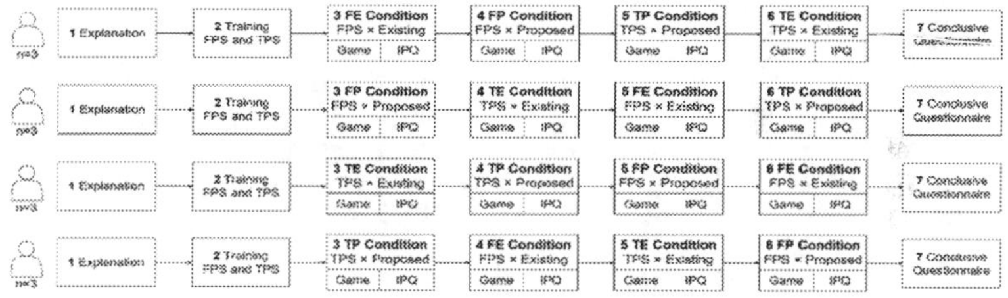

Fig. 5. Flowchart of the study procedure with four different orders of each condition

Analysis Details. We performed two-factor repeated-measures ANOVA for the mean values of the total IPQ score and each subscale score in the IPQ obtained from each subject in the four conditions. There were two independent variables: *Person Perspective* and *Methodology*. In addition, we performed pairwise t tests with Bonferroni corrections as post hoc tests when significant effects were found.

We performed the Wilcoxon signed-rank test, which is a nonparametric test, using the mean values of the operability and gameplay in the conclusive questionnaire. We selected the test because the number of subjects was small, and the results from the Shapiro–Wilk test, which is a test of normality, showed that there was no normality in some scores. In addition, we performed the Kruskal–Wallis test, which is a nonparametric repeated-measures ANOVA, using the mean values of the ease of answering questionnaire in the conclusive questionnaire. We performed the Durbin-Conover test as a post hoc test when significant effects were found.

5   Results

5.1   The Results of the Questionnaire Inside the VR in Each Condition

Figure 6 shows the mean values of each IPQ subscale (general presence, spatial presence, involvement, and realism) and the mean values of total IPQ scores measured in four conditions. From the results of the two-factor repeated-measures ANOVA, we found a significant effect of *Person Perspective* on the mean values of the total IPQ scores ($F = 27.12$, $p < 0.001$, $\eta^2 = 0.71$). Additionally, there was also a significant effect of *Person Perspective* on the mean values of the General Presence, Spatial Presence, and Realism subscales of the IPQ ($F = 23.93$, $p < 0.001$, $\eta^2 = 0.69$, $F = 52.06$, $p < 0.001$, $\eta^2 = 0.83$ and $F = 5.86$, $p < 0.05$, $\eta^2 = 0.35$). However, there were no significant effects of *Methodology* in any results. The results of the pairwise t test are also shown in Fig. 6.

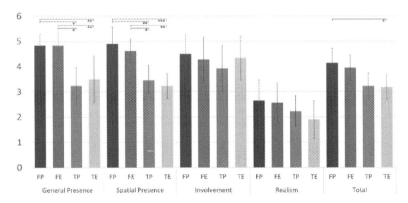

Fig. 6. Results of the IPQ score measured in the experiment. The statistical significances evaluated by pairwise t test are marked with stars ($*** = p < 0.001$, $** = p < 0.01$, $* = p < 0.05$)

5.2   The Results of the Conclusive Questionnaire After Each VR Experience and the Whole VR Experience

Table 1 shows the results of the operability and gameplay in the conclusive questionnaire, and Table 2 shows the results of the ease of answering questionnaire in the conclusive questionnaire. From the results of the Wilcoxon signed-rank test, there was a significant difference in the mean values of operability ($p < 0.01$, $r = 0.88$) and in the mean values of gameplay ($p < 0.01$, $r = 0.76$). From the results of the Kruskal–Wallis test and Durbin-Conover test, there was a significant difference between the proposed method (FPS) and the proposed method (TPS) ($p < 0.05$, $r = 0.61$) and the proposed method (TPS) and the existing method. However, there was no significant difference between the proposed method (FPS) and the existing method ($p < 0.01$, $r = 0.72$). Table 3 shows the results of the mean values of the time from starting the task to completing the questionnaire in each condition.

Table 1. Results of the operability and gameplay in the conclusive questionnaire

Questionnaire items	FPS	TPS
Operability	5.42	1.83
Gameplay	5.17	3.00

Table 2. Result of the ease of answering questionnaire in the conclusive questionnaire

Questionnaire item	Proposed method		Existing method
	FPS	TPS	
Ease of questionnaire	4.08	1.58	4.50

Table 3. The mean values of the time from starting task to completing the questionnaire

	FP	FE	TP	TE
Time [s]	248	228	358	268

6   Discussion

6.1   The Measured Presence During VR Experiences

Comparison of the Proposed Method and Existing Methods. The result from each IPQ score shows that there are no significant effects of *Methodology* in any of the conditions, unlike the results of the first experiment. In other words, we could not find any significant difference in the presence measured by the proposed method and the existing method in the second experiment. We will discuss the reasons for the different results from the first experiment below.

We think the reason is the change in the answer method for the questionnaire. As mentioned in the subjects' opinion in the first experiment, our initial proposed method has a count-up method, and subjects feel that they wanted to shoot down more drones than their answer number. However, subjects select their answer directly by our proposed method in the second experiment, so there is no possibility of selecting a balloon with a higher value than the intended answer. Considering these factors, if we make the consistency of the game experience and the questionnaire be tighter as in the first experiment, the results of the questionnaire may include positive bias by subjects. Alternatively, if we consider the ease of answering the questionnaire too much, as in the second experiment, there is dissociation between the game experience and the questionnaire, and a BIP may occur in the transition from the game experience to the questionnaire.

Comparison of First-Person Perspective and Third-Person Perspective. The result from each IPQ score shows that there are significant effects of *Person Perspective* on the total IPQ score and the subscales of the IPQ, General Presence, Spatial Presence and Realism. In addition, the results from the pairwise t test show that there are significant differences between FP and TE in the total IPQ score and between FP and TE, FP and TP, FE and TP, and FE and TE in the general presence and spatial presence scores.

These results suggest that subjects feel higher presence in the first-person perspective for VR shooting games. This supports the results of Denisova et al. [4], who compare the immersion between the first-person perspective and third-person perspective on a desktop, and the results of Diego et al. [15], who compare the presence between the first-person perspective and third-person perspective in a VR racing game.

Considering that presence is important for having more interesting VR experiences, we should avoid third person shooting game if we create third-person perspective game in VR.

6.2   Subjects' Opinions from the Conclusive Questionnaire

The result from the conclusive questionnaire shows that the FPS is significantly easier to control and better to play than the TPS. Some opinions obtained from subjects include "I was able to operate FPS intuitively", "TPS was slower than I expected", and "I felt cybersickness in the TPS". In terms of the slowness of movement in the TPS, we intentionally created the slowness to reduce cybersickness. However, this slowness was interfering with the gameplay. In addition, the result of feeling cybersickness was contrary to the result of Diego et al. [15], which they found the third-person perspective provides less cybersickness than the first-person perspective. We thought the reason for this result was due to the difference of game genres. Considering the loss of presence due to feeling cybersickness, it is necessary to adopt a game genre that causes less cybersickness when using the third-person perspective.

Additionally, the result from the conclusive questionnaire shows that the proposed method (TPS) is significantly more difficult to answer based on the questionnaire compared to the proposed method (FPS) and the existing method. In terms of the time that passes from starting the task to completing the questionnaire, TP to TE equaled a time ration of 1.34:1.00. From these results, we conclude that our proposed method may not be effective for a game with poor operability, such as TPS, in the second experiment. However, there was no significant difference between the proposed method (FPS) and the existing method. In addition, FP to FE equaled a time ration of 1.09:1.00. These results suggest that the proposed method (FPS) in the second experiment was able to provide a similar ease to the existing method for answering the questionnaire. However, considering that there was no significant difference in the measured presence, there is a trade-off between the ease of answering the questionnaire and the consistency of the game experience and the questionnaire flow. We need to research the optimal design for the proposed method in future work.

6.3   Limitations and Future Work

Optimal Design for the Integrated Questionnaire Inside the VR. As mentioned above, we could not determine the design in which the proposed method can be used most effectively. If we make consistency of the game experience and the questionnaire be tighter as in the first experiment, the proposed method may give a positive bias to the questionnaire or bother users while answering the questionnaire. However, if we consider the ease of answering the questionnaire too much, the consistency of the game experience and the questionnaire flow will not match, and a BIP may occur between the game experience and the integrated questionnaire in the proposed method. Therefore, as future research, we should investigate how far we should keep the consistency of the game experience and the questionnaire flow and how close we should match the ease of answering questionnaire to the existing method.

Mapping the Questionnaire to the VR Experience. First, as Frommel et al. argued [7], when we want to integrate the questionnaire into the VR experience, we still need to resolve how to map the questionnaire for each piece of content of the VR experience. In this study, we used a shooting game for the VR experience, so it was easy to create the questionnaire design with the same flow as the game. In addition, it was easy to integrate the Likert scale into the questionnaire because it was scaled by integers. However, most FPS and TPS games are interpersonal games called person versus person games, with many uncertainties, such as what actions the enemy player will take. Therefore, not all FPS games can be mapped as in this study. Additionally, for VR games and VR experiences other than the FPS and TPS, we need to consider a completely different mapping method. Similarly, there is still the issue of how to map questionnaires not answered by Likert scale.

7   Conclusion

In the development of VR applications and for providing more interesting VR experiences, it is very important to investigate whether users feel a higher presence for the created virtual environment. Currently, questionnaires are the main method used to measure this presence, but there is a dissociation between VR experiences and questionnaires in the existing method, so the sense of presence is already impaired when the users answer. Therefore, in this study, we proposed a method to measure presence in the VR experience by integrating the questionnaire into the VR experience.

To verify the effectiveness of the proposed method, we conducted the first experiment between the existing method and the proposed method. We used the VRQT as the existing method, which was implemented by Feick et al. [6] based on the optimal design for questionnaires inside the VR, as surveyed by Alexandrovsky et al. [1] In addition, we used the IPQ created by Schubert et al. [21] as the questionnaire to measure a presence. The results of comparing the existing method and the proposed method show that the presence measured in the proposed method is significantly higher than the presence measured in the existing method. Therefore, the proposed method can measure the presence felt during the VR experience more accurately without losing it. However, there are some problems: The time for answering the questionnaire by our proposed method is longer than that of the existing method, and the operability of the proposed method is worse; for example, subjects cannot select their answer directly because the proposed method uses the count-up method, and subjects want to shoot down more drones than their answer values. Therefore, after the first experiment, we changed the answer method of the proposed method to make it easier way to answer the questionnaire. We compared the FPS game and the TPS game in VR by using this revised method.

The results from the second experiment show that the presence measured from the first-person perspective is significantly higher than that from the third-person perspective. This supports the results shown in previous studies [4, 15]. However, unlike the results of the previous study [15], we found that subjects feel more cybersickness in the third-person perspective. These results suggest that it is necessary to adopt a game genre that does not cause cybersickness when we create a third-person perspective game in VR. On the other hand, unlike the first experiment, there are no significant differences between the presence measured by the proposed method and by the existing method. We think the reason is the answering method for the questionnaire. If we make the consistency of the game experience and the questionnaire be tighter as in the first experiment, the results of the questionnaire may include positive bias by subjects. Alternatively, if we consider the ease of answering the questionnaire too much as in the second experiment, there is dissociation between the game experience and the questionnaire, and a BIP may occur in the transition from the game experience to the questionnaire.

We believe that further research will enable us to make more accurate measurements in the future.

References

1. Alexandrovsky, D., et al.: Examining design choices of questionnaires in VR user studies. In: Proceedings of the 2020 CHI Conference on Human Factors in Computing Systems, pp. 1–21 (2020)
2. Brogni, A., Slater, M., Steed, A.: More breaks less presence. In: Presence 2003: The 6th Annual International Workshop on Presence, pp. 1–4 (2003)
3. Cipresso, P., Giglioli, I.A.C., Raya, M.A., Riva, G.: The past, present, and future of virtual and augmented reality research: A network and cluster analysis of the literature. Front. Psychol. **9**, 2086 (2018)
4. Denisova, A., Cairns, P.: First person vs. third person perspective in digital games: do player preferences affect immersion? In: Proceedings of the 33rd Annual ACM Conference on Human Factors in Computing Systems, pp. 145–148 (2015)
5. Dinh, H.Q., Walker, N., Hodges, L.F., Song, C., Kobayashi, A.: Evaluating the importance of multi-sensory input on memory and the sense of presence in virtual environments. In: Proceedings IEEE Virtual Reality (Cat. No. 99CB36316), pp. 222–228. IEEE (1999)

6. Feick, M., Kleer, N., Tang, A., Krüger, A.: The virtual reality questionnaire toolkit. In: Adjunct Publication of the 33rd Annual ACM Symposium on User Interface Software and Technology, pp. 68–69 (2020)
7. Frommel, J., et al.: Integrated questionnaires: maintaining presence in game environments for self-reported data acquisition. In: Proceedings of the 2015 Annual Symposium on Computer-Human Interaction in Play, pp. 359–368 (2015)
8. Hodges, L.F., et al.: Presence as the defining factor in a VR application. Technical report, Georgia Institute of Technology (1994)
9. Jensen, L., Konradsen, F.: A review of the use of virtual reality head-mounted displays in education and training. Educ. Inf. Technol. 23(4), 1515–1529 (2017). https://doi.org/10.1007/s10639-017-9676-0
10. Jerald, J.: The VR Book: Human-Centered Design for Virtual Reality. Morgan & Claypool, San Rafael (2015)
11. Kang, H., Lee, G., Kwon, S., Kwon, O., Kim, S., Han, J.: Flotation simulation in a cable-driven virtual environment–a study with parasailing. In: Proceedings of the 2018 CHI Conference on Human Factors in Computing Systems, pp. 1–11 (2018)
12. Lazar, J., Feng, J.H., Hochheiser, H.: Research methods in human-computer interaction. Morgan Kaufmann, Burlington (2017)
13. Lombard, M., Ditton, T.: At the heart of it all: The concept of presence. J. Comput. Med. Commun. 3(2), 321 (1997)
14. Mohamudally, N.: State of the Art Virtual Reality and Augmented Reality Knowhow. BoD–Books on Demand (2018)
15. Monteiro, D., Liang, H.N., Abel, A., Bahaei, N., de Cassia Monteiro, R.: Evaluating engagement of virtual reality games based on first and third person perspective using EEG and subjective metrics. In: 2018 IEEE International Conference on Artificial Intelligence and Virtual Reality (AIVR), pp. 53–60. IEEE (2018)
16. Oberdörfer, S., Heidrich, D., Latoschik, M.E.: Usability of Gamified knowledge learning in VR and desktop-3D. In: Proceedings of the 2019 CHI Conference on Human Factors in Computing Systems, pp. 1–13 (2019)
17. Putze, S., Alexandrovsky, D., Putze, F., Höffner, S., Smeddinck, J.D., Malaka, R.: Breaking the experience: Effects of questionnaires in VR user studies. In: Proceedings of the 2020 CHI Conference on Human Factors in Computing Systems, pp. 1–15 (2020)
18. Razzaque, S., Kohn, Z., Whitton, M.C.: Redirected walking. Citeseer (2005)
19. Scherer, K.R., Ellgring, H.: Are facial expressions of emotion produced by categorical affect programs or dynamically driven by appraisal? Emotion 7(1), 113 (2007)
20. Schiza, E., Matsangidou, M., Neokleous, K., Pattichis, C.S.: Virtual reality applications for neurological disease: A review. Front. Robot. AI 6, 100 (2019)
21. Schubert, T., Friedmann, F., Regenbrecht, H.: The experience of presence: Factor analytic insights. Presence Teleoperators Virt.Environ. 10(3), 266–281 (2001)
22. Schwind, V., Knierim, P., Haas, N., Henze, N.: Using presence questionnaires in virtual reality. In: Proceedings of the 2019 CHI Conference on Human Factors in Computing Systems, pp. 1–12 (2019)
23. Schwind, V., Mayer, S., Comeau-Vermeersch, A., Schweigert, R., Henze, N.: Up to the finger tip: The effect of avatars on mid-air pointing accuracy in virtual reality. In: Proceedings of the 2018 Annual Symposium on Computer-Human Interaction in Play, pp. 477–488 (2018)
24. Skarbez, R., Brooks, F.P., Jr., Whitton, M.C.: A survey of presence and related concepts. ACM Comput. Surv. (CSUR) 50(6), 1–39 (2017)

25. Slater, M., Usoh, M., Steed, A.: Depth of presence in virtual environments. Presence Teleoperators Virt. Environ. **3**(2), 130–144 (1994)
26. Witmer, B.G., Singer, M.J.: Measuring presence in virtual environments: A presence questionnaire. Presence **7**(3), 225–240 (1998)
27. Wolf, M.J., Perron, B.: Immersion, engagement, and presence: A method for analyzing 3-D video games Alison McMahan. The Video Game Theory Reader. Routledge, pp. 89–108 (2013)

Gesture-Based, Haptic and Multimodal Interaction in VAMR

Tabletop 3D Digital Map Interaction with Virtual Reality Handheld Controllers

Adrian H. Hoppe[1,2(✉)], Florian van de Camp[1], and Rainer Stiefelhagen[2]

[1] Fraunhofer Institute of Optronics, System Technologies, and Image Exploitation (IOSB), Karlsruhe, Germany
{adrian.hoppe,florian.vandecamp}@iosb.fraunhofer.de
[2] Karlsruhe Institute of Technology (KIT), Karlsruhe, Germany
{adrian.hoppe,rainer.stiefelhagen}@kit.edu

Abstract. Immersive technologies, such as virtual reality, enable users to view and evaluate three-dimensional content, e.g., geographic data. Besides navigating this data at a life-size scale, a tabletop display offers a better overview of a larger area. This paper presents six different techniques to interact with immersive digital map table displays, i.e., panning, rotating, and zooming the map and indicating a position. The implemented interaction methods were evaluated in a user study with 12 participants. The results show that using a virtual laser pointer in combination with the buttons and joystick on a controller yields the best results regarding interaction time, workload, and user preference. The user study also shows that interaction methods should be customizable so that users can adapt them to their abilities. However, the proposed virtual laser pointer technique achieves a good balance between physical and cognitive effort and yields good results for users with varying experience levels.

Keywords: Virtual reality · Digital map · Tabletop · Controller interaction

1 Introduction

The display of geospatial data in virtual and augmented reality (VR/AR) allows for a whole new use of three-dimensional (3D) data in particular. Such data may be used in the context of data visualization, modeling, designing, or planning [11]. There are first, implemented interactions with this kind of data in VR but due to the multiple options for display—from map displays to virtual walk-through or aerial flight—there is a lack of investigation of the most efficient form of interaction for certain types. To experience and better understand, for example, the height of a building or the width of a road, a life-size scale of the data may be presented to the user. With the help of different methods of locomotion, a user can walk or fly through the digital model and perform a virtual site inspection. Another approach is to present the data on a virtual map display, e.g., a table.

© The Author(s), under exclusive license to Springer Nature Switzerland AG 2022
J. Y. C. Chen and G. Fragomeni (Eds.): HCII 2022, LNCS 13317, pp. 291–305, 2022.
https://doi.org/10.1007/978-3-031-05939-1_19

This allows several users to stand around the map and discuss the data. Also, different zoom stages allow to perceive the content at varying levels of detail and to get a better overview of larger areas.

When dealing with maps that allow world-wide access, the question arises of how to navigate the world and change the current view extent. Basic functionalities, such as panning, rotating, or zooming the map as well as indicating a position are needed. This paper implements several techniques that provide basic map interactions for a virtual map table display. First, related work and the proposed interaction methods are presented. After that, the different techniques are evaluated in a user study and the results are presented and discussed. Lastly, this paper concludes the gained insights and proposes directions for future work.

2   Related Work

The current body of work of virtual map interaction can be grouped by dimensionality (i.e., 2D or 3D), map display (i.e., a vertical/wall, horizontal/tabletop, movable, or immersive display), user perspective (i.e., virtual site inspection or birds-eye view), and interaction device (i.e., personal computer (PC), input, touch, wearable, handheld, gestures, or VR/AR controllers). However, systems can also combine multiple strategies, such as a vertical and a horizontal display [22].

For a virtual site-inspection, most systems rely on navigation techniques that are commonly used for 2D or 3D virtual environment (VE) locomotion. To guide orientation, arrows, or a radar-style mini-map may be used [5]. Especially 3D arrows help users to navigate to a target location more quickly. When using a PC, 6 Degrees of freedom (6DOF) devices or gesture input may be used [18]. VR technology is especially suited for navigating a VE, because the immersive display conveys the feeling of being at the virtual location. Different modes of movement, e.g., flight, teleportation, World-in-Miniature, 3D cone drag, and Walking-in-Place, can be utilized [7,16]. For unrestricted movement, users prefer methods where they can fly up in the air to get an overview and then move quickly towards their target [7]. Continuous movement is faster, as it helps users to orient themselves while moving and correct for any errors. For ground-based movement, walking in place comes close to real-life walking [16]. Depending on the used method, VR navigation can be faster than real-life movement. Yet, PC-based movement can be even quicker [14]. Virtual movement speed may also be adjusted depending on the surroundings [1].

For a birds-eye view on the map, 2D vertical display PC systems use a mouse for drag and drop or button interaction [2] or 3D input devices [4,8]. Mouse interaction is mostly quicker but other methods may be more natural [8]. 2D horizontal PC systems found no differences for a mouse and touch-based interaction [3], while interaction can be further supported by speech and gesture input [19]. Besides static display technology, also movable displays via wearable or handheld devices can support digital map navigation. For this, peephole or magic lens interaction utilizes user's proprioception as additional feedback. Depending on the implementation, the arm movement results in quicker [13] or slower [10] interaction compared to touch or joystick-based interaction. Also the tilt of a device [12] or its position [20] may be used for map navigation. While a 2D display may use a 3D perspective or adaptive terrain shear [21] to provide users with a better perception of the terrain and height, immersive VR/AR displays are much more suitable to convey 3D map information. However, few works actually implement navigation for a birds-eye view 3D map display [6]. Most work focuses on interaction with 2D maps only. For this, direct-grab, joystick, or hybrid methods allow to control the viewport of a horizontal 2D map [15]. Other work uses a physical surface and camera-based touch detection to convey a similar experience as if using a large touch screen monitor [17]. Besides hand interaction, also gaze is used for vertical map displays [9].

We have found a lack in research regarding 3D horizontal map interaction using immersive displays and of-the-shelf input hardware, i.e., VR controllers. Because of this, based on, e.g., [3,9,15,17], we defined common map interactions as requirements for possible interactions with a tabletop digital map:

Pan the map to move the view extent.
Rotate the map to adjust the direction in which the user looks at the data.
Zoom the map to change the level of detail and size of the map section.
Position indication to determine a point on the map, e.g., to select a point of interest (POI) or to communicate a location to other people.

3   Digital Map Table Interactions

Fig. 1. Points of interests and lines displayed on a 3D digital map table.

Three different interaction techniques, i.e., direct-grab, ray-casting, and joystick-control, with two variations were implemented using Unity and an HP Reverb G2. Figure 1 shows the digital map table and Table 1 gives an overview of the input methods.

Using the direct-grab methods, the map is grabbed at the location of the hand. For this, the user presses the trigger button on one or both VR controllers. While performing a one-handed press, a horizontal movement of the hand yields a movement of the map by the same amount. Vertical hand movements are

Table 1. Interaction methods and their controls for the basic map functions panning, rotating, and zooming and position indication.

Method	Pan	Zoom and Rotate at Location	Position indication	Example Image
Direct-grab 1	One-handed grab with any hand	Two-handed pinch at gaze position	Hand position	
Direct-grab 2	One-handed grab with dominant hand	One-handed pinch at hand position	Hand position	
Ray-cast 1	One-handed grab with any hand	Two-handed pinch at gaze position	Ray position	
Ray-cast 2	One-handed grab with dominant hand	One-handed joystick at ray position	Ray position	
Joystick 1	Left joystick	Right joystick at cursor position	Cursor static in map center	
Joystick 2	Left joystick	Triggers and buttons on both controllers at cursor position	Right joystick to move cursor	

ignored. Direct-grab 1 uses the two-handed pinch gesture known from touch devices. If a user grabs the map with both hands and moves them further apart, the map zooms in as it is "stretched" or "pulled apart". If the hands are moved closer together, the map zooms out as it is "compressed". If the user rotates the hands around each other in the table plane, like turning the steering wheel of a car, the map rotates in the direction of the hand rotation. The map zooms and rotates at the location the user is looking at. This position is approximated by the forward vector of the VR headset. To indicate a position, the user simply reaches for a POI and touches it with one hand. For this, the user may move into the table or move the target location closer by panning the map prior to the indication. With direct-grab 2, only the dominant hand is used for panning and position indication. To rotate and zoom the map, the joystick on the VR controller of the dominant hand is used. Pushing the joystick up or down, zooms the map in or out respectively. Pushing the joystick left or right, rotates the map clockwise or anti-clockwise. Zooming and rotating takes place at the location of the hand.

Ray-casting 1 and 2 work similarly. The only difference is that the map is grabbed at the location of the virtual laser pointer and this location is used for all map interactions, i.e., panning, rotating, zooming and position indication.

The joystick-based interaction is inspired by the interaction with gamepads, e.g., from gaming consoles. The map extent is changed by twisting the joysticks or pushing the buttons on the VR controllers. The location of the VR controller does not influence the input. Therefore, users can hold their hands in the way that is most comfortable for them. For joystick 1 and 2, the joystick on the left controller pans the map. With joystick 1, the joystick on the right controller rotates and zooms the map as with direct-grab 2 and ray-cast 2. A static cursor that points from the ceiling to the center of the map is used for position indication. Therefore, POIs need to be moved in the center of the map to highlight them. For joystick 2, the right joystick is used to move the ceiling-cursor. Therefore, additional buttons are used to rotate and zoom the map. The right trigger button, zooms the map in, the left trigger button, zooms the map out. The "A"-button on the right controller and the "X"-button on the left controller rotate the map clockwise or counter-clockwise respectively.

4 User Study

A within-subject user study was conducted to evaluate the previously presented interaction techniques. Users had to interact with the map using the six different input methods. The order of the techniques was reversed based on a Latin square so that learning and fatigue effects are eliminated as much as possible. Before the first task and after each of the 6 tasks, a virtual questionnaire was displayed to the participants so that the users did not have to take off the VR headset between tasks. The test subjects took between 35 and 80 min to complete the tasks.

4.1   Participants

A total of 12 subjects (6 male, 6 female) participated. 11 subjects were right-handed. 2 participants were 18–25 years old, 5 were 26–35 years old, 4 were 36–50 years old, and one was over 50 years old. On a 10-point Likert scale, users indicated that they have a high level of experience using information technologies with 8.8 ± 1.1 on a scale of 1 (none) to 10 (very much). On the same scale, users rated their experience with VR as moderate with 5.0 ± 2.9.

4.2   Tasks and Procedures

Users performed the six different interaction techniques that change the view extent of the map. In order to decouple the interaction from the contents of the map (e.g., knowledge about the location of a city), a task was designed in which users were asked to follow a given parcours. One parcours consists of the four previously defined tasks: Panning, rotating, and zooming the map, as well as indicating different positions. For each technique, each user goes through a training parcours (always the same) followed by a task parcours (different for each technique). To avoid interference between the interaction technique and the task parcours, the order of the task parcours was also randomized accordingly. Each task parcours consists of a mixture of 12 panning movements, 3 map rotations, 10 map zoom level changes (equally distributed between zooming in and out), and finally 7 position indications. Figure 2 describes the different tasks within a parcours in more detail.

4.3   Measurements

Descriptive, objective, and subjective metrics were collected during the user study. The time taken by subjects to complete a task was measured from the display of the first parcours element to the indication of the seventh POI. In addition, questionnaires were filled out directly after each task: A NASA Raw TLX (RTLX) and ratings of the individual interactions panning, rotating, zooming, and position indication were queried. Subjects rated a total of 10 dimensions on a 10-point Likert scale from 1 to 10 with 1 being the corresponding best value (e.g., very low stress, very good rating, etc.) and 10 being the worst value (e.g., very high stress, insufficient rating, etc.). In addition, there was an opportunity for open feedback per technique.

To evaluate the data, a Shapiro-Wilk test was performed to check whether a normal distribution of the data can be assumed. However, this was not the case for any dimension. For this reason, and because of the dependent samples with at least ordinal scaling, the Friedman test was chosen to test for significant differences between the central tendencies. Effect size is reported using Kendall's coefficient of concordance W. For pairwise comparisons between techniques, a Wilcoxon rank test with Bonferroni-corrected p-values was used. Results are also presented as box-whisker plots due to the mostly ordinal scaling.

The start of a task instructs users to zoom out with the label "ZOOM OUT".

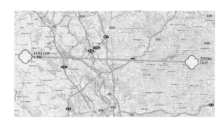

After a user has zoomed according to the previous instruction, a yellow symbol appears with the label "FOLLOW LINE" whereupon the user should follow the line by moving the map until she/he receives the next instruction. In this example, the next task is marked by the yellow symbol "ZOOM OUT". Alternatively, it could be labeled "ZOOM IN". Note: The user sees only a small section and not the full extent of the displayed map.

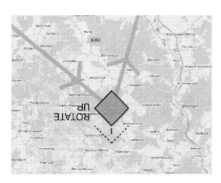

Red icons may also appear on the path along the line, instructing the user to rotate the map. Here, the goal is to rotate the digital map table so that the description text "ROTATE UP" is upright and the dashed arrow on the red symbol points away from the user (relative to the user's view). Two arrows on the line also indicate from which direction the user came and in which direction she/he has to follow the line to minimize any confusion after the rotation.

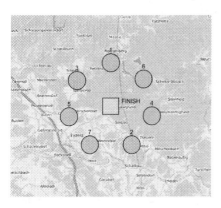

At the end of the parcours, the green "FINISH" symbol appears, indicating the end of the map movement. In addition, seven blue circles appear. These seven positions represent possible POIs and should be indicated by the user one after the other, according to the numbering. To do this, the user first points to the blue circle with the number 1, then to the circle with the number 2, and so on. The task is based on ISO 9241-9. As feedback, the POIs turn green as soon as a user has indicated their position correctly.

Fig. 2. The different tasks within a parcours.

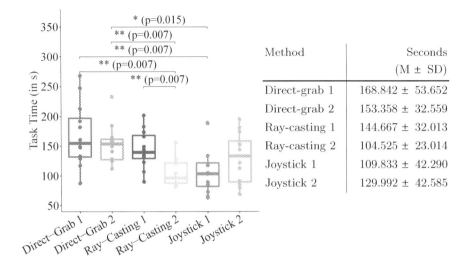

Fig. 3. Task time by interaction technique.

Method	Seconds (M ± SD)
Direct-grab 1	168.842 ± 53.652
Direct-grab 2	153.358 ± 32.559
Ray-casting 1	144.667 ± 32.013
Ray-casting 2	104.525 ± 23.014
Joystick 1	109.833 ± 42.290
Joystick 2	129.992 ± 42.585

4.4 Results

Figure 3 shows the time required by users to complete one parcours. The standard deviation for all techniques is quite high. The mean values indicate that the ray-casting 2 and joystick 1 techniques tend to be the fastest. A Friedman test shows a significant difference for the interaction technique factor ($\chi^2(5) = 31.095$, $p < 0.001$, $n = 12$) with a large effect size (Kendall's W = .518). Pairwise comparisons show that ray-casting 2 and joystick 1 are several times significantly faster than direct-grab 1 and 2 and ray-casting 1 techniques.

Figure 4 shows the workload of the users during the execution of the task parcours. It can be seen that all techniques generate a low to medium workload. A Friedman test shows a significant difference for the interaction technique factor ($\chi^2(5) = 25.549$, $p < 0.001$, $n = 12$) with a medium effect size (Kendall's W = .426). The ray-casting 2 technique produces significantly less user workload than direct-grab 2, ray-casting 1, and joystick 2, and achieves the lowest mean workload. The joystick 1 technique results tend to produce the second-least workload, although there are no significant differences.

Figure 5 shows the users' rating for panning the map with the different interaction techniques. All techniques achieve a satisfactory to very good rating. A Friedman test shows no significant difference for the factor interaction technique ($\chi^2(5) = 9.036$, $p = .107$, $n = 12$. The mean values indicate that the movement with ray-casting 2 and 1 as well as joystick 1 tended to be rated better.

Figure 6 shows the users' rating for the rotation of the map with the interaction techniques. Direct-grab 1 and ray-casting 1 achieve a satisfactory rating, the other techniques a rather good to very good rating. A Friedman test shows a significant difference for the interaction technique factor ($\chi^2(5) = 26.203$, $p < 0.001$,

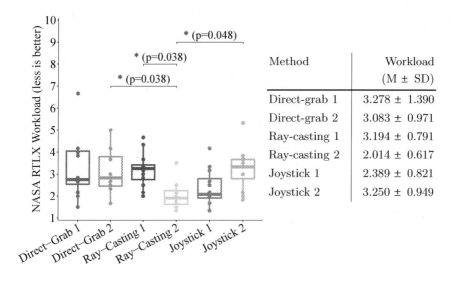

Fig. 4. NASA RTLX workload by interaction technique.

Method	Workload (M ± SD)
Direct-grab 1	3.278 ± 1.390
Direct-grab 2	3.083 ± 0.971
Ray-casting 1	3.194 ± 0.791
Ray-casting 2	2.014 ± 0.617
Joystick 1	2.389 ± 0.821
Joystick 2	3.250 ± 0.949

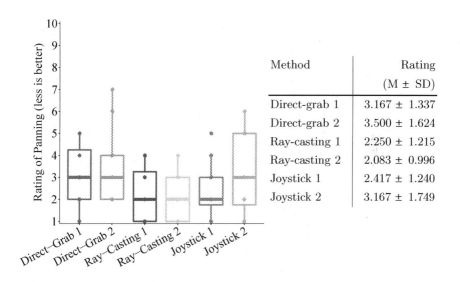

Fig. 5. Rating of panning the map by interaction technique.

Method	Rating (M ± SD)
Direct-grab 1	3.167 ± 1.337
Direct-grab 2	3.500 ± 1.624
Ray-casting 1	2.250 ± 1.215
Ray-casting 2	2.083 ± 0.996
Joystick 1	2.417 ± 1.240
Joystick 2	3.167 ± 1.749

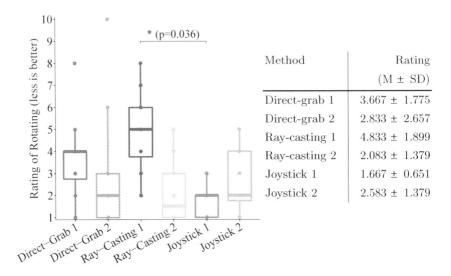

Fig. 6. Rating of rotating the map by interaction technique.

n = 12) with a medium effect size (Kendall's W = .437). Pairwise comparisons show that the joystick 1 technique is significantly better than ray-casting 1. Ray-casting 2 tends to follow in second place.

Figure 7 shows the user ratings for zooming the map with the interaction techniques. The techniques direct-grab 1 and 2, as well as ray-casting 2 and joystick 1 achieve good to very good ratings. Ray-casting 1 and joystick 2 only achieve a satisfactory to good rating. A Friedman test shows a significant difference for the interaction technique factor ($\chi^2(5) = 36.925$, p < 0.001, n = 12) with a large effect size (Kendall's W=.615). Pairwise comparisons show that joystick 1 was rated significantly better than ray-casting 1, with direct-grab 2, ray-casting 2, and joystick 1 tending to share first place.

Figure 8 shows the users' rating for indicating a position on the map with the interaction techniques. The two joystick techniques appear to have been rated significantly lower than the direct-grab and ray-casting techniques. However, there are several outliers in the ratings. A Friedman test shows a significant difference for the interaction technique factor ($\chi^2(5) = 30.068$, p < 0.001, n = 12) with a large effect size (Kendall's W = .501). Pairwise comparisons cannot identify significant differences between the techniques. According to the mean values, ray-casting 2 performs best, followed by direct-grab 2 and ray-casting 1.

In general, the test subjects sometimes state that they find the speed and direction of the interaction techniques unsuitable and would like to have a possibility for configuration. The map panning is described 5 times as too fast, 2 times as too slow, zooming 1 time as too slow, 1 time as too fast and the position indication 6 times as too fast. In addition, users would like to be able to invert the direction of panning 1 time, rotation 5 times and zooming 7 times.

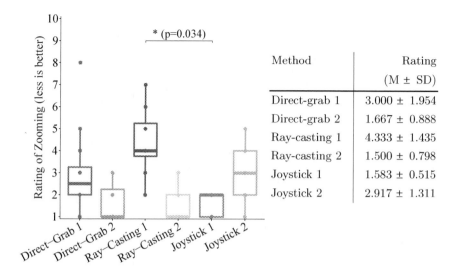

Method	Rating (M ± SD)
Direct-grab 1	3.000 ± 1.954
Direct-grab 2	1.667 ± 0.888
Ray-casting 1	4.333 ± 1.435
Ray-casting 2	1.500 ± 0.798
Joystick 1	1.583 ± 0.515
Joystick 2	2.917 ± 1.311

Fig. 7. Rating of zooming the map by interaction technique.

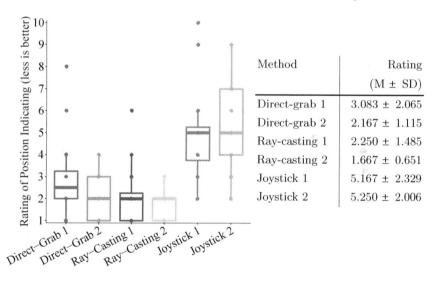

Method	Rating (M ± SD)
Direct-grab 1	3.083 ± 2.065
Direct-grab 2	2.167 ± 1.115
Ray-casting 1	2.250 ± 1.485
Ray-casting 2	1.667 ± 0.651
Joystick 1	5.167 ± 2.329
Joystick 2	5.250 ± 2.006

Fig. 8. Rating of indicating a position on the map by interaction technique.

When moving the map with direct-grab, users mention 6 times that the map should keep moving (by holding on to it or by pushing on it and letting go), otherwise interaction becomes tiring (5 times) or annoying (1 time). It is reported 2 times that the proximity to the map causes a certain discomfort when rotating. With direct-grab 1, rotating is also not easily separable from zooming (1 time) and difficult to use (2 times). For panning, rotating and zooming the map with direct-grab 2 it is mentioned 4 times that the operation is intuitive.

For the position indication, it is mentioned 1 time that the overview is lost due to the proximity to the map.

In the case of ray casting, it was mentioned 2 times that one has to lift one's arm in order to indicate some positions that are otherwise covered by other POIs and that the laser pointer is wobbly (1 time). However, due to the distance to the map, all POIs are visible at the same time (1 time). With ray-casting 1 it is noted 1 time that the map should move on after panning. In addition, it is commented 4 times that the rotation is difficult and 1 time that it is not so easy to separate from zooming. Ray-casting 2 is described as efficient (2 times), easy (1 time) and better than the other techniques (5 times). However, it is noted 2 times that the rotation point around the laser pointer position needs habituation, as it can change during rotation (1 time), is not fixed in the center of the table (1 time), and needs attention (1 time).

Joystick operation is described as easy (3 times), but also as initially difficult (3 times). The position indication of joystick 1 is described as not suitable (1 time) and that of joystick 2 as annoying (1 time). With more distance to the map, rotation is described as being not so disorienting (1 time).

5 Discussion

The results indicate that the ray-casting 2 technique is best suited for interaction with a digital map table, as it performs better than the other techniques in at least one measurement, sometimes significantly, sometimes only trending, but never worse.

For task times, the techniques that allow the map to be panned with as little physical and cognitive effort as possible (i.e., small movements, no large gestures, simple input) are better. The workload measured by the NASA RTLX supports this as well. Techniques with larger movements (direct-grab 1 and 2), more complex controls (joystick 2 and rotation/zoom of ray-casting 1) perform worse.

The ratings of panning the map show that grabbing and moving the map with direct-grab techniques seems too strenuous or slow and thus receives a slightly worse rating. Using the joystick for shifting is very efficient and not very strenuous, but also takes a lot of getting used to, as the interaction needs to be practiced.

The two-handed rotation and zooming of direct-grab 1 and ray-casting 1 causes problems for the participants since sometimes very precise movements have to be executed. Also, as both interactions are combined into one gesture, users have issues separating the controls. The use of the digital buttons of joystick 2 also seems too complicated and imprecise for these tasks. The use of a joystick for rotating and zooming as with direct-grab 2, ray-casting 2 and joystick 1 seems to be better suited. When rotating the map, care should also be taken that the map does not fill too large of an area in the user's field of view (e.g., if the user is looking directly at the map from above, as in direct-grab 1), as this can trigger motion sickness. Providing users with a way to manipulate the map from a greater distance, e.g., with a laser pointer, can reduce this issue.

For the position indication, indirect control via the joystick is too complicated. Here it is better to use the gesture inputs. Direct touching of POIs has the disadvantage that an overview is lost due to the close proximity to the targets. Using a laser pointer preserves the overview and allows interaction with distant objects, although at greater distances precision may suffer.

User comments indicate that configuration options for the speed and direction of the techniques should be given so that they can adapt the interaction to their individual abilities and learning curve.

6   Conclusion and Future Work

In general, it can be said that the implemented interaction techniques and the user study have provided several insights into interacting with geospatial data in VR. Working directly with the hands often leads to larger arm or hand movements and thus promotes fatigue and reduces speed. Operating the map without gesture movements with a joystick is not as intuitive and has a steep learning curve initially, but can be done quickly and with little physical effort. Using ray-casting to pan and point in combination with zooming and rotating via joystick seems to provide a good balance between intuition and efficiency. In general, it should be possible for a user to make certain adjustments (e.g., speed/direction of interaction) to adapt the operation to her/his individual needs.

For future work, we want to explore how well the proposed techniques can be transferred to other display modes, e.g., a wall display. We want to evaluate if the ray-casting 2 technique can also be used for virtual site-inspection locomotion to provide a consistent interaction method across several ways of displaying 3D geographic data. The user study also shows that there is a trade-off between intuitiveness and strain (i.e., physical and cognitive effort). Therefore, future work may focus on optimizing both factors to enable an easy and effortless interaction for new as well as experienced users.

References

1. Argelaguet, F.: Adaptive navigation for virtual environments. In: 2014 IEEE Symposium on 3D User Interfaces (3DUI), pp. 123–126 (2014). https://doi.org/10.1109/3DUI.2014.7027325
2. Battersby, S.E.: User-centered design for digital map navigation tools. In: Proceedings of International Research Symposium on Computer-based Cartography, vol. 17, pp. 1–15 (2008)
3. Beheshti, E., Van Devender, A., Horn, M.: Touch, click, navigate: comparing tabletop and desktop interaction for map navigation tasks. In: Proceedings of the 2012 ACM International Conference on Interactive Tabletops and Surfaces, ITS 2012, pp. 205–214. Association for Computing Machinery, New York (2012). https://doi.org/10.1145/2396636.2396669

4. Bellucci, A., Malizia, A., Diaz, P., Aedo, I.: Don't touch me: multi-user annotations on a map in large display environments. In: Proceedings of the International Conference on Advanced Visual Interfaces, AVI 2010, pp. 391–392. Association for Computing Machinery, New York (2010). https://doi.org/10.1145/1842993.1843072

5. Burigat, S., Chittaro, L.: Navigation in 3D virtual environments: effects of user experience and location-pointing navigation aids. Int. J. Human-Comput. Stud. **65**(11), 945–958 (2007). https://doi.org/10.1016/j.ijhcs.2007.07.003

6. van de Camp, F., Hoppe, A., Unmüßig, G., Peinsipp-Byma, E.: Cooperative and location-independent terrain assessment for deployment planning using a 3D mixed reality environment. In: Jr., M.S.D. (ed.) Virtual, Augmented, and Mixed Reality (XR) Technology for Multi-Domain Operations, vol. 11426, pp. 1–8. International Society for Optics and Photonics, SPIE (2020). https://doi.org/10.1117/12.2558593

7. Danyluk, K., Willett, W.: Evaluating the performance of virtual reality navigation techniques for large environments. In: Gavrilova, M., Chang, J., Thalmann, N.M., Hitzer, E., Ishikawa, H. (eds.) CGI 2019. LNCS, vol. 11542, pp. 203–215. Springer, Cham (2019). https://doi.org/10.1007/978-3-030-22514-8_17

8. Dubois, E., Truillet, P., Bach, C.: Evaluating advanced interaction techniques for navigating google earth. In: Proceedings of HCI 2007 The 21st British HCI Group Annual Conference University of Lancaster, UK 21, pp. 1–4 (2007). https://doi.org/10.14236/ewic/HCI2007.54

9. Giannopoulos, I., Komninos, A., Garofalakis, J.: Natural interaction with large map interfaces in vr. In: Proceedings of the 21st Pan-Hellenic Conference on Informatics, PCI 2017. Association for Computing Machinery, New York (2017). https://doi.org/10.1145/3139367.3139424

10. Kerber, F., Krüger, A., Löchtefeld, M.: Investigating the effectiveness of peephole interaction for smartwatches in a map navigation task. In: Proceedings of the 16th International Conference on Human-Computer Interaction with Mobile Devices and Services, MobileHCI 2014, pp. 291–294. Association for Computing Machinery, New York (2014). https://doi.org/10.1145/2628363.2628393

11. Mazuryk, T., Gervautz, M.: Virtual reality-history, applications, technology and future (1996)

12. Merdes, M., Häußler, J., Jöst, M.: 'slidingmap': Introducing and evaluating a new modality for map interaction. In: Proceedings of the 6th International Conference on Multimodal Interfaces, ICMI 2004, pp. 325–326. Association for Computing Machinery, New York (2004). https://doi.org/10.1145/1027933.1027989

13. Rohs, M., Schöning, J., Raubal, M., Essl, G., Krüger, A.: Map navigation with mobile devices: virtual versus physical movement with and without visual context. In: Proceedings of the 9th International Conference on Multimodal Interfaces, ICMI 2007, pp. 146–153. Association for Computing Machinery, New York (2007). https://doi.org/10.1145/1322192.1322219

14. Santos, B.S., et al.: Head-mounted display versus desktop for 3D navigation in virtual reality: a user study. Multimedia Tools Appl. **41**(1), 161–181 (2009). https://doi.org/10.1007/s11042-008-0223-2

15. Satriadi, K.A., Ens, B., Cordeil, M., Jenny, B., Czauderna, T., Willett, W.: Augmented reality map navigation with freehand gestures. In: 2019 IEEE Conference on Virtual Reality and 3D User Interfaces (VR), pp. 593–603 (2019). https://doi.org/10.1109/VR.2019.8798340

16. Savino, G.L., et al.: Comparing pedestrian navigation methods in virtual reality and real life. In: 2019 International Conference on Multimodal Interaction, ICMI 2019, pp. 16–25. Association for Computing Machinery, New York (2019). https://doi.org/10.1145/3340555.3353741

17. Strentzsch, G., van de Camp, F., Stiefelhagen, R.: Digital map table VR: bringing an interactive system to virtual reality. In: Lackey, S., Chen, J. (eds.) VAMR 2017. LNCS, vol. 10280, pp. 54–71. Springer, Cham (2017). https://doi.org/10.1007/978-3-319-57987-0_5

18. Tscharn, R., et al.: User experience of 3D map navigation - bare-hand interaction or touchable device? In: Prinz, W., Borchers, J., Jarke, M. (eds.) Mensch und Computer 2016 - Tagungsband. Gesellschaft für Informatik e.V., Aachen (2016). https://doi.org/10.18420/muc2016-mci-0167

19. Tse, E., Shen, C., Greenberg, S., Forlines, C.: Enabling interaction with single user applications through speech and gestures on a multi-user tabletop. In: Proceedings of the Working Conference on Advanced Visual Interfaces, AVI 2006, pp. 336–343. Association for Computing Machinery, New York (2006). https://doi.org/10.1145/1133265.1133336

20. Wiehr, F., Daiber, F., Kosmalla, F., Krüger, A.: Artopos: augmented reality terrain map visualization for collaborative route planning. In: Proceedings of the 2017 ACM International Joint Conference on Pervasive and Ubiquitous Computing and Proceedings of the 2017 ACM International Symposium on Wearable Computers, UbiComp 2017, pp. 1047–1050. Association for Computing Machinery, New York (2017). https://doi.org/10.1145/3123024.3124446

21. Willett, W., Jenny, B., Isenberg, T., Dragicevic, P.: Lightweight relief shearing for enhanced terrain perception on interactive maps. In: Proceedings of the 33rd Annual ACM Conference on Human Factors in Computing Systems, CHI 2015, pp. 3563–3572. Association for Computing Machinery, New Yor (2015). https://doi.org/10.1145/2702123.2702172

22. Yoshimoto, Y., Dang, T.H., Kimura, A., Shibata, F., Tamura, H.: Interaction design of 2d/3d map navigation on wall and tabletop displays. In: Proceedings of the ACM International Conference on Interactive Tabletops and Surfaces, ITS 2011, pp. 254–255. Association for Computing Machinery, New York (2011). https://doi.org/10.1145/2076354.2076402

Hand Gesture Recognition for User Interaction in Augmented Reality (AR) Experience

Aasim Khurshid$^{(\boxtimes)}$, Ricardo Grunitzki, Roberto Giordano Estrada Leyva, Fabiano Marinho, and Bruno Matthaus Maia Souto Orlando

Sidia Institute of Science and Technology, Manaus, AM, Brazil
{aasim.khurshid,ricardo.grunitzki,roberto.leyva,fabiano.marinho,
bruno.orlando}@sidia.com

Abstract. Augmented Reality (AR) has gained a lot of attraction in the recent past. Arguably, the most important tool that can make AR a household gadget is its interaction with the user. This may lead to two possible interaction methodologies: (i) Using an extra device for interaction; (ii) Using human hands as interaction. Former is probably the easy method, but it may increase the cost of the AR device, limiting its target users. Therefore, hand gestures are a feasible and efficient mode of interaction. However, for accurate and pleasant interaction, the AR device should be capable of hand gesture understanding. In this direction, we propose a hand gesture classification method, based on Convolutional Neural Networks (CNNs) that takes advantage of the pre-trained network weights for faster and efficient training, which also helps improve the quality of gesture classification. Moreover, the proposed approach takes advantage of hand detection for background elimination and efficient gesture recognition. The proposed approach is evaluated on the Hand gesture classification task for three datasets that differ in terms of the number of data samples, amount of gestures, and data quality. The obtained results show that our method outperforms state-of-the-art methods in most of the experimentation cases.

Keywords: Hand detection · Gesture recognition · Augmented Reality · AR interaction

1 Introduction

The hand gesture recognition task detects the different shapes of hands and classifies them as one of the gesture classes. It is important to accurately detect and recognize these gestures so that they can be utilized in understanding sign

---

This work is partially supported by Sidia institute of science and technology, and Samsung Eletrônica da Amazônia Ltda, under the auspice of the Brazilian informatics law no 8.387/91.

© The Author(s), under exclusive license to Springer Nature Switzerland AG 2022
J. Y. C. Chen and G. Fragomeni (Eds.): HCII 2022, LNCS 13317, pp. 306–316, 2022.
https://doi.org/10.1007/978-3-031-05939-1_20

language, human-computer interaction, and/or Augmented Reality (AR) inter-action through hands.

The literature in hand gesture recognition can be classified into two different approaches: (i) the wearable glove-based sensor approach; and (ii) the camera vision-based sensor approach [20]. Although the wearable glove-based sensor approach provides good results, since it uses multiple sensor values to represent a hand gesture, such techniques have various limitations such as monetary cost, users discomfort, and confusion among older people. These drawbacks led to the development of promising and cost-effective techniques using camera vision-based sensors.

Several studies based on computer vision techniques were published in the past decade [3,6,14]. These strategies essentially involve the replacement of the instrumented glove with a camera, such as RGB, time of flight (TOF), thermal, or night vision cameras. The camera vision-based methods also differ according to the type of the camera, to take advantage of the new features captured by each type of camera. However, the main idea behind them is the same: segment and detect hand features such as skin color, appearance, motion, skeleton, depth, 3D model, deep learning detection, and more [20].

Dealing with hand gesture recognition in a camera vision-based approach evolves certain challenges which are required to resolve for accurate gesture recognition, such as skin color, background, and illumination conditions. Most of these challenges are because of the non-rigid nature of human hands which makes it challenging due to the different shapes it could take. Furthermore, occlusions may occur in some parts of the hand due to other objects or cause by some parts of the hand on other parts of the hand, such as finger(s) occluding other fingers or palm. Moreover, due to limited textural information and contrast differences among hand features, it is more challenging as compared to a human face, as the human face has prominent features and textural structure. Therefore, for accurate and robust hand gesture recognition approach, it should be created considering the above-mentioned issues.

The methods presented in literature [5,10,17] normally consider a two-phase algorithm, that first use segmentation for skin detection (eliminating unnecessary background), followed by a classification algorithm that will perform the hand gesture recognition. Such a strategy is very efficient and may work with limited data samples. However, it is highly dependent on the quality of skin segmentation, which makes it less robust to different skin tones of hand. Another important consideration required in such approaches is background subtraction because objects of similar color tones or similar texture to skin color and texture may be detected as the skin of the background. Another possibility is to directly use the classification of different gestures by training directly on the gesture-based dataset, not considering any local features. Such methods are fairly accurate if there is sufficient data and features are selected carefully that represent different gestures. However, poor features selection may deteriorate the performance of these methods [2,20]. With the resurgence of deep learning techniques and the availability of resources, deep learning is also used for hand gesture classification.

Agrawal et al. trained an end-to-end neural network with images of hands, and their labels without significant pre-processing, such as image-based models for Hand Gesture Recognition using Deep Learning [1]. Also, Deep Learning is used for hand gesture recognition using Representative Frames in videos [7]. Deep learning methods, however, suffer from data scarcity and require a large amount of labeled training data [11,14]. To address the data scarcity issue, we employ the transfer learning approach, which also improves training efficiency in time and resources[1].

In AR devices, the field of view is wide and a large part of the frame is composed of the background. Therefore, we propose to employ hand detection that is followed by a gesture recognition algorithm. This technique has two advantages: (1) Hand detection will make the task of gesture recognition classifier easier, providing only the hand to recognize a gesture; and (2) It would allow gestures to be accurately recognized in varied background conditions. In this approach, the hand detector is trained on a fairly large dataset, which detects hand palm and it is used as input for the gesture classification method. For the classification of hand gestures, a Convolution Neural Network (CNN) is trained for hand gesture recognition. An independent CNN requires very large labeled data which may range from 50k-100k labeled images of hand and hand landmarks belonging to different geographic descent people for the robustness of the algorithm. Also, such methods require much higher training time and computational resources as compared to the previously mentioned methods. For this reason, we propose to use a pre-trained network and customize its weights for gesture recognition using a transfer learning approach. This method proved to be robust and accurate for classification tasks.

As the current AR devices have limited memory, and the models trained using computers do not apply directly to the AR devices, we use Tensorflow lite to convert the model, so that it can execute in the AR device [19]. To solve the issue of memory size, we propose to utilize an optimization technique that allows reducing the size of the model substantially. In this work, we used integer optimization, which is capable of reducing the size of the model to half with insignificant accuracy loss [19]. However, it is important to attach the metadata in the model, so that any pre-processing can be achieved before the received frame can be used to produce classification results.

Furthermore, an AR/android application is created for the utilization of the gesture classifier. The application can be allowed to execute automatically at the start of the AR operating system and can be initiated explicitly.

The rest of the paper is organized as follows. Section 2 details the proposed approach and introduces relevant concepts used along with the conducted experiments (Sect. 3). Section 4 provides the conclusions and future work in this direction.

---

[1] https://www.tensorflow.org/lite/convert/metadata.

2   Proposed Approach

The proposed computer vision-based approach for hand gesture recognition is composed of two parts:

1. A hand detection mechanism; and
2. A gesture recognition mechanism.

For a given image frame containing a hand gesture, the hand detector finds the hand location, removes the unnecessary background, and passes a cropped image frame containing just the hand to the gesture classifier mechanism, which then identifies the hand gesture represented in the image frame.

The details of both hand detector and hand gesture recognition mechanisms are explained next.

2.1   Hand Detection

The proposed approach considers using hand detection before hand recognition/classification of gestures because it improves the robustness of the gesture classification in varied background conditions. Also, it guarantees the availability of a hand in the image frame before calling the gesture classification.

Several methods are proposed in the literature for hand detection [13,18,24]. Kourbane et al. proposed a regression-based hand detection and pose estimation. Teeparthi et al. utilize object-detection and time projections for hand detection in long videos [24]. Moreover, Narasimhaswamy et al. proposed a Hand-CNN method that utilizes a CNN architecture for detecting hand masks and predicting hand orientations in unconstrained images [18]. Hand-CNN extends MaskR-CNN with a novel attention mechanism to incorporate contextual cues in the detection process. Furthermore, Mask R-CNN utilizes Faster R-CNN for hand detection [21]. Faster R-CNN is an object detector that introduces a Region Proposal Network (RPN) with shareable convolutional layers that enable nearly cost-free region proposals by sharing convolutional features with the detection network. Moreover, RPNs are designed as an end-to-end network to generate high-quality region proposals, which are then used by Fast R-CNN [4]. In this work, we utilize Hand-CNN as base hand detection with little changes [18]. As Hand-CNN utilizes region proposals for training, the region proposal network loss is explained below for complementing the hand detection.

For training RPNs, a binary class label (of being hand or not) is assigned to each anchor. The positive label is assigned to two kinds of anchors: (i) the anchor/anchors with the highest Intersection over-Union (IoU) overlap with a ground-truth box, or (ii) an anchor that has an IoU overlap higher than 0.7 with any ground-truth box. it is worth mentioning that a single ground-truth box may assign positive labels to multiple anchors. On the other hand, a negative label is assigned to a non-positive anchor if its IoU ratio is lower than 0.3 for all ground-truth boxes. Moreover, the anchors that are neither positive nor negative do not contribute to the training objective. With these definitions, we minimize an objective function following the multi-task loss in Fast R-CNN [4]. The loss function for an image is defined as [18]:

$$L(\{p_i\}, \{t_i\}) = \frac{1}{N_{cls}} \sum_i L_{cls}(p_i, p_i^*) + \lambda \frac{1}{N_{reg}} \sum_i p_i^* L_{reg}(t_i, t_i^*) \qquad (1)$$

where, i is the index of an anchor in the mini-batch and p_i is the probability of the anchor to be the object. p_i^* is the ground-truth probability $label \in [0, 1]$ and t_i^* is that of the ground-truth box associated with a positive anchor. The classification loss L_{cls} is log loss over two classes (object vs. not object), and L_{reg} represents regression loss of the bounding box. Moreover, The two terms are normalized with N_{cls} and N_{reg}, and a balancing weight λ. For details on the computation of the objective function, we refer to the Faster RCNN paper [21].

Hand-CNN extends MaskRCNN with a novel attention mechanism to incorporate contextual cues in the detection process. This attention mechanism can be implemented as an efficient network module that captures non-local dependencies between features. This network module can be inserted at different stages of an object detection network, and the entire detector can be trained end-to-end. Hand-CNN contains two modules that run in parallel for hand detection and semantic hand segmentation [18]. However, segmentation slows the process, and a hand bounding box is sufficient for the gesture recognition algorithm as it removes the extra background and makes the gesture recognition task easier. Therefore, we propose to use only hand detection and utilize this hand bounding box as input for gesture classification in the next phase.

2.2   Gesture Recognition

For the classification of hand gestures, a Convolution Neural Network (CNN) is trained for hand gesture recognition. An independent CNN requires very large labeled data which may range from 50k-100k labeled images of hand and hand landmarks belonging to different geographic descent people for the robustness of the algorithm. Also, such methods require much higher training time and computational resources as compared to the previously mentioned methods. For this reason, we propose to use a pre-trained network and customize its weights for gesture recognition using a transfer learning approach. This method proved to be robust and accurate for classification tasks [23]. In this work, we used GoogleNet as a base network [23]. For the base network, we utilize pre-trained weights learned using ImageNet dataset [22]. For the details on the base network architecture, we refer to the GoogleNet inception paper [23]. Furthermore, the weights of the first few convolution layers were fixed, and the rest of the weights are allowed to change to adapt to the gesture recognition scenario.

3   Experimental Evaluation

The AR device used in our experiments is the Microsoft HoloLens. For training and evaluation of the models, we used a Macbook Pro machine with a 2.8 Ghz processor core i7, 16 GB RAM 2133 MHz LPDDR3. This setup was used for both the training and the evaluation of the models. The classification models were developed using TensorFlow[2] platform and Tensorflow lite[3]. Moreover, an AR application is created using android studio[4] and Unity development environment[5].

The inference models in the present paper are evaluated according to the following measures: accuracy, training time, and frame rate (number of frames executed per second) during the test. The application is installed on the AR device, therefore dependency on the communication overhead is removed, as was the case in our recently proposed scene classification for AR devices [11].

3.1 Gestures for AR

This section presents some details about basic gestures which can be used to design AR experiences. Figure 1 shows the symbolic representation of such gestures. All these gestures must be supported for both hands individually. The gestures used are "Tap", "FingerUp", "ThumbsUp","ThumbsDown", "Palm", "BackHand".

1. **Tap** happens when the index finger touches any GUI or virtual object. Furthermore, it requires the user's intent to press something, such as pressing a button to commit an action.
2. **Finger up** represents the index finger pointing up. It could be linked to a fuse component to commit actions, such as clicking a button. The fuse component is a kind of timer to trigger events after some seconds.
3. **Thumb up** is defined by the thumb finger pointing up. It could be used as a shortcut to confirm an action, such as the OK option on multiple-choice buttons.
4. **Thumb down** defines the thumb finger pointing down. It could be used as a shortcut to decline an action, such as the CANCEL option on multiple-choice buttons.
5. **Palm** represents keeping the user's palm facing up. It could be used to hold a GUI, such as buttons, etc. It should support both hands individually or both hands at the same time.
6. **Back of hand** is defined by showing the back of the hand, mainly to push any GUI or virtual objects. But it could be used to hold GUI also, like the Palm gesture. It should support both hands individually or both hands at the same time.

3.2 Datasets

The experiments are performed on three different datasets for hand gesture recognition. These include:

---

[2] https://www.tensorflow.org/.

[3] https://www.tensorflow.org/lite.

[4] https://developer.android.com/studio.

[5] https://unity.com/.

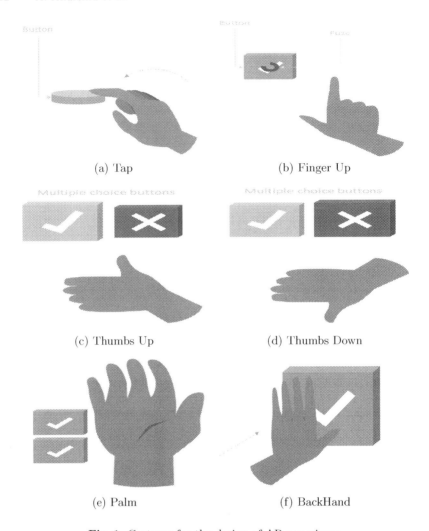

(a) Tap

(b) Finger Up

(c) Thumbs Up

(d) Thumbs Down

(e) Palm

(f) BackHand

Fig. 1. Gestures for the design of AR experience

- **HGR** [9]: contains the gestures from Polish Sign Language (PSL) and American Sign Language (ASL) [9]. HGR1 (PSL) contains 899 images acquired from 12 individuals and contains 25 gestures taken in uncontrolled lighting conditions with image dimensions varied from 174×131 up to 640×480. Similarly, HGR2 (ASL) contains $(85+574)$ images containing 13 gestures of $(3+18)$ individuals among which contains images taken under controlled and uncontrolled lighting conditions with varied image dimensions $(4672 \times 3104$ (uncontrolled) or 3264×4928 (controlled green tone).
- **Senz3D** [16]: dataset acquired with the Creative Senz3D camera [16]. It contains 11 different gestures performed by 4 different people and is available

online[6]. Each gesture has been repeated by each user 30 times for a total of 1320 acquisitions; and

– **Hololens**: dataset created by the authors. The data samples were recorded using Microsoft HoloLens 2[7] AR device and contains 6 gestures mentioned in the Sect. 3.1 recorded as images. Each image contains a dimension of 1920×1080 in RGB color space. The dataset contains close to 2000 images and each gesture has between 300 to 310 images with varied and uncontrolled lighting conditions, which makes it challenging. These images are divided into training, validation, and test datasets, where training contains 240 images, and 30 images for each validation, and 30 or more for test per gesture.

3.3   Quantitative Evaluation

The proposed approach is compared quantitatively with the following methods: Skin detection using spatial analysis with adaptive seed [8] and Self-adaptive algorithm for segmenting skin regions [10], on Hand Gesture Recognition dataset [9]. Skin detection performance is assessed based on 10 metrics, namely: Attack Presentation Classification Error Rate (APCER), Normal Presentation Classification Error Rate (NPCER), Average Classification Error Rate (ACER), True Positive Rate (TPR), i.e. a percentage of skin pixels classified as skin, True Negative Rate (TNR), i.e. a percentage of background pixels classified as background, False Positive Rate (FPR), i.e. a percentage of background pixels misclassified as skin, and b) False Negative Rate (fn), i.e. a percentage of undetected skin pixels, recall, Jaccard similarity measure, accuracy, and F1 score. For details on APCER, NPCER, and ACER, we refer to [12].

Table 1 shows the evaluation of the proposed method and the comparative methods, **representative of the state-of-the-art**.

Table 1 shows the quantitative evaluation of the proposed method and the comparative methods representative of the state-of-the-art on the metrics mentioned above. ApCER, NPCER, ACER, and FPR are error measures, and the lower the values of these metrics, the better, whereas TPR, recall, accuracy, and F1 score require higher values for the algorithm correctness. For the HGR1 dataset, the baseline method performs slightly better than the proposed method. However, for HGR2, the Grzejszczak gesture recognition method [5] outperforms the other methods including the proposed method in terms of correctness. The reason for such behavior is the limited amount of data available to train for each class. On the other hand, the proposed method outperforms the comparative methods in terms of error measures, especially accuracy, APCER, and FPR on HGR2. This is the indication that the proposed method is more resistant to the error as compared to the comparative methods. Moreover, the proposed method performs better than the comparative methods on the SENZ3D dataset [15] on all the metrics except recall. The Kwalok gesture recognition method has 1% higher than the proposed method. Moreover, the proposed method outperforms

---

[6] http://lttm.dei.unipd.it/downloads/gesture2.

[7] https://www.microsoft.com/en-us/hololens.

Table 1. Quantitative evaluation of the proposed and comparative methods.

Method	APCER	NPCER	ACER	FPR	TPR	Recall	Accuracy	F1Score
HGR1 dataset [10]								
Kawlok et al. [8]	**0.0336**	0.0381	**0.03591**	**0.03363**	0.9618	**0.9663**	**0.9660**	**0.9366**
Kawlok et al. [10]	0.0446	0.0444	0.0445	0.04462	0.9556	0.9554	0.9583	0.9298
Grzejszczak et al. [5]	0.257	**0.02674**	0.1419	0.2572	**0.9732**	0.7427	0.8006	0.7886
Proposed	0.0385	0.0431	0.3632	0.0384	0.9533	0.9361	0.9259	0.9217
HGR2 dataset [10]								
Kawlok et al. [8]	0.03088	**0.04342**	0.0372	0.0309	0.9566	0.9691	0.9667	0.8991
Kawlok et al. [10]	0.0381	0.0311	**0.0346**	0.03815	**0.9689**	0.9618	0.9621	0.8770
Grzejszczak et al. [5]	0.0130	0.1046	0.0588	0.0130	0.8954	**0.9869**	0.9769	**0.9074**
Proposed	**0.0094**	0.2757	0.1426	**0.0094**	0.7243	0.7243	**0.9812**	0.7548
SENZ3D dataset [15]								
Kawlok et al. [10]	0.0085	0.0874	0.0479	0.0085	0.9126	**0.9126**	0.9848	0.9146
Memo et al. [16]	x	x	x	x	x	x	0.8991	x
Grzejszczak et al. [5]	0.0473	0.5555	0.3014	0.0473	0.4444	0.7537	0.9173	0.4898
Proposed	**0.0064**	**0.0643**	**0.0353**	**0.0032**	**0.9936**	0.9017	**0.9883**	**0.9326**
HoloLens dataset								
Kawlok et al. [10]	0.0222	0.1142	0.0682	0.0222	0.8858	0.8858	0.9625	0.8825
Memo et al. [16]	0.0562	0.2782	0.1672	0.0562	0.7218	0.7218	0.9107	0.7260
Grzejszczak et al. [5]	0.1747	0.3359	0.25534	0.1747	0.6640	0.7917	0.7690	0.6574
Proposed	**0.0044**	**0.0219**	**0.0132**	**0.0044**	**0.9780**	**0.9569**	**0.9927**	**0.9780**

the comparative methods on the HoloLens dataset on all metrics. Especially on the error metrics, the proposed method is much more resistant to errors than the comparative methods. Therefore, the proposed gesture recognition is more stable and does not identify wrong gestures. In conclusion, the proposed gesture recognition is more suitable for AR devices than the comparative methods representative of the state-of-the-art.

4   Conclusions

This work proposes a gesture recognition approach for the design of Augmented Reality interaction and experience. We propose to utilize hand detection followed by a gesture classification CNN. This approach of hand detection first improves the efficiency of gesture recognition, and also allows gesture recognition to perform effectively in varied background conditions. The most important quality of the proposed method is that it is more resistant to error than the comparative methods, and outperforms comparative methods in terms of error measures on all four tested datasets. In the future, we look to improve gesture recognition by including more gestures and also using temporal information effectively.

References

1. Agrawal, M., Ainapure, R., Agrawal, S., Bhosale, S., Desai, S.: Models for hand gesture recognition using deep learning. In: 2020 IEEE 5th International Conference on Computing Communication and Automation (ICCCA), pp. 589–594 (2020). https://doi.org/10.1109/ICCCA49541.2020.9250846
2. Bao, P., Maqueda, A.I., del Blanco, C.R., García, N.: Tiny hand gesture recognition without localization via a deep convolutional network. IEEE Trans. Consum. Electron. **63**(3), 251–257 (2017)
3. Devineau, G., Moutarde, F., Xi, W., Yang, J.: Deep learning for hand gesture recognition on skeletal data. In: 2018 13th IEEE International Conference on Automatic Face & Gesture Recognition (FG 2018), pp. 106–113. IEEE (2018)
4. Girshick, R.: Fast R-CNN. In: Proceedings of the IEEE International Conference on Computer Vision, pp. 1440–1448 (2015)
5. Grzejszczak, T., Kawulok, M., Galuszka, A.: Hand landmarks detection and localization in color images. Multimedia Tools Appl. **75**(23), 16363–16387 (2015). https://doi.org/10.1007/s11042-015-2934-5
6. Jiang, F., Wu, S., Yang, G., Zhao, D., Kung, S.: Independent hand gesture recognition with Kinect. SIViP **8**(1), 163–172 (2014)
7. John, V., Boyali, A., Mita, S., Imanishi, M., Sanma, N.: Deep learning-based fast hand gesture recognition using representative frames. In: 2016 International Conference on Digital Image Computing: Techniques and Applications (DICTA), pp. 1–8 (2016). https://doi.org/10.1109/DICTA.2016.7797030
8. Kawulok, M., Kawulok, J., Nalepa, J., Papiez, M.: Skin detection using spatial analysis with adaptive seed. In: 2013 IEEE International Conference on Image Processing, pp. 3720–3724 (2013). https://doi.org/10.1109/ICIP.2013.6738767
9. Kawulok, M.: Database for hand gesture recognition (2013). http://sun.aei.polsl.pl/~mkawulok/gestures/. Accessed 30 Oct 2020
10. Kawulok, M., Kawulok, J., Nalepa, J., Smolka, B.: Self-adaptive algorithm for segmenting skin regions. EURASIP J. Adv. Sig. Process. **2014**(1), 1–22 (2014). https://doi.org/10.1186/1687-6180-2014-170
11. Khurshid, A., Cleger, S., Grunitzki, R.: A scene classification approach for augmented reality devices. In: Stephanidis, C., Chen, J.Y.C., Fragomeni, G. (eds.) HCII 2020. LNCS, vol. 12428, pp. 164–177. Springer, Cham (2020). https://doi.org/10.1007/978-3-030-59990-4_14
12. Khurshid, A., Tamayo, S.C., Fernandes, E., Gadelha, M.R., Teofilo, M.: A robust and real-time face anti-spoofing method based on texture feature analysis. In: International Conference on Human-Computer Interaction. pp. 484–496. Springer (2019). https://doi.org/10.1007/978-3-030-30033-3_37
13. Kourbane, I., Genc, Y.: Skeleton-aware multi-scale heatmap regression for 2D hand pose estimation. arXiv preprint arXiv:2105.10904 (2021)
14. Li, G., et al.: Hand gesture recognition based on convolution neural network. Clust. Comput. **22**(2), 2719–2729 (2017). https://doi.org/10.1007/s10586-017-1435-x
15. Memo, A., Minto, L., Zanuttigh, P.: Exploiting Silhouette descriptors and synthetic data for hand gesture recognition. In: Giachetti, A., Biasotti, S., Tarini, M. (eds.) Smart Tools and Apps for Graphics - Eurographics Italian Chapter Conference. The Eurographics Association (2015). https://doi.org/10.2312/stag.20151288
16. Memo, A., Zanuttigh, P.: Head-mounted gesture controlled interface for human-computer interaction. Multimedia Tools Appl. **77**(1), 27–53 (2016). https://doi.org/10.1007/s11042-016-4223-3

17. Nalepa, J., Kawulok, M.: Fast and accurate hand shape classification. In: Kozielski, S., Mrozek, D., Kasprowski, P., Małysiak-Mrozek, B., Kostrzewa, D. (eds.) BDAS 2014. CCIS, vol. 424, pp. 364–373. Springer, Cham (2014). https://doi.org/10.1007/978-3-319-06932-6_35

18. Narasimhaswamy, S., Wei, Z., Wang, Y., Zhang, J., Hoai, M.: Contextual attention for hand detection in the wild. In: Proceedings of the IEEE/CVF International Conference on Computer Vision, pp. 9567–9576 (2019)

19. organization, T.: Model Optimization. https://www.tensorflow.org/lite/performance/model_optimization. Accessed 01 Dec 2001

20. Oudah, M., Al-Naji, A., Chahl, J.: Hand gesture recognition based on computer vision: a review of techniques. J. Imag. **6**(8), 73 (2020)

21. Ren, S., He, K., Girshick, R., Sun, J.: Faster R-CNN: towards real-time object detection with region proposal networks. Adv. Neural Inf. Process. Syst. **28**, 91–99 (2015)

22. Russakovsky, O., et al.: ImageNet large scale visual recognition challenge. Int. J. Comput. Vision **115**(3), 211–252 (2015). https://doi.org/10.1007/s11263-015-0816-y

23. Szegedy, C., et al.: Going deeper with convolutions. In: 2015 IEEE Conference on Computer Vision and Pattern Recognition (CVPR), pp. 1–9 (2015). https://doi.org/10.1109/CVPR.2015.7298594

24. Teeparthi, S., Jatla, V., Pattichis, M.S., Celedón-Pattichis, S., LópezLeiva, C.: Fast hand detection in collaborative learning environments. In: Tsapatsoulis, N., Panayides, A., Theocharides, T., Lanitis, A., Pattichis, C., Vento, M. (eds.) CAIP 2021. LNCS, vol. 13052, pp. 445–454. Springer, Cham (2021). https://doi.org/10.1007/978-3-030-89128-2_43

Natural 3D Object Manipulation for Interactive Laparoscopic Augmented Reality Registration

Tonia Mielke⬤, Fabian Joeres⬤, and Christian Hansen$^{(\boxtimes)}$⬤

Faculty of Computer Science and Research Campus STIMULATE,
Otto-von-Guericke-University, Magdeburg, Germany
{tonia.mielke,fabian.joeres,christian.hansen}@ovgu.de

Abstract. Due to the growing focus on minimally invasive surgery, there is increasing interest in intraoperative software support. For example, augmented reality can be used to provide additional information. Accurate registration is required for effective support. In this work, we present a manual registration method that aims at mimicking natural manipulation of 3D objects using tracked surgical instruments. This method is compared to a point-based registration method in a simulated laparoscopic environment. Both registration methods serve as an initial alignment step prior to surface-based registration refinement. For the evaluation, we conducted a user study with 12 participants. The registration methods were compared in terms of registration accuracy, registration duration, and subjective usability feedback. No significant differences could be found with respect to the previously mentioned criteria between the manual and the point-based registration methods. Thus, the manual registration did not outperform the reference method. However, we found that our method offers qualitative advantages, which may make it more suitable for some application scenarios. Furthermore we identified possible approaches for improvement, which should be investigated in the future to strengthen possible advantages of our registration method.

Keywords: Augmented reality · 3D interaction · Registration · Laparoscopic surgery

1 Introduction

While minimally invasive laparoscopic surgery is gaining significance, the indirect perception and limited field of view during surgery pose challenges. To support surgeons during these operations, intraoperative software support, e.g. using augmented reality (AR), can be helpful [3].

To provide effective software support through AR during surgery, an exact registration is required, which can be achieved by surface-based registration. In surface-based registration, the distance between a point cloud acquired intraoperatively and a point cloud obtained from geometric information of preoperative

© The Author(s), under exclusive license to Springer Nature Switzerland AG 2022
J. Y. C. Chen and G. Fragomeni (Eds.): HCII 2022, LNCS 13317, pp. 317–328, 2022.
https://doi.org/10.1007/978-3-031-05939-1_21

data is minimized. The quality of the registration results depends on an initial transformation, which can be accomplished through an initial registration. Initial registrations can be performed point-based or interactively.

In point-based registration, individual landmarks are selected on both the virtual and physical model, between which the square distances are minimized. As landmarks, intrinsic or extrinsic markers can be selected on the virtual model and subsequently recorded on the physical model, for example, by touching them with a tracked surgical instrument [3]. At least three markers are needed for registration, for example, Conrad et al. [8] use four markers.

In interactive registration methods, the required rotation and translation can be determined by different user interactions. This allows users to iteratively adjust the registration result in real-time [16]. For this, for example, the virtual model can be rotated and translated on a previously captured screenshot of the laparoscopic image until the virtual and the physical model are optimally aligned [7]. It is also possible to manually manipulate fewer degrees of freedom, for example by determining the translation by recording a single landmark and then only manually adjusting the rotation [17]. There are different possibilities for input during manual registration, e.g. by using a touch screen monitor or a mouse [18], a tracked rigid body [21] or gestures [11]. As manual registration is the three-dimensional manipulation of virtual objects, established approaches from virtual reality (VR) can also be used for the required user input. The most promising approach in VR is to mimic natural interactions with real objects [9,15,20]. Based on these concepts, Joeres et al. [13] presented two possibilities to use surgical instruments for natural interactions with the virtual content.

In this work, we investigated an improved interactive, intraoperative AR registration of anatomical kidney models, for which laparoscopic kidney surgery served as an example.

2   Registration Methods

We developed one initial manual registration method that was compared to a point-based approach. Both registration methods act as the initial alignment step prior to surface-based registration.

2.1   Manual Registration

In manual registration, rotation and translation of the virtual model are adjusted until optimal alignment with the physical model is reached. Because the registration aims at mimicking natural interactions, we use surgical instruments that are already part of the workflow as input device. These are tracked optically to allow movement of the instrument to manipulate the virtual model. The interaction is divided into four modes activated by buttons (see Fig. 1). These modes can only be activated when the instrument tip is in the field of view of the laparoscope.

The *start mode* initiates the registration by placing the virtual model 100 mm in front of the instrument tip. Then, three different modes are available for

adjusting the degrees of freedom, which are activated by pressing the corresponding buttons. In *translation mode* the virtual model is translated by mapping the
movement of the instrument tip to the center of gravity of the virtual model
(Fig. 1a). It is visualized by a handle that extends from the virtual model's center of gravity to the tip of the instrument. In *free rotation mode*, rotation is
achieved using a handle $\overrightarrow{MI}$ running from the tip of the instrument to the center of gravity of the virtual model (Fig. 1b). By moving the instrument tip, the
virtual model is rotated according to the rotation of $\overrightarrow{MI}$. This mode is visualized
on the augmented reality screen by displaying $\overrightarrow{MI}$. The last mode is the *axis
rotation mode*, in which the virtual model is rotated around $\overrightarrow{MI}$, defined by the
position of the instrument tip. Therefore, the rotation axis $\overrightarrow{MI}$ is initiated when
the button is pressed. By moving the instrument tip around $\overrightarrow{MI}$, the model is
rotated around this axis (Fig. 1c). This mode is also supported by the visualization of the rotation axis $\overrightarrow{MI}$. Additionally, a handle leading perpendicularly
from the rotation axis to the instrument tip is visualized.

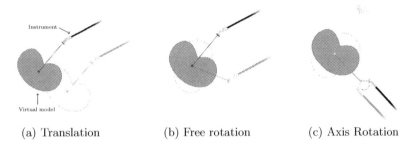

(a) Translation   (b) Free rotation   (c) Axis Rotation

Fig. 1. Overview over different modes for interaction with the virtual model

2.2 Point-Based Registration

As a reference method for manual registration, point-based registration using
anatomical internal landmarks was implemented. The registration consists of two
steps (similar to [13]). In the first planning phase, four characteristic landmarks
are identified. These can be selected on the virtual model's surface by rotating the
model and finally clicking on the desired positions using a mouse. In the second
step, the previously selected points have to be identified on the physical model
by touching them with the tracked laparoscopic instrument. From the resulting
point clouds, the position and orientation of the virtual model is determined [1].

2.3 Surface-Based Registration

To improve the accuracy of the initial registration, a surface-based registration was implemented (similar to [14]). Surface-based registration minimizes the

distance between the point clouds of the virtual and the physical model. There-fore, the point cloud describing the physical model's surface is determined by moving the tracked instrument along different arbitrary paths on the surface. While pressing a foot pedal, points are recorded along these paths. The points describing the virtual model can be extracted from the surface mesh. Then, the required transformation of the virtual model can be determined using the specified points and the Iterative Closest Point Algorithm [4].

2.4   Prototype Implementation

We implemented a video see-through AR prototype in Unity 2018 (Unity Tech-nologies, USA). The laparoscopic video was captured from an Einstein Vision©
3.0 laparoscope (B. Braun Melsungen AG, Germany). The camera was calibrated using the pinhole camera model [22] of the OpenCV library [5]. A ChArUCo pattern [10] was used to determine the internal camera parameters. The exter-nal camera parameters were determined using a tracked calibration body. The laparoscopic video stream is permanently displayed on one screen. On another screen, either the registration GUI or the image captured by the laparoscope overlaid with the AR content is displayed (Fig. 2a). The virtual kidney model was presented as a semi-transparent solid surface. Standard surgical graspers were used as the tracked surgical instrument required for registration. Both the laparoscope's camera head and the surgical graspers (Fig. 2b) are tracked using passive optical tracking markers with an Atracsys fusionTrack 500 infrared track-ing camera. The offset between the tip of the graspers and the attached markers was determined by pivot calibration using NDI Toolbox software (Northern Dig-ital Inc, Canada) and an NDI Polaris Spectra infrared tracking camera.

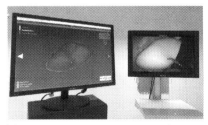 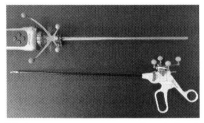

(a) Display Setup. Left screen showing our software during point-based regis-tration. Right screen displays laparo-scopic video

(b) Laparoscopic camera head (top) and surgical graspers (bottom) with passive tracking markers

Fig. 2. Main components of our prototypical laparoscopic AR system

3   Experiment Methods

3.1   Study Design

The user study was conducted in a within-subject repeated measurement design. The independent variables were the registration methods. All participants performed both initial registrations in combination with surface-based registration, the order of initial alignments was counterbalanced. Three dependent variables were examined for the comparison between manual and point-based registration: accuracy, duration, and subjective feedback. In addition, the accuracy of surface-based registration was recorded. Accuracy was determined using the mean target registration error (TRE). The registration time was measured by the task completion time (TCT), which describes the time required to complete the interaction for the initial registration. The perception on the usability of the users was recorded using the System Usability Scale (SUS) by Brooke et al. [6], which was translated to German. In addition, a semi-structured interview was conducted to obtain qualitative feedback on the initial registration methods.

3.2   Sample Design

Twelve subjects participated in the user study. The inclusion criterion was a medical background where participants had to be at least in their 3rd year of medical school. Participants were paid 20€ for participation in the study.

3.3   Study Setup

To simulate the surgical site a partially occluded kidney phantom was positioned in a laparoscopic training torso model (EasyLap Training System, HumanX GmbH, Germany). The 3D-printed kidney models were based on a public computer tomography database [12]. Two healthy kidneys were manually segmented and converted to surface mesh models. The kidney models were rigidly connected to an optical marker that served as a world anchor (Fig. 3a). This world anchor acted as a reference point for all other tracked markers. In addition, the models were covered at one pole by a cloth. This was to simulate the limited access and visibility. It was important that at least 28% of the kidney were accessible for surface-based registration to enable robust registration [2]. One kidney model was positioned in the torso model at a time (Fig. 3b). The marker was guided outward to make it visible to the tracking camera. The torso model was then closed. Instruments were passed through two 12 mm trocars into the interior of the torso model. The laparoscope was passed through the left trocar and rigidly positioned with a tripod. The position of the laparoscope remained constant throughout the procedure. Participants held the surgical instrument that served as a pointing tool in the right hand, while an remote control with four buttons was held in the left hand. The overall study setup is shown in Fig. 3c.

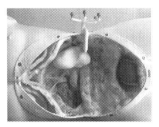

(a) Torso with kidney phantom fixed by tracked clamp

(b) Partly occluded phantom with manual registration GUI

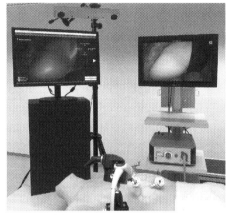

(c) Overall study setup

Fig. 3. Main components of the study setup

3.4 Study Procedure

After the participants were welcomed, they were asked to sign the informed consent form and demographic data were recorded. A brief introduction to laparoscopic AR and registration was then given. Training was provided at the beginning of the study to learn how to use the instruments and to strengthen hand-eye coordination. This consisted of a self-built version of the "Checkerboard Drill" [19] and a task of tracing lines on the surface of a deformable ball. The second task was intended as practice for the later surface recording. Each of the tasks was performed once by each participant, with no measurement or recording of performance. Subsequently, one trial block was performed for each of the two initial registration methods in combination with the surface-based registration. The order of the blocks was counterbalanced. At the beginning of each block, the basic functionality of the corresponding registration method was explained. Each block consisted of three trials to familiarize users with the interactions. In the first trial, step-by-step instructions for the registration methods were given. In the second trial the participants acted independently, but with the opportunity to ask questions. For the third trial, the kidney model was exchanged.

The order of the used kidney models was counterbalanced. In the third execution, the required variables for the evaluation were recorded. Finally, participants were asked to complete the SUS questionnaire for the initial registration previously performed. After the completion of both blocks, a short semi-structured interview was conducted with the participants.

4   Results

4.1   Data Exclusion

Two participants were excluded from the entire evaluation because they each attained very high TREs for one initial registration. One subject achieved a mean TRE of 103.96 mm for manual registration, and the other achieved a mean TRE of 120.21 mm for point-based registration. These two very high TREs indicate the upper and lower kidney poles being interchanged. This suggests problems in visualization, i.e., recognizing the correct placement of the kidney, rather than problems with interaction. One additional participant was excluded for analysis of the TCT only. This participant required 537 s to complete the point-based registration. This high TCT can be attributed to the fact that the participant was very unsure which kidney pole of the virtual model corresponded to which pole of the physical model. Therefor the kidney was rotated 180° several times to identify corresponding landmarks. In the interview, the participant stated they found the spatial imagination challenging and therefore had problems orienting the virtual model. Since this TCT does not influence the registration accuracy, the participant is included in the other aspects of the evaluation.

4.2   Participants Demographics

For the evaluation of the study results, the data of 10 participants (nine female, one male) were included. The participants were medical students between the third and sixth year of their studies. They were between 20 and 34 years old (median = 25 years). Seven of the participants had previous experience in laparoscopy. Of these, four had experience exclusively in the trainer, one exclusively in the OR, and two in both the trainer and OR. These participants had between 1 and 20 h of previous experience (median = 2 h). The two participants excluded from the analysis had no distinctive demographic features.

4.3   Statistical Results

The statistical results of our experiment are stated in Table 1. No significant differences were observed for the TRE (see also Fig. 4a), the TCT (Fig. 4c) and the SUS rating (Fig. 4d). Descriptively, however, the manual method performed slightly better for the TRE and the TCT. Furthermore, both initial registration methods could be significantly improved by the surface-based registration. The results of these surface-based registrations did not differ significantly depending on the initial registration method (Fig. 4b).

Table 1. Statistical results for all depended variables and results of the paired t-test

	Manual	Point-based	T	p	d
TRE	10.40 ± 1.85 mm	11.46 ± 1.50 mm	0.413	0.344	0.13
TCT	159.74 ± 14.67 s	188.08 ± 32.59 s	0.782	0.228	0.26
SUS	65.50 ± 6.63	71.50 ± 4.80	0.658	0.264	0.21

The first two columns are in the format <mean value ± (standard error)>

4.4   Qualitative Feedback

From the qualitative data analysis, six general categories of comments on the registration concepts can be derived. These include comments on general impression, overview during registration, influence of practice on results, depth perception, error correction, and confidence in a correct registration result. It should be noted that the reported data are qualitative and no conclusions should be drawn from the reported frequencies. Due to the open interview format, these are not necessarily representative.

Manual Registration. Four participants reported that they felt very confident during manual registration because they felt in control over the results. According to two participants, errors could be easily recognized, allowing them to be compensated. Generally, the translation and rotation of the virtual model through the interaction are well predictable according to two participants. Three participants reported that the division into different modes led to a division of labor that reduced perceived difficulty. One participant was critical of how the instrument had to be moved in the torso for the interaction. Four participants felt that it is tedious to rotate the model completely, leaving limited overview. Five participants reported difficulty perceiving the topology of the virtual model due to the semi-transparency, which resulted in them mainly using the contour for registration. Additionally, two participants commented on difficulties in depth perception due to the static camera position. Four participants noted that practice was needed to use the different modes. Three participants felt that they would feel more confident with more practice and two participants felt that more experience would also make the interaction faster.

Point-Based Registration. Point-based registration was described by two participants as intuitive and easy to learn. However, two participants indicated that it was difficult to identify corresponding landmarks because the virtual model was displayed on a separate screen, making it difficult to verify the correct orientation. According to five participants, mouse interaction was more intuitive than interaction with the surgical instrument because the use of the mouse was already familiar. One difficulty of the interaction, two participants noted, was that the results were unpredictable. In addition, this final result could not be corrected, which meant that the desired result could not always be achieved.

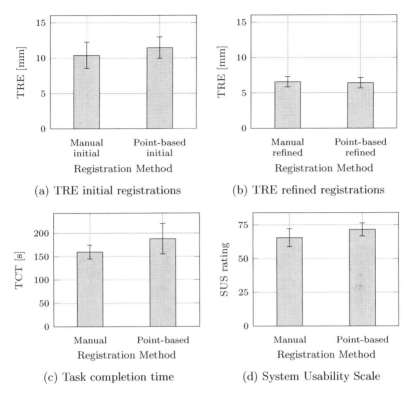

Fig. 4. Statistical results for all dependent variables. Error bars show standard errors

5 Discussion

5.1 Discussion of Results

The results show no significant difference between the registration accuracy of point-based and manual registration. In manual registration difficulties in the accurate positioning of the virtual model can possibly be attributed to problems in visualization. First, depth cues are lost due to the semi-transparent visualization of the virtual model, thus participants mainly relied on contours for registration, making it easier for errors to occur. Possibly, an improved model visualization could ease the alignment between the virtual and physical model and thus improve the accuracy and prevent extreme outliers like the excluded participants. Second, slight inaccuracies in the camera calibration could lead to the virtual content not being displayed at the exact position on the laparoscopic image. Therefore, even though the alignment is perceived as optimal, the results could be shifted.

No significant difference in TCT of the two initial registration methods could be found either. In both point-based and manual registration, a lot of time was required to match the kidney poles of the models. It should be noted that only the time needed for the interaction during initial registration was recorded since only the duration of the key steps of the workflow was to be analyzed. The time required in point-based registration between the selection of the markers and the recording of the points, which is needed for the movement between input devices, was neglected because it cannot yet be determined whether both steps will be performed by the same person. Therefore, possible time advantages of manual registration, which can be performed by one person continuously, are not taken into account.

5.2 General Discussion

During the development and evaluation of the registration methods, deformations of the kidney were neglected. In the study, a rigid kidney model was used, so deformations caused by touch of the instrument were not modeled. This could have influences especially on the point recording in the point-based registration and on the tactile surface recording. In addition, the rigid kidney model could provide haptic feedback, especially during point recording. This could have led to advantages compared to manual registration.

Further limitation results from the selection of participants for the user study. Due to the participation requirements, only a small sample of subjects was able to participate. With more participants, better generalizations could be made. Additionally, the experience among the participants in using laparoscopic instruments was limited. Surgeons with more experience could potentially obtain different results.

One limitation in the study setup lies in the remote control for manual registration being held with the left hand. In practice, this setup might not be possible because the surgeon may need to handle additional instruments. This could be solved by attaching the buttons to the instrument or using non-touch interactions such as voice activation. Alternatively, foot pedal control could be possible, as is already used in point-based and surface-based registration.

A final limitation is given by the general comparison of a manual method with a point-based method. The point-based method was chosen because it is a standard used in practice. However, a comparison of the method evaluated here with existing manual methods could be useful.

The results suggest comparable registration accuracy and registration duration. Therefore, it may be useful to consider further benefits and drawbacks of the registration methods. Manual registration offers the advantage that the entire registration procedure can be performed standing at the patient side. No additional tools are introduced into the workflow except for the buttons, which could potentially be integrated into the instruments. This could reduce the time required for movement between registration input devices and patients. Considering the conditions in the OR, it could be that for sterility reasons surgeons cannot perform the marker positioning themselves. This would cause further difficulties that can be avoided with manual registration. The registration methods were each used as initial alignment but due to the different characteristics, different application scenarios could be applicable. The point-based registration seems to be well suited for getting an initial overview. Thus, this could be used when there is no previous knowledge about the location of the kidney. However, with point-based registration, it is not possible to correct errors in the registration result. Therefore, manual registration could be suitable to manually adjust existing registration results. For example, the scenario presented in Joeres et al. [14] could be a possible application. Here, after tumor resection and resulting deformation and movement of the kidney, the result is to be adjusted. This could overcome the difficulty of tedious large rotations that emerged in the qualitative feedback, as only fine adjustments are necessary.

6   Conclusion

In this work, we presented and evaluated a method for manual AR content registration during laparoscopic surgery using tracked surgical instruments for natural user input. We compared our method to a point-based registration as an initial registration step prior to surface-based registration. Results of the user study indicated that the novel manual registration method could not significantly outperform the reference method in terms of registration accuracy, registration speed, and subjective user feedback. However, possible improvements and application scenarios for this method were identified. Further research is required to address difficulties in visualization and to investigate the potential of our registration method for alternative application scenarios.

References

1. Arun, K.S., Huang, T.S., Blostein, S.D.: Least-squares fitting of two 3-d point sets. IEEE Trans. Pattern Anal. Mach. Intell. **PAMI-9(5)**, 698–700 (1987). https://doi.org/10.1109/TPAMI.1987.4767965
2. Benincasa, A.B., Clements, L.W., Herrell, S.D., Galloway, R.L.: Feasibility study for image-guided kidney surgery: assessment of required intraoperative surface for accurate physical to image space registrations. Med. Phys. **35**(9), 4251–4261 (2008)
3. Bernhardt, S., Nicolau, S.A., Soler, L., Doignon, C.: The status of augmented reality in laparoscopic surgery as of 2016. Med. Image Anal. **37**, 66–90 (2017)
4. Besl, P.J., McKay, N.D.: Method for registration of 3-d shapes. In: Sensor Fusion IV: Control Paradigms and Data Structures, vol. 1611, pp. 586–606. International Society for Optics and Photonics (1992)
5. Bradski, G.: The OpenCV library. Dr. Dobb's J. Softw. Tools Prof. Program. **25**(11), 120–123 (2000)
6. Brooke, J., et al.: SUS - a quick and dirty usability scale. Usability Eval. Ind. **189**(194), 4–7 (1996)
7. Chen, Y., Li, H., Wu, D., Bi, K., Liu, C.: Surgical planning and manual image fusion based on 3d model facilitate laparoscopic partial nephrectomy for intrarenal tumors. World J. Urol. **32**(6), 1493–1499 (2014)
8. Conrad, C., Fusaglia, M., Peterhans, M., Lu, H., Weber, S., Gayet, B.: Augmented reality navigation surgery facilitates laparoscopic rescue of failed portal vein embolization. J. Am. Coll. Surg. **223**(4), e31–e34 (2016)

9. De Araújo, B.R., Casiez, G., Jorge, J.A., Hachet, M.: Mockup builder: 3d modeling on and above the surface. Comput. Graph. **37**(3), 165–178 (2013)

10. Garrido-Jurado, S., Muñoz-Salinas, R., Madrid-Cuevas, F.J., Marín-Jiménez, M.J.: Automatic generation and detection of highly reliable fiducial markers under occlusion. Pattern Recogn. **47**(6), 2280–2292 (2014)

11. Gong, R.H., Güler, Ö., Kürklüoglu, M., Lovejoy, J., Yaniv, Z.: Interactive initialization of 2d/3d rigid registration. Med. Phys. **40**(12), 121911 (2013)

12. Heller, N., et al.: The KiTS19 challenge data: 300 kidney tumor cases with clinical context, CT semantic segmentations, and surgical outcomes. arXiv preprint arXiv:1904.00445 (2019)

13. Joeres, F., Heinrich, F., Schott, D., Hansen, C.: Towards natural 3d interaction for laparoscopic augmented reality registration. Comput. Meth. Biomech. Biomed. Eng. Imaging Visual. **9**(4), 384–391 (2020)

14. Joeres, F., Mielke, T., Hansen, C.: Laparoscopic augmented reality registration for oncological resection site repair. Int. J. Comput. Assist. Radiol. Surg. **16**(9), 1577–1586 (2021). https://doi.org/10.1007/s11548-021-02336-x

15. Mendes, D., Caputo, F.M., Giachetti, A., Ferreira, A., Jorge, J.: A survey on 3d virtual object manipulation: from the desktop to immersive virtual environments. In: Computer Graphics Forum, vol. 38, pp. 21–45 (2019)

16. Nicolau, S., Soler, L., Mutter, D., Marescaux, J.: Augmented reality in laparoscopic surgical oncology. Surg. Oncol. **20**(3), 189–201 (2011)

17. Pratt, P.: An effective visualisation and registration system for image-guided robotic partial nephrectomy. J. Robot. Surg. **6**(1), 23–31 (2012)

18. Schneider, C.: Comparison of manual and semi-automatic registration in augmented reality image-guided liver surgery: a clinical feasibility study. Surg. Endosc. **34**(10), 4702–4711 (2020). https://doi.org/10.1007/s00464-020-07807-x

19. Scott, D.J.: Laparoscopic training on bench models: better and more cost effective than operating room experience? J. Am. Coll. Surg. **191**(3), 272–283 (2000)

20. Song, P., Goh, W.B., Hutama, W., Fu, C.W., Liu, X.: A handle bar metaphor for virtual object manipulation with mid-air interaction. In: Proceedings of the SIGCHI Conference on Human Factors in Computing Systems, pp. 1297–1306 (2012)

21. Thompson, S., et al.: Accuracy validation of an image guided laparoscopy system for liver resection. In: Medical imaging 2015: Image-Guided Procedures, Robotic Interventions, and Modeling, vol. 9415, p. 941509. International Society for Optics and Photonics (2015)

22. Zhang, Z.: A flexible new technique for camera calibration. IEEE Trans. Pattern Anal. Mach. Intell. **22**(11), 1330–1334 (2000)

Generating Hand Posture and Motion Dataset for Hand Pose Estimation in Egocentric View

Hwangpil Park[✉], Deokho Kim, Sunghoon Yim, Taehyuk Kwon, Jiwon Jeong, Wonwoo Lee, Jaewoong Lee, Byeongwook Yoo, and Gunill Lee

Samsung Research, Seoul 06765, South Korea
{hwangp.park,deokho16.kim,sunghoon.yim,taehyuk.kwon,jiwon.jeong,
wonw.lee,jw84.lee,byeongw.yoo,gunill.lee}@samsung.com

Abstract. Hand interaction is one of the main input modalities for augmented reality glasses. Vision-based approaches using deep learning have been applied to hand tracking and shown good results. To train a deep neural network, a large dataset of hand information is required. However, obtaining real hand data is painful due to a large number of annotations and lack of diversities such as skins, lighting conditions, and backgrounds. In this paper, we propose a method to generate a synthetic hand dataset that includes diverse human and environmental parameters. By applying constraints of a human hand, we can get realistic hand poses for hand dataset. We also generate dynamic hand animations which can be used for hand gesture recognition.

Keywords: Hand pose estimation · Hand dataset · Synthetic dataset

1 Introduction

Hand interaction is one of the main tools for people to interact with the external environment, so hand interaction is used as important input modality in virtual reality and augmented reality devices, such as Oculus[1] or Hololens[2]. To get spatial information of hand, vision-based approaches are widely used with camera images. However, the performance of the hand tracking using camera images has been limited due to the lack of key points of hands and varying postures between frames. To overcome such problems, recent studies have adopted deep learning for hand tracking which showed breakthrough performance.

To train a neural network for hand tracking, a large amount of data such as images and key point annotations is required. However, there are some physical restrictions to obtaining a dataset from real human hands. First, manual annotations for joint location are needed. It is time-consuming and difficult to localize the exact joint location. Second, it takes a lot of effort to collect variety of image data in different conditions, e.g., lighting, background, and skin colors, etc.

---

[1] www.oculus.com.

[2] www.microsoft.com/hololens.

© The Author(s), under exclusive license to Springer Nature Switzerland AG 2022
J. Y. C. Chen and G. Fragomeni (Eds.): HCII 2022, LNCS 13317, pp. 329–337, 2022.
https://doi.org/10.1007/978-3-031-05939-1_22

In this paper, we propose 3D simulation-based approach for a large-scale hand pose dataset generation. Our method can generate a dataset to deal with several factors affecting the performance which are body poses, skin colors, lighting conditions, and backgrounds. Furthermore, we generated realistic hand poses and motions under detailed constraints of human kinematics. We also demonstrate the performance of hand pose estimation results on the generated dataset.

2   Related Work

Hand pose estimation is a topic that has been continuously studied in the field of computer vision. With the recent development of deep learning, there have been many advances in vision-based hand pose estimation. There have been many kinds of research using depth images [2], RGB images [16], RGB-D [1], or monochrome image [4] as input.

In order to train the neural network for hand pose estimation, dataset that include image data for the hand and well annotated hand joint position data is required. Several works to obtain such a high-quality real hand dataset are continuously being conducted [3,9,12,14,15]. However, a real hand dataset requires manual annotation and is difficult to generalize to various models, postures, and backgrounds.

In order to compensate the physical limitations of a real dataset, there have been studies that produce and use a synthetic dataset for training a neural network [6,10,11,16]. Zimmermann and Brox [16] firstly introduced a large synthetic hand dataset to train a neural network for hand pose estimation. Mueller et al. [11] generated a synthetic hand dataset that mainly includes hand mesh data occulded with objects. Recently, the work of Lin et al. [6] generated a dataset for two-hand pose estimation from an egocentric view.

3   Approach

Our system consists of 3D human models and virtual environments such as cameras, lightings, and backgrounds. When the user provides the value or range of parameters of each component, the system generates feasible hand data by randomly choosing parameter values within the range. The following sections describe each component in detail.

3.1   Human Model and Environment

We have used MB-Lab [8] as a 3D human simulator, which is an add-on of Blender and provides an articulated and parametric human model (Fig. 1). MB-Lab provides six types of character (Asian, African, and Caucasian for each sex) and several body skin parameters. We use all types of character, and skin parameters for veins, freckles, and complexion to generate diverse skin textures. The characters have 21 joints (wrist and four joints for each finger) in each hand,

and two arm joints are used to express more diverse hand gestures. Each joint has three degrees of freedom, but we use an only a subset of the degrees of freedom to get more human-like poses.

Fig. 1. MB-Lab human models used in our paper. The model can be Asian, African, and Caucasian characters with several skin parameters.

In order to generate the dataset, it is necessary to set the camera and lighting for rendering. We place the camera near the eyes of the human model and simulated it with the configurations of a target augmented reality (AR) glasses device. In addition, in order to express a more diverse relative positions between the camera and the hand, the rotations of the neck and arm joints are changed for each rendering (Fig. 2).

We use the basic lightings provided by MB-Lab and arbitrarily changed the parameters of this lightings for each shot. We obtain scenes about various lighting environments by changing the intensity and location of lighting. The intensity of the lightings is determined by multiplying the basic light intensity to an randomly selected ratio, and the range of ratio is $[e^{-1}, e^{1}]$ in our cases. The location of the lighting is randomly chosen in a range within one meter from the character. The background image is also arbitrarily selected.

Once a human pose, skin color, lighting, and a background image are decided, a hand image is rendered by the virtual cameras. Along with the rendered images, we also record all joint rotations in Euler angles, the position of the hand joints in a set of 2D image coordinates, and a set of 3D coordinates with respect to each camera coordinate system.

3.2 Pose Generation

In order to generate a hand pose, the angle of each joint of the human hand should be determined. One simple way to determine the angle of each joint is to arbitrarily set the angle of the hand joints within a predetermined range. However, among the hand poses obtained by arbitrarily selecting the joint angle value, there are postures that a person cannot take actually. This is because the movement of a human hand is limited by the musculoskeletal structure of the human hand. In particular, the joint angle of a finger is strongly limited to the joint angles of the adjacent fingers. Therefore, in order to obtain a realistic hand

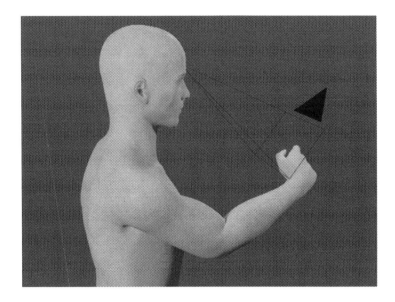

Fig. 2. Our environment for generating hand pose dataset.

pose, these constraints should be considered. We obtained a more realistic hand pose by limiting the range of the hand joints based on the several constraints used in the studies of Lee and T.L. [5] and Lin et al. [7].

There are two types of interdependent constraints; One is *intrafinger*, and the other is *interfinger*. The intrafinger constraint is the relation between distal interphalangeal (DIP) and proximal interphalangeal (PIP) joint angles.

$$\theta_{DIP} = (2/3)\theta_{PIP}. \tag{1}$$

The interfinger constraint is for metacarpophalangeal (MP) joint angles of adjacent fingers.

$$dmin(\theta_{MP}) = \max(\theta_{MP}^{adj} - \theta_0^{inter}, smin(\theta_{MP})), \tag{2}$$

$$dmax(\theta_{MP}) = \min(\theta_{MP}^{adj} + \theta_1^{inter}, smax(\theta_{MP})). \tag{3}$$

where θ_{MP}^{adj} is a MP joint angle of adjacent finger, θ_0^{inter} and θ_1^{inter} are predefined scalar value for each finger pair, $smin(\theta_{MP})$ and $smax(\theta_{MP})$ are minimum and maximum values when ignoring interdependence. We set $smin(\theta_{MP}) = 0$, $smax(\theta_{MP}) = 60^o$ for all fingers.

We obtain hand joint angles whose constraints of real human hands are applied through the following procedure. Firstly, the joint angle of the thumb without interdependence with other fingers was arbitrarily generated within a predetermined range. Secondly, among the fingers with interdependencies, the joint angles of the index finger and the little finger corresponding to both ends were arbitrarily generated within a predetermined angle range. Lastly, the joint angles of the middle finger and the ring finger were arbitrarily generated until the components given in the study of Lee and T.L. [5] were satisfied. Figure 3 shows the hand poses obtained through the procedure.

Fig. 3. Generated hand poses with human hand's constraints [5].

3.3   Animation

Hand animation is a continuous recording of hand poses according to time. In hand animation, a pose in a certain time has a dependency on the front and back poses. Beacause of these characteristics of hand animation, it can be used in hand gesture recognition or hand pose estimation algorithm that use temporal information [4]. For that purpose, we generate and add hand animations to the dataset.

We use two or more key hand poses to generate a single hand animation (Fig. 4). These key hand poses correspond to the hand poses that the character takes at each moment. The key hand poses are created by the method mentioned in Sect. 3.2, or by hand-crafted, or by using the hand joint angle values from an existing real hand dataset. After determining key poses and the times for each key pose, the hand poses for the time between key poses are automatically generated through spherical linear interpolation for rotations of each joints.

4   Experimental Results

Figure 5 and Fig. 6 show the images generated by our method. Our method successfully generated both static hand poses (Fig. 5) and hand motion (Fig. 6) datasets with realistic postures, diverse skin colors, lighting conditions, and backgrounds, as well as consecutive images of feasible hand motion.

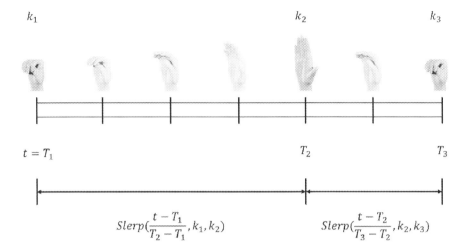

Fig. 4. An example of generating a hand animation from three key poses. k_i are key poses and T_i are corresponding time. Poses in frames between key poses are generated by spherical linear interpolation (slerp) for two adjacent key poses.

Fig. 5. Static hand poses in different environments.

Fig. 6. Dynamic hand motions with randomly selected key poses.

Also, we manually create three different key poses and used the poses for generating hand animation (Fig. 7). In Fig. 7, the first, third, and fifth figures are the key poses. This result verifies that our method can work with either arbitrarily selected pose or existing hand motion data.

We tested a hand pose estimation network trained with the dataset generated by our method. The network was trained to estimate 2D key points and 3D positions of hand joints from a cropped hand image, and EfficientNet-V2 was used as a backbone network [13]. Figure 8 depicts the 2D keypoints estimation results using the trained network, and the average error of 3D joint positions was 15.52 mm. The result shows that our method can generate enough data to be used for learning of pose estimation network.

Fig. 7. Dynamic hand motion with hand-crafted key poses.

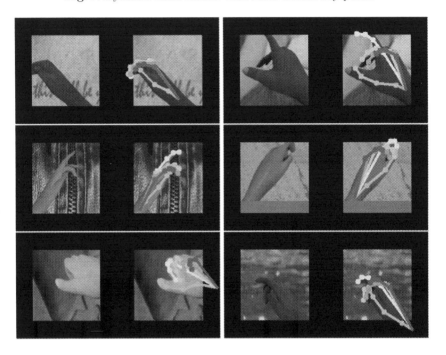

Fig. 8. 2D key points of hand joint estimated by the trained neural network.

5   Conclusion

In this paper, we proposed a method for generating a synthetic dataset for hand tracking. Our method created a human hand dataset that includes various postures, skin conditions, and lighting conditions. Especially, constraints to the human hand joint were added to implement a human hand posture and motion similar to the range of motion of the human hand. In addition, hand animation for hand gesture recognition was also produced by interpolating key poses. Currently, it is not possible to put the hand in the desired position on the image. Using the method of placing the hand in the desired position on the image through inverse kinematics, it will be possible to produce a uniformly distributed dataset with respect to the hand position on the image.

References

1. Dibra, E., Melchior, S., Balkis, A., Wolf, T., Oztireli, C., Gross, M.: Monocular RGB hand pose inference from unsupervised refinable nets. In: Proceedings of the IEEE Conference on Computer Vision and Pattern Recognition (CVPR) Workshops, June 2018 (2018)
2. Ge, L., Liang, H., Yuan, J., Thalmann, D.: Robust 3d hand pose estimation in single depth images: from single-view CNN to multi-view CNNs, June 2016 (2016). https://doi.org/10.1109/CVPR.2016.391
3. Gomez-Donoso, F., Orts-Escolano, S., Cazorla, M.: Large-scale multiview 3d hand pose dataset. CoRR abs/1707.03742 (2017)
4. Han, S., et al.: MEgATrack: monochrome egocentric articulated hand-tracking for virtual reality. ACM Trans. Graph. **39**(4) (2020). https://doi.org/10.1145/3386569.3392452
5. Lee, J., Kunii, T.: Model-based analysis of hand posture. IEEE Comput. Graph. Appl. **15**(5), 77–86 (1995). https://doi.org/10.1109/38.403831
6. Lin, F., Wilhelm, C., Martinez, T.: Two-hand global 3d pose estimation using monocular RGB. In: Proceedings of the IEEE/CVF Winter Conference on Applications of Computer Vision (WACV), pp. 2373–2381, January 2021 (2021)
7. Lin, J., Wu, Y., Huang, T.: Modeling the constraints of human hand motion. In: Proceedings Workshop on Human Motion, pp. 121–126 (2000). https://doi.org/10.1109/HUMO.2000.897381
8. Mb-lab. https://mb-lab-community.github.io/MB-Lab.github.io
9. Moon, G., Yu, S.-I., Wen, H., Shiratori, T., Lee, K.M.: InterHand2.6M: a dataset and baseline for 3d interacting hand pose estimation from a single RGB image. In: Vedaldi, A., Bischof, H., Brox, T., Frahm, J.-M. (eds.) ECCV 2020. LNCS, vol. 12365, pp. 548–564. Springer, Cham (2020). https://doi.org/10.1007/978-3-030-58565-5_33
10. Mueller, F., et al.: GANerated hands for real-time 3d hand tracking from monocular RGB. In: Proceedings of Computer Vision and Pattern Recognition (CVPR), June 2018 (2018). https://handtracker.mpi-inf.mpg.de/projects/GANeratedHands/
11. Mueller, F., Mehta, D., Sotnychenko, O., Sridhar, S., Casas, D., Theobalt, C.: Real-time hand tracking under occlusion from an egocentric RGB-D sensor. In: Proceedings of International Conference on Computer Vision (ICCV), October 2017 (2017). http://handtracker.mpi-inf.mpg.de/projects/OccludedHands/
12. Simon, T., Joo, H., Matthews, I.A., Sheikh, Y.: Hand keypoint detection in single images using multiview bootstrapping. CoRR abs/1704.07809 (2017)
13. Tan, M., Le, Q.: EfficientNetV2: smaller models and faster training. In: Meila, M., Zhang, T. (eds.) Proceedings of the 38th International Conference on Machine Learning. Proceedings of Machine Learning Research, July 2021, vol. 139, pp. 10096–10106. PMLR (2021)
14. Yangang Wang, C.P., Liu, Y.: Mask-pose cascaded CNN for 2d hand pose estimation from single color images. IEEE Trans. Circ. Syst. Video Technol. **29**(11), 3258–3268 (2019). https://doi.org/10.1109/TCSVT.2018.2879980
15. Zhang, X., et al.: Hand image understanding via deep multi-task learning. In: Proceedings of the IEEE/CVF International Conference on Computer Vision (ICCV), pp. 11281–11292 (2021)
16. Zimmermann, C., Brox, T.: Learning to estimate 3d hand pose from single RGB images. In: IEEE International Conference on Computer Vision (ICCV) (2017)

Real-Time Bimanual Interaction Across Virtual Workspaces

Chao Peng[(✉)] , Yangzi Dong , and Lizhou Cao

School of Interactive Games and Media, Rochester Institute of Technology,
Rochester, NY, USA
{cxpigm,yd8608,lc1248}@rit.edu

Abstract. This work investigates bimanual interaction modalities for interaction between a virtual personal workspace and a virtual shared workspace in virtual reality (VR). In VR social platforms, personal and shared workspaces are commonly used to support virtual presentations, remote collaboration, data sharing, and would demand for reliable, intuitive, low-fatigue freehand gestures for a prolonged use during a virtual meeting. The interaction modalities in this work are asymmetric hand gestures created from bimanual grouping of freehand gestures including pointing, holding, and grabbing, which are known to be elemental and essential ones for interaction in VR. The design and implementation of bimanual gestures follow clear gestural metaphors to create connection and empathy with hand motions the user performs. We conducted a user study to understand advantages and drawbacks amongst three types of bimanual gestures as well as their suitability for cross-workspace interaction in VR, which we hope are valuable to assist the design of future VR social platforms.

Keywords: Bimanual gestures · Cross-workspace interaction · VR interface

1 Introduction

Nowadays, people become more dependent on virtual meetings and online collaboration tools to maintain effective communications, demanding for physical-like interactivity while working virtually. VR technologies can help transform the setting of a physical working environment to a virtual reality environment. The latest VR social software applications, such as The Wild, Facebook Spaces, and MeetInVR, can be used by users from remote locations, in support of virtual presentation, remote collaboration, data sharing, and therefore enhance abilities for remote working. One of the evolutionary ideas in VR social platforms is the make of virtual personal workspace and shared workspace [15,28,44]. A *personal workspace* usually acts as a repository storing a user's personal data and controlling choices (e.g., drag & drop, swipe, button press, etc.), which are accessible only by the owner user. A *shared workspace* acts as a public space, where invited users are granted with access to view and explore the shared social environment, or upload and download data from this space. In VR, these workspaces are no longer physical. MeetInVR, for example, allows that, *"using your virtual tablet you can access your files, cast them on screens, share them with other meeting participants and even detach them from the tablet and stick them to walls"*. Here, the virtual tablet is a personal workspace, and the screens and walls are shared workspaces.

© The Author(s), under exclusive license to Springer Nature Switzerland AG 2022
J. Y. C. Chen and G. Fragomeni (Eds.): HCII 2022, LNCS 13317, pp. 338–356, 2022.
https://doi.org/10.1007/978-3-031-05939-1_23

One fundamental requirement for cross-workspace interaction in VR is the capability to move data items between a person's personal workspace and the shared workspace, with reliable, intuitive, low-fatigue interaction modalities, so that it could support a prolonged use during a virtual activity. This work investigates bimanual gestures for cross-workspace interaction in VR. It can be analogized to cross-device interaction, which facilitates ubiquitous computing in physical environments and intends to understand co-located interactivity across wearable devices, smartphones, tablets, large displays, etc. [6,31]. In VR, cross-workspace interaction has the following characteristics that the physical cross-device interaction does not provide:

– *Freehand metaphors.* The user's hand motions are directly mapped to object manipulating operations without being associated with any touchscreen or handheld device [35,36,43].
– *Ergonomic personalization.* Intuitive freehand gestures comfort to user expectation and thus likely improve user experience and presence [9,33].
– *Portability.* Head-mounted, wireless tracking techniques permit "anywhere" access to the virtual environment without a spatial limit from hardware constraints [29,34].

To assist the design of VR social platforms, it is important to understand the advantages and drawbacks of bimanual gestures as well as their suitability for cross-workspace interaction in VR. We have performed an empirical study of three types of bimanual gestures for moving objects across virtual workspaces. The gestures are asymmetric [13], and they are created from grouping of elemental, conscious freehand gestures, including *pointing*, *holding*, and *grabbing* [12,19,27,42]. A preliminary evaluation based on this study was published in [32]. This work provides much more details on the bimanual gestural design and experiment setup, and gives a comprehensive analysis of user data collected during the study. The efforts of analysis lead us towards new findings on participants' performance, engagement and measurement of VR sickness. Our findings are the contribution of this work in relation to bidirectional operations across virtual workspaces.

2   Related Work

2.1   Cross-Device Interaction in Physical Environments

Our work can be analogized to physical cross-device interaction, which allows users to use portable devices to share information onto a public device or edit a digital document with others through networked devices, devoting to a mix of personal and social usages. Such interaction can be cast back to the 1980s, when Bolt proposed the "Put-That-There" system [5]. Lee et al. [24] presented simple selection and pointing gestures for controlling multiple devices and sharing information. Their system improved the interaction in a ubiquitous computing environment, but there was a lack of evidence on user acceptance of *Select-and-Point* gestural functions. Schmidt et al. [40] proposed mobile interaction styles across all displays, but further evaluation would be needed to understand benefits when using in tasks. Paay et al. [31] presented four bi-directional interaction gestures between a handheld device and a large display, but the gestures were primarily on one hand. Badam and Elmqvist [1] presented the Visfer framework for visual exploration between handheld devices and a large display. They studied gestural actions elicited by participants, but there was a lack of supporting bi-directional communication beyond transferring a QR code.

This work adopts the concept from cross-device interaction and enable bimanual gestures between workspaces in VR. Different from cross-device interaction, the gestures and interaction across virtual workspaces are not associated with any physical display or device. This work focuses on in-air bimanual interaction in VR in a harmony with naturalness of human arm and hand movements.

2.2   Bimanual Interaction Design for VR

Bimanual interaction has been seen in many VR applications that is more efficient than one-handed interaction [10,17,18,22]. There are two types of bimanual interaction: *symmetric bimanual interaction* and *asymmetric bimanual interaction*. In symmetric bimanual interaction, two hands are assigned an identical role during the interaction [3, 43]. The asymmetric bimanual interaction was presented in Guiard's Kinematic Chain (KC) model [13], with which a task is usually performed by dependent movements between two hands. The dominant hand usually leads the non-dominant hand in tasks.

Diliberti et al. [12] trained a gesture recognition model using 3D hand and finger motion data. Their method demonstrated the capability to detect and recognize gestures from new hand and finger motion sequences. Shanthakumar et al. [42] proposed an angular-velocity method to recognize symmetric gestures of each hand. Both works [12,42] contributed to symmetric bimanual interaction and considered authoritative gestures [46]. Researchers found that the two hands often have different roles during the interaction. Even when the user is given an identical, symmetric task for each hand, he or she may not always perform it in a symmetric manner [3,25,43].

In regards to the study of asymmetric bimanual interaction, Levesque et al. [26] designed a two-handed gestural interface based on the principles in Guiard's KC model. The interaction relied on static hand and arm gestures. Kim et al. [20] and Bai et al. [2] studied asymmetric bimanual interaction, where the controller is held in the dominant hand and the non-dominant hand performs freehand motions. Such a combined modality tended to cause fatigue faster than a mono-modality. Cao et al. [7] presented bimanual gestures in combining with body movements for sport-like interaction. Their work promoted exercising engagement; however, the gestures were not easy to be re-purposed for the use in a generalized manipulation task.

Although asymmetric bimanual interaction has been made available in modern VR devices and interfaces [16], there are also cases where asymmetric bimanual interaction may decrease performance or may not be preferred by users due to poor gestural metaphors in a given scenario [14,30]. In this work, we employed simple, low-fatigue, finger-level freehand gestures. Users were able to learn the gestural interaction modalities without having to learn an entirely new way of using gestures. We used asymmetric bimanual interaction to study users' experience and the matter of metaphors on cross-workspace tasks in VR. The interaction can be performed with three different combinations of freehand gestures on each hand.

3   Cross-Workspace Interaction

3.1   Elemental Freehand Gestures for VR

With a Head-mounted display (HMD), interacting with virtual objects can be difficult with handheld controllers, filling with obscure buttons. Freehand movements tracked by cameras or wireless data gloves will be less fatiguing and free from worries to fall controllers off the hands. Simple finger-level freehand gestures have been found to be beneficial to users in VR experiences [9,37]. We have identified three elemental freehand gestures for 3D user interaction in VR, described as *pointing*, *holding*, and *grabbing*, though they may be named differently in the papers from the literature. These elemental gestures express conscious movements of hands and arms. They have meanings by themselves, as opposed to spontaneous movements whose meanings associate with the context of speech [8].

Pointing (P). The pointing gesture can be performed in mid-air by extending one, two fingers or the arm towards something. It is the most basic way for people to convey something to another [11]. With the state-of-the-art HMDs, such as Oculus Quest, its front cameras track the user's hands. The hand and fingertip pointing movements can be mapped precisely to a shadowy hand avatar, creating the feeling of true presence in the virtual environment. For our study, the pointing gesture is applied to interact with the shared workspace, indicating the target location in the shared workspace, to which the user will move a personal item, or from which a shared item is retrieved to the personal workspace.

Holding (H). The holding gesture retains a virtual object in the palm or makes it follow the movement of the hand. For our study, the holding gesture corresponds to a gestural status that manages the personal workspace. Suitable to our study, the holding gesture is applied only to interact with the personal workspace, which can be implemented as a touchable tablet/container-like platform [44]. The user can hold and move it to view items it contains, as well as adjusting its relative location to comfort the hands when grabbing an item.

Grabbing (G). The grabbing gesture is an important interaction technique to manipulate virtual objects remotely in VR. For our study, the grabbing gesture represents a combination of "pick-up" and "drop-off" actions. It is used to interact with both personal and shared workspaces. We compute finger movements to detect swipe, pinch and fist motions as the implemented forms of the grabbing gesture, because they are well supported by precise and stable movements of limb segments [4]. For example, the user can bring thumb and forefinger together to pick up a personal item, and apart the fingers to drop it to the shared space.

3.2   Bimanual Gestures

Bimanual interaction refers to the use of two hands in a collaborative way to achieve the goal of object manipulation. According to Guiard's study of the asymmetry of bimanual actions [13] and the design of bimanual gesture-based VR interfaces presented by Levesque et al. [26], the dominant hand is more suitable to perform precise and fast hand gestures, such as pointing, while the non-dominant hand is more suitable to perform gestures that support the dominant hand. Thus, in our study, the pointing gesture is always performed by the dominant hand, and the other two gestures, holding and grabbing, can be performed by either hand. We designed three types of asymmetric bimanual gestures, as shown in Table 1, each of which requires one hand to perform two gestures and the other hand to perform just one gesture.

There are potentially two types of cross-space interaction tasks, defined as follows:

- **P-to-S task:** the user moves an object from the personal workspace (P) to the shared workspace (S).
- **S-to-P task:** the user moves an object from the shared workspace (S) to the personal workspace (P).

Table 1. Three bimanual gestures. The words in parenthesis describe the metaphor a gesture provides.

Bimanual gestures	Dominant hand	Non-dominant hand
PH+G (Swipe Throw)	Pointing and Holding	Grabbing
PG+H (Force Push/Pull)	Pointing and Grabbing	Holding
P+HG (Pinch & Release)	Pointing	Holding and Grabbing

PH+G (Swipe Throw). The *Swipe Throw* stimulates the use of a virtual tablet as the personal workspace, which is held in the dominant hand. It is also used as a virtual pointer to point at a target location in the shared workspace, as shown in Fig. 1. A metaphor is created when performing this gesture: the user thinks of throwing an item with a finger-added pseudo force, so that the force pushes the item on the swiping direction to the target location.

To move a personal item to the shared workspace, the non-dominant hand selects an item in the personal workspace by touching it with the index finger of the non-dominant hand. After that, the user performs the swiping with the index finger towards the pointing direction to move the selected item to the target location. If the selected item is not the one the user intends to move, the user can deselect the item by touching it again, and then touch to select a different one.

To move a shared item to the tablet, the user uses the non-dominant hand to select an empty slot in the personal workspace. Then, the user points at an item in the shared workspace using the dominant hand. After that, the user swipes the non-dominant hand backwards to move the selected item to the empty slot in the personal workspace. If the selected empty slot is not what the user wants, he or she can deselect by touching it again, and then touch to select a different slot.

PG+H (Force Push/Pull). The *Force Push/Pull* reminds of a Jedi force push & pull motion from the movie of *Star Wars*. As studied in [45], the force push & pull motion is suited for manipulating objects at a distance. As shown in Fig. 2, the dominant

Fig. 1. The illustration of *Swipe Throw*. Assume that the right hand is the dominant hand and the left hand is the non-dominant hand. The first row images are gestures for the P-To-S task, and the second row images are gestures for the S-To-P task.

hand does the pointing and grabbing while the non-dominant hand holds the personal workspace. Performing this gesture creates a metaphor: the user thinks of the force-push as pushing air so that the airflow moves an item from the hand to the target location and thinks of the force-pull as pulling air so that the airflow sucks the item to the hand.

To move a personal item to the shared workspace with the force push, the user uses the dominant hand to grab a personal item. Then, the user clenches the dominant hand to pick it up. After that, the item follows the movement of the dominant hand. The user straightens the dominant arm to point at a target location in the shared workspace. At this moment, the user releases the hand so that the item is pushed to the target location.

To move a shared item to the personal workspace with the force pull, the user straightens the dominant arm to point at an item in the shared workspace, and then clenches the dominant hand to select it. The selected item is then sucked into the hand. After that, the user clenches the dominant hand to move it to the personal workspace. The user drops it into an empty slot by releasing the hand.

***P+HG* (Pinch & Release).** In the *Pinch & Release*, the dominant hand points at a target position, an item, or an empty slot. The personal workspace follows the movement of the non-dominant hand. As shown in Fig. 3, the non-dominant hand performs the pinch gesture to select the item that is being pointed by the dominant hand. To deselect, the non-dominant hand pinches again while the dominant hand is pointing at the selected item. Performing this gesture may create a metaphor: the user thinks of having the

Fig. 2. The illustration of *Force Push/Pull*. Assume that the right hand is the dominant hand and the left hand is the non-dominant hand. The first row images are gestures for the P-To-S task, and the second row images are gestures for the S-To-P task.

trigger on the non-dominant hand and using the dominant hand to aim at the target. The user triggers to launch the item like shooting with a crossbow.

To move a personal item to the shared workspace, the dominant hand points at an item in the personal workspace. While pointing, the non-dominant hand does the pinch to select the item. After that, the dominant hand points at the target location in the shared workspace, and the non-dominant hand does the pinch to move the selected item to the target location.

To move an item from the shared workspace to the personal workspace, the dominant hand points at an empty slot in the personal workspace. While pointing, the non-dominant hand does the pinch to select the slot. After that, the dominant hand points to the item in the shared workspace, and the non-dominant hand does the pinch to move the item to the selected empty slot in the personal workspace.

4   Method

We developed a virtual interior environment composed of three cubby shelves (left, right, and center) around the user avatar. Each shelf contains 6×5 storage units. There are three types of objects: a red sphere, a yellow box, and a blue cone. They can be held on the user's hand, selected, and moved between the hand and shelf. We conducted the study on the *P-To-S* and *S-To-P* tasks. Participants were required to accomplish the tasks

Fig. 3. The illustration of *Pinch & Release*. Assume that the right hand is the dominant hand and the left hand is the non-dominant hand. The first row images are gestures for the P-To-S task, and the second row images are gestures for the S-To-P task.

by using the proposed bimanual gestures. Figure 4 shows the images of a participant wearing the HMD and doing the tasks. For the *P-To-S* task, a hint icon displaying the object type appears in a storage unit on a shelf. The user selects the corresponding object in the hand, and move it to the specific storage unit. If the user selects a wrong object or moves it to a wrong place, he or she has to redo it until the correct object is moved to the correct location. For the *S-To-P* task, a hint icon appears on the selected empty slot in the hand. The user selects the corresponding object from the shelf and moves it to the hand. The user has to redo it if a wrong object is picked. The user repeats each task for 10 times.

4.1 Apparatus

We used Oculus Quest, which is a VR HMD installed with four fisheye mini cameras on the front corners of the HMD surface. The camera is able to track hand movements in real-time, instantly reconstruct 3D virtual hand avatars, and then render them in the virtual environment.

4.2 Gesture Implementation

The positions and rotations of 24 joints for each hand are captured by Oculus Quest and mapped onto virtual hand avatars. The method to implement hand gestures is same

P-To-S Task   S-To-P Task

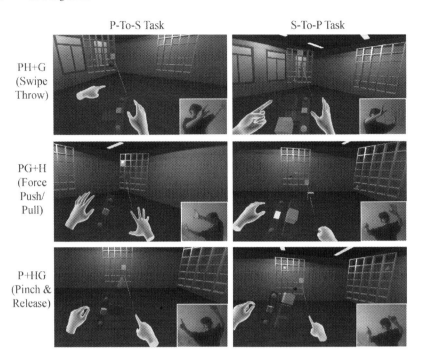

PH+G
(Swipe
Throw)

PG+H
(Force
Push/
Pull)

P+HG
(Pinch &
Release)

Fig. 4. The photos and screenshots taken in the user study.

as the angular velocity method presented in [42]. The pointing in *Swipe Throw* and *Force Push/Pull* is implemented on the dominant arm, where a laser-like ray is cast along the forward direction of the dominant forearm. The pointing in *Pinch & Release* is implemented on the dominant hand's index finger, where a laser-like ray is cast along the forward direction on the index finger's distal phalanx. In *Swipe Throw*, the swiping direction is determined by the moving offset between two successive frames on the index finger tip of the non-dominant hand, towards either shared or personal workspace. In *Force Push/Pull*, a fist-like grabbing gesture is implemented on the dominant hand, where an average position is computed from all finger tips. If the average position is close enough to the wrist joint, the grabbing gesture is recognized and kept, until the average position becomes far enough from the wrist to trigger a release gesture. For the pinch gesture in *Pinch & Release*, the distance between index finger tip and thumb tip is checked. If they are close enough to each other, a pinch gesture is recognized and kept, until they separate to trigger a release gesture.

4.3 Participants

Participation in this study is voluntary. We recruited 18 participants, including 12 males and 6 females. Their ages are between 18 and 29 years, and the average age is 24.06 years. 14 participants had VR experience using an HMD and 4 participants did not have any VR experience in the past. The three bimanual gestures make six possible orders to perform. There are two orders in which *Swipe Throw* is performed first, so they are (1) *Swipe Throw, Force Push/Pull, Pinch & Release* and (2) *Swipe Throw, Pinch & Release, Force Push/Pull*. Similarly, there are two orders in which *Force Push/Pull* is performed first and two orders in which *Pinch & Release* is performed first. Three participants were randomly selected for each order.

4.4 Study Procedure

Due to COVID-19, the study was performed remotely. The VR application developed for this study was installed in an Oculus Quest HMD. Each participant signed the consent form electronically and came to the research center at the university to pick up the sanitized HMD. The participant took it home and communicated with the investigator in an online video meeting during the study. The study lasted 40–60 minutes. After the study, the participant returned the HMD to the university.

Through the online meeting, the participant was first guided by the investigator to check the surroundings for safety and set up necessary connections for the HMD. Then, the participant watched a 5-minute tutorial video to know how to move hands and arms. The tutorial video remained open during the study in case needing to watch again. Then, the participant was guided to wear the HMD and launch the VR application. The participant performed the two tasks with three bimanual gestures in the order assigned. At the end of the study, the participant filled a Virtual Reality Sickness Questionnaire (VRSQ) [21], a User Experience Questionnaire (UEQ) [23], and a Post-Study Questionnaire (PSQ). Participants filled the questionnaires in Google forms.

The questions in the PSQ are as follows:

- *Q1: Among the three bimanual interaction methods, which one do you prefer to use, and which one would you not choose? Please tell us why.*
- *Q2: Did you have any trouble in performing any of those three interactions? If yes, please describe your feeling.*
- *Q3: Do you think gesture-based interaction modalities could be a substitution of current methods for online communication experience? Please describe your thoughts.*
- *Q4: What other hand-based interaction modalities with virtual objects would you suggest, beyond the three you have experienced?*
- *Q5: Please leave any comments about this study.*

Table 2. Participants' performance data on the tasks across three bimanual gestures. For each data category we reported mean and standard deviation (SD) values from all participants.

Bimanual gestures	Tasks	Time (sec.)		# of Misses		Hand moving distance			
		Mean	SD	Mean	SD	Non-dominant hand (m)		Dominant hand (m)	
						Mean	SD	Mean	SD
PH+G (Swipe Throw)	P-To-S	98.66	24.47	1.61	0.92	15.62	4.13	15.41	3.88
	S-To-P	86.40	12.89	1.06	0.64	13.08	2.01	12.87	1.90
PG+H (Force Push/Pull)	P-To-S	86.78	17.67	0.83	0.62	13.18	3.44	10.18	2.39
	S-To-P	75.59	13.54	0.89	0.68	11.05	3.09	10.59	2.22
P+HG (Pinch & Release)	P-To-S	145.87	38.82	2.72	1.74	21.96	4.91	22.49	4.75
	S-To-P	65.27	11.47	0.61	0.61	10.03	1.89	10.39	1.96

5   Results

We conducted a one-way analysis of variance (ANOVA) to analyze the task completion time, accuracy in placing objects, hand moving distances, and participants' answers in the questionnaires, among three types of bimanual gestures. All statistical results were based on the significance value of $\alpha = 0.05$. Although Task completion time and accuracy in pacing objects were listed in our preliminary evaluation [32], this work gives them a more detailed analysis with indications and participant feedback.

5.1   Performance Data Analysis

Participants' performance data are shown in Table 2. The column of "Time (sec.)" is the mean time of accomplishing the tasks. The column of "# of Misses" is the mean number of objects that participants either selected wrongly or placed in a wrong location. With each gesture, the participant placed ten objects in the P-To-S task and ten objects in the S-To-P task. The column of "Hand Moving Distance" lists the mean values of hand moving distances in meters.

In the P-To-S task, the participant chose one of three objects in the personal workspace, and put it in a particular location in the shared workspace. In the S-To-P task, the participant chose an object in the shared workspace, and fetched it back to one of three locations in the personal workspace. Regardless of gesture types, participants' performance in the S-To-P task was better than their performance in the P-To-S task in terms of task completion time and hand moving distances. This could be because in the P-to-S task participants sometimes moved the dominant hand cautiously as they felt the target location is hard to point. One participant commented that *"'From' exercises (S-To-P task) were easy and satisfying to perform."*

Task Completion Time. We did the one-way ANOVA analysis for every pair of comparison in the three bimanual gestures. For the P-To-S task, *Swipe Throw* and *Force Push/Pull* were performed significantly better than *Pinch & Release* in terms of task completion time, where $F(1, 34) = 34.545, p < 0.001$ and $(F(1, 34) = 19.054, p < 0.001$, respectively. This could be due to the observation that many participants spent most of operating time on choosing the object in the personal workspace rather than on moving it to the shared workspace, and they expressed that pointing to an object in the personal workspace using *Pinch & Release* consumed more time than using other bimanual gestures. We did not found any significant difference between *Force Push/Pull* and *Swipe Throw* in terms of task completion time for the P-To-S task, since $F(1, 34) = 2.786, p = 0.104 > 0.05$. This indicates that the participants were comfortable to perform these two bimanual gestures likely at the same comfort level. For the S-To-P task, *Pinch & Release* was performed significantly better than *Swipe Throw* and *Force Push/Pull* in terms of task completion time, where $F(1, 34) = 6.089, p = 0.019$ and $F(1, 34) = 26.986, p < 0.001$, respectively. This could be because of the observation that many participants spent most of operating time on choosing the object in the shared workspace rather than on fetching it to the personal workspace, and they seemed to feel that *Pinch & Release* was faster than the other modalities when picking the object in the shared workspace.

Accuracy in Placing Objects. In regards to the accuracy in placing objects at target locations, we found that *Force Push/Pull* resulted in the lowest number of misses in the P-To-S task, whose accuracy was 8.40% higher than *Swipe Throw*, and 18.9% higher than *Pinch & Release*. In the S-To-P task, *Pinch & Release* resulted in the lowest number of misses, whose accuracy was 2.80% higher than *Force Push/Pull*, and 4.50% higher than *Swipe Throw*. Statistically, the difference between *Force Push/Pull* and other two bimanual gestures in the P-To-S task is significant, where $F(1, 34) = 8.909, p = 0.005$ compared to *Swipe Throw*, and $F(1, 34) = 18.788, p < 0.001$ compared to *Pinch & Release*. In the S-To-P task, we found that *Pinch & Release* outperformed *Swipe Throw*, where $F(1, 34) = 4.571, p = 0.040$, but there was no significant difference between *Pinch & Release* and *Force Push/Pull* since $F(1, 34) = 1.680, p = 0.204$. This could be due to the observation that *Force Push/Pull* likely provided more stable actions for the hands. When the non-dominant hand was swiping for *Swipe Throw* or pinching for *Pinch & Release* in order to confirm the action to move the object, the postures of the dominant hand or the upper body pose was affected. This observation was consistent to a participant's comment read as *"I feel some of the task(s) are not user friendly technical(ly), hard to align the ray."*

In the S-To-P task, *Pinch & Release* outperformed other bimanual gestures, likely because *Force Push/Pull* did not provide a stable dropping action to the personal workspace. We observed that some participants shaked the dominant arm unconsciously when fisting to grab the object from the shared workspace. Participants commented on *Force Push/Pull* that *"Force pull (is) hard to pull with natural gesture"*, and *"hand steadiness requirement in the 'grabbing' model is high."*, and consequently it might cause uneasiness to select the object. This was not observed when participants were performing *Pinch & Release* in the S-To-P task.

Hand Moving Distances. The difference in moving distance between two hands was not large among three bimanual gestures. Although the pointing gesture was performed by the dominant hand in all three bimanual gestures, requiring to move the hand frequently across two workspaces, the dominant hand did not always end up with a larger moving distance than the non-dominant hand, as evidenced in Table 2. This could be due to an observed tendency that the participants moved the non-dominant hand to conform to the movement of the dominant hand in order to balance out the body. We tended to agree that larger moving distances on hands likely indicate a higher chance to cause people feel fatigued in a task [7, 39]. We found that *Force Push/Pull* and *Swipe Throw* advanced *Pinch & Release* significantly in terms of reducing movements on two hands in the P-To-S task, where $F(1, 34) = 21.440, p < 0.001$ and $F(1, 34) = 67.169, p < 0.001$, respectively; in the S-To-P task, *Pinch & Release* advanced *Swipe Throw* significantly in terms of reducing movements on two hands, where $F(1, 34) = 20.332, p < 0.001$, but no evidence to show *Pinch & Release* could advance *Force Push/Pull*, where $F(1, 34) = 0.678, p = 0.416$.

From the analysis above in regards to time efficiency, accuracy improvement, and movement fatigue mitigation, in the P-To-S task, *Force Push/Pull* outperformed other bimanual gestures, and *Pinch & Release* might be the least favorable one; and in the S-To-P task, *Pinch & Release* outperformed other bimanual gestures, and *Swipe Throw* might be the least favorable one. Also, people should likely perform more effectively when fetching items to their personal workspace than when moving or displaying personal items to the shared workspace.

5.2   Questionnaire Analysis

We analyzed the VRSQ and UEQ that are composed of subjective answers.

VRSQ. We calculated the scores for the two components in VRSQ. The scores were scaled to the range of $[0, 100]$. For oculomotor, which is related to symptoms of general discomfort, fatigue, eyestrain, and difficulty in focusing, the average score was 25.93 (min: 8.33 and max: 66.67). For disorientation, which is related to symptoms of headache, head fullness, blurred vision, dizziness, and vertigo, the average score was 13.33, (min: 0.00 and max: 73.33). The scores of both components were at the low end of the range. There was not an indication on the consideration of VR sickness. This was consistent to our observation during the user study. No participant reported any discomfort after the study. This could be because the VR environment was composed of static objects. An object moves only when the user interacts with it, so the occurrence of unexpected perceptional motions are mitigated to a large extent in user experience.

UEQ. Participants answered all 26 questions by giving each a Likert scale score between -3 (negative extreme) to 3 (positive extreme). The results were average from all participants, as shown in the top chart of Fig. 5. In accordance with the UEQ's standard interpretation [41], values in $[-0.8, 0.8]$ represent a neural evaluation for the corresponding category, values in $[-3.0, -0.8)$ represent a negative evaluation, and values in $(0.8, 3.0]$ represent a positive evaluation. Answer tendencies discussed in the literature have indicated that values more than 1.5 are considered to be very good [38]. Our findings as illustrated in the bottom chart of Fig. 5 show that the scores of all six categories are good (> 0.8). The scores for Efficiency (1.57), Stimulation (1.97), and Novelty (1.72) are very good. These indicate that the participates highly agreed that the bimanual interaction approach was interesting and exciting, and motivated them to use the system (as interpreted by Stimulation). They also agreed that bimanual interaction approach was efficient and innovative to perform cross-workspace interaction tasks (as interpreted by Efficiency and Novelty). The score for Perspicuity was the lowest among the six categories, which likely indicates that the bimanual gestures were not very easy for participants to learn. This appears to be consistent to our observation that there was some rigidity in some participants' hand motions when they were doing tasks (see Sect. 5.3), though they did not have difficulties to understand the use of bimanual gestures.

5.3   Other Observations and Discussions

We observed that the non-dominant hand tended to comfort to the movement of the dominant arm and hand when participants were performing *Swipe Throw* and *Force Push/Pull*, more frequently than when performing *Pinch & Release*. It seems that the

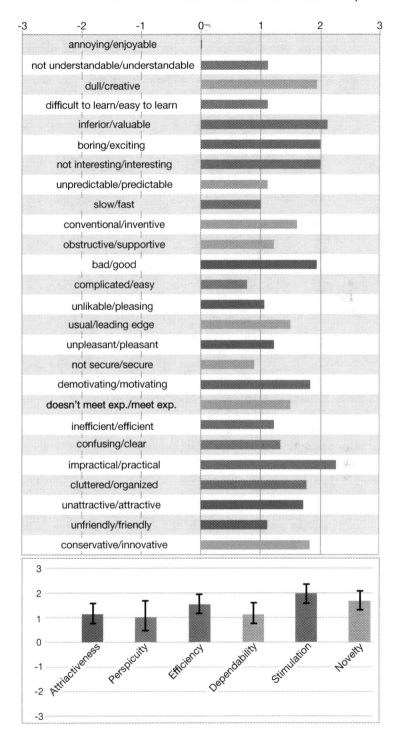

Fig. 5. The UEQ result based on the participants' rating on the entire system. The items in the same color belong to the same UEQ category.

participants did it unconsciously and they felt natural to do so. In *Pinch & Release*, participants often remained the non-dominant arm and wrist stationary while performing the gestures using fingers. Even with the state-of-the-art hand motion tracking capability in Oculus Quest, we found that, when performing *Pinch & Release*, the non-dominant hand was often out of the tracking range of the Quest, as the participant's body and dominant hand were moving away from where the non-dominant hand tended to stay. When this happened, it caused the gesture recognition approach was not functioning on the non-dominant hand and even lost track of the hand. This likely caused a poor experience since participants might feel clueless on why the non-dominant hand was lost track and not functioning to their expectation, as evidenced in participants' feedback in PSQ for *Pinch & Release*, which is read as *"I cannot see my hands sometimes."*

Participants mentioned that they felt the fatigue on the non-dominant arm worse than the fatigue feeling on the dominant arm at the end of the study. Most participants liked using *Force Push/Pull* to do the tasks, where 12 out of the total 18 participants chose *Force Push/Pull* to be their preferred gesture, *Swipe Throw* was ranked to the second, and *Pinch & Release* was ranked to the third. In the PSQ, a participant provided feedback, read as *"Hard to remember pinch or not pinch, gesture is a little complicated in pinch and release"*. We observed that, when some participants performed *Pinch & Release*, they moved the non-dominant arm up and remained a posture in the air all the time. This could make them feel uncomfortable on the non-dominant hand or possibly draw them to the fatigue feeling quickly.

The Oculus Quest uses computer vision algorithms to track hand movements and construct virtual hand avatars during the system's run-time. If two hands are too close to each other, one hand may block the view of the other hand and therefore cause the view of the hand is occluded. We observed that the occlusion problem occurred in *Pinch & Release* when participants pointed and pinched to the personal workspace. In that case, they sometimes unconsciously move the hands closer to each other and therefore caused the view of one hand was blocked by the other hand. The participant had to move the hands apart to restore real-time tracking. Although we observed that the participants were no problem to adjust the hands to restore the tracking, it made participants feel unnatural to move hands after they learned that they had to consciously keep two hands apart, like one participant commented in PSQ for *Pinch & Release*, which is read as *"One hand interfere(s) with another in two-hand(ed) interaction."* We did not observe such unnaturalness in *Swipe Throw* and *Force Push/Pull*.

6   Conclusion and Future Work

This work studied how different combinations of elemental hand gestures in bimanual gestures would affect users' performance and experience in interaction across virtual workspaces. The bimanual gestures were designed and implemented with clear gestural metaphors. In the user study, we were particularly interested in the characteristics and differences of those bimanual gestures in relation to task completion effectiveness (time and accuracy) and hand moving fatigue. This is an important research question as bimanual gestures are introduced to VR social platforms for doing virtually situated collaborative work, requiring a significant amount of dynamic operations to move data items between a personal workspace and a shared workspace. The data and questionnaires collected during the user study were analyzed to understand statistical differences amongst the proposed bimanual gestures. Also, the observations from the study were discussed.

The user study in this work considered the personal workspace as a tray-like container depositing hand holdable objects, and assumed the shared workspace to be a large shelf. Variations on shapes and sizes of workspaces could possibly make users perceive differently on how to move hands as well as on the speed of motions. The interaction in the study was along the depth direction. The work evaluated different bimanual gestures in this specific cross-workspace design. In the future, it would be valuable to study the suitability of a particular bimanual gesture in different cross-workspace designs, such as doing pick & drop for a vertical interaction.

From design perspective, we believe the bimanual gestures in this work have demonstrated clearly ways to group the elemental freehand gestures and perform them asymmetrically. More considerations could be added for the design in the future. It would be beneficial to consider the sense of hand movement and harmony, which are also related to intuitiveness and effectiveness of bimanual interaction.

References

1. Badam, S.K., Elmqvist, N.: Visfer: camera-based visual data transfer for cross-device visualization. Inf. Vis. **18**(1), 68–93 (2019). https://doi.org/10.1177/1473871617725907
2. Bai, H., Nassani, A., Ens, B., Billinghurst, M.: Asymmetric bimanual interaction for mobile virtual reality. In: Proceedings of the 27th International Conference on Artificial Reality and Telexistence and 22nd Eurographics Symposium on Virtual Environments, pp. 83–86. ICAT-EGVE 2017. Eurographics Association, Goslar, DEU (2017)
3. Balakrishnan, R., Hinckley, K.: Symmetric bimanual interaction. In: Proceedings of the SIGCHI Conference on Human Factors in Computing Systems, pp. 33–40. CHI 2000, Association for Computing Machinery, New York, NY, USA (2000). https://doi.org/10.1145/332040.332404
4. Balakrishnan, R., MacKenzie, I.S.: Performance differences in the fingers, wrist, and forearm in computer input control. In: Proceedings of the ACM SIGCHI Conference on Human Factors in Computing Systems, pp. 303–310. CHI 1997. Association for Computing Machinery, New York, NY, USA (1997). https://doi.org/10.1145/258549.258764
5. Bolt, R.A.: "Put-that-there": voice and gesture at the graphics interface. In: Proceedings of the 7th Annual Conference on Computer Graphics and Interactive Techniques, pp. 262–270, SIGGRAPH 1980. Association for Computing Machinery, New York, NY, USA (1980). https://doi.org/10.1145/800250.807503
6. Brudy, F., et al.: Cross-device taxonomy: survey, opportunities and challenges of interactions spanning across multiple devices. In: Proceedings of the 2019 CHI Conference on Human Factors in Computing Systems, pp. 1–28, CHI 2019. Association for Computing Machinery, New York, NY, USA (2019). https://doi.org/10.1145/3290605.3300792
7. Cao, L., Peng, C., Dong, Y.: Ellic's exercise class: promoting physical activities during exergaming with immersive virtual reality. Virtual Reality **25**(3), 597–612 (2020). https://doi.org/10.1007/s10055-020-00477-z

8. Cassell, J.: A framework for gesture generation and interpretation. In: Computer Vision in Human-Machine Interaction, pp. 191–215 (2003)
9. Chan, E., Seyed, T., Stuerzlinger, W., Yang, X.D., Maurer, F.: User elicitation on single-hand microgestures. In: Proceedings of the 2016 CHI Conference on Human Factors in Computing Systems, pp. 3403–3414, CHI 2016. Association for Computing Machinery, New York, NY, USA (2016). https://doi.org/10.1145/2858036.2858589
10. Chastine, J., Franklin, D.M., Peng, C., Preston, J.A.: Empirically measuring control quality of gesture input. In: 2014 Computer Games: AI, Animation, Mobile, Multimedia, Educational and Serious Games (CGAMES), pp. 1–7. IEEE (2014)
11. Cooperrider, K.: Fifteen ways of looking at a pointing gesture (2020). https://psyarxiv.com/2vxft/download?format=pdf
12. Diliberti, N., Peng, C., Kaufman, C., Dong, Y., Hansberger, J.T.: Real-time gesture recognition using 3D sensory data and a light convolutional neural network. In: Proceedings of the 27th ACM International Conference on Multimedia, pp. 401–410, MM 2019. Association for Computing Machinery, New York, NY, USA (2019). https://doi.org/10.1145/3343031.3350958
13. Guiard, Y.: Asymmetric division of labor in human skilled bimanual action: the kinematic chain as a model. J. Motor Behav. **19**, 486–517 (1987)
14. Guimbretière, F., Martin, A., Winograd, T.: Benefits of merging command selection and direct manipulation. ACM Trans. Comput.-Hum. Interact. **12**(3), 460–476 (2005). https://doi.org/10.1145/1096737.1096742
15. Hansberger, J.T., Peng, C., Blakely, V., Meacham, S., Cao, L., Diliberti, N.: A multimodal interface for virtual information environments. In: Chen, J.Y.C., Fragomeni, G. (eds.) HCII 2019. LNCS, vol. 11574, pp. 59–70. Springer, Cham (2019). https://doi.org/10.1007/978-3-030-21607-8_5
16. Hillmann, C.: Comparing the Gear VR, Oculus Go, and Oculus Quest, pp. 141–167. Apress, Berkeley (2019). https://doi.org/10.1007/978-1-4842-4360-2_5
17. Hough, G., Williams, I., Athwal, C.: Fidelity and plausibility of bimanual interaction in mixed reality. IEEE Trans. Visual. Comput. Graph. **21**(12), 1377–1389 (2015). https://doi.org/10.1109/TVCG.2015.2480060
18. Jerald, J., LaViola, J.J., Marks, R.: VR interactions. In: ACM SIGGRAPH 2017 Courses. SIGGRAPH 2017. Association for Computing Machinery, New York, NY, USA (2017). https://doi.org/10.1145/3084873.3084900
19. Kang, H.J., Shin, J., Ponto, K.: A comparative analysis of 3D user interaction: how to move virtual objects in mixed reality. In: 2020 IEEE Conference on Virtual Reality and 3D User Interfaces (VR), pp. 275–284 (2020)
20. Kim, H., Park, J.: DuplicateSpace: enhancing operability of virtual 3D objects by asymmetric bimanual interaction. In: 2014 11th International Conference on Ubiquitous Robots and Ambient Intelligence (URAI), pp. 324–327 (2014)
21. Kim, H.K., Park, J., Choi, Y., Choe, M.: Virtual reality sickness questionnaire (VRSQ): motion sickness measurement index in a virtual reality environment. Appl. Ergonomics **69**, 66–73 (2018). https://doi.org/10.1016/j.apergo.2017.12.016, http://www.sciencedirect.com/science/article/pii/S000368701730282X
22. Kotranza, A., Quarles, J., Lok, B.: Mixed reality: are two hands better than one? In: Proceedings of the ACM Symposium on Virtual Reality Software and Technology, pp. 31–34, VRST 2006. Association for Computing Machinery, New York, NY, USA (2006). https://doi.org/10.1145/1180495.1180503
23. Laugwitz, B., Held, T., Schrepp, M.: Construction and evaluation of a user experience questionnaire. In: Holzinger, A. (ed.) USAB 2008. LNCS, vol. 5298, pp. 63–76. Springer, Heidelberg (2008). https://doi.org/10.1007/978-3-540-89350-9_6

24. Lee, H., Jeong, H., Lee, J., Yeom, K.W., Shin, H.J., Park, J.H.: Select-and-point: a novel interface for multi-device connection and control based on simple hand gestures. In: CHI 2008 Extended Abstracts on Human Factors in Computing Systems, pp. 3357–3362, CHI EA 2008. Association for Computing Machinery, New York, NY, USA (2008). https://doi.org/10.1145/1358628.1358857

25. Leganchuk, A., Zhai, S., Buxton, W.: Manual and cognitive benefits of two-handed input: an experimental study. ACM Trans. Comput.-Hum. Interact. 5(4), 326–359 (1998). https://doi.org/10.1145/300520.300522

26. Lévesque, J.-C., Laurendeau, D., Mokhtari, M.: An asymmetric bimanual gestural interface for immersive virtual environments. In: Shumaker, R. (ed.) VAMR 2013. LNCS, vol. 8021, pp. 192–201. Springer, Heidelberg (2013). https://doi.org/10.1007/978-3-642-39405-8_23

27. Lin, W., Du, L., Harris-Adamson, C., Barr, A., Rempel, D.: Design of hand gestures for manipulating objects in virtual reality. In: Kurosu, M. (ed.) HCI 2017. LNCS, vol. 10271, pp. 584–592. Springer, Cham (2017). https://doi.org/10.1007/978-3-319-58071-5_44

28. Luxenburger, A., Prange, A., Moniri, M.M., Sonntag, D.: MedicalVR: towards medical remote collaboration using virtual reality. In: Proceedings of the 2016 ACM International Joint Conference on Pervasive and Ubiquitous Computing: Adjunct, pp. 321–324, UbiComp 2016. Association for Computing Machinery, New York, NY, USA (2016). https://doi.org/10.1145/2968219.2971392

29. Mistry, P., Maes, P., Chang, L.: WUW - wear ur world: a wearable gestural interface. In: CHI 2009 Extended Abstracts on Human Factors in Computing Systems, pp. 4111–4116, CHI EA 2009. Association for Computing Machinery, New York, NY, USA (2009). https://doi.org/10.1145/1520340.1520626

30. Nanjappan, V., Liang, H.N., Lu, F., Papangelis, K., Yue, Y., Man, K.L.: User-elicited dual-hand interactions for manipulating 3D objects in virtual reality environments. Human-Centric Comput. Inf. Sci. 8(1), 31 (2018). https://doi.org/10.1186/s13673-018-0154-5

31. Paay, J., Raptis, D., Kjeldskov, J., Skov, M.B., Ruder, E.V., Lauridsen, B.M.: Investigating cross-device interaction between a handheld device and a large display. In: Proceedings of the 2017 CHI Conference on Human Factors in Computing Systems, pp. 6608–6619, CHI 2017. Association for Computing Machinery, New York, NY, USA (2017). https://doi.org/10.1145/3025453.3025724

32. Peng, C., Dong, Y., Cao, L.: Freehand interaction in virtual reality: bimanual gestures for cross-workspace interaction. In: Proceedings of the 27th ACM Symposium on Virtual Reality Software and Technology, VRST 2021. Association for Computing Machinery, New York, NY, USA (2021). https://doi.org/10.1145/3489849.3489900

33. Peng, C., Hansberger, J., Shanthakumar, V.A., Meacham, S., Blakley, V., Cao, L.: A case study of user experience on hand-gesture video games. In: 2018 IEEE Games, Entertainment, Media Conference (GEM), pp. 453–457. IEEE (2018)

34. Peng, C., Hansberger, J.T., Cao, L., Shanthakumar, V.A.: Hand gesture controls for image categorization in immersive virtual environments. In: 2017 IEEE Virtual Reality (VR), pp. 331–332. IEEE (2017)

35. Ren, G., O'Neill, E.: 3D selection with freehand gesture. Comput. Graph. 37(3), 101–120 (2013). https://doi.org/10.1016/j.cag.2012.12.006, http://www.sciencedirect.com/science/article/pii/S0097849312001823

36. Riecke, B.E., LaViola, J.J., Kruijff, E.: 3d user interfaces for virtual reality and games: 3d selection, manipulation, and spatial navigation. In: ACM SIGGRAPH 2018 Courses, SIGGRAPH 2018. Association for Computing Machinery, New York, NY, USA (2018). https://doi.org/10.1145/3214834.3214869

37. Sagayam, K.M., Hemanth, D.J.: Hand posture and gesture recognition techniques for virtual reality applications: a survey. Virtual Reality 21(2), 91–107 (2016). https://doi.org/10.1007/s10055-016-0301-0

38. Santoso, H.B., Schrepp, M., Isal, R., Utomo, A.Y., Priyogi, B.: Measuring user experience of the student-centered e-learning environment. J. Educators Online **13**(1), 58–79 (2016)
39. Sarupuri, B., Chipana, M.L., Lindeman, R.W.: Trigger walking: a low-fatigue travel technique for immersive virtual reality. In: 2017 IEEE Symposium on 3D User Interfaces (3DUI), pp. 227–228 (2017). https://doi.org/10.1109/3DUI.2017.7893354
40. Schmidt, D., Seifert, J., Rukzio, E., Gellersen, H.: A cross-device interaction style for mobiles and surfaces. In: Proceedings of the Designing Interactive Systems Conference, pp. 318–327. DIS 2012. Association for Computing Machinery, New York, NY, USA (2012). https://doi.org/10.1145/2317956.2318005
41. Schrepp, M.: User experience questionnaire handbook (2019). https://www.ueq-online.org/Material/Handbook.pdf
42. Shanthakumar, V.A., Peng, C., Hansberger, J., Cao, L., Meacham, S., Blakely, V.: Design and evaluation of a hand gesture recognition approach for real-time interactions. Multimedia Tools Appl. **79**(25), 17707–17730 (2020). https://doi.org/10.1007/s11042-019-08520-1
43. Song, P., Goh, W.B., Hutama, W., Fu, C.W., Liu, X.: A handle bar metaphor for virtual object manipulation with mid-air interaction. In: Proceedings of the SIGCHI Conference on Human Factors in Computing Systems, pp. 1297–1306, CHI 2012. Association for Computing Machinery, New York, NY, USA (2012). https://doi.org/10.1145/2207676.2208585
44. Surale, H.B., Gupta, A., Hancock, M., Vogel, D.: TabletInVR: exploring the design space for using a multi-touch tablet in virtual reality. In: Proceedings of the 2019 CHI Conference on Human Factors in Computing Systems, pp. 1–13, CHI 2019. Association for Computing Machinery, New York, NY, USA (2019). https://doi.org/10.1145/3290605.3300243
45. Yu, R., Bowman, D.A.: Force push: exploring expressive gesture-to-force mappings for remote object manipulation in virtual reality. Front. ICT **5**, 25 (2018). https://doi.org/10.3389/fict.2018.00025, https://www.frontiersin.org/article/10.3389/fict.2018.00025
46. Zhai, S., Kristensson, P.O., Appert, C., Andersen, T.H., Cao, X.: Foundational issues in touch-screen stroke gesture design - an integrative review. Found. Trends Hum. Comput. Interact. **5**(2), 97–205 (2012). https://doi.org/10.1561/1100000012, https://hal.inria.fr/hal-00765046

Typing in Mid Air: Assessing One- and Two-Handed Text Input Methods of the Microsoft HoloLens 2

Emily Rickel[✉], Kelly Harris, Erika Mandile, Anthony Pagliari,
Jessyca L. Derby, and Barbara S. Chaparro

Department of Human Factors and Behavioral Neurobiology,
Embry-Riddle Aeronautical University, Daytona Beach, FL 32114, USA
{rickele, harrik28, mandilel, pagliara,
derbyjl}@my.erau.edu, chaparbl@erau.edu

Abstract. The Microsoft HoloLens 2 is a mixed reality (MR) headset that overlays virtual elements atop a user's view of their physical environment. To input text, the device has the ability to track hands and fingers, allowing for direct interaction with a virtual keyboard. This is an improvement over the HoloLens 1 device, which required head tracking and single-finger air-tapping input. The present study evaluated the performance (speed and accuracy), perceived usability, mental workload, and physical exertion of one-handed and two-handed text entry. A sample of 21 participants (12 male, 9 female) aged 18–32 years typed standardized phrases presented in random order. Typing with two hands was faster and more preferred than one-handed input; however, this input method was also less accurate. Exertion in some body parts was also higher in the two-handed condition. Findings suggest that while two-handed text input was better than one-handed, there is room for improvement to approximate typing on a physical or mobile device keyboard.

Keywords: Human factors · Mixed reality · Mixed reality headset · Microsoft HoloLens 2 · Text input

1 Introduction

Virtual Reality (VR), Augmented Reality (AR), and Mixed Reality (MR) are becoming increasingly popular for use in education and other domains [1]. This research focused on the Microsoft HoloLens 2, an MR headset that anchors virtual elements over a user's view of their physical environment, allowing users to complete a variety of tasks while maintaining an awareness of their surroundings. VR gives the user the feeling of "being there" and simulates a realistic environment [2], and AR allows users to see their physical surroundings but overlays virtual elements that move as the user moves, such as in phone applications [3]. MR differs in that virtual elements are anchored in the user's environment, and remain stationary if the user moves, as an object would if it was physically present [3]. As the user moves their head, the virtual elements appear larger or smaller depending on the user's orientation.

© The Author(s), under exclusive license to Springer Nature Switzerland AG 2022
J. Y. C. Chen and G. Fragomeni (Eds.): HCII 2022, LNCS 13317, pp. 357–368, 2022.
https://doi.org/10.1007/978-3-031-05939-1_24

The Microsoft HoloLens 2 is diverse in its uses and can launch over 300 applications, including games, business, and productivity applications [4]. Consequently, text entry is a key component for many HoloLens 2 tasks. Prior research on the first version of the device, the Microsoft HoloLens 1, showed text input controlled by head movements and air-tap hand gestures was slow, fatiguing, and frustrating for users [5]. The HoloLens 2 improved upon these concerns with the implementation of functionality to track users' hands and individual fingers, enabling direct interaction with a virtual keyboard. Users can press individual keys using their fingers on one hand or both hands at the same time and receive an audio cue when touching the virtual keyboard that closely mimics that of a physical keyboard.

Although the Microsoft HoloLens 2 provides changes from the first model, there are still challenges facing text input on head-mounted devices. Mid-air keyboards that have the ability to track ten fingers while typing are the "holy grail" of virtual text entry [6]. A study done by Sears [7] showed that participants typing on a traditional QWERTY keyboard averaged 58 words per minute (WPM); almost 10 times faster than the averages calculated in the Microsoft HoloLens 1 study, where speeds averaged from 5.41 WPM for gesture typing and 6.58 WPM for clicker typing [5].

This study aimed to evaluate performance (speed and accuracy) and preference of one-handed and two-handed text entry on the Microsoft HoloLens 2, along with perceived workload, usability, exertion, and eye fatigue.

2   Method

2.1   Participants

The study sample consisted of 21 participants (12 male, 9 female) recruited from a university located in the southeastern United States. Participant ages ranged from 18 to 32 years ($M = 21.62$, $SD = 3.87$). Sixteen participants reported prior use with VR or AR headsets, and four participants reported owning a VR or AR headset. Number of hours for prior VR or AR use ranged from 0 to 50 h ($Mdn = 2$, $IQR = 9.25$). Four participants reported being non-native English speakers. Two participants reported being left-handed. Participants were screened for disabilities or movement problems associated with their hands.

2.2   Experimental Design

A repeated-measures experimental design was utilized for this study. Qualitative and quantitative data was collected through this study. Participants were asked to input text using two conditions: 1) one-handed (i.e., using their dominant hand), and 2) two-handed. The conditions were presented in a counterbalanced order. The independent variable was the input method being used (one-handed or two-handed) and the dependent variables included: typing speed, typing accuracy, perceived workload, perceived exertion, perceived eye strain, perceived usability, and preference.

2.3   Measures

Text Input Speed and Accuracy. Words per minute (WPM), adjusted words per minute (AdjWPM), and word error rate (WER) were calculated to evaluate the impact that each text input method had on performance. Measures for text input accuracy (WER) were examined by type of error made: substitution, insertion, and omission. Substitution errors occurred participants completely replaced a word with another word. Insertion errors were marked when participants typed an additional word not already a part of the phrase. Omission errors occurred when participants excluded a word from the given phrase.

Perceived Workload. The NASA Task Load Index (NASA-TLX-R) is a 6-item questionnaire that determines participants' subjective workload and perceived performance [8]. Each statement in the questionnaire represents one of the six dimensions: physical demand, mental demand, temporal demand, performance, effort, and frustration. Participants rated each statement on a 21-point scale. A higher rating signifies that the participant perceived the task as being more demanding or that they performed poorly.

Perceived Usability. The System Usability Scale (SUS) was used to gain insight into the participants' perceived usability of each text input method [9]. The SUS is a standardized 10-item questionnaire. Participants rated each question on a scale of 1 (strongly disagree) to 5 (strongly agree). A final score between 0–100 was calculated and placed on an adjective rating scale that ranges from worst imaginable (a score of 0 to 25) to best imaginable (a score of 100) [9, 10]. The questions on the SUS were modified to fit the subject of the study, therefore "system" was changed to "input method".

Perceived Exertion. The Borg Category Ratio Scale (Borg CR10) was used to evaluate the participants' perceived exertion with each text input method [11]. Participants were presented with an upper-body map consisting of 33 areas that were rated based on an exertion scale starting from "nothing at all" (0) to "extremely strong" (10) or even "absolute maximum" which can be rated as a 12, 13, or higher. If participants rated a specific area of their body above "moderate" (3), they were asked to explain their rating.

Perceived Eye Fatigue. A 6-item questionnaire was used to assess the participants' ability to concentrate, their ease of reading text, text clarity, physical fatigue, mental fatigue, and level of eye strain. The questions were rated on a 5-point likert-scale. Higher scores indicated an easier ability to read text, higher satisfaction with text clarity, higher ability to concentrate, and lower levels of fatigue and eye strain.

Preference. Participants were asked at the end of the study to indicate their preferences on the text input methods. Participants were asked to rate the text input methods on a preference scale (from 0 - Least Preferred to 50 - Most Preferred) independently of one another and to explain their rating. Participants were also asked to indicate with which input method they believed they typed the fastest and most accurately.

2.4   Materials

Microsoft HoloLens 2. The Microsoft HoloLens 2 is a wireless MR headset that was first released in 2019. The headset uses spatial mapping technology to create a three-dimensional model of the user's physical environment and to display digital content that users can manipulate through hand tracking, eye tracking, and voice commands [12]. The software version used for this study was Windows Holographic for Business, operating system (OS) build 10.0.19041.1154.

Phrases. Participants were presented with pre-selected phrases of text that originated from a subset of MacKenzie & Soukoreff's [13] standardized set of 500 phrases using Qualtrics, an online survey platform (see Fig. 1). These phrases were designed to evaluate text entry techniques and are characterized as being moderate in length, easy to remember, and representative of the English language.

Fig. 1. Participants' view of the text input task, which consisted of using a virtual keyboard to type pre-selected phrases of text using Qualtrics, an online survey platform.

2.5   Procedure

Participants were recruited from a university located in the southeastern United States. After participants provided their consent to participate in the study, they completed a demographic questionnaire. Participants were then fitted with the Microsoft HoloLens 2 headset, given a brief tutorial on how to use the device, and prompted to complete the device eye calibration procedure.

All participants completed both the one-handed and two-handed study conditions in counterbalanced order. Participants typed a total of 40 unique phrases from MacKenzie & Soukoreff's [13] phrase set that were presented in random order. For each condition, participants typed 5 practice phrases and 15 experimental phrases that were later evaluated for text input speed and accuracy. Timing for text input speed was measured by tracking when participants said "start" after they adjusted the virtual keyboard to a comfortable size and position and as they began typing each phrase, and "finish" as they completed inputting each phrase. Participant performance was monitored by a researcher who observed a television screen that showed the participant's view of the task using a screen mirroring device (see Fig. 2). As they typed each phrase, participants were instructed to input text as quickly and as accurately as possible, without using predictive text or abbreviated language (e.g., typing "u" instead of "you"). Participants also were directed not to worry about capitalization or punctuation and were given the option to make corrections, but they were not required to do so. After each condition, participants were asked to complete a series of questionnaires to capture perceived workload (NASA-TLX-R), usability (SUS), exertion (Borg CR10), and eye fatigue. After both conditions were completed, participants rated their preference for one- and two-handed input methods independently of one another and provided suggestions for improving text input using the Microsoft HoloLens 2. The study took approximately 60–90 min per participant.

Fig. 2. Layout of experimental set-up, showing the participant completing the text entry task while wearing the HoloLens 2 (left) as the researcher (right) observes the participant's performance using the television screen and screen-mirroring device (top).

3   Results

Paired samples t-tests were conducted to compare text input speed and accuracy, as well as perceived workload, usability, exertion, eye fatigue, and preference between one- and two-handed text input.

3.1   Text Input Speed and Accuracy

There was a statistically significant difference in typing speed between the one-handed (M = 12.07, SD = 1.78) and two-handed (M = 13.91, SD = 2.62) conditions, $t(20)$ = –3.43, P = 0.003 (two-tailed), D = –0.75. Participants typed faster with the Microsoft HoloLens 2 keyboard when using two hands compared to using one hand (see Fig. 3).

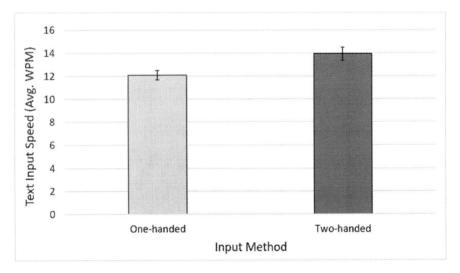

Fig. 3. Comparison of text input speed (average words per minute) between one-handed and two-handed text input. Error bars represent ±1 standard error.

Word error rate (WER), substitution error rate (SER), insertion error rate (IER), and omission error rate (OER) were calculated to assess text input accuracy (see Fig. 4).

Word Error Rate (WER). There was a statistically significant difference in WER between the one-handed (M = 0.05, SD = 0.06) and two-handed (M = 0.08, SD = 0.09) conditions, $t(20)$ = –2.70, p = 0.014 (two-tailed), d = –0.59. Participants made more word errors while typing with two hands compared to one hand.

Substitution Error Rate (SER). There was a statistically significant difference in SER between the one-handed (M = 0.04, SD = 0.05) and two-handed (M = 0.06, SD = 0.08) conditions, $t(20)$ = –2.40, p = 0.026 (two-tailed), d = –0.52. Participants made more substitution errors while typing with two hands compared to one hand.

Insertion Error Rate (IER). There was no statistically significant difference in IER between the one-handed and two-handed conditions.

Omission Error Rate (OER). There was a statistically significant difference in OER between the one-handed ($M = 0.004$, $SD = 0.007$) and two-handed ($M = 0.009$, $SD = 0.01$) conditions, $t(20) = -2.35$, $p = 0.029$ (two-tailed), $d = -0.51$. Participants made more omission errors while typing with two hands compared to one hand.

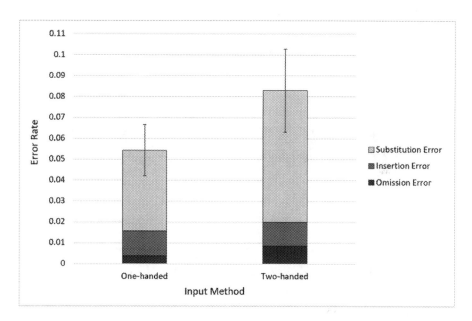

Fig. 4. Comparison of text input accuracy (word error rate). Error bars represent ±1 standard error.

To summarize, participants typed significantly faster using two hands compared to one hand; however, participants made significantly more errors using two hands.

3.2 Perceived Workload

There was a statistically significant difference in mental demand scores between the one-handed ($M = 6.52$, $SD = 4.46$) and two-handed ($M = 8.52$, $SD = 4.90$) conditions, $t(20) = -2.49$, $p = 0.022$ (two-tailed), $d = -0.54$. Participants reported higher mental demand when typing with two hands compared to one hand.

There was a statistically significant difference in physical demand scores between the one-handed ($M = 10.95$, $SD = 5.04$) and two-handed ($M = 8.95$, $SD = 5.04$) conditions, $t(20) = 2.28$, $p = 0.033$ (two-tailed), $d = -0.50$. Participants reported lower physical demand when typing with two hands compared to one hand.

There was no statistically significant difference between one-handed and two-handed conditions for temporal demand, performance, effort, and frustration subscales (see Fig. 5).

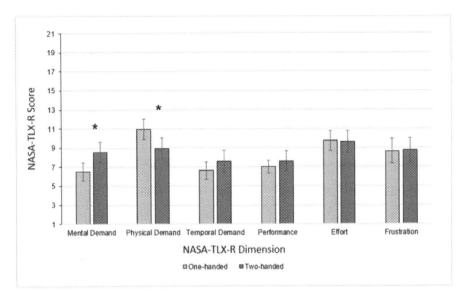

Fig. 5. Comparison of perceived workload (NASA-TLX-R) between one-handed and two-handed text input. Error bars represent ±1 standard error. * indicates $p < 0.05$.

3.3 Perceived Usability

There was no statistically significant difference in perceived usability between the one-handed ($M = 62.02, SD = 19.02$) and two-handed conditions ($M = 65.13, SD = 17.39$). Participants perceived the usability of one- and two-handed typing to be similar and falling within the adjective rating scale of "ok" (see Fig. 6).

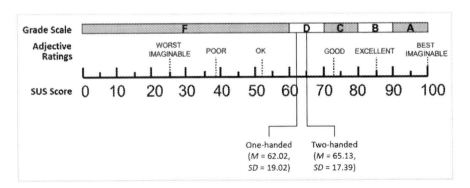

Fig. 6. Comparison of perceived usability (System Usability Scale). Figure adapted from [10].

3.4 Perceived Exertion

Participants reported significantly greater exertion in their left hand and left index finger when typing with two hands than with one hand (palm of left hand: $t(19) = -2.33$, $p = 0.031$ (two-tailed), $d = -0.52$; back of left hand: $t(20) = -2.13$, $p = 0.046$ (two-tailed), $d = -0.47$; left index finger: $t(20) = -2.69$, $p = 0.014$ (two-tailed), $d = -0.59$). In general, perceived exertion was minimal across all body parts.

3.5 Perceived Eye Fatigue

There was no statistically significant difference in reported eye strain ratings between one-handed and two-handed typing conditions for ease of reading text, text clarity, ability to concentrate, physical fatigue, mental fatigue, or level of eyestrain.

3.6 Preference

Participants reported their preference for each text input method (one-handed, two-handed) on a scale from 0 – Least Preferred to 50 – Most Preferred. There was a statistically significant difference in preference ratings between the one-handed ($M = 19.90$, $SD = 10.97$) and two-handed ($M = 32.81$, $SD = 11.94$) conditions, $t(20) = -3.54$, $p = 0.002$ (two-tailed), $d = -0.77$. Participants preferred inputting text with two hands compared to one hand (see Fig. 7).

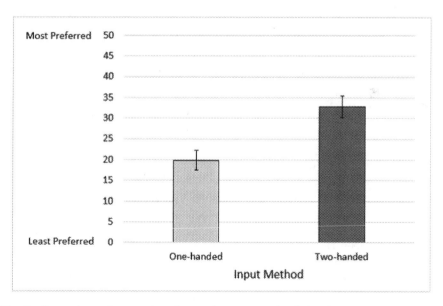

Fig. 7. Comparison of reported preference between one-handed and two-handed text input. Error bars represent ±1 standard error.

Several participants liked the auditory feedback provided by the system when they clicked a key, as some relied on this feature to determine whether the system recognized each keystroke. Several participants, however, reported they would like to use more than their index finger on each hand and recommended that the system accommodate the ability to type with all of their fingers. They also did not like how the keyboard reset its size and position between each phrase, and recommended that there be an option to save the size and position when users close the keyboard and then open it again within a short period of time. In addition, participants reported difficulty in typing double letters (e.g., "ee") and suggested this could be improved by reducing the system's lag after clicking a key.

4   Discussion

Overall, participants typed faster using the two-handed input method and preferred this method to one-handed input. Interestingly, the two-handed input method was more prone to error. Participants often stated that they sometimes accidentally clicked wrong keys because they were typing faster with two hands and perhaps being less precise. Additionally, participants occasionally attempted to use more than one finger on a single hand to type, which resulted in accidental touches of keys.

Many participants commented that the keyboard should allow detection of all fingers, making it more realistic to typing on a physical keyboard. Participants commented that having the keyboard fixed at a downward angle, similar to a physical keyboard, could prevent users from reaching out to type, reducing the amount of exertion for upper extremities.

The two-handed method had a higher perceived usability score, however it is only considered to be "ok" [10], meaning there is room for improvement. Overall, participants' preference for the two-handed method may suggest that they may be willing to sacrifice accuracy for speed and less exertion both mentally and physically. Participants reported that typing using two hands required a higher mental demand ($M = 8.52$, $SD = 4.89$) than typing with just one hand ($M = 6.52$, $SD = 4.46$). Many participants indicated that they had less accuracy typing two-handed. One participant thought it was easier to concentrate on the text input task when typing one-handed, whereas typing two-handed was distracting since they would often get confused about which hand was typing which letter. Another participant suggested that typing two-handed is something they had to get used to because they had to be aware of their hand placement. This higher degree of concentration may have contributed to the higher level of mental demand in two-handed typing.

Results in this study demonstrate speeds twice that reported by Derby et al. [5] for HoloLens 1 text input ($M = 5.41$ WPM, $SD = 0.89$, for gesture method; $M = 6.58$ WPM, $SD = 0.75$, for clicker method). While this comparison shows marked improvement in typing speeds for the HoloLens 2, typing speeds are not yet comparable to that of a physical keyboard (see Table 1).

Table 1. Comparison of different typing speeds across device types.

Device	Method	Average WPM
Microsoft HoloLens 1 [5]	Gesture	5.41
	Clicker	6.58
Microsoft HoloLens 2	One-handed	12.07
	Two-handed	13.91
Touchscreen Keyboard [7]	Two-handed	25
Physical Keyboard [7]	Two-handed	58

4.1 Limitations and Future Research

There were some limitations involved in this study. Our sample only included college-aged students. This limited generalizability and therefore it may have been beneficial to have a more diverse and robust sample of participants. Another limitation to this study was the system would sometimes automatically correct text input mistakes, which potentially could have affected error rates if incorrect words were substituted, submitted, and evaluated. Additionally, participants were instructed to not use speech-to-type or predictive text while typing. By restricting participants in this way, the process of typing may not have been representative of how an everyday user may type with the device.

In the future, research examining text input performance of the HoloLens 2 with other populations should be conducted. Other HoloLens 2 text input methods (e.g., voice-to-text, swiping gesture) should also be investigated, as well as scenarios that are more representative how an everyday user may input text with the headset. Additionally, text input performance should be continuously evaluated as new iterations of the HoloLens are developed. Improvements to future versions of the HoloLens are expected to focus on three key areas: improvement in immersion, improvement in comfort and social acceptability, and increasing the value of what can be accomplished using the headset [14]. These modifications could change the efficiency and effectiveness of typing using the MR headset, as well as increase consumer acceptance for a variety of applications and use cases.

References

1. Milman, N.B.: Defining and conceptualizing mixed reality, augmented reality, and virtual reality. Distance Learning **15**(2), 55–58 (2018)
2. Zheng, J.M., Chan, K.W., Gibson, I.: Virtual reality. IEEE Potentials **17**(2), 20–23 (1998). https://doi.org/10.1109/45.666641
3. Brigham, T.J.: Reality check: basics of augmented, virtual, and mixed reality. Med. Ref. Ser. Q. **36**(2), 171–178 (2017)
4. Browse All HoloLens Apps: https://www.microsoft.com/en-us/store/collections/hlgettingstarted/hololens. last accessed 25 Jan 2022
5. Derby, J.L., Rarick, C.T., Chaparro, B.S.: Text input performance with a mixed reality head-mounted display (HDM). Hum. Fac. Ergono. Soc. Ann. Meet. **63**, 1476–1480 (2019)

6. Dudley, J.J., Vertanen, K., Kristensson, P.O.: Fast and precise touch-based text entry for head- mounted augmented reality with variable occlusion. ACM Trans. Comp.-Hum. Interac. **25**(6), 1–40 (2018)

7. Sears, A.: Improving touchscreen keyboards: design issues and a comparison with other devices. Interac. Comp. **3**(3), 253–269 (1991)

8. Hart, S.G., Staveland, L.E.: Development of NASA-TLX (task load index): results of empirical and theoretical research. Human Mental Workload, 139–183 (1988)

9. Brooke, J.: SUS - a quick and dirty usability scale. Usabi. Eval. Indus. 189–194 (1996)

10. Bangor, A., Kortum, P., Miller, J.: Determining what individual SUS scores mean: adding an adjective rating scale. J. Usability Stud. **4**(3), 114–123 (2009)

11. Borg, G.: Borg's Perceived Exertion and Pain Scales. Human Kinetics, Champaign, IL (1998)

12. Microsoft: https://www.microsoft.com/en-us/hololens/hardware . last accessed 23 Jan 2022

13. MacKenzie, I.S., Soukoreff, R.W.: Phrase sets for evaluating text entry techniques. In: CHI '03 Extended Abstracts on Human Factors in Computing Systems, pp. 754–755. Association for Computing Machinery, New York, NY, USA (2003)

14. Microsoft is working on Hololens 3: Consumer version. https://mspoweruser.com/microsoft-is-working-on-hololens-3-consumer-version/. last accessed 25 Jan 2022

Learning Effect of Lay People in Gesture-Based Locomotion in Virtual Reality

Alexander Schäfer[1]([✉])[ID], Gerd Reis[2], and Didier Stricker[1,2]

[1] TU Kaiserslautern, Gottlieb-Daimler-Strasse Building 47,
67663 Kaiserslautern, Germany
Alexander.Schaefer@dfki.de
[2] German Research Center for Artificial Intelligence, Trippstadterstr. 122,
67663 Kaiserslautern, Germany
{Gerd.Reis,Didier.Stricker}@dfki.de

Abstract. Locomotion in Virtual Reality (VR) is an important part of VR applications. Many scientists are enriching the community with different variations that enable locomotion in VR. Some of the most promising methods are gesture-based and do not require additional handheld hardware. Recent work focused mostly on user preference and performance of the different locomotion techniques. This ignores the learning effect that users go through while new methods are being explored. In this work, it is investigated whether and how quickly users can adapt to a hand gesture-based locomotion system in VR. Four different locomotion techniques are implemented and tested by participants. The goal of this paper is twofold: First, it aims to encourage researchers to consider the learning effect in their studies. Second, this study aims to provide insight into the learning effect of users in gesture-based systems.

Keywords: Virtual Reality · Locomotion · Hand gestures ·
Gesture-based interaction · Learning effect

1 Introduction

Intuitive locomotion is an essential part of VR research and its applications. Usually a controller is used for virtual locomotion [1,5,8], but more recent work uses other techniques such as vision-based tracking [7] or sensors that are attached to the body [4,6]. The controller-based methods are extensively researched and already in commercial use. Gesture-based locomotion is getting more attention lately and requires more research to find out which methods are adequate. Many studies focus entirely on subjective user preference in researching and developing such locomotion systems. Moreover, studies related to locomotion in VR usually use a single "ease-to-learn" question for participants to find out if the technique is easy to learn. This article addresses another important factor that is often neglected. Namely, how quickly people can learn such a system. Complicated

© The Author(s), under exclusive license to Springer Nature Switzerland AG 2022
J. Y. C. Chen and G. Fragomeni (Eds.): HCII 2022, LNCS 13317, pp. 369–378, 2022.
https://doi.org/10.1007/978-3-031-05939-1_25

methods lead to longer times to achieve objectives and ultimately to user frustration. Therefore, attention should be paid to whether or not users can quickly adapt to implemented techniques.

To investigate the learning effect, a user study with 21 participants was conducted. Four different locomotion techniques based on hand gestures were implemented and tested by each participant. People with minor and no background in VR were recruited in order to remove additional bias or knowledge regarding VR systems. This article focuses on the learning effect that can be observed among these lay people. More concrete, this work answers the following research questions:

Do lay people significantly improve their task completion time when using hand gesture based locomotion during a second session compared to the first?

How much do lay people adapt to the limitations of a hand tracking device after a first trial session?

Will lay people significantly improve their efficiency (less number of teleportations) when using hand gesture based locomotion during a second trial session?

This article is organized as follows: In Sect. 2 relevant articles about the learning effect in VR locomotion are provided. The locomotion techniques used for the experiment are introduced in Sect. 3. In Sect. 4 the experiment is described and Sect. 5 the research questions are answered. Finally, the results are discussed in Sect. 6 and concluded in Sect. 7.

2   Background and Related Work

To the best of our knowledge, no paper was published that is focused on investigating the learning effect of lay people for hand gesture based VR locomotion. However, some work mentions learning effect during their studies.

Zhao et al. [9] investigated different techniques to control locomotion speed. The gestures included Finger Distance, Finger Number, and Finger Tapping. Users were asked within a questionnaire to subjectively evaluate the ease-to-learn. According to the results, users found the proposed techniques easy to learn. However, no quantitative analysis was performed to gain insights into the learning effect of participants.

Zielasko et al. [10] implemented and evaluated five different hands-free navigation methods for VR. The techniques included Walking In Place, Accelerator Pedal, Leaning, Shake Your Head, and Gamepad. Using a questionnaire, the authors came to the conclusion that the introduced techniques are easy to learn.

Kitson et al. [3] introduced NaviChair, a chair based locomotion technique for virtual environments. Users were required to move within the chair to get different locomotion effects. The authors compared this technique with a technique based on a joystick. During exit interviews, it was revealed that the joystick variant is preferred by users because it was more accurate and easier to learn.

The work of Keil et al. [2] used VR locomotion techniques to measure users' learning effect in distance estimations. The authors found a significant decrease in distance estimation errors after a subsequent task.

This paper does not rely on a subjective questionnaire to answer whether techniques are easy to learn. Instead, gathered data was quantitatively analysed to measure the learning effect of users.

3   Locomotion Techniques

In this section the locomotion techniques used for the experiment are introduced. Four different locomotion techniques, two two-handed and two one-handed, were implemented. All techniques are hand gesture-based and do not require controller or other handheld hardware. For details of the implementation of the proposed techniques, the reader is referred to the work of Schäfer et al. [7]. In the following text these four techniques are referenced as TwoHandIndex, TwoHandPalm, OneHandIndex, and OneHandPalm. These techniques are depicted in Fig. 1.

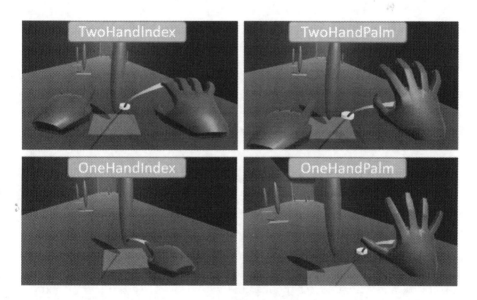

Fig. 1. The four locomotion techniques used for experiments. The two-handed techniques use one hand for choosing a destination and the other hand for activating the teleport via gestures. The one-handed techniques use one hand to choose the destination and the teleport is activated if the hand is kept still.

TwoHandIndex. This method requires the user to use both hands for moving through a virtual environment. The index finger on the right hand is used to choose a teleport destination. If the left hand performs a certain gesture, teleportation to the chosen destination is performed. The gesture consists of bending and straightening the index finger, similar to a pointing gesture.

TwoHandPalm. This method is similar to the TwoHandIndex technique. However, instead of using the index finger for navigation, the palm is used.

OneHandIndex. Only one hand for navigation as well as performing teleportation is used for this technique. When a pointing gesture is found, a ray emanating from the tip of the index finger is activated. After the ray is visible, teleportation will be performed after the hand is held still for 1.5 s.

OneHandedPalm. Similar to OneHandIndex, only one hand is used for locomotion. Instead of a pointing gesture, this technique uses the palm for navigation. As soon as the user opens his hand, a ray emanates from the centre of the palm. The teleportation is triggered after the hand is held still for 1.5 s.

4   Experiment

4.1   Objectives

The objective of the experiment was to answer the question whether users are able to quickly learn hand gesture based locomotion. More precise, the research questions mentioned in Sect. 1 should be answered. Four techniques to control locomotion in VR with hand gestures were implemented and performed by users. Task completion time was used to measure the efficiency of the user with different techniques. Additionally, the number of teleportations required to reach the goal and the number of times the hand tracking failed was collected to measure improvements by the users.

4.2   Participants

The study was performed with 21 volunteers (15 Male, 6 Female). The subjects' age ranged between 25 and 60 years ($M = 35.4$, $Median = 31$). A 5-point Likert-scale (1 denotes less knowledge and 5 expert knowledge) was used as a preliminary questionnaire to assess the experience of participants within the relevant subject areas. 81% of participants answered that they have good experience in software and computer (they answered with 4 or 5). Regarding VR experience, 86% of users have never worn a VR-HMD before and the remaining 14% used a VR headset at least once.

4.3   Apparatus

The experiment was performed by using a gaming notebook. Hand tracking was provided by the Leap Motion Controller. Samsung Odyssey+ was used as the VR-HMD.

4.4   Experimental Task

Participants had to touch ten pillar-like objects in a virtual environment. These objects were placed at fixed positions in a large corridor (10 m high, 10 m broad and 100 m long) with no obstacles other than the touchable pillar-like objects as depicted Fig. 2A.

Participants were required to move towards the pillars with the locomotion techniques proposed in Sect. 3. Once the user was close enough, a pillar could be touched and its color changed to indicate it was touched (Fig. 2B). The task was completed once the participant touched all 10 pillars in the VE. The task was repeated for each technique. The experiment was conducted in seating position.

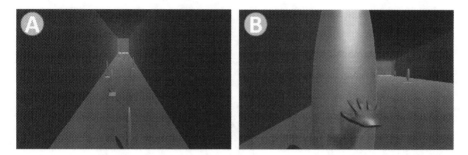

Fig. 2. (**A**) Overview of the virtual environment. 10 pillars are placed inside a large corridor. (**B**) Participant touching a pillar and changing its color to green. (Color figure online)

4.5   Procedure

The experiment had a within-subjects design. Each trial session was performed individually with the 21 subjects. The experiment was split into two phases: Learning phase and evaluation phase. In both phases, the participants had to move through the environment and perform the experimental task. In the learning, as well as the evaluation phase, all four techniques were used by the participants. Both phases are identical in terms of task and VE. The difference between the two phases is the order of techniques, which was counterbalanced between participants in the evaluation phase. In the learning phase, participants have performed each technique for the first time. Therefore, data is collected where users performed each technique for the first and the second time. A trial session lasted about 43 min.

5   Answering the Research Questions

Data was collected during the experiment to answer the research questions. No questionnaire regarding learning experience was given to the participants and our findings are based solely on quantitative results. Task completion time measured the time a participant required to complete the task. More precisely, it represents the time from touching the first pillar to the last inside the VE. Additionally, the number of times the hand tracking was lost was collected. This value represents the tracking failures of the chosen device. The tracking failed if the participant moved a hand out of the reliable tracking range of the device. For two-handed locomotion techniques, both hands had to be tracked by the sensor and for one-handed techniques only the dominant hand had to be tracked. This measure is particularly useful to measure the adaption of the user to overcome the limitations of the tracking device. Furthermore, the number of teleportations a user required to reach the goal was collected. The raw values such as mean, median, standard deviation, minimum, and maximum are shown in Table 1. One-way ANOVA was used for statistical analysis and throughout the paper significance at the 0.05 level is reported.

Table 1. Raw data collected during the experiment. Task completion time, number of times the hand tracking was lost during a session, and number of teleportations required to complete the task is shown.

Task	Mean	MDN	SD	MIN	**MAX**
Task Completion Time					
M1 - Learning	33.19	31	18.51	17	102
M2 - Learning	25.61	23	8.78	15	47
M3 - Learning	23.00	22	4.38	18	36
M4 - Learning	22.19	20	5.87	17	41
M1 - Evaluation	25.76	24	4.21	18	37
M2 - Evaluation	25.52	23	8.07	16	48
M3 - Evaluation	23.04	22	5.21	18	44
M4 - Evaluation	22.33	21	4.62	17	35
Hand Tracking Failures					
M1 - Learning	26.14	22	16.21	8	78
M2 - Learning	19.57	15	10.68	7	46
M3 - Learning	12.14	11	8.48	2	42
M4 - Learning	6.80	6	3.84	2	14
M1 - Evaluation	12.90	11	5.21	7	29
M2 - Evaluation	13.28	11	5.55	6	28
M3 - Evaluation	9.19	7	4.40	3	18
M4 - Evaluation	8.95	7	6.0	3	29
Number of Teleportations					
M1 - Learning	33.19	31	18.51	17	102
M2 - Learning	25.61	23	8.78	15	47
M3 - Learning	23.00	22	4.38	18	36
M4 - Learning	22.19	20	5.87	17	41
M1 - Evaluation	25.76	24	4.21	18	37
M2 - Evaluation	25.52	23	8.07	16	48
M3 - Evaluation	23.04	22	5.21	18	44
M4 - Evaluation	22.33	21	4.62	17	35

5.1 Do Lay People Significantly Improve Their Task Completion Time When Using Hand Gesture Based Locomotion During a Second Session Compared to the First?

To answer this question, the task completion time was taken into account. Levene's test was conducted in order to ensure homogeneity of the input data ($p > 0.05$). One-way ANOVA was used in order to answer whether users are faster at completing the given task after performing a training. A comparison was made between the learning phase of each technique and the corresponding evaluation phase. The average values are depicted in Fig. 3. The results of the ANOVAs are: TwoHandIndex: $F(1, 40) = 12.38, p = 0.001$; TwoHandPalm: $F(1, 40) = 8.298, p = 0.006$; OneHandIndex: $F(1, 40) = 2.04, p = 0.161$; OneHandPalm: $F(1, 40) = 0.144, p = 0.707$.

The results showed significant difference in the task completion time for the techniques TwoHandIndex and TwoHandPalm with $p < 0.05$. The techniques OneHandIndex and OneHandPalm did not show significance with $p > 0.05$. Therefore, it can be concluded that users performed significantly faster after conducting a learning phase for the two-handed techniques. The one-handed techniques however did not show significant improvements.

5.2 How Much Do Lay People Adapt to the Limitations of a Hand Tracking Device After a First Trial Session?

Today, hand tracking devices have several limitations such as occlusion, low field of view, and tracking range. Scientists working in this field know these limitations and already avoid them unconsciously. Non-experts who have never been exposed to this technology will discover many of these limitations. This inevitably leads to many tracking errors until the user becomes aware of why the system has problems. For this reason, the number of times the hand tracking failed during a session was used as an indicator to answer this research question. Once the

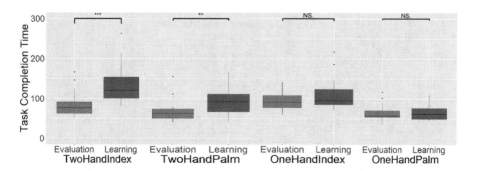

Fig. 3. Boxplot comparing task completion time between learning and evaluation phase. The values represent the time users required to fulfill the given task in seconds. Significance Levels: *** = 0.001; ** = 0.01; * = 0.05; NS = No Significance.

user's hands were no longer tracked, it was considered a loss of hand tracking. It can be said that users unconsciously and unintentionally move their hands out of the sensor's FOV because they are not accustomed to the technology. Therefore, this metric was used as an indicator of lay peoples learning effect of the chosen techniques. The average values are depicted in Fig. 4. One-way ANOVA was used to find significant improvements between the learning and evaluation phase. Levene's test assured homogeneity of the input data.

The result of the ANVOAs are: TwoHandIndex: $F(1,40) = 12.69, p = 0.001$; TwoHandPalm: $F(1,40) = 5.727, p = 0.021$; OneHandIndex: $F(1,40) = 2.003, p = 0.165$; OneHandPalm: $F(1,40) = 1.898, p = 0.176$.

These results indicate, that the two-handed techniques showed significant improvements between the learning phase and the evaluation phase. The one-handed techniques did not show significance. The two-handed techniques show overall increased tracking errors compared to the one-handed techniques. Therefore, it can be concluded that people perform better when using one-handed techniques. However, users are also able to significantly improve with the two-handed techniques by only doing one prior session with the technique.

5.3 Will Lay People Significantly Improve Their Efficiency (Less Number of Teleportations) When Using Hand Gesture Based Locomotion During a Second Trial Session?

To answer this question, the number of teleportations was considered. Levene's test was conducted in order to ensure homogeneity of the input data. One-way ANOVA was used to identify significant differences between the learning and evaluation phase of the experiment. The learning phase of each technique was compared with the corresponding evaluation phase. The average values are depicted in Fig. 5. The result of the ANOVAs are: TwoHandIndex: $F(1,40) = 3.214, p = 0.08$; TwoHandPalm: $F(1,40) = 0.001, p = 0.971$; OneHandIndex: $F(1,40) = 0.001, p = 0.975$; OneHandPalm: $F(1,40) = 0.008, p = 0.931$.

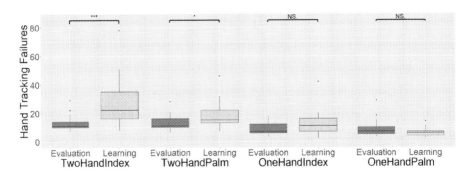

Fig. 4. Boxplot comparing the number of times the tracking has failed between learning and evaluation phase for each technique. Significance Levels: *** $= 0.001$; ** $= 0.01$; * $= 0.05$; NS $=$ No Significance.

According to the one-way ANOVAs, there was no significant improvement observed for individual techniques between learning and evaluation phase ($p >$ 0.05). Therefore, no learning effect could be observed in teleportation behavior.

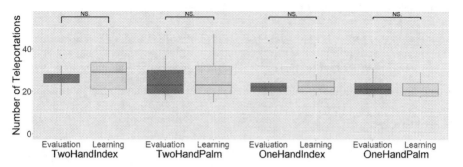

Fig. 5. Boxplot comparing the number of teleportations required to reach the goal between learning and evaluation phase. Significance Levels: *** = 0.001; ** = 0.01; * = 0.05; NS = No Significance.

6 Discussion

The participants showed a significant improvement in task completion time for the two-handed techniques. The use of one-handed techniques showed no significant improvement between the first and second phase of the experiment. During the experiment, subjects already expressed that one-handed techniques seem to be more intuitive and henceforth would explain these results. However, after performing the two-handed techniques for a second time, there was already significant improvement noticeable. This result is also backed by the fact that users significantly improved in regards to hand tracking failures. In the first phase, the users were uneasy because they first had to understand the limitations of the hand tracker. In the second phase, a clear improvement was noticeable. The number of teleportations required to reach the goal did not significantly vary between learning and evaluation phase. This could mean that the users understood how to achieve the goal and the task was straightforward to understand.

7 Conclusion

This paper investigated the learning effect of lay people performing hand gesture-based locomotion. A user study with 21 participants was conducted. In this study, four locomotion methods were utilised and the experiment was divided into a learning phase and an evaluation phase. All four methods were carried out twice by the subjects. The first time a method was performed was referred to as the learning phase and the second time as the evaluation phase. The study revealed significant improvements for the subjects while using two-handed techniques. The participants were considerably faster and significantly improved at using the hand tracking device. Therefore, it can be said that users struggle at first and then, with just one more trial run, they can significantly adapt to gesture-based systems with two hands. Furthermore, no significant learning effect was observed using one-handed techniques.

Acknowledgements. Part of this work was funded by the Bundesministerium für Bildung und Forschung (BMBF) in the context of ODPfalz under Grant 03IHS075B. This work was also supported by the EU Research and Innovation programme Horizon 2020 (project INFINITY) under the grant agreement ID: 883293.

References

1. Frommel, J., Sonntag, S., Weber, M.: Effects of controller-based locomotion on player experience in a virtual reality exploration game. In: Proceedings of the 12th International Conference on the Foundations of Digital Games, pp. 1–6 (2017)
2. Keil, J., Edler, D., O'Meara, D., Korte, A., Dickmann, F.: Effects of virtual reality locomotion techniques on distance estimations. ISPRS Int. J. Geo Inf. **10**(3), 150 (2021)
3. Kitson, A., Riecke, B.E., Hashemian, A.M., Neustaedter, C.: NaviChair: evaluating an embodied interface using a pointing task to navigate virtual reality. In: Proceedings of the 3rd ACM Symposium on Spatial User Interaction, pp. 123–126 (2015)
4. Pai, Y.S., Kunze, K.: ArmSwing: using arm swings for accessible and immersive navigation in AR/VR spaces. In: Proceedings of the 16th International Conference on Mobile and Ubiquitous Multimedia, pp. 189–198 (2017)
5. Rantala, J., Kangas, J., Koskinen, O., Nukarinen, T., Raisamo, R.: Comparison of controller-based locomotion techniques for visual observation in virtual reality. Multimodal Technol. Interact. **5**(7), 31 (2021)
6. Sarupuri, B., Hoermann, S., Steinicke, F., Lindeman, R.W.: TriggerWalking: a biomechanically-inspired locomotion user interface for efficient realistic virtual walking. In: Proceedings of the 5th Symposium on Spatial User Interaction, pp. 138–147 (2017)
7. Schäfer, A., Reis, G., Stricker, D.: Controlling teleportation-based locomotion in virtual reality with hand gestures: a comparative evaluation of two-handed and one-handed techniques. Electronics **10**(6), 715 (2021)
8. Weißker, T., Kunert, A., Fröhlich, B., Kulik, A.: Spatial updating and simulator sickness during steering and jumping in immersive virtual environments. In: 2018 IEEE Conference on Virtual Reality and 3D User Interfaces (VR), pp. 97–104. IEEE (2018)
9. Zhao, J., An, R., Xu, R., Lin, B.: Comparing hand gestures and the gamepad interfaces for locomotion in virtual environments. arXiv preprint arXiv:2104.12182 (2021)
10. Zielasko, D., Horn, S., Freitag, S., Weyers, B., Kuhlen, T.W.: Evaluation of hands-free hmd-based navigation techniques for immersive data analysis. In: 2016 IEEE Symposium on 3D User Interfaces (3DUI), pp. 113–119. IEEE (2016)

Flick Typing: A New VR Text Input System Based on Space Gestures

Tian Yang$^{(\boxtimes)}$, Powen Yao, and Michael Zyda

University of Southern California, Los Angeles, CA 90089, USA
{tyang863,powenyao,zyda}@usc.edu

Abstract. Text Entry is a significant topic in human-computer interaction in Virtual Reality. Most common text entry methods require users to interact with a 2D QWERTY keyboard in 3D space using a ray emitting from their hands or controllers. This requires the user's head and hands to be in a specific position and orientation to do text entry. We propose a new text entry input method that we call Flick Typing that is agnostic to user posture or keyboard position. Flick Typing utilizes the user's knowledge of a QWERTY keyboard layout, but does not explicitly provide visualization of the keys. To type with Flick Typing, users will move their controller to where they think the target QWERTY key is with respect to the controller's starting position and orientation, often with a simple flick of their wrists. We provide a manually defined gesture-key mapping model of the QWERTY keys in 3D space. Experiments containing both quantitative and qualitative measurements are conducted and discussed this paper, which shows the potential of our method.

Keywords: Text input · Virtual Reality · Human-computer interaction

1 Introduction

1.1 Background

Virtual Reality (VR) technologies has been enjoying rapid development in multiple fields, such as game industry, film production, stage performance and mobile application. In these applications, text input systems play a significant role. Currently, using a virtual representation of a standard QWERTY keyboard in some form is the most common way to input alphabetical letters, which is consistent with the most popular QWERTY based input methods in reality. However, these input systems suffer from different drawbacks and limitations in VR applications.

Traditional virtual keyboard based input systems present a visual QWERTY keyboard to the user, such as SteamVR input system. A conventional VR text input method (we call it Point and Click in this paper) is that users point the laser emitted from their hand controllers at the key they want to input and then click a specific button, for example, the trigger button on HTC Vive controllers. This kind of input system is straightforward and easy to handle, but studies have

© The Author(s), under exclusive license to Springer Nature Switzerland AG 2022
J. Y. C. Chen and G. Fragomeni (Eds.): HCII 2022, LNCS 13317, pp. 379–392, 2022.
https://doi.org/10.1007/978-3-031-05939-1_26

shown that it results in less than half the average typing speed on a standard physical keyboard [22]. In addition, a floating QWERTY keyboard taking up a large area of the user's field of view may be problematic. In real-time VR games and experiences, users may need to type while keeping an eye on the surrounding, and a big floating keyboard makes the interaction inconvenient. If the keyboard is made small, however, it would be difficult to select the keys, as a slight movement of the user's hand would result in a considerable change of the cursor. Therefore, visual keyboard may hinder user experience for VR applications. There has been solutions to alleviate this issue, such as dynamically changing key visuals [25]. Researchers has also been exploring and proposing other methods to facilitate text input in VR applications.

1.2 Flick Typing System

Developing new input mechanisms with better interaction experience and relatively high speed remains to be a research area with potential. We propose a new framework of alphabetical typing system called Flick Typing which utilizes 3D gestures in space to uniquely input alphabetical keys. Our aim is to develop a typing system with friendly user interaction experience, high accuracy, high speed, high degree of freedom and better immersion feeling. The mechanism is similar to the Punch Typing system proposed by Yao et al. [26]. It is called Flick Typing since users can perform gestures by just slightly rotating their hand controllers by flicking their wrists. When using our Flick Typing system, users are allowed to be in any body postures while typing, including sitting, standing, lying, or even walking. It only requires users to have knowledge about the layout of standard QWERTY keyboard, and proficient users can even type without looking at any visual aid. We construct a mapping from space gestures to key entries utilizing the rotation of hand controllers. This paper introduces the mechanism of Flick Typing, analyzes its performance comparing with the other two popular text input system: point and click and drum typing [4], and discuss our plan for future version of Flick Typing with personal-customized functionalities. Both qualitative and quantitative evaluation metrics are applied.

2   Related Work

Other alternatives to typing and text input in VR have been offered and explored in recent years. We look at 4 common types of virtual typing solutions:

- Visualize hands and keyboard in VR scenes. These methods use cameras on the HMD to track the position and motion of user's hands and visualize them in VR scenes [1,13,16,21]. There would be a virtual keyboard in the scene with which users can interact. Users can type as if on the physical keyboard with high speed using these methods. However, as mentioned before, the virtual keyboard should be large enough for users to interact easily with, which takes a large area in the scene, and the user need to be stationary and look at the keyboard.

– Design specific usage on hand controllers. These methods focus on making fully use of 2 hand controllers contained by most popular VR equipment set. Zigang et al. constructed a mapping from specific thumb movements on the touchpad of controllers to keys [28]. Ryan et al. applied a 3 * 4 telephone numpad keyboard in VR scenes and used different operations on hand controllers to specify which key to input [11]. Janis implemented a Swype-like typing system which input words using swiping-like gestures [10]. Costas and Stian proposed a typing mechanism using controllers as 'drum sticks' to press a virtual keyboard underneath like a 'drum' [4]. These methods enable users to type using just their controllers with high speed. However, users are required to learn a specific ways for typing, which might not be easy to start with.
– Using additional equipment. These methods use hardware equipment other than HMD and hand controllers to help typing. Some utilize a smartphone as a finger tracking sensor [5,12], some use thumb sticks of a game controller joystick [27], and some design customized hardware equipped on user's hands [8,24] or controllers [14]. These extra devices can improve the speed and accuracy for VR typing, though it might be inconvenient and add an additional cost for users to equip such equipment.
– Eye tracking. Research has gone into use gaze-tracking technology to type words instead of using hands [17,20]. The keys are specified by the movement of user's eyes. Even though controllers are no longer needed in these methods, users are required to pay extra attention to control their head and eyes, and the input speed is relatively slow using current solutions.

3   Flick Typing Input Mechanism

Flick Typing is based on the QWERTY keyboard layout. As shown in Fig. 1, a simplified QWERTY keyboard containing 30 keys is divided to 2 parts, the left and right hand responsible for each part. In order to enter a key, the user would need to use one of the controller to perform a specific space gesture according to the layout of QWERTY keyboard. The mapping from gestures to keys is based on the relative relationship between the transformation of the starting state and the end state of the controller.

In detail, at the beginning of the gesture, the user should hold the controller straight forward, imagining that the controller is pointing at the central key of the corresponding sub-keyboard, namely the left controller pointing at 'D' and the right controller pointing at 'K'. These are treated as the starting states, and the user needs to set up a start state reference for the gesture here by pressing a button once on the controller (in our case, the grip button on the side of the HTC Vive controller). After setting up the start state reference, the user can start text input with gestures. In order to input a letter, the user rotates the controller, as if the key it points at transfers from the starting key of the sub-keyboard to the target key. Upon reaching the target key, the user would click the other button (in our case, the trigger button of the HTC Vive controller) and the key will be inputted. The system will set up an end state reference

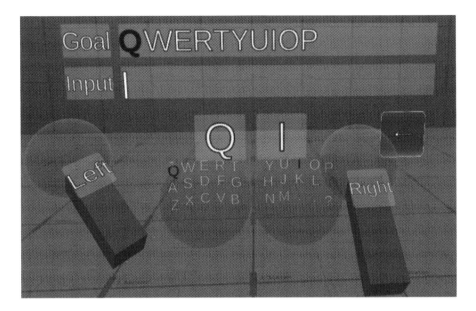

Fig. 1. Simplified QWERTY Keyboard layout for Flick Typing. The left controller is typing key 'Q', and the right controller is typing key 'L'.

when clicking the trigger button, and compute the space transformation of the controller's end state relative to the start state. Each key is assigned with a unique space transformation of the gesture according to the QWERTY layout. Such movement can be performed easily by slightly flicking and rotating the user's wrists. For example, flick the left hand to the left substantially and to around 10 o'clock direction to type 'Q' (as shown in Fig. 2), while flick the left hand slightly to around 11 o'clock with little motion of wrist to type 'W'; flick the right hand substantially to the right to type ';', while flick the right hand slightly to the left with little motion of wrist to type 'L'; to type 'D' or 'K', the user just need to let the controller back to the start state and click. Users do not need to care where the key exactly is. The only need is to move the controller smoothly according to their spatial memory of the QWERTY keyboard.

Since gestures are distinguished only by its relative transformation from the start state to the end state, Flick Typing allow users to type freely at any position, to any direction and in any body postures. Users can type while sitting in front of the computer, standing aside the window, or lying on the bed; with their hands holding in the front, beside the waist, etc. Users only need to set up appropriate start state reference and perform correct motions on their wrists.

User interface-wise, we provide two sphere keyboard to visualize the rotation of the two controllers. The indicator inside the sphere removes as the controller rotates, and key it arrives at is the key being input, meanwhile will change to a highlight color, as the Fig. 1 shows. We also provide two panels showing the real

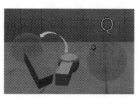

(a) Locate at right, facing forward

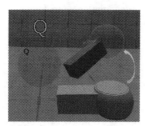

(b) Locate at right, facing right

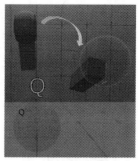

(c) Locate at middle, lying with head towards right

Fig. 2. Typing Q in different body postures and orientations

time key prediction as soon as the user set up the start states. The sphere keyboards and panels provide feedback on what is being typed if needed for better accuracy. However, theoretically, users familiar with Flick Typing mechanism can type without looking at the sphere keyboards or the panels, simply relying on spatial memory and muscle memory of the QWERTY keyboard.

3.1 Rotation Based Key Mapping

Aiming at enabling users to type letters with any body posture, we propose a set of data features used by the mapping model using the local rotation of the hand controllers in order to avoid the influence of the orientation of the body or the position of the hands. 'Local' means that it considers the space rotation of the controller with respect to their start state rather than the world coordinate system during a gesture. In other words, the feature that is the input of the mapping model is the controller rotation in the coordinate system fixed on the start state reference, i.e. the controller at the moment the gesture begins. Considering that what actually decides the corresponding key of a gesture is only its rotation with respect to its start state, meanwhile users can set up the start state reference of the gestures without any limitation, it is feasible for users to type freely with any body posture, orientation or hand position, as long as their gestures are correct with respect to the start state reference. For example, in order to type key 'E', users can just let the start reference points to their front, and slightly flick their left wrist upward, no matter he is actually facing which direction.

We use quaternion as the representation for space rotation since it is straightforward to compute rotation revolving in coordinate system conversion (in our case, from world system to the coordinate system fixed on the start state reference) using quaternion, and it does not suffer from problems such as the Gimbal Lock problem in Euler Angle representation.

We assign each key of each sub-keyboard with a unique local rotation value as a standard for comparison and prediction. Considering the coordinate system fixed on the controller as Fig. 3 shows, we model the rotation of a gesture as first rotating around the x axis and then rotating around the y axis. We set the 'Vertical Angle' namely the standard for rotating angle along the x axis as 20°, 'Outer Angle' along the y axis as 40°, and 'Inner Angle' along the y axis as 20°. 'Outer' means keys further from the sub-keyboard center on the x direction including 'Q' 'A' 'Z' 'T' 'G' 'B' and 'Y' 'H' 'N' 'P' ';' '?', and 'Inner' means keys nearer from the sub-keyboard center including 'W' 'S' 'X' 'R' 'F' 'V' and 'U' 'J' 'M' 'O' 'L' '.'. For each sub-keyboard, considering that 'D' and 'K' require no rotation, the standard rotation degrees of other keys along the x axis and the y axis in left-hand coordinate system are decided by the following rules:

– Keys in the top line: negative Vertical Angle along the x axis
– Keys in the middle line: no rotation along the x axis
– Keys in the bottom line: positive Vertical Angle along the x axis
– Keys in the left outer column: negative Outer Angle along the y axis
– Keys in the left inner column: negative Inner Angle along the y axis
– Keys in the middle column: no rotation along the y axis
– Keys in the right outer column: positive Outer Angle along the y axis
– Keys in the right outer column: positive Outer Angle along the y axis

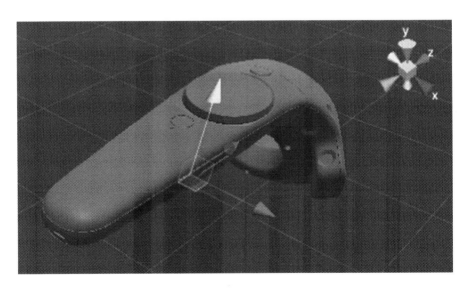

Fig. 3. Local coordinate system fixed on the controller. Screenshot from Unity.

There are totally 15 standard rotations applied to both the two sub-keyboard, and all of them are restored in quaternion representation in the system. In order to predict a key being entered, we compute the angle between the current rotation of the controller with each standard rotation by the following equation:

$$angle = 2\arccos|Q_{current} \cdot Q_{standard}|$$

The $Q_{current}(w, x, y, z)$ denotes the current rotation quaternion value, and $Q_{standard}(w, x, y, z)$ denotes the standard rotation quaternion value. The key with the smallest angle is treated as the key being input.

4   Experiments and Results

4.1   Typing Performance Evaluation

In order to evaluate the performance of Flick Typing, we conduct a series of experiments considering both quantitative and qualitative metrics. Additionally, we implement two widely used VR typing method, drum-like typing and point-and-click, and apply the same evaluation metrics on them in order to make a comparison among the three methods.

Typing Test Baseline. In the typing test stages of our experiment, participants will be provided with several English sentences on a user interface, and they need to type these sentences with the given typing method. Test sentences in all experiments are randomly selected from sentences containing 20 to 25 characters, from a widely used phrase set for text input method evaluation published by MacKenzie and Soukoreff [18].

Software Platform. We implement a experiment software platform which can run on most VR equipment, including HTC Vive series, Oculus series, etc. The software is implemented and built with Unity 2019. Flick Typing and point-and-click are implemented totally by ourselves, and drum-like typing is modified from a open source drum-like keyboard in Unity Asset Store. The user interface for three typing methods are shown in Fig. 4. In order to keep the fairness, keyboards for all three methods are simplified QWERTY keyboards containing 30 keys. Auto completion or correction mechanism are not applied in the software. The software provides haptic impulse on controllers and visual feedback on visual keyboards when a keystroke is performed to improve user experience. During the experiments, data used for calculating quantitative metrics is collected in the background.

Quantitative Metrics. We apply three quantitative evaluation measures for typing tests: typing speed, average moving distance of controllers and error rate.

Typing Speed. The typing speed is measured by Words-per-minute (WPM), which is the most widely used metrics for typing speed evaluation [2]. Typically 5 consecutive characters are treated as one word [2]. WPM is calculated by the following formula [2]:

$$WPM = \frac{\|T\| - 1}{S} \times 60 \times \frac{1}{5}$$

(a) Flick Typing

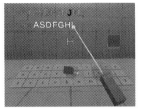
(b) Drum-like Typing

(c) Point and Click

Fig. 4. UI for the three typing methods

S denotes the seconds taken for typing given characters, and T denotes the number of final submitted characters [2]. The "-1" means that the first character is not taken into consideration [2].

Error Rate. We use three error rate metrics to evaluate the accuracy of the three typing methods: Corrected Error Rate (CER), Uncorrected Error Rate (UER) [6] and Total Error Rate (TER). Denoting the number of character deletions as CD, target sentence length as TL, submitted sentence length as SL, the Levenshtein Edit Distance between target sentence and submitted sentence as LD, CER is calculated by the following formula [6]:

$$CER = \frac{CD}{TL}$$

UER is calculated as follow [6]:

$$UER = \frac{LD}{max(SL, TL)}$$

TER is simply the sum of CER and UER:

$$TER = CER + UER$$

Qualitative Metrics. In order to evaluate user experience with the three typing methods, we require participants to fill in three questionnaires, one is before and the other two are after the testing experiments. The pre-experiment questionnaire collects participants' demographic data and experience on VR. The System Usability Scale (SUS) [3] and NASA Task Load Index (NASA-TLX) [9] are used as post-experiment questionnaires.

Pre-Experiment questionnaire. The pre-experiment questionnaire contains the following questions:

- Participant's name
- Participant's age
- Participant's gender

- What is the VR equipment you are using?
- How familiar are you with Virtual Reality?
- How often do you use VR equipment?
- Are you familiar with different types of VR Text Entry Solutions?
- What is your familiarity with QWERTY keyboard?
- Do you think blind typing without the help of a visual keyboard is useful in VR applications?

SUS. SUS is a simple and reliable measurement of the subjective usability of computer systems [3]. It contains 10 questions measuring user experience in different aspects. There are 5 response options: strongly disagree, slightly disagree, neutral, slightly agree and strongly agree, assigned with value 1 to 5 respectively. To calculate the overall value, we first subtract 1 from the response value of odd number questions (positive experience), and subtract the response value of even number questions (negative experience) from 5. Finally by adding all yielded values together and multiply it by 2.5, we can get the final SUS score in range from 0 to 100 [15].

NASA-TLX. NASA-TLX is a useful measurement for assessing the subjective work load when using human-machine interface systems. It includes 6 questions assessing work load in Mental Demand, Physical Demand, Temporal Demand, Performance, Effort and Frustration [9]. For simplification, we assign 5 options to each NASA-TLX question: very low, low, medium, high and very high, with value 0, 25, 50, 75, 100. We applied a unweighted TLX pattern (a.k.a Raw TLX, RTLX), whose usability has been proved in [19].

Experiments Procedure. Participants will first be given a brief introduction of the experiments, meanwhile be made aware that they can refuse to take the experiments if they feel uncomfortable being recorded or otherwise do not wish to participate, and can stop at any point if they feel like cannot or do not want to finish the experiments. Then they will fill in the pre-experiment questionnaire. After they enter the experiment software, they are required to read detailed instructions for the experiments before starting to test. For each typing method, participants will be first offered a playing around stage, where they can get themselves with this typing method. They can keep practicing until they feel ready for the actual experiment, and nothing will be recorded in this stage. For each typing method, there are 4 testing stages, each requiring participants to type a sentence block containing 5 sentences of 20–25 character long randomly chosen from MacKenzie and Soukoreff's phrase set [18], totally 20 different sentences. Quantitative metrics values and their raw data will be recorded for each testing stage. When participants complete all testing stages for one typing method, a text file in csv (Comma-Separated Values) format recording all data for this method will be generated. If participants feel tired after completing experiments for one method, they can take a rest, and re-enter the software for the experiments with other methods at any time, so that their fatigue will not influence their performance when using different methods. Finally participants are required to fill in the SUS and NASA-TLX questionnaires based on their experience on Flick Typing, and send all questionnaires and data files to us.

4.2 Results

Pre-experiment Survey. There were 9 participants taking part in our experiments. The average age of participants is 26. 8 of them are Male and 1 is Female. The VR devices they use includes Oculus Quest 1 and 2, Valve Index, Vive Cosmos Elite, HTC Vive and HTC Vive Pro. The results for other questions are listed in Table 1, where Ct. (Count) means the number of participants choosing this option:

Table 1. From left to right: (1) Results for familiarity with VR, (2) Frequency using VR, (3) Familiarity with different VR typing methods, (4) Familiarity with QWERTY keyboard and (5) Attitude to the necessity of blind typing in VR.

Option	Ct.	Option	Ct.	Option	Ct.	Option	Ct.	Option	Ct.
No	0	Never	0	No	1	No	0	Not helpful	0
Little	1	Hardly	2	Little	2	Little	0	Little helpful	0
Medium	2	Sometimes	6	Medium	5	Medium	0	Neutral	4
Much	5	Often	1	Much	1	Much	4	Helpful	4
Skillful	1	Skillful	0	Skillful	0	Skillful	5	Very helpful	1

Quantitative Metrics. Results for average WPM, CER, UER and TER of each typing method are listed in Table 2:

Table 2. Results for quantitative metrics.

Method	WPM	CER	UER	TER
Flick Typing	9.77	7.73%	3.32%	11.05%
Drum Typing	17.56	6.57%	1.17%	7.74%
Point and Click	15.57	2.88%	0.23%	3.11%

Qualitative Metrics. The average score for SUS questionnaire from all participants is 73.75, which exceeds the average SUS score reported by an analysis from Saura et al. [15]. This reveals the subjective usability of Flick Typing is above average level. The average score for NASA-TLX questionnaire is 35.42. As the survey from Rebecca [7] reports an average score of RTLX to be 45.29, we conclude that the subjective work load using Flick Typing is below average.

4.3 Discussion

Although the results above show that the typing speed of the current version Flick Typing is worse than the two popular VR typing method Drum-like Typing and Point-and-Click, Flick typing still outperforms various controller based typing methods, such as 8.55 WPM of 2-Thumb Typing [28], 8.49 WPM of telephone-numpad-like VRKeyboard [11], 5.3 WPM of discrete-joystick-like typing and 8.4 WPM of continuous-joystick-like typing [23].

Considering that the input mechanism of Flick Typing is new to most participants, and participants are provided only 20 short sentences to type, the unfamiliarity with Flick Typing may have considerable impact on typing speed and error rate performance. Practice on Flick Typing can improve typing performance significantly, since the average typing speed from sentence block 1 to block 4 grows from 8.52 WPM to 10.61 WPM. In addition, the two developers of Flick Typing who has tested the system a lot can gain an average typing speed of 14.26 WPM and total error rate of 6.94%, which substantially outperform the average level of all participants (all other participants are completely new to Flick Typing).

A unique characteristic of Flick Typing is that it does not necessarily need to interact with a visual keyboard while taking advantage of the QWERTY layout which is familiar to most users. Although the test software for Flick Typing implemented in this paper provides two sphere keyboards to facilitate typing, theoretically experienced users can type letters without of the help of sphere keyboards as long as they get used to applying their mental memory of QWERTY layout to their space gestures, and finally achieve blind typing in VR applications. According to the pre-experiment survey, more than half participants think that blind typing would be helpful in VR, and no participant believe that it would not help, which to some extent confirms our work. Furthermore, as the subjective survey through SUS and NASA-TLX questionnaires reveals, Flick Typing is a system with acceptable usability and work load.

4.4 Future Work

The current version of Flick Typing has a lot of room for improvement. We plan to improve Flick Typing in 3 directions:

User Interaction with Higher Usability. According to feedbacks from the participants, current version of Flick Typing is relatively not friendly enough to users. For example, new users may feel hard to type some keys at corner because of their unfamiliarity with the appropriate rotation for those keys, and the prediction may jump to weird keys far from the correct one if they perform large gestures or apply some angle of rolling on the controller. In addition, since the simplified QWERTY keyboard is divided into left part and right part, it takes more time when typing words whose most keys are in the same sub-keyboard, since users just use one hand in this case. We will find proper ways to alleviate these problems and provide better user interaction experience.

Applying Machine Learning Methods in Order to Provide Personal Customized Typing Experience. Current gesture-key mapping model is defined manually, which require users to adapt themselves to the system. We aim to develop VR typing system with tailored user interaction experience, where users are able to have personal customized typing system accommodating to their own habits. We have conducted preliminary experiments for such system by applying machine learning method. Multi-layer Perceptron (MLP) neural network has been applied to construct gesture-key mapping. However, according to feedbacks from participants, the experience of using the model generated by MLP is not as fluent and comfortable as manually defined model, and the typing speed and error rate of MLP model based Flick Typing cannot exceed manually defined model, so this paper does not discuss results of machine learning method in detail. We plan to make modifications to current machine learning method and conduct more experiments in future version of Flick Typing, in order to implement a typing method taking advantage of both current Flick Typing and user-customized experience.

Introducing Full QWERTY Keyboard. Current version of Flick Typing applies a simplified QWERTY keyboard which contains only alphabetical keys and four punctuation marks used frequently, in order to simplify implementation and experiments for usability. It is necessary to introduce the whole QWERTY keyboard including number keys, more punctuation marks, space key, backspace, enter key, etc. so that Flick Typing can be used in practical applications.

5   Conclusion

We propose a new VR text input system Flick Typing, which utilize space gestures of hand controllers based on the layout of QWERTY keyboards, and can enable users to type in any body postures or hand positions. To type a key, user will first set up a start state reference for each hand, and then slightly rotate the controller to perform a gesture. The rotation of the controller with respect to the start state will be input to a gesture-key mapping model and the corresponding key is typed. Different keys are differentiated by different rotations, and the value of rotations are designed based on the QWERTY layout. Users do not need to interact with a visual keyboard when using Flick Typing. Experiments are conducted to evaluate the performance of Flick Typing, containing both quantitative metrics including WPM and error rate, and qualitative metrics including SUS [3] and NASA-TLX [9] questionnaire. The typing speed of Flick Typing reaches an average of 9.77 WPM, and the total error rate is 11.05%. SUS and NASA-TLX surveys reveal acceptable usability and work load.

References

1. Adhikary, J., Vertanen, K.: Typing on midair virtual keyboards: exploring visual designs and interaction styles. In: Ardito, C., et al. (eds.) INTERACT 2021. LNCS, vol. 12935, pp. 132–151. Springer, Cham (2021). https://doi.org/10.1007/978-3-030-85610-6_9

2. Arif, A.S., Stuerzlinger, W.: Analysis of text entry performance metrics. In: 2009 IEEE Toronto International Conference Science and Technology for Humanity (TIC-STH), pp. 100–105. IEEE (2009)

3. Bangor, A., Kortum, P.T., Miller, J.T.: An empirical evaluation of the system usability scale. Int. J. Hum. Comput. Interact. **24**(6), 574–594 (2008)

4. Boletsis, C., Kongsvik, S.: Text input in virtual reality: a preliminary evaluation of the drum-like VR keyboard. Technologies **7**(2) (2019). https://doi.org/10.3390/technologies7020031. https://www.mdpi.com/2227-7080/7/2/31

5. Boustila, S., Guégan, T., Takashima, K., Kitamura, Y.: Text typing in VR using smartphones touchscreen and HMD. In: 2019 IEEE Conference on Virtual Reality and 3D User Interfaces (VR), pp. 860–861 (2019). https://doi.org/10.1109/VR.2019.8798238

6. Fashimpaur, J., Kin, K., Longest, M.: PinchType: text entry for virtual and augmented reality using comfortable thumb to fingertip pinches. In: Extended Abstracts of the 2020 CHI Conference on Human Factors in Computing Systems, pp. 1–7 (2020)

7. Grier, R.A.: How high is high? A meta-analysis of NASA-TLX global workload scores. Proc. Hum. Factors Ergon. Soc. Annu. Meet. **59**, 1727–1731 (2015)

8. Gupta, A., Ji, C., Yeo, H.S., Quigley, A., Vogel, D.: RotoSwype: word-gesture typing using a ring, pp. 1–12. Association for Computing Machinery, New York, NY, USA (2019). https://doi.org/10.1145/3290605.3300244

9. Hart, S.G.: Nasa-task load index (NASA-TLX); 20 years later. Proc. Hum. Factors Ergon. Soc. Annu. Meet. **50**, 904–908 (2006)

10. Jimenez, J.G.: A prototype for text input in virtual reality with a Swype-like process using a hand-tracking device. University of California, San Diego (2017)

11. Kim, R., Donahoe, K., Sriram, P.: A survey and implementation of fast-input typing methods in virtual reality

12. Kim, Y.R., Kim, G.J.: HoVR-type: smartphone as a typing interface in VR using hovering. In: 2017 IEEE International Conference on Consumer Electronics (ICCE), pp. 200–203 (2017). https://doi.org/10.1109/ICCE.2017.7889285

13. Knierim, P., Schwind, V., Feit, A.M., Nieuwenhuizen, F., Henze, N.: Physical Keyboards in virtual reality: analysis of typing performance and effects of avatar hands, pp. 1–9. Association for Computing Machinery, New York, NY, USA (2018). https://doi.org/10.1145/3173574.3173919

14. Lee, Y., Kim, G.J.: Vitty: virtual touch typing interface with added finger buttons. In: Lackey, S., Chen, J. (eds.) VAMR 2017. LNCS, vol. 10280, pp. 111–119. Springer, Cham (2017). https://doi.org/10.1007/978-3-319-57987-0_9

15. Lewis, J.R., Sauro, J.: The factor structure of the system usability scale. In: Kurosu, M. (ed.) HCD 2009. LNCS, vol. 5619, pp. 94–103. Springer, Heidelberg (2009). https://doi.org/10.1007/978-3-642-02806-9_12

16. Lin, J.W., et al.: Visualizing the keyboard in virtual reality for enhancing immersive experience. In: ACM SIGGRAPH 2017 Posters, SIGGRAPH 2017. Association for Computing Machinery, New York, NY, USA (2017). https://doi.org/10.1145/3102163.3102175

17. Ma, X., Yao, Z., Wang, Y., Pei, W., Chen, H.: Combining brain-computer interface and eye tracking for high-speed text entry in virtual reality. In: 23rd International Conference on Intelligent User Interfaces, IUI 2018, pp. 263–267. Association for Computing Machinery, New York, NY, USA (2018). https://doi.org/10.1145/3172944.3172988

18. MacKenzie, I.S., Soukoreff, R.W.: Phrase sets for evaluating text entry techniques. In: CHI'03 Extended Abstracts on Human Factors in Computing Systems, pp. 754–755 (2003)

19. Moroney, W.F., Biers, D.W., Eggemeier, F.T., Mitchell, J.A.: A comparison of two scoring procedures with the NASA task load index in a simulated flight task. In: Proceedings of the IEEE 1992 National Aerospace and Electronics Conference@ m_NAECON 1992, pp. 734–740. IEEE (1992)

20. Rajanna, V., Hansen, J.P.: Gaze typing in virtual reality: impact of keyboard design, selection method, and motion. In: Proceedings of the 2018 ACM Symposium on Eye Tracking Research & Applications, ETRA 2018. Association for Computing Machinery, New York, NY, USA (2018). https://doi.org/10.1145/3204493.3204541

21. Richardson, M., Durasoff, M., Wang, R.: Decoding surface touch typing from hand-tracking. In: Proceedings of the 33rd Annual ACM Symposium on User Interface Software and Technology, pp. 686–696 (2020)

22. Speicher, M., Feit, A.M., Ziegler, P., Krüger, A.: Selection-based text entry in virtual reality. In: Proceedings of the 2018 CHI Conference on Human Factors in Computing Systems, CHI 2018, pp. 1–13. Association for Computing Machinery, New York, NY, USA (2018). https://doi.org/10.1145/3173574.3174221

23. Speicher, M., Feit, A.M., Ziegler, P., Krüger, A.: Selection-based text entry in virtual reality. In: Proceedings of the 2018 CHI Conference on Human Factors in Computing Systems, pp. 1–13 (2018)

24. Wu, C.-M., Hsu, C.-W., Lee, T.-K., Smith, S.: A virtual reality keyboard with realistic haptic feedback in a fully immersive virtual environment. Virtual Reality 21(1), 19–29 (2016). https://doi.org/10.1007/s10055-016-0296-6

25. Yang, Z., Chen, C., Lin, Y., Wang, D., Li, H., Xu, W.: Effect of spatial enhancement technology on input through the keyboard in virtual reality environment, vol. 78, pp. 164–175 (2019). https://doi.org/10.1016/j.apergo.2019.03.006. https://www.sciencedirect.com/science/article/pii/S0003687019300596

26. Yao, P., Lympouridis, V., Zhu, T., Zyda, M., Jia, R.: Punch typing: alternative method for text entry in virtual reality. In: Symposium on Spatial User Interaction, pp. 1–2 (2020)

27. Yu, D., Fan, K., Zhang, H., Monteiro, D., Xu, W., Liang, H.N.: PizzaText: text entry for virtual reality systems using dual thumbsticks. IEEE Trans. Vis. Comput. Graph. 24(11), 2927–2935 (2018). https://doi.org/10.1109/TVCG.2018.2868581

28. Zhang, Z., Sun, M., Gao, B., Wang, L.: 2-thumbs typing: a novel bimanual text entry method in virtual reality environments. In: 2021 IEEE Conference on Virtual Reality and 3D User Interfaces Abstracts and Workshops (VRW), pp. 530–531 (2021). https://doi.org/10.1109/VRW52623.2021.00147

Social, Emotional, Psychological and Persuasive Aspects in VAMR

A Design Framework for Social Virtual Reality Experiences: Exploring Social and Cultural Dimensions for Meaningful and Impactful VR

Vanessa Cui[1]([⊠]), Thomas Hughes-Roberts[2], and Nick White[1]

[1] Birmingham City University, Edgebaston Campus, Birmingham, UK
vanessa.cui@bcu.ac.uk
[2] University of Derby, Markeaton Street Campus, Derby, UK

Abstract. Virtual Reality has often been described as providing a means to "walk a mile in another's shoes" offering powerful interventions for experiential learning. Such experiences can, for example, provide a safe and controlled means of engaging with often difficult, unsafe or emotionally charged situations. Crucial to this experience is the sense of presence, informed by place and plausibility, of the simulation design. However, past studies often create such experiences through the lens of the developer, and they may therefore lack the authenticity and social nuance of the situations they are attempting to model. Health care students, for example, will often face difficult conversations with seriously ill patients during their placement time when in study. Currently, there is an under-preparedness associated with placement shock when students' previous assumptions and the reality of patient care do not match. VR would seem well suited to preparing students for this reality but only if the simulations capture the complexity and social nuance. As currently there is little consideration of the social and cultural dimensions for developing social VR experiences, this paper proposes a framework for designing such socially oriented VR applications. We case study the framework by designing a social VR application for health care students to prepare for placement.

Keywords: Social virtual reality · User centered design · Health care education

1 Introduction

Virtual Reality (VR) provides a powerful medium within which to create complex learning environments and contexts. VR can result in the illusion of presence, where a participant believes they are in a virtual place and the events occurring are really happening to their virtual self (Slater 2017). Through body ownership, where the participant takes cognitive control of their virtual body (Slater et al. 2009), implicit learning in VR can lead to changes in perception, attitudes, cognition, and behaviour. Throughout the design process, developers will seek to explore how they can maximise the feeling of presence an application provides with the goal that a strong sense of presence will lead to a believable and potentially impactful experience.

Central to achieving presence are the related concepts of place, which describes the environment or setting, and the sense of plausibility, which describes the believability

© The Author(s), under exclusive license to Springer Nature Switzerland AG 2022
J. Y. C. Chen and G. Fragomeni (Eds.): HCII 2022, LNCS 13317, pp. 395–409, 2022.
https://doi.org/10.1007/978-3-031-05939-1_27

of the actions that take place in the virtual world (Slater 2007). What is unclear, from a development perspective, is how to maximise the quality of these factors when seeking to create social VR applications; particularly, where the applications model real world experiences for others to share in. Such experiences are likely to be complex and nuanced, the subtleties of which a developer alone may not be able to capture.

Health care education provides a case study for the challenging task described. Effective conversational interactions are key for providing patients with compassionate, respectful care safely (Pollard et al. 2019), yet it is a challenging area for healthcare student's learning and development. In England, the 'Reducing Pre-registration Attribution and Improving Retention' (RePAIR) report highlighted a major contributing factor to first-year healthcare students (adult, child, learning disabilities and mental health nursing, midwifery and therapeutic radiography) discontinuing their course is a perceived lack of preparedness to deal with seriously ill patients (Health Education England, 2018). As part of a higher education healthcare programme, students complete clinical practice placements where they are faced with seriously ill patients (*e.g.* cancer patients), for many, often for the first time. This under-preparedness is associated with "placement-shock" (Society and College of Radiographers 2013) as they deal with emotional patient interactions that may not match students' previous assumptions regarding their placement (Leducq 2019). A challenge for educators and students is that these encounters are situational, dynamic, and difficult to prepare for without first-hand experience from which to reflect and learn from.

This would therefore appear to be an ideal area of application for VR to provide pre-exposure and reduce placement shock. However, capturing the dynamic, nuanced and social complex situations they may find themselves in is a challenge. This paper seeks to extend the concepts of presence, place and plausibility and present a design methodology that captures the social nuance of lived experiences through a user-centred design approach. Using radiotherapy education as a case study, we outline the design of a VR application the intends to prepare students for some of the encounters they may face in their placement. The remainder of the paper is structured as follows: a literature review of related applications, a presentation of the theoretical framework to be utilized, an outline of the methodology and data collection activities, findings from user interviews and a proposed VR application design. It is intended that this paper provide initial steps towards a methodology for capturing social nuance in VR development.

2   Review of Relevant Literature

2.1   User-Centred Design to Generate Meaningful Social VR Content for Professional Learning

There is past work demonstrating VR has a history in experiential learning (see Bailenson 2018). As suggested by Gillies and Pan (2018), the experiential learning environment provided by a VR application can assist learning and teaching of social skills and decision making in situ that cannon be gaining from books, taught sessions or two-dimensional multimedia (e.g. video). The potential power of using VR in experiential learning of complex social activities in professional education such as medical/healthcare education has been widely acknowledge by scholars and practitioners (see Bracq et al. 2019 for summary) and in recent years, studies have tested the VR environment, interaction and the hardware to optimise its effectiveness (e.g. O'Connor et al. 2021).

In the context of health and medical care education, VR has been widely used for skills-based training and learning (see Slater and Sanchez-Vives 2016 for summaries). Studies (*e.g.* Samosorn et al. 2020; Rajeswaran et al. 2018; Gunn et al. 2018) have highlighted the effectiveness of using VR in health care skills learning and training where trainees could undertake complex procedures in a safe place. As highlighted by Samosorn et al. (2020), the main strengths of a well-designed VR for training healthcare professionals include allowing for computational offloading thus trainees can concentrate on learning material rather than imagining details of the scenario and allowing skills and content to be repeated through deliberate practice. A number of VR applications focus on developing social skills: Mpathic VR, for example, is an application aims to teach 'effective, empathic communication skills' to medical students that uses virtual human patients for difficult conversations. Many of these applications on using VR for effective communication in healthcare/medical care education focus on teaching – what skills/attributes should be taught and how they should be taught to learners. These applications use previous research and/or professional knowledge by practitioners on what effective communication should be like and how it could be development in healthcare students. In the limited publications which share how the content is designed and developed, patient-centred perspective tends to be the lens through which the content is generated (*e.g.* Hannans 2019). The healthcare students' perspective and their experiences of difficult conversations they had are often not considered when designing the content of these new learning tools.

Capturing such perspectives and generalising them in a VR application to be relevant experiential learning experiences for new audiences is a challenge. Such lived experiences are often nuanced and situated based on the social and cultural contexts of persons involved. As such, understanding of this nuance and situated-ness is required during content creation and application development, something which developers are likely to lack without the input from users. User-centred design of such VR applications provides a meaningful and relevant solution whereby unique insights can be obtained from users directly by placing them at the core of the design process (Chayutsahakij and Poggenpohl 2002). Specifically, including users in the process of co-creation by capturing their narratives and iteratively developing with them through consultation not only ensures the authenticity of the final designs but also empowers users by giving them the opportunity to influence interventions (Dietrich et al. 2021).

2.2 Theoretical Framework

Like all VR applications, immersion, presence and interactivity are the core characteristics (Radianti et al., 2019) for social interaction VR. The impact of an experience on an individual can be considered from two perspectives: the level of immersion offered by the VR platform and the feeling of presence within the generated 3D worlds. Slater (2009) suggests that presence is a cognitive perception based on the place and plausibility of simulations. However, work is needed to show how these concepts be utilised when creating complex and nuanced social simulations so that they accurately and authentically represent the subject matter. As pointed out by Riva and Mantovani (2000), experiences in VR is subjective to the individual. They (2000) argued that VR could be seen as an advanced communication tool in which the social and cultural dimensions of user's experiences are as important as the quality of sensory experiences such as visual and sound in the VR. Viewing VR from this perspective opens up inquiries over the importance of considering social and cultural factors in the design, development and evaluation of VR scenarios that involve or are for social interactions. This is central to the methodological design and development of this study.

In this study, works from microsociology on social interactions (Hochschild 1979; Blumer 1969; Berger and Luckmann 1966; Goffman 1959) are used to create a framework for identifying detailed social and cultural components of social interactions. These works are underpinned by the philosophical view that social interactions are socially and culturally constructed and subjective to the individual. Moreover, social interactions such as conversations are situated which means the social and cultural circumstances of the interaction are key to such experience (Haugh 2012). During a social interaction, the *social environment*, the *social and cultural context*, *communication* and the *social and cultural situation* are fundamental to the actions, reactions and feelings of participants of this social interaction. In the proposed framework for social VR, the virtual social interactions are intended to capture the authenticity of real-world social interactions. There is an expectation that if these interactions are meaningful to their participants, they would have powerful immediate and possible long-term impact on these participants.

Table 1. Social and cultural dimensions of the design framework for social VR

Dimension	Description
Social Environment	Where the interaction takes place and who are there
Social and Cultural Context	The relationship between persons involved and the wider social and cultural context of such relationship
Communication	Verbal and non verbal languages, facial expressions and tones of verbal communication
Social and Cultural Situation	The identities of the persons involved and how they are perceived by each other

3   Methodology and Methods

A user-centred design approach necessitates the identification and involvement of user representatives throughout the design and development process deployed by this project. This section describes the methodology and methods the project used to ascertain placement experiences and learning from therapeutic radiography students which were then turned into the scenarios in the VR application.

An interpretive phenomenological approach (IPA) (Larkin et al. 2009) to capture students' lived experiences and emotions when encountering challenging conversations with patients is utilised. IPA is used as it is the methodology for understanding lived experiences and exploring how individuals make sense of their personal experiences in the social world. The foundation of IPA is the phenomenological philosophical understanding of human experiences in the way in which things are perceived as they appear to consciousness (Langdridge 2007). In this study, student therapeutic radiographers' memories and reflections of their encountered challenging conversations with patients form the basis for the content of the VR application. The underpinning philosophy of IPA regarding the subjectivity of human making sense of lived experiences aligns with Riva and Mantovani's argument about the subjectivity of VR experiences (2000) and the pedagogical view of reflective learning that learning experiences is subjective to individual learners.

To ensure the content can engage users in meaningful experiences, the use of IPA allows the researchers to gather and analyse data to understand the meanings individual students attach to their experience. Participants are encouraged to tell their own story in their own words which means the data collection and analysis provide an outline of themes for creating the VR content that is not too rigidly scheduled and structured. By focusing on interviewees telling their own experiences, the data collection and analysis design allows the project team to capture the authentic situated accounts and nuanced details (Larkin et al. 2009) of the challenging conversations interviewees had with patients.

These interpretive phenomenological interviews focused on students recalling and reflecting on challenging conversations they had with patients during their first year clinical placement. The interview schedule is underpinned by Gibbs' reflective model (1988) in order to capture what students experienced, how they felt about their experiences and what they learnt from it. Students were given the interview questions prior to the interview in preparation for recalling the experiences. The interview questions involved:

- **Descriptive recall** of these challenging encounters – a detailed sketch of the event, the environment where it took place, the people involved and the interactions (verbal and non-verbal) took place – to capture the environment (social and physical) and the social and cultural situation of the scenarios;
- Reflection by student on how they **felt** at the time during the interaction and immediately afterwards to capture the perceived social and cultural context; and
- Reflection on what the student **learnt** from these experiences about themselves as a student healthcare professional and how these experiences connect with their learning and development in clinical settings and at university.

Telling the experiences through their own words, these students offered authentic understandings of '*What conversations do students find challenging? And Why?*' '*Where and when did the conversation take place?*' '*Who was at the scene and what was their involvement?*' '*How did they feel during and after these encounters with patients?*' '*How did they go about managing and negotiating during these conversations?*' and '*How did they manage their emotions during and after these conversations?*' which are essential to the creation and development a VR experiential learning tool that is meaningful for medical/healthcare learners in similar context.

For the interviews to ascertain student placement experiences and learning, a total of six participants were recruited through convenience sampling. Recruitment emails were sent to all second-year students from course leaders inviting their participation. All six participants were female and from a range of age, race and nationality groups with some being mature students who had previous professional experience (not in healthcare) prior to their course and some young students who came straight to higher education from school/college. The range of social and cultural backgrounds represented by interview participants is essential in collecting scenarios that are relevant and meaningful to the target user group in similar social and cultural contexts. One limitation of this study is the lack of male student participation in the interview.

Interviews were recorded and transcribed verbatim. Data analysis followed the approach designed by Larkin et al. (2009). Two researchers first read transcripts independently and took notes on the initial themes which include characteristics of difficult/challenging conversations, the environment where the conversation took place (physical and social), the social and cultural context and situation of the conversation. Coding of social and cultural aspects (Table 1) of the interactions was produced in the notes. Notes from each researcher then collected and formed a table of themes and findings. This was refined by one of the researchers to create a final table of themes and findings.

Findings from these themes formed the scenario vignettes representing the range of experiences encountered by participants. Scenario vignettes were presented back to participants to confirm they broadly represented a key experience. From the interview data, scripts were also developed that would form the potential character interactions. Scripts were drawn in collaboration with the participants for to ensure representation of their experience.

The work was fully ethically approved by the university's research ethics committee and it followed the research ethics guidelines provided by the British Education Research Associated (BERA 2018). Three particular potential research ethical issues regarding participant anonymity, participant in distress and reporting poor practice or risk of harm were dealt with caution. As the interview aimed to find out as much detail as possible about these specific incidents, there was a potential of revealing the identities of those individuals involved and the clinical practice. In order to protect their anonymity, the scenarios created are not based on any one particular student's experience but an amalgamation of different incidents. The validity of the content is underpinned by the shared characteristics from the thematic analysis of each incident. The amalgamated scenarios were presented back to interview participants to confirm they broadly represented their experience. As participants were asked to reflect on difficult situations they encountered, the protocol allowed them to stop at any time and further support service provided if required. The interview was not aimed at discovering poor practice or risk of harm/s that took place during student placements. Participants were asked to not disclose any issues that might be considered as poor practice or risk of harm/s as the interview is not the appropriate forum. Should participant start to disclose such information, the researcher would stop the recording and ask the participant to stop and advise the participant to report the issue to an appropriate authority. Because therapeutic radiography is governed by a set of professional standards, the researcher made it clear to participants that if there were possible disclosure of poor practice or risk of harm, the research team would inform the programme leader of the course participating students belonged to.

4 Interview Findings

Between six participants, thirteen scenarios of difficult conversations with patients were reported. Analysis of the thirteen reported scenarios enabled the research team to generate a number of potential scenarios for the VR application.

Findings from the interviews identified five broad characteristics of difficult conversations (Image 1). In all these situations, at least two of these characteristics were involved, *e.g.* being in an unexpected and overwhelming situation as such a patient having a cardiac rest. In addition, a number of these examples also involved situations where students were performing technical/medical tasks while carrying out social interactions. Findings from these interviews clearly indicate these students experienced complex situations that required quick professional decision making and communication with patients under pressure.

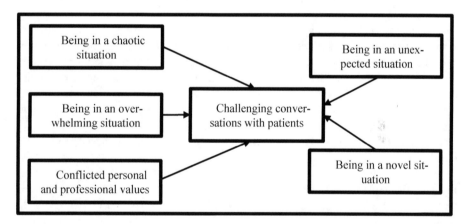

Image 1. Key characteristics of challenging conversations with patients based on student experiences

Analysis using the framework on the social environment, the social and cultural context, communication and the social and cultural situation (Table 1) across the thirteen scenarios revealed a number of key findings that are essential to students' perceptions of their interactions with patients.

The presence of persons involved is an important aspect of the social environment. In this study, students reported that who else were present and their involvement matter significantly to how they acted and perceived the situation. When there were others present, such as another staff member or the patient's family, all students felt they had to consider how the others might judge their actions. While some students preferred having a senior colleague with them to ask for guidance, reassurance and/or support, some students felt that having the opportunity to deal with challenging conversations by themselves helped them grow and establish their professional identity.

The perceived relationships and professional identities between persons involved play a part in students' feelings towards the interaction as one participant revealed 'you know you can have a laugh with some senior colleagues about an embarrassing situation but it's not being professional to some other colleagues'. However, the relationships between persons involved impact on the interactions as a longitudinal quality. A characteristic of therapeutic radiographer's work is working with patients during the course of their treatment thus having the opportunity and time to know them and their families. Such kind of relationship development led some students to grow a deep empath with their patients which meant having conversations about their treatment became challenging. This is a challenging area for short, episodic VR scenarios to convey. As such, this project did not incorporate this finding into its design. Nevertheless, it is an important social and cultural aspect for social VR applications to be mindful of.

The identities of persons involved (such as their age and gender) matter to how participant perceives the situation and how they act during the interaction. In this study, students' empathy led them to make personal connections with people in the personal lives with similar age and gender. For example, one student reported a challenging conversation with a female patient who reminded her of her sister due to their age similarity; several students also reported that older patients made them thinking about their own grandparents. Some students reported encounters with male patients that were either awkward or made them feeling slightly intimidated due to the voice or the physical size and presence of a male.

Age and maturity of the students were important factors to their perceptions of these challenging conversations they had. This is where the situated-ness and subjectivity of social interactions matter to consider participants' experiences. Students who were more mature with previous experiences of working in other professions reported challenging conversations that shared similar characteristics as their younger peers. The nature of a therapeutic radiographer's work with cancer patients meant conversing with empathy and compassion for students is an emotional experience. Sometimes, the situation requires the student to act counterintuitively to how they would acted in other social situations. Nevertheless, mature students revealed more effective recovery strategies after a challenging encounter with a patient where younger students required more support from their peers or more experienced colleagues. This is a key area for student to have experiential learning using the VR application to carry out reflections and professional discussions safely with their peers and/or tutors.

The other environmental factor that played an important part in student's perception of the situation is the physical materials they were working with while conversing with the patients. As these were student's initial placement experiences, familiarising and operating the equipment, technologies and/or materials for technical tasks were high on their training priority. Even a task like reading the patient's report, which experienced therapeutic radiographer can skillfully perform routinely, added complexity to the situation. In some cases, students were anxious about having to do this while talking to the patient when often the conversation is emotionally charged. While the physical environment and materials can be seen as outside the scope of social and cultural factors, clearly it is an integral part of radiographer's work and should be considered with the other factors. Therefore, having an interactive technical task for the participant to do during the VR experience is also incorporated in our design.

5   Scenario Design and Development

Based on the time scale, resource and skillset of the project team, after consultation with the therapeutic radiography programme team, this pilot project decided to develop three scenarios for the VR application: an introduction scenario that introduce participant to the VR environment, interaction and equipment, a scenario with an upsetting patient and a scenario with an angry patient. Each scenario combined at least two of five difficult conversation characteristics illustrated in Image 1 and incorporated the social, cultural and physical factors identified from interview data. Vignettes were developed to detail the setting, personals involved, the interaction (including scripts of verbal and non-verbal communication) and how each scenario starts, develops and ends. This was the starting point of how the amalgamation of different incidents from interviews was created. Table 2 is the vignette of scenario two - the angry patient which is presented here as an illustrative example.

5.1   Scenario 1: Introduction and Training

The student (*i.e.* the user) is placed in a consultancy room with a senior radiographer and asked to read the patients treatment sheet (Image 2). This scenario is for student to:

- test the hardware and settings of the VR
- familiarise themselves with wearing the VR headset and using the controllers
- experience the virtual environment
- carry out virtual interaction with a senior radiographer
- perform a technical skill of reading patient's treatment sheet

This scenario is for student and researcher to ensure the student does not experience any discomfort during the simulation. The student can interact with a clipboard containing the patient information. This has been modelled on real treatment sheets so students can familiarise themselves with it. This had the aim of grounding them quickly into the simulation.

Image 2. Introduction and training

5.2   Scenario 2: Upset Patient

Scenario 2 covers an upset patient vignette. Here, the user is placed in the same consultancy room as in the training scenario. This scenario involves the student radiographer (*i.e.* the user), an approximately 60 year old female patient with breast cancer and a senior radiographer. The decision on the profile of the patient was made based on students found talking to patients who remind them about their own elderly relatives while remaining professional can be really challenging. This is an important social situation from interview findings.

The treatment sheet reveals to the student the cancer has metastasised to the patient's bones and it was a hip that was being treated. The patient had her CT scan and this was the first appointment to discuss her scan and treatment. While the senior radiographer was talking about the scan result, the patient suddenly looked at the student anxiously and start asking '*Will I be cured?*' '*How long will it take for me to die?*' then starting to cry. As mentioned earlier, these statements were designed during scripting using the interview data and they are generic enough to be repeatable.

The virtual agent will focus on the user during this portion of the scenario, with their head amination tracking the users HMD position. Similarly, during the emotive exchange, the senior member of staff will also look at the user. This was a design decision based on interview findings as the participants highlighted that the scrutiny of senior members of staff was often just as disconcerting as the pressure of the situation they found themselves in. Furthermore, this is an example of a social dimension informed by the framework; specifically, the social environment and social situation where the individuals involved, and their role impact the emotion of an encounter (Image 3).

Image 3. Upset patient

5.3   Scenario 3: Angry Patient

The final scenario for the proof-of-concept prototype was based on an angry patient vignette (Table 2). The premise is a patient who has been waiting for his appointment for over 20 min with a full bladder (a requirement for the particular scan).

This scenario involves the student radiographer and two male patients (Mr. Allen and Mr. Bridge) with prostate cancer. The student is at the waiting area to collect one patient (Mr. Allen) for his appointment, while the other patient (Mr. Bridge) barged in front of the student and started asking '*When will I being seen?*' '*I have been here for ages, before this gentlemen, how is it not my turn?*' Suddenly, Mr Bridge starts to swear loudly and moving close to the student. This scenario design used interview data of some students finding dealing with male patients can be challenging in particular when they raise their voices. The design of the character's look and body language is intended to make students feel unconformable or even a little intimidated. Unlike the first two scenarios, there is no senior staff present but another patient. Again, it addresses the findings of the social environment, the communication and the social and cultural context of these challenging conversations (Image 4).

These three scenarios provided the initial proof-of-concept prototype for a VR application that has been co-designed with key stakeholders. This was necessary in order to ensure the authenticity of the scenarios such that the experiences they are based on can be provided to new students in a safe and controlled environment. However, prior to testing with new students to assess if these experiences have the desired impact, it was necessary to close the co-creation loop and ascertain if these simulations are close approximations of the vignettes defined by participants.

Image 4. Angry patient

Table 2. Scenario two, the angry patient, vignette

Scenario and setting	Script	Notes for developer
A patient in pain and anger at the waiting area: This scenario involves the student radiographer and two over male patients (Mr. Allen and Mr. Bridge) with prostate cancer. The student is at the waiting area to collect one patient (Mr. Allen) for his appointment, while the other patient (Mr. Bridge) barged in front of the student and started asking 'When will I being seen?' 'I have been here for ages, before this gentleman, how is it not my turn?' It transpires the patient have been waiting with a full bladder as required for his treatment for over 20 min as the previous treatments were over run. **Note, this is not a reception but a waiting area specifically for these patients – more privacy than a reception area that would be found in a hospital.** **Student position and body:** Participant will be standing as will the patients. No full body avatar is necessary for the participant character, but should have visible hands	In waiting area, two males sitting across the area, the one sitting nearer to the consultation room across the corridor is Mr Bridge, and the one sitting across at the far end of the waiting area is Mr Allen (who the student radiographer is coming to collect). Mr Bridge is the "Angry Patient" who will ultimately cause a scene. Student radiographer standing close by Mr Bridge, holding Mr Allen's report, the student calls for the patient. Student radiographer "…" Mr Allen standing up, walking towards the student radiographer. Mr Bridge suddenly standing up, very close to the student, (Tall – 6 foot +, big built), looking contempt "I've been here for ages!" Student radiographer "…" Mr Bridge: "I can't wait! I am bursting" Student radiographer "…" Mr Allen standing next to the two, watches the proceedings, waiting patiently but focussed on the drama. Mr Bridge: "Are you not hearing me! I was here first." He snaps… "It's MY turn NOW!" "I am bursting" "I can't bloody wait!" Student radiographer "…" Mr Bridge: "For fucks sake". Then he storms off	As per scenario 1, these scripted elements are not concerned with high fidelity implementations on the interactions but serve to set the scene. The student will need to call for Mr Alan in this first part which starts the simulation. A UI widget should make this clear to the participant as per training scenario. When the response has been made, **the simulation progresses through a button press triggered by the director.** The goal here is to set-up what ultimately will be an intimidating simulation. A UI widget should make this clear to the participant as per training scenario. When the response has been made, **the simulation progresses through a button press triggered by the director**

6   Initial User Feedback

After the VR application was developed, the six students and a member of staff from the programme were invited back to review it. Two students and the staff were able to take part in this review evaluation. Participants received the narrated video captions of the VR scenarios a week before the interview. The narration explained the differences between the video captions and the VR experience, walked the participants through the VR application, and highlighted key features to participants. The participants were asked to note down their thoughts on their initial impression about the VR scenarios and application and to what extent do they feel they represent the students' real world experiences. The group interview used these questions as prompts to co-evaluate the application and its potential pedagogical use. It took place on Microsoft Teams and it was recorded and transcribed for analysis.

The two students and one staff member though the scenarios are very realistic. They captured the environment well. Details such as the filled in treatment sheet which users can interact with provided users with the sense of realism, as well as a purpose for student to experience what they do on a radiotherapy ward.

Users also commented on the authenticity of the interactions which reflect real world experiences of student radiographers. The user can learn from the conversations taking place in the scenarios between the senior radiographer and the patients, modelled on real conversations, thus developing their professional knowledge and skills. Most importantly, the challenging conversational interactions between the patients and the user felt very emotionally charged and put the student radiographers on the spot to react quickly and professionally. The changing tones of their voices, their eye contact, their physical appearances and their language (verbal and non-verbal) all play an important part in making the interaction feel realistic. For instance, the users commented on how the angry patient's body language, his stare and the use of swear words brought the situation to life and made them feel they were challenged by this person.

The students commented on the appearances of the characters in the scenarios are similar to what they encountered during their placements. The upset patient in particular reminded students someone they saw or cared for during placements. Students also commented on the presence of others (the senior radiographer in scenario 1 and 2 and another patient in scenario 3) as an important factor of these experiences. They believed these characters would impact on how users react in these situations. Again, they felt the inclusion of these characters was authentic.

7   Conclusion

Based on user feedback, for future development of VR applications for and with social interactions, the nuanced details of the social and physical environment, the characters (their age, gender, ethnicity and appearances), their expressions, languages (verbal and non-verbal) and their movements are key to ensure the realism of the scenarios. While creators and developers of the application can pay close attention to such details during the design and development process, this project shows working closely with users to capture the details from their experiences and including their input into the design of these details is essential to ensure the authentic nuances are faithfully captured and included in the application.

Ultimately, in order for a socially oriented VR scenario to be believable to participants, there is a need to extend the concepts of place, plausibility and presence based on the social and cultural considerations outlined in this paper. What this study demonstrated is that social environment (where the interaction takes place and who are there) and social and cultural situation (the identities of the persons involved) are part of the concept of place. Communication and social and cultural context (the relationship between persons involved) are the essence of a conversational interaction that must be considered to create a plausible scenario. These social and cultural considerations should be rooted in the authentic experiences of those informing the design process in order for future participants to effectively "walk a mile" in another's shoes.

The next step for this project is to run the VR application with first year students to see whether it provides them with believable experiences which can influence their views and behaviours of patient care. After this initial pilot case study with the healthcare programme, future studies ought to test and refine the social and cultural dimensions outlined in this paper to see their impact on the sense of presence in VR. Furthermore, the relationship of these factors to other key design considerations requires exploration through research. For example, how these factors work with other aspects such as graphical fidelity, animation quality, voice acting *etc.* to provide a meaningful and impact experience.

References

Bailenson, J.: Experience on demand: What virtual reality is, how it works, and what it can do. W.W. Norton & Company (2018)

British Education Research Association: Ethical Guidelines for Educational Research. 4th edition. BERA (2018)

Berger, P.L., Luckmann, T.: The social construction of reality: A treatise in the sociology of knowledge. Anchor Books, New York (1966)

Blumer, H.: Symbolic interactionism: Perspective and method. Prentice-Hall, Englewood Cliffs, NJ (1969)

Bracq, M.-S., Michinov, E., Jannin, P.: Virtual reality simulation in non-technical skills training for healthcare professionals. Simulation in Healthcare: J. Soc. Simula. Healthcare **14**(3), 188–194 (2019)

Chayutsahakij, P., Poggenpohl, S.: User-centered Innovation: The Interplay Between User-research and Design Innovation (2002)

Dietrich, T., et al.: Co-creating Virtual Reality Interventions for Alcohol Prevention: Living Lab vs. Co-design. Frontiers in Public Health, p. 9 (2021)

Gibbs, G.: Learning by Doing: A guide to teaching and learning methods. Further Education Unit. Oxford Brookes University, Oxford (1988)

Gillies, M., Pan, X.: Virtual reality for social skills training. In: Proceedings of the Virtual and Augmented Reality to Enhance Learning and Teaching in Higher Education Conference 2018, 8, pp. 83–92 (Sep 2018)

Goffman, E.: The presentation of self in everyday life. Anchor Books, New York (1959)

Gunn, T.M., Jones, L.V., Bridge, P., Rowntree, P., Nissen, L.: The use of virtual reality simulation to improve technical skill in the undergraduate medical imaging student. Interact. Learn. Environ. **26**(4), 1–8 (2018)

Hannans, J.: Virtual reality: a strategy to improve patient-centered care. American Nurse. Online: https://www.myamericannurse.com/virtual-reality-a-strategy-to-improve-patient-centered-care/ (2019)

Haugh, M.: Conversational interaction, In: Allan, K., Jaszczolt, K.M. (eds.) The Cambridge Handbook of Pragmatics. CUP, Cambridge (2012)

Health Education England: Reducing Pre-registration Attrition and Improving Retention Report. Available at: https://improvement.nhs.uk/resources/reducing-pre-registration-attrition-and-improving-retention-repair/ (2018)

Hochschild, A.: Emotion work, feeling rules, and social structure. Am. J. Sociol. **85**, 551–575 (1979)

Langdridge, D.: Phenomenological Psychology: Theory, Research and Method. Pearson Education, London (2007)

Larkin, M., Smith, J.A., Flowers, P.: Interpretative Phenomenological Analysis: theory, method and research. SAGE, London (2009)

Leducq, M.: A key transition for student nurses: The first placement experience. Nurse Educ. Today **32**, 779–781 (2019)

O'Connor, M., Stowe, J., Potocnik, J., Giannotti, N., Murphy, S., Rainford, L.: 3D virtual reality simulation in radiography education: the students' experience. Radiography **27**(1), 208–214 (2021)

Pollard, N., Lincoln, M., Nisbet, G., Penman, M.: Patient perceptions of communication with diagnostic radiographers. Radiography **25**, 33–338 (2019)

Rajeswaran, P., Hung, N.T., Kesavadas, T., Vozenilek, J., Kumar, P.: Airwayvr: learning endotracheal intubation in virtual reality. In: 2018 IEEE Conference on Virtual Reality and 3D User Interfaces (VR), pp. 669–670 (2018)

Riva, G., Mantovani, G.: The need for a socio-cultural perspective in the implementation of virtual environments. Virtual Reality **5**, 32–38 (2000)

Samosorn, A.B., Gilbert, G.E., Bauman, E.B., Khine, J., McGonigle, D.: Teaching airway insertion skills to nursing faculty and students using virtual reality: a pilot study. Clin. Simul. Nurs. **39**, 18–26 (2020)

Slater, M.: 2009. Place illusion and plausibility can lead to realistic behaviour in immersive virtual environments. Philoso. Transa. Royal Soc. B: Biologi. Sci. **364**(1535), 3549–3557 (2009)

Slater, M., Sanchez-Vives, M.V.: Enhancing our lives with immersive virtual reality. Frontiers in Robotics and AI, 3 (2016). https://doi.org/10.3389/frobt.2016.00074

Society and College of Radiographers: Improving retention of the radiotherapy workforce - the role of practice placements in student attrition from pre-registration programmes in England: Full report. Available at: https://www.sor.org/learning/document-library/improving-retention-radiotherapy-workforce-role-practice-placements-student-attrition-pre (2013)

Designing Virtual Environments for Smoking Cessation: A Preliminary Investigation

Elham Ebrahimi$^{(\boxtimes)}$, Dana Hajj, Matthew Jarrett, Anastasiya Ferrell, Linda Haddad, and Marc Chelala

University of North Carolina Wilmington, Wilmington, NC 28403, USA
{ebrahimie,hajjd,mdj7111,ferrella,haddadl,mgc6040}@uncw.edu

Abstract. The recent pandemic of COVID-19 is placing smokers at a high risk of death as a result of the combination of smoking and COVID-19. This signals a need to address this problem among dual users (cigarette and vape users) and provides them with successful tools to quit tobacco. This pilot project aims to test a novel tool, a Virtual Reality and Motivational Interviewing combined approach that will assist dual users to quit tobacco products. The investigators wanted to pilot test the equipment and scenario for user-friendliness and interface. For the first phase of the pilot, we developed four Virtual Reality scenarios that contain different triggers for smoking, such as noise, stress, and cigarettes. We used Oculus Quest 2 for the hardware because the equipment does not require towers or connections to computers, operates utilizing WIFI, and is mobile. To develop the Software, we used the "Unity3D" game engine. A total of 21 participants tested the equipment and scenarios. The participants ranged between ages 18–71 with various gaming and virtual reality experience. The majority of the participants felt immersed in the Virtual reality environment. Some participants had some challenges with the equipment and the Software and provided valuable feedback to enhance the scenarios. The virtual reality environment promises to be a novel tool to assist tobacco users, mainly dual users, in quitting tobacco.

Keywords: Smoking cessation · Virtual reality · Usability testing

1 Introduction

In the United States (U.S.) and globally, COVID 19 has killed thousands of individuals of all ages via severe cardio-pulmonary complications. However, tobacco use remains the number one cause of mortality and morbidity among adults in the United States and globally. It is a major contributor to pre-existing cardio-pulmonary conditions that increase COVID-19 risk. E-cigarettes and vape products are advertised as healthier alternatives to traditional cigarettes and as an option for quitting smoking, leading many smokers to dual use of traditional and

Supported by University of North Carolina Wilmington.

© The Author(s), under exclusive license to Springer Nature Switzerland AG 2022
J. Y. C. Chen and G. Fragomeni (Eds.): HCII 2022, LNCS 13317, pp. 410–422, 2022.
https://doi.org/10.1007/978-3-031-05939-1_28

electronic cigarettes. Recent literature on e-cigarettes has shown that dual use is associated with adverse health outcomes, including cardiovascular and pulmonary diseases. To date, no treatment protocol exists for dual users other than the traditional evidence-based treatment, including nicotine replacement and behavioral modification. The recent pandemic of COVID-19 is placing smokers at a high risk of death as a result of the combination of smoking and COVID-19. This signals a need to address this problem among dual users and provide them with successful tools to quit tobacco. This pilot project aims to test a novel tool that will assist dual users to quit tobacco products. We will use a combined Virtual Reality and Motivational Interviewing approach to assist dual users in quitting tobacco products. MI is a goal-oriented client entered counseling style that enhances intrinsic motivation to assist individuals in changing their behaviors. MI has been shown to be effective in helping patients abstain from negative behaviors by helping a person resolve their ambivalence to change [37].

Virtual reality (VR) technology is rapidly evolving to support prolonged exposure (PE) therapy, proven treatment in different areas such as anxiety disorders, and has been tested in limited research to be successful in the area of smoking cessation [10,11,35]. Virtual Reality (VR) is becoming a powerful tool in the areas of addictive behaviors and pain control as well [26,28]. In the area of smoking cessation, VR has successfully assisted smokers in quitting, but the research was limited to traditional cigarette use. This pilot study will test the feasibility, acceptability, and preliminary effectiveness of Virtual Reality using Cue Exposure Therapy (CET) to assist dual users to quit dual tobacco use.

This study aims to pilot test the equipment and the software for user-friendliness and evaluate the interface design. For the first phase of the pilot, we developed four Virtual Reality scenarios with increasing smoking triggers: Museum, Beach, Living Room, and Bar environments. Each scene/environment included different triggers for smoking, such as noise, stress, alcohol, ashtrays, and traditional and electronic cigarettes. We used Oculus Quest 2 for the hardware because of its ease of use and ease of portability (the equipment does not require towers or connections to computers, operates utilizing WIFI, and is mobile). To develop the software, we used the "Unity3D" game engine.

1.1 Paper Organization

The remainder of this paper is organized as follows. Section 2 discusses related research in integrating virtual technologies for smoking cessation, Sect. 3 details the design of our investigations, including hardware used and software implementation and design, Sect. 4 covers experiment's procedure and participants, and administered surveys. Sections 5 and 6 discuss our results, general observations of the investigation, lessons learned for the next stages of development, and conclusion.

2   Background

In the United States, tobacco use accounts for more than 480 thousand deaths every year, or one in five deaths [20]. Smoking is associated with increased risk of different types of cancer, respiratory disorders such as chronic obstructive pulmonary disease, cardiovascular disease, complications of pregnancy as well as low birth weight [5]. Despite all the efforts to reduce cigarette use, other forms of tobacco use, such as electronic cigarettes (e-cigarettes), have been increasing, especially among youths and young adults. The popularity of e-cigarettes increased over the past few years, changing the current e-cigarette use rate from 5.1% (2014) to 7.6% (2018) for young adults [7]. Results from the baseline data from the Health eHeart Study showed that among 39,747 participants, 573 (1.4%) reported e-cigarette only use, 1,693 (4.3%) reported cigarette only use, and 514 (1.3%) dual-use [43]. Results from the 2016 Behavioral Risk Factor Surveillance System (BRFSS) showed that the prevalence of current e-cigarette use was highest among individuals aged 18 to 24 years at 9.2% [30]. Results from the National Health Interview Survey (NHIS), 2017, reported a prevalence of 2.8% for e-cigarettes [43]. An epidemic level (27.1%) of e-cigarette use among high school students is likely to increase this rate in the next few years [15]. Although e-cigarettes and other vaping products are not officially promoted by the Food and Drug Administration (FDA), they are commonly advertised by tobacco companies and used by smokers as cessation materials [42]. Smokers, who try to quit, start vaping, but for many, these cessation attempts lead to dual use of vaping and smoking [33]. Furthermore, some studies have found that vaping can be a gateway to using conventional cigarettes, especially among young individuals [6,31].

Although e-cigarettes are relatively novel tobacco products and the evidence about this product is still emerging, vaping is not safe. Nicotine in e-cigarettes is addictive, and vaping can lead to smoking in non-smokers [8,17]. E-cigarette use can lead to cell mutations (that can potentially lead to cancer), increased inflammatory response, delayed recovery from respiratory infections, cardiovascular diseases, and an increased risk for e-cigarette, or vaping, product use-associated lung injury (EVALI) [2,8]. Recent literature reveals that dual use is associated with adverse health outcomes, including cardiovascular and pulmonary diseases [36]. Smoking in all its forms has been associated with negative outcomes, and severe adverse effects of COVID 19 [40]. Dual users are also at risk of severe outcomes of COVID-19. The current smoking and vaping cessation practice utilize a behavioral approach coupled with pharmacologic therapy. Since the pandemic, cessation attempts among tobacco users increased [23,41]. This signals an urgent need to develop successful cessation tools such as virtual reality games that can be sustainable outside of a clinical or study setting - especially during social distancing - and help save lives.

To date, no treatment protocol exists for dual users other than the behavioral approach coupled with pharmacologic therapy. One of the emerging alternatives to current practice is virtual reality (VR). Over the past 20 years, VR has been predominately used for psychological disorders, and health assessment [25]. Although research on VR and smoking cessation is limited, recent studies show that VR coupled with Motivational Interviewing (MI) can be effective for smokers of traditional cigarettes [1,3,44,45]. This success can be indicative of the potential for dual users, as well. VR's promising results in behavior modification are also replicated in interventions for addictive behaviors, weight loss, pain management, and substance abuse [12,16,18,22,24,34]. Results of these studies demonstrate VR's applicability to participants of a wide age range: youth to older adults. For interventionists, VR has shown improvement in counseling proficiency and assessing clients' psychological and emotional status. For clients, VR is effective in psychomotor training, dissociation from reality, and more vivid delivery of information [38,39]. Interventions involving VR showed improvement over the control group and were comparable to a traditional practice (e.g., Cognitive Behavioral Therapy). García-Rodríguez et al. [13] showed that VR environments with smoking-related cues increase subjects' craving for smoking, whereas the neutral environment did not affect the user's craving for cigarettes, which validates the use of VR for simulating scenarios capable of eliciting craving. The success of an intervention can be amplified in the absence, or at least reduction, of the attrition rate.

Young adults' attraction to vaping products can be explained in part by their affinity for technological innovation [21,29]. The same affinity for technology can benefit clients' participation and adherence to the VR intervention. With recent improvements in VR technology, this intervention can be replicated for home – during and after the study – on materials that are affordable and are likely to be available in one's possessions: a smartphone (<\$200) or a VR headset (~\$300). Therefore, clients can reuse the intervention long after the study ends to prevent relapse and promote maintenance.

3   Experiment Design

This investigation is designed as a virtual reality simulation. The subject wears a virtual reality head-mounted display to observe and interact with the virtual environment and virtual agents/avatars. For this investigation, we designed and tested four scenarios that took place in different virtual locations (a museum, a household, a beach, and a bar) inspired by the work of García-Rodríguez et al. [13]. Each scenario had a few smoking-related cues such as increased noise and stress, alcohol, ashtrays, and traditional and electronic cigarettes. Stimuli within these scenarios were designed to trigger a desire to smoke with varying degrees of intensity. Scenes use a mixture of dialogue, location, and visual and audio cues to increase or decrease a subject's desire to smoke a cigarette. The scenes are designed to be immersive, with realistic settings and virtual avatars for the subject to see and interact with. Additionally, sounds and music are implemented to increase the subject's immersion, and occasionally, as a tool to either strengthen or weaken the subject's habitual desire to smoke.

3.1   Virtual Reality Scenarios

Museum Environment: This virtual environment consists of two rooms for the subject to explore. One contains soft classical music in the background, neutral lighting in the room, and neutral images and exhibits modeled after the Cameron Museum in Wilmington, NC. The second room contains slightly more stressful images, such as people with masks that may trigger the participant's desire to smoke in order to relieve their stress (Fig. 1). The museum scene has the least number of smoking-related cues. The rooms are not congested and only have two-three individuals/avatars. These two rooms are designed to help the participants acclimate to the simulation - how to navigate and interact with the objects and avatars. Additionally, we will be using the museum scenes as a baseline for our future studies to measure participants' desire to smoke after their first exposure to VR.

Fig. 1. Examples of different views within the museum scene. The top two images display the neutral museum scene, and the bottom image shows slightly more stressful arts in the second museum scene.

Household Environment: In the household scenario (Fig. 2), the subject is shown a stressful family situation - that of a couple worried about their jobs, COVID, and their health and future. In this scenario, one of the virtual avatars (the male on the left side of the Fig. 2), is a 45-year-old dad of 2 teenage children and a wife who is a nurse who could not handle working in the hospital, afraid of the virus and bringing it home to her children. He works as an engineer at a big company, and his job is very stressful. He began smoking at age 15 and has smoked for 25 years. None of his children smoke. He has made 3 quit attempts in the past, both within the last five years and using NRT (21 mg patch) and bupropion (150 mg/day). His most recent quit attempt was about six months ago, after he had pneumonia, at which time he was diagnosed with early emphysema. He reports success managing cravings with the medications until the relapse at three months due to a series of stressful events and COVID-19 changing the way we view the world. He describes his life as very stressful, with a long commute, juggling work, family, school, and financial struggles. John is on his fourth attempt to quit, and he is in his second-month smoke-free.

Fig. 2. Examples of different views within the living room scene. *Left:* Inside the Living Room Environment. *Right:* Outside Environment

At the beginning of the scenario, John is watching the news with his wife and listening to the increasing number of COVID patients. There are not enough kits to test for the virus. They are both stressing over the situation and their kids. The couple starts conversing with the participants in this virtual living room. Items that might trigger a smoke craving can be found throughout the house, such as alcohol at the living room minibar, a scented candle jar with a lighter, and an ashtray on the table. They both occasionally like to drink and ask the participant to drink with them. The participant is instructed to interact with the virtual avatars to proceed in the simulation. Later in the simulation, the participant is asked to walk outside with John to talk to a neighbor. During the living room scenario, the participant is asked twice if they would like to smoke. The participant is asked by the wife to vape first. Then the participant is asked by the neighbor to smoke when they are outside. The participant is discouraged from doing so by John throughout the scenario.

Beach Environment: The beach provides two paths the subject can pursue at their leisure and are not mutually exclusive. One path involves partaking in beach sports activities (such as volleyball), while the other involves joining a group of people drinking and smoking. If the user participates in a sports activity, other virtual avatars will join the participant. After a few minutes of playing, the participant is asked to join other friends around the bonfire. If the participant joins the smokers, they are offered cigarettes twice, making use of peer pressure to tempt the participant.

In this scenario, some people are dancing to music, while others are gathered around the fire. There is a grilling station, where people prepare greasy food such as burgers and hotdogs, which are another trigger for smoking. One virtual avatar gets drunk enough to start causing trouble and bothering others. The participant is not offered a cigarette or tempted if they avoid this group or choose to partake in the sports activities fully (Fig. 3).

Fig. 3. Examples of different views within the beach scene. The top left image shows some of the sports activities. The top right image displays the bonfire and the virtual avatars drinking and smoking. The bottom image shows the entire scene.

Bar Environment: The bar scene does not directly offer the subject a chance to smoke a cigarette. The subject is shown a bar, where multiple patrons are shown drinking or smoking. This scenario includes all of the smoke-triggering items. These items can be found and interacted with in the bar by the participants. Background music and conversation provide the sense of immersion and being in an actual bar. The virtual avatars converse with the participant if they get close to them. In this scene, the environment is designed to tempt the participants to smoke (Fig. 4).

All these scenarios are timed, and once the subject has reached a scene's time limit, they are moved to a neutral transitory scene before being shown the next simulation. Additionally, neutral beginning and ending scenes introduce the subject to the simulations and indicate their completion. While every scenario will progress without subject input, the subject has the option to interact with their environment in certain ways and converse with the virtual avatars. Often this includes choosing whether to respond to the stimuli by accepting or rejecting a cigarette. The experiment proctor records the subject's choice.

Fig. 4. Examples of different view within the bar scene.

4   Procedure

All participants in this investigation started the experiment by viewing the museum scene first that was designed to help the participants acclimate to the experience. All participants completed a standard informed consent form and demographic survey upon arrival. Participants were instructed on how to select different scenes in VR and how to use the controller and interact with the environment. Each participant experienced all four scenarios and completed a scripted interview with the experimenters after the VR experience. This simulation was created using the Unity 3D game engine and deployed as an Oculus Quest 2 head-mounted display app. Figure 5 shows a participant exploring and interacting with objects in the virtual Beach scene.

4.1   Participants

For the initial phase of this pilot study, we tested the equipment on a total of 21 participants who are non-tobacco users. The rationale of using non-tobacco users was that we did not want to taint the equipment testing results with the intervention itself. The sample included ten females and 11 males. The age of the participants ranged between 18–72 years old. Eight of the participants had no prior exposure to virtual reality or any form of gaming. The participants provided valuable feedback and recommendations about the equipment and the VR scenarios discussed in the results section.

Fig. 5. This image show a participant interacting with balls in the Beach scene.

5   Results

The participants provided valuable feedback and recommendations about the equipment and the VR scenarios. The investigators in this study utilized the recommendations to enhance and provide improvements on the scenarios as well as the equipment use. The results were as follows.

During this investigation, participants felt immersed in the virtual environment. The avatars' details were reported clear and realistic, such as facial creases, hair, and eyes. The different scenarios' images, interactions, and tasks were self-explanatory and detailed, and participants needed little to no extra instruction to complete the scenarios. The participants were able to feel immersed in the environment by interacting and teleporting within the VR setting. The participants could pick up different items such as beer bottles, a beach ball, a surfboard, and food items and converse with virtual avatars. These interactions helped participants be grounded in the virtual environment and created a strong place-, self-, and social-presence. Most of the participants efficiently and quickly understood and used the device and handheld joysticks/controllers.

However, a few participants had some difficulty using the handheld joystick/controllers. Another issue some participants had was that they kept using the inside of the joystick buttons for teleporting and rotating the scenes instead of the trigger finger button, which will be disabled in the next version of the software. Other issues with the software include having to exit the app and log back into the app to move from one scene to another. These issues have been remedied and tested with a small group of pilot users. The menu bar sometimes appeared behind the participants instead of showing in front. That could have been due to the orientation of the participants, which might require more instructions on the screen to point them in the right direction. During the different scenarios, the cigarette in the hand of the avatar was going through his index finger, which made the scene seem unrealistic and broke the immersion. This issue has been addressed in the latest version of the software. In the Living Room scene, the participants can go outside before being prompted by the avatar. The lack of proper instruction left the participants in a state of "not sure what to do next." Thus, the team redesigned the Living Room scene and added more constraints to user interaction. In the new layout, the participant will not be able to move outside before prompted.

The participants provided valuable recommendations for the investigators to enhance technology and user-friendliness. Most of the participants suggested the development of a tutorial on the use of the equipment, mainly the handheld device. Another suggestion was a guide on "what to expect" with a Start menu as participants go through the scenarios. At least seven participants stated, "I felt I did not know what to do next" at some point in the simulation. The investigators created a guide in the Start menu to assist the participants to better navigation through the different scenes. The investigators also limited the timeframe for each scenario with guided prompts on the next step, so participants do not spend more time within the scenario unnecessarily.

Overall, most of the participants felt immersed in the scenarios. They reported that the experience felt very real and that the capacity "to move around as if I am really there was just amazing." We have taken feedback from the testers/participants and have incorporated the changes and made several adjustments to enhance the quality of the scenarios for the next round of testing. The next phase of the pilot is to start the Motivational Interview/ Virtual Reality combination approach with the target population of smokers who want to quit.

6   Discussion and Conclusion

The present pilot study provided a valuable first step towards developing a tobacco cessation intervention through virtual reality (VR). It incorporated previously established smoking cues, and social situations that increase heart rate and skin conductance levels [28]. Unlike most of the VR studies that only focus on pleasant environments and group use (e.g., bar scene), the present tobacco cessation intervention also incorporates stressful situations, such as walking through a tobacco-free museum with stressful arts and exhibits [28]. As with many other behavioral studies that incorporate VR, ours also faced user and technology challenges [14]. To address these issues, we plan to continue periodic assessment of subjects' experience and inclusion of brief pre-intervention training to enhance participants' engagement. Meanwhile, the technology challenges are continuously assessed in our weekly meetings and taken care of by our VR experts.

Despite the hurdles, our study subjects found this immersive experience enjoyable overall, echoing participants of prior VR studies [4,32]. Unlike some of the other VR studies, participants in our intervention did not experience cybersickness [4]. This might have been avoided due to our limited participants' presence at each scene and allowing for breaks between the scenes. In addition, most of our subjects were younger adults, and there were not sufficient older adults in our sample to definitively refute that older subjects are more likely to experience cybersickness, as it is indicated in prior research [27]. In addition, unlike previously published studies, our team noticed similar levels of engagement between different genders of participants [9]. Further investigation may be needed to quantify these observations.

Similar to prior studies, our current VR interventions were favored among even first-time, and novice users [19]. Consequently, uptake of this method for motivational interviewing continues to be of prime interest in the tobacco control field and our team. Federal grants for tobacco control have been looking for innovative methods for tobacco cessation, and this study holds a promise towards that offer. The development process involved in the first phase of this project can be helpful for studies that plan to create similar interventions. This phase has also served as a learning process for our team as we listened to our study subjects' recommendations. As we apply participants' suggestions, we anticipate having a solid foundation for the next step, incorporating motivational interviewing scenarios.

Acknowledgement. The project is supported by an internal grant by University of North Carolina Wilmington. The authors would like to acknowledge the following students and faculty who have also contributed to the development and testing of this project: Hannah Vuncannon, Kole Bostic, and Lisa Cook.

References

1. Borrelli, B., O'Connor, G.T.: E-cigarettes to assist with smoking cessation (2019)
2. Cao, D.J., et al.: Review of health consequences of electronic cigarettes and the outbreak of electronic cigarette, or vaping, product use-associated lung injury. J. Med. Toxicol. **16**(3), 295–310 (2020)
3. Caponnetto, P., Maglia, M., Lombardo, D., Demma, S., Polosa, R.: The role of virtual reality intervention on young adult smokers' motivation to quit smoking: a feasibility and pilot study. J. Addict. Dis. **37**(3–4), 217–226 (2018)
4. Carroll, J., Hopper, L., Farrelly, A.M., Lombard-Vance, R., Bamidis, P.D., Konstantinidis, E.I.: A scoping review of augmented/virtual reality health and well-being interventions for older adults: redefining immersive virtual reality. Front. Virtual Real. **2**, 61 (2021)
5. Centers for Disease Control and Prevention: Health effects of cigarette smoking. National Center for Chronic Disease Prevention and Health Promotion (2021)
6. Chien, Y.N., et al.: Electronic cigarette use and smoking initiation in Taiwan: evidence from the first prospective study in Asia. Int. J. Environ. Res. Public Health **16**(7), 1145 (2019)
7. Dai, H., Leventhal, A.M.: Prevalence of e-cigarette use among adults in the United States, 2014–2018. JAMA **322**(18), 1824–1827 (2019)
8. Eaton, D.L., Kwan, L.Y., Stratton, K.: Harm reduction. In: Public Health Consequences of E-cigarettes. National Academies Press (US) (2018)
9. Felnhofer, A., Kothgassner, O.D., Hauk, N., Beutl, L., Hlavacs, H., Kryspin-Exner, I.: Physical and social presence in collaborative virtual environments: exploring age and gender differences with respect to empathy. Comput. Hum. Behav. **31**, 272–279 (2014)
10. Ferrer, M.F.G., Gutiérrez Maldonado, J.: The use of virtual reality in the treatment of eating disorders. Studies in Health Technology and Informatics, vol. 181, p. 17–21 (2012)

11. Ferrer-García, M., García-Rodríguez, O., Gutiérrez-Maldonado, J., Pericot-Valverde, I., Secades-Villa, R.: Efficacy of virtual reality in triggering the craving to smoke: its relation to level of presence and nicotine dependence. Stud. Health Technol. Inform **154**, 123–127 (2010)

12. Gance-Cleveland, B., et al.: Technology to support motivational interviewing. J. Pediatr. Nurs. **35**, 120–128 (2017)

13. García-Rodríguez, O., Pericot-Valverde, I., Gutiérrez-Maldonado, J., Ferrer-García, M., Secades-Villa, R.: Validation of smoking-related virtual environments for cue exposure therapy. Addict. Behav. **37**(6), 703–708 (2012)

14. Garrett, B., et al.: Virtual reality clinical research: promises and challenges. JMIR Serious Games **6**(4), e10839 (2018)

15. Gentzke, A.S., et al.: Vital signs: tobacco product use among middle and high school students-United States, 2011–2018. Morb. Mortal. Wkly Rep. **68**(6), 157 (2019)

16. Ghiţă, A., Gutiérrez-Maldonado, J.: Applications of virtual reality in individuals with alcohol misuse: a systematic review. Addict. Behav. **81**, 1–11 (2018)

17. Glasser, A., Abudayyeh, H., Cantrell, J., Niaura, R.: Patterns of e-cigarette use among youth and young adults: review of the impact of e-cigarettes on cigarette smoking. Nicotine Tob. Res. **21**(10), 1320–1330 (2019)

18. Greene, D.D., Heeter, C.: Personal stories within virtual environments: a cancer patient information software case study. CyberPsychol. Behav. **1**(3), 201–211 (1998)

19. Huygelier, H., Schraepen, B., Van Ee, R., Vanden Abeele, V., Gillebert, C.R.: Acceptance of immersive head-mounted virtual reality in older adults. Sci. Rep. **9**(1), 1–12 (2019)

20. Jamal, A.: Tobacco use among middle and high school students-United States, 2011–2016. MMWR Morb. Mortal. Wkly Rep. **66**(23), 597 (2017)

21. Keamy-Minor, E., McQuoid, J., Ling, P.M.: Young adult perceptions of JUUL and other pod electronic cigarette devices in California: a qualitative study. BMJ Open **9**(4), e026306 (2019)

22. Kehle-Forbes, S.M., et al.: A randomized controlled trial evaluating integrated versus phased application of evidence-based psychotherapies for military veterans with comorbid PTSD and substance use disorders. Drug Alcohol Depend. **205**, 107647 (2019)

23. Klemperer, E.M., West, J.C., Peasley-Miklus, C., Villanti, A.C.: Change in tobacco and electronic cigarette use and motivation to quit in response to COVID-19. Nicotine Tob. Res. **22**(9), 1662–1663 (2020)

24. Kubica, A.: Self-reported questionnaires for a comprehensive assessment of patients after acute coronary syndrome. Med. Res. J. **4**(2), 106–109 (2019)

25. Luxton, D.D., Pruitt, L.D., Osenbach, J.E.: Best practices for remote psychological assessment via telehealth technologies. Prof. Psychol. Res. Pract. **45**(1), 27 (2014)

26. Maples-Keller, J.L., Bunnell, B.E., Kim, S.J., Rothbaum, B.O.: The use of virtual reality technology in the treatment of anxiety and other psychiatric disorders. Harv. Rev. Psychiatry **25**(3), 103 (2017)

27. Matas, N.A., Nettelbeck, T., Burns, N.R.: Dropout during a driving simulator study: a survival analysis. J. Safety Res. **55**, 159–169 (2015)

28. Mazza, M., Kammler-Sücker, K., Leménager, T., Kiefer, F., Lenz, B.: Virtual reality: a powerful technology to provide novel insight into treatment mechanisms of addiction. Transl. Psychiatry **11**(1), 1–11 (2021)

29. McDonald, E.A., Ling, P.M.: One of several 'toys' for smoking: young adult experiences with electronic cigarettes in New York city. Tob. Control **24**(6), 588–593 (2015)
30. Mirbolouk, M., et al.: Prevalence and distribution of e-cigarette use among us adults: behavioral risk factor surveillance system, 2016. Ann. Intern. Med. **169**(7), 429–438 (2018)
31. Morgenstern, M., Nies, A., Goecke, M., Hanewinkel, R.: E-cigarettes and the use of conventional cigarettes: a cohort study in 10th grade students in Germany. Dtsch. Arztebl. Int. **115**(14), 243 (2018)
32. Mouatt, B., Smith, A.E., Mellow, M.L., Parfitt, G., Smith, R.T., Stanton, T.R.: The use of virtual reality to influence motivation, affect, enjoyment, and engagement during exercise: a scoping review. Front. Virtual Real. **1**, 39 (2020)
33. Olfson, M., Wall, M.M., Liu, S.M., Sultan, R.S., Blanco, C.: E-cigarette use among young adults in the US. Am. J. Prev. Med. **56**(5), 655–663 (2019)
34. Park, W., et al.: Comparable long-term efficacy, as assessed by patient-reported outcomes, safety and pharmacokinetics, of CT-P13 and reference infliximab in patients with ankylosing spondylitis: 54-week results from the randomized, parallel-group planetas study. Arthritis Res. Ther. **18**(1), 1–11 (2016)
35. Pericot-Valverde, I., García-Rodríguez, O., Ferrer-García, M., Secades-Villa, R., Gutiérrez-Maldonado, J.: Virtual reality for smoking cessation: a case report. Annu. Rev. Cyberther. Telemed. **10**, 292–296 (2012)
36. Qasim, H., Karim, Z.A., Rivera, J.O., Khasawneh, F.T., Alshbool, F.Z.: Impact of electronic cigarettes on the cardiovascular system. J. Am. Heart Assoc. **6**(9), e006353 (2017)
37. Rollnick, S., Miller, W.R.: What is motivational interviewing? Behav. Cogn. Psychother. **23**(4), 325–334 (1995)
38. Saidel-Goley, I.N., Albiero, E.E., Flannery, K.A.: An evaluation of nonclinical dissociation utilizing a virtual environment shows enhanced working memory and attention. Cyberpsychol. Behav. Soc. Netw. **15**(2), 112–116 (2012)
39. Tieri, G., Morone, G., Paolucci, S., Iosa, M.: Virtual reality in cognitive and motor rehabilitation: facts, fiction and fallacies. Expert Rev. Med. Devices **15**(2), 107–117 (2018)
40. Vardavas, C.I., Nikitara, K.: COVID-19 and smoking: a systematic review of the evidence. Tob. Induc. Dis. **18**, 20 (2020)
41. Volkow, N.D.: Collision of the COVID-19 and addiction epidemics (2020)
42. Wallace, A.M., Foronjy, R.E.: Electronic cigarettes: not evidence-based cessation. Transl. Lung Cancer Res. **8**(Suppl 1), S7 (2019)
43. Wang, T.W., et al.: Tobacco product use among adults-United States, 2017. Morb. Mortal. Wkly Rep. **67**(44), 1225 (2018)
44. Woodruff, S.I., Conway, T.L., Edwards, C.C., Elliott, S.P., Crittenden, J.: Evaluation of an internet virtual world chat room for adolescent smoking cessation. Addict. Behav. **32**(9), 1769–1786 (2007)
45. Woodruff, S.I., Edwards, C.C., Conway, T.L., Elliott, S.P.: Pilot test of an internet virtual world chat room for rural teen smokers. J. Adolesc. Health **29**(4), 239–243 (2001)

Social-Emotional Competence for the Greater Good: Exploring the Use of Serious Game, Virtual Reality and Artificial Intelligence to Elicit Prosocial Behaviors and Strengthen Cognitive Abilities of Youth, Adolescents and Educators – A Systematic Review

Patrick Guilbaud[1](✉), Carrie Sanders[2], Michael J. Hirsch[3], and T. Christa Guilbaud[4]

[1] Winthrop University, Rock Hill, SC, USA
guilbaudp@winthrop.edu
[2] Radford University, Radford, VA, USA
csanders27@radford.edu
[3] ISEA TEK LLC, Maitland, FL, USA
mhirsch@iseatek.com
[4] UNC at Charlotte, Charlotte, NC, USA
tguilbau@uncc.edu

Abstract. This study sought to understand the learning benefits, impacts, and opportunities involved with the use of serious games (SG), extended reality (XR), Artificial Intelligence (AI) and other advanced technologies in the classroom and other educational settings. We conducted a systematic literature review focusing on the potential benefits of utilizing those technologies to build and strengthen prosocial behaviors and cognitive abilities of students and other learners. Results of the study reveal that those modern technologies can be used to improve students' academic experiences and interactions with their peers while in school. In our rapidly changing global knowledge society, it is clear there is a need to develop and build the capacity of students to work effectively and cooperatively with all people including those from diverse socio-cultural and educational backgrounds. This paper highlights ways in which advanced technologies can support ongoing efforts to enhance students' knowledge while building more inclusive and emotionally supportive learning environments in school settings.

Keywords: Serious game · Gamification · Esports · Extended reality · Mental-Agility · Artificial intelligence · Social-emotional competence

1 Introduction

Currently, there exists significant debates in many facets of society regarding ways in which to best help children and young adults develop greater awareness, understanding and knowledge of their feelings and those of other individuals [1, 2]. This challenge is

© The Author(s), under exclusive license to Springer Nature Switzerland AG 2022
J. Y. C. Chen and G. Fragomeni (Eds.): HCII 2022, LNCS 13317, pp. 423–442, 2022.
https://doi.org/10.1007/978-3-031-05939-1_29

particularly acute for educators and professionals who work closely with students during the early and developmental stages of their lives [3, 4]. At the same time our society continues to be more diverse – ethnically, culturally, and linguistically. Consequently, today's students are increasingly taking part in learning activities, both formal and informal, that involve collaboration, teamwork, and cooperation with peers and classmates who have different abilities, ancestry, and backgrounds [5].

The good news is that there is great awareness of the need for students to develop the ability to negotiate situations that are uncomfortable or threaten their sense of belonging in their classes or bonding with their peer groups [6]. This is because such knowledge allows students to relate better with their classmates and peers irrespective of their backgrounds, abilities, and personalities. Thus, within a given school system, students have a variety of resources and support systems (e.g., teachers, counselors, and principals) to help them navigate a host of issues and challenges they face on any given day. These challenges may be related to academic, emotional, social, behavioral, and physical safety concerns [7–9].

School counselors, in particular, are called to respond to the socio-emotional needs and concerns of students. As a result, these counselors strive to proactively explore new approaches and strategies to help students under their care cope with adverse or unfamiliar situations [10–12]. Some of the approaches being explored include the use of advanced technologies in teaching and learning. Thus, there is strong interest in exploring how extended reality (XR), serious game or gamification (SG), and artificial intelligence (AI) can be leveraged to present learning experiences that offer diverse, inclusive, and pluralistic perspectives [13–15]. In the same vein, esports, or electronic sports combined with competitive gaming, is being used in schools and universities and even offered as an academic subject at many institutions of higher learning [16–18]. As a result, researchers and practitioners in the field of human development, learning sciences, cognitive psychology, and computer engineering have been examining how these new technologies can be utilized to help students, educators, and professionals develop and sustain the ability to be more compassionate, kind, and connected to their classmates, peers and colleagues [19, 20].

This paper examines how SG, XR, and AI technologies are being investigated and used for the purpose of strengthening the cognitive skills and prosocial behaviors of students – most specifically young children and adolescents. We conducted a systematic literature review (SLR) to: (a) Identify key cognitive and emotional benefits to introducing SG, XR and AI technology in both K-12 and post-secondary school settings; (b) Explore how novel implementations, approaches, and practices of advanced technology such as SG, XR, and AI can be used in K-12 and post-secondary schools to facilitate the development of prosocial behaviors e.g. empathy and compassion of learners, particularly those from underserved and underprepared backgrounds; and (c) Determine whether learning environments in K-12 that incorporate SG, XR, AI and other advanced technology foster affective and cognitive outcomes. In the remaining sections of this paper, we present an overview on current and recent uses of advanced technology to help improve mental agility and non-cognitive skills of K-12 and post-secondary learners. We also highlight modern theory, pedagogy, and instructional practices focused on the affective and behavioral aspects of teaching and how to support learners, most specifically youth and adolescents. We then delineate the results, findings, and conclusion from peer-reviewed articles that explore ways in which SG, XR, AI, and similar advanced technologies might be used to support the development of academic skills and prosocial behaviors.

2 Background

2.1 Prosocial Behaviors and Cognitive Abilities of Youth and Other Learners

Young children experience the world very differently than adults. This because they have yet to develop contextual awareness, appreciation, or sensitivity to properly recognize and understand emotions in themselves and others [21]. According to Yeager [22], "Adolescence is a period of tremendous learning exploration, and opportunity. Yet it's also a time when behavioral and health problems can emerge or worsen with negative consequences that last long into adulthood" (p. 74). Therefore, it is important to introduce lessons and experiences that highlight prosocial behaviors and practices to help guide our youths as they grow and develop into young adults. In today's very diverse, multi-lingual, and multicultural American society, there is a greater need to not only understand the perspectives of others but to also develop a sense of compassion and empathy in pluralistic interactions and dialogues [23–25]. Questions have been raised on whether human emotions like empathy can actually be taught to children and youth. This is a major challenge because empathy, or the ability to recognize and share other people's emotions, involves a host of internal and external factors that affect and influence a child's development, identity and sense of belonging [26–28].

To succeed in school, particularly in classes that require advanced reading and mathematical skills, students must demonstrate capability and competency in the three main learning domains, which are cognitive, affective and psychomotor [29, 30]. As noted by Bloom [31] cognitive ability is the learning domain of focus for skills such as problem solving, decision making and abstract thinking. In contrast, affective and psychomotor learning domains relate to human emotions (empathy) and physical ability (e.g., ballet dancing), respectively. Further, research shows that the three main learning domains need to be at the center of educational goals in student-centered instructional activities and classroom practices see [29, 32, 33, 34].

According to Ackerman & Heggestad [35] cognitive ability, which is also referred to as intelligence, allows individuals to make generalizations and abstractions. By so doing, cognitive ability makes it possible for learners to apply knowledge they acquire to new situations and unfamiliar contexts [29–31]. Consequently, a focus on helping students strengthen their cognitive abilities will stand to facilitate the growth, build-up, and/or bolstering of their mental agility, problem solving, and critical thinking skills.

Recently there has been keen interest in understanding how affective factors or behaviors such as emotions, feelings, and dispositions (e.g., motivation, self-efficacy and responsible-decision making) influence students' cognitive ability and consequently their academic achievement [36–38]. As presented by Eccles & Wigfield [39], achievement-related behaviors can be fully explained by an individual's expectancies about future success. Further, Steinmayr & Spinath [40] offered that affective factors or prosocial behaviors such as empathy, teamwork, and cooperation play a significant role in facilitating greater scholastic achievement. Newer and student-centered pedagogical approaches and strategies such as social emotional learning (SEL) and culturally responsive teaching, are thus placing a strong emphasis on helping students, most specifically youth, build connections and relationships and therefore cooperative disposition with their classmates and peers [41–43]. These newer approaches can help with the achievement of cognitive, prosocial, and socio-emotional learning outcomes.

From a teaching and pedagogical standpoint, socio-emotional learning has emerged as a potential guiding theory that can be used to facilitate the implementation of educational activities, programs and processes that meet the needs, interests, and orientations of a diverse student body [22, 29–31]. The ecological systems theory by Bronfenbrenner [44, 45] provides a comprehensive framework and an expansive lens to examine contextual factors that influence the development of a child or adolescent [36, 37]. As depicted in Fig. 1, these factors include the main social dynamics that impact a child, such as family, school, peers, neighborhood, and general culture, within which they are situated and immersed.

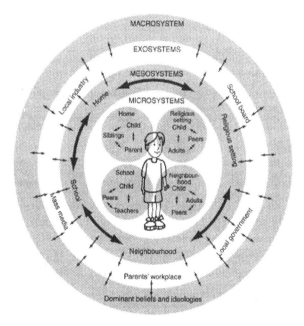

Fig. 1. Layers of influence on a child [25]

Recently, much attention has been placed on how advanced technologies can be used to improve learning and knowledge development [14, 15]. For example, research studies and field practices have shown that popular SG, XR, and AI tools and applications such as Microsoft's Hololens, Meta's Oculus Quest, Pokémon Go, Amazon Alexa, Apple Siri, Omni-Immersion Vision, Microsoft Cortana, and Google Cardboard offer multi-faceted and interactive learning experiences to students. Through combining the real and virtual worlds, these tools allow the presentation of learning situations that take into account cognitive differences as well as pluralistic points of view. Therefore they foster opportunities for critical reflection as well as appreciation for diverse perspectives to students and other learners.

2.2   Socio-emotional Learning and Social Cohesion in Schools

Social Emotional Learning (SEL) is defined by The Collaborative for Social and Emotional Learning [46] as "the process through which all young people and adults acquire and apply the knowledge, skills, and attitudes to develop healthy identities, manage emotions and achieve personal and collective goals, feel and show empathy for others, establish and maintain supportive relationships, and make responsible and caring decisions" [46]. In order for young people to be prepared to successfully enter the world of work or begin other post-secondary plans, they need to possess core SEL skills, which include cognitive and emotional regulations as well as social and interpersonal skills. Research indicates we can promote students' social emotional competence, which not only increases their SEL skills, but also academic achievement [47]. The intrapersonal skill of a growth mindset and the interpersonal skills of empathy and motivation contribute to positive outcomes. Underlying beliefs people have about learning and intelligence contribute to their mindset, which can be conceptualized as a fixed mindset or a growth mindset [48]. As Bronfenbrenner [44] offers, factors in and out of school work together to impact students' level of educational attainment. Neuroscience research on brain plasticity has shown that with practice, neural networks grow new connections and can be strengthened. When a growth mindset exists, the individual behaves differently and there is an increase in motivation and achievement. Those with a growth mindset view an obstacle as a chance to use creativity to innovate in order to solve problems; conversely, a fixed mindset associates the obstacle with a reason to give up on a challenging task [48]. Mindset standards also provide a framework to address SEL skills and promote social emotional competence. Corcan and Tormey [50] suggest that social emotional competence (SEC) can be defined as the ability and disposition to use emotional capabilities in a situated context.

2.3   Social Emotional Competence and Advanced Technology

The ASCA [49] standards provide a framework to address SEL skills and promote social emotional competence (SEC) on the part of students and other learners. Corcan and Tormey [50] noted that SEC can be defined as the ability and disposition to use emotional capabilities in a situated context. More specific definition of SEC highlights that it involves an individual's (i) ability to express, receive and manage emotions; (ii) effective formation and maintenance of relationships; (iii) general interactions with others; (iv) ability to make good life choices; and (v) dealing with internal and external challenges that occur over their life [51, 52]. There have been numerous studies showing the potential for making use of XR environments to improve feelings of empathy and compassion, which are two of the core tenets of SEL [53]. While it is not possible to completely capture non-objective experiences of others, XR does offer the opportunity to provide new and empathy-enhancing qualities from users of XR [54,

55]. At present, there are many outlets for people to learn new topics and skills (e.g., Khan Academy for mathematics and YouTube for playing the guitar [56, 57]. Academics, educators, and technology companies are beginning to explore how advanced technologies, like SGs, XR, and AI can help with strengthening SEC.

Many people and specifically youth enjoy video games and use them as entertainment. In contrast, SGs are video games that are specifically designed to be more than pure entertainment [58]. For instance, the military uses video games or SGs to train soldiers in realistic combat environments [59, 60]. This is because SGs can be single-player as well as multi-player. Multi-player SGs, like those used in esports, favor team-building, quick decision making, collaboration, and cooperation in facing challenges and issues. They do this by explicitly fostering an environment where working together results in more efficiently solving the problems encountered and/or achieving the goals of the game. Over the past few years and in light of the COVID-19 pandemic, many companies have moved to virtual working. Some have made use of multi-player SGs, and esports in particular, to keep the spirit of team-work and work-place camaraderie in place (58). Moreover, esports are being used in academic institutions to build prosocial skills and reduce isolation of the increasing number of students, who for one reason or another, do not feel that they fit in to the school environment academically or socially [16, 18]. Extended Reality (XR) is a general term to encompass the umbrella of all immersive technologies. These include Augmented Reality (AR) and Virtual Reality (VR). AR refers to a three-dimensional user interface that provides the user with an interactive environment [61]. VR is the use of computer technology and software to create a simulated environment [62]. While AR simulates objects within the users' real environment, VR envelops the user within a fully artificial environment.

AI is the field of science and engineering concerned with making smart machines [63]. AI leverages computers and machines to mimic the problem-solving and decision-making capabilities of human beings. Machine Learning (ML) is the subset of AI focused on analyzing data and employing algorithms to learn intelligent processes [64]. ML can be further be partitioned into the sub-category of deep learning, which does not need a pre-defined model (e.g., linear regression) by which to learn, but is able to learn based on the data itself (as opposed to a human assuming a model upon which to learn or fit the data). Deep learning is usually employed using an approach with multiple layers within which patterns, structure, or insight about the data is discovered.

As the realism and first-person viewpoint of the XR improves, the user is better able to 'imagine' themselves as part of this world, experiencing events and promoting greater empathy to others in this same situation. While other mediums (e.g., watching videos or reading articles) also promote these qualities, they do so to a much lesser impact than does an immersive first-person XR environment [55]. One of the biggest benefits of XR technology and educational learning is the direct interaction, and hence immediate feedback, with the environment, promoting active learning. It is noted that empathy can be purposefully increased and decreased, much like a muscle which one can work to increase its strength [65]. With the right exercises, through use of XR and other mediums, over time feelings of empathy and SEL skills can be strengthened across many different individuals and groups.

3   Methodology

3.1   Context

The Social Emotional Competence for the Greater Good research was undertaken to understand how educators and researchers (within and outside academia) are using or testing SG, XR, AI and other advanced technologies for the purpose of helping learners, and most specifically K-12 students, develop prosocial behaviors and strengthen their cognitive abilities. The research also sought to gauge the benefits and challenges of implementing those technologies to achieve greater social cohesion in schools.

3.2   Research Approach

According to Dewey & Drahota [66] a SLR, identifies, selects, and then critically appraises articles and studies in order to answer clearly formulated research questions. Moreover, the SLR needs to follow a clearly defined protocol or plan where the criteria is clearly stated before the review is conducted [67–69]. For this paper, we conducted a SLR on SG, XR, AI, and advanced technologies that are currently being used in academic institutions to improve students' socio-emotional skills (prosocial behaviors) and cognitive abilities of students and other learners.

3.3   Research Questions

Our study is guided by the three following questions:

1. What are the cognitive and socio-emotional benefits to introducing SG, XR and AI technology in both K-12 and post-secondary school settings?
2. Can advanced technology such as SG, XR, and AI be used in K-12 and post-secondary schools to facilitate the development of prosocial behaviors E.G. empathy and compassion?
3. How can advanced technologies best be used by teachers and educators to foster positive affective and cognitive learning outcomes in K-12 settings?

3.4   Data Collection

The literature search was conducted between November 2021 and January 2022, from two popular databases, JSTOR and ERIC through EBSCO host. We started the initial literature search through JSTOR within the 2015–2021 timeframe. The search keywords used were "Technology or Virtual and Serious Game, Emotion, Empathy, and Cognitive Abilities", which yielded 8,298 results as shown in Fig. 2.

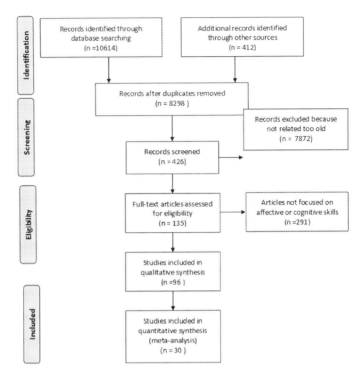

Fig. 2. Adapted from: Moher D, Liberati A, Tetzlaff J, Altman DG, The PRISMA Group [70].

The search result helped us gain a preliminary understanding of the scope and type of research conducted in the field that are related to our research questions. We then excluded 7,872 articles from the data collected. These involved studies and research that were deemed too old or did not have a strong focus on teaching and learning. Grey literature (e.g., reports, theses, projects, conference papers, fact sheets, and similar documents that are not available through traditional bibliographic sources such as databases or indexes) were also excluded during this step. The team then removed 291 articles that were unrelated to issues such as affective, cognitive, or emotional behaviors. Studies in the workplace that did not involve pre-service, certified teacher training, and continuing professional development were also excluded. The remaining 135 articles were closely examined by 2 reviewers to gauge whether their titles, abstracts, and research questions were in congruence with the focus of this study. The reviewing team and the other authors of this paper skimmed through the full-text articles to further evaluate the quality and eligibility of the studies. This led to the selection of 96 journal articles to be relevant for further analysis. Discrepancies between the reviewers' findings were discussed and resolved. Lastly, 30 articles were included for detailed review and analysis. These were put in a spreadsheet along with the full reference, author, year, title, and abstract for detailed examination and evaluation.

4 Results and Discussion

4.1 Dataset Categorization

The first learning category developed for the data is Learning Domain, which are Cognitive Ability, Prosocial Behaviors in Schools, and SEC. Knowledge, Skills, and Abilities (KSAs) was the second category that was determined for the study. Nine KSA's were identified from the data collected. Tables 1 and 2, respectively, present the Learning Domains, KSA, and technology cluster for each article.

Table 1. Domain and KSA categories.

Learning domain	KSA	Description
Cognitive Ability and Processes (CAP)	MEA	Mental agility
	PSO	Problem-solving
	CRT	Critical thinking
Prosocial Behaviors and Attitudes (PBA)	EMP	Empathy
	TWS	Team-working skills
	COO	Cooperation
Socio-Emotional Competence (SEC)	MOT	Motivation
	SEF	Self-efficacy
	RDM	Responsible-decision-making

Table 2. Technology Cluster (TC).

Cluster	Definition
SG	Serious game/gamification
XR	Extended reality
AI	Artificial intelligence
OT	Other: learning management systems, artificial intelligence, mobile, social media, videos, robotics etc

Table 3 presents the complete list of articles reviewed for the study along with the learning domains, KSA, technical cluster (TC), and date of publication for each of them. As is shown in the Table 3, articles that met the selection criteria for the study range from 2014 to 2021. Further, the overwhelming majority of the selected articles (88%) were published between 2018 and 2021.

As shown in Fig. 3, the articles selected for the SLR used a wide variety of technologies and placed focus on a range of learning domains. SG was used the most in studies that focus on cognitive abilities (CAP). On the other hand XR appeared in a lot of studies dealing with prosocial behaviors (PBA) and that involved KSA such as empathy, team-working skills, and cooperation, which were defined in the study. Further there has been an increasing level of research on the topic of the study e.g., use of advanced technology to strengthen cognitive ability and prosocial behaviors from 2014 to 2021 with 2020 being the peak year of article production activity.

Table 3. Selected articles.

| Ref | Year | Learning focus | | |
		DOM	KSA	TC
[71]	2022	PBA	EMP	SG
[72]	2018	PBA	EMP	XR
[73]	2017	PBA	EMP	XR
[74]	2020	PBA	EMP	XR
[19]	2021	CAP	PSO	SG
[75]	2018	CAP	PSO	SG
[76]	2016	CAP	PSO	SG
[77]	2016	CAP	MEA	SG
[78]	2018	CAP	CRT	SG
[79]	2016	CAP	CRT	SG
[80]	2021	PBA	EMP	SG
[81]	2016	CAP	MEA	SG
[82]	2019	CAP	MEA	SG
[83]	2021	SEC	RDM	XR
[84]	2020	SEC	RDM	XR
[85]	2018	PBA	EMP	XR
[86]	2018	SEC	RDM	XR
[87]	2020	CAP	PSO	AI
[88]	2018	PBA	EMP	XR
[89]	2018	CAP	MEA	XR
[90]	2019	CAP	MEA	OT
[91]	2020	SEC	RDM	AI
[92]	2018	SEC	RDM	SG
[93]	2014	CAP	MEA	SG
[94]	2017	CAP	PSO	SG
[95]	2021	SEC	PBA	SG
[96]	2017	PBA	COO	OT
[97]	2015	CAP	PSA	OT
[98]	2019	PBA	EMP	XR
[99]	2016	PBA	TWS	OT

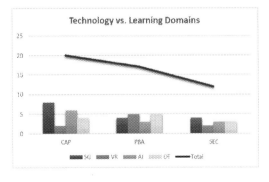

Fig. 3. Technology and LD of Focus.

5   Question 1: What Are the Cognitive and Socio-emotional Benefits to Introducing SG and XR Technology in Both K-12 and Post-secondary School Settings?

As shown in Fig. 4, the KSA of most interest to researchers are empathy (EMP), mental ability (MEA), responsible decision making (RDM), and cooperation (COO).

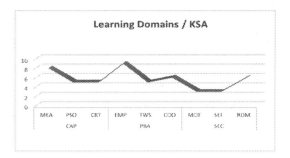

Fig. 4. LD/KSA areas.

The research studies that were reviewed suggest that advanced and experiential technologies and applications such XR, SG, and AI combined with learner-centered pedagogies have positive effects on lower-level cognitive processes [71–73]. However, there is weak evidence that SG and similar technologies strengthen higher-order cognition such as executive functioning [40, 74]. Nonetheless, there are some clear benefits associated with introducing the use of advanced technologies, and most specifically SG and XR, in the classroom or other learning contexts. In a study that examines the ethical aspects of using VR to enhance empathy Rueda and Francisco [19] offer that digital embodiment through the use of an avatar in conjunction with gaming and other experientially-oriented VR applications can foster empathic abilities. According to the authors, such an activity supports empathic response by "allowing people not only to metaphorically walk a mile in another person's virtual shoes, but also to literally embody the virtual representation of the specific social target in whom they wish to increase empathy," [p. 8]. In a similar vein, Garcia, Ferguson, and Wang [40] note there is some evidence that SG or gaming supports positive learning experiences and prosocial behaviors. It is offered however, that outcomes such as empathy and cognitive processes may not be long lasting as there have been few longitudinal studies examining the duration or transferability of skills learned in a VR or gaming activity. Schutte and Stilinovic [75] also found the use of VR in classroom-related activities supports greater student engagement and connection to the learning materials or scenarios due to the "sense of presence" that the technology offers. Based on their findings, the researchers recommended that future training studies could "utilize virtual reality to create even more effective empathy training…tailored to specific purposes [such as] for those entering professions in which empathy is desirable" [p. 711]. As Southgate et al. [76] highlighted, studies that involve Immersive VR (IVR), which allows a user to perform normal human activities and interactions with objects in the digital environment (e.g., avatars, goods, office equipment, and buildings), also offer important learning opportunities. Their project involved the use of Facebook/Meta's Oculus Rifts head-mounted display (HMD) system located in designated VR rooms attached to classrooms involved in an 8th grade science study. The IVR set-up used in the study is often preferred because the Oculus HMD offers sophisticated tracking systems, allowing a very intense feeling of presence in the digital environment. Notably, the authors found that IVR can be used to help strengthen learners' collaboration, critical thinking, and ethical perspectives. Further, the mixed-gender science study showed some degree of differences regarding how the students relate to the attractiveness of IVR as a learning tool [p. 28]. Nonetheless, the researchers concluded that targeted and facilitated use of IVR in the classroom will tend to promote student's attention, engagement, motivation to learn, and self-regulated behavior, irrespective of their prior knowledge and skills with the technology.

6   Question 2: Can Advanced Technology Such as SG, XR, and AI Be Used in K-12 and Post-secondary Schools to Facilitate the Development of Prosocial Behaviors e.g. Empathy and Compassion?

Van Loon et al. [65] perform experiments to determine the degree of effectiveness of immersive virtual environments to helping an individual take the perspective of, and empathize with, someone else. The results indicated IVR influence empathy at the group level. Allcoat et al. [77] sought to determine how VR learning influences performance, emotion, and engagement, compared with other learning mediums. Findings indicate that the emotional outlook improved the most for students using the VR technologies to learn the material, which has a direct impact on empathy and compassion for others. Flogie et al. [78] examined the impact and effectiveness of Information and Communication Technology (ICT) on engagement of youth and their interest in collaborating with peers and teachers, on the level of interpersonal relationships. The overall result of the study showed that both parents and teachers had the same view: the use of ICT in the classroom had a positive impact on the engagement and motivation of the students in school and learning.

Salas-Pilco [79] try to find out how AI and robotics impact multiple aspects of learning; specifically, from the physical, SEC, and intellectual perspectives. Results from the study showed that students showed significant improvement across the physical, SEC, and intellectual domains, as a result of interaction with AI and robotics. While this study was quite small, there was definite improvement among the three students with respect to the dimensions of empathy and compassion. Hafner et al. [80] performed a study on player's experience and persuasive SG. The authors made use of two immersive games, My Life as a Refugee (MLR) and PeaceMaker (PM). For the PM game, more than half of the players did not feel they played the game long enough to be immersed (hence, not persuaded either). The authors also noted t the influence of immersion on emotion and identification are areas of future research. Barrera et al. [82]

conducted a study to analyze the effectiveness of EmoTIC, a game-based SEC program designed for adolescents in a school context. EmoTIC is focused on developing SEC in adolescents. This program was designed as a space adventure, with the goal of the player rebuilding a spaceship in order to return to Earth. Experimental results showed that adolescents who participated in this study had more self-esteem, empathy toward others, and affect balance, with fewer emotional symptoms and behavioral problems as compared with those that did not use the EmoTIC program. Overall, the results showed that the adolescents interacting with EmoTIC had consistently higher positive change and lower percentages of negative change. The authors note that EmoTIC did not improve emotional intelligence. While there have been some studies done attempting to determine a relationship between advanced technologies and their impact on empathy and compassion, this area of research is still in its infancy.

7 Question 3: How Can Advanced Technologies Best be Used by Teachers and Educators to Foster Positive Affective and Cognitive Learning Outcomes in K-12 Settings?

Positive relationships between teachers and learners are central to successful human interaction and learning [84]. Teaching and learning grounded in an understanding of social and emotional skills is critical for the success of all learners, of all ages, in all environments [85, 86]. SEL skills can be taught and measured and can support the positive development of students from diverse family backgrounds and geographic contexts [13, 87]. SEL may be more important now than ever because it helps educators, families, and students manage stress, develop resilience, and maintain a sense of optimism during challenging times [46, 86]. Jones et al. [85] found statistically significant associations between social and emotional skills in kindergarten and key outcomes for young adults years later. Empathy, a SEL skill, has a strong moral effect by impacting learning and development [84]. It facilitates understanding and communication between people and combines both affective and cognitive understanding, which are continually interrelated (p. 265).

Stavroulia and Lanitis [88] indicate empathy is an "integral part of education and must be an integral part of the pedagogical process to assist with the social and emotional development of students" (p. 24). This involves the development of empathy skills for teachers, learners and other stakeholders in the educational process. The sudden move to remote learning due to the COVID-19 pandemic impacted students and educators throughout the world without warning. For example, preservice teachers in their senior year were torn from the P-12 classroom, where they were practicing the craft of teaching, to adapt and change their practices immediately. They were not trained to teach in a virtual environment; however, those possessing a growth mindset collaborated with their clinical educators and continued their work by planning, instructing and assessing their students remotely [89]. Although many transitions to remote teaching and learning that happened due to the pandemic utilized advanced technologies, there were many aspects of the design process that were not able to be implemented due to the unexpected nature of the crisis. Well-informed and ethical decisions need to be made at all levels of technological implementation and usage [84]. There are intentional and systematic ways to incorporate advanced technologies for teaching and learning. Opportunity exists to develop a design-based education paradigm that uses design thinking and design-based education to develop the cognitive skills of curiosity, innovation and critical thinking as well as social skills of empathy, facilitation and collaboration [90]. For example, Stavroulia et al. [88] support the five-phase process used in instructional design for the development of the VR system. These phases include an analysis of the training needs, designing a competency framework, designing the scenarios, developing the VR system, and implementing and evaluating the effectiveness of the VR system. SEL interventions show the largest effect size when the intervention is designed with a specific context or culture in mind [91]. J. Han et al. [92] conducted an exploratory study with 81 five and six year old children in a kindergarten setting in Korea.

Overall, results suggested significantly more positive perceptions in interest in dramatic play, interactive engagement, and empathy with media. The enhanced use of the multi-modal approaches of changing facial expressions and physical actions of the robot-mediation system designed and employed in this study where children become more emotionally attached to the media with which they were interacting [92]. Vossen and Valkenburg [93] conducted a longitudinal study of the relationship between social media use as it relates to empathy and sympathy. Stavroulia et al. [88] wanted to know if the use of VR promotes the cultivation of reflection and empathy skills. Results of the study indicated the VR experience can contribute to a higher level of change in beliefs and ideas regarding multiculturalism and bullying, change the way teachers attend to the needs of their students and react to disruptive behavior of students. Empathy was cultivated in both groups; however, there was a significant difference between those who used the VR system and those who were trained in the real classroom, related to the ability to put themselves in the position of someone who is racially and/or ethnically different from themselves. The technological evolution is reshaping teaching and learning by providing new and innovative strategies to be implemented in classroom environments including VR. Multisensory learning is powerful in raising achievement as it expands and satisfies the brain and senses [84]. VR environments can be useful in complex and difficult to master domains and VR has the potential to become an innovative and essential tool in teacher training. Technology can provide engaging, efficient ways to support content learning in all areas [71]. For example, digital technology increases children's empathy when its content and use are prosocial [94]. Advanced technologies provide opportunities for teachers to refine their practice within a XR environment rather than in the real classroom context. They encounter real-life situations and respond to them, reflect, and revise their approach in the virtual environment as a way to prepare for success in the real classroom. Digital technology that uses prosocial approaches can be enhanced by use of interactive coherent learning environments [94]. Developing reflection and empathy skills through a XR system that targets the cultivation of specific competencies for teachers as part of their professional development could benefit the teaching and learning taking place in K-12 [88]. Moreover, XR offers users the opportunity to view a scenario from multiple lenses, making their experience a unique learning opportunity. It should be mentioned, however, that IVR is not a replacement for video lessons or other types of instructional media. Benefits of IVR could be domain specific and might improve learning. However, extraneous sounds, animations and interactions not pertinent to learning the information could distract from learning [95].

8 Conclusion

With the increasing use of advanced and emerging technologies in schools, the opportunity exists to continue exploring how SG, XR, and AI can be leveraged to elicit prosocial behaviors and strengthen cognitive abilities of youth, adolescents and educators. As noted by Scholtes et al. [100] and Wimmer et al. [101] esports helps students make new friends, build community, and become more engaged in their schools. Consequently, the introduction and use of SG, XR, and AI in schools, particularly as part of esports-related initiatives offer strong opportunities to help students strengthen their social-emotional competence or positive prosocial behaviors. As the study shows, when use of advanced technologies are linked with solid pedagogy to help promote SEC and improve behavioral outcomes, there is a strong likelihood of enhancing KSAs for all students, irrespective of their academic, personal, or social backgrounds.

References

1. Brownell, C.A., Hazen, N.: Early peer interaction: a research agenda. Early Educ. Dev. **10**(3), 403–413 (1999)
2. Lewis, M., Michalson, L.: Children's Emotions and Moods: Developmental Theory and Measurement. Plenum Press, New York (1983)
3. Hyson, M.: The Emotional Development of Young Children: Building an Emotion-Centered Curriculum, 2nd edn. Teachers College Press, New York (2004)
4. Webster-Stratton, C.: How to Promote Children's Social and Emotional Competence. P. Chapman, London (1999)
5. Dewar, G.: Raising helpful kids: the perils of rewarding good behavior. Parent. Sci. (2014 Aug 20)
6. Pizarro, D.A., Salovey, P.: Being and becoming a good person: the role of emotional intelligence in moral development and behavior. In Aronson, J., Cordova, D. (eds.) Improving Academic Achievement: Impact of Psychological Factors on Education, pp. 247–266. Academic Press, San Diego, CA (2002)
7. Kremenitzer, J.P., Miller, R.: Are you a highly qualified emotionally intelligent early childhood educator? Young Child. **63**, 106–112 (2008)
8. Liew, J., Eisenberg, N., Losoya, S.H., Fabes, R.A., Guthrie, I.K., Murphy, B.C.: Children's physiological indices of empathy and their socioemotional adjustment: does caregivers' expressivity Matter?" J. Fam. Psychol. **17**(4), 584–597 (2003)
9. Catalano, R.F., Oesterle, S., Fleming, C.B., Hawkins, J.D.: The importance of bonding to school for healthy development: findings from the social development research group. J. Sch. Health **74**(7), 252–261 (2004)
10. Constantine, M.G.: Theoretical orientation, empathy, and multicultural counseling competence in school counselor trainees. Prof. Sch. Couns. **4**(5), 342–348 (2001)

11. Gunawan, I., Wibowo, M.E., Purwanto, E., Sunawan, S.: Group counseling of values clarification to increase middle school students' empathy. Psicología educativa (Madrid) **25** (2), 169–174 (2019)

12. Osterman, K.F.: Students' need for belonging in the school community. Rev. Educ. Res. **70** (3), 323–367 (2000)

13. Guilbaud, P., Bubar, E., Langran, E.: STEM excellence and equity in K-12 settings: use of augmented reality-based educational experiences to promote academic achievement and learner success. In: HCI International 2021 – Posters, pp. 45–50 (2021)

14. Patterson, T., Han, I.: Learning to teach with virtual reality: lessons from one elementary teacher. TechTrends **63**(4), 463–469 (2019). https://doi.org/10.1007/s11528-019-00401-6

15. Dalgarno, B., Lee, M.J.W.: What are the learning affordances of 3-D virtual environments? Br. J. Educ. Technol. **41**(1), 10–32 (2010)

16. Hilvoorde, I.V., Pot, N.: Embodiment and fundamental motor skills in eSports. Sport Ethics Philos. **10**(1), 14–27 (2016)

17. Taylor, T.L.: Raising the Stakes e-Sports and the Professionalization of Computer Gaming. MIT Press, Cambridge, Mass (2012)

18. Martoncik, M.: e-Sports: playing just for fun or playing to satisfy life goals? Comput. Hum. Behav. **48**, 208–211 (2015)

19. Rueda, J., Lara, F.: Virtual reality and empathy enhancement: ethical aspects. Front. Robot. AI **7**, 506984 (2020)

20. Schaber, P., Wilcox, K., Whiteside, A., Marsh, L., Brooks, D.: Designing learning environments to foster affective learning: comparison of classroom to blended learning. Int. J. Scholarsh. Teach. Learn. **4**(2) (2010)

21. James, A.: Childhood Identities: Self and Social Relationships in the Experience of the Child. Edinburgh University Press, Edinburgh (1993)

22. Yeager, D.S.: Social and emotional learning programs for adolescents. Future Child. **27**(1), 73–94 (2017)

23. Koppelman, K.L., Goodhart, R.L.: Understanding Human Differences: Multicultural Education for a Diverse America. Pearson/Allyn and Bacon, Boston (2005)

24. Martin-Beltrán, M., Guzman, N.L., Kidwell, T.: Building a community of practice to counter the marginalisation of adolescent language learners. Lang. Cult. Curr. **32**(2), 142–156 (2019)

25. Cutter-Mackenzie, A.: Multicultural school gardens: creating engaging garden spaces in learning about language, culture, and environment. Can. J. Environ. Educ. **14**, 122–135 (2009)

26. Angel, B.Ø.: Foster children's sense of sibling belonging: the significance of biological and social ties. SAGE Open **4**(1) (2014)

27. Brownell, C.A., Hazen, N.: Early peer interaction: a research agenda. Early Educ. Dev. **10** (3), 403–413 (1999)

28. Penn, H.: Unequal Childhoods: Young Children's Lives in Poor Countries, 1st edn. Routledge, London (2005)

29. Ackerman, P.L., Kanfer, R., Beier, M.E.: Trait complex, cognitive ability, and domain knowledge predictors of Baccalaureate success, STEM persistence, and gender differences. J. Educ. Psychol. **105**(3), 911–927 (2013)

30. Del Missier, F., Mäntylä, T., de Bruin, W.B.: Decision-making competence, executive functioning, and general cognitive abilities. J. Behav. Dec. Mak. **25**(4), 331–351 (2012). https://doi.org/10.1002/bdm.731

31. Bloom, B.S.: Taxonomy of Educational Objectives; the Classification of Educational Goals, 1st edn. Longmans, Green, New York (1956)

32. Carroll, J.B.: Human Cognitive Abilities: A Survey of Factor-Analytic Studies. Cambridge University Press, Cambridge (1993)
33. Krathwohl, D.R.: A revision of bloom's taxonomy: an overview. Theory Pract. **41**(4), 212–218 (2002)
34. Bandura, A.: Self-efficacy: toward a unifying theory of behavioral change. Psychol. Rev. **84**(2), 191–215 (1977)
35. Ackerman, P.L., Heggestad, E.D.: Intelligence, personality, and interests: evidence for overlapping traits. Psychol. Bull. **121**(2), 219–245 (1997)
36. Hagenauer, G., Hascher, T.: Early adolescents' enjoyment experienced in learning situations at school and its relation to student achievement. J. Educ. Train. Stud. **2**, 20–30 (2014). https://doi.org/10.11114/jets.v2i2.254
37. Murayama, K., Pekrun, R., Lichtenfeld, S., vom Hofe, R.: Predicting long-term growth in students' mathematics achievement: the unique contributions of motivation and cognitive strategies. Child Dev. **84**(4), 1475–1490 (2013). https://doi.org/10.1111/cdev.12036
38. Jin, M., Ji, L., Peng, H.: The relationship between cognitive abilities and the decision-making process: the moderating role of self-relevance. Front. Psychol. **10**, 1892 (2019). https://doi.org/10.3389/fpsyg.2019.01892
39. Eccles, J.S., Wigfield, A.: In the mind of the actor: the structure of adolescents' achievement task values and expectancy-related beliefs. Person. Soc. Psychol. Bull. **21**(3) 215–225 (1995)
40. Garcia, S., Ferguson, C.J., Wang, C.K.J.: Prosocial video game content, empathy and cognitive ability in a large sample of youth. J. Youth Adolesc. **51**(1), 62–73 (2021). https://doi.org/10.1007/s10964-021-01512-1
41. Garner, P.W., Mahatmya, D., Brown, E.L., Vesely, C.K.: Promoting desirable outcomes among culturally and ethnically diverse children in social emotional learning programs: a multilevel heuristic model. Educ. Psychol. Rev. **26**(1), 165–189 (2014)
42. Yoder, N.: Teaching the Whole Child: Instructional Practices that Support Social and Emotional Learning in Three Teacher Evaluation Frameworks. American Institutes for Research Center on Great Teachers and Leaders, Washington, DC (2013)
43. Dobyns, K.: Building Empathy through Social-Emotional Learning in Advisory. Education: Student Scholarship & Creative Works (2019)
44. Bronfenbrenner, U.: The Ecology of Human Development Experiments by Nature and Design. Harvard University Press, Cambridge, MA (1996)
45. DeAnn Marsh, A.K., et al.: What is Bronfenbrenner's ecological systems theory? The Psychology Notes Headquarters, 27 Jul 2021
46. Collaborative for Academic Social and Emotional Learning.: Fundamentals of SEL. CASEL, 26 Oct 2021
47. Durlak, J.A., Weissberg, R.P., Dymnicki, A.B., Taylor, R.D., Schellinger, K.B: The impact of enhancing students' social and emotional learning: a meta-analysis of school-based universal interventions. Child Dev. **82**(1), 405–432 (2011)
48. Dweck, C.: Mindset: The New Psychology of Success, p. 2016. Ballantine Books, New York, NY (2016)
49. American School Counselor Association (ASCA).: ASCA Student Standards; Mindsets and Behaviors for Student Success. Alexandria, VA; Author (2021)
50. Corcoran, R.P., Tormey, R.: How emotionally intelligent are pre-service teachers? Teach. Teacher Educ. **28**(5), 750–759 (2012)
51. Halberstadt, A.G., Denham, S.A., Dunsmore, J.C.: Affective social competence. Soc. Dev. **10**(1), 79–119 (2001)
52. Calaguas, G.M., Dizon, C.S.: Development and initial validation of the social competency inventory for tertiary level faculty members. Int. J. Hum. Soc. Sci. **5**, 1043–1048 (2011)

53. Daccord, T.: Using Virtual Reality for Social and Emotional Learning, 5 Mar 2020
54. Nazerian, T.: How VR is Being Used to Teach SEL, 29 May 2018
55. Bailenson, J.: Experience on Demand: What Virtual Reality Is, How It Works, and What It Can Do. W.W. Norton & Co. (2018)
56. Murphy, R., Gallagher, L., Krumm, A., Mislevy, J., Haer, A.: Research on the Use of Khan Academy in Schools – Sri. Research on the Use of Khan Academy in Schools, Mar 2014
57. Juhasz, A.: Learning from YouTube. The MIT Press, Cambridge, MA (2011)
58. De Gloria, A., Bellotti, F., Berta, R.: Serious games for education and training. Int. J. Ser. Games **1**(1) (2014)
59. Shaban, H.: Playing War: How the Military Uses Video Games. The Atlantic, 10 Oct 2013
60. Romaniuk, S., Burgers, T.: How the US military is using 'violent, chaotic, beautiful' video games to train soldiers. The Conversation, 7 Mar 2017
61. Asai, K.: Visualization based on geographic information in augmented reality. In: Maad, S. (ed.) Augmented Reality, pp. 185–204 (2010)
62. Bardi, J.: What is Virtual Reality? (Definition and Examples), 21 Sep 2020
63. Russell, S., Norvig, P.: Artificial Intelligence: A Modern Approach, 2nd edn. Prentice Hall (2002)
64. Hua, W., Cuiqin, M., Lijuan, Z.: A brief review of machine learning and its application. In: Proc. of the International Conference on Information Engineering and Computer Science (2009)
65. van Loon, A., Bailenson, J., Zaki, J., Bostick, J., Willer, R.: Virtual reality perspective-taking increases cognitive empathy for specific others. PLoS ONE **18**(8) (2018)
66. Dewey, A., Drahota, A.: Introduction to systematic reviews: online learning module cochrane training (2016)
67. MacKenzie, H., et al.: Systematic reviews: what they are, why they are important, and how to get involved. J. Clin. Prevent. Cardiol. **1**(4), 193–202 (2012)
68. Page, M.J., et al.: Explanation and elaboration: updated guidance and exemplars for reporting systematic reviews. BMJ (Online) **372**(2021), n160–n160 (2020)
69. Harris, J.D., Quatman, C.E., Manring, M.M., Siston, R.A., Flanigan, D.C.: How to write a systematic review. Am. J. Sports Med. **42**(11), 2761–2768 (2014)
70. Moher, D., Liberati, A., Tetzlaff, J., Altman, D.G.: Reprint—preferred reporting items for systematic reviews and meta-analyses: the PRISMA statement. Phys. Ther. **89**(9), 873–880 (2009)
71. Bruno, C., Donaldson, C.: Combining the best aspects of humanity with the best of technology. Child. Educ. **94**(6), 25–32 (2018)
72. Habig, S.: Who can benefit from augmented reality in chemistry? Sex differences in solving stereochemistry problems using augmented reality. Br. J. Edu. Technol. **51**(3), 629–644 (2020)
73. Alizadeh, M.: Virtual Reality in the Language Classroom: Theory and Practice (2019)
74. Kirschner, P.A., Kreijns, K., Phielix, C., Fransen, J.: Awareness of cognitive and social behaviour in a CSCL environment. J. Comput. Assist. Learn. **31**(1), 59–77 (2015)
75. Schutte, N.S., Stilinović, E.J.: Facilitating empathy through virtual reality. Motiv. Emot. **41**(6), 708–712 (2017)
76. Southgate, E., et al.: Embedding immersive virtual reality in classrooms: ethical, organisational and educational lessons in bridging research and practice. Int. J. Child Comput. Interact. **19**, 19–29 (2019)
77. Allcoat, D., von Mühlenen, A.: Learning in virtual reality: effects on performance, emotion and engagement. Res. Learn. Technol. **26**, 1–13 (2018)
78. Flogie, A., Aberšek, B., Pesek, I.: The impact of innovative learning environments on social competences of youth. Res. Learn. Technol. **27** (2019)

79. Salas-Pilco, S.Z.: The impact of AI and robotics on physical, social-emotional and intellectual learning outcomes: an integrated analytical framework. Br. J. Edu. Technol. **51** (5), 1808–1825 (2020)

80. Hafner, M., Jansz, J.: The players' experience of immersion in persuasive games. Int. J. Serious Games **5**(4), 63–79 (2018)

81. Bogost, I.: Persuasive Games: The Expressive Power of Videogames. MIT Press (2007)

82. Barrera, U., Monaco, E., Postigo-Zegarra, S., Gil-Gomez, J., Montoya-Castilla, I.: EmoTIC: impact of a game-based social-emotional programme on adolescents. PloS ONE **16**(4) (2021)

83. Hirsch, M.: Situation alignment for distributed operations. In: IEEE Conference on Cognitive and Computational Aspects of Situation Management (CogSIMA), pp. 7–11 (2020)

84. Cooper, B.: Empathy, emotion, technology, and learning. In: Tettegah, S.Y., McCreery, M. P. (eds.) Emotions, Technology, and Learning, pp. 265–88. Elsevier Academic Press (2016)

85. Jones, D.E., Greenberg, M., Crowley, M.: Early social-emotional functioning and public health: the relationship between kindergarten social competence and future wellness. Am. J. Public Health **105**(11), 2283–2290

86. Summers, L.L.: The right blend: SEL skills support teacher learning in person and online. Learn. Professional **41**(4), 32–36 (2020)

87. Taylor, R.D., Oberle, E., Durlak, J.A., Weissberg, R.P.: Promoting positive youth development through school-based social and emotional learning interventions: a meta-analysis of follow-up effects. Child Dev. **88**(4) 1156–1171 (2017)

88. Stavroulia, K.E., Christofi, M., Baka, E., Michael-Grigoriou, D., Magnenat-Thalmann, N., Lanitis, A.: Assessing the emotional impact of virtual reality-based teacher training. Int. J. Inf. Learn. Technol. **36**(3), 192–217 (2019)

89. McIntosh, N.A., Nenonene, R.L.: In this spirit: helping preservice teachers thrive during the pandemic through adaptation and change. J. Catholic Educ. **23**(1), 162–174 (2020)

90. Noel, L.A., Liu, T.: Using design thinking to create a new education paradigm for elementary level children for higher student engagement and success. In: Lloyd, P., Bohemia, E. (eds.) Future Focused Thinking – DRS International Conference 2016, 27–30 June, Brighton, United Kingdom

91. Wigelsworth, M., et al.: The impact of trial stage, developer involvement and international transferability on universal social and emotional learning programme outcomes: a meta-analysis. Cambridge J. Educ. **46**(3), 347–376 (2016)

92. Han, J., Jo, M., Hyun, E., So, H.-J.: Examining young children's perception toward augmented reality-infused dramatic play. Educ. Tech. Res. Dev. **63**(3), 455–474 (2015)

93. Vossen, H.G.M, Valkenburg, P.M.: Do social media foster or curtail adolescents' empathy? A longitudinal study. Comput. Human Behav. **63**, 118–124 (2016)

94. Flecha, R., Pulido, C., Villarejo, B., Racionero, S., Redondo, S., Torras, E.: Effects of the Use of Digital Technology on Children's Empathy and Attention Capacity: Analytical Report. Vol. 4/2019. Luxembourg: Publications Office (2020)

95. Parong, J., Wells, A., Mayer, R.E.: Replicated evidence towards a cognitive theory of game-based training. J. Educ. Psychol. **112**(5), 922–937 (2020)

96. Arnab, S., Clarke, S., Morini, L.: Co-creativity through play and game design thinking. Elect. J. e-Learn. **17**(3), 184–198 (2019)

97. Avgousti, M.I., Hadjistassou, S.: ReDesign: Redesigning Learning through a New Learning Management System (2019)

98. Blau, I., Weiser, O., Eshet-Alkalai, Y.: How do medium naturalness and personality traits shape academic achievement and perceived learning? An experimental study of face-to-face and synchronous e-learning. Res. Learn. Technol. **25**, 1–23 (2017)

99. Bower, M., DeWitt, D., Lai, J.W.M.: Reasons associated with preservice teachers' intention to use immersive virtual reality in education. Brit. J. Educ. Technol. **51**(6), 2214–2232 (2020)

100. Scholtes, V., van Hout, M., van Koppen, L.: Can people develop a sense of belonging through playing league of legends?" In: Proceedings of the 13th International Conference on Advances in Computer Entertainment Technology, pp. 1–6. ACM (2016)

101. Wimmer, S., Denk, N., Pfeiffer, A., Fleischhacker, M.: On the use of esports in educational settings. How can esports serve to increase interest in traditional school subjects and improve the ability to use 21st century skills? In: ICERI2021 Proceedings, IATED, vol. 8, pp. 5782–5787 (2021)

Body-Related Attentional Bias in Anorexia Nervosa and Body Dissatisfaction in Females: An Eye-Tracking and Virtual Reality New Paradigm

José Gutierrez-Maldonado[1]([⊠]) ⓘ, Mar Clua i Sánchez[1],
Bruno Porras-Garcia[2] ⓘ, Marta Ferrer-Garcia[1] ⓘ,
Eduardo Serrano[3] ⓘ, Marta Carulla[3] ⓘ,
Franck Meschberger-Annweiler[1] ⓘ, and Mariarca Ascione[1] ⓘ

[1] Department of Clinical Psychology and Psychobiology,
University of Barcelona, Passeig de la Vall d'Hebron, 171,
08035 Barcelona, Spain
jgutierrezm@ub.edu
[2] Department of Population Health Sciences, School of Medicine,
University of Utah, 295 Chipeta Way, Room 1N490, Salt Lake City,
UT 84108, USA
bruno.r.porras@hsc.utah.edu
[3] Department of Child and Adolescent Psychiatry and Psychology,
Hospital Sant Joan de Déu, Passeig de Sant Joan de Déu, 2,
Esplugues de Llobregat, 08950 Barcelona, Spain
eserrano@sjdhospitalbarcelona.org

Abstract. According to recent research, eating disorder (ED) patients tend to check unattractive body parts. However, few studies have studied this attentional bias (AB) phenomenon combining virtual reality (VR) with eye-tracking (ET). This study aims to examine whether anorexia nervosa (AN) patients have a longer fixation time and a greater fixations number on the weight-related body areas compared to the healthy sample with high body dissatisfaction (HBD) and low body dissatisfaction (LBD). It will also examine whether the HBD group will have more fixations and spend more time looking at weight-related areas than those with LBD. Forty-three college women (18 with HBD and 25 with LBD) and 23 AN patients were immersed in a virtual environment and then embodied in a virtual avatar with their real body measurements and body mass index (BMI). Eye movement data were tracked using an ET device incorporated in the VR headset (FOVE). The number of fixations and the complete fixations time were registered on the weight-related areas of interest (W-AOIs) and non-weight-related areas of interest (NW-AOIs). The results showed that AN patients have a longer fixation time and a greater fixations number on W-AOIs than both HBD and LBD groups, who did not show any statistical differences in the visual selective attention to NW-AOIs and W-AOIs.

Keywords: Attentional bias · Body dissatisfaction · Anorexia nervosa · Virtual reality · Body image

© The Author(s), under exclusive license to Springer Nature Switzerland AG 2022
J. Y. C. Chen and G. Fragomeni (Eds.): HCII 2022, LNCS 13317, pp. 443–454, 2022.
https://doi.org/10.1007/978-3-031-05939-1_30

1   Introduction

Anorexia nervosa (AN) is one of the most common eating disorders (ED), and its prevalence among women has increased over the previous two decades (Dahlgren et al. 2017). The peak onset of AN occurs throughout adolescence and early adulthood, with a higher prevalence in women (Treasure et al. 2020), and in higher-income groups (Boushey et al. 2001). AN is recognized as a significant cause of mortality in young people (Arcelus et al. 2011), with a high suicide rate and chronic courses: less than half of patients are fully recovered, and just 33% improve (Steinhausen 2009). This disorder is characterized by an intense fear of gaining weight, a disturbance in the way body size or weight is perceived, and obsessive symptoms consisting of intrusive thoughts about food, weight, and shape (Toro 2001).

Regarding the treatments, only 20% of ED patients seek treatment, and generally at advanced stages of the disease's course, reducing the possibilities of treating and managing the illness (Treasure et al. 2020). Frequently, AN treatment services lack the necessary equipment to deal with such a severe, long-term disorder (Hudson et al. 2007), and AN patients frequently do not respond to treatment (Herzog et al. 1992). According to Hudson et al. (2007), innovation and progress are critical to improve the treatment of AN.

Body image (BI) is a multidimensional model that is developed by the effect of various judgments that an individual makes about his or her body (Banfield et al. 1994). The dimension of body dissatisfaction (BD) includes cognitive and affective components (Banfield and McCabe 2002), and it relates to perceived overestimation of one's body size and strong negative feelings toward one's appearance (Gleaves et al. 1995; Wilhelm et al. 2018). BD is emphasized and maintained by the phenomena of body checking: the activity of continuously checking one's body, scoping selective body parts, frequently weighing oneself, and repeatedly staring in the mirror (Reas et al. 2002). Body image distortion (BID) is another core symptom of AN (Beato-Fernández et al. 2004), and it is one of the primary risk factors for the disease's development (Gaudio et al. 2014). As described in the DSM-5, AN patients see their bodies or body parts as being too fat, even if they are severely underweight (APA 2013).

Previous studies have confirmed that body checking practices and cognitions, which are currently neglected in treatment programs (Rosen 1997), may contribute to the etiology and maintenance of ED (Mountford et al. 2006). These behavioral patterns, however, are also observed in the non-clinical female population (Haase et al. 2011). It is critical to consider these signals since they may suggest pathological conduct and may result in the development of ED.

Previous research has found that it is possible to identify and convert to analyzable data this specific behavioral pattern. People with different levels of BD have different visual scanning behaviors (Gao et al. 2014). These comparisons can be made by assessing attentional bias (AB). In ED, AB refers to the tendency of paying more attention to body-related information compared to other information or stimuli (Williamson et al. 2004). Previous studies have shown this visual selective bias towards the body or food-related information in ED patients using AB assessment techniques such as the emotional Stroop paradigm, the dot prove paradigm (Lee and Shafran 2004), or the visual research paradigm (Smeets et al. 2008). However, these paradigms have significant limitations (Lee and Shafran 2004).

AB can now be examined more accurately because of new technologies applied to the clinical field (Myers et al. 2004). Eye-tracking (ET) is a technology that measures eye movement and has been recently applied to provide insights into cognitive, social, and emotional factores related to psychopathological disorders (Kerr-Gaffney et al. 2019). Despite its popularity, ET has some limitations, such as those related to validity (Godfroid and Hui 2020; Lai et al. 2013), which are particularly pronounced regarding ecological validity (Gegenfurtner et al. 2018). New technologies, thanks to advances in gestural recognition hardware of 3D avatars in virtual reality (VR) and using VR-based embodiment techniques, can capture full-body motion to facilitate an immersive experience [e.g. the rubber hand illusion (Newport et al. 2010)] and producing the feeling that the artificial body is the participant's body, known as the paradigm of the full body ownership illusion (FBOI). Thus, by combining ET with VR, the ecological validity improves. Also, there is evidence that FBOI applied in VR produces cognitive changes in BD (Ferrer et al. 2018).

It has been demonstrated in previous studies that there are differences in eye movement patterns between AN patients and non-clinical samples with different BD levels: women with high levels of BD (HBD) showed sustained attentional maintenance to thin bodies (Gao et al. 2014), while ED patients have a longer fixation time for body areas they find unattractive (Bauer et al. 2017; Tuschen-Caffier et al. 2015), especially the stomach and hips (George et al. 2011). It is important to note that previous studies have focused on dividing areas of interest (AOIs) into attractive and non-attractive body parts. However, this is a subjective measure that can be affected by different types of errors. Alternatively, by dividing the body into weight-related areas and non-weight-related areas, the potential AB studied will be towards the areas objectively related to weight.

Currently, only a few studies examine eye movements in ED (Kerr Gaffney et al. 2019), and there are even fewer that study this variable using VR. Combining ET and VR can provide a new method to investigate AB in clinical and non-clinical individuals with BID, leading to more reliable results.

This study aims to provide further information about the differences in the AB between AN patients and healthy individuals with different levels of BD by combining these two technologies. According to previous studies, it is expected that AN patients should have a gaze pattern focused on weight-related body areas, as well as HBD individuals (lesser extent than the AN patients), compared to low levels of BD (LBD) participants, that should show a more general gaze scanning behavior of their own body. Adding the contribution of the new techniques to analyze this phenomenon, more valid conclusions can be drawn.

2   Method

2.1   Participants

A sample of 43 college women (M_{age} = 21.12, SD = 1.56, M_{BMI} = 21.94, SD = 2.53) from the University of Barcelona was recruited via social media and campus flyers, as well as 23 AN patients, 9 adults and 19 adolescents (M_{age} = 16,54, SD = 4.13, M_{BMI} = 17.58, SD = 0.51), diagnosed at the Eating Disorders Unit of the Hospital Sant Joan de Déu of Barcelona and the Hospital of Bellvitge. The exclusion criteria for healthy participants were a self-reported diagnosis of a current ED, a BMI < 17 (moderate thinness) or BMI > 30 (obesity), according to the World Health Organization (2004), or a self-reported current severe mental disorder diagnosis (e.g., schizophrenia or bipolar disorder), visual deficits that prevent exposure, epilepsy, pregnancy, or clinical cardiac arrhythmia.

The inclusion criteria for patients were a primary diagnosis of AN (DSM-5 criteria), a BMI < 19, and age of 13 years or over. Exclusion criteria included visual deficits that prevent exposure, severe mental disorder diagnosis, pregnancy, epilepsy, and clinical cardiac arrhythmia. Among the AN patients, 18 were diagnosed with a restricted AN type (AN-R), while 5 were diagnosed with purgative AN type (AN-P). Regarding clinical or subclinical comorbidity with other mental health disorders, two patients had mood-related disorders, two had a borderline personality disorder, three had anxiety disorders, one had a borderline personality disorder and post-traumatic stress disorder, one had major depressive disorder, and one had both anxiety and mood-related disorders. Eight patients were also receiving pharmacological treatment, including antidepressants (2 of them), anxiolytics (3 of them), and a combination of antidepressants and anxiolytics (3 of them). They were all enrolled in a day patient intensive treatment program at the Eating Disorder Unit, which consisted of 11-h sessions allowing them to sleep at home.

2.2   Instruments

Hardware and Software. Each participant was exposed to an immersive virtual scenario using a head-mounted display (HTC-VIVE Pro HMD) and was assigned a virtual avatar. In addition to the HTC-VIVE Pro HMD, four body trackers (two on the feet and two in the hands) were used to achieve full-body motion tracking. The moves of the head, the arms, and the feet were captured within the playing area delimited by two base stations. To induce the full-body illusion (FBI) with the virtual body, a visual-motor procedure and a visual-tactile stimulation was used. A second headset with incorporated ET systems (FOVE VR-HMD) was used to detect and register eye movements while participants viewed their virtual avatar in the virtual environment. The FOVE VR-HMD has a resolution of 2560 * 1440 pixels and creates 70 frames per second. Infrared ET sensors create 120 frames per second with an accuracy level of less than $1°$.

Virtual simulations were developed by two software: the Blender 2.78.v software was used to create a 3D female avatar wearing a white t-shirt, jeans, brown shoes, and a swim cap to avoid any influence of hairstyle (see Fig. 1); and the Unity 3D 5.5.v. software was used to develop the object-oriented programming code and integrate the elements in the virtual environment, which consisted of a grey and brown empty room with a large mirror placed 1.5 m in front of the participant.

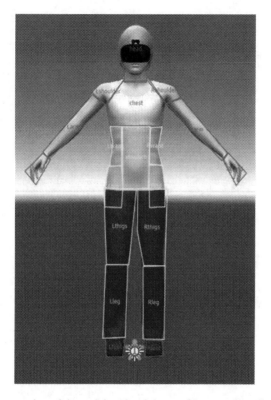

Fig. 1. Visual representation of the weight-related Areas of Interest (in yellow) and non-weight related Areas of Interest (in blue) in the virtual avatar (Color figure online)

2.3 Measures

Eating Disorders Inventory (EDI-3; Garner 2004) is a self-report inventory consisting of 12 scales and 91 items, in which the answers are provided on a 6-point Likert scale. In the current study, the Spanish version of the Body Dissatisfaction Scale (EDI-BD) was used. The EDI-BD scale, with 10 items, measures the negative subjective attitude or evaluation of one's body or specific body areas, including their shape, weight, and fitness (e.g., "I think my butt is too big"). This EDI-3 Spanish version presents robust validity and reliability indices, with a Cronbach's alpha ranging from 0.74 to 0.96. (Elosua et al. 2010).

2.4   Eye-Tracking Measures

Body-related AB was recorded by an ET device integrated into the FOVE headset, determining the participant's visual fixation on their own body. The participant's visual fixations are defined as the involuntary act of maintaining the gaze on a single location for a minimum duration, usually 100–200 ms (Jacob and Karn, 200). The measurements used in the study were the number of fixations (NF) and complete fixation time (CFT). CFT refers to the sum of the fixation time, measured in milliseconds, for the specified AOI, while NF is used to refer to the total number of fixations on the AOIs. Using the Physical Appearance State and Trait Anxiety Scale (PASTAS; Thompson 1999), two areas of interest (AOI) were defined: weight-related AOIs (W-AOIs) included waists, stomach, hips, thighs, and legs, and non-weight related AOIs (NW-AOIs) included the remaining areas. The segmentation of the AOIs was drawn in a 3D female avatar (Fig. 1). ET data was collected to obtain the records focused on W-AOIs and NW-AOIs, as used in previous studies (Mountford et al. 2006; George et al. 2011; Porras-Garcia et al. 2018).

2.5   Procedure

This study was approved by the ethics committee of the University of Barcelona. Participants or the legal guardians (if under the age of 18) had to provide informed consent before entering the study. Each participant was informed of the procedure, the data confidentiality, and the possibility of dropping out of the study at any point without consequences. Confidentiality was ensured by assigning a different identification code to each participant.

Before starting the study, the healthy participants were asked orally about their weight and height to figure out their BIM [weight (kg)/height (cm)], which was needed for the inclusion/exclusion criteria and to create a more accurate avatar for each participant's shape. For AN patients, the clinical doctors of the ED units responsible for the patients were requested information to assess the exclusion and inclusion criteria: patient's current BMI, AN subtype diagnosis, and prior history of the disorder.

To create a personalized avatar, each participant was taken a frontal and a lateral photo of the whole body by a camera connected to the computer. All participants were placed two meters from the camera standing up with their legs slightly separated and extending their arms at shoulder height. The participants completed the EDI-BD questionnaires while the researchers overlapped manually each participant's photo and virtual avatar by adapting the different dimensions of the virtual avatar (e.g., arms, legs, hip, waist, chest, stomach, breast, shoulder, etc.) to fit the silhouette of the participant.

Once ready, the participants were exposed to the VR scenario where each participant was able to observe himself in the first-person perspective and to look at himself in the mirror (in the third-person perspective). Then, a visual-motor and a visual-tactile stimulation were done to evocate the FBI by increasing identification with the virtual avatar, and the feeling that the virtual body was the participants' own body. The visual-motor stimulation procedure consisted of synchronizing the movement of the participant with that of the avatar using motion capture sensors placed on the hands and feet (e.g., "move your left arm doing little circles in front of you", "pretend that you are walking without moving from your position", etc.). The visual-tactile stimulation procedure consisted of synchronizing participants' visual and tactile stimulations: while the different areas of the body (arms, legs, and stomach) were touched on the participant, each participant observed the same areas being touched on the avatar at the same time by a tactile controller of the HTC- VIVE Pro. Both procedures lasted for 1 and a half minutes.

Finally, to assess the body-related AB the HTC-VIVE Pro HMD was replaced with the HMD FOVE ET headset that displayed the same virtual room as that in the previous VR environment, with the participant's real-size avatar reflected in the mirror. After the calibration and validation procedure of HMD-FOVE-ET, participants were instructed to gaze at the avatar reflected in the mirror for 30 s while spontaneous eye movements were recorded. As a cover story, they were told to remain still while the virtual avatar position was being recalibrated; this was necessary to avoid any bias in the participants' gaze orientation due to knowledge of the real objective and was only explained after the completion of the procedure.

2.6   Statistical Analysis

The Open Gaze and Mouse Analyzer (OGAMA) software were used to transform the ET raw data into suitable quantitative data. An additional data transformation was conducted by subtracting the difference between W-AOI and NW-AOIs (e.g., in fixation points: 25 (W-AOIs) – 10 (NW-AOIs) = 15). Therefore, a positive outcome would mean that the participant had been looking more at the weight-related body parts than at the non-weight-related body parts, while a negative outcome would mean the opposite. It is important to note that if there is a tendency it does not imply the existence of an attentional bias.

The healthy sample was divided into high versus low BD levels using the median score of the EDI-BD as a cut-off point ($Me_{BD} = 8$). All participants with a score equal to or less than the median were classified in the low body dissatisfaction group. Since several healthy participants scored at the median value, this resulted in a different sample size in the high and low body dissatisfaction groups, with a higher number in the low than in the high group. This distribution seemed more valid to us than assigning the same number of participants to each of the two groups into which the sample of healthy participants was divided, since this would have required that some participants whose score were equal to the median of the distribution had been classified in the low body dissatisfaction group and others, with the same score, would have been classified in the high body dissatisfaction group.

All the statistical analyses were performed using the software IBM SPSS v.26. One-way between-groups analysis of variance (ANOVA) was conducted to determine if there was a difference between the three different groups (AN, HBD, and LBD participants) in the attentional bias measures (NF and CFT). Data were normally distributed in all the variables assessed by the Kolmogorov-Smirnov test, except for the LBD group. However, one-way ANOVA has performed anyway since it has been considered a robust test even in the case of a deviation from normality (Schmider et al 2010).

3 Results

3.1 Descriptive Results

Participants were classified into three groups: AN patients (n = 23), healthy participants with HBD (n = 18), and healthy participants with LBD (n = 25). The descriptive
analysis of ET data related to CFT and NF is shown in Table 1. Regarding the EDI- BD
scale, the AN patients showed a score of BD = 24.03, women with LBD = 4.04, and
women with HBD = 14.61.

Table 1. Descriptive analysis of ET data

	AN (n = 23)	High BD (n = 18)	Low BD (n = 25)
Measure	Mean (SD)	Mean (SD)	Mean (SD)
CFT	7,190.79 (7180.13)	965,56 (7578,91)	−2,858.48 (10589.35)
NF	22.00 (12.99)	5.22 (15.49)	2.20 (15.88)

Note: Body Dissatisfaction (BD), Anorexia Nervosa (AN), Complete
Fixation Time (CFT), Number of Fixations (NF)

3.2 Visual Selective Attentional Bias

A statistically significant difference ($p < .05$) between the groups on both ET variables
was found: for CFT $F_{(2,64)} = 8.258$, $p < .001$, partial $\eta2 = 0.20$; and for NF
$F_{(2,64)} = 12,297$, $p < .001$, partial $\eta2 = 0.27$. The effect size between groups was
medium in both ET variables according to Cohen (1988). Descriptive analysis show that
CFT scores increased from the LBD (M = −2858,48, SD = 10589,35) to the HBD
(M = 965,56, SD = 7578,91) and to AN patients (M = 7190,97, SD = 7180,13) groups,
in that order. Similarly, NF score increased from the LBD (M = 2,20, SD = 15,88) to the
HBD (M = 5,22, SD = 15,48) and to AN patients (M = 22,00, SD = 12,99) groups, in
that order (see Table 1). Tukey post hoc analysis revealed that the difference between
LBD group and AN patients in the CFT variable was statistically significant ($p < .001$),
as well as the difference between LBD group and AN patients ($p < .001$), and between
HBD group and AN patients in the NF variable ($p = .002$) (see Table 2).

Table 2. Post hoc analyses (pairwise comparison) between groups in ET data

	LBD vs. HBD			AN vs. LBD			AN vs. HBD		
	Mean deviation (SD)	p	d^{cohen}	Mean deviation (SD)	p	d^{cohen}	Mean deviation (SD)	p	d^{cohen}
CFT	−3824.03 (2691.92)	0.33	0.20	10049.27 (2488.61)	<0.001*	1.11	6225.23 (2715.30)	0.64	0.84
NF	−3.02 (4.57)	0.78	0.19	19.80 (4.23)	<0.001*	1.37	16.77 (4.61)	0.002*	1.17

Note: Low Body Dissatisfaction (LBD), High Body Dissatisfaction (HBD), Anorexia Nervosa (AN),
Complete Fixation Time (CFT), Number of Fixations (NF)
*Significant p values <.05.

4 Discussion

The current study aimed to assess body-related AB toward W-AOIs and NW- AOIs in women with AN and healthy participants by using an ET device for the AB measurements, a virtual idiosyncratic avatar, and an embodiment illusion. In contrast to previous studies, the AB measurements were collected using a VR headset with an ET device (FOVE), in which patients observed their own body in a virtual avatar designed specifically for them using their real BMI rather than seeing printed photographs or other people's bodies. It also differs from previous studies in the methodology used to divide the AOI into W-AOIs and NW-AOIs rather than dividing body parts based on self-reported attractive vs. unattractive criteria. Because the body attractiveness measure has been used in several AB studies (Bauer et al. 2017; Tuschen-Caffier et al. 2015; George et al. 2011), to compare this study with others the attractive areas would be considered as NW-AOIs and the unattractive areas as W-AOIs, because these areas are reported almost identically [e.g., stomach, hips and thigs as unattractive body areas (George et al. 2011)].

The results showed that AN patients had longer and more frequent gazes towards weight-related body parts than healthy participants. Between HBD and LBD groups no significant differences in the AB to body areas were found. The results observed in the AN group regarding the AB are in line with previous studies (Bauer et al. 2017; Tuschen-Caffier et al. 2015; George et al. 2011; Mountford et al. 2006; Jansen et al. 2005; Freeman et al. 1991).

The study's findings reveal that AN patients and healthy controls process information differently. One possible explanation for these findings could be that AN patients have an altered capacity of processing and integrating body representations, perceiving their body parts not in a holistic way, but in a dissociated view (Gaudio et al. 2014). This could create a vicious circle: a stronger AB to the unattractive body parts may lead to an emphasis in the negative body image, creating unfavorable cognitions and so furthering the disease (Williamson et al. 2004), These findings also support previous research (Tuschen-Caffier et al. 2015; Jansen et al. 2005; Mogg et al. 2004) that found ED patients to be hypervigilant about specific body areas that cause them dissatisfaction.

It's also crucial to consider how AN patients store body experiences in memory, particularly in sensory-motor/proprioceptive memory. According to research, AN patients have a negative allocentric view of their body, which may lead to insufficient egocentric and somatosensorial body updating, resulting in an alteration in the way they experience and remember their shape (Riva and Gaudio 2012). Furthermore, this alteration will be also associated with biased long-term memory because the orientation and position of body parts will be stored incongruously between presentation and recall (Burgess et al. 2001). These findings are supported by brain imaging studies, which show a deterioration in the areas between the parahippocampus and the precuneus in AN patients, the same areas that process an allocentric and egocentric view of the body. Body image-related cognitive biases can be manipulated (Rodgers and DuBois 2016), and according to the latest findings, VR therapy could treat biased information processing compensating this brain malfunction as the patients see their virtual avatar in an allocentric position towards the mirror.

As young girls are more susceptible to cultural and social messages and pressures concerning the body, this alteration of the space experience may lead females, particularly adolescents, to perceive negative areas of their bodies as defining of themselves. It should also be noted that in today's Western societies the ideal body is characterized by extreme thinness, almost grazing the sick body, encouraging the female population (e.g., through the media) to maintain constant attention on the body (e.g., body checking) to keep it slim, making them more vulnerable to developing ED.

There are several limitations to this exploratory study. The first and is that the age variable was not considered. If the ED of adolescents and women were studied separately, conclusions could be drawn at these critical stages of development. Adolescents, as previously stated, have a more pronounced tendency to check body parts related to weight. No attentional bias was measured in the first point of attachment. This measurement could provide more precise information about approach-avoidance behavior. Another limitation is that women were classified as having HBD or LBD levels based on the EDI-BD median score. This is justified because the healthy sample had very similar test scores, so there were only a few extreme values.

Future research should test the possibility of modifying attentional patterns using VR technology, which could serve as an innovative therapy with ecological validity, assisting patients in becoming more conscious of their AB. It may also be used as a reference to objectively determine the improvement after therapy. Furthermore, it could be used as a preventive function in HBD females at risk of developing ED. Future initiatives should investigate this paradigm in a broader and more representative sample of AN patients and of participants with different levels of BD.

Funding. This study was funded by the Spanish Ministry of Science and Innovation (Ministerio de Ciencia e Innovación, Spain. Project PID2019-108657RB-I00: Modification of attentional bias, with virtual reality, for improving anorexia nervosa treatment) and by AGAUR, Generalitat de Catalunya, 2017SGR1693.

References

American Psychiatric Association: Diagnostic and Statistical Manual of Mental Disorders. American Psychiatric Association (2013). https://doi.org/10.1176/appi.books.9780890425596

Arcelus, J., Mitchell, A.J., Wales, J., Nielsen, S.: Mortality rates in patients with anorexia nervosa and other eating disorders: a meta-analysis of 36 studies. Arch. Gen. Psychiatry **68**(7), 724–731 (2011)

Banfield, S.S., McCabe, M.: An evaluation of the construct of body image. Adolescence **37**(146), 373–393 (2002)

Beato-Fernández, L., Rodríguez-Cano, T., Belmonte-Llario, A., Martínez-Delgado, C.: Risk factors for eating disorders in adolescents. Eur. Child Adolesc. Psychiatry **13**(5), 287–294 (2004)

Boushey, C.J., Coulston, A.M., Rock, C.L., Monsen, E.: Chapter 43: eating disorders: anorexia nervosa, bulimia nervosa and binge eating disorder. In: Rock, C.L., Kaye, W.H. (eds.) Nutrition in the Prevention and Treatment of Disease. Amsterdam: Elsevier (2001)

Burgess, N., Becker, S., King, J.A., O'Keefe, J.: Memory for events and their spatial context: models and experiments. Philos. Trans. R. Soc. Lond. B Biol. Sci. **356**(1413), 1493–1503 (2001)

Dahlgren, C.L., Wisting, L., Rø, Ø.: Feeding and eating disorders in the DSM-5 era: a systematic review of prevalence rates in non-clinical male and female samples. J. Eat. Disord. **5**(1), 56 (2017)

Elosua, P., López-Jáuregui, A., Sánchez-Sánchez, F.: Adaptación Española del Eating Disorder Inventory-3. Normalización y Validación. TEA, Madrid (2010)

Ferrer, M.F.G., Porras Garcia, B., Moreno, M., Bertomeu, P., Gutiérrez Maldonado, J.: Embodiment in different size virtual bodies produces changes in women's body image distortion and dissatisfaction. Annu. Rev. Cyberther. Telemed. **16**, 111–117 (2018)

Freeman, R., Touyz, S., Sara, G., Rennie, C., Gordon, E., Beumont, P.: In the eye of the beholder: processing body shape information in anorexic and bulimic patients. Int. J. Eat. Disord. **10**(6), 709–714 (1991)

Gao, X., Deng, X., Yang, J., Liang, S., Liu, J., Chen, H.: Eyes on the bodies: an eye tracking study on deployment of visual attention among females with body dissatisfaction. Eat. Behav. **15**(4), 540–549 (2014)

Garner, D.M.: Eating Disorder Inventory-3 (EDI-3). Professional Manual. Psychological Assessment Resources, Odessa, FL (2004)

Gaudio, S., Brooks, S.J., Riva, G.: Nonvisual multisensory impairment of body perception in anorexia nervosa: a systematic review of neuropsychological studies. PloS ONE **9**(10) (2014)

George, H.R., Cornelissen, P.L., Hancock, P.J., Kiviniemi, V.V., Tovee, M.J.: Differences in eye-movement patterns between anorexic and control observers when judging body size and attractiveness. Br. J. Psychol. **102**(3), 340–354 (2011)

Gleaves, D.H., Williamson, D.A., Eberenz, K.P., Sebastian, S.B., Barker, S.E.: Clarifying body-image disturbance: analysis of a multidimensional model using structural modeling. J. Pers. Assess. **64**(3), 478–493 (1995)

Godfroid, A., Hui, B.: Five common pitfalls in eye-tracking research. Second Lang. Res. 026765832092121 (2020)

Haase, A.M., Mountford, V., Waller, G.: Associations between body checking and disordered eating behaviors in nonclinical women. Int. J. Eat. Disord. **44**(5), 465–468 (2011)

Herzog, D.B., Keller, M.B., Zucker, M.E., Strober, M., Yeh, C., Pai, S.Y.: The current status of treatment for anorexia nervosa and bulimia nervosa. Int. J. Eat. Disord. **12**(2), 215–220 (1992)

Hudson, J.I., Hiripi, E., Pope, H.G., Jr., Kessler, R.C.: The prevalence and correlates of eating disorders in the national comorbidity survey replication. Biol. Psychiat. **61**(3), 348–358 (2007)

Kerr-Gaffney, J., Harrison, A., Tchanturia, K.: Eye-tracking research in eating disorders: a systematic review. Int. J. Eat. Disord. **52**(1), 3–27 (2019)

Lai, M.L., et al.: A review of using eye-tracking technology in exploring learning from 2000 to 2012. Educ. Res. Rev. **10**, 90–115 (2013)

Lee, M., Shafran, R.: Information processing biases in eating disorders. Clin. Psychol. Rev. **24**(2), 215–238 (2004)

Mogg, K., Bradley, B., Miles, F., Dixon, R.: Brief report time course of attentional bias for threat scenes: testing the vigilance-avoidance hypothesis. Cogn. Emot. **18**(5), 689–700 (2004)

Mountford, V., Haase, A., Waller, G.: Body checking in the eating disorders: Associations between cognitions and behaviors. Int. J. Eat. Disord. **39**(8), 708–715 (2006)

Myers, T.C., Swan-Kremeier, L., Wonderlich, S., Lancaster, K., Mitchell, J.E.: The use of alternative delivery systems and new technologies in the treatment of patients with eating disorders. Int. J. Eat. Disord. **36**(2), 123–143 (2004)

Newport, R., Pearce, R., Preston, C.: Fake hands in action: embodiment and control of supernumerary limbs. Exp. Brain Res. **204**(3), 385–395 (2010)

Reas, D.L., Whisenhunt, B.L., Netemeyer, R., Williamson, D.A.: Development of the body checking questionnaire: a self-report measure of body checking behaviors. Int. J. Eat. Disord. **31**(3), 324–333 (2002)

Riva, G., Gaudio, S.: Allocentric lock in anorexia nervosa: new evidences from neuroimaging studies. Med. Hypotheses **79**(1), 113–117 (2012)

Rodgers, R.F., DuBois, R.H.: Cognitive biases to appearance-related stimuli in body dissatisfaction: a systematic review. Clin. Psychol. Rev. **46**, 1–11 (2016)

Schmider, E., Ziegler, M., Danay, E., Beyer, L., Bühner, M.: Is it really robust?: reinvestigating the robustness of ANOVA against violations of the normal distribution assumption. Methodology **6**(4), 147–151 (2010). https://doi.org/10.1027/1614-2241/a000016

Smeets, E., Roefs, A., van Furth, E., Jansen, A.: Attentional bias for body and food in eating disorders: increased distraction, speeded detection, or both? Behav. Res. Ther. **46**(2), 229–238 (2008)

Steinhausen, H.C.: Outcome of eating disorders. Child Adolesc. Psychiatr. Clin. N. Am. **18**(1), 225–242 (2009)

Thompson, J.K.: Physical Appearance State and Trait Anxiety Scale: Trait 1996. APA, Washington, DC (1999)

Toro, J.: Anorexia nervosa. Med. Clin. **117**(9), 334–335 (2001)

Treasure, J., Duarte, T.A., Schmidt, U.: Eating disorders: innovation and progress urgently needed. Lancet **395**(10227), 840 (2020)

Tuschen-Caffier, B., Bender, C., Caffier, D., Klenner, K., Braks, K., Svaldi, J.: Selective visual attention during mirror exposure in anorexia and bulimia nervosa. PLoS ONE **10**(12), e0145886 (2015)

Wilhelm, L., Hartmann, A., Cordes, M., Waldorf, M., Vocks, S.: How do you feel when you check your body? Emotional states during a body-checking episode in normal – weight females. Eating and Weight Disorders – Studies on Anorexia, Bulimia and Obesity **25**(2), 309–319 (2018)

Williamson, D.A., White, M.A., York-Crowe, E., Stewart, T.M.: Cognitive – behavioral theories of eating disorders. Behav. Modif. **28**(6), 711–738 (2004)

Enhancing Emotional Experience by Building Emotional Virtual Characters in VR Exhibitions

Yangjing Huang and Han Han[✉]

Shenzhen University, Shenzhen, China
han.han@szu.edu.cn

Abstract. Virtual digital exhibitions attract public attention as they can provide an immersive aesthetic experience augmented by virtual reality (VR) technologies. However, since each visitor is placed in an isolated virtual environment while using VR devices, the exhibitions lose the immediate emotional perception between visitors. In order to enable visitors to perceive the communicative value of the digital exhibitions, increasing the user's feeling of immersion and engagement in the virtual environment is crucial. Existing experience designs of VR exhibitions put more effort into developing the imitation of physical exhibited space, rather than display instant emotional facial expressions of visitors. Thus, a supporting system design on how to enhance the visitor's real-time emotional communication in the VR exhibitions experience is needed at present. An emotional color label of visitors in exhibitions and an emotaion recognition and display model in the virtual environment are proposed to alleviate this issue. Our research has the potential to enhance the user's emotional experience and engagement in VR exhibitions and other forms of virtual digital exhibition.

Keywords: Virtual digital exhibition · Virtual reality · Emotional experience

1 Introduction

1.1 Background

Art museums now open digital exhibitions to provide an immersive experience and maximize user interaction in order to serve a broader public on a larger scale of space and time. Virtual reality (VR) has the potential to support rich experiences and has been widely used in digital art exhibitions. In traditional exhibitions, emotions play a crucial role in an aesthetic experience [1]. During an aesthetic experience, while visiting exhibitions, visitors often gain emotional experience through interacting with the artworks and the physical exhibition environment. At the same time, the emotion of visitors is always influenced by the expressions and behaviors of their companions or peers who visit the exhibition together. Under the circumstances, the recognition of other people's emotions in an exhibition is as importantly influencing the emotional experience of visitors as the direct feedback during interaction with the physical artworks and space. Existing experience designs of the exhibitions applying virtual reality

© The Author(s), under exclusive license to Springer Nature Switzerland AG 2022
J. Y. C. Chen and G. Fragomeni (Eds.): HCII 2022, LNCS 13317, pp. 455–464, 2022.
https://doi.org/10.1007/978-3-031-05939-1_31

put effort into developing the technical aspects to build a virtual environment, which leads to the ignorance of the emotional experience of visitors in digital exhibitions and the absence of the communicative value of museums. Thus, a supporting system design on how to enhance the visitor's real-time emotional communication in the VR exhibitions experience is needed at present.

1.2   Virtual Digital Exhibition

'The virtual museum is the all-round communicative projection of the real museum' [2]. As a common means of displaying exhibitions, virtual digital exhibition (VDE) presents different paths based on two types of venues: online and offline. However, whether it is an online or offline digital exhibition, the purpose is to combine audio-visual media to mobilize the senses of touch, smell, and taste to create sensory interoperability and to let the viewers experience a panoramic virtual situation beyond reality under the same effect of multi-dimensional media [3].

At present, building virtual exhibition space scenes to replicate the panoramic space of offline exhibitions is the main presentation method of online exhibitions in major art museums. If you want to create sensory interoperability in the virtual exhibition space scene, you can build a 'virtual display environment' with the help of digital technologies such as virtual reality techniques. The most common technical features of virtual museums are as follows:

1. based on a combination of media, visitors can use different expressions (images, texts, sounds) to communicate;
2. being interactive by providing the ability to act, choose and actively construct various paths;
3. being connected or part of a network system that facilitates access to one or more museums realities;
4. in live time.

These technical characteristics emphasize how virtual museums can use all the physical and conceptual methods to become real museums, without the physical constraints of entity space. Some scholars have argued that these attempts to construct virtual spaces sometimes seem to be simple and poor replications of real spaces, without expressing the exact same spatial concepts as the physical museum, with the aim of deepening unpublished knowledge and presenting the exhibitors in their original and complete forms. The focus on technological reproduction highlights the risk of neglecting the overall meaning of the museum: the focus is on the immediate gratification from digital and three dimensions visuals rather than the study of elements of the cognitive and relational nature of traditional exhibitions. This suggests that to better realize the nature of virtual museums, we need to clarify the function of the museum itself, so that we can build towards the goal set by virtual digital exhibitions [2].

The online exhibitions that appear on the market today, realized through various technical means and media, provide personalized, thematic, and immersive viewing scenarios that visitors can freely choose from, allowing them to independently choose to view the exhibition through mobile roaming, image manipulation, voice explanation, and angle switching [4]. The seemingly novel experience, but exhibitors often give negative comments and even choose to exit the exhibition between the halfway point of the visit because of the bad interactive experience, these phenomena indicate the lack of consideration from the essential purpose of the exhibition when designing the virtual exhibition, so that the virtual implementation of the exhibition is oriented to various technical solutions.

The virtual museum experience is not a replacement for the real one, but it can still provide new learning experiences that are bound to change the way visitors interact with each other. The goal is to allow visitors to experience the artworks in their own unique way, so they can then share their initial views and develop their own personalized path. In addition, the virtual experience can still provide new learning opportunities that are bound to change the way people interact with each other [5]. In this sense, the learning or visiting path should allow viewers to not only know the artworks from the perspective of the exhibition settings, but also to form their own feedback, interpretation, and research based on individual interests and personalized path motivation, so that visitors can exchange their initial views and finally form an emotional interaction with the other visitors in the museum. If the data of these views can be effectively collected by the staff involved in the virtual exhibition If the data from these perspectives can be effectively collected by the staff of the virtual exhibition, visitors will have the opportunity to become the contributors and creators of new paths to the exhibition and to continuously optimize the emotional experience of exhibition visiting.

1.3   Learning and Communitive Value of VDE

In fact, the Italian Museum Institute and many scholars from related sectors and industries have recognized that the communicative value of virtual museums is more important than their traditional exhibition functions: learning, education, and entertainment.

Currently, virtual exhibitions are mainly using existing social media as communication tools in order to realize their communicative value. The communication between museums and their visitors and spectators, both real and potential, takes place through social networks [2]; Virtual exhibitions that use other social platforms as supplementary communication methods do realize their learning and communicative value to a certain extent. However, there is a certain lag in the interaction on social platforms, and the views on social platforms come from the viewers who have viewed the exhibition in all previous time periods. The virtual space scene of the virtual museum restores the physical scene of the physical museum in real time online, but its viewers rely on other social platforms to communicate in a way that does not restore the real-time communication between the viewers in the viewing phase in real time. Based on the existing technology that can perfectly restore the physical space of the exhibition, we hope to continue to restore the real-time communication among the visitors when visiting the exhibition, improve the interactive experience of the existing virtual digital exhibition, and realize the learning and communicative value of the virtual exhibition. Our research tries to explore more possibilities in this direction.

In our paper, we propose a design model for emotional experience in VR exhibitions. We first determine that VR technology is currently the application technology with the highest degree of restoration of physical space and senses in virtual digital exhibitions, and select VR exhibitions as our research object. Second, by drawing on the facial emotion classification method used for immersive virtual environment interaction and conducting a case study of the emotion model in existing VR games, we propose and describe an emotional experience design model applied to VR exhibitions, and we conclude with research conclusions and future work.

2   Related Works

2.1   VR Exhibition

The previous section has explained that the research direction of this paper is to explore ways to enhance the user experience of virtual digital exhibitions from the perspective of realizing the learning and communicative value of virtual exhibitions. In order to reduce the intervention of other elements, we choose virtual digital exhibition based on virtual reality (VR) technology as the research type.

Virtual reality is a technology that uses computers to create artificial virtual environments. It enhances the users' perception and allows them to restore the maximum interactivity in the physical space in a virtual environment close to the real physical world. As a result, many exhibitions have begun to experiment with the integration of virtual reality technology to ensure a deep restoration of the physical exhibition display content.

From the theoretical point of view of the product service system, no matter what medium is used for content presentation, the basic principle of 'human-centered' is indispensable. Human are the core of the service [6]. Virtual reality exhibition is based on the virtual display system, the core of concern is the user of the exhibition - the viewer. In the study of virtual display system proposed, virtual display system is based on virtual reality technology to achieve the main features of virtual reality technology is also virtual display system has. 1993, the U.S. scientists Berdie in the world of electronics annual meeting published 'virtual reality systems and their applications', proposed a virtual reality technology triangle used to describe the three main features of virtual reality technology: (1) immersion; (2) interactivity; (3) imagination.

An ideal virtual display system should have the following points:

(1)   The ability to create a virtual environment that is almost indistinguishable from the real scene.
(2)   Need to have good human-computer interaction characteristics.
(3)   Have the characteristics that enable users to play more imaginative [7].

In order to improve the user experience of VR exhibition, there have been many attempts and studies on the first two points from the technical point of view. This article focuses the second and third characteristics of the user, i.e., the exhibition experience of the viewers as the starting point.

2.2   Virtual Display System

First of all, the viewers should be able to interact well with the products in the virtual display system. The acquisition of good interactivity in virtual display system needs to apply to the research method of user experience map in service design, find all the physical contacts and interpersonal contacts of users in traditional display system, and transform them into interactive contacts in virtual display system, and further make good interactive experience design for these contacts. Secondly, the reason why users can get good imagination in the virtual display system is because in the virtual display system, the users imagine the system according to the information they get in the system and combine with their own judgment, analyze and explore its laws, such process can bring users a feeling of exploring something new [8]. Therefore, we need to consider how to design each touchpoint in order to make visitors play more imagination.

Based on the service design contacts for the physical display system and the virtual display system, combined with the characteristics of VR technology, we supplemented the production of a comparison chart of the contacts in the service model of the display system for the physical display system and the virtual reality exhibition (shown in Fig. 1). By comparing the service design contacts of these two systems, it is found that in the current virtual reality exhibition in the process of interactive contact transformation, the transformation of interpersonal contacts appears to have the absence of two parts: users and service providers and users and other users. Since VR devices only require staff assistance to put them on before and after viewing the exhibition, and do not affect the user experience in the viewing phase, the lack of the user-other-user part actually causes a loss of communication between the viewers in the virtual reality exhibition, which corresponds to the above, which may cause the users to lose the perception and imagination of other users who are viewing the exhibition together, ultimately leading to the lack of the virtual exhibition in terms of communicative value.

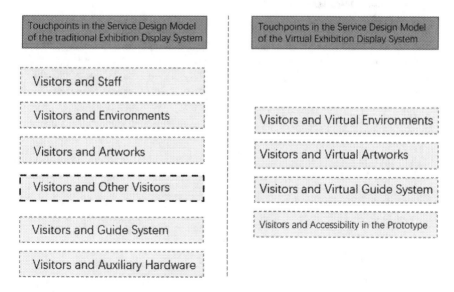

Fig. 1. Comparison of touchpoints in the service model of the physical display system and the display system of the virtual reality exhibition.

For a normal visitor, in order to promote the communication with other users in a virtual reality exhibition, the first step is to restore the affordance of other users in the virtual reality environment. The concept of Affordance was first introduced by the ecological psychologist Gibson to discuss a set of attributes in the environment that can be perceived and used by actors [9]. Norman [10] introduced it to the field of human computer interaction by arguing that there are two possible types of affordance for products: real affordance, which is the actual property of the component that requires action, and Perceived Affordance, which is the user's perception or understanding of the action that the component can take. which is the user's perception or understanding of the actions that can be taken by a component. In a virtual exhibition environment, all visitors should be able to perceive at least the attributes of 'seeing' visually. In a traditional physical exhibition, visitors can naturally form a sensory intention for other visitors through their physical senses during the viewing stage, thus forming a natural and potential communication and interaction with other visitors.

Neuroimaging studies have identified significant overlap in the neural circuits involved in action execution and observation of others' actions (e.g., seeing another person smile activates the same facial muscles at the subthreshold level of the viewer), as well as imagining one's own actions and those of another person. Reproducing images of somatic and motor components is a means for individuals to recognize the emotions of others [11]. When applied to VR technology, it has been suggested that by engaging the sensory components of these technologies (primarily visual and auditory media) that are not directly stimulated through simulation, and by amplifying these actual stimuli, mental imagery can enhance the impact of these technologies through content-based sensory trigger elements [12].

2.3   The Emotional Types of Visitors

Museums have recognized the role of emotion in increasing user engagement, and Perry categorized users' engagement behaviors when visiting exhibitions into four types: physical, intellectual, social, and emotional. Among these, emotional expressions of engagement include being moved by beauty, wonder, amazement, excitement, and hope, but also by sadness, fear, or anger. Contemporary museums not only want to convey knowledge, or stimulate interest and awareness, but often also want visitors to develop empathy and reflect on values [13]. Thus, virtual reality exhibitions also need to enhance the emotional engagement of the viewers.

2.4   Emotion Model in VR Sport Games

Games are also a frontier area for VR technology applications. Virtual reality games and virtual reality exhibitions are similar in that they are both products of traditional strong interactive entertainment scenes after undergoing digital transformation [14]. In the application of VR technology, both attach great importance to how to use technology to achieve sensory transfer and emotional communication from physical scenes to virtual space. Games have very much research in the field of emotion research, such as creating virtual characters with richer, more vivid and believable behaviors in VR games, making VR games have many ways to transfer these two elements.

Therefore, our research first analyzes the basic types of emotions of viewers in the exhibition, and with the perspective of emotional experience, we try to build an emotional model in virtual exhibitions for users by referring to the process of building emotional models in virtual reality games, in order to enhance the emotional communication and user experience of viewers in the digital exhibitions that apply virtual reality technology. The framework structure of our paper can be demonstrated by the following diagram (Fig. 2).

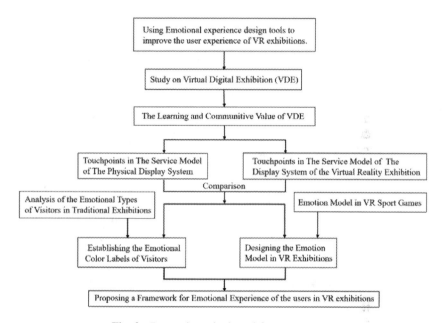

Fig. 2. Research methods and framework map

3 Framework Development

3.1 The Emotional Color Label of Visitors

A large body of empirical research has shown that emotional information can be conveyed through different colors. Researchers have begun to investigate the relationship between emotional vocabulary and color and have constructed a large database of color-coded emotional stimuli for researchers in other fields to use in studies related to perceptual, linguistic, memory, and cognitive research paradigms [15]. We choose and define eight emotion-laden words from the dataset to distinguish the six target emotional states (Beautiful, surprised, admired, inspired, hopeful, unhappy, terrified, and anger).

Emotional color labels for exhibition visitors were established by corresponding the types of emotional expressions of the visitors during the exhibition visit phase to the colors representing such emotions in the database (shown in Fig. 3).

Exhibition Visiting State Virtual Environments	Visitors Emotional Engagement category							
	Beauty	Surprise	Wonder	Excitement	Hope	Sadness	Fear	Anger
Emotion-laden Word	Beautiful	Surprised	Admired	Inspired	Hopeful	Unhappy	Terrified	Anger
Color	36% (Pink)	32% (Red)	43% (Red)	23% (Yellow)	29% (Blue)	42% (Blue)	38% (Red)	83% (Red)

Fig. 3. Emotional color labels of visitors (Color figure online)

3.2 Framework for Emotional Experience in VR Exhibitions

There is research that proves that in VR volleyball games, the emotional experience of users can be enhanced by building emotional virtual characters [16]. This has been achieved through a data-driven framework. In VR volleyball games, frameworks that inspire and express emotional avatars based on the game state have considerable benefits in increasing user emotional experience and user stickiness. noted that if there is an emotional element in the non-player character, the variation in character behavior increases, creating a more interesting game [17].

In the case of virtual reality exhibitions, it can be assumed that the viewer can personalize the viewing path and enhance the user experience by reacting emotionally when confronted with the interactive touchpoints of the exhibition and simultaneously adjusting his or her cognition and behavior under the influence of recognizing the emotions of other viewers. Through a case study of a user facial emotion recognition system in a virtual environment, and combined with our established color labels for viewer emotions, we derive a framework for emotional experience in virtual reality exhibitions with existing technical support, the details of which are shown in the following illustration.

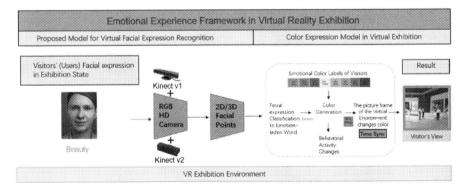

Fig. 4. Emotional experience framework in VR exhibitions

The facial expression recognition framework is shown in the left part of Fig. 4. A two-stage hierarchical model is designed to map exhibitionstate to emotion states of visitors. The first stage of the model is responsible for predicting the visitor's emotion based on the exhibition visiting state, while the second stage outputs the emotion of visitor in the virtual environment.

The expression model is implemented to render emotional expression for each visitor according to the predicted emotion states as shown in Fig. 4. The total generation process is split into three consecutive parts: facial expression classification to emotion-laden words, generating the color corresponding to certain facial expression, and time synchronization of changing the color of user's view in the virtual environment. In the first place, we use the techniques of Kinect to extract facial features for user's facial emotion recognition. It is a widely used approach to collect facial data due to the proliferation of affordable commodity depth sensing devices [18].

Figure 4 shows the process of an emotional experience of a visitor through our proposed model. For example, a visitor put on the VR equipment and enter the VR exhibition. When the user interacts with the virtual artworks or environment and make some reaction to them, Kinect sensors will recognize the visitor' emotions base on different expression features. If the person considers the artworks are beautiful and display facial expression, the model will classify it into the corresponding color pink based on emotional color labels for exhibition. At the same time, a pink border will appear in the other existing user's view of the virtual exhibition. At last, visitors are able to show their inner thoughts of their moods/feelings with others through the changing of colors, and gain greater interactive communication and improve their user experience in virtual exhibition.

4   Conclusion

After combing through the relevant literature, we found that although domestic and international studies have carried out preliminary explorations on the user experience of various online exhibitions such as those applied with VR technology, most of them focus on the stage of technical characteristics of physical and sensory elements of physical exhibitions, this study proposes that the immersion and participation of online exhibition users can be enhanced from the perspective of emotional experience to promote the realization of the communication value of future online exhibitions.

Although this study constructs a model of users' emotions in the virtual reality exhibition, considering the different socio-cultural backgrounds of the exhibition viewers, it may cause some variability in the correspondence between emotions and colors among people in different regions. Meanwhile, factors that may affect user experience evaluation such as age, occupation as well as other identity characteristics of the viewers should be taken into consideration in the follow-up study. In our future works, we plan to extend the emotional expression of the viewers to a variety of ways, such as body posture, body movement, etc. In addition, we will consider conducting actual research on virtual reality exhibitions and more in-depth user interviews to discover more interaction touchpoints and factors that affect the emotional experience of virtual digital exhibitions, and continue to improve the flowchart our emotional experience framework.

Acknowledgment. The author Yangjing Huang and corresponding author Han Han would like to express sincere appreciation to all the participants who contribute advise and data to this study.

References

1. Guazzaroni, G.: Digital heritage: new ways to provoke an emotional response to art. Int. J. Art Cult. Des. Technol. (2021)
2. Panciroli, C., Russo, V., Macauda, A.: When technology meets art: museum paths between real and virtual. Proc. **1**, 913 (2017)
3. Huang, J., Zhang, Y.: The logical strategy and design translation of virtual digital exhibition: by the clue of 2020 online graduation exhibition of global art colleges. Art Des. Res. 65–72 (2020)
4. Huang, Y.: Online virtual art exhibitions help to study the experience of scene presence. Beauty Times **4**, 2018–2020 (2021)
5. Panciroli, C., Veronica, R., Anita, M.: I musei come luoghi per l'educazione permanente: l'esempio del MOdE-Museo Officina dell'Educazione dell'Università di Bologna. in L'educazione permanente a partire dalle prime età della vita. Educazione Per Tutta La Vita, 404–413 (2016)
6. Wolstenholme, D.: Service design: from insight to implementation. Des. J. **19**, 183–186 (2016)
7. Sun, R.: Design and Realization of Virtual Display System Based on Internet. Beijing University of Posts and Telecommunications (2007)
8. Ziying, T.: The research and application of service design about virtual display system (2016)
9. Gibson, J.J.: The ecological approach to visual perception: classic edition. Ecol. Approach to Vis. Percept (2014). https://doi.org/10.4324/9781315740218
10. Norman, D.A.: The Psychology of Everyday Things (1988)
11. Decety, J., Jackson, P.L.: The functional architecture of human empathy. Behav. Cogn. Neurosci. Rev. **3** (2004)
12. Bertrand, S., Vassiliadi, M., Zikas, P., Geronikolakis, E., Papagiannakis, G.: From readership to usership: communicating heritage digitally through presence. Embodiment Aesthetic Experience. Front. Commun. **6**, 1–11 (2021)
13. Wang, Y., et al.: An emotional response to the value of visualization. IEEE Comput. Graph. Appl. **39**, 8–17 (2019). https://doi.org/10.1109/MCG.2019.2923483
14. Huawei Technologies Co. L.: Cloud VR User Experience Evaluation White Paper (2019)
15. Sutton, T. M., Altarriba, J.: Color associations to emotion and emotion-laden words: a collection of naorms for stimulus construction and selection. Behav. Res. Methods **4a8** (2016)
16. Bai, Z., et al.: Enhancing emotional experience by building emotional virtual characters in VR volleyball games. Comput. Animat. Virtual Worlds **32**, 1–11 (2021)
17. Popescu, A., Broekens, J., Van Someren, M.: GAMYGDALA: an emotion engine for games. IEEE Trans. Affect. Comput. **5**, 32–44 (2014)
18. Amara, K., et al.: Towards emotion recognition in immersive virtual environments: a method for facial emotion recognition. CEUR Workshop Proc. **2904**, 253–263 (2021)

The Island of Play: Reflections on How to Design Multiuser VR to Promote Social Interaction

Lasse Juel Larsen [ID], Troels Deibjerg Kristensen,
Bo Kampmann Walther [ID], and Gunver Majgaard[(✉)] [ID]

University of Southern Denmark, Campusvej 55, 5230 Odense M, Denmark
gum@mmmi.sdu.dk

Abstract. This article consists of reflections and considerations concerning a virtual reality design case: *The Island of Play*. It is a multiuser virtual reality prototype aimed at maintaining and encouraging social relationships between long term hospitalized children and their friends. The motivation behind this design is the dire situation long term hospitalized children often find themselves in. They experience isolation and marginalization due to constraints from hospitalization. A consequence hereof is a limited access to social interaction as well as a reduced opportunity to play with friends from either home or school. *The Island of Play* was essentially designed to set up a virtual meeting place to stimulate socialization through play. This article sits at the intersection between game design theory and actual design impressions, with a particular focus on how real-world design interweaves with theoretical considerations. The argument that follows is structured over five sections: 1) First, we contemplate the design of the player's character. 2) Second, we scrutinize the relationship between game objects and playful interactions. 3) Then we move on to consider the design of social experiences, 4) followed by the fourth section where we inspect the value of the magic circle as a design metric. 5) Finally, in the fifth section, we reflect on the importance of weighing the player's sensation of purpose and skill against interacting with the application. Overall, this design case pivots around design issues and considerations involved in the development of play and game scenarios in a multiuser VR-application aimed at bolstering the social fabric between long term hospitalized children and their friends.

Keywords: Virtual reality · Multiplayer VR · Design issues and theory · Development · Virtual playground · Game design theory

1 Introduction

Children and adolescents with long term or chronic illnesses suffer not only from the consequences of their illness, but also from the solitary experience of living apart their known communities. A study made by the Danish state council to ensure childrens' rights, examined the social ramifications of patients who undergo long time hospitalization [35]. The hospitalizations greatly impact the childrens life: they become separated from their school setting and isolated from their friends. The study showed that

© The Author(s), under exclusive license to Springer Nature Switzerland AG 2022
J. Y. C. Chen and G. Fragomeni (Eds.): HCII 2022, LNCS 13317, pp. 465–484, 2022.
https://doi.org/10.1007/978-3-031-05939-1_32

25% of the children found their friendships and social relations negatively affected during their hospitalization. Two conclusions were drawn from this: on the one hand, it is important that hospitalized childrens' classmates and friends show understanding, interest, and empathy during their hospitalization [29]; on the other hand, it is vital that the same classmates and friends make an effort to keep in touch with their hospitalized friend. But classmates and friends of the hospitalized children find it difficult to maintain the social bond and share everyday experiences due to constraints imposed by the entire situation of isolation and separation. This dual challenge presents a situation, which we aim to mitigate by creating a third place: a virtual reality playground where the hospitalized child can meet up with their friends and vice versa.

Additionally, the expanding technical possibility of designing interesting multi-player virtual reality applications open new opportunities for design cases [2, 14, 32, 50]. The designs of multiuser virtual reality applications prompt new directions and trajectories for the development of educational games and play oriented scenarios.

In passing, it should be noted that immersive [5, 6, 11, 37, 39] multiuser virtual reality applications herald three-dimensional experiences viewed from a head mounted display [31]. We used wireless and standalone Oculus Quest virtual reality headsets so that no additional equipment was needed, and so that wires wouldn't get in the way and unnecessarily complicate the players' experience. The Oculus Quest headsets use eye-gaze and/or controllers (joysticks) to interact with the content of the virtual world. On a technical note, the oculus quest equipment registers head movements, and the two screens inside the head mounted display support the stereoscopic vision giving the user a sense of depth. The development of *The island of Play* aimed to take advantage of this newest design wrinkle. The methodology known as Design Thinking [3, 26, 27, 33, 34, 56], which forms the base of the following reflections, and which assists and guides the decision making in the development process, is enveloped by a long and wide range of game designers together with insights from formal game design theory [12, 16, 36, 44]. However, the offset of the development of *The Island of Play* was directed toward uplifting social and playful interactions aimed at maintaining and expanding the social networks between physically separated friends. In other words, the reflections and considerations of this design case focuses of the in-situ decision making directed and informed by the existing corpus of game design theory together with the intended users' evaluation (we could not test on actual long term hospitalized children during the corona pandemic). Instead, we play tested on four adolescents 12–19 years of age plus a variety of 4–6 adult users including both software developers and non-technical adults. The tests were done in iterations as part of the development process to guide the design decisions. The software developers were experts and provided feedback on the design and technical details, while the non-technical adults provided feedback on the usability. The feedback we got from the adolescents was mainly centered on playability, while all test informants provided feedback on bugs. This solution was obviously far from perfect; it did however yield important insights on the design.

In the following we shall dive more into how the design of *The Island of Play* combines playfulness, exploration, and character-driven world interaction, and how all this catapult social and meaningful experiences for hospitalized children. First by 1) reflecting on the player's character; 2) second, by thinking about the intersections between game objects and playful interactions; 3) third, by scrutinizing how to best design social experiences; 4) fourth, by inquiring the value of the concept of the magic circle; and finally, 5) by weighing the importance of the purpose and skill acquisition in relation to the overall design of the island. Thus, each section, from player character to play purpose (see Fig. 1 below), is devoted to the entanglement of a specific aspect of game design theory and how it might influence or direct actual design – which will run parallel to continuous play and game tests.

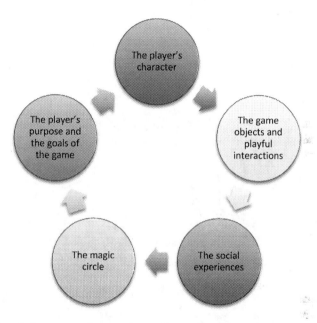

Fig. 1. The five design perspectives on the multiuser virtual reality playground *The Island of Play.*

However, striking an informed balance between theory and praxis is no easy feat. Nevertheless, the driving force behind the design of *The Island of Play* was the aforementioned aim of empowering friendships by enabling social relationships between the long-term hospitalized children and their friends in and out of school. The aspiration was to develop a multiuser virtual reality playground to alleviate the sensation of loneliness and isolation among hospitalized children by bridging the physical distance and the emotional separation between the everyday life of school and the secluded life lived in the hospital. The following sections highlights our design case, *The Island of Play*, and associated reflections on the challenges of designing playfulness to propel social relationships between physically distanced and isolated friends.

2   The Island of Play

The design of *The Island of Play* showcases an isolated and uninhabited tropical Island. The rationale for choosing this setting for the playground was to establish an emotional warm, evocative, and welcoming place distinctively different from the sterile atmosphere of traditional hospital surroundings. We drew inspiration from the computer game *The Witness* [66], which also features an island filled with natural and man-made structures and a bunch of hidden puzzles. Another inspiration was the game *The Legend of Zelda Breath of the Wild* [62]. Both games present relaxing puzzles for the players to investigate and explore. On top of that, these puzzles are embedded in worlds the players can move freely around in. Noteworthy in these games is also the perception of the color green [24]; as an inspirational tool we designed a mood board to get a sense of how players felt about the green color (see Fig. 2 below).

Fig. 2. Mood board to investigate the players' emotions and responses.

The result of our investigation of the mood board showed that players correlated the green color with relaxation, summertime, holidays, and spending happy days with friends. Those results convinced us to emphasize the green color in the design of *The Island of Play,* since those feelings were exactly the responses we were looking for. Finally, we hoped that such design would create an embracing space where children could interact, socialize, fool around, and have fun.

A top view of *The Island of Play* (see Fig. 3 below) showcases not only the entire island, but also the four main areas of embedded activities; a beach volley site, a labyrinth, woods, and the area where players arrive and depart from the island (start camp and helicopter pickup).

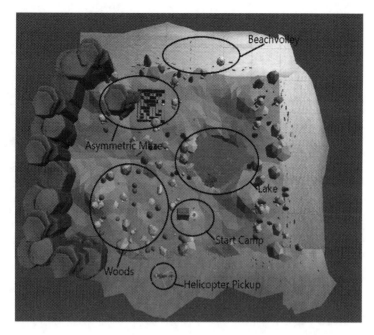

Fig. 3. An overview of the entire area of *The Island of Play*.

Our preliminary play tests demonstrated that when entering the application for the first time players looked around to familiarize themselves with the site followed by curiously moving about while figuring out how to interact with the surroundings. A general finding of ours was that players experimented with the surroundings to determine if and how objects responded. Simultaneously, the children were enthusiastic about navigating the spatial layout of the island.

On *The Island of Play* children locate activities based on the assumption that interactional objects create activity and become playful [15, 18, 48] if they abide to explicit rules and goals. For instance, one such activity has to do with finding and plucking cartoonish looking red and white mushrooms. This activity invites self-organized play scenarios, as our observations attested. Children plucked the mushrooms and in an elevated mood began to either playfully throw them up into the air or into the water; or they would teasingly throw them at each other while simultaneously jumping and crouching to avoid being hit by the incoming mushrooms.

Another example of a self-organized play activity happened around the game of beach volley. Either the children approached this in-game activity formally; or they utilized the game of volleyball in a multitude of unforeseen ways. The latter involved throwing the ball high into the air; balancing the ball on their fingertips; and bouncing the ball from one hand to the other and back again. As part of the island's design there is a radio placed on a table next to the beach volleyball. Here, children can listen to different kinds of music while playing around or spontaneously take up dancing on the beach, which, by the way, wasn't constrained by the lack of a bodily presentation: weaving hands and a moving head sufficed as 'dance'.

The labyrinth in the center of the island is filled with intriguing interactive obstacles. However, the children must work together to successfully navigate the maze. Thus, we introduced several techniques of interaction to facilitate cooperation; equipping and embedding twist and turns within the labyrinth as well as adding puzzle elements on top of the navigational challenge. The goal of the labyrinth, of course, is to safely navigate from the entrance to the exit, but in order to do so the child situated inside the labyrinth depends on assistance from the other child, which have to walk to the top of a hilltop next to the maze. From this vantage point the child can assists and guide her fellow playmate. The maze is therefore designed asymmetrically. One child must be inside the labyrinth while the other child assists in solving the challenging tasks. The intention behind this design was teamwork; to spark social interactions and a playful atmosphere between players.

Furthermore, the development of *The Island of Play* was intended to follow a scrum-based framework [46, 54] coupled with an agile iterative approach [25], user-testing [30], a continuous attention to design matters. However, the development process was - as noted above - disrupted by the arrival of covid-19. This obviously meant that playtesting in the hospital setting was out of the question.

3   Understanding Play

Since the development of *The Island of Play* focuses on play and game elements to promote playful, purpose-driven social interactions it is necessary to come to grip with what is meant by 'play' and 'games'.

In ludology, the (formal) study of computer games, a multitude of definitions and explanations of 'play' and 'gameplay' prevail often resulting in a confusing and rather non-consensual conceptualization [18, 21, 53]. However, within the scope of the present case, play is regarded as a free and voluntary activity that strengthens social relations and personal empowerment [19]. This understanding of play is inspired by Huizinga's [15] definition of play as "a free activity standing quite consciously outside "ordinary" life as being "not serious", but at the same time absorbing the player intensely and utterly. It is an activity connected with no material interest, and so no profit can be gained by it. It proceeds within its own proper boundaries of time and space according to fixed rules and in an orderly manner. It promotes the formation of social groupings which tend to surround themselves with secrecy and to stress their difference from the common world by disguise or other means" (p. 13 [15]).

In *The Island of Play* players engage in voluntary activities, which Huizinga most probably would regard as 'not serious' and without any 'material interest', such as plucking funny looking mushrooms and throwing them either around or after each other. Not only can players take on different roles and act accordingly whether outsiders view them as secretive or not; the can also involve themselves and engross their activities in situated social happenings: ephemeral social groupings such as oscillating between interacting socially or exploring the island while others are engaged in other activities.

Nonetheless, in contrast to play, games are usually considered goal dependent, relying on challenges, establishing clear rules together with indisputable procedures, concise feedback, and variable and quantifiable outcomes, which secure uneven results. This means that games should end differently each time they are played and with varied outcomes [10, 12, 22, 36].

Surely, play possesses the ability to evolve into games, which by some researchers' standards [57] insert games as a subset to play or as a natural evolutionary continuation of an initial formation of play. The tropical island of *The Island of Play* inspires formations of play outlined by Huizinga and to instill a playful attitude [43] in the players together with an opportunity for play to evolve into gameful [20] activities; the latter would happen through stricter and more rule driven activities [4], such as the beach volley and labyrinth activities both of which can be engaged with either playfully or as part of a structured, goal-oriented gameplay. We designed *The Island of Play* with this flexible dynamic in mind. The overall aim was to uplift essential play and game design elements and bring them front and center.

Our play-centric approach was inspired by Tracy Fullerton [12], Jesse Schell [45], and Robert [59] who all highlight the divide between formal and dramatic game design elements. This distinction is far from trivial. The formal game design elements place emphasis on players' patterns of interaction, the objectives of the game, the rules, and procedures of the game together with the resources of the system, the emerging challenges, and unpredictable outcomes. In light of formal game design elements our design took into account not only the number of players, but also their pattern of interaction. We aimed to create cooperative patterns of interaction to promote social interactions between players. This feature is especially apparent in the asymmetrical objectives build into the labyrinth at the center of the island. Asymmetrical objectives present players with different goals and mechanics [4, 47] defined as methods for interacting with the game state. These objectives and mechanics define what players aim toward within the rules or frame of the labyrinth. In *The Island of Play* rules act as a framework around the game, while the procedures dictate the agency of playing the game: who does what and when to achieve the objective(s) of the game. For instance, are players allowed turn taking? Turn taking between two cooperating players intro-duces social interaction and creates a sense of purpose, especially if the activity centers on realizing a common goal. Our play-testers underscored this assumption, i.e., they exhibited a heightened social interaction. Afterwards they said that the lack of stress together with turn taking greatly increased social interactions.

The dramatic elements, on the other hand, are concerned with the fictional fantasy and story of the game as they provide a context for gameplay [8, 9]. Not all games are mounted on narrative in their designs. This is evident in games such as Tetris [63], while other games like *The Stanley Parable* [65] build their entire gameplay experience [16] around characters, plots, and story [59].

Within the confines of this design case, we focused on the game design elements that assisted players in reaching goals as well as the play elements and structures of interaction. Of particular interest was the combination of play and game elements that fused into an experience that strengthened and enriched the players' social bonds – such as open-ended mushroom plucking and the asymmetrical design of the labyrinth.

4   Reflections on the Design of the Player's Character in *The Island of Play*

This section pivots on reflections on the design of playfulness regarding the player's character (avatar). In particular, we will look into the emotional connection between the player and her representation inside The Island of Play and further discuss how this representation fuels the commitment to play within the game world activities. Our findings showed that the bonds between avatar and player was both necessitated by and expressed through the players' commitment to playful activities. When players took on new identities, they assigned values and a certain intentionality to their avatars. According to game design theory, this happens regardless of whether the player becomes a hero in a fairytale or plays the role of a volleyball player. In the case of The Island of Play, the player was represented inside the virtual playground as an abstract shape and not as a well-crafted character. We equipped the player with an avatar in the shape of a three-dimensional cube together with two 'Stickmen'-like, 'free flowing' and moving hands ready for interaction (see Fig. 4 below).

Fig. 4. The character as the other player perceives it. The character is shaped by a 3D cube with free floating hands.

A few considerations regarding the shape of the avatar deserves to be mentioned. Character shapes are not as value free as one would assume. Most avatars are based on fundamental geometrical shapes: circle, square, and triangle [51]. Each shape encloses a range of symbolic values. The circle points toward innocence, youth, energy, movement, positivity, freedom, and relaxation. The square, on the other hand, makes symbolic reference to maturity, balance, stubbornness, strength, rest, restraint, rationality, conventionalism, and calmness. Lastly, the triangle is associated with aggression, force, instability, pain, sorrow, and tension. Of course, the primary shapes together with their identified symbolic values and sensations allow for a multitude of combinations and compositions expanding from the characters' shapes, their poses, the objects of the game, the lines of movement within the game environment, as well as the formation and contours of the surrounding milieu including the possible pathways laid out for the character. In line with this thinking *The Island of Play*-cube represents balance, stability, strength, and rationality. In the early phases of the design process the cube was thought of as a placeholder for later re-design. Luckily, we observed how the play testers took to and relished the raw cubic shape. The raw cubic shape allowed the play testers to inscribe and project their own fantasy onto the avatar. In other words, we thought the play testers would dislike the cube, but the opposite happened. The cube gave room to assign imaginary roles to the play activities, which falls well in line with theories of play and make-believe in the field of ludology [15, 18, 49]. Conclusively, the game designers decided to stick with the cube. In all fairness, this wasn't the only reason behind our decision: our project suffered, as is the case with so many others, of lack of development time, which in turn constituted a less inspiring second reason for leaving the character in its present cubic shape. In future iterations, however, taking the design theory and target group into account, an avatar of circular shape would most likely be preferable, especially since the circle easily accentuates youth, energy, movement, freedom, and perhaps most importantly, playfulness.

We accommodated the cube with free floating hands. The idea behind this design choice was that free floating hands would support non-verbal communication in the form of gestures: weaving, pointing, saluting, and so forth. From a practical perspective, the free-floating hands manifested the primary passageway of interaction with the objects of the virtual playground. The hands are maneuvered by physical controllers, which are translated into hand gestures inside the play world. The play testers seemed to relate to the hands as they function in real life, i.e., as 'tools' to grab, move, lift, throw, and catch objects inside the play world.

Beyond these design choices other unexplored options are available. In particular, that character designs can be integrated into schematic story arcs such as the Hero's Journey [7], in such a way that players could act out and play the characters of a multitude of different known stories. Other design possibilities could be 3D-scans of the actual real-world player, which would bridge and remix virtual reality representations with the player's appearance in actual reality. However, interpolating the player's real-world presence onto the virtual representation could prove to be an unsound strategy. Especially since, from a theoretical viewpoint at least, such a strategy could conflict with the players' behavior of projecting their own fantasies onto the shape of an avatar. In conclusion, it remains an open question whether it would work to 3D-scan the players to create avatars; perhaps it would strengthen the social bond between players; or perhaps it would undermine their playful behavior. However, as is always the case with the development of interesting artefacts, playtests are required to determine whether such reservations are right or wrong.

5 Reflections on the Design of Game Objects and Playful Interactions in *The Island of Play*

The design of engaging gameplay [8, 9] is far from easy: it requires insight, careful calibration, and meticulous balancing [10] with a firm focus on the players' experience during play [16, 58]. Research shows that players' exertion of what they feel during gameplay can be translated into exciting game mechanics [4, 47, 59]. Game mechanics are interesting since they constitute the ways players interact with the game state; walking, running, crouching, jumping, swimming, swinging, shooting etc. Game mechanics are the 'verbs' of the game: all the stuff the player can do. Game mechanics should not be confused with game feel, which is defined as "real-time control of virtual objects in a simulated space, with interactions emphasized by polish" [55 p. 6]. Game feel is contrary to game mechanics, as the former evolves around player sensations derived from the interactions with a responsive game system [58]. However, both game mechanics and game feel direct design intentions: on the one hand they outline the formal ways of interacting with a game state (game mechanics), and on the other hand they demonstrate how such interactions feel (from a player-centric perspective). In The Island of Play, game mechanics and game feel both primed and guided our design decisions. We focused on creating game objects that allowed for a wide range of uses – such as plucking the aforementioned mushrooms.

A common design complication is the tension between freedom and control. This involves the tension between, on the one hand, the player's ability to roam around freely while exploring the surroundings and interacting with the objects in the surroundings, or, on the other hand, to feel boxed in; to be inserted into a rigid structure without ample space for self-directed maneuvering [43]. Our design approach valued the players' self-directed and free movement as opposed to a task-laden structure that places emphasis on a structure which dictates 'do x' before you can 'do y' and before 'z' happens, and so on. This design choice, we hoped, would inspire intriguing play scenarios since the players were left to figure out how to move about and use the available objects. The approach turned out to be right: players did move about freely and felt inspired to explore in their own pace and by their own volition.

However, beyond the complicated tension between freedom and control, we faced other design challenges, first and foremost how to design proper patterns for playful interactions with the game objects. This design challenge hinges on the creation of an environment rich with objects, we discovered. It is important to note, that game objects should be understood by their properties, behaviors, and relationships, as defined by Fullerton [12]. For instance, "Mario's properties, behaviors, and relationships in the Super Mario-series [62] are centered around his ability to run, jump [game mechanics], and collect coins, mushrooms, nuts, and flowers (game objects), which in turn provide the player with an extra life, make Mario glide through the air, or shoot fireballs" [21 p. 5]. All these properties available to the player affect how she chooses to traverse the obstacles of the levels. Hence, players' interactions with objects within the frame of gameplay and within the game world should feel meaningful, which is to say, they should be both discernable and integrated. "Discernable actions mean that the result of a game action is communicated to the player in a perceivable way [while the other] component of meaningful play requires that the relationship between action and outcome is integrated into the larger context of the game" [43, p. 34–35]. The quote above signals that interactions with objects should be clearly communicated while simultaneously affecting the game state now and later. Chess is a prime example of this case: the player moves a chess piece, which is discernable, and the action creates meaning here and now; but the move also dictates meaning later on: it is a move that directly influences the future game state.

Another design challenge concerns the pattern of interaction that arises from how players choose to interact with each other. Here, designers should explore and consider the following questions: Are players equipped with the same mechanics or do they interact with the game state through different means (different mechanics)? Also, how do these interaction mechanics tie into the social dynamics of players? How can the players interact with each other? Does communication consist in using gestures, chat messaging, or perhaps voice commands? Or is the interaction rather mediated by game objects where one player picks up a ball and throws it to the other player who in turn could catch the ball and/or return it to the first player? Questions such as these uncover the spatial game environment instrumental in developing The Island of Play. We populated the island with game objects which we hoped would create playful and social interactions. In other words, players should be able to interact with the game object – and then things would happen. Two play testers demonstrated this case when they explored the intricacies of the objects present on the island. In Fig. 5 below, the players engaged with the beach volley opportunity by throwing the ball to each other, which in this case ended up in the water: presenting a problem to solve together.

Fig. 5. The two players throw a beach ball to each before it ends up in the water. Luckily, the players can easily fetch the ball. If they choose not to fetch the ball it will drift to shore.

Yet another design consideration behind the ambition of enriching the *The Island of Play* with plentiful objects to interact with was the notion of the empowered agent [13]. This should be understood within the context of an affordance network: the digital playground presents game objects to be acted on with socially agreed upon trajectories.

These considerations of game design rest on the notion that players shouldn't be viewed as game consumers, but as producers of play experiences. We observed that players attuned themselves to the environment of *The Island of Play*, in that they developed *effectivity sets*, i.e., means for interacting with the surroundings and each other, thereby activating and enhancing their *life-worlds* [1]. The non-directed game objects did what we hoped for: they created self-directed play, which oscillated between individual enquiries and social interaction. In conclusion of this section, we would have liked to populate the island with even greater numbers of interesting game objects, since they seem to drive a host of inspiring social play scenarios that enhance the bond between the players. The following section will tune in and focus more on the social experience of *The Island of Play*.

6   Reflections on the Design of Social Experiences in *The Island of Play*

For most children and teens gaming is a social activity and a major component in their social life [28]. Teens play games in a variety of ways and for numerous reasons, which include inviting others to join in game sessions in person, online (through Discord or by phone or sometimes both depending on connectivity), and of course by themselves. Studies have found that three-quarters of teens play games with others some of the time [28]. Close to half of the teens who play online games do so with people they know in their offline lives. Keeping in touch with friends and maintaining friendships are done by social media and through multiplayer games. In *The Island of Play* the players can socialize with each other in a playful manner using the present game objects: the beach ball, the music device, and the mushrooms. In multiplayer games players often can decide from various types of user interaction patterns: player vs player; cooperative play; team competition, and multiple individual players versus game [12]. In *The Island of Play* players can use voice-chat, gestures, and game objects to communicate.

However, designing social experiences in computer games and virtual reality hinges on several things. For one, multiplayer play or game worlds must invite social interactions: the possibility for establishing *and* maintaining social relationships. When players engage in multiplayer games, they find themselves participating in and expanding each other's "life-worlds". In other words, multiplayer games possess the ability to influence each other's experience of play. This seemingly innocent insight is important since it calls for thinking about how, why, and when players influence each other's experience of play.

In *The Island of Play*, we tried to incorporate cooperative play activities together with player versus player interaction patterns (voice-chat, gestures, interacting with game objects). When players fooled around with the pluckable mushrooms or joyously threw the volleyball into the air or out to sea, we observed, they found themselves engaged in inclusive play. The opposite was true, we discovered, when the players engaged in a formal game (match) of beach volley, in which case the players partic- ipated in a player versus player game-like structure. Consequently, the players became more competitive and less forgiving of each other. It deserves to be mentioned that, in the game of beach volley, the players had the opportunity to either follow preestab- lished rules or develop their own set of rules, values, and countable outcomes [23, 41], which they did on more than one occasion. Still, neither the play nor the game-like activities were fixed and predetermined; they existed only as options and not as points or places that had to be conquered to progress further into the game world.

However, when players engaged with the labyrinth at the center of the island they had to asymmetrically work together to explore and unearth the hidden secrets of the labyrinth. Thus, when players explored the labyrinth they cooperated against the game system, so to speak. And they did so by different means: players occupied different roles and used diverging methods for interacting with the game state. I.e., player one walked through the maze in an effort to discover the needed key codes, while player two, from the mountain top afar, oversaw the labyrinth and punched in the key codes received by voice-chat. This meant that player two, in the receiving end, acted upon the verbal inputs from player one.

This asymmetric pattern of interaction design instantiated the desired form of cooperative play. In other words, if players desired to combat the labyrinth they could do so, but they would have to work with the other player; they would have to communicate with each other to complete the task (see Fig. 6).

Fig. 6. To the left a screenshot of the labyrinth from the perspective of player two. The picture to the right is viewed from the perspective of player one.

The interaction patterns of *The Island of Play* hold potential to be developed even further by including more players and/or more diverse challenges and obstacles with even more player roles. However, the play test revealed that longer lasting activities were the self-directed play scenarios driven by the objects of *The Playful Island*. Thus, further development should focus on developing a wider range of diverse options of playful interactions with objects that inspire solitary *and* cooperative play.

7 Reflections on Using the Magic Circle for Design in *The Island of Play*

We set out with an idea of play derived from Huizinga [14]. His explanation of how play takes place inside what he coined 'the magic circle' [43] seemed to resonate well not only with our understanding of play, but also with our design challenge of making a virtual playground within which children would play and socialize. However, Hui-zinga's concept of the magic circle deserves an introduction. Broadly speaking, 'the magic circle' circumferences and outlines the conceptual, mental, and physical experiences as well as the boundaries of a play space [38], which in our case is the conceptual and digital geography of *The Island of Play*.

The conceptual framework of the magic circle highlights how two different places (spaces or states) are separated by a clear boundary [14, 17]. The segregation distinguishes an 'inside' of a game or play activity from an 'outside' of the selfsame game or play activity. This distinction is attributed to Huizinga's characterization of play as an activity separated from ordinary life.

In computer games as well as in virtual reality game worlds, the physical boundaries between the game world and real world are obvious and easy to distinguish. However, the boundaries quickly blur when the experience of taking part in a make-believe play scenario meshes with the physical surroundings. Here, the experience of make-believe play can conjure up magical scenarios where players find themselves immersed in serious play activities in otherwise ordinary surroundings. Thus, make-believe play becomes quite fantastic; especially when we think of our ability to create and enter vivid scenarios driven entirely by a mental simulation. Here, we should remember that we have no problem of convincingly imagining something while simultaneously knowing that the imagery isn't real at all. We move in and out of such scenarios with ease.

Nonetheless, the ambition of *The Island of Play* was to inspire make-believe play inside a virtual playground advanced by compelling imagery and interesting objects to interact with. To achieve this lofty ambition, *The Island of Play* is populated, as already mentioned, with several playful objects designed to animate flexible, negotiable, and 'open ended' activities as opposed to traditional game-like structures, which focus on goals, challenges, feedback, and quantifiable outcomes. But accentuating playful activities within *The Island of Play* is not the same as stating that game-like activities, such as the labyrinth, do not hold a place there as well. Thus, both playful interactions and game-like activities may populate the magic circle; our play testers easily shifted between modes of play and modes of gaming.

Moreover, the virtual playground could easily integrate more game-like features similar to those found in e.g. *Minecraft* [60]. We could introduce building options as well as a mechanic for killing hostile zombies, or perhaps running deep into dangerous dungeons, as in *Minecraft Dungeons* [61]. In short, a future design option could be to present players with a common goal, introduce several challenges, and further implement a variety of upgradable options to choose from. All of this, however, should be designed in such a way that players would have to work together. We should never abandon the socializing aspects of the play world, as it speaks directly into the vision of the game: to promote and sustain friendship.

Traditionally, game goals provide players with a sense of purpose, while challenges hinder the progress of reaching said goal. Upgradable options underscore progression and merge both intrinsic and extrinsic motivation [42]. When limitations are added to the mix, they can inspire players' perseverance and the evolution of creative strategies for reaching a particular goal [36]. Another design option could be to integrate quest-like structures like the ones found in the mobile game *Animal crossing: Pocket Camp*

[64]. Here, players engage in a social simulation where they customize their avatars and inhabit their living spaces; furnish camp sites with utilities not forgetting the option of gathering tradeable materials such as cotton and wood. All in all, a target group identical to that of *The Island of Play*.

When we look at the simulated 'physical' boundaries of the magic circle of *The Island of Play* it is constituted by the surrounding ocean of the island. The Island itself figures as a mixture between a playground and a deserted tropical island. The overall ambience of the Island is intended to elicit a vacation-like sensation, a promising, pleasant, and cozy experiences. Indeed, the players shouldn't expect monster encounters. Instead, *The Island of Play* radiates safeness, tranquility, and a playful atmosphere. Birds are singing, the sea is calm, and the world is at peace (see Fig. 7).

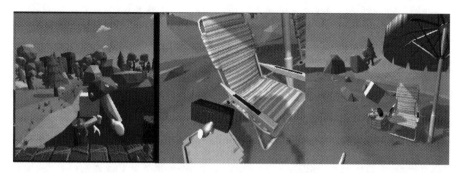

Fig. 7. The screenshot to the left show players having fun picking mushrooms, while the beach scenario on the screenshot to the right depicts the players' search for music through the airwaves of the music box. The music quickly fades when players leave the area.

Considering the Players' Sensation of Purpose and Development of Skills in The Island of Play

When we designed and play tested *The Island of Play* we gave attention to the possible goals of the activities of play. Goals in games, as already noted, present players with targets to strive for, which instils a sense of purpose. Furthermore, goals provide players with trajectories toward accomplishments within the confines of the rules of the game. Moreover, goals and challenges grant players the time and place to practice interactions and sharpen their skills [21] – all to reach the end goal of the game. Additionally, the goals of a game activity tend to set the tone and atmosphere of the entire game. All in all, goals are important; they establish a complex web of aspirations, purposes, and possibilities for navigating the game space.

We wanted to tap into those dynamics, and especially emphasize the sensation of purpose. We discovered to our surprise that play scenarios where the players interacted with objects also instantiated a sense of purpose. For instance, when players discovered how to pick mushrooms and afterwards learned how to throw them, they experienced purpose while simultaneously gaining insight into the operations of the game system. Also, when players embraced the teleport ability – yes, we included such a device to maneuver the island – they immediately felt purposeful, as the device was instrumental in navigating the landscape of the game world. Later, when players figured out how to collaboratively manage the different player roles to successfully penetrate the labyrinth, they again felt a sense of purpose. The players got this sensation when they communicated and assisted each other in a mutual effort to unveil the secret digits and hidden keys inside the labyrinth. Especially the labyrinth provided the players with a shared goal and therefore a shared purpose. Important, however, the rules of operating and navigating the labyrinth are fixed and unchangeable. Thus, the rules are not negotiable. But players are, of course, not prevented from inventing their own rules ('house rules'). Playtesting revealed how players placed they own inventions on top of the existing parameters. If, for instance, some players found traversing the labyrinth amusing while listening to the music box while carrying mushrooms. Such behavior has no bearing on solving the mysteries of the labyrinth. Nonetheless, we went to great length to make sure that the parameters for and the rules themselves attuned or aligned with the players' opportunity for interaction and progressing their skill levels.

In *The Island of Play* we also ensured that players were presented with amble opportunities to enthuse playful activities – collecting and tossing objects around, as previously mentioned – while simultaneously training and honing the players' abilities for teleporting, griping, and letting go of collected objects, and, finally, accustoming themselves with the physics of the world. Certifying that players learn in incremental steps – whereby they gradually expand their knowledge of the game space [20] – constitutes a vital component in the design of an immersive [6] experience. Additionally, in-game goals also prepare players for future challenges; they must plan, negotiate directions, and come to terms with their choices. The labyrinth sets the stage for applying the learned abilities, so that players must work together toward a common goal, which in turn inspires social interaction between the players.

In carefully crafted games, players gradually learn new abilities and mechanics in clear successive steps. However, these games must also present the players with opportunities to practice and sharpen their skills by engrossing them in challenges they need to accomplish if they want to continue. Normally, players regard their skills first and foremost as strategies for accomplishing desired goals and only secondarily as a set of discrete and discernable skills [13]. In *the Playful Island*, the playful activities were some of the most successful ones of the entire game. In general terms, our observations prompted a call to redesign and rethink the exact overall number of interactable objects, as they both encompass and promote play, and thus highlighting a key takeaway of this project: that play objects should be favored over game-like scenarios.

Reflections on Designing The Island of Play: A Summary

In essence, our reflections on the design case of *The Island of Play* have focused on five design considerations. Together they encompass a matrix that focus not only on the design of the game itself but also on the player's experience of the interaction with the game. These reflections engross both a game-centric and a play-centric approach to design, which spring from a sometimes diffuse and elusive understanding of what play is, as dealt with in the above. Nevertheless, the five considerations of design can be summed up as follows: 1) Reflections on the design of the player's character. 2) Thinking about the playfulness of the game objects. 3) Questions of how to accelerate the social interaction between the players. 4) Reflecting upon the magic circle. And, finally, 5) diving into the player's sense of purpose of the game.

8   Conclusion

The description of our design case, *The Island of Play*, stressed several hands-on design considerations in the design of a playful multiuser virtual reality playground: *The Island of Play*. These experiences and considerations constitute the bulk of this article. Reflections sprung from the in-house development of a multiplayer Virtual Reality application, which we have dubbed *The Island of Play*. As described and discussed above, the ambitions behind *The Island of Play* was to create a virtual play space where long term hospitalized children could socialize and play with their friends from school and home. We anticipated, from our research into play, that playful activities could be created from open-ended interactions as well as using game-like structured designs. We hope and think our considerations of design are applicable to a host of design cases, which focus on virtual play worlds entailing playful interactions – whether driven by the ambition to develop virtual reality sites for playful social interactions; or whether they are novel spaces in the ever-expanding field of Serious Games.

References

1. Barab, S.A., Roth, W.-M.: Curriculum-based ecosystems: supporting knowing from an ecological perspective. Educ. Res. **35**(5), 3–13 (2006)
2. Boling, E.: The need for design cases: disseminating design knowledge. Int. J. Des. Learn. **1** (1), 1–8 (2010). http://scholarworks.iu.edu/journals/index.php/ijdl/index
3. Brown, T.: Design Thinking. Harvard Business Review, pp. 1–10 (2010)
4. Burgun, K.: Clockwork Game Design, 1st edn. Focal Press, Burlington, MA (2015)
5. Calleja, G.: In-Game – From Immersion to Incorporation. The MIT Press Cambridge, Massachusetts, USA (2011)
6. Calleja, G.: Revising immersion: a conceptual model for the analysis of digital game involvement. In: Situated Play, Proceedings of DiGRA. http://www.digra.org/digital-library/publications/revising-immersion-a-conceptual-model-forthe-analysis-of-digital-game-involvement/ (2007). Retrieved 10 Nov 2020
7. Campbell, J.: The Hero with a Thousand Faces. New World Library, California, USA (2008)
8. Costikyan, G.: I have no words & i must design: toward a critical vocabulary for games. In: Proceedings of Computer Games and Digital Conference, Tampere University Press. http://www.digra.org/digital-library/publications/i-have-no-wordsi-must-design-toward-a-critical-vocabulary-for-games/ (2002)
9. Larsen, L.J., Walther, B.K.: The ontology of gameplay: toward a new theory. Games Cult. **15**(6), 609–631 (2020). https://doi.org/10.1177/1555412019825929
10. Elias, G.S., Garfield, R., Gutschera, K.R.: Characteristics of Games. MIT Press, Cambridge (2012)
11. Frasca, G.: Immersion, outmersion & critical thinking. http://www.dream.dk/uploads/files/Gonzalo%20Frasca.pdf (2008)
12. Fullerton, T.: Game Design Workshop, 3rd edn. Elsevier, Morgan Kaufmann Publishers (2014)
13. Gee, J.P.: Learning by design: good video games as learning machines. E-Learn. Dig. Media **2**(1), 5–16 (2005)

14. Howard, C.D.: Writing and rewriting the instructional design case: a view from two sides. Int. J. Des. Learn. **2**(1), 40–55 (2011). http://scholarworks.iu.edu/journals/index.php/ijdl/index

15. Huizinga, J.: Homo Ludens—A Study of the Play-element in Culture. Martino Publishing, Mansfield Centre (2014)

16. Isbister, K.: How Games Move us—Emotion by Design. Playful Thinking Series MIT Press, Cambridge and London, England (2017)

17. Larsen, L.J., Majgaard, G.: The concept of the magic circle and the Pokémon GO phenomenon. In: Geroimenko, V. (ed.) Augmented Reality Games I, pp. 33–50. Springer, Cham (2019). https://doi.org/10.1007/978-3-030-15616-9_3

18. Larsen, L.J.: Play and space—towards a formal definition of play. Int. J. Play **4**(2), 175–189 (2015). https://doi.org/10.1080/21594937.2015.1060567

19. Larsen, L.J., Majgaard, G.: Expanding the game design space: teaching computer game design in higher education. Designs Learn. **8**(1), 13–22 (2016)

20. Larsen, L.J.: Play and gameful movies: the ludification of modern cinema. Games Cult. **14** (5), 455–477 (2019). https://doi.org/10.1177/1555412017700601

21. Larsen, L.J.: The play of champions: toward a theory of skill in eSpor. Sport Ethics Philos. **16**(1), 130–152 (2020). https://doi.org/10.1080/17511321.2020.1827453

22. Juul, J.: The game, the player, the world: looking for a heart of gameness. In: Copier, M., Raessens, J. (eds.) Level Up: Digital Games Research Conference Proceedings, pp. 30–45. Utrecht University, Utrecht (retrieved 10–04–2018) http://www.jesperjuul.net/text/gameplayerworld/ (2003)

23. Juul, J.: Half-Real—Video Games Between Real Rules and Fictional Worlds. The MIT Press, Cambridge, Massachusetts, London, England (2005)

24. Kaya, N., Epps, H.H.: Relationship between color and emotion: a study of college students. Coll. Stud. J. **38**(3), 396–405 (2004)

25. Keith, C.: Scrum rising—Agile development could save your studio. Retrieved 21 Nov 2020, from http://www.clintonkeith.com/resources/ScrumRising.pdf (2007)

26. Kimbell, L.: Rethinking design thinking: part I. Des. Cult. **3**(3), 285–306 (2011)

27. Kimbell, L.: Rethinking design thinking: part II. Des. Cult. **4**(2), 129–148 (2012)

28. Lenhart, A., et al.: Teens' gaming experiences are diverse and include significant social interaction and civic engagement. Pew internet & American life project 1615 l st., nw– suite 700, Washington, D.C. 20036 (2008)

29. Li, W.H., Chung, J.O., Ho, E.K.: The effectiveness of therapeutic play, using virtual reality computer games, in promoting the psychological well-being of children hospitalised with cancer. J. Clin. Nurs. **20**(15–16), 2135–2143 (2011)

30. Macklin, C., Sharp, J.: Games, Design and Play: A Detailed Approach to Iterative Game Design. Addison-Wesley, US (2016)

31. Majgaard, G., Weitze, C.: Virtual experiential learning, learning design and interaction in extended reality simulations. In: Proceedings of the European Conference on Games-based Learning (2020). https://doi.org/10.34190/GBL.20.010

32. Lyk, P.B., Majgaard, G., Dietrich, T., Stock, C.: Co-Designing an immersive and interactive alcohol resistance training tool using 360-degree video. In: Proceedings of the 13th European Conference on Game Based Learning, ECGBL 2019. Academic Conferences and Publishing International, pp. 450–458. (2019) https://doi.org/10.34190/GBL19.081

33. Majgaard, G.: Quick and dirty group testing of mobile app for educators teaching digital literacy and production. In: Proceedings of the 15th European Conference on Game Based Learning ECGBL 2021. Academic Conferences and Publishing International, pp. 509–515. (2021) https://doi.org/10.34190/GBL.21.048

34. Majgaard, G.: The playful and reflective game designer. Electron. J. E-Learn. **12**(3), 271–280 (2014)
35. Malm, T., er al.: Jeg er ikke min sygdom, ed. I am not my illness. Børnerådet (2017)
36. McGonigal, J.: Reality is broken. Jonathan Cape, London, England (2011)
37. McMahan, A.: Immersion, Engagement, and Presence: A Method for Analyzing 3-D Video Games in The Video Game Theory Reader. Routledge, UK (2003)
38. Montola, M., Stenros, J., Waern, A.: Pervasive Games: Theory and Design. CRC Press (2009). https://doi.org/10.1201/9780080889795
39. Murray, J.: Hamlet on the Holodeck. MIT Press, Cambridge (1997)
40. Natalie, A., Williams, A.B.: Importance of Play for Young Children Facing Illness and Hospitalization: Rationale, Opportunites and a Case Study Illustration. Early Child Development and Care. Taylor and Francis, UK (2019)
41. Rogers, S.: Level Up—The Guide to Great Video Game Design, 2nd edn. Wiley, UK (2014)
42. Ryan, R.M., Deci, E.L.: Intrinsic and extrinsic motivations: classic definitions and new directions. Contemp. Educ. Psychol. **25**(1), 54–67 (2000)
43. Salen, K., Zimmerman, E.: Rules of Play—Game Design Fundamentals. The MIT Press, Cambridge, Massachusetts, London, England (2004)
44. Salmond, M.: Video Game Level Design. Bloomsbury, London, New York, Oxford, New Delhi, Sydney (2021)
45. Schell, J.: The Art of Game Design: A Book of Lenses, 2nd edn. CRC Press, Boca Raton, FL (2008)
46. Schwaber, K.: Agile Project Management with Scrum. Microsoft Press A Division of Microsoft Corporation, US (2004)
47. Sicart, M.: Defining game mechanics. Game Studies, 8. http://gamestudies.org/0802/articles/sicart (2008)
48. Sicart, M.: Play Matters. The MIT Press, Cambridge, Massachusetts, London, England (2014)
49. Dorothy, G., Singer, J.L.: Reflections on pretend play, imagination, and child development. Interview Am. J. Play **6**(1), 1–14 (2013). https://www.journalofplay.org/sites/www.journalofplay.org/files/pdf-articles/6-1-interview-relections-on-pretend-play.pdf
50. Smith, K.M.: Producing the rigorous design case. Int. J. Des. Learn. **1**(1), 9–20 (2010). http://scholarworks.iu.edu/journals/index.php/ijdl/index
51. Solarski, C.: Interactive Stories and Video Game Art—A Storytelling Framework for Game Design. CRC Press, Taylor and Francis Group, London and New York (2017)
52. Squire, K.: Video games in education. Comput. Entertain. **2**(1), 49–62 (2005)
53. Stenros, J.: The game definition game: a review. Games and Cult. **12**(6), 499–520 (2017). https://doi.org/10.1177/1555412016655679
54. Sutherland, J.: Scrum Handbook. Retrieved 23 Nov 2020, from http://www.scrummaster.dk/lib/AgileLeanLibrary/People/JeffSutherland/scrumhandbook.pdf (2010)
55. Swink, S.: Game Feel: A Designer's Guide to Visual Sensation. CRC Press, Taylor & Francis Group, Boca Raton, London, New York (2009)
56. Tonkinwise, C.: Design studies—what is it good for? Des. Cult. **6**(1), 5–43 (2014)
57. Walther, B.K.: Playing and gaming - reflections and classifications. Game Studies the Int. J. Comput. Game Cult. 3(1) (2003). Available at: http://www.gamestudies.org/0301/walther/
58. Walther, B.K., Larsen, L.J.: Bicycle kicks and camp sites: towards a phenomenological theory of game feel with special attention towards 'rhythm.' Convergence: The Int. J. Res. into New Media Technol. **26**(5–6), 1248–1268 (2020). https://doi.org/10.1177/1354856519885033
59. Zubek, R.: Elements of Game Design. The MIT Press, Massachusetts, London, England (2020)

Ludography

60. Minecraft. Mojang Studios (2011)
61. Minecraft Dungeons. Mojang Studios (2020)
62. Super Mario Series. Nintendo (1985–2015)
63. Tetris. Infogrames (1984)
64. The Legend of Zelda Breath of the Wild. Nintendo (2017)
65. The Stanley Parable. Galactic Café (2011)
66. The Witness. Thekla (2016)

Development of an Invisible Human Experience System Using Diminished Reality

Maho Sasaki$^{(\boxtimes)}$, Hirotake Ishii, Kimi Ueda, and Hiroshi Shimoda

Graduate School of Energy Science, Kyoto University,
Yoshida Honmachi, Sakyo-ku, Kyoto 606-8501, Japan
{sasaki,hirotake,ueda,shimoda}@ei.energy.kyoto-u.ac.jp

Abstract. In this study, we have been developing a diminished reality system that allows users to experience becoming invisible human in order to reduce self-awareness and to improve their self-esteem. The system employs a camera to capture the user's view and replaces his/her body images with background images in real time. These processed images are shown with a head mounted display to realize the immersive experience of becoming invisible human. The image inpainting is performed by a deep learning network. We also created a training and validation datasets and compared three networks. These networks are designed for image inpainting in this study. Moreover, we have made a hypothetical model of how psychological states and self-awareness will change when experiencing the developed system. In the future work, we are planning to conduct an experiment and confirm whether use of the system improves self-esteem. Also, we will investigate the process of changing the psychological state based on the hypothetical model by questionnaire surveys.

Keywords: Diminished reality · Deep learning · Invisible human · Psychological model

1 Introduction

It is important to have high self-esteem for living healthy and fulfilling life, however, some people have low self-esteem and it is difficult for them to improve their self-esteem by themselves. Although some studies on improving self-esteem [1] have focused an idea that people can improve their self-esteem by taking initiative and working with others, people with low self-esteem sometimes have trouble in working and communicating with others in the long term. Then, if a system is developed which can improve self-esteem easily, it will help people with low self-esteem to live happy life. Low self-esteem might be caused by estimating a large gap between real-self and ideal-self and hating themselves or evaluating themselves excessively low. For these reasons, we have focused on the possibility of changing the perceived self and improving self-esteem when people become invisible and experience diminished existences of themselves [2].

© The Author(s), under exclusive license to Springer Nature Switzerland AG 2022
J. Y. C. Chen and G. Fragomeni (Eds.): HCII 2022, LNCS 13317, pp. 485–494, 2022.
https://doi.org/10.1007/978-3-031-05939-1_33

In this study, we have developed a diminished reality system that allows people to experience becoming invisible and to reduce their self-awareness and improve their self-esteem. After we build this system, we are planning to conduct some experiments to evaluate the developed system. Also, we aim at revealing how people change their perception of themselves when they use the invisible human experience system based on the hypothetical model of psychological change.

2   Development of an Invisible Human Experience System

2.1   Overview of the Proposed System

In this study, we have proposed a system that provides an invisibility experience. In other words, this system provides the sense of becoming invisible human by making their body invisible to themselves (Fig. 1).

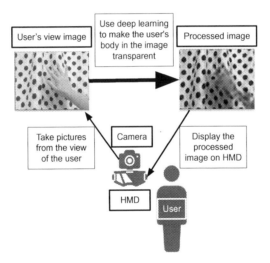

Fig. 1. Overview of the proposed system.

This system equips a head mounted display(HMD) to show the images in order to realize an immersive experience. A camera is attached to the HMD to capture the field of user's view. The camera acquires images in real time and uses them as input images. The next step is to eliminate the body images of the user from the input images and replace them with background images. There are two main possible ways of removing the user's body and replacing with the background. The first one is to detect objects within a certain distance from the camera based on depth information and replace the objects with a 3D model of the experience environment created in advance. However, there are some problems in this method that it is difficult to create an accurate 3D model and the quality of the experience may be low because it cannot deal with a dynamically changing environment. In particular, it is difficult to reproduce under the hand when the user lifts an object with their hand. The second way is to employ inpainting technique using deep learning in order to generate realistic images. In this method, detecting body regions and replacing with the background images might deal with dynamically changing environments. For this reason, we decided to apply the deep learning for inpainting images.

2.2   Outline of Body Region Inpainting Using Deep Learning

In this section, the specific method of body region inpainting using deep learning is described.

First, we introduce the method of inpainting using deep learning in conventional studies. There are mainly two methods which use Generative Adversarial Network(GAN) [3–5] and the encoder-decoder model [6,7]. Although GAN can be used to generate images that looks realistic. Due to the large network size of GAN, processing time will be long and it may be difficult to realize the real-time processing.

In the encoder-decoder model, the model using an autoencoder consisting of an encoder and a decoder part is trained by the dataset consisting of the pairs of input images and grand truth images, which enables us to recover a natural background image based on the surrounding images after eliminating body regions such as hands. Nian Cai et al. realized the real-time inpainting using CNN [6]. In this method, it is possible to infer the location of the images to be inpainted even when the location is not known in advance. The problem with using CNNs is that the repaired part of the images may be blurred [7].

In this study, we use encoder-decoder network because GAN is not suitable for the system that requires real time processing. Also, we create a new training dataset and train the models with it instead of using some existing datasets. Then, we compare multiple networks and use the best network for the purpose of improving the quality of the invisible human experience.

The networks are shown in the Fig. 2. The explanation of each network is described below. First, Fig. 2(a) is a simple network with combined encoder and decoder. The former part, the encoder, is a two-layered network with the first layer being a combination of convolutional layers and activation functions repeated three times until Max pooling is performed. The size of the image is halved in one layer, so that an input image of 120×160 is down sampled to 30×40. In the latter part, the decoder, unpooling is repeated twice to bring the output image back to the size of the original input image. It is assumed that the encoder part extracts the information of the background area excluding the body area.

Then the decoder part restores the background image based on the information obtained through the encoder part. Next, Fig. 2(b) is a slightly customized version of the network (a). In network (a), only the decoder part is used to generate the output image, while in network (b) it is expected that the output image is generated using the raw data of the input image by implementing a shortcut connection using the add layer. Also, we add batch normalization layers between convolutional layers and activation function layers. We expected that this would allow us to generate more appropriate background images, since the decoder part can concentrate on recovering only the background of the user's body. Finally, Fig. 2(c) is almost the same network as (b), however, it uses concatenate layer instead of add layer in the shortcut connection. By using concatenate, it would be possible to generate images keeping both the data that passed through the encoder-decoder part and the raw data of the input images. In other words, it would be possible to generate the output images using the raw data of the input images for the region except the body and using the image recovered by the encoder-decoder part for the body region. The Rectified Linear Unit function (ReLU function) is used as the activation function in the all networks.

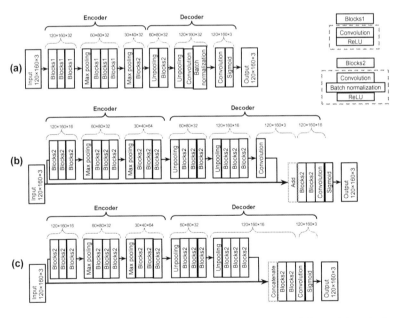

Fig. 2. The structure of networks (a) Encoder-decoder model (b) Model with shortcut connection using add layer (c) Model with shortcut connection using concatenate layer.

2.3 How to Create Dataset

Figure 3 shows how to create dataset. We prepare images with a part of the body as input images and images without the body as grand truth images. Specifically, the grand truth images are taken from various distances and angles of the environment and objects that the users will see during the experience of being invisible. Then, the images of only a part of body are randomly superimposed on the grand truth images. The image with only a part of the body was created by taking pictures of the body such as hand on a green background from various directions and then removing the green regions like chroma key processing. The image size is 640 pixels wide and 480 pixels high. 2500 images of the background and 1000 images of the hands were taken. In order to remove the similar images, we employed the method as described in the reference [8]. The Hamming distance was 0.1 for the background images and 0.05 for the hand images, and the images above these values were held. After that, 400 and 300 images were randomly selected from the remaining images respectively and they were used to create the dataset. As a result, 120,000 pairs of images were prepared for the training dataset, which is a combination of these images. The examples of the images used in the dataset are shown in Fig. 4.

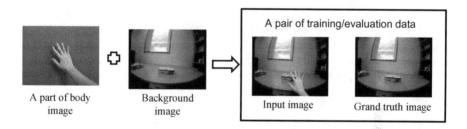

Fig. 3. How to create the training dataset.

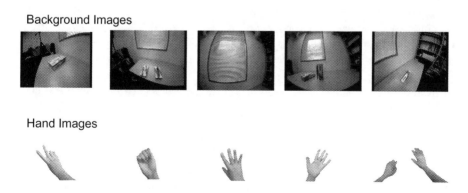

Fig. 4. Example of the images used for creating dataset.

Image augmentation was also performed to the training dataset. Specifically, we first expanded the background images in the range 1.1 to 1.5 times with a probability of 70% and cropped them to be 160 pixels wide and 120 pixels high at random positions. The luminance was also changed in a range of 0.5 to 1.5 times with a probability of 80%. In addition to this, the hand images were flipped horizontally with a probability of 50% and expanded with a probability of 70% in the range 1.1 to 1.5 times and cropped them to the same size, and modified to have the same luminance as the background images. The aim of such image augmentation is to improve the generalization performance. In particular, we expected that it would be possible to respond to changes in brightness by learning images with widely varying brightness since the skin colour changes greatly depending on the camera angle. The evaluation dataset was also created in the same way and the number of prepared images was 324 pairs.

2.4   Comparison of the Networks

In this section, the performance of each network is compared. We evaluate them by comparing the results of training with the dataset described in Sect. 2.3. The training iteration epochs were 50 and the batch size was set to 128. Our environment for processing is the following: OS, Windows 10 Pro 64bit; CPU, Intel Core i7-10700; RAM, 32 GB; GPU, NVIDIA GeForce RTX 3060 12 GB; CUDA version, 11.0; Neural Network Console, version 2.1; Neural Network Libraries, version 1.22.0 [9]; Python, version 3.6.12; OpenCV, version 3.4.2. The results to be compared are the training errors and validation errors at the end of training. Training errors and validation errors represent the mean squared error between the output images and the grand truth images. Figure 5 shows the training errors and validation errors of the three networks. The network (a) finishes training with a much larger error than (b) and (c). In other words, the images generated by the network (a) is not very close to the grand truth image. On the other hand, the results of network (b) and (c) are similar. Figure 6 also shows some of the output images using networks (b) and (c). It can be seen that both networks are able to generate the background image with the similar quality. Table 1 shows the time taken by each network to generate one image. The run time is of network (a) is the shortest and it is 0.2 [ms] shorter than those of (b) and (c), and all the networks are fast enough to process the images in real time.

From the above, it was found that the networks (b) or (c) are superior in terms of error, and there was no significant difference between the output images of (b) and (c).

2.5   The Examples of the Images Processed in Real Time

The examples of the image processing are shown Fig. 7 and Fig. 8. As shown in the figures, the hand on top of the tissue box in the input image is replaced by the background image in the output image and appears to be transparent.

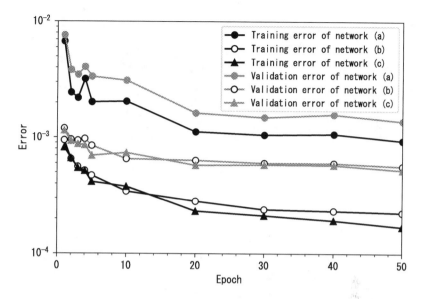

Fig. 5. Training errors and validation errors of network (a), (b), (c).

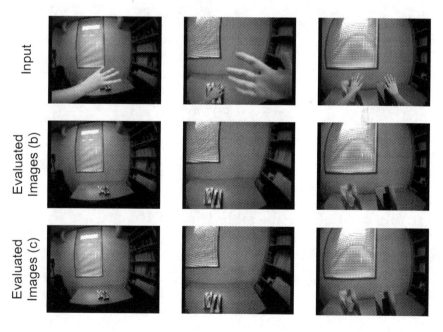

Fig. 6. Examples of input images and processed images by network (b) and (c).

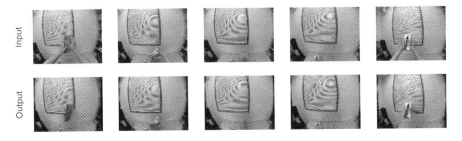

Input

Output

Fig. 7. The examples of the images processed in real time using network(c)

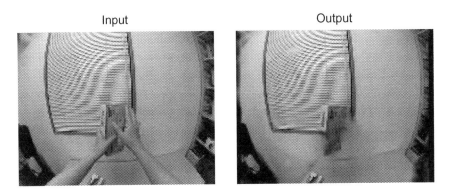

Input

Output

Fig. 8. The larger images of the Fig. 7

Table 1. Run time of network (a),(b),(c)

Network	Run time [ms]
(a)	2.34
(b)	2.42
(c)	2.40

3 Evaluation of the Invisible Human Experience System

3.1 Outline of the Evaluation

The purpose of the evaluation is to confirm whether the system developed in this study reduces self-awareness and improves self-esteem and to examine the process by which the psychological state changes in detail. The first step in the evaluation is to find out whether the developed system improves self-esteem. Next, in order to analyze the results more deeply, we build a hypothetical model of psychological change and investigate the process by a covariance structure analysis. In order to carry out this study, we will prepare questionnaire to investigate the changes in each psychological variable presented in the hypothetical model and conduct an experiment. We recruit participants with low self-esteem and ask them to experience the developed system, and then conduct a questionnaire survey. Each psychological variable of the hypothesized model will be measured. Based on this results, we will conduct a covariance structure analysis to investigate whether the cause-consequence between each psychological variable exists or not.

3.2 Hypothetical Model of Psychological Change

The hypothetical model of psychological change is shown as Fig. 9. In this figure, the rectangles represent the psychological variables for measurement, arrows represent cause-consequence paths and the sign in the arrows represent the positive or negative correlation between the variables.

First, it is known that experiencing of becoming invisible human reduces the presence of user's body [10]. This is the first item of Fig. 9. In the upper path, we built the hypothesis that the reduction in the presence of one's own body would reduce one's awareness of dislike points about oneself and improve one's perception of the real self. When we perceive the real self better than usual, we will be closer to the ideal self and the gap between the ideal self and the real self will become smaller, which will eventually lead to self-acceptance and we can expect to improve our self-esteem [11].

In the lower path, the experience of becoming invisible human leads to a lower awareness of the evaluating oneself [2]. Therefore, we also built the hypothesis that negative awareness of oneself would be reduced and this leads to self-acceptance. In the future, we are planning to confirm the validity of this model by conducting experiments.

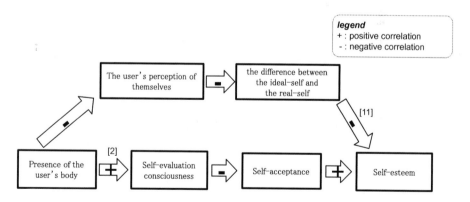

Fig. 9. The hypothetical model of psychological change.

4 Summary

In this study, we have developed a diminished reality system that enables invisible human experience and the hypothetical model of psychological change when using this system in order to improve self-esteem. In the system, body images are replaced with background images by image inpainting. The image inpainting is performed by a deep learning network and we have created networks and training datasets. Also, we have built two hypotheses when users experience the system. In the future work, we will conduct a experiment to investigate whether self-esteem improves when using the system.

References

1. Shirai, T.: Rethinking of educational practice targeting promotion of self-esteem. Memoirs Osaka Kyoiku Univ. **64**(1), 147–156 (2015)
2. Mizuta, K., The effect of objective self awareness on self-evaluation. Japan. J. Exp. Social Psychol. **27**(1), 59–67 (1987–1988)
3. Pathak, D., Krähenbühl, P., Donahue, J., Darrell, T., Efros, A.: Context encoders: feature learning by inpainting. In: Proceedings of the IEEE Conference on Computer Vision and Pattern Recognition, pp. 2536–2544 (2016)
4. Yang, C., Lu, X., Lin, Z., Shechtman, E., Wang, O., Li, H., High-resolution image inpainting using multi-scale neural patch synthesis. In: Proceedings of the IEEE Conference on Computer Vision and Pattern Recognition, pp. 6721–6729 (2017)
5. Seychell, D., Debono, C.J.: An approach for objective quality assessment of image inpainting results. In: 2020 IEEE 20th Mediterranean Electrotechnical Conference (MELECON), pp. 226–231 (2020)
6. Cai, N., Su, Z., Lin, Z., Wang, H., Yang, Z., Ling, B.W.-K.: Blind inpainting using the fully convolutional neural network. Visual Comput. **33**(2), 249–261 (2015). https://doi.org/10.1007/s00371-015-1190-z
7. Salem, N.: A survey on various image inpainting techniques. Fut. Eng. J. **2**(2), 1 (2021)
8. Glocker, B., Izadi, S., Shotton, J., Criminisi, A.: Real-time RGB-D camera relocalization. In: 2013 IEEE International Symposium on Mixed and Augmented Reality (ISMAR), pp. 173–179 (2013)
9. Hayakawa, A., et al.: Neural network libraries: a deep learning framework designed from engineers' perspectives (2021)
10. Martini, M., Kilteni, K., Maselli, A., Sanchez-Vives, M.V.: The body fades away: investigating the effects of transparency of an embodied virtual body on pain threshold and body ownership. Sci. Rep. **5**(13948), 1–8 (2015)
11. Mizuma, R.: A study of relationship between an ideal self and self-esteem, and consciousness to self-formation. Japan. J. Educ. Psychol. **46**(2), 131–141 (1998)

Towards a Social VR-based Exergame for Elderly Users: An Exploratory Study of Acceptance, Experiences and Design Principles

Syed Hammad Hussain Shah[1]([⊠]) [iD], Ibrahim A. Hameed[1] [iD],
Anniken Susanne T. Karlsen[1] [iD], and Mads Solberg[2]

[1] Department of ICT and Natural Sciences, Faculty of Information Technology
and Electrical Engineering, Norwegian University of Science and Technology,
Larsgårdsvegen 2, 6009 Ålesund, Norway
`syed.h.h.shah@ntnu.no`
[2] Department of Health Sciences in Aalesund, Faculty of Medicine and Health
Science, Norwegian University of Science and Technology, Larsgårdsvegen 2,
6009 Ålesund, Norway
`https://www.ntnu.edu/employees/syed.h.h.shah`

Abstract. For many elderly individuals, the aging experience is associated with a lack of social interaction and physical exercise that may negatively affect their health. To address these issues, researchers have designed experiences based on immersive virtual reality (VR) and 2D screen-based exergames. However, very few have studied the use of social VR for elderly, in which users can interact remotely through avatars in a single, shared, immersive virtual environment, using a head-mounted display. Additionally, there is limited research on the experience of elderly in performing interactive activities, especially game-based activities, in social VR. We conducted an exploratory study with 10 elderly people who never experienced VR before, to evaluate an avatar-mediated interaction-based social VR game prototype. Based on a mixed-methods approach, our study presents new insights into the usability, acceptance, and gameplay experience of elderly in a social VR game. Moreover, our study reflects upon design principles that should be considered when developing social VR games for elderly to ensure an engaging and safe user experience. Our results suggest that such games have a potential among the user group. Direct hand manipulation, based on hand tracking for interaction with 3D objects, presented an engaging and intuitive interaction paradigm, and the social game activity in VR was found to be enjoyable.

Keywords: Social VR · Avatar-mediated interaction · Metaverse · Eldercare · Immersive VR · Health games · COVID-19

© The Author(s), under exclusive license to Springer Nature Switzerland AG 2022
J. Y. C. Chen and G. Fragomeni (Eds.): HCII 2022, LNCS 13317, pp. 495–504, 2022.
https://doi.org/10.1007/978-3-031-05939-1_34

1   Introduction

In recent years, the proportion of adults over the age of 65 in the overall population has increased in many parts of the world, and this number is expected to grow. New research has correspondingly focused on the potential of ICT to socially connect the elderly with family and peers [1]. For many elderly individuals, the aging experience is associated with the lack of social interaction and little physical activity, which can negatively affect their health in various ways [2]. Regular physical activity in daily life is recommended by health professionals to avoid the functional decline, as it positively impacts peoples' physical fitness and overall health situation, including their cognitive abilities [3–5]. Moreover, the COVID-19 pandemic has forced many communities to physically isolate themselves through various measures for social distancing. This has highlighted the role of technology as a rich medium for communication [6–8]. Previous studies have reported on the use of avatar-mediated communication in virtual worlds, but these applications have been limited to a 2D screen rather than immersive virtual reality (VR) [9–12], except one recent report [13]. In their study, Baker et al. [13] investigated communication between older adults through avatar-mediated interactions in social VR. Avatar-mediated communication in social VR involves the use of a head-mounted display to facilitate communication through interaction with representative avatars from remote locations, while being immersed in the same virtual three-dimensional space. This study suggested that elderly participants, under some conditions, are comfortable when communicating on the platform, suggesting that a closed social VR environment is a suitable platform where users can discuss sensitive topics. COVID-19 has raised awareness about the impact of social isolation and the significance of meeting face-to-face with family and friends [8]. Aging is also associated with a decline in mobility, which can negatively impact health outcomes [14]. Various gaming applications have therefore been made to promote physical exercise among elderly. Such digital games, designed to engage people in physical activity, are known as 'exergames'.

Exergames take place in a digital environment, but entails vigorous physical movements in the real world, scaled to the abilities of participants [15]. These digital games frequently rely on an array of sensors to capture and simulate body movements, and can be based on various display technologies, such as 2D screens, VR, augmented reality and mixed reality. Several studies have demonstrated that VR interventions may support physical exercise among the elderly [16]. The social effects of exergames on this user group have also been investigated [17], suggesting that they can potentially support social connection between participants. Although several exergames have been dubbed as 'VR exergames', these have been limited to virtual worlds projected on to 2D screens. In this paper, we report on a feasibility study to examine the usability and acceptance of a multiplayer social VR game based on avatar-mediated communication using head-mounted display for primarily elderly users. We focus on elderly outpatients and patients living in a short-term care facility due to a decline in functional capacity. We also outline key design principles that can affect the efficacy and safety of social VR-based games tailored to the needs of this user group. We also offer some suggestive guidelines, which can be helpful in designing enjoyable games for this user group in the future. Our study is part of an ongoing effort of co-designing and developing a social VR-based exergame in collaboration with physiotherapists from a rehabilitation center in Western Norway.

A challenge for studies on social VR, is a general unfamiliarity with, and skepticism towards, advanced technologies like virtual reality headsets, among aging users. Moreover, healthcare professionals and other caretakers are sometimes skeptical about the value of VR for elderly users, due to perceived risk factors and safety concerns, such as poor balance and control of the body. A feasibility study like the one we have conducted provides useful insights into user perspectives, design requirements, and safety critical factors when developing social VR-based games for elderly users, which can also be implied to the exergames.

2   Literature Review

Our research builds on previous studies that have investigated two-dimensional screen-based exergames for play and social interaction, and VR for the elderly [15,18,19]. Jorge et al. [15] introduced a bowling exergame that can be played as either single- or multi-player. This exergame was based on a 2D screen and the Kinect motion sensor. Their findings suggest that the exergame could improve adherence of elderly individuals to the exercise. In another study, Maja et al. [20] presented an arm rehabilitation exergame which had two modes of playing game: competitive and cooperative. This game was also based on a virtual environment with 2D screens and hand trackers. Overall, the authors found that both modes contributed to increased motivation to perform arm exercise, and the competitive mode had potential for functional improvements. Sara et al. [21] proposed a 2D screen-based application, where elderly users could interact with each other while cycling. Ather et al. [22] presented an exergame design for the same target group, based on a concept called 'Out in Nature'. The idea of doing exercise immersed in a forest was well-received by the study's participants. Carina et al. [23] presented an intelligent exergame based on 2D screens and gestural sensors, which could recommend exercises to users, based on gestural interactions. In another study, Imad et al. [24] personalized and adapted the needs of elderly players and directed them towards suitable activities in the exergame. O'Brien et al. [25] studied social interaction among older adults through avatars in 'Second Life', with the anonymity afforded by avatar-mediated communication being highly appreciated by some users. Other studies include interventions whereby VR-based exergames has been used for balance rehabilitation [26]; memory functioning [27,28]; and improvements in mobility and strength [29,30].

3   Method

3.1   The Game Prototype

We developed a prototype of social VR-based game that allowed participants to meet each other in an immersive environment through VR headset. The game entails a multiplayer activity, which allows two participants to meet and play together. An important feature was the support for avatar-mediated communication, so participants could interact with each other's avatars and communicate via audio. We included direct hand manipulation as the primary mechanism to interact with 3D objects in the virtual space. On basis of user feedback and previous research [22], the gaming environment was based on a concept of 'Out in Nature'. This environment was designed to resemble the outdoors, decorated with grass, trees, water, a blue sky, and birds with sound effects. The idea was to immerse users in a pleasant outdoor environment that can be otherwise inaccessible for many users due to reduced mobility. The prototype was based on the 'Unity3D' game engine, and the setup for each participant consists of a standalone Meta Quest (formerly Oculus Quest) VR system with tracking sensors to allow control of the avatar's body, head and hand movements.

The game activity consists of picking objects from one virtual table through direct hand manipulation and arranging the objects on a different table. In the game, participants stand around the tables, facing each other, and each participant will pick an object with the color assigned to the user, as shown in Fig. 1. The participant who first completes the activity wins the game.

Fig. 1. First person view of participants while playing social VR game

3.2   Participants

10 participants were recruited, aged between 64 and 82 years (Mean (M): 71.6). Five were residing in a rehabilitation center within a short-term care facility, and the remaining five were living independently in their own homes. Six women, and four men participated. Inclusion criteria were as follows: above 64 years of

age, not visually impaired, could hear and speak, able to stand, not physically disabled, and with an interest in trying out novel technology. Two participants relied on supporting aids to walk but could stand upright without support. Moreover, two physiotherapists were involved in testing out the prototype, assessing suitable activities, ensuring safety and assessing risks. They would also suggest improvements in game design. Notably, none of the participants had any previous experience with VR-interfaces. Due to COVID-19 restrictions, it was only possible to recruit a small number of participants for the study. The research project was assessed and recommended by the Personal Data Official, at the Norwegian Centre for Research Data (project number 508625).

3.3 Procedure

We conducted five social VR gaming sessions in total, in the building of the rehabilitation center. All sessions were conducted on the same day, due to safety restrictions at the care facility (related to COVID-19). Each session included two participants and lasted between 5 and 20 minutes (average = 13.2 min). Participants were a mix between strangers and acquaintances: those who resided in the short-term care facility were somewhat familiar with each other, while participants living on their own were unfamiliar with the other players.

During gaming sessions, participants were physically dispersed across different rooms within the same building. Figure 2 shows two of the participants playing with the prototype.

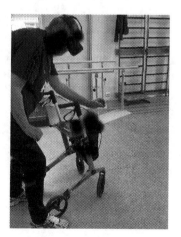

Fig. 2. Two participants while participating in social VR gaming session

Physiotherapists received detailed instructions from a researcher before they facilitated sessions with the participants. These instructions were then provided to each participant at the beginning of each session, and the physiotherapist remained present with each player throughout the session for support. A member of our research team was also present at the site, to closely observe and survey each participant's response at the end of each session.

At the beginning of each user's session, a member of the research team launched the game in the headset, and assisted participants when putting it on. Players were then asked to check the synchronization between actual and tracked hands in VR, to get familiar with the hand tracking interface. By default, both participants automatically joined the game room at the beginning of the session. After getting comfortable within the virtual environment, participants were asked to start the game. Having completed the game activity, the researcher then helped participants to remove the headset.

A mixed-methods approach, based on a questionnaire, semi-structured interviews and field-observations, was adopted to collect users' feedback. The semi-structured interview was carried out at the end of each session, and participants were requested to fill out a questionnaire.

4   Results and Discussion

The questionnaires (N=10), interviews (N=10), in addition to observations of how the participants interacted within (and outside) the gaming environment, offered valuable insights about future design choices. Despite this event being their first experience with an immersive virtual environment, participants assessed the game prototype in positive terms, and their feedback provided critical suggestions about how to better design future interaction paradigms for social VR. Notably, participants found the social aspect of the game less engaging, due to the sphere-shaped appearance of avatars. This suggests that improvements should be made in the game design, including making the avatars more human-like in terms of embodied movements and facial expressions, for instance. A contextual understanding of these aspects was acquired from observations during gaming sessions, along with participant feedback. In the present study, we adapted the questionnaire from USEQ (User Satisfaction Evaluation Questionnaire) [31] to Norwegian language, to evaluate user-satisfaction with the game. Responses were rated on a Likert scale, where 1 = 'not at all', and 5 = 'very much'. Table 1 shows the results in terms of mean (M), the standard deviation (SD) and standard error (SE) for questionnaire responses.

Table 1. Means and standard deviations for questionnaire responses

Question	M	SD	SE
1. Did you enjoy your experience with the system?	4.30	1.13	0.36
2. Did you feel comfortable during your experience with the system?	4.80	0.42	0.13
3. Was it easy to interact with virtual 3D objects?	3.50	0.70	0.22
4. Did you feel comfortable in interactions with the avatar of your fellow player?	3.70	0.60	0.19
5. Was avatar-mediated interaction with fellow player engaging and natural?	3.50	1.10	0.35

As a measure of how closely or widely distributed are the individual responses, SD is calculated as shown in Table 1. Low values of SD and SE indicate towards the close distribution among responses and sharing of same views among participants. Overall, participants found the gaming experience positive and engaging. A participant mentioned that, *I felt very active and lost track of time while playing the game.* Another commented that *the motivation and involvement of players in the game was mutually dependent on each other's actions.* It was also mentioned that playing the game with acquaintances would be more engaging, fun, generating lots of conversation. One player mentioned that *it felt a little strange to interact with the avatar of the fellow player at first, but after some time, we felt comfortable when interacting with the avatars.* The elderly participants mentioned that they found the interaction with virtual objects, in terms of grabbing, throwing, and touching etc., easy and that it demanded less effort compared to using the hand controllers. Furthermore, players noticed that direct hand manipulation stimulated the movement in wrist and fingers which was considered good exercise. One participant considered the use of hands for interaction and grabbing in-game objects as beneficial for those with weak fingers and that it supported easy interaction. The majority of participants also reported that they felt safe when interacting with the virtual objects, if they were stationary. They did not, however, like that the target objects where dynamic and moving, potentially due to a risk of motion sickness and loss of balance. It should, however, be noted that participants did not report general discomfort or motion sickness. Physiotherapists were confident that VR could be helpful for elderly users, seeing it as useful for engaging elderly users in exercise, and providing a platform for improving social connectedness and exercise motivation.

In addition to these self-reports from participants, information was also collected through close observations of participants by the physiotherapists and the researcher who was present during gaming-sessions. One insight that emerged from these observations, was that there ought to be an introductory session for the participants, before they proceeded with the actual game activity. Such a small social ritual, could potentially help decrease hesitations towards interacting with strangers. Moreover, we observed several issues that should be considered when designing VR-based games for elderly. First, external hardware, such as hand controllers, should be avoided, as this introduces unnecessary complexity to the user interface. For instance, users tend to forget how the interaction controls work (e.g., what are the functions of buttons in hand controller). Instead, direct hand manipulation with the help of hand tracking through cameras embedded in the VR headset offers a more convenient interaction paradigm. Furthermore, different color schemes should be used for provisioning feedback to users upon touching and grabbing the virtual objects. According to self-reports by participants, this supports 3D perception of objects and user interaction in the virtual environment. It was also noted that moving objects should be avoided in the virtual game, because this was seen as confusing, and potentially nauseating.

Furthermore, the game design and mechanics should be kept simple, with large, high-contrast objects and text for better visibility.

5   Conclusion

In this paper, we examined the usability and acceptance of avatar-mediated communication among elderly users in a social VR-based game through a head-mounted display. Based on qualitative data from our pilot-study with 10 users aged between 64 and 82 years, we conclude that there is a potential for the use of social VR games among elderly to support participation in physical exercise. Participants showed no adverse response to participating in social VR-based activities. Moreover, our feasibility study highlights future opportunities for designing enjoyable and engaging exergames for an aging target group. In this case, participants expressed engagement when playing with a partner. But some players were less engaged, possibly due to their partner player being a stranger. This suggests that some multiplayer exergames are primarily applicable for use among people who are already acquaintances. Further research is necessary to investigate the effects from repeated use of such applications on the social well-being of this user group. We were also able to learn some lessons regarding user interface and interaction design to improve the ergonomics of social VR-based exergames for elderly users. Participants preferred direct hand manipulation for interaction with virtual objects in an immersive 3D-environment, finding it more engaging and less cumbersome.

Acknowledgement. The authors are grateful to the Norwegian University of Science and Technology (NTNU) for supporting the project, and all the cordial participants and professionals who made this study possible.

References

1. Baker, S., et al.: Combatting social isolation and increasing social participation of older adults through the use of technology: a systematic review of existing evidence. Australasian J. Ageing **37**, 184–193 (2018)
2. Manini, T.M.: Mobility decline in old age: a time to intervene. Exercise Sport Sci. Rev. **41**, 2 (2013)
3. Van Santen, J., et al.: Effects of exergaming in people with dementia: results of a systematic literature review. J. Alzheimer's Disease **63**, 741–760 (2018)
4. Cacciata, M., et al.: Effect of exergaming on health-related quality of life in older adults: a systematic review. Int. J. Nurs. Stud. **93**, 30–40 (2019)
5. Wu, Y.-Z., Lin, J.-Y., Wu, P.-L., Kuo, Y.-F.: Effects of a hybrid intervention combining exergaming and physical therapy among older adults in a long-term care facility. Geriatrics Gerontology Int. **19**, 147–152 (2019)
6. Chen, A.T., et al.: Reactions to COVID-19, information and technology use, and social connectedness among older adults with pre-frailty and frailty. Geriatric Nurs. **42**, 188–195 (2021)
7. Morrow-Howell, N., Galucia, N., Swinford, E.: Recovering from the COVID-19 pandemic: a focus on older adults. J. Aging Soc. Policy **32**, 526–535 (2020)

8. Seifert, A.: The Digital Exclusion of Older Adults during the COVID-19 Pandemic. J. Gerontol. Soc. Work **63**, 674–676 (2020)
9. Cook, N., Winkler, S.L.: Acceptance, usability and health applications of virtual worlds by older adults: a feasibility study. JMIR Res. Protocols **5**, e5423 (2016)
10. Reed, D.J., Fitzpatrick, G.: Acting your age in second life. In: Markopoulos, P., de Ruyter, B., IJsselsteijn, W., Rowland, D. (eds.) Fun and Games 2008. LNCS, vol. 5294, pp. 158–169. Springer, Heidelberg (2008). https://doi.org/10.1007/978-3-540-88322-7_16
11. Siriaraya, P., Ang, C.S.: In Perspectives on Human-Computer Interaction Research with Older People, pp. 101–117 Springer, Switzerland (2019)
12. Siriaraya, P., Ang, C.S., Bobrowicz, A.: Exploring the potential of virtual worlds in engaging older people and supporting healthy aging. Behav. Inf. Technol. **33**, 283–294 (2014)
13. Baker, S., et al.: Avatar-mediated communication in social VR: an in-depth exploration of older adult interaction in an emerging communication platform. In: Proceedings of the 2021 CHI Conference on Human Factors in Computing Systems, pp. 1–13 (2021)
14. Peixoto, S.V., et al.: Physical activity practice among older adults: results of the elsi-brazil. Revista de Saude Publica **52**, 5s, e5423 (2018)
15. Júnior, J.L.A.D.S., et al.: A bowling exergame to improve functional capacity in older adults: co-design, development, and testing to compare the progress of playing alone versus playing with peers. JMIR Serious Games **9**, e23423 (2021)
16. Gao, Z., Lee, J.E., McDonough, D.J., Albers, C.: Virtual reality exercise as a coping strategy for health and wellness promotion in older adults during the COVID-19 pandemic (2020)
17. Li, J., et al.: The social effects of exergames on older adults: systematic review and metric analysis. J. Med. Int. Res. **20**, e10486 (2018)
18. Li, J., Theng, Y.-L., Foo, S.: Play mode effect of exergames on subthreshold depression older adults: a randomized pilot trial. Front. Psychol. **11**, 2912 (2020)
19. Cyarto, E. V., Batchelor, F., Baker, S. Dow, B.: Active ageing with avatars: a virtual exercise class for older adults. In: Proceedings of the 28th Australian Conference on Computer-Human Interaction (2016), 302–309
20. Goršič, M., Cikajlo, I., Novak, D.: Competitive and cooperative arm rehabilitation games played by a patient and unimpaired person: effects on motivation and exercise intensity. J. Neuroeng. Rehabilitation **14**, 1–18 (2017)
21. Arlati, S., et al.: A social virtual reality-based application for the physical and cognitive training of the elderly at home. Sensors **19**, 261 (2019)
22. Nawaz, A., et al.: Designing simplified exergame for muscle and balance training in seniors: a concept of 'Out in Nature'. In: Proceedings of the 8th International Conference on Pervasive Computing Technologies for Health- care, 309–312 (2014)
23. González-González, C.S., Toledo-Delgado, P.A., Mu noz-Cruz, V., Torres-Carrion, P.V.: Serious games for rehabilitation: gestural interaction in personalized gamified exercises through a recommender system. J. Biomed. Inf. **97**, 103266 (2019)
24. Afyouni, I., Murad, A., Einea, A.: Adaptive rehabilitation bots in serious games. Sensors **20**, 7037 (2020)
25. O'Brien, C.J., Smith, J.L., Beck, D.E.: Real relationships in a virtual world: social engagement among older adults in second life. Gerontechnology **15**, 171–179 (2016)
26. Kim, A., Darakjian, N., Finley, J.M.: Walking in fully immersive virtual environments: an evaluation of potential adverse effects in older adults and individuals with Parkinson's disease. J. Neuroeng. Rehab. **14**, 1–12 (2017)

27. Hayhurst, J.: How augmented reality and virtual reality is being used to support people living with dementia—design challenges and future directions. In: Jung, T., tom Dieck, M.C. (eds.) Augmented Reality and Virtual Reality. PI, pp. 295–305. Springer, Cham (2018). https://doi.org/10.1007/978-3-319-64027-3_20

28. La Corte, V., Sperduti, M., Abichou, K., Piolino, P.: Episodic memory assessment and remediation in normal and pathological aging using virtual reality: a mini review. Front. Psychol. **10**, 173(2019)

29. Lange, B.S., et al.: The potential of virtual reality and gaming to assist successful aging with disability. Phys. Med. Rehab. Clinic. **21**, 339–356 (2010)

30. Skæret, N., et al.: Exercise and rehabilitation delivered through exergames in older adults: an integrative review of technologies, safety and efficacy. Int. J. Med. Inf. **85**, 1–16 (2016)

31. Gil-Gómez, J.-A., et al.: USEQ: a short questionnaire for satisfaction evaluation of virtual rehabilitation systems. Sensors **17**, 1589 (2017)

Relative Research on Psychological Character and Plot Design Preference for Audiences of VR Movies

Lingxuan Zhang[1]([✉]) and Feng Liu[2]

[1] School of Public Communication and Mass Media, Kede College of Capital Normal University, Beijing, P.R. China
[2] Shandong College of Tourism and Hospitality, Shandong Jinan, P.R. China

Abstract. VR movies have been a new trend in recent years, and interactive VR films are getting popular among young audiences. The high-tech environment, sense of immersion and participation and decision in making choices at fork points in the story are all so appealing the audience are part of the movie, and their decision may change the flow and even the ending of the plot. Outstanding interactive VR movies can provide chances that can go up to a hundred choices, and more than 10 different endings, which would be heavy workload and huge budget for the producing team, including the screenwriters. The thesis reviewed and collected the development of VR movies and relevant theories on personality test and screenwriting, to find the barriers that hinder VR movie script and plot development. The purpose is to investigate the audience's intuitive feelings and expectations of watching VR movies, as well as their understanding and acceptance of the story, to explore the relationship between personality and decision making at turning points of each fork of the pitchfork bifurcation structure plot. The authors hope to find an efficient way to lead the audiences to an ending which seems to be chosen by themselves rather than the writers, although it is within the designer's expectation.

Keywords: Personality · Plot design · Screenwriters

1 Introduction

Traditional movies tell stories through Montage and professional film languages, hence it is widely accepted that movies can break the shackles of time and space and have gained narrative freedom in spatial dimensions. VR (Virtual Reality) movies based on digitization, which have currently become a film making trend, are originated from classical film arts and still enjoy common narrative features with traditional ones, although the transcendence and differences are in plain sight.

With the development of VR and AR(Augmented Reality) technologies, VR and interactive movies have become a new type of experience and interactive method for both film makers, audiences, and the professionals as well.

© The Author(s), under exclusive license to Springer Nature Switzerland AG 2022
J. Y. C. Chen and G. Fragomeni (Eds.): HCII 2022, LNCS 13317, pp. 505–518, 2022.
https://doi.org/10.1007/978-3-031-05939-1_35

1.1   The Origin and Development of VR Movies

Created by Czech New Wave directors Radúz Cincera and Vladimír Svitácek in 1966, lověk a jehodm is recognized as the first interactive cinema in the world. After being screened at the Offscreen Film Festival & Bozar Cinema Present at the World Expo in Montreal, Canada in 1967, it has aroused hot discussions among industry insiders. It is a brand-new experience. The audience decides the follow-up development of the film's plot at key branches of the story by pressing red or green handles in their hands. Whereas the audience's reaction was not as hot. After decades of development, interactive movies maintain calm for a long time, without significant breakthroughs. The turning point comes with the rapid development of the Internet and virtual reality and augmented reality technology, virtual movies are booming and have received more and more attention from people in the industry.

The 69th Cannes International Film Festival and the 74th Venice Film Festival have added "VR Film Competition Unit" separately. Public audience can watch and experience *Invasion!* directed by Eric Darnel, and Giant by Milica Zec in 2016. The team grew fast in 2017 and 22 CVRs (Cinema Virtual Reality) were on show, including Milita by Ncolas Alcala, La Camera Insabbiata by Laurie Anderson & Huang Hsin-Chien, and 4 Chinese CVR products, all joined the competition to win Best VR, Best VR Experience and Best VR Story. In the past, the audience could only watch on screen from 360-degree perspective, but now they are in the movie.

1.2   Basic CVR Devices

VR has become a widely used and popular technology because it can create an interactive 3D or Virtual Environment (VE) that is generated through computer graphic display system with various reality and control interface equipment. In August, 2020, Chinese government issued a white paper on 5G high tech VR videos, indicating that VR videos are panoramic ones that users will be visually and personally on the scene with the help of virtual equipment, like Head-Mounted Display (HMD) or VR glasses.

360-degree virtual reality cameras or panoramic cameras are basic to make any VR Video, from different perspectives. All the videos made will be edited, compressed and integrated into a multi-channel fusion and transmitted to clients with high digital technology that combines VR and AR.

To watch a VR movie, generally you need a set of HMD machines, or 3D glasses with two handles. A qualified VR all-in-one case is more convenient to get a more comfortable wearing experience. It is normally equipped with 4–8 core CPU operation, batteries with long time charging support, built-in shaft precision gyroscope for more stable movement, more accurate and high definition eye care blue lenses, multi-function keys with the menu list, switch machine key, volumes, main interface, object distance adjustment key, smart sensor to automatically play, external USB card reader and USB support, charging socket, about pd regulating key, etc…, currently audience can even play with their own hands to change the lights, play music, and identify gestures, completely leaving handles alone.

The following photographs are taken in Sandbox X while watching paper birds in Musicfans Art Space located in Sanlitun, Beijing (Figs. 1, 2, 3, 4 and 5).

Fig. 1. Watching environment of CVR

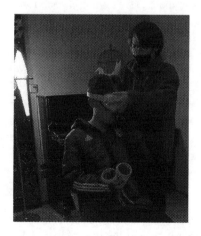

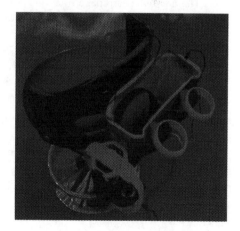

Fig. 2. Helping the audience to wear devices   **Fig. 3.** All-in-one 3D glasses

1.3   Categories and Typical Works

With the rapid development of VR movies, all kinds of theme and genres are on show, or on the way. To make it clearer, the authors tried to clarify them into the following categories.

Cartoon and Interactive. *Hangman at home*, a 45-minute-VR Movie, tells what a hangman thinks after work at night. 5 stories are combined together in the movie, and the audiences become peeper, observer and accomplice at the same time. It was named as finalists for 2020 Venice VR Expanded.

Non-verbal Interactive. In *Buddy*, a 25-minute-VR movie made in Korea, the audiences can touch and stroke buddy to make friends with it, and can play the musical instrument as their will.

Jellyfish, is a 15-minute voice interactive movie produced in 2020, the audiences are beckoned by Jellyfish to control the fish with their eyes and hear various voices and create a surrealistic self-made choir in the movie.

Narrative Experience. *The Line*, directed by Ricardo Laganaro, has won a series of international awards, including Outstanding Innovation in Interactive media of 70th Emmy Awards. It is the first VR narrative experience movie that is integrated with Oculus Quest hand manual tracking function.

Multiple Endings. The 8-minute-VR Chinese movie named the *cutest scar*e, is a multiple endings experience to explore the world from other creatures perspective, instead of human beings.

The most famous one should be *Black mirror: Pandersnatch* produced by Netflix in 2018. With the pitchfork bifurcation narration approach, it improved narrative interactive movies into a higher level. It is said Netfllix is trying to make it a VR movie. The movie bears giant narrative clues and 30 interactive plot design, which leads to 16 endings of the story. The audience can make their own choices at the crossing point of each fork (or bifurcation) of the story, and it takes the audience 5 h to experience all the possibilities. Most audiences were shocked by it, but some audiences think the plot is not so logic and most either-or choices are unnecessary and boring, it gives too many branches and they are not satisfied with the endings at all. To them, it is more like a full-motion video game (FMV game), rather than an interactive movie [1]. The most impressive thing about it is the audiences are controlling the running and ending of the story.

Games. VR games are successful recently, like *Night Shift* developed by Steam. There are 180 choices designed for the players, leading to 7 different endings, even so, the main structure and outline keep the original design very well. Although it is called an interactive suspense movie game, it is written by Michael R. Johnson and played by professional actors. What's more, it joined the competition of many film awards in the world.

Goliath: Playing with Reality is also a VR movie game, being a real player in the movie, the audience can experience multiple reality through the perspective of Joe, a PRU (Psychos R Us). It was named as finalists for 2021 Venice VR Grand Prix.

Others. *Space Explorers: The ISS Experience*, is a documentary VR movie, episodes 1-2 have been on.

*Is Anna OK?*Is a BBCVR Hub based on real story, two participants can play together in the movie to experience different effects caused by brain trauma.

LE BAL DE PARIS is a live show movie that lasts 35 min. Led by the dancer in the movie, audience can put on the clothes they like and join in a love story.

Madrid Noir is a detective movie in which the player goes deep into her memory, discovers the clues to the puzzle and finds the truth by herself.

The list is so long that we cannot name them one by one in accurate category, but there are so many newcomers in the field that we can wait and watch in the near future.

1.4   Comments, Features and Challenges

From the audiences' perspective, although a VR movie plot is not so attractive as that in VR games, they can be surrounded by 360-degree viewing environment and completely immersed in the story, as an observer staying at the place where the story happens, rather than watching an outside world before a scene. After getting familiar with the story, the audience can play the lead role, speaking the actor's lines and even improvise or deduct the development of the movie plot, which is brand new and inviting!

Audiences enjoy marvelous watching experience because VR movies provide more clarified and higher quality images, they can touch, move and even draw arbitrarily. Few audiences feel dizzy because they can turn their bodies and change visual angels at their will. They described it with words like amazing, novel, romantic, shocked, within reach and interactive, while watching long hours (even if over 30–40 min) would be a tiring burden for most viewers because the heavy HMD equipment, an all-in-one glasses cannot make it easier.

Although Steven Spielberg, the great director, considered CVR"a dangerous media", more and more studios are joining in the new field and constantly experimenting and creating. VR movies have become the coming trend of modern filmmaking development. The most fantastic thing about it lies in the magic feeling of joining in the movie plot and experience a real film within one's control.

The three key characteristics of VR technology are immersion, interaction and simulation. Audiences can enjoy systems immersion, spatial immersion, empathic/social immersion, and narrative/sequential immersion [2]. That is to say, in a system built on VR image, players seem to be transmitted to a 360-degree virtual world, enjoying a taste of the roles' emotions and social activities, and try three-dimensional, real-time and infinite narrative possibilities.

While watching 3 dimensional VR movies, audiences can take options and impetus plot development. The movie is in high similarity with VR games, but mainline of it is always the narrative story, the audiences' choices influence the way they experience, interactive and participate in each other's remodeling procedure [3].

Many researchers have tried to analyze interactive movies on the possibilities of movie narration and technology, to explore interactive effects caused by building inner structure of the story on the suspense design and audience participation through comprehension of the plot [4].

Interactive movies will combine the advantages of movies and games, and become a new catchy narrative media [5]. That is an interactive narrative that belongs to the primary tree-like bifurcation and has many limitations. The technology platform provided by VR can break through the primary interactive narrative, bring a more authentic and interactive viewing experience, and form a more advanced interactive and immersive narrative [6].

The tree network (pitchfork bifurcation) narration in VR movies requires tremendous plot materials from screenwriters to meet the demands of audiences, to support every option from each branch of the structure and make all choices go smoothly in a logic and catchy way, which means millions of dollars of investment and a great burden, or even a disaster for producers.

CVR (Cinema Virtual Reality), an interactive narrative movie which is set on a tree bifurcated structure, gives users more interactive permissions and choices. The result is that both the audience and the screenwriter become implicit co-authors of the film, and the audiences will be part of instant plot generation, creating a sense of co-telling the story, which would fulfill the participants' creative willingness, thereby leading to changes towards personal psychological status of users by generating with different shooting angels and transition techniques. However, the mode is facing many limitations. In terms of script writing, the living environment and role experience of characters in the play provide sources and base for their personality and choice. In CVR, the emotional structure varies from person to person with the changes of individual selection of the plot, hence the fate of the roles becomes changeable, and it is getting more difficult and complicated to create a sense of reality. In addition, there is a natural and inherent contradiction between telling stories to the audience and letting the audience have fun. The challenges are more than that, in what degree can audience participant in the creation of the story so as to distinguish from other types of game arts? How to establish a real connection among the characters in the film and the outside users, with the help of creative techniques such as VR, AR, and MR? How well can users understand the story while participating in the co-construction of a new film? What is the theme that the director expects to convey? All of them have become key elements restricting its development at the moment.

2   Literature Review

2.1   Big-Five Theory

Systematic and scientific research on human personality were formed in the 1820s, leading to 5 major schools to explore the regular patterns of personality traits of human beings, from different angles. After nearly two hundreds of years development, the

Big-Five theory has been considered relatively stable in one's lifetime and widely used in recent years, in a range of fields like career options and lifelong development, psychotherapy, human resources management, and so on. They are also known to predict life outcomes that are crucial important for human beings, such as education and health.

The theory is based on lexical hypothesis, to sum up the most accurate adjectives to describe the respondents' human personality traits from all the word lists in the dictionary, trying to statistical analyze the most typical character features. In nearly a hundred years, a lot of psychologists and researchers contributed to the forming of Big-Five theory. Baumgaten, Allport & Odbert were considered the pioneers who put the hypothesis into practice in the 1930s, Cattell, R.B. (1945) collected 16 source personality traits that can cover almost all the personality styles and improved the theory a lot [6]; Fiske (1949) discovered that 5 factors were marked in his list of statistics all the time, indicating they probably can describe the most meaningful features of personality [7]. In the 1960s, Tupes & Christal, Norman, Borgata pushed the theory a lot forward, and in 1981 Digman & Takemote Chock summed up 5 key factors with similar statistical approach of vocabulary repetition, in the 1980s, Goldberg defined Big-Five Personality traits on the basis of Norman's research [8]. Soto and John's (2009) further quantification of the Big Five from 5 dimensions into 10 facets [9], two for each dimension, but the number of items and scoring methods for the degree remain unchanged. The inventory was further advanced in generations, and BFI (MIT version) grows to be the most popular and convenient one in the world.

As time goes, a large amount of scale/inventory appeared to measure human personality in psychological field. The most popular ones are as follows: MBTI Personality Test Indicators, Holland Vocational Hobby Test, Big Five Personality, the Riso-Hudson Enneagram Type Indicator (RHETI), Cattel 16 Personality Factor Questionnaire, and Eysenck Personality Questionnaire (EPQ). As for Psychometric validation, Big- Five is more valid and reliable, and a widely used model. It was raised by Paul Costa and Robert McCrae in 1992, as a Five-Factor Model, or OCEAN model, indicating individual personality can be described by five factors that bear the basic traits on psychological structures. The acronym of this model is "OCEAN". Goldberg(1992) considered Big Five as a revolutionary in personality psychology [10]. Studies show no matter who does the test, the participants themselves, or their relatives or partners, there is merely no difference of certain individual personality result.

Big-Five inventory has become the most widely accepted personality traits model. The human personality structure consists of five core factors including "Openness to Experience, Conscientiousness, Extraversion, Agreeableness and Neuroticism, each trait represents a continuum and is divided into several factors, which is more related to the words below (Table 1):

Table 1. Descriptions of big-five model

Personality dimensions	Description
Openness to Experience	Fantasy, aesthetics and rich feelings into consideration, actions, ideas and values
Conscientiousness	Competence, order, dutifulness, achievement striving, self-discipline and deliberation
Extraversion	Warmth, gregariousness, assertiveness, activity, excitement seeking and positive emotions
Agreeableness	Trust, straightforwardness, altruism, compliance, modest and tender-mindedness
Neuroticism	Anxiety, angry or hostile,feelings like depression, low self-consciousness, impulsiveness and vulnerability

When measuring a certain factor, one would be placed on a scale determining their level of the factor. By ranking individuals on each of these traits, it is possible to effectively measure individual differences in personality [11].

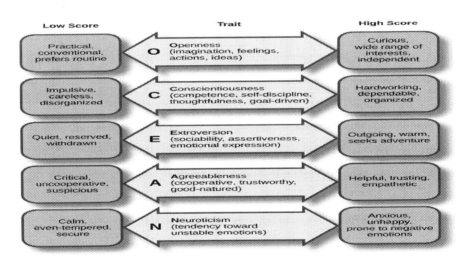

Fig. 4. The big five personality traits [12]

2.2   VR Movie Screenwriting

Unlike linear narrative and one-way communicative in traditional movies, VR movie audiences will take a role in the interactive plot and enjoy high sense of participation. Apart from professional and technological work like filming, producing, editing and playing, creative and productive team is facing a great challenge to make the story more inviting and immersive with various routes that lead to lots of catchy endings, which would be a great burden for screenwriters. No idea could grow well unless it is supported by fancy story and attractive roles.

Film Genres. It is crucial for modern movie producers to pull target audiences into the cinema, by cooperating with all partners, like creative team, agents, and studio managers, in an effective and efficient way. The truth is a good logline and a lead would attract players just because the character or the story is appealing.

"There is nothing new under the sun" (Ecclesiastes, the old testament, Bible), so is screenwriting. Same Goldwyn, the studio executive, once mentioned he needs something similar, and different as well. A Movie is just like a complex machine that produces emotions, and it is also like an accurate Switzerland -made watch with precise gears and reels that can be broken up and assembled again [13].

A successful logline can be conceptualized and is usually combined with several elements: unexpected irony, strong mental image about inspiring possibilities, least cost with most audiences and eye catching movie title. The purpose is to make movies worthwhile for all sides, the producer, writer, filmmaker, studio and audience as well.

Scholars and insiders generally classify movie creations according to their genre to make clear a specific category and decide how to set unusual twists. Most famous playwrights, even Steven Spielberg, the great director, would borrow ideas from other movies, to seek for appropriate tricks in designing their own genre and task design.

Robert Mckee [14] divided all movies into 25 categories, namely Romantic Comedy, Epic, Biography, Western, Cartoon, Crime, War, Fiction......, which is widely used among audiences and sellers.

But for screenwriters, the 25 categories failed to give basic information on the story itself. That is why Blake Snyder sorted movies into 10 film genres: Monster in the House; Golden Fleece; Out of the Bottle; Dude with a Problem; Rites of Passage; Buddy Love; Whydunit; The Fool Triumphant; Institutionalized and Superhero [14].

This approach is more helpful for screenwriters, especially when they are facing audiences with various tastes and designing more interactive pitchfork bifurcation narrative.

Lead Character Archetype. Swiss psychologist Jung [15] believed that once a writer expresses the archetype, "the voice of a thousand people is expressed", and at the same time "the destiny of the individual is incorporated into the destiny of mankind, and the awakening form inside encourages mankind to escape danger," The power to get through the long night slowly." Character archetypes are the refinement of typical characters. The use of archetypes can turn accident into necessity, and individual as the whole. It is not the one-sided experience of a certain author, but the collective experience of mankind.

Victoria Lynn Schmidt [16] defined archetypes as "a blue print for building well-defined characters, be they heroes, villains, and supporting characters" "each archetype has her own set of motivations, fears and cares that push her as well as the plot forward".

She also marked that the most common male and female archetypes are actually the mythic, cross-cultural models from which all characters originate. To print a wide variety of character profiles, including heroes, villains, and supporting can help to make characters and their stories more compelling, complex, and original .

We all know great heroes and villains are the keys to bring any story to life. Victoria created altogether 45 female and male heroes with villains in her book (in pairs, with heroes and anagonist) 32 out of them are for heroes.

Writers usually care more about what he/she wants to express instead of what the readers really need. To touch others' heart, it is important for screenwriters to give audiences as much power as possible to teach, help and guide. When designing a story, character's motivation, fears and goals are supposed to be carved in his/her nature. With regular human motivations, abilities and dysfunction, it is easier to build well-rounded characters that readers everywhere are related to and learn from to drive the story forward to the way they expect. The turning point and options they make at the fork would be a reaction to the situations those plot points put him/her in, the decision is from deep inside because it is in his nature to do so. By creating real people that arouse the audience's coherence and empathy, the writer will invoke strong emotion and satisfying immersive experience or even learn and grow from the life story within the movie interactive.

2.3   Unique Task for VR Movie Screenwriters

Designed story genre and character choice/assignment are in close relation to the pitch. A good genre would inspire both the producing team and the buyers. The leading role in the world of the story carries the theme of the movie, the protagonist serves the story. We need to create an audience stand-in that can resonate with the target audience and satisfy the storyteller as well. A rebelling conflict can go the farthest emotionally, be loved by the most audience and meet their needs and goals. VR movies mainly attract young audiences whose original impulse is waiting to release. The biggest problem facing screenwriters at present is how to solve the contradiction between the audience's dominance and the development of the plot and the director's creation. There are too many forks in the story for an interactive VR movie. If the needs of all audiences are met, the storyline will be very huge and go easily out of control.

3   Hypothesis

People with similar personality share many commonalities and preferences in the choice of fork in stories with multiple endings. These preferences can be used as key points in the plot design of VR writers to guide the audience to make choices and gradually approach the intention of the story designer. From the audience's point of view, his/her decision is just he/she, the decision is for the hero with strong partici-pative movie experience. The choice conforms to his/her own wishes, enhances watching experience and participation, and meets the idea that the director wants to convey.

4 Survey

The survey will be done with 260 participants (to 50 CVR audiences and 210 college students) from three angels. Firstly, the respondents will be tested online to get their personal personality trait chart; secondly, the choices of each group member on story genre and character archetypes (profile of 10 genres and 32 lead female and male characters) will be collected; thirdly, the 260 subjects will make choices at the flow-chart of typical interactive movies *Black mirror: pandersnach* and interactive VR movie *Night Shift* separately, people share the same highest personality traits will be tested for preferences in making choices at key points in tree bifurcated design from story tellers.

4.1 Questionnaire

Through observation, the author found that most audience watching VR movies in Sanlitun, Beijing are young people in their 20s, and a great majority of whom are college students or newcomers to the workplace. Therefore, we distributed 50 questionnaires to the audience outside the theater and 210 questionnaires to college students.

The personality test was done online, inventory and test result are from the website https://apesk.com/bigfive/index.asp?language=cn, at the same time, respondents are asked to tick out the top 3 that they like most from Blake Snyder's 10 film genres and the first 3 favorite female and male characters they are willing to play as will separately, from Blake Snyder's 46 character archetypes listed in test paper, and the last survey is to make their own choice at each turning point of black mirror and night shift, the story flowchart was downloaded from https://movie.douban/rewiew/9856170/, https://www.ign.com/wikis/black-mirror/Bandersnatch_Map_-_All_Choices_and_Outcomes, and https://indienova.com/u/asukalin/blogread/3712.

4.2 Data Statistics and Analysis

Personality Classification. Of all the 260 questionnaires, we got 249 back. Data collected was classified into 5 groups, according to each subject's personality trait at the highest level. Cronbach α value of OCEAN is .64, .66, .65, .70, .71, respectively.

The result shows that 48.80% of all the respondents are high agreeableness personality (means altruistic and docile), 33.60% of the 249 people are of high conscientiousness (represents organization and self-discipline), the other three takes only poor percentage, extravertion (0.09%), openness (0.07%) and Neuroticism (0.01%), tells that most people are of low confidence and active, aesthetic and creative level are even lower, the lowest trait is Neuroticism, shows most respondents' depression and anxiety are at the lowest level.

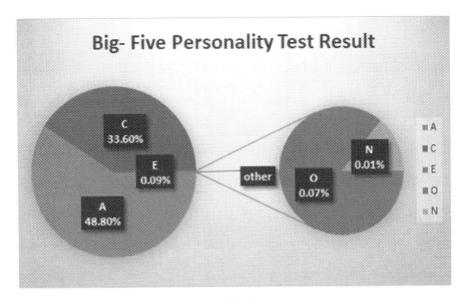

Fig. 5. Personality classification among respondents

Personality and Film Genre Selection and Character Options. After the test paper was analyzed, we found it difficult to find a meaningful relationship between a specific personality type and choices on their favorite story and characters. That is to say, there is no correlation between personality and story or role options. However, all the subjects showed similar options in this part. Of the 10 film genres created by Blake, the most popular ones are Rites of Passage (facing sudden change in life, a reluctant but hardworking lead successes in the end), Whydunit (detective to deep mind of human beings), Golden Fleece (long journey to seek for sth. special, overcome obstacles all the way and won growth in him/herself), and Monster in the House (a supernatural monster generated due to sin of the human, full of hiding and killing, scary, thrilling and tension story) in turn. Nearly 30% of them take Mystic (a sensitive woman who enjoy peaceful and comfort of life, although a little isolated) as the first choice, the Nurturer (helpful and generous mother full of love and sense of belongs) and troubled teen (rebelling girl as a teenager) are the second and third options. As for male characters, top 1 is the protector (who offers shelter for all his beloved with power of wisdom), businessman and warlock are also popular choices, and most male respondents enjoy to be women's man.

4.3   Correlation Analysis

The authors found that in average, nearly 60% of the people share the same highest personality traits are ticking out the same choice at each fork of the flowcharts of both *Black Mirror* and *Night Shift*, it can be seen as a positive correlation between personality and turning-point option in interactive movies with pitchfork bifurcation plot structure.

5   Conclusion

The above analysis illustrates that it is possible for VR movie screenwriters to create interactive connection with layers and layers of choices in a pitchfork bifurcation structure, hence the audience enjoys a real participative experience from which he/she can make his/her own decision and push the story forward to an ending that seems to be drawn by the player him/herself. Actually, related researches on interactive VR movies are still in the initial stage and the materials we can find are so limited that the sample and data collected are not big enough to make the research more valid and reliable. The result is the content and research designed in this paper are not logic or comprehensive enough to put the research into practice. However, the relationship between the audience's personality traits and option preferences exists, and audience's participation desire in VR movies is growing rapidly. Option preference of target audiences based on big data analysis and AI writers are technologically in reach, and RivetAI, a smart screenwriter too, has been successfully developed in the U.S.. More targeted fork point design and plot structure would become bestsellers in the near future.

To attract target audiences with stable personality, big data and AI writers can help in designing turning point in layers, and each goes to the direction that would be attractive and enjoyable for the player. Screenwriters and creative team are free to decide certain film genre and character model and keep their original theme and idea in control. The plot can be created on big data analysis, which is a heavy workload for film script writers. That will significantly reduce design blindness and more effectively mobilize the audience's awareness of participation and interaction, so as to obtain better audience feedback and market expectations. We believe the future of VR interactive movies are even brighter than ordinary VR movies.

References

1. Bo, X., Peng, S.: Boundaries between the interactive possibilities and the real world: on the boundless interactive films. Contemporary Cinema **09**, 119–126 (2020)
2. Bo, X., Peng, S.: Boundaries between the interactive possibilities and the real world: on the boundless interactive films. Contemporary Cinema **09**, 121–126 (2020)
3. Glorianna, D.: Interactive cinema. In: Ryan, M.-L., Emerson, L., Robertson, B. (eds.) Johns Hopkins University Press, The Johns Hopkins Guide to Digital Media, MD, p. 278 (2014)
4. Elsaesser, T.: The mind-game film. In: Buckland, W. (ed.) Puzzle Films, pp. 13–41. Wiley-Blackwell, Oxford, UK (2008). https://doi.org/10.1002/9781444305708.ch1
5. Huang, X.Y., Jiu, Z.: On the ontology characteristic of interactive films - the fusion, collision and rebirth of film and game. Contemporary Cinema **01**, 167–171 (2020)
6. Cattel, R.B.: The description of personality: principles and findings in a factor analysis. Am. J. Psychol. **58**(1), 69–90 (1945)
7. Fiske,D.W.: Consistency of the factorial structures of personality ratings fromdifferent sources. J. Abnorm. Soc. Psychol. **13**, 667–673(1949)
8. Qiming, L., Zhixia, C.: Survey on the personality of Chinese aged between 15–75 with 5 dimensions and 10 facets of Big Five Theory. Psychol. Sci. **01**(20), 131–138 (2015). https://doi.org/10.16719/j.cnki.1671-6981.2015.01,015

9. Soto, C.J., John, O.P.: Ten facet scales for the Big Five Inventory: convergence with NEO PI-R facets, self-peer agreement, and discriminant validity. J. Res. Pers. **43**(1), 84–90 (2009)

10. Goldberg, L.R.: The structure of phenotypic personality traits. Am. Psychol. **48**(1), 26–34 (1993). https://doi.org/10.1037/0003-066X.48.1.26

11. Annabelle, G.Y.L.: The big five personality traits. 06 www.simplypsychology.org/big-five-personality.html (2020)

12. Reprinted from PennState, by R. Gray. https://sites.psu.edu/leadership/2017/09/02/the-importance-of-personality-trait-screening-for-todays-organizations-application-of-the-five-factor-model-ffm/ (2017)

13. Blake, S.: Save the Cat: the Last Book on Screenwriting You'll Ever Need. Zhejiang University Press 04, pp. 6–17; 21–38; 42–48 (2018)

14. Mckee, R.: Story-Substance, structure, style and the principles of screenwriting. Tianjin Renmin Press **06**, 3–109 (2017)

15. Jung, C.G., Mcguire, W.: Archetypes and the collective unconscious. Princeton University Press **8**, pp. 1-109 (1969). (the collected works of C.G. Jung Pt.1)

16. Victoria, L.S.: 45 Master Characters: Mythic Models for Creating Original Characters. China Renmin University Press 06, pp. 4–5, 41–43 (2014)

Author Index

Printed in the United States
by Baker & Taylor Publisher Services